contents

2	Editorials
6	Streaming Sin

ARTICLES & INTERVIEWS

8	The Subersive Submissions of Amy Hesketh
21	Japanese Pink Films: The Japanese Wife Next Door!
25	Bionic Guts And Exploding Huts!
39	Massacre Mitchell Style
42	Tuesday Night Grindhouse Nights at the New Beverly
47	Telefilm Terror: My Made-for-TV Life
	Jess Franco & Soledad Miranda: Made in Euro-Cult Heaven
	...mentary, My Dear Whatsit: ...es Vs. The Red Planet Mars
	...ion of the Legend Of John: Balladeer to Hillbilly Hippie
	The Other Side Of Madness: Creepy-Crawl Through the Cinema of Charles Manson
97	A Body-Slamming Look at the Horrific Relationship Between Wrestling and Horror
101	Horror on the Airwaves: Doomed Disc Jockeys
107	Release Spotlight: Last Exit Entertainment
109	Take It to the Limit: Karate Warrior, Larry Ludman and 'Eighties Italian Trash Cinema
115	The Stupendous Cinema of SyFy: The Maneater Films
129	A Few Early Films by Umberto Lenzi
133	Steve's Video Store: Lost-in-the-Shuffle DVD Era Edition
136	Greek VHS Mayhem 5: Troma
147	Pimping Godfrey Ho
153	Stephen Biro Interview: American Guinea Pig
155	REVIEWS
193	THE BOOKSHELF
209	ABOUT THE CONTRIBUTORS

Brian Harris, Editor & Publisher
Tony Strauss, Editor & Proofing
Timothy Paxton, Editor & Design

WENG'S CHOP is published quarterly. © 2015 Wildside Publishing / Kronos Productions. All rights reserved. No part of this publication may be reproduced, distributed, or transmitted in any form or by any means, including photocopying, recording, or other electronic or mechanical methods, without the prior written permission of the publisher, except in the case of brief quotations embodied in critical reviews and certain other noncommercial uses permitted by copyright law. For permission requests, write to the publisher, addressed "Attention: Permissions Coordinator," at the address below.
4301 Sioux Lane #1, McHenry, IL 60050, United States
wengschop@comcast.net

Volume #3 / Issue #2 / Number 8
September 2015 1st Printing

IT'S AN E&J GALLO™ KINDA LIFE!

Welcome to Wildside-Kronos' 11th issue of *Weng's Chop* Magazine! For those of you grabbing issue #8, allow us to sincerely thank you with yet another money-grabbing gimmick guaranteed to starve your children and send you into delirium tremens…our first-ever full-color issue! In the past we've offered up two or three covers per issue, giving dedicated readers and veracious art lovers a variety to choose from, but this time we figured we'd try something new with the *interior* instead. One B&W issue for the currency disabled, and a **More Expensive Color Edition** for those that often take to the streets in maximum skip mode, tossing money to the adoring peons. If you wipe your button with money, it's for you. If you consider your accountant to be your best friend, it's for you. If *Weng's Chop* is the boxed wine of exploitation cinema mags, our **More Expensive Color Edition** is a chilled box of wine, with the drunken cougar thrown in for your three-and-a-half-minute pleasure.

Unless, of course, you were being a cheap bastard and you purchased the **Standard Edition**. In that case, you still kick ass but we can only let you peek up the cougar's khaki shorts.

Another major achievement is we're the *very first* book out there to be printed in 4K dpi, a resolution so advanced it took three months just to render the cover and interior.[1] Every word and picture will be crystal clear and razor sharp. The process was so impressive, the European Coalition of Free and Independent Periodicals (ECFIP) said, "We are astounded at this new process and look forward to a new future of print."[2] How is that for an accolade? We're calling this process **ULTIMOPRINT**™ and all of our upcoming releases will be printed in it.[3] Not only do we hold all the rights to this process, we've licensed it to well over a dozen publications![4] Wildside-Kronos is indeed the future of print.

One last, final, bit of amazing news…we have signed our first book author, Troy Howarth! Let the envy fly, bitches! While we're not yet at liberty to say what the book will be about—because to let it slip that it will be a ~~Kinski filmography~~ [5] will give our competitors a devastating head-start—but expect an outstanding publication with the high quality you've come to expect from Wildside-Kronos. BRING IT ON 2016! *~Brian Harris*

1 We believe this comment to be false. - Scurnfield, Jameson & Sapstein Legal
2 "The ECFIP categorically denies ever having said such a thing. Please cease and desist all false or erroneous statements made on our behalf." (ECFIP Legal Counsel)
3 As far as we know, yet another false comment. - Scurnfield, Jameson & Sapstein Legal
4 We no longer represent Wildside-Kronos Publications. - Scurnfield, Jameson & Sapstein Legal
5 Dear Competitors, please ignore this comment. - Brian

THE OPTIONS ARE SEXY, BUT CAN WE MAKE THEM VIOLENT?

Welcome back to the Wild and Wonderful World of *Weng's Chop*, The Incredible Cinema Megazine—now 100% gluten-free! (Of course, in order to achieve this, we've had to load it to the gills with arsenic and strychnine…but hey, no fuckin' gluten! So gorge yourselves to the fill-line, hippies!)

As my esteemed colleague, Prof. Brian Harris, Esq., DDS, OB/GYN, Jr. (*Ret.*), has already indicated, this issue of our pernicious publication represents our first offering of two distinct editions:

First is our **Standard Edition**, which will look familiar to you all, presented in all its greyscale glory at the usual cover price, jam-packed with myriads of marvelous movie muck that you marvelous movie mucklovers have come to expect—nay, *demand*…because that's just the kind of sophisticated, erudite, suave and sexy motherfuckers you all are.

Also available is our ultra-deluxe **More Expensive Color Edition**, jam-packed with all the same wonderful material as our Standard Edition…but more expensive, and in color. You see, many of our "High Society" readers in places like Wall Street, The Hamptons, Buckingham Palace, and Cleveland have been constantly asking if we're ever going to publish in color…so we've decided to give it a try, because we'd hate to get any kind of scornful mention in the Society Pages—we just couldn't weather the scandal.

Regardless of which edition you decide to purchase, you will have your lives thoroughly enriched by the glorious content contained within, knowing full well that merely *holding* the magazine will cure you of any bone-related ailments you may suffer, and that actually *reading* the material inside will give you psychic healing powers which you can use in any manner—good or evil, we don't judge—you see fit. What you may *not* know is that if you buy one **Standard Edition** and one **More Expensive Color Edition**, and hold one in each hand facing True North at the exact moment of the vernal equinox whilst dressed in traditional Russian folk dance attire, you will not only cause eternal peace between Eskimos and Peruvians, but you will also receive one extra life for your current saved game in *Zelda II: The Adventure of Link*! The combination possibilities are limitless, but we cannot go into too much detail here, lest the more powerful incantations and effects fall into the hands of the Illuminati and/or the Reptilians…or worse, the 4-H Club, those bastards who *really* control us all.

IMPORTANT SIDEBAR:

To know if you have actually bought our **More Expensive Color Edition**, please check to see if the image of Jet Jaguar and Godzilla are indeed in Fujicolor. If they are, then congratulations are in order on purchasing our **More Expensive Color Edition**. If the photo is a greyscale construct then you have purchase our **Standard Edition**, which is just as fun and cool, but *not* in color. Thank You for you time, and helping support independent publishing the world over.

So in the interest of pleasing as many of our illustrious readers as possible, we are giving you all the choice of two editions. Rest assured, the **Standard Edition** will always remain as such, and will always be there for you. The **More Expensive Color Edition** is a bit of an experiment, and will be made available for each issue for as long as there are fat-walleted readers out there to buy it (or until our merciless 4-H Club overlords demand its cessation, in which case we'll have no choice in the matter).

In the meantime, please do book your face on over to our Facebook page (*facebook.com/wengschopmagazine*) or twiddletwaddle us on Twitter (@WengsChop) and let us know your thoughts on the B&W/Color options…if we're lucky, we'll get some real venomous animosity going between the two camps that we can elevate into some kind of awesome organized back-alley rumble with knives and bicycle chains and lots of people with greasy duck's-ass. Damn, that would be fuckin' awesome…let's try for that.

At any rate, please delight in our first gluten-free excursion into the heavenly world of incredible cinema, and enjoy mixing and matching editions and rituals to create new and exciting explosions of earth-shattering power…also the complimentary 24-oz. packet of black-licorice-flavored nacho sauce on page 61, as per usual. ~*Tony Strauss*

Bonus Editorial Rant

I Miss the Good Old Days when People Weren't So Nostalgic

by Tony Strauss

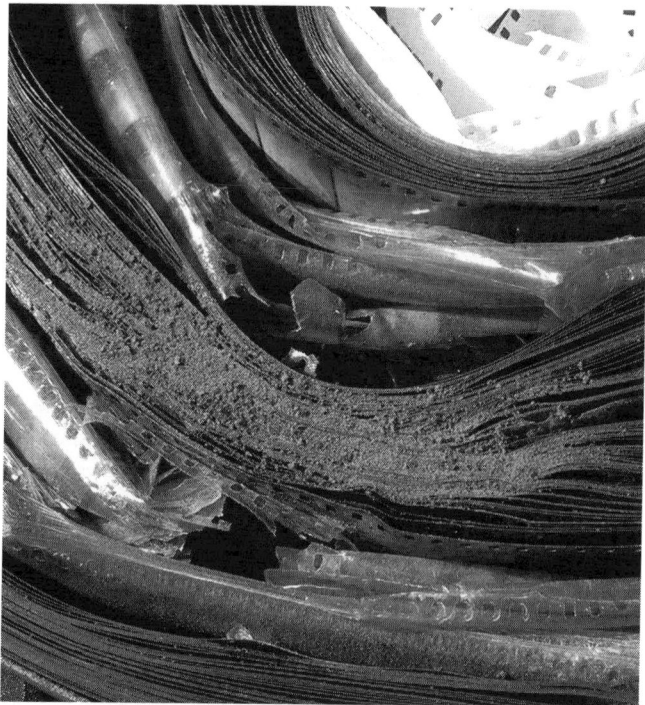

Did you know that there are more original independent films being produced now than at any other point in cinema history? It's true. Never before has there been a time when more movies were being made. Not ever.

So, you'll have to excuse me when I don't show much sympathy for you "fans" who rant and rave about there being no original movies coming out any more, about how everything is a remake or reimagining, and about how much better movies were when you were growing up.

I've noticed that if you grew up in the 1980s in America, you are particularly prone to this type of whining.[1]

But regardless of the generation hollering these self-pitying complaints, this kind of whining baffles and befuddles me (*vexes* me, even). This complaining about sequels and remakes and no new ideas. In this day and age? From people that claim to be *movie fans*? You've got to be kidding me.

I hate to sound like an old fart, but I think your problem is laziness.

No, hear me out…I'm not here to just bash on you—I'm here to help you. Miserable fuckin' whiners that you are.

I don't think the laziness is entirely your fault (does that make you feel better?)…the world changes so fast in so many ways that we don't even notice most of them, and the fact that the proper method of seeing good movies has also changed seems to have missed the notice of many a movie fan. Sure, you can still go to the theatre every weekend and see "all the latest movies" until you're blue in the face, but the general nature of the choices you're being offered at that theatre has changed dramatically since you were a kid. It's a bigger ballgame now.

I'll skip the tired old rant about the movie industry being a profit-seeking business…I can assume you already know that part. So, in order to maximize profits, a business that wishes to remain successful must pay attention to their customers' tastes. And, just like any product on the market, customer tastes are first and foremost determined by what sells and what doesn't, plain and simple. Sure, companies generally have a passing interest in what the customers *say* about their products, but the bottom line is *sales*. So you can complain until you are once again blue-faced about how much you hate remakes and reboots and sequels (oh my), and shout about how stupid you think such-and-such upcoming blockbuster looks on every public forum you can find…but if you buy a ticket to see it, the studio thinks you fucking loved it. And they're going to think you want more just like it.

And if we're being perfectly honest, they're sort of right. In general, people *do* want to see the same familiar and safe entertainments over and over, repackaged into the parameters of the latest trends *du jour*. And that's understandable for the casual moviegoer; from childhood through death, humans have *always* found comfort in the familiar when it comes to stories—from the earliest campfire gatherings to the biggest modern multiplexes—and the bulk of what most people want from a movie is just to be entertained for a couple nice hours of reality-free escapism. But *these* are not the people I'm addressing here—these people don't really complain much, so long as they're entertained by a steady flow of A-lister-filled fodder that doesn't step too far outside their comfort zones.

No, the people I'm talking about consider themselves *more* than just casual viewers, but genuine movie-lovers; people who grew up with movies being an important part of their lives, and remember the Hollywood blockbusters of their childhoods to be some of the greatest experiences of their days on Earth. But now they've grown up (-ish), and are upset that these modern-day blockbusters don't give their adult (-ish) brains the exact same sense of wonder and amazement that the films' predecessors gave their 10-year-old selves.

Well, no fuckin' shit—really?! Who'd'a thunk it! I'm just gonna go out on a limb here and guess that you aren't learning all kinds of new stuff from recent episodes of *Sesame Street*, either.

---

[1] I don't know…maybe my sample group is skewed because that's my generation so I notice it more. Maybe every generation whines like that…but I really don't hear a *fraction* of the amount of cries of "they don't make movies like **THE STING/GREASE/EVERY WHICH WAY BUT LOOSE** anymore," as I do rallied over **BACK TO THE FUTURE, GHOSTBUSTERS** and **THE GOONIES**.

Weng's Chop

Do you see what I'm getting at here? What makes you think you can go back to the same tree season after season and expect the fruit to ever taste any different?

It's *mainstream* cinema, ferfucksake—do you think it's referred to as such because it's a category looking to be fresh and new? No, silly…it's looking to be safe and profitable. Hollywood has maintained its gluttonous existence by taking as few chances as possible, and it doesn't care how much you howl about wanting new and creative material…so long as you keep buying those tickets in vain hope.

Nor is it interested in your childhood memories or sense of nostalgia…any further than it can exploit them. Now, *that* is where Hollywood might listen to you every now and then: if it thinks you're waxing nostalgic for one of your favorite movies or shows of yesteryear, it will do its best to repackage that same successful formula and give it to you, all polished up with the latest bells and whistles. And statistics show that you tend to hate it…but you still *watch* it.

Hell, sometimes you don't even have to *see it* to hate it. Your rush-to-judgment at the product Hollywood is desperately scrambling to churn out in order to keep up with your ever-increasing, confused and self-contradictory demands is almost cartoonish in its selfishness. Your lust for nostalgia combined with your desire for variation (not to mention an ever-shortening attention span in this instant-gratification age) creates a cognitive dissonance that makes you act…well, *insane*. You want something fresh and new and different—but only if it's exactly like stuff that you've loved before. And you want it fucking now, before you get distracted by something else. And dammit, it had better be perfect, or there'll be hell to pay.

You know, I'd almost feel sorry for Hollywood, struggling like mad to keep up with your outrageous demands…if it weren't for the fact that you keep financially rewarding it for stoking your ire.

Because ultimately, they don't *have* to care if you hate their newest big-budget blockbuster, for they know from experience that you'll go see it right along with all the rest of the casual-viewing masses. They've got your number, you know…and your dollars. So whine all you want about lack of originality in Hollywood, because Hollywood knows what it's doing. Originality doesn't sell—familiarity sells. And your dollars keep telling it that you want familiarity.

So what does this all have to do with laziness, you might ask?

Well, going back to the tree analogy, you're just plain too lazy and set in your ways to walk to a different tree. You're surrounded by a thousand orchards, but you keep walking to the same damn tree and complaining that it's the same damn fruit. Seriously…what are you *thinking*?

I know that the Hollywood tree presents a vast, easy-to-reach expanse of branches weighted down by shiny, pre-polished, familiar-tasting fruit…but you want something more, remember? Let me restate that there are more movies coming out now than ever before: Films being made outside the big ol' Hollywood system. Films that cost less money and can therefore take more chances with regards to originality. And they're not too difficult to find… you've just gotta try some new trees, my friends. So stop shouting at that one damn tree, and follow me to some different parts of the orchard.

One of the more common complaints I encounter from frustrated film fans is that there's "nothing good on Netflix". While I myself would *love* for the Netflix digital library to include every movie ever made, I've always puzzled at this particular complaint, because I've always found it to be so patently untrue. Then I came to realize that what this complaint *really* means is, "There's nothing on Netflix that I've heard of that I haven't already seen," which is an entirely different problem, but an easy one to solve, if you're not too lazy, and not afraid to—*GASP*—try new things.

A great way to beef up your queue with new entertainments is to spend some time rating films on the Netflix site to improve your recommendations. Their software has a great algorithm for recommending films to your tastes, but you have to spend some time using it to make it work for you. So sit down and spend an hour or so giving star-ratings on Netflix to films you've seen, and telling it which films you are aware of but have no interest in, then go browse through the films Netflix recommends to you. Don't be a wuss about movies that you've never heard of, just read the synopses and see what's there…I'll bet you'll find something that sounds worth trying. And the more time you're willing to spend rating films, the better their ability to recommend others to you that are likely to be up your alley.

Another great recommendation-generating algorithm can be found on Amazon's site; this is one that can be affected in multiple ways. The basic generating is done based on what you've already purchased in the past, but you can enhance it similarly to the way it's done on Netflix by just rating some movies you've seen and enjoyed (whether you've purchased them through Amazon or not), then head over to the recommendations. One particularly useful option that Amazon offers is the ability to tell it *not* to use a particular film to generate recommendations, which goes a long way toward thinning out undesirable suggestions. Just browse through the recommendations, rate, delete, and refresh to refine.

Yet another method of finding new and worthwhile watchables is the method you are currently engaged in right at this moment: reading cinema-related publications! In addition to your beloved *Weng's Chop* and *Monster!* tomes, there are a great number of worthwhile repositories of recommendation out there just waiting to be mined, from books organized by genre or theme (just pick a category you like and get perusing!) to the myriad mags and 'zines that focus on cinematic roads less travelled (again, pick a mag that looks up your alley and dive in!). Not to mention the numerous websites, 'blogs and podcasts out there dedicated to spreading the word about lesser-known productions waiting to be discovered.

But perhaps the most important and effective key to discovering new and different cinema is to *not be a fucking pussy about trying new shit*. Seriously… does it really *matter* if you don't recognize any of the actors? If it looks interesting, give it a try—if you're not entertained 15 or 20 minutes in, turn it off and try a different movie. It's super easy to turn off a movie that doesn't entertain you…try it sometime and reap the sweet rewards of minimal effort!

Now, if the thought of at least *attempting* some of these things sounds like too much effort for you, then maybe "new and different" isn't what you really want. Maybe you're happier just re-watching the treasures of your youth, basking in nostalgia and pretending that they don't make 'em like the used to. I see the comfort in that; there's security in the familiar, and maybe the fruit on that one tree isn't so bad after all…at least you already know what it tastes like.

But I'm telling you, there's some wonderful and amazing fruit out there ripe for the pluckin'…if you're willing to just take a little stroll.

Cover and interior illustration:
Art by Megh

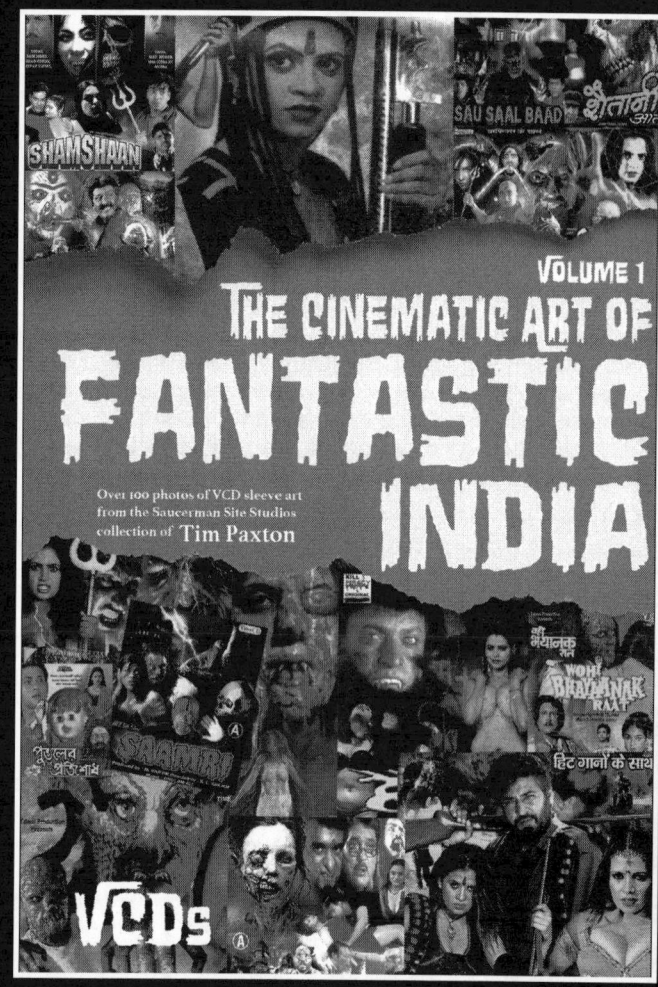

STREAMING SIN:
YET ANOTHER REASON TO CUT THE CORD

by Brian Harris

Netflix for exploitation fans? Fuckflix? Well, yeah, close. Welcome to Vinegar Syndrome's newest labor of super sleazy love, the streaming channel, *Exploitation.tv*! Now, exploitation fans can head to their Roku, or other streaming device, and furiously spank it to classics (**CASTLE OF BLOOD** [*Danza macabra*, 1964]), not-so-classics (**MASSACRE MAFIA STYLE** [a.k.a. **LIKE FATER, LIKE SON**, 1974][1]) and flat-out crap (**VIXENS OF KUNG FU** [1975]); truly a smorgasbord for the cult connoisseur.

Now, I'm sure some of you are wondering why you should pay $10 a month for the kind of cinema you can find on some of those free streaming channels. For starters, there's stuff on *Exploitation.tv* that you will simply not find on other channels. Being a Roku junkie, I can state with full confidence that most of the "grindhouse/cult/horror" channels are mainly comprised of public domain films, or the kind of low budget, Z-grade indie horror carried by companies like Brain Damage and Chemical Burn. I rarely use most of the channels I've installed on my Roku for that very reason. While I love and embrace crappy cinema, I do have my limits, even if it's free. So, just what do we get for sawbuck then?

THE GOOD

Exploitation.tv offers categories like "Action", "Arthouse", "Comedy", "Drama", "Horror", "Thriller", and "Shorts"...but take it from me, a large portion of those can be lumped into three categories: "Porn", "Horror", and "Sleaze". That's a good thing, readers, a very good thing.

I see films from VinSyn, DistribPix, Massacre Video, and one of my favorite companies, Severin Films. I'm hoping Bill Lustig's Blue Underground and whomever holds the digi-rights to Something Weird Video eventually jump ship from Band's Full Moon Streaming and Erotic Movie House. Not wishing failure on Ol' Charlie or anything, but divvying up the FM, BU and SWV catalogs between two channels and charging subscribers almost $20 is...well, sleazy. *Exploitation.tv* would be *killer* with Troma, Blue Underground, Synapse, 88 Films, SWV and Scorpion added to their lineup. Seriously.

My initial count of films (including shorts) being offered right now: 27 Action, 34 Arthouse, 75 Comedy, 80 Drama, 75 Horror, 33 Thriller, 20 Shorts. That's 344 flicks. That breaks down to a little under 30 films a month, at 35 cents per film. And with anywhere from five to seven new films promised to be added each month, that $10 is damn good value.

THE BAD

What could possibly be bad about watching two chicks go at one another's cookies like starving Ethiopians in a Chinese buffet? Nothing, but there are some places *Exploitation.tv* could use a bit more TLC. Considering they've just launched and are making adjustments on the fly, I feel bad for pointing out these issues but potential subscribers should know about them anyhow.

Menu. Oh Christ. Simple, sleek...and clunkier than two wooden legs. You scroll across the top, from category to category, and are forced to wait for each category to load before you're allowed to go to the next. It takes a bit of patience, and it's a total boner-killer. It's basically the Windows Vista of streaming channel navigation. It needs improvement. Big time.

Search function. There is none. You're flying blind here. Want something with black chicks, get scrolling. Puffy nipples, get guessing. Martial arts featuring nude female ninjas, yeah right...me and you both. Unfortunately, there's no keyword search of any kind, so it's all a guessing game and it's frustrating.

Rating. There are star ratings on the films, just like Netflix. The only difference is, you can't actually use them here. If you want to rate films, you've gotta log in to the *Exploitation.tv* website.

Watchlist. You cannot use this feature, like the rating system, unless you're logged in online. That sucks for subscribers that rarely go online.

Once again, I'm sure VinSyn is already working to address these issues, so hopefully by the time this review sees print, they'll be moot.

THE UGLY

There isn't much "ugly" here. Outside of a need for the designers to do some proof-reading, I find nothing truly objectionable about *Exploitation.tv*. I'm seeing all kinds of grammar issues, but I'm sure they just stem from coding errors.

One thing I consider to be an "ugly"—*but it is not at all an* Exploitation.tv *issue*—is Roku's adult entertainment restrictions. If you want this channel, you have to seek it out and add it manually. You will not find it on the Roku website. I foresee *years* of people whining and bitching about this. So, if you're wondering why you cannot find it on the Roku site, there's your answer.

While it may seem like there's more "bad" than "good" in my review, that's not at all the case. I cannot recommend *Exploitation.tv* enough. If your entertainment is primarily streamed and you're a hardcore ex/sexploitation fan, *you will* need this channel. Full stop.

With more films on the way and probable updates galore, this is going to be *the* cult cinema channel to watch. Here's to *Exploitation.tv* 2.0!

---

1 See p.39

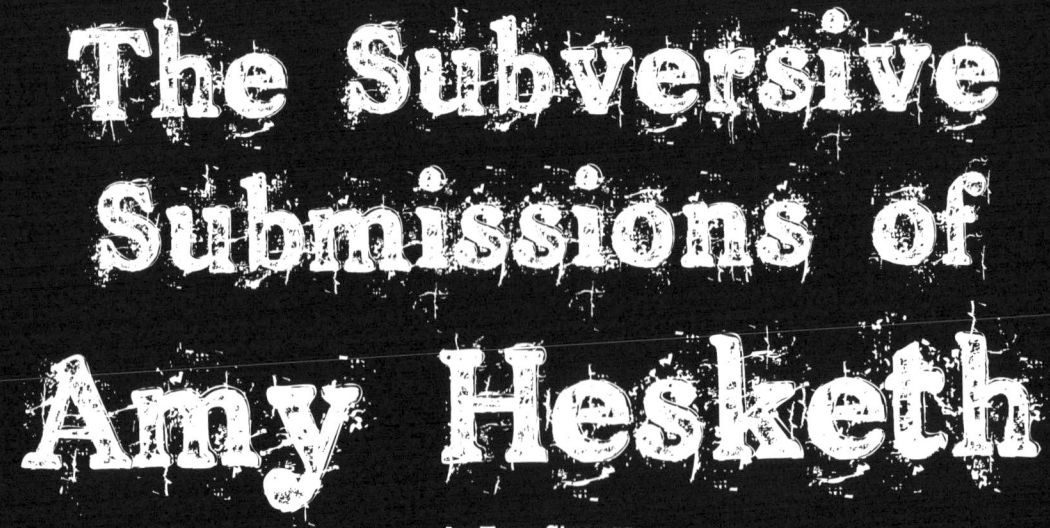

The Subversive Submissions of Amy Hesketh

by Tony Strauss

Weng's Chop *readers are probably at least aware of the name Amy Hesketh—I reviewed her 2012 film* **BARBAZUL** *(a.k.a.* **BLUEBEARD***) back in issue #5[1]—but probably not as familiar with her body of work as a* Weng's Chop *reader should be. I mean, her films have so much of what a proper Chopper craves: sex, violence, suspense, horror, drama, rich atmosphere… along with a familiarity with and passion for of all those great Euro genre films of yesteryear that make us all so weak in the knees and kick our nostalgia glands (among others) into overdrive. Honestly, we should all be ashamed of ourselves for not already knowing volumes about this right-up-our-alley talent. ASHAMED, I tells ya!*

Well fear not, dear reader…I'm here to ameliorate your vicissitudes of unfamiliarity, and enlighten you to the painful passions of a filmmaker whose work should feature prominently in your library of weird and wonderful cinema. So sit back, pay attention, and let the enlightenment begin—just be sure to have a bucket of cold water handy, because this is some hot stuff, right here!

1 – The Artist

I met Amy Hesketh in 2013 at the PollyGrind Underground Film Festival in Las Vegas, while covering the event for *Weng's Chop*.[2] It was the first time I'd covered *any* event in *any* journalistic capacity, and I was nervous as hell, since I pretty much had no idea what I was doing. I just figured if I went to as many screenings as I could and introduced myself to as many people as I could, something worth reading would have to come out…or so I hoped. So that's what I did—I schmoozed it up with anyone wearing a PollyGrind pass and got to know as many filmmakers and performers as I could.

After one screening (I forget which block of films), I approached a young woman wearing a festival pass and asked her if she had a film in the festival. She did indeed, and introduced herself as Amy Hesketh, inviting me to attend the screening of her feature, **BARBAZUL**, in a couple days. The film's poster was hanging outside the theatre and had already caught my eye, so it was a pretty easy sell.

Sadly, my erratic day-job schedule yet again reared its ugly head on the day of the screening, so I didn't even make it to the festival until Amy's after-film Q&A session was well underway. After it was over, I approached her and apologized for missing the movie, and she smiled and said "No problem," and handed me the **BARBAZUL** Blu-ray that had just been screened! *Sweet!* We chatted for a few more minutes then she had to get going, and I told her I'd contact her after I'd watched the film.

I always have these moments of anxiety when I meet a filmmaker who's a really cool and friendly person (as the vast majority of indie filmmakers I've met thus far have been)…and then they hand me their film to watch and review. I'm constantly terrified that I'm going to hate the film worse than anything I've ever endured, and then, not being one to bullshit folks, have to find a diplomatic way to tell this really cool and friendly person that their artistic vision and hard work made me want to spoon out my eyes and burn them. Seriously, I have this fear each and every time a friendly indie filmmaker hands me their movie. Maybe I'm in the wrong line of work.

Fortunately, I needn't have worried, because I not only liked the movie, but it ended up being one of my favorite PollyGrind films that year. It tapped into this nostalgic vein that took me back to the days of Mom and Pop video shops, when I was just discovering the works of Jess Franco, Jean Rollin and Mario Bava. Sure, **BARBAZUL** was shot on HD video, so the image quality was completely different than the classic films of those directors, but Hesketh's filmmaking style evoked the spirit and feel of their works from their heyday, and gave me as a viewer the same sense of "otherworldness" that their films did. Video medium aside, this felt like '60s/'70s Euro genre cinema, through and through—full of exotic locales, creepy characters, beautiful women and intense eroticism—and I loved it.

Naturally, I immediately sought out the rest of Amy's films, and as I began to become more familiar with her work, I became fascinated with several aspects of her auteurist style. All of her films are overtly, aggressively sexual in nature, with plot-lines unanimously involving the sexual subjugation and peril of women to at least some degree, depicted in frank and unflinching—even fetishistic—detail. Indeed, the pervasive sexual subjugation of females in her oeuvre could at first glance lead many a casual viewer to label her work as misogynistic. But if you look closer, you'll see that there's something else going on here, something entirely subversive.

On the surface, it might be tempting for some to dismissively label Amy's work as mere erotic thrillers aimed at the BDSM crowd (and there are plenty who have), what with all the tying-up and flogging and whatnot—because there is a *lot* of tying up and flogging and whatnot—but that would just be a lazy surface analysis, and missing much of what makes her films so unique and interesting. Because amid all the tying-up and flogging and whatnot is a series of works that are subversively feminist.

Yeah, that's right, I said *feminist*.

But how, you ask, can all this whipping of naked, screaming women be considered anything *close* to feminist? And in reply, I answer to you: Stop interrupting and just read the damned article…I'm about to explain right now, ferchrissakes!

---

[1] Reprinted below for your convenience. You're welcome.
[2] See coverage in *WC#5*, p.32

Amy's oeuvre is an extremely interesting arena, in which the gender of the filmmaker and viewpoint of the narrative establishes a distinct moral context for the films' more provocative content. If these films had been written and directed by a male, they would likely be viewed by many as borderline offensive—the films are extremely voyeuristic in nature, with an intimate, lingering fascination with the humiliation, submission, pain and torture of women—and viewers would have a tendency to perceive the films as the sadistic fantasies of some sicko dude who wanted to torture and humiliate women. But because the films were written and directed by a woman, told with a woman's voice and from a woman's perspective, the interpretation of the content is patently redirected into a completely different moral context and viewpoint, which, ironically, lends to a subtextual display of female *empowerment*, rather than subjugation. By guiding the viewers to feel greater identification with the female victims rather than focusing on the perspectives of the depraved male aggressors, Hesketh's films introduce a surprisingly frank element of sexual submissive fantasy, played out in elaborate dramatic and emotional detail, in an environment where such "dangerous" fantasies can be safely explored. During the scenes of torture and humiliation of the female characters, in which we as viewers are sharing the point-of-view and by extension that same torture and humiliation of said female characters, there is always the safe specter of a *woman* orchestrating the action, calling the shots, pulling the strings, directing our gaze, and making it okay for these images and acts to be witnessed and shared. I know the general rule is that the work should speak entirely for itself, uncontaminated by outside factors like who the filmmaker is, but these films take on a brilliantly subversive, boldly feminist aspect when you *do* consider who made them. They become a confident expression of dangerous desires, desires which would likely be considered hostile, unsafe and unacceptable—or, at best, exploitative to the extreme—if expressed by a member of the opposite sex.

On the other side of the coin, there *is* a deliberate, overtly provocative misogynistic element to her films, as well—I mean, these *are* women being tortured by men, after all. But that's just another part of her skill as a filmmaker: she doesn't let the viewer off the hook easily, never clearly telling us how we *should* feel about what we're watching. Are we watching BDSM titillation? Are we watching commentary on men's cruelty to women? Are we watching women's submissive fantasies? Are we watching men's fantasies of domination? Are we watching mature psychological dramas unfolding in the universal arena of sexual politics?

Well, I ask you this: Why can't it be all of the above? That's the challenge we're presented with as viewers: there's no clear-cut single way to interpret an Amy Hesketh film, and no rulebook informing us on the "proper" way to view it. It's up to us to determine how we feel about them...and how we feel about the way they make us feel. Is it okay to be turned on by these beautifully-filmed scenes of gorgeous naked women being bound and flogged against their will? Is it proper to be appalled by them? There are no easy answers to validate nor scorn the strong feelings the films elicit from you, but you *are* forced to have these strong feelings, nonetheless.

Like I said: brilliantly subversive. Amy Hesketh may dabble in submissive fantasies, but she's definitely a woman in charge.

That is not to say that the peril and subjugation is the defining element of her films; there's much more going on, both subtextually and overtly. There's not only psychosexual drama, but also plenty of sociopolitical commentary, historical context, morality tales, comic irony as well as deep tragedy to be found in her body of work. But in the end, her films are ultimately about the characters that populate them, each telling a story of a woman who is at some manner of a great crossroad or turning point in her life—whether it be returning to her roots in search of self-identity (**SIRWIÑAKUY** [2010]), marrying a near-stranger in hopes of improving her family's station in life (**BARBAZUL**), selling herself to a known deviant to avoid the guillotine (**LE MARQUIS DE LA CROIX** [2012]), or breaking family bonds to sate personal desires (**OLALLA** [2015])—where the choices each makes will change her life forever, frequently in violent, even fatal, ways.

Hesketh's worlds are populated by characters that are rich and complex, and her films ask that we become acquainted with them rather than being told who they are through archetype or simple expository means, giving us a much greater sense of empathy and emotional investment in their stories and the trials they face. Forcefully immersed in their world, we are obliged to experience their pleasures, pains, victories and tragedies as our own, before being released back to our own reality to deal with those experiences and the feelings they give us, for better or worse. This is what art is meant for—to challenge us and make us feel things we normally wouldn't, or to consider our own relatable experiences in new ways—and make no mistake about it, Amy Hesketh's films are *art*, in the truest sense; they're beautiful, intelligent, engaging and provocative. And for a jaded movie junkie like me, encountering a filmmaker out to make real, honest *art* in my most favorite of artistic mediums is such a refreshing experience in a cinematic world infected by so much spectacle with so little substance, wherein "art" is the furthest thing from too many filmmakers' minds.

Weng's Chop had the tremendous privilege to acquire (read: kidnap) Amy for a proper interrogation, in hopes of getting to the heart of this passionate and gifted talent. No stranger to bondage and inquisition, our intimidation tactics didn't rattle her in the least, but she was kind enough to humor our amateurish attempts long enough to discuss her history, tactics, passions and perturbations in some amount of detail before easily slipping our sorry bindings and carrying on her merry way. We consider ourselves fortunate and enlightened by the experience...hopefully, you will be, too.

---

2 – *The Artist's Interview*

Hi, Amy! Thanks so much for taking time out and agreeing to be interrogated by a licensed **Weng's Chop** *representative...I apologize if the restraints are too tight, but our knot guy called in sick today. At any rate, I intend to get you through this as smoothly as possible and have you delivered back to your loyal followers in time for tea.*

Behind the scenes of **OLALLA**: (**Left**) Amy discusses a scene from the flashback subplot with actor Christian Del Rio. (**Right**) Setting up a shot with DP Miguel Inti Canedo

I'd like to start by going over your Secret Origin Story, back before the world became aware of your super-powers. You're originally from Maine, yes? What initially led you out of the New England territory and started you down the path to the life of an expat in Bolivia?

I am originally from rural Maine, yes. I left when I went to college, in upstate NY, then left for Paris to live the Bohemian life there for some time. In 2005, I traveled to Bolivia, at the behest of a friend who was working here. I figured I needed an adventure at that time in my life. After traveling around South America for a month, I was cast in a National Geographic docudrama that Jac Avila[3] was producing in Beni, Bolivia (*Vientos Negros* [2006]). A couple of weeks after that wrapped, I saw Jac's film, **MARTYR** [2005], in a film festival here, and got talking with him about independent cinema. I realized that Bolivia was a great place to produce indie films, and that if we teamed up, as a company we could do a lot here. Jac agreed to stay in Bolivia, we became business partners, and the result is ten years of hard work.

Rural Maine is an interesting place. It's Gothic, people are spare with showing their emotions, and winter lasts five months out of the year (at least). Growing up there forced me to create a very strong internal world of my own, through books, movies, and imagination.

Was the National Geographic docudrama something you auditioned for? Did you already have acting aspirations/experience at the time?

I had acted in a few films and shorts before that. I was working more as a photographer at the time, and thought it would be fun to audition for the role in the docudrama. What I really wanted was an entry into the film scene here, to see what it was like, to know more about it. Bolivia seemed like a great place to make films.

Most people probably don't think "film scene" when they think of Bolivia... what is it that makes it such a great place for filmmaking?

I quickly learned that, at the time, there wasn't much of a film scene here. There's been a huge growth in indie films in Bolivia over the past ten years, and our company is responsible for quite a few of those films. People here joke about how prolific we are.

As for making films here, it's the people (talent and crew), the amazing and diverse locations (haciendas, cliffs, jungle, you name it), and the help from sponsors, institutions (like the mayors' offices, museums, etc.) that make it a great place to work.

There are also difficulties that come with the territory—like bureaucracy, blockades, and the rainy season—that can make it less optimal to work here sometimes, but it all balances out in the end.

Do you encounter many problems making erotic films in such a predominantly Catholic country? It seems to me that alone could present its own set of obstacles from time to time.

I don't think I make erotic films. I make films that have some erotic (depending on your brand of eroticism) scenes. And they always have a point or pur-

3 See review of Jac's film **DEAD BUT DREAMING** on p.174

Amy shows off what the cool kids read!

pose to being in the film—they're not the point of the film. In an "erotic" film, the entire point of its plot/storyline is the sexy scenes.

Like anywhere, here there is a mix of conservatives, and more liberal, open-minded people. I'm lucky to have mostly encountered the more open-minded types, who appreciate independent cinema, new ideas and concepts. Catholics tend to grow up with a set of very violent, sexual iconography. Take into consideration that Bolivia is a very mixed culture. It's a colonized country, in the midst of a lot of change. The cosmovision here is an amalgam of cultural influences.

I certainly meant no offense nor dismissiveness with the "erotic" label... quite the opposite, in fact. But let's talk about that label for a moment, because I'm interested in your take on it.

The term "erotic film" is a bit of a slippery slope in modern parlance, due mainly, in my view, to pornographers' attempts to appropriate the word for their own work in an effort to make it sound more relevant and less "threat-

BARBAZUL: (Left) Amy directs one of the film's many sexy scenes. **(Right)** The stunning Mila Joya as Soledad, makin' hot whoopee with Bluebeard

ening", when in actuality, erotica is and has always been a historically valid—and even vitally important—category of fine art...a category too-often sidestepped for discussion due to prudish post-Victorian sensibilities. At the risk of splitting hairs, I do indeed see your work as erotica—very much in the same vein as D.H. Lawrence, Anaïs Nin, the Marquis de Sade, etc.—in the classic sense of the term as it applies to fine art: using sexually-themed stories and situations to address higher psychological and sociopolitical issues in a more subversive, less didactic fashion.*

Do you resist the label of "erotic films" due to a stigma associated with the more modern appropriation? Because your films seem consciously and deliberately set apart from other films within the genres you work in by their starkly frank and fetishistic depictions of sexual subjugation and peril—which, on one level of reading your films, elevates and distances them somewhat from mere "drama", "horror", etc.

Yes, you're right in thinking that I avoid the label "erotic" when applied to my work because of its association with pornography. I also think that it's a label that oversimplifies my films, and sometimes can create a stigma.

But, based on your comparisons of my films, then yes, we can call them "erotica". Especially if you're comparing my work to D.H. Lawrence, Anaïs Nin, and the Marquis de Sade. Because they're some of my favorite authors, and have influenced my artistic sensibilities a great deal.

BARBAZUL: (**Top**) Amy Hesketh as Jane, at the moment she becomes one of Bluebeard's ex-wives. (**Middle**) Soledad isn't quite sure she's made the best decision in her marriage. (**Above**) Amy and Jac working behind the camera

To me, sexuality is inseparable from higher issues—it underlies many of the decisions we make in our lives, our psychology, the way we behave with others, whether we choose to buy this or that material object, etc. I think that viewpoint is heavily reflected in my work.

It's sad that there's such a stigma attached to such an important category of art, because as you suggested, sexuality is inseparable from life itself—it's a vital part of the human condition (not to mention, pretty important to the propagation of the species), and one of the few truly universally accessible themes for exploration in art. But alas, it seems most people would rather attempt to relate to giant robots or spandex heroes than to face far more relevant issues of sexuality head-on...which is fine, if you're just in it for the escapism.

However, there seems to be more and more hope for the "mature" side of the medium nowadays, and your work seems to be in fairly promising company, with filmmakers such as Catherine Breillat, Gaspar Nöe, Peter Greenaway, Michael Winterbottom, Pedro Almodóvar, Borja Brun and many others pushing not only the boundaries of frank and honest sexuality in film, but by extension the very medium itself. Greenaway has famously observed that film as an art form, if compared to painting, hasn't even reached its relative "cubism stage", even after more than 100 years; we are for the most part still in the infancy stages of the medium, with the majority of films being little more than illustrated novels, almost never daring to use film as a genuine art form in which the observer/viewer can be challenged and motivated to consider higher concepts and ideas than "whodunit" or "will he/she live happily ever after".

Not to point too direct of a light at your creative process, but is this something you're conscious of when writing and directing? Do you actively push yourself to challenge viewers with the medium, and make something more than "just a story about stuff that happens"? Or is it more subconscious for you, something that comes naturally as a byproduct of your particular inspirations, influences and interests?

I actively push viewers with the medium. Something that I often do, for instance, is make a shot or scene go on for "too long". I want my audience to feel uncomfortable, like the scene will never end.

I studied fine arts, so for me cinema really is an art medium. You can't force an audience to look at a painting for so long that the colors bleed together (like one should when viewing a Rothko, for example), but in film, I can force my audience to exceed their comfort level.

Much of that process is done in the editing, but also in the scenes I present, the framing/composition, where I want to force the gaze to go, and for how long.

Part of my process is always, also, subconscious. Sometimes the audience picks up on things after the fact, which is part of my style, which even I am unaware of in the moment.

Your films have a very dreamlike quality to them--often feeling as if they take place in a slightly different, alternate reality, even when they're clearly purporting to occur in "modern day"—but they also have a very "literary" feel to them. Who are some of your biggest influences—in any medium—and how do you feel they inform your work?

Some of that alternate reality/dreamlike quality is created through the limited demonstration of technology. I don't like to show people using more than a rotary phone in my films. **OLALLA** has an exception to the rule, mostly because I wanted to show juxtaposition between the family and the outside world.

My films are very direct representations of how my dreams are structured, how they look in my head when I'm asleep. I try very hard to make them look like what is in my mind's eye when I'm writing the script, imagining them.

I think that everything I've ever read, seen, listened to...all input in the many forms of art have influenced me in some way or another. I don't consciously inform my work with that of others. I think it's easier for someone from the outside to pinpoint influences. The other day I was talking with a friend who sees the 1932 film **FREAKS** in some of my work. Which is interesting, because I was obsessed with that film when I was eight. I must have seen it dozens of times.

I tend to think that any and all artists that we have been exposed to influence our work, like an artistic ancestry. What I have noticed is that my expression is very similar in any medium; the same kind of composition, humor, darkness.

My favorite artists have changed over time, and are too numerable to count, so I'll just give two of each in a few categories…

    Photography: Joel-Peter Witkin, Diane Arbus
    Filmmakers: Luchino Visconti, Pier Paolo Pasolini
    Painters: Cy Twombly, Hieronymus Bosch
    Writers: Anaïs Nin, Ernest Hemingway

I'd love for you to expand a little on what you mean by a "literary" feel.

I'll attempt to clarify what I mean by "literary feel", though it's tough for me to put too distinct a definition on it without sounding pretentious…but here goes: Your films always give me a feeling similar to being drawn into the rich tapestry of a dense novel—particularly of the Victorian or Gothic traditions—thick with atmosphere, deliberately paced, with generally sparse dialogue, wherein characters speak and interact with subsumed levels of interpretation that is more "felt" than delivered straightforward through simple narrative. The conversation between your characters often seems to mask or evade the full intent or emotions behind what is being said (or not said), leaving the viewer to interpret the full meaning from a much wider context. The dialogue generally has the feel of being from a novel rather than casual "real-world" conversation—and that's something I rarely see filmmakers pulling off without it coming across as awkward or stiff…yet in your films it feels like the "right" way for them to speak, and just adds to the overall lushness of the film.

Or maybe I'm just reading too much into your technique, and all of this is just a cumulative result of your intuitive style of storytelling…I don't want to make you too self-conscious about it, because whether intended or subconscious, it really works in the films' favor.

Thank you! You're not reading too much into my technique. I'm conscious of how I intuitively tell a story, and I work with that, build on it.

I'd like to go back to your very beginnings as a filmmaker, if you don't mind. How long had you aspired to write and direct films before you actually found yourself on that path?

I always wanted to make films, since I first understood what they are. Instead of showing me children's films (Disney, etc.) when I was a kid, my father would show me Peckinpah, and Chaplin, and Keaton.

I began writing my first script in 2000. This later turned into my first film, **SIRWIÑAKUY**, which I directed in 2008.

When I started out, digital cinema was new; only a few filmmakers were beginning to work in that medium, Hal Hartley, etc. With the dawn of the digital format, I realized that making a feature film would be so much easier for a first-time filmmaker. When I saw Jac Avila's **MARTYR** in a film festival here in Bolivia, the format, production values, and subject matter made me believe that forming a company with him would be just what I was looking for to start my career.

Could you walk us through what the process was like for you with SIRWIÑAKUY? I'm always interested in how an indie filmmaker gets their first film made. How did the project ultimately come together for you, and what kind of things did you learn as a first-time filmmaker during that process?

It was just after I partnered up with Jac, and I told him about this script I had started writing a few years before. It was set in France. He really liked the idea, so I finished the script and changed the setting to Bolivia, with all of the sociopolitical implications that includes. This turned into my first film, **SIRWIÑAKUY**.

I had seen Veronica Paintoux act with Jac Avila in his film, **MARTYR**. I loved the onscreen tension between those two. We contacted her, and she agreed to act in the film, and flew over from France. Her family's house was the main location. It's a very old house in La Paz, owned by the Bedregal family for generations. In order to shoot in the house, we had to provide lodgings for the family for two weeks, so we contacted the Radisson here, and they sponsored us with two suites for two weeks, plus the suite to shoot the hotel scene for the film. The other locations belonged to friends and Jac's family. An airline company gave us discounts for Veronica's plane ticket.

Olalla's cravings make it a bit difficult to keep a boyfriend for long

I learned a great deal with my first film, working with people I had never worked with before, how to ask for difficult scenes from an actress. I had never met Vero before, and I had to ask her to act in several nude scenes. I wasn't sure if she would understand the character as I saw her. I lucked out with Vero. She's an amazing actress, immediately understands a character, and does not have any false modesty. She also always has wonderful suggestions for art design in the film, wardrobe, small changes in dialogue or character. She's an amazing person all around.

It would be difficult to define everything I learned from that first film. Each film is a learning process. Now that I'm directing my 5th feature, what I've learned through the entire process is not to wear too many hats. You end up burning out very fast. Interns are awesome!

On the release of **SIRWIÑAKUY**: When I released the film in theaters here in Bolivia, I anticipated a bit of press, and two weeks maximum run. What I got was five months in theaters, a major slam from critics accusing me of everything from promoting domestic violence to inhabiting the 10th circle of hell, and a huge amount of press. It was overwhelming. From that, many more actors and crew contacted me, wanting to work with me on my next project. It was essentially how I found all of the ladies for **BARBAZUL**.

I could see it arising more commonly if your films were directed by a male, but do you ever get accusations of misogyny leveled at you for the more extreme sexual content? And overall, how much does criticism—positive or negative—affect you personally?

Apparently, being accused of misogyny is not something exclusive to men. I received it more with my first film, **SIRWIÑAKUY**. I was accused by critics, in Bolivia of, respectively, "living in the last circle of hell", "promoting domestic violence", and misogyny. One critic also accused me of being a front for Jac. That a woman could not possibly have directed a film like that. Utterly ridiculous.

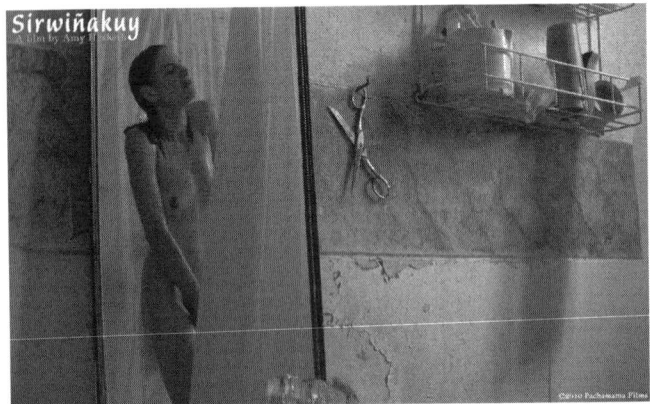

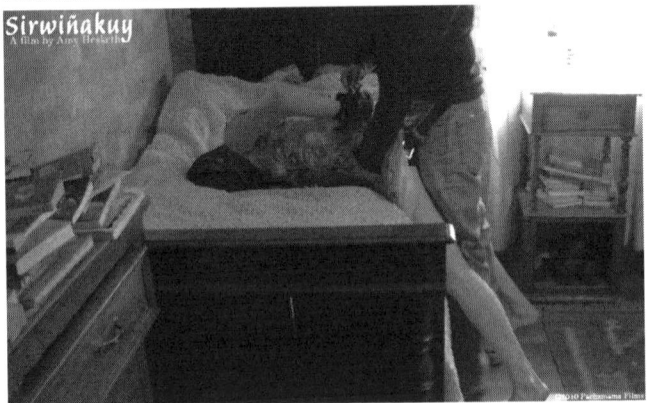

SIRWIÑAKUY: (Top) Anouk is surprised to find herself aroused by the "punishment" she's received. **(Middle)** Getting acquainted over a meal. **(Above)** Luis shows his peculiar brand of disciplinary affection

The criticism from **SIRWIÑAKUY** affected me much more; I was a "virgin", so to speak, and didn't know how to handle it. I later received a bevy of wonderful criticism from the USA and Europe for that film, as well as my later ones.

Now, I realize that criticism has its place. They're opinions, and I mostly benefit more from the way my films and their subjects can make new friends, bring about a discussion, and/or unite my fans and I.

Do you find there's a significant divide between those who "get" your films and those who don't? And do you feel that audience and critical perception of you as an artist evolves in any noticeable way as your body of work increases?

All of my films have had a polemic reception for some reason. Audience members either love or hate them. For those who follow my work, critics and audiences, they tend to have an increasingly positive perception of my growth as an artist.

I feel that my films have connected me more with people. Those who love my films understand the incredibly emotional subtext and issues I put into my work.

Speaking of divisions, do you find it difficult to promote or advertise your work with regards to the subject matter? I mean, your work tends toward the serious and melodramatic, but the overt sexuality must be considered in terms of promotion, to both draw in the right audience as well as "warn away" the prudish who might be put off by the material. It seems that would be a tough tightrope walk sometimes...owning the proudly frank (and sometimes wickedly playful) sexuality while at the same time avoiding the implication that you're advertising an exploitative softcore film.

"Tightrope" is the appropriate word. Some of my audience is drawn only to the naughty bits of my films, while others are drawn to them for more intellectual reasons, and others for a combination of the two.

So we tend to advertise in varied social networks, forums, magazines, and whatnot, approaching each audience with a slightly different slant.

One of the great things that has happened over the years is that people who love our films advertise for us on their own sites, the forums they frequent, 'blogs, etc. When you're a tiny production company like ours, this is one of the greatest gifts you can hope to receive.

An advantage we have is that we're making truly independent and personal cinema, *cine d'autor*, and our subject matter is unique; those who long for a resurgence of films that they loved from the '60s and '70s often find us because we're like a post-modern resurgence of that kind of cinema.

Is this one of your motivating reasons for choosing to go the route of self-distribution through your own company, in lieu of trying to find distributors to release your work? What do you feel are some of the major pros and cons of self-releasing vs. finding a distribution house?

I guess I just never took the usual route of finding a distributor. That might come later, but it doesn't have much to do with the content. A distributor could go any number of ways in marketing my films.

I suppose one of the reasons I can scrape out a living (most of the time) from making films is because I self-distribute. A distributor would have to make me a good offer for me to want to go with them.

With self-distribution, if you have a good film, the more effort you put into promoting the film, the more you can make, and not just potentially, but immediately.

The new reality of distribution for small indie companies is that it's no longer absolutely necessary to have a third party between a film and its audience.

You and Jac seem very fortunate to have found in each other a rather like-minded, symbiotic partnership with Pachamama Films, wherein you can each offer your own talents to each other's projects. What is the collaboration process like for the two of you? Do you have much influence/interaction with each other during the development process of each film, or do you each kind of work on your own ideas until a new script is ready? How do you decide whose idea is the next to move forward?

Jac has his process, and I have mine. We bounce ideas off of each other on a daily basis. There's a lot of work that's done separately, and then we talk about an issue/snag/block with the development as it arrives.

Generally we naturally come to a decision about what film to make next. If a script is ready, and we have resources, and everything is coming together, we make that one.

I think that our collective enthusiasm—and not just Jac and I, but our whole crew—keeps us moving forward. We're all artists, and we work collectively, so that is one of the major driving forces of our work.

So, you're currently hard at work on your next feature, PYGMALION. What can you tell us about it to get us all eagerly champing at the bit with anticipation?

We're now in post-production on **PYGMALION**. It's a film, within a film, within a film—a movie about a film crew making an adaptation of George Bernard Shaw's *Pygmalion*. It's written by Jac Avila, and directed by yours truly. A first for both of us; we normal write and direct our own films.

It has two parallel stories of *Pygmalion*: a film director training his new actress, who is playing Eliza Doolittle, and both the actress and her character have the same arc.

I was very rigorous with shooting this film. I did as many takes as I needed to get it right—I made 107 takes in Scene 51, as an example. I think it was a bit of a torture to make this film; we had a tight shooting schedule, and I demanded a lot more from everyone than I normally do.

This is my first true comedy, but it also has a sadomasochistic theme, which is implied in the play; I just bring it to the fore.

That sounds like a really interesting take—can't wait to see it! Speaking of which, I should probably let you get back to work—you know, so I can see it sooner…I am nothing if not selfless and altruistic. We here at **Weng's Chop** *really appreciate you taking time out, Amy, and we hope that you'll come back and chat with us again once PYGMALION is released!*

Thank *YOU*, Tony, for one of the greatest, in-depth interviews I could ever hope to have! I'm overwhelmed by your insight into my films. You can count on me to come back and dish about **PYGMALION**…and **JUSTINE** (for which we are just about to begin production)!

3 – The Art

SIRWIÑAKUY

Amy Hesketh's debut feature is a bold, challenging film right out of the gate, presenting us with the story of a chance meeting that escalates into an unusually intense relationship, and a sexual battle of wills. One sunny day in a café in La Paz, a middle-aged Bolivian man (Jac Avila) spots a beautiful young French woman (Veronica Paintoux) and approaches her, wasting no time in very matter-of-factly asking if she wants to leave with him. Surprising herself as much as we viewers, she obliges, and allows this stranger to take hold of her wrist and lead her away into a strange—and kinky—new world.

He takes her home with him, and immediately begins nitpicking her behavior, telling her not to talk with her mouth full ("it's disgusting"), then after dinner ordering her upstairs to brush her teeth, use the bathroom, then wait for him in bed. When he comes into the bedroom, he doesn't try to fuck her, just bids her goodnight.

The next morning over breakfast, they introduce themselves. She's a translator named Anouk, and he's a media consultant named Luis…who could use a translator—*quelle coincidence!* He hires her, and things go well, until she comes home late for dinner that evening…after he had *specifically* told her *not to be late for dinner*. He explains that she must be punished, and asks her how her parents used to punish her when she was little. She tells him with spankings…so he bends her over, pulls down her pants and spanks her.

Again surprising herself, she goes along with it, and finds she even might actually sort of like this disciplinary form of affection; Anouk is at a stage in her life where she feels it's time to stop bouncing around and actually start trying to figure out who she really is…perhaps this is why she's allowing herself to even consider this strange sexual behavior at all, let alone allow herself to enjoy it. But as Luis' affections grow increasingly more intense and painful, and his expectations of her submission rise, Anouk's rebellious nature comes bubbling up to the surface. Is this what she really wants, or has she gotten herself entangled in a situation she vastly underestimated with a man she hardly knows? And how far is she willing to go before she reaches her breaking point?

It's depressing that in this day and age, **SIRWIÑAKUY** (2010), by the very nature of its kinky content, will inevitably and unfairly be compared by some to that Fifty-Shady nonsense that has ubiquitously and malodorously infected the entertainment arena of late…it's really sad, but you know it will. Though really, that would be much akin to comparing *Dracula* with *Twilight*, so if that's the sort of person you are, I'm very sorry you purchased this magazine by mistake. Now please leave so we can all make fun of you.

Really, what we get here is more of an intense and kinky love story, somewhat in the spirit of **TIE ME UP! TIE ME DOWN!** (1989) and **SECRETARY** (2002)—though decidedly more serious in tone, quieter in its approach, and voyeuristic in its delivery—filtered through a Jess Franco vision of **LAST TANGO IN PARIS** (1972). Challenging in its frankness, the film is deliberately paced, often using its sometimes leisurely tempo and textural sensuality (this is an extremely tactile film, portrayed with such an intimate atmosphere and immersion of environment that you can practically feel, smell and taste what you're watching) to draw you gradually into situations of extreme intensity before you've even realized it.

In the opening of the film, we learn that a *Sirwiñakuy* is an old tradition in which a man "takes" a woman he desires, brings her home, and the two attempt to determine if they are compatible for marriage. This process, it is said, can last weeks or even years. Hesketh's vision displays that concept perfectly, albeit refracted through a somewhat sadomasochistic filter (although the *Sirwiñakuy* can be viewed as a master/servant act by its very nature), in an impressively relatable demonstration—when you first learn what a *Sirwiñakuy* is, you scoff at such an outlandish proposition, but when you see it played out before you in Hesketh's film, it seems far less preposterous and shocking. In fact, what may surprise you most about this film is how *frightfully romantic* it all is (provided, of course, that you are not put off by the depicted lifestyle of

Luis leads Anouk away to attempt their own kinky version of a *Sirwiñakuy*

the characters)…I honestly was taken aback by how charmingly sentimental and heartfelt the overall tone of the film was when all was said and done. This is an outstanding and complex debut that should not be missed.

2010, BOLIVIA. D: AMY HESKETH
AVAILABLE FROM VERMEERWORKS

BARBAZUL
(a.k.a. BLUEBEARD)

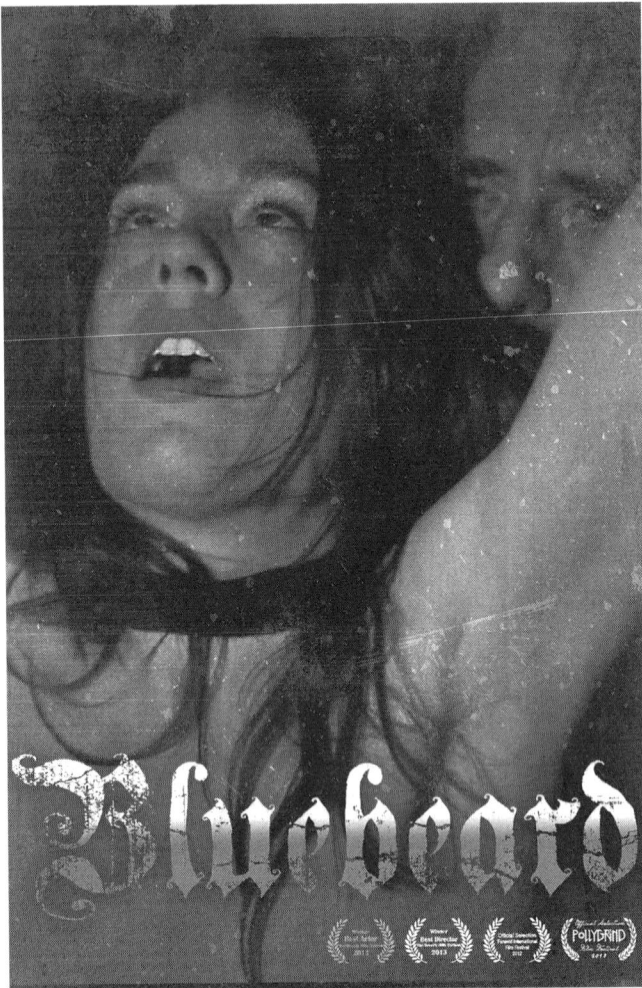

NOTE: I've reprinted this review from WC#5 in its entirety rather than writing a new review and re-working my original thoughts, as I felt this best conveys my initial reaction to seeing my first Amy Hesketh film.

Employed as an expendable, verbally abused, up-and-coming fashion model in order to provide for herself and her younger sister (Mariela Salaverry) who is in her charge, Soledad (Mila Joya) one day meets the client of a shoot she's working on, a mysterious and wealthy man (Jac Avila) who shows her kindness and respect that she hasn't encountered before. His charm quickly wins her over as he begins to court her, and when he asks for her hand, she eagerly accepts, with his assurance that both she and her sister will be well provided for (though her sister scoffs at the whole affair, believing Soledad is letting herself be bought). He takes Soledad to his beautiful countryside villa to live, giving her free reign of the place and a master set of keys to unlock every door. But he warns her to never use one particular key to his private study, assuring her that there is nothing for her in there, and to honor the trust he is putting in her. But the moment he is away on business, she lets her curiosity get the better of her and enters the forbidden room, where she finds a journal detailing the stories of all the women who have come before her, and the horrible manners in which they all died. She can't help but think that she is to share a similar fate.

Have you ever wondered what would happen if Mario Bava, Jean Rollin and Jess Franco had somehow defied the laws of nature and biology and produced a lovechild who became a filmmaker? Yeah, me too! Well, now we have our answer in the form of writer/director Amy Hesketh. With the exception of its being shot on HD video, everything about this film has the look and feel of much of the '70s output of the aforementioned three filmmakers—from the direction to the editing to the music to the production design. This erotic reimagining of the *Bluebeard* legend is like a sexy little time machine that gloriously transports your spirit back to the Euro-horror glory of days past, and manages to effectively one-up all the other adaptations of a popular legend in the process. Here we have a Bluebeard that is less of a monster than he is a tortured soul haunted by a compulsion he cannot control, giving him a sympathetic dimension rarely associated with the character, allowing the film to achieve a deeper-level examination of emotional and sexual interrelation, social manipulation, and even addiction. More films from Amy Hesketh, please!

ADDITIONAL THOUGHTS: With this film, Hesketh displays an adaptive interest that continues as a theme throughout her work from this point forward, drawing on well-known historical/literary sources and references to create something new, and completely her own. Her interests in both literature and classic Euro genre films come to the forefront with **BARBAZUL**, which, though it deviates greatly from the traditional *Bluebeard* folk tale in many ways, could be considered her most direct adaptation of a source material. Her next two films, while both drawn directly from literary sources (the Marquis de Sade and Robert Louis Stevenson, respectively), would use their source material more as mere launching-off points for completely original stories, using those authors' worlds as sand-boxes in which to play, rather than taking a directly adaptive approach *per se*, and would show the development of a storytelling style (dare we call it "Heskethian"?) that is, by nature of her interests and obsessions, truly unique in genre film, and well deserving of being viewed within the parameters of the auteur theory, despite the obvious collaborative effort that begat them. Though there may be some minor faltering moments here and there along the way, each film forms a clear stepping stone in the path to a distinct filmmaking voice truly worthy of attention.

2012, BOLIVIA. D: AMY HESKETH
AVAILABLE FROM VERMEERWORKS

(**Middle**) The suave and sophisticated Bluebeard woos Soledad.
(**Above**) Doin' the dangerous dirty

LE MARQUIS DE LA CROIX

A tourist (Amy Hesketh) traveling in Bolivia hunts down a museum of torture she read about in her guidebook, a museum that was once a dungeon cell where the legendary Marquis de la Croix, a notorious aristocratic sexual deviant, was allegedly held prisoner. As the tour guide explains the history of the place, the tourist watches a playful couple toying flirtatiously with the instruments of torture, and we flash back to the days of the Marquis' residence in this cell...

A beautiful young gypsy woman named Zynga (Mila Joya) who's been arrested and condemned to death, has consented, in lieu of facing the guillotine, to be sold to the imprisoned Marquis (Jac Avila) as a plaything. The Marquis has been incarcerated as a deviant, but due to his social status and wealth is permitted some approximation of the life he lived on the outside. The guards put a nice dress on Zynga and deliver her to the Marquis' comfortable cell, replete with a writing desk, wine and other creature comforts...as well as various shackles, whips and medieval torture devices.

The Marquis at first seems like he might be a charming, erudite, gentlemanly aristocrat—he knows she's starving, so he offers her an apple. But as she comes close to accept the gift, he roughly grabs her and forces her to fellate him, and afterward crams the apple in her mouth to further the humiliation. He then continues to reveal his deviant cruelty to her and upon her in measures of domination and pain, focusing the entirety of his attentions on her subjugations for his pleasure. Ever taunting and implying mercy might be granted if she only endures certain humiliations (but never really promising such), poor Zynga submits to his cruel demands in hopes of at some point earning her freedom. He chains her up and flogs her...and flogs her...and flogs her. He occasionally breaks up the flogging with some stretching out on the rack or perhaps some different flogging, always administering his humiliation and torture with an unnerving air of loving yet disdainful respect for his new possession.

If Zynga can just endure this humiliation, rape and torture awhile, the Marquis will surely tire of his new toy, and she'll avoid the terrible fate sentenced to her. But which sentence is actually worse?

I'll admit that upon first viewing, I didn't think much of this film. Despite the great location and often beautiful photography, it didn't connect with me. Sure, it was sexy and intense at times, but I initially saw it as being too repetitive and lacking in character development, and more of a catalogue of sexual humiliation and torture than an actual story.

But upon rewatching the film in preparation for this review, I had a rather different reaction to it...perhaps due to better understanding the intent of the film itself with repeat viewing. I had initially expected more story and character due to my previous experiences with Hesketh's first two films, which were generous on both accounts, however, this film—socio-historical commentary aside—isn't interested in the complexities of story and character, but rather in the focus of the relationship between predator and prey, and the cruel mindgames of a perilous relationship. In a way it could be seen as the malicious evil twin of Hesketh's debut feature, **SIRWIÑAKUY** (2010), depicting a relationship that is caustic rather than connective. In both films the male pushes the female to see how far she can handle it, but whereas **SIRWIÑAKUY**'s Luis pushes and punishes Anouk out of kinky-but-genuine affection, in the present film the Marquis is out to push Zynga to her physical, emotional and psychological breaking point; he respects her as a plaything, but not as a person. However, he is extremely interested in examining and exploiting her own humanity, to see how much her blind hope will lead her to submit to his dark desires in the face of bold-faced betrayal and pain. The film is indeed repetitious, but that's part of the point—how much repeated punishment will Zynga endure before she recognizes the Marquis' game?

Although clearly and deliberately inspired by the works of the Marquis de Sade, perhaps it will better prepare the viewer going into this film for the first time if it is approached as an homage to the Marquis rather than any kind of biography or direct adaptation. Sure, there are definitely elements within the film from both his life and his work, but this is more of a "what if" fantasy than any attempt to coalesce his life or work into a definitive context. It serves more as a speculation upon a possible fantasy or desire the imprisoned Marquis might have entertained or even wrote during his incarceration, intended to capture the "spirit" of the man and his work more than anything. And at this, it succeeds tremendously. Though it may be lighter in story and character development than her other works, it could be argued that this is the most challenging and complex of her films, rewarding those viewers willing to dig beneath its deceptively simple surface.

2012, BOLIVIA. D: AMY HESKETH
AVAILABLE FROM VERMEERWORKS

(Middle) The tourist seeks out an off-the-beaten-path attraction.
(Above) The Marquis taunts his beautiful new plaything

OLALLA

Robert Louis Stephenson's short story *Olalla*, first published in 1885, told the story of an English soldier who, upon the recommendation of his doctor, goes to stay with a local family to recover from his wounds sustained in the Peninsular War (1807-1814) in Spain. There he falls in love with the once-noble family's beautiful daughter, Olalla, who despite or because of her love for him, warns him to flee from her and her family. Of course he ignores this warning, until, one night, he accidentally cuts his wrist, and Olalla's mother, upon seeing the blood, attacks him and bites his arm! Olalla's brother Filipe pulls his mother off of the soldier, who promptly decides that leaving isn't such a bad idea after all.

Less of an adaptation than a continuation of the story and its implied mythology, Amy Hesketh's film opens in modern times with Olalla's daughter—also named Olalla (Hesketh)—watching Murnau's **NOSFERATU** (1922) on TV with her boyfriend. She becomes aroused by the famous knife-cut-at-dinner scene, and the couple starts to make out…but arousal soon turns to insatiable hunger, and Olalla suddenly and savagely bites into his jugular, sating on his blood as his life leaves him. Suddenly coming to her senses and realizing with horror what she's done, she calls her family for help.

Olalla's reclusive, weirdo family (merely calling them eccentric would be stressing the term well beyond its means) is furious with her, and her spiteful sister Ofelia (Mila Joya) sends for Uncle Filipe (Jac Avila) to come help deal with Olalla's behavioral problems before she exposes the family's bloodthirsty secret to the world. Filipe's methods of discipline consist of sexual domination and humiliation—which is no great shakes to this obviously long-incestuous family—and he immediately goes to work on…ahem, whipping the dangerously compulsive Olalla into submission.

In the meantime, a handsome young photojournalist named Nathan (Luis Almanza) has been recommended by his doctor to stay with the strange family to recover from his PTSD sustained while on assignment as a combat photographer. Naturally, he becomes immediately smitten by the beautiful and mysterious Olalla, and begins to become uncomfortably curious about the kooky family's bizarre behavior, nosing around where his attention is far from desired. Will Uncle Filipe and Ofelia succeed in keeping the family's secrets safe from nosy houseguests while getting Olalla's impulses under control, or will Olalla have to be killed, as Ofelia seems to want? More importantly, who are these doctors who keep sending their troubled patients to recover in the home of the most hated and feared family around? Is there no respect for the Hippocratic Oath anymore?!

Hesketh's fourth feature is her most accomplished work to date, directed with a kinetic, stylish confidence that is a clear culmination of the progress of her first three outings, and is just an all-around terrific genre film. Alternating back and forth between the modern story and flashbacks to Olalla's childhood over 100 years before—a parallel plotline that is a more direct continuation of Stevenson's tale, wherein another doctor-sent lodger (*Seriously, Doc?!*) is endangered by his infatuation with the first Olalla (also played by Hesketh), despite warnings from both his priest and the locals—we begin to puzzle together the dark history of this eternally damned, vampiric family, piece by piece, and slowly discover the horrific depths of their centuries-old secret. The characters are bizarre and fascinating, and the story peels away in layers that are each more intriguing than the last; you're pulled into this strange and secretive family's world as you watch like a terrified voyeur in fear of discovery, sometimes aroused, sometimes repelled, but always unable to look away. Hesketh plays Olalla's incarnations with a repressed, smoldering sexual intensity mixed with a fearful innocence that is powerfully alluring, and makes it easy to believe the hold she has on the men who become infatuated with her, and Mila Joya's Ofelia just sizzles off the screen with her cat-like smile and wickedly cruel sensuality…not to be overly pedantic, but: *hubba-hubba!* Jac Avila gives an unnerving presence to the dominating Uncle Filipe (as does Alejandro Loayza as the young Filipe in the flashback scenes), and you'll swear the room gets a couple degrees colder whenever he's onscreen.

Toward the end of the film there is a scene in which Olalla's family puts on a record and dances around the room together with an inappropriately joyful abandon that must, given their circumstances at the moment it occurs, be more than a little forced, emotionally speaking; it is a moment which brilliantly balances the surreally comic and horrific, and serves as a perfect emotional microcosm of the entire film…you're touched by the humanity of these strange people, but unnerved by the way they pursue it. Such is the fate of both Olallas each in their own time—they desperately want to live as normal people do, but are so far from normal that they are incapable of it, not really having the slightest clue of how to go about their desired normalcy even if the opportunity arises. As much as we feel for these passionate women who desire to live and love in ways their tragic stations in life cannot allow, we come to understand that the controlling, dominating family may be the ones who understand the situation far better, and are in fact making the wisest decisions for the survival of the family. That doesn't stop us from hoping that Olalla will find a way to break free of her familial bonds and find a way to love and be loved without endangering everyone close to her.

Though it is a continuation of a literary source, the film stands perfectly well on its own—indeed, its mysterious mythology and atmosphere are arguably enhanced by seeing the film before reading the short story (as I did)—and is in this reviewer's opinion Hesketh's best film thus far. This one comes with the highest of recommendations for the lovers of the sexy, the creepy and the bizarre…pretty much everyone who reads this publication.

2014, BOLIVIA. D: AMY HESKETH
AVAILABLE FROM VERMEERWORKS

All of Amy Hesketh's films can be purchased at *vermeerworks.com*, and you can keep up with her ongoing adventures at *amyhesketh.blogspot.com*, as well as check in on the dynamic duo of Amy & Jac at *pachamamafilms.com*!

All photos courtesy of Vermeerworks/Pachamama Films.

Pachamama Films

"Pull-no-punches art undared by ordinary filmmakers... they crawled under my movie radar and jumped me from the inside."

—C. Dean Andersson (author of Torture Tomb)

VERMEERWORKS.COM

TELLURIDE HORROR SHOW

OCT 16-18 2015

3-DAY HORROR FILM FESTIVAL

Elev. 8,750

Named one of the "20 Coolest Film Fests" by Movie Maker Magazine

3-DAY PASSES ONLY $94
FILMMAKERS: SUBMIT YOUR FILM BY SEPTEMBER 20TH
ROOMS STARTING AT $92/NIGHT

WWW.TELLURIDEHORRORSHOW.COM

JAPANESE PINK FILMS:
THE JAPANESE WIFE NEXT DOOR!

by Louis Paul

Pink Eiga is an American-based indie DVD company that has released a number of Japanese pink films to disc and to online streaming. I have selected two of what I consider their showcase titles for review: **THE JAPANESE WIFE NEXT DOOR** *(*Inran naru ichizoku: Dai-ni-shô - zetsurin no hate ni*, 2004) and its follow-up,* **THE JAPANESE WIFE NEXT DOOR: PART 2** *(*Inran naru ichizoku: Dai-isshô - chijin-tachi no tawamure*, 2004).*

First, I wanted to offer a primer on what exactly "pink" movies are, and how they figure into the world of offbeat genre cinema.

Pink films, or pinku eiga*...or pink* eiga*, are common terms applied to Japanese movies that feature quite a bit of sex or sexual situations. Far from most R-rated softcore movies, the carnal activities on view featured in pink movies runs the gamut from steamy simulated sexual situations to full-on hardcore, but the latter is nearly always censored with the close-ups (and medium shots) of sexual activity obscured by in-camera soft filters, or digitally pixelated squares (usually done in post-production) and such that are supposed to obscure the X-rated scenes before our eyes...but sometimes, filmmakers do a poor job of this and its quite clear what is going on. Pink films run the gamut from comedies to thrillers, full-on exploitation to costumed female ninja adventure movies. Not all are successful in their entertainment value, and very few of them manage to titillate. Those that do, and manage to transcend their paltry budgets, manage to find their way to my collection.*

Most of the pink films were produced by a variety of small independent studios, the most well-known of them are Nikkatsu (their "Roman Porno" series), Toei ("Pinky Violence"), and Shochiku (who distributed movies produced by their sub-production company, Tokatsu).

The heyday for pink movies lasted quite long. The bastard step-children of Japanese genre cinema, many popular titles were produced during the genre's heyday which lasted from the mid-1960s through the mid-1980s. Some of the movies produced during the latter period are well-known worldwide for their sadism and bondage ingredients (and amassed quite a cult following, especially among genre enthusiasts who were burned out during the waning days of European thrillers and *giallos*). The *Angel Guts* (*Tenshi no Harawata*) series (nine films produced by Nikkatsu; Japan, 1978-1994), **WATCHER IN THE ATTIC** (*Edogawa Ranpo ryôki-kan: Yaneura no sanposha*, 1976 [Nikkatsu]), **SCHOOL OF THE HOLY BEAST** (*Seijû gakuen*, 1974 [Toei]), **WIFE TO BE SACRIFICED** (*Ikenie fujin*, 1974 [Nikkatsu]), and **ENTRAILS OF A VIRGIN** (*Shojo no harawata*, 1986 [Nikkatsu]) are just some of the more notorious pink film titles with a sadistic bent.

Almost all of the pink movies were filmed exclusively on 35mm film, but due to a waning interest in the genre, some titles were shot on digital video. However, in my opinion, most of the titles I have seen in this format pale in comparison to the filmed ones.

The two titles I am writing about here were produced by Shin-Toho and were directed by Yutaka Ikejima (known for such titles as **S&M HUNTER** (*Kinbaku - SM*, 1986 [Shin-Toho]) and the bizarrely-titled **SEXUAL DESIRES IN THE LADIES RESTROOM: DRIPPING!** (*Shikijô joshibenjo: Shitataru!*, 1995 [XCes]).

THE JAPANESE WIFE NEXT DOOR
(*Inran naru ichizoku: Dai-ni-shô - zetsurin no hate ni*)
2004, Japan. D: Yutaju Ikejima
S: Naohiro Hirakata, Reiko Yamaguchi, Akane Yazaki, Koji Makimura, Kaoru Akitsu

This movie begins with voiceover narration from Takashi (Hirakata), a young, seemingly nebbish, spectacled businessman who is attending a company party in a restaurant. Having recently ended a relationship, Takashi appears reluctant and perhaps hesitant to enter into another one. As the drinks flow and female companions Sakura (Yamaguchi) and Ryoko (Yazaki) become loose with their conversation, Takashi has an inner monologue about which woman he might prefer to be his lover. Glasses-wearing Ryoko seems to like him (she's the

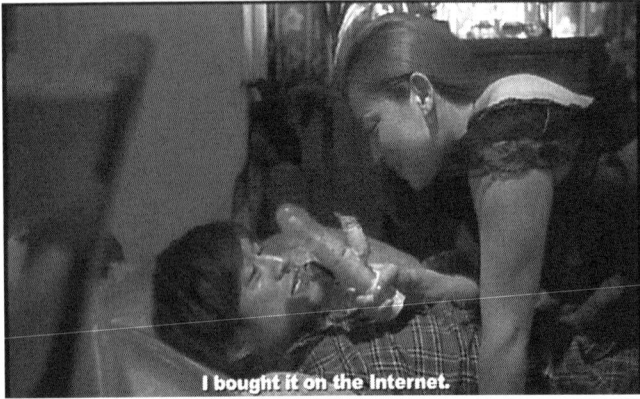

Top to bottom: Reiko Yamaguchi entices hubby, enjoys the rest of the family, and takes a well-deserved break in these hot scenes from **THE JAPANESE WIFE NEXT DOOR**.

daughter of the company president) but Takashi thinks she may be a little more proper, and perhaps it might be dangerous to entertain any more thoughts of her. Sakura asks Takashi to accompany her to the bathroom because she's too drunk to go on her own. At first Takashi debates this—and Ryoko tries to interfere, sensing something is going to happen—but he goes along. Experiencing a first-class enthusiastic blow job, we then find ourselves in Takashi's apartment where he and Sakura go at it for a lengthy, world-class, all-positions imaginable fuck session. Sakura is obviously a nymphomaniac, but Takashi appears to enjoy the attention…and the sex.

Six months later and Takashi and Sakura have married. What happened to Takashi's bachelor apartment is anyone's guess, but for some reason, he states that the couple has to move in with his parents and relatives. Sakura does not seem to have a problem with this, and at first the family appears to be reluctant to welcome the new family member. Takashi's father (Kikujiro Honda) is a businessman who is often off to work, grabbing a quick bite prepared by the often scantily clad, pointy-nipples baring daughter-in-law of his. He also does not appear to notice her attempts at seduction much. Takashi's grandfather (Koji Makimura, wearing aging make-up to make him appear much older than Honda) seems to be an aged but still sharp man who suffers from some sort of illness, or possibly senility. He nearly always seems to inhabit a small corner of the family's living room in their duplex apartment. Granddad is attended to by Takashi's sister Yayoi (Akitsu), a spectacled librarian who has come out of a bad marriage and returned, like Takashi, to the family home. Yayoi seems bitter and a bit spinster-ish, a real hard-ass to poor Sakura, who always wears a bright smile, while donning the shortest dresses and nighties while attending to chores and cooking.

At night, Takashi and Sakura's sex sessions rock the house as she loudly orgasms and say's things like "Fuck me in the ass hard hubby". The men smile, and go about their routine life, but sister Yayoi seems to suffer greatly, debating how she can make life horrible for the newcomer.

Oddly enough, Takashi begins to drift away from his sexual firecracker of a wife Sakura (only in the movies, folks!), her wild untamed libido proving to become an annoyance to him. He even begins to spend late nights at work, and takes a secret apartment in the city near his job…just so he doesn't have to go home.

What is poor Sakura to do with her insatiable libido? Why, she seduces every member of the family, of course. Mere masturbation does not work for her, so it's a lovely meal for grandfather, followed by a hand job, blowjob, then a royal fuck. Sister-in-law Yayoi fares better with a hot lesbian seduction then a really torrid fuck session featuring dildos. While he's away pouting about his highly-sexed wife and wondering why he's no longer attracted to her, who does Takashi run into but the seemingly staid Ryoko from the movie's beginning. After a brief conversation the two of them retreat to Takashi's apartment for a no-holds-barred round of sex. Of course, Sakura is happy as a kitten with her new family, as they all enjoy each other's newly acquired swinger's paradise, and when Takashi returns home, well…he has decisions to make.

If you've not already figured it out yet, this is a warped sex comedy, comparable to nothing else I've seen in the pink genre. Naohiro Hirakata makes a fine handsome leading man with a touch of bewilderment (and later, guilt). Reiko Yamaguchi as Sakura literally burns up the screen with a performance that can be charitably called "electric". A sex film actress (she has scores of credits in Japanese hardcore films, both censored and uncensored…and yes, if you want to see more of her, just search the Internet), she really shines in the comedic moments, and reveals a natural talent for exhibitionism and hedonism. Akane Yuzaki in the minor role of Ryoko, Sakora's rival for the affections of Takashi, disappears after the movie's beginning but returns near the end to finally end up in a carnal adventure with Takashi. Attractive, but not as exhibitionistic about her sexuality, the actress appears to have few credits besides this film (and its immediate sequel), unless of course she changed her name and performed elsewhere under a pseudonym. The real find here is Kaoru Akitsu as Yayoi, Takashi's sister, who challenges Reiko's firecracker performance with one that begins first as a bit nerdy, perhaps a repressed bookworm type, who becomes an unleashed dynamo in first lesbian trysts, and then in imaginative couplings with the other family members.

If you were wondering just how hardcore the sex in the film is, despite obvious soft filter camera tricks, and the occasional fogging, all the activity onscreen is obvious full-on hardcore taking place.

Pink Eiga's DVD features a fine representation of the film, where all the colors appear natural and the flesh-tones (something which is important in a movie like this) are naturalistic. The English subtitles (the disc's audio is in Japanese only) seems accurate, without too many ridiculous typos. Extras include a 14-minute interview with Reiko Yamaguchi, who discusses the differences between working in pink movies and full-on pornographic fare. And oh yes, she profoundly reveals her love of cock…no joke. She mentions it quite a few times. This interview is subtitled, so reading this stuff as it's spoken is…well, humorous.

Mr. Pink Exposed: What Happened Next Door is a 15-minute interview with director Yutaju Ikejima. Shot inside the Shin-Toho vaults (reels of film in canisters can be seen stacked in the room). It is a brief but revealing conversation—or rather, a monologue—about working in the pink film industry. He reveals a lot about the Japanese attitudes towards censorship in sex films and how he goes about filming them. Oddly enough, Ikejima believes that his sex scenes show less with his camera eye than what we know we are actually viewing. It all seems to be smoke and mirrors concerning the very weird and tricky ideology of being a filmmaker working in the sex business in a country where actual penetration onscreen is frowned upon for the most part.

Personally, I find this all rather bizarre, as Japan is among the forefathers for sexual expression. Sexually explicit imagery is contained in literature, graphic textural prints, paintings and wood block screenings from centuries before the Iron Age. As time went on there would be numerous other categories of sexual expression, most emanating from Japan. Whilst softcore pornography thrived in illustrated magazines in the U.S. in the 1960s and 1970s, Japan was experimenting with more graphic variations. Pornographic *manga* (Japanese comics), computer games, and even animated films (called *hentai*) appear to be quite common, with the *manga* and *hentai* even garnering fans worldwide, with women among the audience.

There is a Japanese law that any lawfully-produced pornography must censor the genitals of both actors and actresses (there were a few notable exceptions, like art movies). Forbidden until the mid-1990s was the depiction of pubic hair and vaginal sex for the women. Anal sex, for some reason, was only censored at the point of contact or penetration with a penis; hence, the birth of the popular series of titles featuring girl-girl action with strap-ons and dildos. Since it was not a male member penetrating, anything could be shown. As the Japanese laws surrounding censorship began to relax, it was ok to show *bukkake* (cum on face, or facial gangbangs), and even tentacle erotica (something that grew out of the most perverse *hentai*)…usually rubbery special FX house-created tentacles of a monster penetrating some nubile maiden. But for the pink films and those filmmakers experimenting with stories set inside a sexual milieu, they were stymied by not being able to show everything…so they had to get around that in challenging ways.

THE JAPANESE WIFE NEXT DOOR: PART 2

(*Inran naru ichizoku: Dai-isshô - chijin-tachi no tawamure*)
2004, Japan. D: Yutaju Ikejima
S: Naohiro Hirakata, Akane Yazaki, Reiko Yamaguchi, Azuska Sakai, Koji Makimura, Kaoru Akitsu

Most of the cast from the previous film return in this delirious and harder-edged *Twilight Zone*-style "what if" follow-up. **PART 2** begins with events that mirror those of the first movie. There's the company dinner where Takashi (Hirakata) meets both Sakura (Yamaguchi) and Ryoko (Yazaki), but this time events change, as Takashi does not end up leaving with Sakura but with Ryoko, who turns out to be pretty much a demon in bed who delivers a bit of deliciously energetic fellatio herself. Although not as hot sexually or a looker like Yamaguchi, Yazaki does reveal a certain edge about her in a portrayal that can be called simmering, perverted sensuality. Takashi and Ryoko get married (much like Takashi and Sakura did in the previous film) and this time they move in with her wealthy, perverted family who live on a large estate. Even his mother is invited to move in. But oddly enough, both he and his mother are encouraged to purchase the company's questionable life insurance policy.

Happy to be frolicking and fucking all over a large estate, Takashi's bliss is brief, as he learns his mom died in an accident, but the beneficiaries of the insurance policy are a bit hazy, as it looks like the monies go to the company. As time goes on, we learn that Ryoko's parents are a perverted pair, and that her father is involved with gangsters who do his bidding. Also, Ryoko has a sister, Mina (Lemon Hanazawa), who appears to be mentally unstable, and possibly a victim of incest.

Takashi keeps running into Mina by the palatial pool outside of the house, the girl usually clutching a stuffed animal. At one point she attempts an awkward seduction and masturbates in front of him, but Takashi (much like the viewing audience) appears to be puzzled…whether he should be sexually excited, or repelled.

Far removed from the sexually explosive antics of the story and the performance delivered by Reiko Yamaguchi in the first film, **PART 2** is a different beast entirely. Ryoko's parents use the life insurance monies they scam by murdering policy owners to fund their own criminal empire and drug-running. Tokunaga (Kikijiro Honda) is the family's sadistic drug mule who has a wild three-way with Ryoko and her mother. Probably the film's best sex scene then goes into a hyper-realistic S&M mode, and we find that Tokunaga has been carrying the drugs in plastic bags hidden in his body, which he releases from his bowels.

Transposing events from the finale of the first movie, a now-depressed Takashi meets Sakura in a park, and they have amazing torrid sex (it's a relief to see

Middle: Akane Yazaki, who portrayed the demure "other woman" in the first movie, scorches the screen and disturbs her newlywed husband in the sordid **THE JAPANESE WIFE NEXT DOOR : PART 2**. **Above:** With the aid of her even more sexually hyper mom, Yazaki seeks to sexually torture the gangster family's drug mule by draining him of bodily fluids.

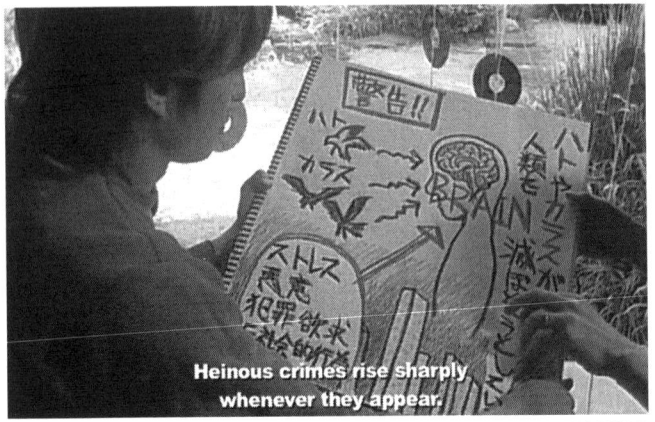

Just what does it all mean? Find out when you watch **THE JAPANESE WIFE NEXT DOOR: PART 2**

Foregoing the comedic events of the first film, **PART TWO** is a different animal altogether. More sexually deviant, more downbeat, and a tad sadistic. Still, if you are willing to view a one-two punch of pink movies, I highly recommend these two films.

The Pink Eiga DVD features a 10-minute interview with Reiko Yamaguchi, but since she's barely in this movie, she discusses the differences (again) of working in the purely adult video biz and the pink movies. Since she spoke so energetically of loving to fuck and suck in the interview on the previous DVD, her comments are kept to a minimum. The director Yutaju Ikejima returns in another 15-minute chat about working in the pink film genre, and the challenges of making an explicit film while being hindered by governmental censorship. Like that previously mentioned disc, the only language option is Japanese, but the English subtitles are clear, easy to read, and generally free from hilarious typos.

2004, JAPAN. D: YUTAJU IKEJIMA
AVAILABLE FROM PINK EIGA

Yamaguchi onscreen again) but twisting things around, she reveals that she is happily married and only had sex with him because he seemed so depressed. Sakura moves on and Takashi returns to the house of deviates…where he is drugged, kidnapped and awaits his fate.

When in Las Vegas, be sure to visit...

Alternate Reality Comics

4110 S. Maryland Pkwy. #8
Las Vegas, NV 89119
702.736.3673
alternaterealitycomics.net
ichliebecomics.blogspot.com

BIONIC GUTS AND EXPLODING HUTS!

The Filipino Pulp Factory of Bobby A. Suarez
Part One: From Manila Boy's Town to Hong Kong and Back to Manila, 1942-1975

by Andrew Leavold

*It wasn't just the drive-in exploitation market, but popular culture the world over that would see a huge kick to the head in 1973: the kung fu phenomenon, personified by **ENTER THE DRAGON** (1973) exploding across screens worldwide, and the subsequent death of its star Bruce Lee. The demand for Eastern action films was as instantaneous as it was global in nature. Audiences wanted Asian faces, martial arts action, palm trees as scenery—no longer an exotic backdrop, Asia graduated to the foreground.*

For the Philippines, the effect was electric. In the same fashion the Spanish desert would stand in for Texas or Mexico during the spaghetti western cycle of the 'Sixties and early 'Seventies, the Philippines could double effortlessly for any Asian country you'd care to name. Its traditional martial arts—eskrimina and arnis—were usurped for a while by the Japanese-influenced karate craze in the early to late 'Sixties, and this was reflected in karate-themed action films aimed at 'Sixties Pinoy moviegoers already dizzy on goon punch-ups. Enter "The Dragon" himself, Bruce Lee, and a second wave of action stars emerged—Ramon Zamora, Rey Malonzo, Ulysses Tzan, Robert Lee (who had happily traded karate kicks for kung fu chops, becoming known affectionately as the "Bruce Lees of the Philippines"). Thus the Filipino "goon" film morphed with little effort from the spy films and karate adventures of the 'Sixties into the kung fu revenge operas of the 'Seventies.

Hong Kong naturally led the Asian charge into the international market, with local producers not far behind, providing facilities, forming co-productions or making distribution deals with Hong Kong companies for their own kung fu movies. Bobby A. Suarez of BAS Films was without a doubt the most successful of all Filipino producers of kung fu films in the 'Seventies. Working his way to salesman at the Rank Organization's Film Exchange in Manila, he moved to Hong Kong at the start of the kung fu boom, learning the international film trade from working with the Shaw Brothers before starting his own companies, Intercontinental Film Distributors based in Hong Kong, and RJR Film Exchange in Manila. He quickly moved into producing his own martial arts films, then formed BAS Films and started to direct, commencing with a series of kung fu/super-spy combos, the Bionic Boy and Cleopatra Wong series (1977-79).

By splicing together then-popular genres and utilizing an already-established network of pan-Asian funding and global distribution, Bobby managed to sell his action movies the world over—an incredible feat, considering most Filipino producers relied on outside help, primarily from Hong Kong or the United States. Bobby was a first amongst Filipino filmmakers: he

Producer Bobby Suarez chats with **COSA NOSTRA ASIA** star Chris Mitchem

Lobby card for Suarez's early international hit **CLEOPATRA WONG**, featuring all the excitement that you would expect in the film and more

became a one-man export factory for almost fifteen years. All of Bobby's impressive achievements, it should be noted, were created on miniscule budgets, without government financing, and without courting favours with local critics and audiences. Bobby's eye was on the prize, and that prize was screening his modest populist genre films on cinema screens the world over.

I've forgotten how long I've been watching Bobby's movies, and how I'd been aware of the "Bobby A. Suarez" tagline as a film's badge of lunacy. I had certainly trawled the Internet looking for the tiniest scraps of information about him—along with the two-foot-nine "Pinoy James Bond", Weng Weng, Bobby's female kung fu-kicking super-spy creation, Cleopatra Wong, was my favourite Filipino film icon.

At the start of February 2006 I chanced upon an Internet listing for a **CLEOPATRA WONG** (a.k.a. **THEY CALL HER CLEOPATRA WONG**, 1978) screening in Switzerland. The film's star Marrie Lee would be in attendance, along with the French cultural attaché in Singapore, a Monsieur Raphael Millet. I Googled the French Embassy in Singapore and called the number. They put me through to Raphael. "Do you know either Marrie Lee or a Bobby A. Suarez?" I asked breathlessly. "I have both their telephone numbers," he said in a matter-of-fact manner. "Would you like them?"

Raphael suggested he forward an email to both Bobby and Marrie (Raphael *is* a diplomat, after all). Bobby's reply came almost immediately:

(Email 8/2/06)

Dear Andrew:

Hi... Letting you know that my good friend Raphael (Millet) of the French Embassy in Singapore wrote to me about your wanting to talk to me even by phone, and he even furnish me your e-mail letter. How nice to know you, Andrew and your being a film writer, archivist and researcher and a big fan of this lowly producer-director from a very small country. Thanks and definitely I would like to be your friend and vice versa.

I am now writing the script with my friend and brother, British scriptwriter Mr. Mike Cassey a magical-action-packed comedy adventure "family type movie" entitled – THE WANDERING SAMURAI which will bring together Mr. Franco Guerrero ('One-Armed Executioner' fame) and Ms. Marrie Lee ('Cleopatra Wong' fame) to play the lead roles, to be supported by American and Asian talents. My director of photography is no other than my good Australian Hong Kong based friend, Ross (Clarkson).

The Wandering Samurai is what I referred to as the "prelude" to the come backing of Ms. Marrie Lee (Cleopatra Wong) who will play the lead role to a bigger budgeted action-packed-police-drama entitled – "VENGEANCE OF CLEOPATRA WONG", together with my good and personal friend, Mr. Gary Daniels, the Hollywood based British actor and European kickboxing champion.

Hoping that one of this days, we will meet each other personally.

Thanks and take care.

BOBBY A. SUAREZ
President-Producer-Director

We did indeed meet, many times. Bobby believed in divine fate, and would often say that destiny had brought us into each other's orbit; he had already decided that I would one day write the Bobby A. Suarez story, it seemed, and I readily agreed. He practically adopted me, opened his office, his film archive and his home to me; treated me like a member of his family. He used to call me his "white monkey-faced brother", much to his wife Gene's annoyance. "How is our mother in Australia?" was one of his running jokes. I'd laugh and reply, "Well, thank you Bobby, if a little disturbed that she has a child in the Philippines who's almost as old as she is."

Family was paramount to Bobby, the orphan from Manila Boy's Town, to the extent that he had two families: the Suarez clan, and the BAS Films cast and crew. "I care about my people," Bobby told me, "the lowest—the coffee boy, the staff, the crew. If I treat my actors and actresses—what I eat, what they eat, is the same food that my people eat. If they drink coffee, three or four cups of coffee, everything's the same. So I treat them like human beings. And it's forever. Like now, if I'm going to shoot another movie, it's the same people who will be working with me. Not for me, but WITH me. Because they are my family."

To Bobby, it's all about dedication: dedication to an ideal, an almost impossible standard to live up to even for the determined Bobby, in both his work and his familial loyalty. Think what you will about his movies, but there's no denying Bobby's immersion in his work, his fascination with the mechanics of filmmaking. He is a true auteur, involved in every single stage of the filmmaking process, from concept to marketing, even editing his movies himself on an old Moviola table. He was a perennial dreamer, always concocting new projects, and never short of a treatment to dust off, retool and relaunch. He was a true independent, a self-made business man with the world in his sights, but strictly on his terms. Like many Asian producers he could be a brazen opportunist ready to capitalise on the filmic flavour *du jour*; from kung fu actioners to post-apocalypse and 'Namsploitation, on the surface a familiar-sounding catalogue of 'Seventies and 'Eighties genre hijacking. Once filtered through Bobby's utterly unique sensibilities, however, weaned on pulp cinema of the 'Sixties and honed by invaluable years in the trenches during Hong Kong's kung fu boom, his films are anything *but* predictable. One thing we can all agree upon, I'm sure, is that Bobby never let propriety and internal logic get in the way of telling one of his outrageous stories.

"You are the first person that I've ever talked with," Bobby told me during our initial phone conversation, not even a week after the first email exchange. He had a way of making you feel privileged to be taken into his confidence. "But it's not just me. Forget about me. It's about the film industry of Asia." Bobby then launched into a monologue declaring the end of the Filipino film industry, at the time languishing with no hope or direction forward, and at less than fifty features completed in 2006, a mere shadow of its former 300-a-year glory.

"You don't know me," he suddenly interjected. "So why are you running after me now?"
"I beg your pardon?" I was taken slightly aback.
"But you are running after me. Why?"
I made sure my answer was as direct and honest as possible. "Because I love movies," I told him.
You could hear Bobby beam down the phone line. "I am a Filipino director and you like my movies. And that is something, you know? I'm very grateful, I'm happy. But if only my fellow countrymen could feel what I'm feeling now."

Doris Young, a.k.a. Marrie Lee, Bobby's iconic lead actress in his *Cleopatra Wong* films, once tried to pin down his reclusive nature. "He's a very private person. He doesn't relate very fast to people, so he doesn't want to tell people much about himself. He feels a bit uncomfortable. And he's a great writer; you see that a lot of the time, he writes a lot of his own scripts. And another thing is, a friend of his—one of the Shaw brothers—got kidnapped back in the '60s [possibly Vee Ming, in 1964]. Back when I knew him Bobby had two boys; he didn't have his girl yet. And I think he was very worried for his family, because some of these people, they can kill for a bottle of beer. So he doesn't want his family nor himself to be seen or be filmed. He just wants to protect his family."

Over the course of five visits to the Philippines over four years, plus countless phone calls and emails, Bobby would entrust his life story to me, often within conversations which would be scribbled down later on the back of San Miguel beer coasters. Despite the volumes of information he bestowed upon me, we only ever sat down to two formal interviews, first over the phone in February 2006, the second on-camera outside his home in Bulacan, not far Metro Manila. Bobby was a fiercely private man who preferred his film to do the talking; he was also a man of many secrets, some of which he entrusted to me, and which I will never tell, and some were from those closest to him, who evidently felt like I needed the full picture in order to paint him in an honest light.

I'm certainly not going to betray anyone's confidence, nor am I going to indulge in one-sided eulogies. During those four years I came to know a man of a great many contradictions. Bobby the orphan, for one, who perhaps overcompensated for an unhappy childhood by becoming the uncompromising patriarch of two somewhat dysfunctional families—one a surrogate film family—and then almost wilfully setting out to sabotage both, sometimes by testing the loyalty (not to mention endurance) of its members to breaking point. Bobby the paragon of modesty, almost pathologically so, who nevertheless had constructed a self-aggrandising personal narrative of sacrifice, honour, betrayal and forgiveness worthy of a South American telenovela.

I loved the guy, and still do. But I see the real man, riddled with imperfections, not to mention soured dreams, a life well-lived but with a mountain of unfinished business. Bobby's restless soul may still be prowling the BAS Films office looking for Mike Cassey's email address to shoot off additions to his THEY CALL HER…FATSO script.

Many of the words I've used here are Bobby's. I must point out they represent "the truth" as he perceived it, or as he chose to remember it. I'm not saying he's wrong *per se*, but in the immortal words of one of Australia's greatest scribes, never let the truth get in the way of a good story.

They Call Him Bobby A. Suarez

BAS Film Company Profile:
ROBERTO A. SUAREZ (BAS) as a person and as a filmmaker can be compared to a rattan vine that grows wild in the Philippine rain forests. Like a rattan pole that can be crafted into a durable but elegant piece of furniture, is hard but pliant like a police baton, Bobby's career was honed and seasoned by sheer hard work since early childhood.

Roberto A. Suarez, the eldest of four siblings, was born in Manila on 27th November 1942, almost a year into the Japanese occupation of the Philippines. Juanito Suarez, son of a wealthy Spanish family, married Jenecia Suarez Alonzo against his family's wishes. Two more brothers, Rogelio and Virgilio, followed one after the other—while Jenecia actively fought the Japanese as a Captain in the guerrillas. Juanito became separated from his family and died before Liberation, leaving Jenecia widowed, and pregnant with fourth child Erlinda.

Jenecia, the only educated member of her family, clearly had enough of a determined, fiery spirit to have survived World War II looking after three small children. Immediately after the war she used her contacts in the guerrilla underground to help her start up a business importing second-hand army trucks and heavy military equipment. From all reports she was good at making money. She also had a prodigious gambling habit, encouraged by Juanito's family, who she doubtlessly wanted so hard to impress. Before long Jenecia had frittered away her new fortune, and the family was destitute.

In a candid conversation with me, Virgilio estimated that around 1950, he was adopted out to the Velasco clan, friends of his mother's family. His only sister Erlinda, no more than five years old, was also left with family members. Roberto and Rogelio, however, were brought to Manila Boy's Town, the city's refuge and shelter for abandoned and orphaned children, by a friend of their mother's who had become ill, and passed away soon after. Boy's Town was their home until they turned eighteen. Mayor Laxa assisted Bobby in finding

work via City Hall; he was assigned to Manila Zoo, taking care of the residents of the snake house for a year.

Once he left the zoo, Bobby worked as a janitor for a commercial building. It's possible the building housed the J. Arthur Rank Film Distribution (P.I.) Exchange in Manila, one of the largest distributors of British and European films in the Philippines in the early 'Sixties, run by Australian boss Digby Davidson, an early mentor and father figure. Bobby would often cite his time around the Rank offices as a turning point in his life. "Cleaning the office, the toilet, everything! I tried my best to do the best I can. As a telephone messenger, and then they gave me the position of assistant to the booker. Assistant Sales Manager. And they helped me to finish my studies." Barely 20, Bobby already showed his steely reserve to become a self-made man. "'If you want a good life,'" Virgilio remembered Bobby telling him at the time, "'you must be the best at everything you do. Like, for example, I am a janitor. I must be the best janitor they will ever have.'" "That is his motto," Virgilio, now a successful businessman, recalls. "And I listen to that kind of philosophy."

Studying Commerce at FPU, Bobby would also do typewriting for storytellers in the *komik*, film, and TV businesses, occasionally selling one of his own storylines (none of these early credits have surfaced as yet). His college classmate was future filmmaker Danny L. Zialcita, for whom Bobby would also type stories. Danny's father was a relative of Bobby's boss at In Chem, where he worked in the personnel department, and as, in Virgilio's words, In-Chem's "pet employee", Danny asked Bobby to ask Don Zialcita if he would fund a film enterprise. He agreed, and **LADY KILLER** was released by DLZ Productions in November 1965 at the height of the James Bond craze, starring Romano Castellvi as a Filipino secret agent determined to crack a crime syndicate threatening the female population with a sterility drug. According to Virgilio, both Danny and Bobby worked together on the story, editing, and much of the behind-the-scenes business. The result was pure, glorious pulp, as much inspired by the cheap Italian, Spanish and French knock-offs as the actual Bond films themselves, and sounding like Bobby's own spy-centric creations of the 'Seventies and 'Eighties. Bobby, future purveyor of Pinoy pulp, was clearly taking notes.[1]

---

1 Danny L. Zialcita directed three more spy films in 1966 - **CABONEGRO**, **TARGET: DOMINO** and **TIGER LADY**—all starring Romano Castellvi—and it's possible Bobby worked on some or all of these titles.

1965 soundtrack release from Mainstream Records (S/6072)

He still found time to wed his sweetheart Gene on 21st June 1967. Gene was a high school student when she met Bobby in Bulacan in 1965, while he was looking at an apartment owned by her father. "A very serious man," she described him to me. "He cannot smile at all." His entire life consisted of work, and travelling to and from his In-Chem office job. Bobby romanced her from Cutabato by mail; two years into her college degree, they eloped. Three children—Roberto II, John and Richard—followed in quick succession.

Bobby then worked for an independent company, Fortune Films, as a booker and sales manager before asking his manager, Gener Peralta, to allow him to travel abroad. (Virgilio was involved with a company known as Diamond International Films for several months, but left due to the "incompatibility of the proponents".) Bobby first went to Japan, then Hong Kong, looking for action films to import. "I went to work going to buy Chinese pictures," Bobby told me, "as a sideline. So I come back to the Philippines, re-sell the picture, I make 500 dollars or 1,000 US dollars, I'm happy already."

From the start of his career in the movie distribution business, Bobby had no interest whatsoever in the films made and distributed locally. "Here if you say 'action film', it's action from the start to the end without any let-up," Bobby said. "When you say 'drama', it's a crying picture from beginning to end. I wanted to introduce the kind of little movies that you can sell even to the Fiji Islands or West Indies. But Filipinos are very hard-headed. They didn't want anybody to tell them what to do and what not to do." The films Bobby later produced and directed would differ from the local films in a number of ways, not least their ambitious scope and internationalist approach. They were sharp, punchy and moved like a bullet train, much like their European inspirations and the Hong Kong films he imported. Before long other local outfits were jumping on the martial arts bandwagon—a loose confederation of Chinese-Filipinos, such as distributor and later producer Conrad "Boy" Puzon of Cinex Films, who initially helped run his father's film exchange in the late 'Sixties—and supplemented their local titles with Cantonese-language chop-sockeys. "Since my money was short," Conrad related to me in a 2010 interview, "my kind of kung fu films that I purchased in Hong Kong were those kung fus that are cheap, and those without subtitles." It wasn't only in the rabbit warren of cinemas around Manila's Chinatown, next to the old entertainment precincts of Escolta and Quiapo, that un-dubbed Chinese action films—alongside the established staples of Japanese karate, samurai and ninja films—would screen. "In the provinces, where I am expert in booking, they usually enjoy these action, karate [films], even if they don't understand the dialogue." Conrad smiled. "It worked for a while. You can get away with things for not that long."

But there is an extra dimension to Bobby's relationship with local films: that of class and prestige. Bobby deliberately translated his imported Cantonese-language films into English, rather that Tagalog, thus anticipating the explosion of English-dubbed kung fu films in the early 'Seventies. "He was the first dubber of Chinese films into English," Virgilio recounted. "In the 1960s, people here preferred the English films than the Tagalog films. People here pretend to be educated simply by speaking the English language. If you see Tagalog movies, you belong to the '*bakya*' [wooden clogs worn by the poor] crowd. And if you speak Tagalog you are low class, you are not educated. That is the kind of mentality that we have here." The former inmate of Boy's Town was announcing to the world in unambiguous terms: he was a citizen of the world, and not some parochial, Manila-centric underclass. Bobby was forging his way through the world, whether the world was ready for him or not.

Around late 1967, Bobby decided to base himself in Hong Kong and formed his own company, Intercontinental Film Distributors [HK], with Miss Terry Lai. "I started Intercontinental so we would have movies to distribute," Bobby said. **THAT MAN IN ISTANBUL** [1965], a Spanish spy film directed by Antonio Isasi, was one of two films Bobby initially bought for the Far East and made a small fortune on it. "I would go to America to buy movies for Hong Kong. And then I went to Italy, and Paris, and I'd buy the Alain Delon movies which were in France, have them dubbed into English and sell them to the whole of the Far East. Then later on I'd sell the film territory by territory in the Far East."

According to Virgilio, Terry was a secretary to the British Consul in Hong Kong. "She's a very nice girl," he said of his meeting with Terry in Manila in the late 'Sixties. "Their cooperation took some time, I think a span of ten years. Terry is a prime mover of this [film] business." Virgilio then looked introspective. "She doesn't know Bobby is married."

Although based in Hong Kong, the company had offices throughout the Far East and South East Asia. Through Intercontinental, Bobby and Terry would buy the South East Asian and Far East rights to movies from all over the world. Distribution of Bobby's purchases in the Philippines was through the family's RJR Film Exchange—named after the three sons Roberto, John and Richard—which Gene looked after. "R stands for the name of my eldest son Roberto Jr.," said Bobby, "J stands for the name of my second eldest son, John, and the last, R stands for the name of Richard whom, as you know, is the youngest." In turn, Intercontinental purchased the worldwide rights to Hong Kong-produced kung fu movies—just prior to the kung fu boom—for a modest amount, dub them into foreign languages and on-sell them to international markets: Avco Embassy in the United States, Atlas Films GmbH in Germany, and smaller operators in Scandinavia and the Middle East. Intercontinental was both his film school and laboratory, and Bobby, like a wire-haired alchemist with mad spirals in his eyes, kept tinkering with the elements.

"I was a salesman. I would buy Chinese pictures, dub it into English and sell it to the Middle East. And don't laugh, I would bring with me a 16mm print—because I would buy European pictures for the Far East—so I'd bring with me 16mm prints of Chinese movies. And I tried to convince my friends to buy them, and nobody wanted Chinese pictures! They said, 'Bobby, you're crazy.' There's one crazy guy, he bought the movie for the whole of Scandinavia, and the rest is history. He made a lot of money."

Next stop for Bobby was Spain. "I went there because I was fighting with another importer from Continental Films of Hong Kong, I was Intercontinental Films. I was there to buy **SUMMERTIME KILLER** [*Un verano para matar*, 1972] for the Far East. And when Señor Isasi, the director and producer, asked me how much I can pay, I said, 'How much do you think I should pay?' He said, 'Look, I don't have any money. Pay $50,000. Cash now.' I said yes, so I called up Hong Kong, 'Send me $50,000.' I thought that was only a down-payment. But what he asked me was the rights to the Far East, and I was surprised because it's only a third of what I'm expecting to ask. But he said, 'I feel we have become friends.' I said, 'Mr. Isasi, can you teach me to direct a movie?' Because not so many people know that Señor Isasi is the same producer and director of **THEY CAME TO ROB LAS VEGAS** [*Las Vegas, 500 millones*, 1968], a beautiful and commercial movie, and **THAT MAN IN ISTANBUL** [*Estambul 65*, 1965]—that picture outgrossed James Bond in so many countries in the world. He only makes one or two of these movies in five years. I didn't know anything about movie production and direction, just slowly I learn it. Señor Isasi already told me, 'Keep your eyes, ears open, but your mouth closed. Just look and listen.'"

"Don't laugh, I learnt a lot from Señor Isasi, but prior to that the Chinese pictures, if I feel they're talking too much I'll just ask somebody to trust it to me, and I edit the movie. The sound and everything, if you edit a finished movie, a 35mm print, if you cut it and you put it together it goes 'pop' so I have to erase that. I'm going to try to edit it the way it should be done without destroying the movie. So before I became a director, I know already how to edit movies. I learn."

Bobby was also "producer" on early Meng Fei hits **THE KING BOXER** (*Xiao quan wang*, a.k.a. **KING OF BOXERS**, a.k.a. **HANDS OF DEATH**, 1972)[2] and **PRODIGAL BOXER** (*Fang Shi Yu*, 1972), which he sold to Avco Embassy for a tidy profit, as well as the Bobby-friendly title **THAT MAN FROM SINGAPORE** (a.k.a. **THE LIFE FOR SALE**, 1973) featuring a young Sammo Hung in a small role. **KING BOXER** and **PRODIGAL BOXER** were also big money earners in the Philippines, and amongst the most influential non-Bruce Lee titles in the new Kung Fu craze; there were Filipino parodies (both 1973: **IKING BOXER**, with Chiquito, and **THE RADICAL BOXER CHALLENGES THE BIG BOSS**, with, according to the ads, Ramon "Bruce Lee" Zamora and Rey "Meng Fei" Malonzo!) and starring roles for Meng Fei in a number of Filipino/Hong Kong co-productions. He would even marry Filipina actress Elizabeth Oropesa and base himself in Manila for a substantial part of the 'Seventies. For all of this influence and notoriety, Bobby's name is never listed in the films' opening credits, no doubt for legal reasons, as a Filipino could never technically "own" a Hong Kong company—hence Terry's name on Intercontinental's public interface.

Bobby's first *bona fide* film credit, along with Terry Lai, is on Intercontinental's first foray into film production, the Hong Kong-lensed martial arts film **THE BLACK DRAGON** (1974)[3], starring Filipino action star Tony Ferrer. "'Attorney' Laxa," Bobby told me, "is the brother of Tony Ferrer. He approached me and said, 'Bobby, this market that you are selling these Chinese pictures in, why don't you buy our old X-44 movies?' I thought, 'I'm sorry, I cannot do anything.' How can I explain to them that the quality is not saleable?"

Laxa also asked Bobby to create an overseas vehicle for Ferrer, who was by then a veteran of almost 100 local features but was, aside from a bit role in **THE VENGEANCE OF FU MANCHU** (1967) with Christopher Lee, virtually unknown outside the Philippines. From his early days as supporting player in Fernando Poe Jr. and Joseph Estrada action vehicles for his older brother Espiridon Laxa's (a former lawyer, known affectionately as "Attorney") Tagalong Ilang-Ilang Productions, he became a leading man in a series of James Bond derivations playing Tony Falcon, Agent X-44. Thick-bodied and thick-lipped, hair seemingly cast in polyurethane, his trademark white suit was ever-present in a series stretching over fifteen years and more than thirty film appearances. Astoundingly, X-44 became the most popular and enduring

THAT MAN FROM SINGAPORE German Beta tape

of the Pinoy James Bonds, and Ferrer feted himself as a real-life action diva and devout ladies' man to the point where the public and private personas became inseparable. The mid-'Sixties spy craze gave way to the karate kick, and from 1967 to 1969 Ferrer smartened his chops as a "karatista". Along with brothers Roberto and Rolando Gonzales (sons of renowned karate instructor Valentino Gonzales) Ferrer redefined the late 'Sixties Pinoy action star as a flurry of lightning kicks and film titles such as **KARATE KID** (1967) and **BLACKBELT AVENGERS** (1969). But despite a more-than-modest personality cult and several reasonably high-profile stabs at the international market, his non-Falcon roles never had quite the same impact.

---

[2] Not to be confused with the much-more-popular **FIVE FINGERS OF DEATH** (*Tian xia di yi quan*), from Hong Kong that same year, which saw English-language release under the name **KING BOXER**. –ed.

[3] Not to be confused with the same-year HK/Philippines coproduction **XIA NAN YANG**, which is widely distributed under the title **THE BLACK DRAGON**, directed by Chin-Ku Lu under the alias "Tommy Loo Chung". –ed.

By 1973, even his domestic success as Agent X-44 was on the decline. "Now Tony is not up there anymore, he's kaput." Bobby delivered on Laxa's request; Filipinos Ferrer, Alona Alegre, and Ferrer's frequent co-star, stuntman Rey Sagum, arrived in Hong Kong around May 1973 to begin work on **THE BLACK DRAGON**. Tony Ferrer stars as Lam Chi Tong, a.k.a. Jimmy, one of three brothers investigating the brutal murder of their father, undercover cop Lam Senior. A tell-tale ring is left next to the body suggesting his death was the work of "the most ruthless gang in Asia", the fearsome Black Dragon syndicate. Their goons operate on the waterfront where Jimmy's brother Lam Chih Yat (Jimmy Lee) works as a police informer, smuggling heroin in phoney pottery. Other brother Lam Chih Chao (Dick Chan) meanwhile defends a nearby neighbourhood from the mob's protection racket (they call it "squeeze", as in "Pay me some *squeeeeze*…you bastard!") The Black Dragons' master suspects either cops or a rival gang afoot, and orders his men to eliminate them. The brothers' superior, Inspector Pang (Kiu Wan), wants them all to go deeper to flush out the syndicate's leader, who may be one of his own policemen—or even the Police Chief (Tong Ching) himself.

In retrospect, Bobby's official film debut is a competently shot if somewhat unremarkable and conventional karate thriller, directed by the film's Gatling gun editing machine Lo Gio. All three leads share efficient fight scenes with Hong Kong's goons and random snatches of jazz and bombastic bongo-driven funk, and Ferrer, a veteran of the Filipino Action Film's trenches, more than holds his own in the combat scenes (a bloody beatdown with Filipino super-goon Rey Sagum is perhaps the film's highlight). Less convincing is his stint as a dockside lothario, literally sliding from one concubine's boat to pretty Alona Alegre's in one oily move. Alegre's racy nude scenes with Ferrer would have caused a riot in the Philippines, assuming it was allowed by the censors, due to the recently declared martial law outlawing all nudity—not to mention gratuitous violence, a staple in kung fu—from all local films.

THE BLACK DRAGON was released in Manila in March 1974, at a time when practically every second film was a kung fu film from Hong Kong, or a Filipino production starring "the Bruce Lees of the Philippines", Ramon Zamora and Rey Malonzo. Amidst the scores of "Prodigal Boxers", "New Fists of Fury", and the latest ballets of blood from Wang Yu, Meng Fei, Chen Xing, Angela Mao *et al*, "Did **THE BLACK DRAGON** make any kind of impact and revive Tony's career?" I asked Bobby. "I released it here, nobody wanted to come. They said, 'Tony Ferrer? He's already dead! He won't make a cent.' If you are the theatre owner you should get one date, and if the picture doesn't make money, what happened to your movie house? They're going to close it. So what I did was rent the biggest cinema at that time, Cinerama, the biggest and the best, and don't laugh—at that time I paid 5,000 pesos a day, but I have to have a theatre to show Tony Ferrer's movie. And by God, I was lucky the picture went *VOOM!* It opened, first day, nothing. Second day, full house. Third day, overflowing. And Tony Ferrer again came alive, and he made movie after movie, and then died again a natural death. Then he approached me again and said, 'Bobby…' I said, 'No. I helped you once, I told you don't destroy your name, make good quality movies. I spent a fortune to revive your career. And you yourself destroyed it.'"

International sales were negligible, mostly because it was a case of "Tony Who?" "That is the problem with me. People buy my movies because I produce it. Suppose I open my movie like **BLACK DRAGON**, you don't know anything about it. Who is Tony Ferrer? I said, 'Look, for the whole of Scandinavia, I'm only asking $10,000. If you lose money, let me know and I will return it to you. You want to include it in the contract? Sure.' So people trusted me."

If Bobby wanted a name actor for the Asian market on his next projects, he couldn't have picked a hotter one than Chris Mitchum. Son of veteran actor Robert Mitchum, a young Chris found himself unofficially blackballed in Hollywood following roles in two John Wayne pictures, and relocated with his family to Spain where the only paying jobs were. A surprise international hit was 1972's **SUMMERTIME KILLER**, in which Chris plays a psycho on a motorbike; suddenly Chris found himself one of the top action stars in Asia, no doubt partly due to Bobby releasing the film through Intercontinental. The offer to star in Bobby's next two productions soon followed.

Chris Mitchum's soft drawl came down the phone line like cigar smoke; I'd been listening to his voice since I was a kid, so interviewing him was a real honest-to-goodness kick. It was early January 2010, only a month before I had to email Chris with the bad news of Bobby's passing.

"I was kinda run out of the United States because I'd worked with John Wayne. And there was—it was kind of bizarre. I did **CHISUM** [1970], that was a small part, and I did **RIO LOBO** [1970] and **BIG JAKE** [1971] with him." And John Wayne was not cool at the time. This was **THE GREEN BERETS** [1968]-era John Wayne, right? "Exactly. And Hollywood, you know, there was all these people burning flags and booing soldiers returning from the war. And Hollywood could not differentiate between supporting the troops and supporting the war. So they thought he was pro-war. He wasn't—he was pro-American soldier. They were out there taking orders. And they basically set up a policy that anyone who worked with John Wayne was blackballed in Hollywood. Duke was noted for having friends work in his pictures. You watch twenty John Wayne films and you'll see faces repeat, you know; film after film after film the same actors in character roles. A lot of that had to do with the fact that they were of the same political bent. And Hollywood took the position that if you worked with John Wayne, they would not promote you in Hollywood because they did not want a second voice coming out, you know, talking about the Vietnam protesters."

BLACK DRAGON: Tony Ferrer and some sweet lovin' seduction with co-star Alona Alegre between kung fu battles and general bloodshed

So basically it was McCarthyism in reverse. "Exactly. After I did **BIG JAKE**, I was on the Johnny Carson show. I was given the *Photoplay* Gold Medal award. *Photoplay* was a magazine which—their awards were sort of a people's choice award, their readers voted on it. And it was a pre-runner to the Academy Award. They came out before the Academy Awards ceremony. And they actually gave out a medal, about five inches across, of solid fourteen carat gold. And this is back when gold was still thirty-two dollars an ounce." My God, I said, that's a lot of teeth! "Oh yeah, I got that baby sitting on my shelf. I got that for being the best new actor of 1972. I was on the cover of *Seventeen* magazine three times that year, and I couldn't get a job interview. And I got this job offer while I was actually doing promos around the country. Me and Patrick Wayne were doing a twenty-one city tour in nineteen days, flying around doing interviews. And my agent said this director and producer were in New York, and we had a Sunday rest in Houston. So they flew me up from Houston to New York to have lunch, they gave me the script, told me about the project—it was called *Un verano para matar*—**SUMMERTIME KILLER**—and they flew me back down and offered me five times what Duke was paying me. And I said yes before I read the script. And it was a great script; we had Karl Malden, Olivia Hussey, Claudine Auger, Gerard Barry, Raf Vallone…a great cast. And yeah, in L.A. I went to a cast interview, and the casting director looked at me and said, 'Oh, you're *that* Chris Mitchum.' I said, 'What do you mean?' And she said 'I can't cast you because you starred with John Wayne.'"

And that's how you found out! "Yeah. So I went off and did this film in Spain, and I came back, and again I couldn't get an interview. The guy who did the stills photography on the film called me up and said, 'I would like to send you a script. The producer contacted me and wants me to get a script to you. Would you be interested in coming back to Spain?' I said, 'Yeah, sure.' So I went back and I found out that **SUMMERTIME KILLER** was the biggest-grossing film in Spain's history. It won something like seven Spanish awards, and I was a major star in Spain. My second day there I got offered another film in Spain, so I think, 'Screw this.' I go back after the first film, rent out my house, pack up my family and move to Spain for three years. And everything I did there, when Franco was alive—I mean Rosso [*Bronson?*] was living north of Barcelona, Eastwood was shooting all of his spaghetti westerns down at Almeria—it was a happening place. All the stuff I did there was being exported to Asia, and it turned out I was a big star in Asia. There was Eastwood, Bronson, Alain Delon and myself. I mean, Alain Delon was always number one. And the other three of us were two, three and four…depending on who had the latest release. So I started getting job offers over there, and that's when I moved back to the United States, because I figured, what the hell am I doing living in Spain and working in Asia. And I wanted a hamburger and a milkshake.

"So I went back there and I started doing stuff, the first one being the one in Thailand, so I started working there a lot. And the one in Thailand, it was the first…actually, I think **SUMMERTIME KILLER** was the first film Olivia Hussey did after **ROMEO AND JULIET** [1968]. Because that was so successful over there, they brought her over to star in **H-BOMB** [*Dtàt lìam pét*, 1971]."

CHINESE DAREDEVIL COMMANDOS (a.k.a. **CHINESE COMMANDOS**) and **COSA NOSTRA ASIA** (released 1974) were slated to be filmed back-to-back in Taiwan between September and November 1973. **CHINESE…** was up first, with Bobby for the first time—according to Chris—in the director's chair. "We were shooting down in Taiwan, and Tony Ferrer was on it. And it was absolutely hysterical. I mean tragic, but hysterical. We're down there, and we have two typhoons coming in. The hotel we're in is divided in half. One half is a functioning hotel, the other half is a whorehouse. The girls, the whores, they're also operating the hotel; they're at the front desk. And the town, it's this little dinky town with the open sewers running down the street and everything, and every single evening, around 4:30 or 5, a busload of Japanese tourists would come in. And they're all hung over, you'd see them with the big bottle of Johnny Walker Black Label, they'd go up to their room and have a big drunken party all night long screwing the whores. Then at nine in the morning they'd all get up with blood-red eyes and crawl onto the bus to go to the next site for sight-seeing.

"But we were hit with two typhoons when we were there, so we just sat on our asses for God knows how long, waiting for the storms to go through. I decided to do something nice, so I thought I'd throw a party for the crew, because they're all going stir crazy in there. [Actor] Larry Chiu helped me decide the meals, you know, some of them can eat this, and some can have this… And one of the meals they had was Tiger Dragon Soup. And Larry told me, 'This is wonderful. They can't afford to buy this at a restaurant.' So at the night of the party there's this huge soup tureen, and I look in, and the dragon is a snake,

and it's wrapped around a pheasant, some bird they trapped on the roof, and the tiger is an alley cat. And as the host and the guest of honour, I got to have the eyes of the alley cat. But I said, 'No, you set up this party, I'm just writing the cheque. You get the eyes.' He was ecstatic. He was so appreciative.

"**CHINESE DAREDEVIL COMMANDOS**, that was a story that took place during WWII, and it's about a bunch of Chinese and Americans who go up against the Japanese. But they didn't—and I understand this is the way with Chinese thinking, I'm told there is no future tense in their language. And that pretty much exists in the way they think, they don't think ahead at all. And we get out there, and they said, 'Chris, do you think you could go to the American base here, and get some uniforms? And maybe some jeeps and some troop trucks.' All that kind of stuff. So I go down to the base, you know, and talk to the base commander, and he says he'll be happy to do this, the military does co-operate with film companies, but you have to go to Washington; it starts at the Pentagon, you fill in some forms, and then it comes through here and we try to accommodate it. And that takes about three months. So I said, 'Oh well. Is there anything you can do for me?' He says, 'Well, I can give you a camouflage uniform for you to wear.' And I wore that uniform with the sewn-on captain bars. And we had no guns. Guns are outlawed in Taiwan. So we got these toy guns, and they got the special effects guy to put firecrackers up the kazoo. The gun was like an M-1 carbine, and it had a light, and when you pulled the trigger it would light up. So they took out the light and packed it full of fireworks.

"We get to the first real shot, and here comes this Japanese troop carrier, which is just a flatbed farm truck with a plastic machine gun mounted on it, and it's got these guys hanging off it, and it's coming across the field towards us, and they're going to engage us in battle. But there are guys falling off the truck, you know, the road is so bumpy, and they open fire with a machine gun and you see this big purple cloud… So then when the car hits this ditch, it's about five feet wide and six inches deep, they hit the embankment and we all have our M-1s and start to fire, and when we fire, it's like, yellow, poof! Orange, poof! Purple, poof! Coming down to the end of the line, every different colour. And Tony Ferrer, he pulls the trigger and nothing happens, he tries two more times but it doesn't work—he's supposed to shoot the driver of the truck—he tries two more times, then he brings it up to look at it and it goes swoosh! [Laughs.] Cloud of smoke comes over and for like four seconds you can't even see his head. I said 'Cut, cut,' and turned to Bobby and told him, 'Bobby, this isn't

Filipino theatrical newspaper ad

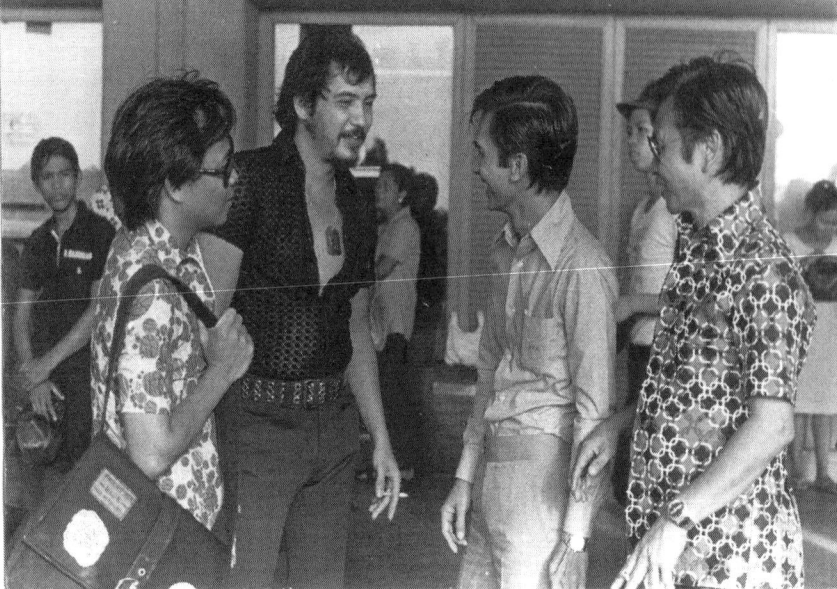

Behind the scenes for the filming of **MASTER SAMURAI**: Bobby with popular Filipino actor Von Serna. Serna had been in the business since 1960, and having made over fifty films, **MASTER SAMURAI** was his next-to-last.

working. It looks like a rainbow coming out of these guns.' He said, 'Okay, you're right. Let's all go back to the hotel to see what we can do.' So we have another four or five days off. And Tony's room is a few doors down from the special effects guy's room. So I'm sitting in Tony's room having a beer, and I hear a big swoosh! I said, 'What the hell is that?' Tony says, 'You've got to see this!' and we go out into the hallway. The door at the end of the hall opens, and a huge cloud of smoke drifts out. [Laughs.] And the special effects guys' standing there coughing his lungs out. And he's been working on it for three days!

"But then [Bobby] comes in and says 'We're not going to do it. We can't make this picture. We'll pay your salary and send you home.' I said, 'I'll tell you what, Bobby. When you can get the act together, I'll come back and do another film for you if you pay my expenses and five grand. I'll do another for you.' And he said, okay, that's great. And the following February I came back to the Philippines and did what at that time was **THE AGENCY** but became **MASTER SAMURAI** [1974]."

In the credits for the second film, **COSA NOSTRA ASIA**, Bobby is once again listed as writer. "Truth is," Chris told me, "when I got to Taiwan, they gave me a 20-page synopsis and said that was the script. I told them it wasn't a typewriter. I wrote a script. Terry Lai's brother also sat down and wrote a script…mostly by changing pages I handed in. Bobby wrote the 'story', Terry's brother Joseph Lai and I wrote the script. We were shooting **CHINESE DAREDEVIL COMMANDOS** at the time."

I attempted to contact Terry and Joseph Lai back in 2006 when doing initial research on Bobby and hit a brick wall. Joseph formed his own distribution company, IFD , in 1973; IFD now list several of Bobby's Intercontinental films in their catalogue. I can only guess at the degree of mutual co-operation between the siblings' companies, and the extent of Bobby's involvement in Intercontinental following his departure from Hong Kong, on paper and in a very real sense.

Chris: "At the beginning, everyone thought [Terry] was kind of like this inscrutable Chinese. Just wouldn't talk to anybody. But the more I got to know her—I mean, she was a very sharp businesswoman. But I think socially she was just very shy and not sure of her English, and was just very reserved because of that. Last year or the year before I went down to the International Film Market down at Santa Monica and stopped by the IFD office to say hi to Joseph and Terry. We chatted for a few minutes, and had a catch-up on old times. They went ahead and did more films with Bobby…"

"Was he ever married to Terry Lai?" he asked me.
"That's a very good question," I replied as diplomatically as I could. "They were definitely 'together'. And for that reason he got in a lot of trouble."

"I thought so. Even though she still went under the name of Terry Lai, she was introduced to me as his wife.

"I think Bobby moved **MASTER SAMURAI** to the Philippines to get away from Terry. That was my take on the whole thing. And once he was able to do that and get the money into the Philippines, it was '*adios*'. Because he already had a wife in the Philippines, and that didn't go down very well. The whole thing got really messy. So I think she was a little stand-offish with me because I had worked with Bobby."

COSA NOSTRA ASIA is a vintage Bobby conceit, a laudable pairing of **THE GODFATHER** (1972) and Bruce Lee's **THE BIG BOSS** (*Tang shan da xiong*, a.k.a. **FISTS OF FURY**, 1971): a kung fu-charged Mafioso thriller of double- and triple-dealing amongst Italian and Asian crime families. In "Chicago", Don Claudio Reynes calls the Families together to choose their Hong Kong successor, and it's a three-way face-off between the Big Boss of Hawaii, Tony Dee (Tony Ferrer), a dangerous cat in a bowler hat named Dy Sy Chung (Wong Sai Lap) who runs the "Yellow Mafia", and the treacherous Italian-American Angellini (Michael Kaye). Chris Mitchum plays mysterious stranger Chris Bellinger who breezes into the volatile mix and plays one side against the other. The result is superior to **THE BLACK DRAGON** in every department: script, fight choreography, original music, and Mitchum and Ferrer work well on-screen together, as do **BLACK DRAGON**'s Dick Chen—playing himself, head of his own (real life?) Martial Arts studio—plus Jimmy Lee as a rival Hong Kong gang leader, and Rey Sagum as Angellini's henchman Pietro. Newcomer Ellie Chow is likeable as Nancy Wong, niece of the mob's reluctant Hong Kong connection, but the standout is Wong Sai Lap, the greasy, cigar-chomping Yellow Mafia boss wielding a deadly blade inside his walking cane—a neat touch from Bobby's head, or perhaps Wong Sai Lap's himself, a veteran villain *and* Bobby's co-writer.

COSA NOSTRA ASIA was the first action film for Bobby's Hong Kong director John Liao after a string of comedies and dramas. "John Liao spoke beautiful English," said Chris, "and from what I understand he studied film and film history at Stanford, or Berkely, or wherever he was. And somewhere in San Francisco he went to film school. And he really had it together, you know.

"That scene where I walk into the dojo and I fight everybody in the room. Then I go in and fight the two girls with the sai, and then I go and fight Dick Chen. That was my first day on the set. And they kind of roughly choreographed the first run-through, fighting the guys. And they said 'Cut!' And they're looking at me like someone farted. They say 'Chris,' and we walk off to the side and he goes 'It doesn't look like you're hitting them,' so I said, 'Yeah, but they're not taking the punch, you know, if I punch at the head they gotta snap their head back, if I hit them in the stomach, they gotta double over.' He says, 'No, I mean really hitting them.' I said, 'Well, no wonder it doesn't look like it.'

MASTER SAMURAI cast and crew

He says, 'That's what they're there for. Hit them!' I said, 'You mean really hit them?' He says, 'Yes!' I said, 'That'll hurt them.' He said, 'Yes! That's what they're here for!' So, I said okay, we go back in the room and do it again. And I'm trying to pull my punches, but if somebody moves forward a half-inch, then you crack a rib. And we get through the shot, and there's a couple of guys moaning and groaning, the director yells 'Cut!' and they all applaud. And it got worse. For my fight scene with Dicky, I knew he was something like that year's Hong Kong kung fu champion. And we would work out a routine, and every time the camera came on, he would change the routine a little. Just haul off and went. So I think, 'Is he just stupid, or is he trying to hit the round-eye on camera?'"

He's trying to one-up you, by the sounds of it? "Yeah, that's what he's doing. So I had to basically get in a fight with him, to protect myself. And I'm, you know, guarding myself from punches and kicks, using my arms and shins. When I finished that first day's work, from my knee to my ankle and from my wrist to my elbow on both legs and arms were black and blue from taking punches."

And it really comes across as brutally realistic. "Believe me, it was," Chris agreed. "And later on we had another fight scene; again he was thinking he was really going to do me in. And while we were mapping it out I had my fight instructor there, Larry Chiu. And word was getting around, you know, because some of the crew actually liked me and they said Dicky was really trying to give me a hard shot, beat me out. And I said to Larry, 'If he takes me down, don't let him stomp on me when I'm unconscious.' He said 'Oh yeah, you're joking.' So we're doing the thing and he throws a punch to my stomach, in slow motion 'cause we're working it out for the camera, and suddenly he steps in and whacks me on the side of the head with his elbow. So I drop to one knee and I come back up to hit him, and he says, 'Sorry, Chris, I just got carried away. It was an accident, please forgive me.' Well, now we get to about five shots later and I'm about to do a side kick into his chest, and he can see the look in my eye, he knows I'm looking for a chance… We come in to do the shot, and we rehearse it and everything's fine, and he braces his hand across his chest to protect it from a hard kick, and I change my kick a little bit, and do a knife-edge hand to his throat. [Imitates painful choking noise.] I said, 'Oh, I'm sorry, I'm really sorry, it was really an accident, I'm really sorry.'" Chris laughed. "And that's the last time he took a swing at me!"

At Dick Chen's dojo, Chris faces off against former school friend and now adversary Tony Dee in another long scene, in the film at least lasting hours. After pummelling each other with fists and kicks, Mitchum and Ferrer switch to medieval swords and shield, and turn the lights off: an odd idea, very Post-Modern, and even post-Tarantino. The film ends in a martial arts free-for-all in Taiwan's harbour as Chris, Dick Chen and Tony Dee face off against Angellini and his goons, to an almost cartoon reveal—"I'm a cop." "But I'm a cop!" "I, too, am Interpol."

"We're doing this scene on a ship," remembered Chris, "and the wanted me to get knocked off one deck down to another deck. And it's like a twelve-foot fall. And I think, 'Hey, that's a steel deck, I don't want to do this.' So I said 'I'll tell you what, get me like twenty cardboard boxes, and two twin bed mattresses and we'll do the shot tomorrow.' They're looking at me like I'm nuts. But they bring them, and I set the boxes up myself, stacking them up, then put the mattress on top. I say, 'Put the camera down here right by the mattresses, get another camera up there for when I go over.' And I go up and do the shot, I go over the rail, fall down, drop out of frame of the camera below, land on the mattress. I say, 'Okay, get this stuff out of here, bring me an apple box.' I get up on the box, I say, 'Put the camera right here, that's where I'm going to land.' They roll camera, boom. I fall down on my back. They're like, 'Oh… He's such a good actor!' Two shots! Wow! It's such a revelation to 'em. You know, Jackie Chan still does this stuff. And these guys, they'll drop you out of a three-storey window and wonder why you couldn't get up off the cement."

As promised, Chris Mitchum took the lead in **MASTER SAMURAI**, Bobby's first production to be filmed in the Philippines. It was February 1974, less than 18 months after President Marcos declared martial law; while a curtain of fear hung over the scarier places in the Philippines, Chris was ensconced in the General MacArthur Suite at the Manila Hotel, with his wife and two kids join-

COSA NOSTRA ASIA: group shot of cast and crew

Michael Kaye and John setting up.

Dick jumps.

Chris.

Chris and thugs.

This page and opposite reprinted from *Clash! Kung Fu* issue 2 (1975), pp. 4-5

Angelita.

Tony.

tive West Virginian Joe Zucchero, born 1940, was a USC graduate from its Director's program and recipient of the George Cukor Award before working throughout Asia—including the Philippines—throughout the 'Sixties. By the start of the 'Seventies he had made Manila his home base while working as writer, editor, production manager and occasional actor on projects as far away as India and Guam. "I was editing a picture called **THE KILL** [released 1975], produced by a good friend of mine, Rolf Bayer, who had also done a lot of pictures in the Philippines. He had shot the film in Hong Kong and we're doing the post in Hong Kong, and I was working in an editing room in the same building where Bobby Suarez had his office upstairs. I would usually be one of the last people out of the building every night, and I would take the elevator down; it would stop on his floor, the door would open and there would be Bobby. After bumping into him on several occasions we started up a conversation and that's when he said, 'I'll bet you're in the film business, because no-one else would be working these crazy hours!' We went out, we had a couple of drinks, got to know each other, and I found out that he was coming back to the Philippines at that time to start up a production company.

"When I finished the edit of the picture I was doing in Hong Kong, I came back to the Philippines, got in touch with him—I recall he was doing a picture at that time, and asked me to participate as an actor. So myself and another good friend and associate of mine, Ken Metcalfe, worked on that show with Bobby, and Ken and I got involved with him, doing scripts for him from time to time, even did post and did editing a couple of times." Joe and Ken became a kind of pantomime horse—where you saw one head, the other was bound to follow. Ken was the tall, white-haired *gwaillo*, frequently taking directions from Eddie Romero and Cirio Santiago; Joe was shorter and rounder, at home playing a crazed scientist or American diplomat, or commander of a post-apocalypse army.

ing him several weeks later. Naturally, Bobby seemed to be a law unto himself. "Whether it was because it was the film business," remembered Chris, "or because Bobby was tied in, we were never really affected. You know, with the curfew, if you wanted to go to a club after curfew—curfew was ten o'clock, and we could drive back at one in the morning. And my driver had an M-16 there on the seat with him. So we had pretty much privileged access."

MASTER SAMURAI was directed by tag-team Cesar "Chat" Gallardo and his son Jun. "Chat" was a hardened survivor of the Philippines' film trenches, notching an impressive hundred-plus features for the local market in just over thirty years, and was said to be super-goon Joseph Estrada's favourite director. He also directed two entertaining export features with Cirio H. Santiago as producer, the blaxploitation kung fu flick **BAMBOO GODS AND IRON MEN** (1974) and the hookers-as-**DIRTY DOZEN**-themed **HUSTLER SQUAD** (a.k.a. **THE DIRTY HALF DOZEN**, 1976). Jun Gallardo was being groomed by his old man to take over the family mantle, and father and son approached Bobby to make the film together.

The result is a Philippines goon actioner with a distinctly Euro-crime flavour, and with the pacing, crash zooms, lightning edits and bone-crunching fights of an export-quality Hong Kong production. Mitchum plays James Peterson, a private detective and former spook for "the Agency" in Manila investigating a kidnapping by the People's Liberation Organization. With the help of disgraced former cop Vargas (Von Serna) and enigmatic Hong Kong MI5 Agent Sing (Larry Chiu), the trail of dead bodies—including Peterson's friend Bruno (Rey Sagum)—lead to American expat George Pomeroy (Ken Metcalfe), dubious associate Jensen (Joe Zucchero), and their well-organized international crime syndicate, who are exploiting weak-willed politician Don Benigno Zapante (Leopoldo Salcedo) and his daughter Cecille (Rosemarie Gil) as their respectable front. The seedy side of Manila is seedier than ever, martial law is effectively woven into the narrative ("It's not a big step from the old politics to syndicate crime," the jaded CIA operative Bill Daniels [Jim Babb] remarks), and there's a fight scene or car chase every five to ten minutes, keeping the action speeding along nicely.

Bobby needed white goons for **MASTER SAMURAI**, and brought into the Suarez film family two faces who would become very important allies. Na-

When did Ken Metcalfe make it to the Philippines? I asked Joe. "This would have been around 1966. I was still here at that time on that ship that we were making a TV show on. Ken came into the country to do a film for the Air Force, it was a training film called *Jungle Survival*; he was playing the pilot who gets shot down in the jungle. While he was in town, the cameraman that they were using was also a friend of ours from a show that we were doing, and they introduced him to us. After he finished that, he became friends with the kids on the ship and myself. And about the time he was finished with that and it was time to go back to the US, another associate of mine, Ken Loring, who was putting a feature film together, asked if Ken would stay and play a part in the film called **COMBAT KILLERS** (1968). Ken agreed, because he didn't particularly want to go back to Hollywood and wait on tables and pump gas waiting for the next opportunity to come along! In the meantime he'd met a lady here who was working for Pan Am, and they got romantically involved, and she was happy to see that he'd stick around for a while, as well. We did that picture, and shortly after that's when I went back to the States and Ken went back later—he and his wife Maria got married, and from that point he was living in the Philippines." The couple set up home in Makati and established Central Casting, following a successful gig coordinating the Caucasian extras on Coppola's **APOCALYPSE NOW** (released 1979).

"Ken had a really good business going," recalled Chris. "He was in charge of all the round-eye extras. And what he would do is, he would line up the various expatriate Americans and have them play these parts. And part of the deal was he would get a part in the film. So he had it pretty well covered. But he would get parts not so much because of the actor he was, but because he could supply

THEY CALL HIM CHOP SUEY: billboard display in downtown Manilla (**left**), and (**right**) Ramon Zamora as the inscrutable Chop-Suey

all these round-eye actors." But he was actually an actor, though. A trained actor. "Well…self-made, yeah. I don't think he ever went to the Neighbourhood Playhouse in New York and studied."

When I met Joe in February 2007 he and his wife Josephine, or "Little Jo", were in the midst of packing up their apartment in Makati before relocating to Las Vegas. It had been forty years, on and off, for Joe in the Philippines, and I remarked how the country certainly allowed a person to reinvent themselves. To an extent, Joe agreed. "In my own particular case I liked it because if I'd stayed in Hollywood, I probably would have compartmentalised; I'd have put myself in one situation which would probably have been the editing room, but I would never have had the opportunity to do other things—write, act, eventually produce. The Philippines was also a wonderful learning experience, because you can only get so much out of film school, and then suddenly you're thrown into it. Here we used to call it the Guerrilla Warfare School of Filmmaking! You just had to jump in, be ready for anything, and go for it."

I mentioned to Chris there were some moments in MASTER SAMURAI that were *very* reminiscent of SUMMERTIME KILLER. "I rode a bike all throughout that. And after that when I'd make a film in Asia, I'd read the synopsis, but after I'd signed up, there'd be an extra eight pages with me on a motorcycle!" Chris laughed. "It must have been MASTER SAMURAI; there was a car chase in it, and they have to blow up the car so they get the worst car they could possibly get. And if you look at that, you'll notice that the car chase isn't very fast. They're going along at twenty-five miles an hour. Because it's completely shot. The transmission's gone, the engine's gone. Everything. I hit a guy on a motorcycle, I jump out, do I help the guy? No, I take his motorcycle! I'm in a car, for Christ's sake—what do I need with a motorcycle? But that's how it was, Chris Mitchum on a motorcycle, that's what sells."

Bobby's second film in the Philippines, THEY CALL HIM CHOP-SUEY (1975), is dramatically different to Bobby's previous potboilers. For starters, it's a comedy, and quite a painful one at times, with grating goofs courtesy of an unlikely but quintessentially Filipino hero, Ramon Zamora. While doing stunts and bit parts in movies, Zamora was both a comedian and song-and-dance man in the dying stages of the vaudeville circuit—the Clover Theatre and the Grand Opera House—where the previous generation of comedians hit their stride. It was while he was treading the boards, the story goes, that he was discovered by Rollie Grande, one of the creators of the cult TV show *Super Laff-In*, which premiered on ABS-CBN in 1970. Amongst the stellar cast and variety of characters, one stood out: Ramon Zamora as a cripple possessed by the spirit of a dead Nazi in full storm trooper outfit and Hitler moustache, spouting a barrage of German-ese gibberish. Oh, and he could do kung fu—thanks to his dance background—and possessed mystical powers. The one decipherable phrase, if you can call it that, was to be Zamora's famous catchphrase, "*Isprakenhayt!*"

After a series of kung fu parodies—most notably on Bruce Lee's THE BIG BOSS, entitled THE PIG BOSS (1972)—Pinoy wunderkind Celso Ad. Castillo featured Zamora as the titular dreamer in ANG MAHIWAGANG DAIGDIG NI PEDRO PENDUKO ("*The Mystical Adventures Of Pedro Penduko*", 1973) and mythical kung fu epic RETURN OF THE DRAGON (a.k.a. REVENGE OF THE DRAGON, 1974), the latter cementing him in the Philippines' collective consciousness as the Pinoy successor to Bruce Lee's Dragon mantle. Zamora would be known for the next decade—only half-jokingly, and without a trace of irony, as befitting the country from which he sprung—as "the Bruce Lee of the Philippines".

THEY CALL HIM CHOP-SUEY has essentially the same premise of THE WAY OF THE DRAGON (*Meng long guo jiang*, 1972)[4], Bruce Lee's sole directorial effort, in which Lee travels to Rome to help his family's restaurant, only to face off against Chuck Norris in the final epic battle. In CHOP SUEY, Zamora plays an awkward Chinoy (half-Chinese, half-Filipino) named Choi, or "Chop Suey" after his mixed heritage, working like a slave in a Hong Kong kitchen alongside his grandfather (Bayani Casimiro), and "haunted" by the spirit of his hero Bruce Lee. In an impressive opening fantasy sequence, Choi as the channelled Bruce levels a nightclub filled with kung fu experts; between kissing the club's singer and cutting down one good after another, he's in reality back in the mundane world choking a chicken carcass towards a twice-killed meal.

On the sudden death of his grandfather, Choi travels to Manila to find the Chinese restaurant of his Aunty Ming (Patria Plata), and discovers she and her helper Shu Mai (bald, sparrow-bodied comedian Pugak) are being fleeced for protection money. Sound familiar? The film even gives the game away by zooming in on a poster featuring Lee and Chuck Norris! Choi then offers his services, along with his grandfather's secret recipe for Chop Suey, and the dish's regenerative, aphrodisiac qualities ignite a restaurant war with local gangster sadist Jackson (MASTER SAMURAI's Romeo Rivera) and Aunty's rival, Mr. Tan. Jackson's moll Jenny (Malaysian beauty Jennifer Kaur), kept as a virtual prisoner and sex slave, manages to escape with incriminating documents from Jackson's safe, and takes refuge with Choi and Shu Mai. Along with pretty, blind, lovestruck girl Celia (Eva Linda), they take a cook's job in the country, at the home of Jackson's American partner-in-crime Hopalong (Mark Le Buse, also in MASTER SAMURAI as "white fat bald goon"). Jenny is recognized by some of Jackson's visiting henchmen, and they all escape to the jungle, with police officers (Arnold Mendoza, and Tony Ferrer's real-life brother Nick Romano) in hot pursuit, and Choi stalking Jackson and Hopalong's armies with bow-and-arrow and bare fists, this time channelling Bruce Lee's cat howls for real.

Now flying solo, director Jun Gallardo cuts frequently between Zamora's "Pinoy Bruce Lee" persona and his Pedro Penduko's hapless dreamer shtick—

---

[4] To make matters nice and confusing, this 1972 Bruce Lee film has seen US release under both the names RETURN OF THE DRAGON and REVENGE OF THE DRAGON, the same two release titles of Castillo's 1974 mythical. *–ed.*

Lobby card for another early, zany Bobby A. Suarez hit from 1977, about the time that "Bionic" became a brief cultural word for SF cool

distinctly Asian in its silliness and somewhat alien, no doubt, to a Western audience, for whom the kung fu comedy of Jackie Chan was still a number of years away. Indeed, Choi's journey from bumbling kitchen hand to jungle predator triggers so many dizzying shifts in tone it's sometimes hard to believe you're still watching the same film. The inclusion of Pugak as comic Ramon Zamora's bonus comic relief defies explanation, other than he's strictly for lazy yuks from the home crowd; with a head that could only be described as a cut thumb, Pugak was a staple of both vaudeville ("bob-a-bil") stage shows and comedy films, sometimes teamed with the chubby Tugak, and often paired with other single-named jokers Tugo, Bentot, and the equally bald pate of Pugo. Again, Pugak engenders a kind of culture shock only comprehensible in the Philippines, making **THEY CALL HIM CHOP-SUEY** the worldly Bobby's most intrinsically "Filipino" film. Nevertheless **CHOP-SUEY** rode on Bruce Lee's coattails and sold well in Europe—released in West Germany as **BRUCE LEE: DIE GROSSE KAMPFMASCHINE** ("*The Big Fighting Machine*")—giving a martial arts spin on the similar knockabout comedies of Terence Hill and Bud Spencer (Bobby's title is a direct nod to their *Trinity* films), and in its strange roundabout way, it foreshadowed the phenomenal success of Jackie Chan's kung-fool fusions. In final analysis, despite its attempts to cover many bases at once, it's an enjoyable if somewhat confused and occasionally jarring romp through Brucesploitation territory.

It was around 1975 that Bobby embarked on a disastrous project with actress Rita Gomez, a real Philippine marquee-blazer of the early 'Seventies. Her manager sought out Bobby as producer due to his connections to overseas distributors; she insisted on Ishmael Bernal, now regarded as one of the finest filmmakers of his generation, as her director. It was a match made in Hell: **SCOTCH ON THE ROCKS TO REMEMBER, BLACK COFFEE TO FORGET** (1976) ended up as a mountain of negatives in a trash can outside Bobby's office. Generations of film scholars may wring their hands over the perceived loss to Philippines' cinema, but Bobby remained unrepentant. "He shot a jeepney ride to Quiapo for half an hour. *Half an hour!* How was I supposed to edit that?"

I remember as if it was yesterday, sitting next to Bobby at the South East Asian Cinema Conference in November 2008. I'd just delivered my "Bamboo Gods and Bionic Boys" paper, and now Pinoy B Films panel moderator Dr. Tilman Baumgartel was trying to reel in an aggressive Bobby who was browbeating his stunned twenty-something audience with lines like "Don't waste your parents' money on your shitty digital features!"

From the auditorium, leading Filipino film archivist Teddy Co stood and addressed Bobby in a reverential tone. "Mr. Suarez…can you please tell us what you did with the negatives that Mr. Bernal had shot?"

Bobby looked at him squarely and defiantly. "I burnt them." The audience and Mr. Co sharply inhaled as one. I had to laugh; I remember Bobby telling me the same story in his office, motioning towards the alleyway where the early work of a master filmmaker would have gone up in spiralling plumes of smoke joining the blanket of smog above Plaza Santa Cruz.

After Bobby died, I asked Gene and sons Richard and Bobby II if Bobby did in fact set fire to the negatives. He certainly told the family he had, but not one of them had seen any evidence of a fire. So the film may still exist, I asked? "It may be in Hong Kong…" was their cryptic response. And until Ms. Lai forgives Bobby and opens up Intercontinental's vaults, **SCOTCH ON THE ROCKS TO REMEMBER, BLACK COFFEE TO FORGET** will remain an intriguing blind alley in the catacombs of Filipino film history.

The fiercely independent Bobby also claimed he was approached by drive-in distributor New World Pictures even before Roger Corman began his long association with Cirio H. Santiago. "Because I'm close with Roger Corman," said Bobby. "So I said, 'No, I only work for myself.' I said, 'Look, we are friends. But I don't want to work for anybody.' Because when you line produce, you know, there is the matter of money. And I don't want that friendship to be ruined by one cent or dollar. And some people say that's crazy. I say, 'Look, I'm no super-producer.' I turned him down because of friendship." To date, Mr. Corman has been unavailable for comment.

At this point in his career, it would be tempting to compare Bobby with fellow Filipino directors Cirio Santiago and Eddie Romero—two towering figures in Filipino cinema whose combined efforts cracked the international market with their cheap and colourful drive-in shockers. Bobby was in fact closer in spirit to Luis Nepomuceno—producer of self-funded Filipino epic war films and martial arts actioners such as **MANILA, OPEN CITY** (1968) and **THE PACIFIC CONNECTION** (a.k.a. **STICKFIGHTER**, a.k.a. **SOUTH PACIFIC CONNECTION**, 1974)—or, more specifically, Jimmy L. Pascual of Emperor Films, whose years spent successfully producing kung fu films in Hong Kong in the post-Bruce Lee boom allowed him to return to the Philippines and craft films such as **DEVIL WOMAN** (*She yao jing*, a.k.a. **MANDA THE SNAKE GIRL**, a.k.a. **THE EVIL SNAKE GIRL**, 1974)[5] and **BRUKA: QUEEN OF EVIL** (*Ren tou she*, a.k.a. **DEVIL WOMAN PART 2**, 1975)[6] for both local and overseas audiences. Both Romero and Santiago's export ambitions were utterly dependent on their relationships with American producers and distributors, and were often treated as subordinates on the payroll of Corman's New World, AIP, Crown Pictures and others; Bobby, on the other hand, had fashioned his own links with Hong Kong financiers and was never once *not* in control. During his time in Hong Kong and while travelling the globe, Bobby envisaged a pan-Asian film empire—with Bobby, naturally, on the emperor's throne. And to Bobby's credit, across the remainder of the 'Seventies and into the 'Eighties, he came closer than any Filipino filmmaker to realizing his ambitious, fevered internationalist fantasies.

IN PART TWO: The B.A.S. Film Family and the Bionic Boy, Marrie Lee becomes Cleopatra Wong, and the "Malaysian Incident" almost ends in bloodshed!

---

[5] IMDb lists this as a 1970 release, which appears to be incorrect, a seeming confusion between the Pascual-scribed film and a 1970 Tagalog film called **DEVIL WOMAN**, reportedly directed by Jose Flores Sibal, and displaying on IMDb a French-language poster bearing the title **KUNG-FU AUX PHILIPPINES**, which research shows was an alternate poster for the Pascual-scribed film. The mysterious 1970 Tagalog film's given synopsis is suspiciously similar to that of Pascual's script, so we suspect major clerical errors with regards to the accuracy of its database entry. –*ed.*

[6] IMDb lists this as a 1973 film, but it appears to have been released in June of 1975. –*ed.*

MASSACRE MITCHELL STYLE
Or: How Grindhouse Releasing Rescued the Pope
by Jeff Goodhartz

Grindhouse Releasing: the little exploitation Blu-ray/DVD company that could.

A Hollywood-based distributor that bowed in 1996, this extremely small operation is devoted to the restoration of classic '70s and '80s exploitation films. To be honest, it does take an exceptionally long time for each of their releases to see the light of day (which, given the circumstances, is understandable), but when one of their titles do finally hit the market, they are always well worth grabbing up. This past spring, they've outdone themselves with a pair of titles from the one and only Duke Mitchell; first restoring his legendary mob opus, **MASSACRE MAFIA STYLE** *(1974) and then going several steps further by actually editing together his never-before-released follow-up,* **GONE WITH THE POPE** *(1976/2010).*

A little background info on our subject: Duke Mitchell (birth name Dominic Micelli) spent much of his professional life as a nightclub singer/entertainer based primarily in Palm Springs, California, leading him to proclaim himself "The King of Palm Springs". Early on in his crooning career, Mitchell formed a popular two-man stage act with comedian Sammy Petrillo. Since Petrillo's main act was doing Jerry Lewis impressions, it made sense for the duo to do approximations of mega-popular Martin and Lewis. By all accounts, they were quite good at it, even going as far as occasionally surprising their audiences by playing each others' characters! Their popularity grew until they found themselves blackballed by Jerry himself (who apparently to this day doesn't want to hear the name Sammy Petrillo). The act was cut short, but not before our dynamic duo found themselves cast in the "Bizarro World" jungle comedy, **BELA LUGOSI MEETS A BROOKLYN GORILLA** (a.k.a. **THE BOYS FROM BROOKLYN**, 1952), directed by the infamously efficient William "One Shot" Beaudine. Parting amicably, the two spent the next couple decades continuing their respective stage acts while also finding sporadic work in front of the camera. Petrillo wound up in Doris Wishman's 1972 sexploitation pic, **KEYHOLES ARE FOR PEEPING**. Duke for his part got a gig as Fred Flintstone's singing voice (yep, that's him as "Hi-Fi" singing the "Listen to the Rocking Bird" song). And just when you thought things couldn't get much more outré…

By the '70s, Duke found his ambitions growing and expanding. Having seen **THE GODFATHER** (1972) and reportedly resenting the Italian stereotype in films in general, he decided in 1974 to tell it like it is (or something approximating it) by writing, producing, directing and starring in **MASSACRE MAFIA STYLE** (originally titled **LIKE FATHER, LIKE SON** before quickly being changed to its more popular and exploitative moniker; it later experienced a brief VHS run where it was re-christened yet again as **THE EXECUTIONER**). Featuring the catchy tagline, "You're in or you're in the way!", his opus begins in mid-film with an epic, bloody mass slaughter in an office building which includes the infamous "urinal execution moment". Set to this spectacular yet clumsily shot sequence is a music track featuring a particularly cheery Italian ditty sung by our hero. So memorably bizarre is this opening that an edited version was used for the trailer (which has gone on to become a legend unto itself).

We then settle into our story. Mitchell plays Mimi Miceli, a first-generation Italian American who, due to his activities in New York, was sent packing back to Sicily. His father, The Don (Lorenzo Dodo), doesn't approve of his son's shenanigans, but Mimi is determined to keep the family business alive. Returning to the US he sets up shop in Hollywood, the place of his childhood dreams. Connecting with old friend Jolly Rizzo (played by Vic Caesar), Mimi intends to take over the town. Having gone honest and currently running a bar, it takes only the slightest bit of coaxing from Mimi to get Jolly to return to the original biz ("Tonight we eat, tomorrow, we shoot!"). And our somewhat dynamic duo proceeds to do just that: shoot, shoot and then shoot some more. At one point, they kidnap one of the local Mafia bosses, Chuck Tripoli (Louis Zito), and hold him for ransom. To show they mean business, they send his finger to

Right: Duke Mitchell chews the scenery with delightfully ham-fisted gusto every chance he gets!

Right: Duke and Sammy Petrillo yuk it up in **BELA LUGOSI MEETS A BROOKLYN GORILLA**. **Middle:** Even the Messiah's excited about the restoration of **GONE WITH THE POPE**! **Right:** Duke lets the sideburns do the talkin' in **GWTP**

the other bosses in a jewelry box (leading to one of the most memorably inane lines in the film, "That's his finger alright. I've seen it on him a million times."). Though some of The Dons object to this hostile takeover, cooler heads prevail and ultimately Mimi gets what he wants. That is until Don Miceli back home becomes aware of his son's doings and orders one of his men to send Mimi a message; essentially slapping some sense (quite literally) into the out-of-control offspring. It works at least temporarily, as Mimi and Jolly attempt to move on from their initial plans and get into the profitable porn industry instead (probably the seediest section of the film). Quickly they realize that the only way to turn over a profit is to make the films themselves. This includes getting the women for the roles, and to this end, they run afoul of top pimp, Super Spook (Jim Williams). When he refuses to deal with them, our heroes first threaten him (featuring some squirm-inducing racist dialogue) and then kill him outright by crucifying him on Easter Sunday (possibly the most jaw-dropping moment in a movie full of them). Getting nowhere with this new would-be enterprise, the pair restart their all-out war with the other mob bosses.

I've seen **MASSACRE MAFIA STYLE** many times over the last two decades ever since I first watched a dupe of the VHS (under the re-title, **THE EXECUTIONER**). My initial reaction was that I was watching an earlier filmed version of **GOODFELLAS** (1990) as directed by Ed Wood. That isn't a put-down as much as it is a backhanded compliment, as I found myself extremely entertained by it all and wanted to watch it again the very next day (not something I could often claim). Some of the most unprofessional and awkwardly shot shootouts ever are to be found here. On more than one occasion, you can see someone getting shot and not dying correctly or quickly enough (the opening massacre is a perfect example of this). The dialogue tends to be all over the place, coming at you from any and all angles. Highlight among this is Duke's diatribe on the plight of the Italian woman. It's obviously heartfelt, but just comes out of nowhere in-between slaughters and comes across with a distinct (though maybe unintended) "do as I say, not as I do" feel. The entire film from first frame to last, left me (and I assume many others) in a decidedly off-kilter state. Speaking of which, I've yet to mention the many catchy tunes that populate Duke's pic (other than the opening sequence, of course), most of which are sung by the man himself; they function as an entity unto themselves. Permeating the whole project is a distinct documentary feel. As wild, over the top and exploitative as the film is, the viewer will also feel like they're being privy to the genuine article. This should be no surprise, as Mitchell based his characters and much of the dialogue on the real life mobsters that often frequented the nightclubs he was performing in. This air of authenticity, which, when combined with the film's other aforementioned "qualities" and the awkward structure of the whole thing (it took a couple of viewings on my part to realize that well over a decade passes at one point), makes for irresistible viewing. This was obviously a labor of love for Duke, and his enthusiasm shows through on every wobbly frame. It succeeds as both a gory, grungy grindhouse classic and (perhaps) as a slice of genuine Mafioso life, the likes of which could only be achieved through this kind of low budget, off-the-cuff filmmaking.

Originally released on DVD by Duke's son, Jeffrey Mitchell as "The Family Edition" (which though inferior, does come with some interesting special features and commentaries and is worth picking up for that reason), it was finally given the full-blown Blu-ray/DVD makeover it so badly needed by Grindhouse Releasing. Presented in all its 1.85:1 glory, the film has never looked better. I can't imagine it having looked half this rich and sharp even during its initial theatrical run. Chief among the extras is the documentary *Like Father, Like Son* (2009), which interviews son Jeffrey along with friends and stalwarts George Jacobs and Frankie Ray. Though none worked on the film itself, they all paint an interesting and intimate portrait of its do-it-all star. A true maverick and real-life tough guy unwilling to take any crap from anyone, Duke did it *his* way whether it won or cost him a few gigs (I'd wager more often the latter). It's a good listen as the group talk freely about the great man's friendships with the likes of Frank Sinatra, Sammy Davis Jr. (who apparently shot him with a gun filled with blanks!), Shecky Greene and even the great Henry Fonda. Also brought up is the difference in father and son's musical tastes (Jeffrey champions Jimi Hendrix; Duke...not so much). A true eyebrow-raiser is when we are told that the urinal sequence from the opening massacre was based on an actual incident! One of the most interesting conjectures was when Mitchell and Jacobs contend that much of the racist atmosphere of the film (the shooting of so many black actors and particularly the aforementioned verbal and physical abuse wrought on Super Spook) would have been considerably less offensive had they stuck with the original idea of Jacobs playing the Jolly character (which likely would have lent the film a JohnTravolta/Samuel Jackson-**PULP FICTION** vibe). There's also "Duke Mitchell Home Movies", plus *An Impressionistic Tribute to Jimmy Durante*—an unaired TV special in which Duke performs an amazing Durante impression. One big surprise among the extras on the Blu-ray is the inclusion of **BELA LUGOSI MEETS A BROOKLYN GORILLA** in its schlocky entirety, making this release an unannounced double-feature.

"Then God said, 'Let there be man,' and he fucked the whole thing up".

While **MASSACRE MAFIA STYLE** was nearing completion, Duke Mitchell had his next brainstorm: a film centering on no less than the kidnapping of the Pope. Given the irresistible re-title **GONE WITH THE POPE** (original shooting title: **KISS THE RING**), it was a million-dollar concept with nary a budget to shoot it on. Once again wearing every cinematic hat imaginable, Duke proceeded to spin a long and winding tale, the likes of which would rarely be considered, much less attempted by most anyone else. Duke plays a jailed hit-man named Paul who, after serving a twenty-year sentence, is paroled just in time for his next job: earning one hundred thousand dollars for rubbing out seven casino owners (three in Vegas and four in Los Angeles) who refuse to sell out to the Chicago mob. The plan by the bosses is to then get rid of Paul once the deed is done. Being made aware of the scheme, Paul enlists his brother Giorgio (Giorgio Tavolieri) and offers him half the money to take care of the Vegas owners. By doing this, Paul is letting his employers (and would-be assassins) know that he has a partner who will squeal should anything happen to him. Once the mission is completed (it should be noted here that the slayings while still awkward, are more efficiently done than in the previous film), Paul decides to take his share of the money and borrow a yacht that belongs to his special lady friend, Jean (Jeanne Hibbard). After bidding farewell to the US (a howler of a rant; the trailer opens with it), Paul sets sail. Along for the cruise are three of Paul's recently released cellmates, Peter (Peter Milo), Luke (Jim Lo Bianco) and "The Old Man" (Lorenzo Dardano). Sailing around the world, our quartet of ex-cons lands themselves in Rome where Paul fills his cronies in on his grand scheme: to kidnap the Pope and demand one dollar from every Catholic in the world (Paul cuts the ransom demands in half when informed that there are over eight hundred and fifty million Catholics in the world—Paul's a fair man if nothing else). Donning a disguise, Paul infiltrates the Vatican and somehow manages to switch The Old Man for The Pope ("Take off your clothes, Your Holiness."). Back on the yacht, The Pope attempts to reform his trio of captors. Paul resists, leading to one of the most jaw-dropping speeches ever heard on film as he drills the exalted one over the hypocrisy of Catholicism and in particular, not preventing Mussolini from helping Hitler kill six million Jews! His two cronies, however, are completely won over by the holy man, one even experiencing a miracle (a prized necklace given by his mother went overboard only to be found in the belly of a caught fish!). After arguing against the idea, Paul reluctantly returns with his two chums and The Pope to the Vatican. Hooking back up with Jean, Paul decides to settle down...but first he must settle the score with his jilted employers who may still have it out for him.

Coming directly on the heels of **MASSACRE MAFIA STYLE**, **GONE WITH THE POPE** represents a surprising departure for our do-it-all man of the hour. The nearly constant carnage, gore and griminess of the previous entry are largely replaced here with a more subdued (and certainly more surreal) atmosphere. It would seem that Duke grew somewhat as a filmmaker, apparently moving on from the Ed Wood style of directing to something akin to Ray Dennis Steckler. Despite the film's inescapably hurried look (he shot the thing on weekends and there was no shooting script!) and some hysterically awful acting (Duke employed his friends, none of whom had any acting experience and then had them read their lines from cue cards), this was an extremely well-filmed and well-lit mini-epic. Sure, it was still a glorified home movie, but it was an often strikingly beautiful one. Some may feel disappointed (initially, anyway) with the lack of action throughout much of it, but there is something oddly hypnotic about it all. The film flows with a stream-of-consciousness feel that kept me locked into it from beginning to end (pretty much, anyway). The story is an increasingly fluid one, and just when you think it's settled down into its "main story", it just casually "sails" off in another direction (see what I did there? ...yeah). The actual Pope plot, for instance, doesn't occur until nearly midway into the picture and then is promptly pushed aside as little more than an afterthought. Oddly, none of this seems to negatively affect the picture, with the one exception being (perhaps) the scene with the obese woman. But even this "yechh!" moment if nothing else is good for revealing Mitchell's eccentric (to put it politely) sense of humor. Punctuating it all is a couple of terrific rockin' tunes courtesy of Duke's son, Jeffrey Mitchell. It boosts many of the travelogue scenes wonderfully and gives the overall movie the extra kick it needed.

The story of how this Holy Grail of lost exploitation movies finally saw the light of day is as fascinating as the movie itself, if not more so. While searching for original elements for **MASSACRE MAFIA STYLE**, luminaries Sage Stallone, Bob Murawski and Bill Lustig were handed boxes of reels from Jeffrey Mitchell that turned out to be the long-lost second film of his father's (under the **KISS THE RING** moniker). At the time, it was considered something of an urban legend and our threesome were floored by what they were so casually handed. It was seventeen reels long, but (again) unscripted and not in any particular order. Worse still was that it was an incomplete film. Determined to assemble what they had and unleash it onto its eagerly awaiting audience, Murawski (the most qualified individual that this project could have possibly hoped for, having edited Sam Raimi's films from **DARKMAN** [1990] on, before landing an Oscar for **THE HURT LOCKER** [2008]) spent a decade and half working on the rough elements (done in-between his Hollywood work as a sort of side project), performing what has to be one of the most painstaking cleanup jobs ever afforded for a genre film. The finished project looks and sounds absolutely stunning. The extras on the Blu-ray/DVD are nearly as numerous as on the previous release. The documentary, *Gone With the Pope: The Players*, features interviews with actor Jim Lo Bianco and actor/producer John Murgia, joined by cinematographer Peter Santoro, editors Robert Florio and Bob Leighton, and filmmaker Matt Climber. This is maybe the most interesting and illuminating extra to be found on either disc as the group recall the great man in one head-shaking story after another; things like how Duke somehow convinced a prison to move all its inmates so a scene could be shot, the editors having to work in shifts in Duke's living room while his wife watched TV, the scene with the black actress ("looks like Brillo"), and most interestingly (to me, at any rate), the reason(s) why they feel the film was never finished (some said he ran out of money while others contend that he chose to do the Durante special over finishing his feature). "Shooting Gone with the Pope" has Santoro sharing his experiences on making the film, in particular the shooting style where Mitchell would improvise many scenes as he went. Also included among the extras are seven deleted scenes (some of which are silent), including a sequence in which Peter overcomes his fear of water in order to save a boy in Mexico. There is also a revealing outtake reel which features Duke yelling and freaking out over airplanes ruining shots and actors blowing their lines. It also shows Duke guiding the actors he's working alongside by simply telling them to say their line again rather than going for another take. There was also the consideration of marketing the film to the porn industry (which makes for an interesting callback to a sequence from the previous film). To that end, Mitchell actually attempted to shoot a soft-core sequence showing him getting his freak on with a woman. The scene is ruined by the actress breaking down in tears and Mitchell's inability to...well, you get the idea. Both titles come equipped with Easter Eggs that are worth the extra effort of finding, particularly **POPE**.

"Why me?" "Why not?!"

One cannot overemphasize the absolutely incredible job that Grindhouse Releasing performed on these two '70s artifacts. They are releases worthy of the Criterion Collection and then some. **GONE WITH THE POPE** in particular should win an award for restoration of the year. Incredible work put in by all involved that would have made the late Duke himself proud.

Now if some enterprising YouTuber would just be kind enough to dub "Listen to the Rocking Bird" tune over the trailer to **MASSACRE MAFIA STYLE**, I'd deeply appreciate it...

Smoke 'em if you got 'em!

BE GOOD OR BE DEAD!

A SHAW BROTHERS PRESENTATION

The kid with the GOLDEN ARM

A W RLD NORTHAL FILM

R RESTRICTED
Under 17 requires accompanying Parent or Adult Guardian

TUESDAY NIGHT GRINDHOUSE NIGHTS AT THE NEW BEVERLY

Starring Bennie Woodell!

January 13th, 2015

The first film of the night was **FIVE ELEMENT NINJAS** (五遁忍術 / *Ren zhe wu di*, 1982), and no martial arts director has made more amazing films than Chang Cheh—and **FIVE ELEMENT NINJAS** (or **CHINESE SUPER NINJAS** to some) is by far one of Cheh's greatest. It starts out with one of the greatest moments in kung fu movies, where the Samurai loses his sword and is reminded by the Chinese that a Samurai who loses his sword loses his life, and he must commit seppuku right then and there. This sets the tone for an insanely bloody film where the Chinese kung fu-ists must seek revenge against the Japanese and defeat the five element ninjas: gold, wood, fire, earth, and water. Each set of ninjas utilizes their element perfectly, hiding in trees, using golden shields to blind their opponents to stab them, hiding under water, etc. This is also one of the Venom Mob's films, so right there you know how spectacularly acrobatic this film will be. Quite honestly, I would put this right under the **CRIPPLED AVENGERS** (殘缺 / *Can que*, a.k.a. **RETURN OF THE 5 DEADLY VENOMS**, 1978) for my favorite Venoms film. This is a must-see!

The second film of this week's double-feature was **THE KID WITH THE GOLDEN ARM** (金臂童 / *Jin bei tong*, 1979), another film from the wonderful Chang Cheh and the Venom Mob. This film is one of those Shaw Brothers films that I have to watch when it's on, but while watching it I always wonder why I hold it so dear to my heart. Yes, there are some fantastic kung fu sequences in it, and some great characters, like Brass Head (Hsiung Yang) and such, but this falls into the trap that a number of Shaw Brother films did, in my opinion, where they took a simple storyline and tried to make it way deeper than it needed to be and gave up on having enough action to keep us interested in the film. We have the Venoms on the screen, the greatest martial arts group on film together, and we spend so much time in the story. And maybe I would have gotten into the story more if the version was subtitled, but it was a dubbed print, and that always takes me out of the film too, so lots of unnecessary story with bad dubbing makes it hard to sit through. This is a must-see though for the fight between Lo Meng and Kuo Chue.

January 20th, 2015

Up first this week was **SUPER MAN CHU: MASTER OF KUNG FU** (烈日狂風 / *Lie ri kuang feng*, 1973). I had seen the trailer a couple of times weeks prior at the New Beverly and I was very much looking forward to this film. It looked like a hell of a good time, as what seemed like an American spoof of kung fu films at the time in the '70s. The joke was on me though as I found out this was a very serious and legit kung fu movie that was imported to the states. This could be one of the hardest kung fu movies I've ever sat through. The dubbing was atrocious and the martial arts were nothing to write home about. Pretty much everything shown in the trailer was the best parts of the fighting; the rest was very ho-hum mediocre martial arts that made B-level martial arts look like A-pictures. I really can't write much about this film except to avoid it at all costs.

Next up was **DUEL OF THE IRON FIST** (大決鬥 / *Da jue dou*, a.k.a. **THE DUEL**, 1971), which completely redeemed the night. Another Chang Cheh masterpiece that had David Chiang and Ti Lung starring in it. This is a Shaw Brothers martial arts film that was not a kung fu flick, but set in more like a modern, 1930s China, so the fight sequences resemble more of a modern feel and flow as opposed to a regular Shaw Brothers kung fu sequence. The knife fights in this film are nothing less than spectacular, and show why Chiang and Lung were the greatest martial artists of their era.

February 24th, 2015

Having had a very, very small background in spaghetti westerns, I was very excited for this week's double-feature. **A BULLET FOR SANDOVAL** (*Los desesperados*, 1969), starring Ernest Borgnine as Don Pedro Sandoval, was the first film of the evening, and I have to say I enjoyed the hell out of this flick. I loved how the hero, John Warner (George Hilton), decided to desert his fellow soldiers the night before a major battle to wed his pregnant girlfriend, who ends up dying, and he becomes a fugitive who forms his own gang/posse. There were some great gunfights in this flick, but most importantly were the final moments of the film where Sandoval and Warner were fighting each other on top of a bull's pen and end up in there with the bull himself. Myself and many other moviegoers were cringing in our seats and worried about the poor stuntman who had to take the hits by the bull. It was a pretty intense ending that did not disappoint.

Next up was another film the New Beverly had been showing the trailer to for weeks leading up to the screening, **CUT-THROATS NINE** (*Condenados a vivir*, a.k.a. **BRONSON'S REVENGE**, 1972), the trailer for which boasted the film was so violent that the theater would provide terror masks so you could look away if need be. Well, the New Beverly did something very fun and gave everybody a barf bag just in case. By today's standards, the film's violence is very tame, but I sat there knowing for the time how crazy the film would have been and really appreciated everything I saw. I felt that the story itself was slow-moving and nothing I'd probably ever go out of my way to watch again, but it was great for a one-time viewing for some great gore sequences from a time where all you had were practical effects, so it was a breath of fresh air to watch that as opposed to anything CG-related that was playing in other cineplexes.

March 10th, 2015

Tonight's double-feature is a very special one to me, as Wong Kar-Wai is one of the people who has inspired me to become a filmmaker, and a chance to see two of his films in 35mm back-to-back was just amazing. **CHUNGKING EXPRESS** (重慶森林 / *Chung Hing sam lam*, 1994) was the first film of the double-feature, and this is one of those gems of cinema. Everything about this film is perfect, from Brigitte Lin's final performance, throwing off her symbolic wig and walking away from the spotlight, to Takeshi Kaneshiro eating thirty days worth of pineapple, to Tony Leung buying fish and chips as opposed to a salad. And let's not forget Faye Wong bouncing back and forth to "California Dreamin'". Combine that with some of the best voiceover narration ever on screen and hyper-stylized cinematography by the great Christopher Doyle, and you have a recipe for lightning in a bottle. Every time you watch this film, you will see something new, and that's what makes it so magical.

The second Wong Kar-Wai film for the double-feature was his second film, **DAYS OF BEING WILD** (阿飛正傳 / *Ah fei zing zyun*, 1990). I thought this was a wonderful choice as not many people have ever seen or heard of this film. It was amazing to see a young Leslie Cheung in his prime on the big screen wooing Maggie Cheung by forever remembering their one minute together. Though this film has a very slow pace and implies a lot more of what happens than it shows, I feel that the characters are so engrossing, suave, and interesting that you just can't help but want to watch the flick again to try and figure out what you might have missed. It is confusing, and the ending doesn't explain anything outside of a symbolic reference really, but that's the beauty of the film—it's what you make of it. I love the movie, and think it's something every cinephile should watch.

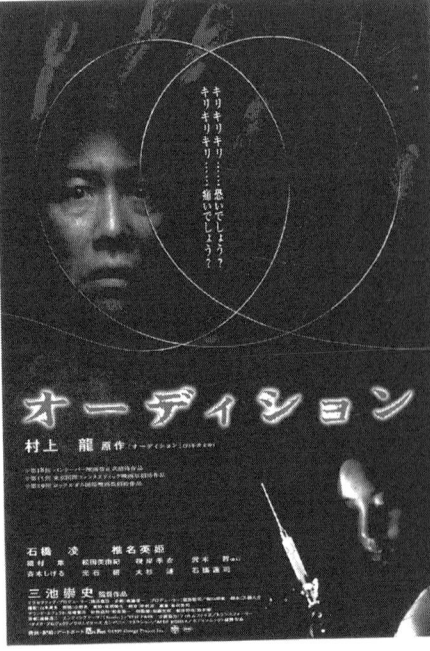

March 17th, 2015

Tonight's double-feature consists of two John Woo classics, the first being the film that made me decide to become a filmmaker, **THE KILLER** (喋血雙雄 / *Dip huet seung hung*, 1989). I don't think you get any better than Chow Yun-Fat when it comes to suave heroes. I wish I had a tenth of a percent of the coolness that he exudes, and this film is where he is the coolest. I would go so far as to say this is the greatest action film ever. It has the perfect anti-hero who's a cold-hearted killer but wants to do the right thing and save the sight of the woman he blinded, a cop who wants to get his man but understands they're in this mess together, and a thousand bad guys who all want them both dead. I don't think a single action sequence has ever been filmed that is more exciting, memorable, or powerful than the final shootout in the church. There's not much more to say; if you have not watched this film yet, put this magazine down right now and buy a copy or you cannot say you're a fan of cult cinema!

After **THE KILLER**, we got ten minutes to catch our breath before **ONCE A THIEF** (縱橫四海 / *Zong heng si hai*, 1991) was shown. I've always said this is a gem. It's John Woo doing a *Mission Impossible*-esque heist film, all the while it still being a slick, '90s Hong Kong action extravaganza. This time we not only get the suave awesomeness of Chow Yun-Fat, but we get the one-two punch of Leslie Cheung being his partner-in-crime. Though the film has some excellent action in it with traps and security systems that are reminiscent of Indiana Jones, I think what I love most about it is the love triangle (that isn't really), and the brotherhood that is forged even deeper from it, which we all know is a theme that Woo loves most. Definitely seek this film out if you haven't; it is, I believe, Woo's least-talked-about film. And get ready for Chow Yun-Fat to return to his comedic roots at the end of the movie!

March 31st, 2015

Tonight's double-feature was an interesting one, with two films that are completely opposite of one another. The first film is a film I have never seen, and have never been able to find a copy of: Tsui Hark's **THE BLADE** (刀 / *Dao*, 1995). I'm so happy I got to see this film for the first time on the big screen as there's no way a small screen could contain its depth. Tsui Hark has a very frenetic shooting style; pretty much all *wu xia pian* films from the '90s did, but this is on a whole different playing field, as that style really was a great juxtaposition of what could be one of the darkest Hong Kong films I've ever seen—and not as in I can't see what's happening, just the tone of the film itself was very dark. The style shouldn't have fit with the emotions, but it added a whole other character onto what I was seeing. And the fights themselves were just absolutely brutal, with the main villain being truly scary. I don't know if this film is available anywhere, but if you get a chance to check it out, do yourself the favor.

On a lighter note, Stephen Chow's **KING OF BEGGARS** (武狀元蘇乞兒 / *Mo jon yuen So Hat-Yi*, 1992) was up next, and a light-hearted comedy was definitely what the doctor ordered after having limbs hacked off in **THE BLADE**. I don't know about you, but I think Stephen Chow is the funniest man in cinema, period, and **KING OF BEGGARS** is one of the best. Chow tries to win the title of Kung Fu Scholar, but is cheated out of it and he and his father have to learn to live like beggars as opposed to royalty. Although **KING OF BEGGARS** is a comedy, you could be fooled into thinking it's a standard '90s HK swordplay flick, as there are many great fight sequences that I would put right up there with anything Tsui Hark, Yuen Woo Ping, or any of the other greats of the time were putting on film. **KING OF BEGGARS** is currently streaming on Netflix for those of you who need a good laugh tonight!

April 7th, 2015

Japanese cinema was the forefront of Grindhouse Night tonight, with Takashi Miike's **AUDITION** (オーディション / *Ôdishon*, 1999) being the first film of the evening. This is one of those very weird flicks that no matter how many years in-between viewings, you can't help but get chills just thinking of what you see on the screen. It had been about a decade since I saw it last, but when Asami Yamazaki (Eihi Shiina) started putting in the acupuncture needles and made this weird sound, the goosebumps came back and I remembered exactly how I felt the first time I saw it. The film stays with you. Although the pacing is on the slower side, it builds into something that just gets more and more intense and freaky. This is a psychological thriller at its finest. Watching **AUDITION** really makes you think twice about meeting anybody anywhere and letting them into your home.

Takeshi Kitano's **SONATINE** (ソナチネ, 1993) was the second film of tonight's double-feature, and though this film touts itself as a gangster film, to me it's more about the guys bonding while trying to stay low while the heat was on back home during a gang war. I found this film very confusing, actually, and if there was more to the story, I didn't catch it. They spent a lot of time on the beach, and not a lot of time shooting at anybody. The trailer I had seen the week before, and it looked like an action packed thrill ride, but instead this was a very Japanese film to me, with small bursts of action and then long bouts of nothing happening. I do really like Takeshi Kitano, especially in **BATTLE ROYALE** (バトル・ロワイアル / *Batoru rowaiaru*, 2000); he's got this rough aura to him that makes him a great on-screen tough guy, but I think there was more comedy in this film than action. Maybe if I hadn't been led to believe it was an action thrill-ride, I might have enjoyed it differently, but I was falling asleep during it, I was so bored.

April 21st, 2015

Hong Kong was at the forefront again for tonight's double-feature, with **BIG BULLET** (衝鋒隊—怒火 街頭 / *Chung fung dui liu feng gaai tau*, 1996) leading the way out of the gate. **BIG BULLET** is a fantastic '90s Hong Kong cop flick that stars two of the great B-movie HK actors, Lau Ching Wan and Anthony Wong. Everything they touch is gold, and **BIG BULLET** is no exception. Jordan Chan also has a role in this, and he always puts in a top-notch performance as well. Wan leads the Emergency Unit team as a punishment after a raid went sour, and turns them into the most badass unit on the force as the team bands together to take down Wong and his men. There is nothing held back here in terms of action; anything goes and this was an absolute pleasure to watch. This came out right before the Hong Kong handover to China, so there is very much an underlying tone of worry about that, as nearly every HK film had at the time. Aside from John Woo and Jackie Chan films, I would put **BIG BULLET** up against any action film that was made in the mid-'90s, and I feel it would hold its own.

The second film, **DOWNTOWN TORPEDOES** (神偷諜影 / *San tau dip ying*, 1997), really let the air out of the crowd, I felt. Teddy Chan has made some great films, most recently **KUNG FU KILLER** (一個人的武林 / *Yi ge ren de wu lin*, a.k.a. **KUNG FU JUNGLE**, 2014), but this was one of his low points for sure. The film stars Takeshi Kaneshiro and Jordan Chan, so on paper this should be outstanding with those three talents together, but the film really has no central focus on a storyline. Outside the theater I heard comment after comment about how people were confused what they just saw, myself included. There was some okay action, but nothing to write home about or make the previous two hours worthwhile. It felt like Kaneshiro and Chan dialed-in their performances, or were also unsure what their direction was, and everything just fell flat. It seemed like they cared more about making it look cool than making a good movie.

FIVE ELEMENT NINJAS
1982, HONG KONG. D: CHEH CHANG
AVAILABLE FROM MBL

THE KID WITH THE GOLDEN ARM
1979, HONG KONG. D: CHEH CHANG
AVAILABLE FROM TOKYO SHOCK

SUPER MAN CHU: MASTER OF KUNG FU
1973, TAIWAN/HONG KONG. D: MIN-HSIUNG WU

DUEL OF THE IRON FIST
1971, HONG KONG. D: CHEH CHANG
AVAILABLE FROM MR. FAT-W and EAST-WEST

A BULLET FOR SANDOVAL
1969, SPAIN/ITALY. D: JULIO BUCHS
AVAILABLE FROM VCI

CUT-THROATS NINE
1972, SPAIN. D: JOAQUÍN ROMERO MARCHENT
AVAILABLE FROM EUROVISTA and VIACOM MN [VOD]

CHUNGKING EXPRESS
1994, HONG KONG. D: KAR WAI WONG
AVAILABLE FROM CRITERION and MIRAMAX [BOTH OOP]

DAYS OF BEING WILD
1990, HONG KONG. D: KAR WAI WONG
AVAILABLE FROM KINO LORBER

THE KILLER
1989, HONG KONG. D: JOHN WOO
AVAILABLE FROM WEINSTEIN COMPANY

ONCE A THIEF
1991, HONG KONG. D: JOHN WOO
AVAILABLE FROM SONY

THE BLADE
1995, HONG KONG. D: HARK TSUI
AVAILABLE FROM MIA [R2]

KING OF BEGGARS
1992, HONG KONG. D: GORDON CHAN
AVAILABLE FROM KAM & RONSON

AUDITION
1999, JAPAN. D: TAKASHI MIIKE
AVAILABLE FROM SHOUT! FACTORY

SONATINE
1993, JAPAN. D: TAKESHI KITANO
AVAILABLE FROM MIRAMAX [OOP] and LIONSGATE [VOD]

BIG BULLET
1996, HONG KONG. D: BENNY CHAN
AVAILABLE FROM TAI SENG

DOWNTOWN TORPEDOES
1997, HONG KONG. D: TEDDY CHAN
AVAILABLE FROM TAI SENG

TELEFILM TERROR: MY MADE-FOR-TV LIFE

by George Pacheco

The current state of made-for-TV movies may be solely relegated to the Hallmark and Lifetime channels these days, but older readers of Weng's Chop *may remember an older, golden age for the medium; a time where all three of the major networks were vying for those Nielsen ratings on a weekly basis with their homegrown "movies of the week".*

This golden age arrived at the tail end of the 1960s, as the modern day telefilm began to find its creative feet with such examples as **SEE HOW THEY RUN** *(1964) and the Don Siegel-directed flick* **THE HANGED MAN** *later that year. It wasn't until the 1970s and '80s where the TV movie truly began to come into its own, however, as CBS, ABC and NBC encouraged all of their viewers to hunker down on the couch to watch one of their "first run" features.*

It makes sense, then, that—given the competition between the networks—many of these made-for-TV movies focused on excitement as their main draw. Horror, mystery, natural disasters and science fiction storylines were all major selling points for these films, many mirroring the major motion picture tropes of the day, albeit with the budgetary and content restrictions of network television.

One aspect of the telefilm which *was* shared with the motion picture industry happened to be talent, however, as many modern day masters of their craft cut their teeth on the made-for-TV circuit, such as Curtis Harrington, Dan (*Dark Shadows*) Curtis and, most infamously, a pre-**JAWS** (1975) Steven Spielberg. The network telefilm also proved itself worthy of netting some major star power, as the medium gained increased exposure and popularity during its 1970s heyday. Bette Davis, Jack Palance and Farrah Fawcett all lent their respective talents to the telefilm at one point another, while standout TV fright as *The Night Stalker* broke ratings records at the time during its momentous debut in January of 1972.

This column for *Weng's Chop* will hopefully shed some light upon this oft-maligned corner of the television world. We will discuss some of the major telefilm players with regards to writing, directing, acting and producing, and hopefully unearth some obscure gems of the genre, while also revisiting all of the well-worn classics once again for a new appraisal. So strap in, grab a snack and settle in for a smooth 'Seventies ride to where TV films ruled the roost!

DEVIL DOG: THE HOUND OF HELL
Air Date: October 31st, 1978
D: Curtis Harrington / W: Steven Karpf, Elinor Karpf
C: Kim Richards, Yvette Mimieux, Richard Crenna, Martine Beswick

Devil Dog: Hound of Hell is very much indicative of what has come to be known as the "typical" made-for-TV tropes of the day. Awkward acting? Check. Cheesy music? Double check. A ridiculous concept, usually dealing with devil, or some derivative thereof? Aw hell yeah.

This telefilm originally aired on Halloween night, 1978, and promised tons of terror to its audience, as director Curtis Harrington sheepishly organizes a script which details the exploits of a Satanic litter of puppies, one of which comes to the Barry family after their family dog is hit by a car. If this all

"I'm gonna hump the *Hell* outta your leg!"

sounds sublimely silly, then you're on the right track with these kinds of Halloween telefilms, yet this flick is anything but boring in its stone-faced and serious take on the Satanic possession theme.

This lack of pretension ultimately works in the film's favor, as the psychic dog attacks and predetermined accidents all work their way throughout the Barry family and their assorted friends. The fact that **DEVIL DOG** doesn't play the kitsch card means that we can simply enjoy the film for what it is: a cheap but breezy ride which may not arrive with any legitimate chills, yet nevertheless leaves a huge impression on the viewer which remains long after the movie is over.

Indeed, **DEVIL DOG: HOUND OF HELL** (the film's home video title, *sans* definite article) has endured to this very day, receiving VHS, DVD and even Blu-ray releases to the home video market, complete with extras and interview footage from the crew and cast. Speaking of which, the acting from lead Richard Crenna is straight-forward and without irony here, while Bond girl Martine Beswick provides some sex appeal in a brief-but-appreciated cameo as a devil-worshiping cult leader.

Bravo fans might also find it interesting to note that future *Housewife*[1] and former child star Kim Richards (**ESCAPE TO WITCH MOUNTAIN** [1975]) appears here as Crenna's young daughter. Richards' acting isn't the greatest, and very much hammers home the "made for TV" ideal in its stunted feel, but this can really be forgiven seeing how very young she is here, of course. One particularly memorable image occurs at the film's climax, as Crenna faces hand-to-paw with the demonic dog itself in an abandoned warehouse, complete with reverse negative effects galore! One can only imagine what the actor felt like after watching the finished product.

I love this movie. It's a great entry level picture to turn friends on to the made-for-TV model, presenting an energetic pace and a memorable premise for those just discovering the telefilm. I also have a personal feeling of nostalgia associated with **DEVIL DOG**, as I have a vivid memory of hearing the television ad for it as a kid from my grandmother's room. It scared the devil out of me (pun intended), and I got up out of bed and begged her to change the channel!

Of course, years later I've realized there was nothing really to be scared about, but that memory remains, with **DEVIL DOG: HOUND OF HELL** serving as one blast of a TV telefilm.

1978, CANADA/USA. D: CURTIS HARRINGTON
AVAILABLE FROM MEDIA BLASTERS

DYING ROOM ONLY

Air Date: September 18th, 1973
D: Philip Leacock / W: Richard Matheson
Cast: Cloris Leachman, Ned Beatty, Dabney Coleman

DYING ROOM ONLY stands in strict opposition to **DEVIL DOG: HOUND OF HELL**, in that this 1973 film is a no-joke, nerve-wracking and tension-filled masterpiece which deserves to be seen by those who deny that the TV movie is just a wasteland for bad taste and cheese.

---
1   *The Real Housewives of Beverly Hills* (2010-2015)

This simple yet effective telefilm tells a straightforward mystery story, but tells it oh so well, thanks to a cracking teleplay from famed genre writer Richard Matheson (*I Am Legend, Stir of Echoes*). **DYING ROOM ONLY** deals with a married couple, Bob and Jean—played by Dabney Coleman and Cloris Leachman (who absolutely *owns* this film)—making their way back home on a car trip. They decide to stop at a small diner in the middle of nowhere for a bite to eat, after bickering a bit in the car.

Tensions rise even further when the couple is greeted with incredible disdain and rudeness by the diner chef and the one patron. Derided as "city folk", the chef antagonizes Bob to the point where the *Drexel's Class* (1991-1992) and **NINE TO FIVE** (1980) actor lets loose with a number of verbal barbs of his own, after which he stomps off to the men's room…leaving Jean alone at the table.

Here's the rub, however: Bob never returns. He disappears. Jean is understandably upset, and the rednecks in the diner are no help. The motel next door is equally dismissive of Jean's pleas as to her husband's whereabouts, while the town sheriff (Dana Elcar) isn't sure which side to trust. It's here where **DYING ROOM ONLY** ceases being a character piece and really turns to focus on Leachman's absolutely immense performance as a panicked, stricken wife who is forced to do some detective work in order to understand just what exactly is going on behind the scenes in this small, isolated town.

The actress is intense, vulnerable and affecting as we the audience become increasingly invested in her plight, while the supporting cast of Ned Beatty, Ross Martin and Louise Latham are equally excellent as the town locals who are hiding a secret. The strength of this acting lifts the film beyond its lean running time restrictions and set locations, as we ride along with Leachman/Jean every step of the way in her quest to find her husband. The actress looks beautiful here—a flower in the otherwise dusty dirt hole off the highway—and her desperation, strength and determination are palpable, right up to the film's satisfying conclusion.

DYING ROOM ONLY is one hell of a telefilm; one which demands some serious attention and reappraisal. Thankfully, Warner Archive has released a great made-on-demand DVD-R of the film (available on Amazon as well as directly from Warner), so do yourself a favor, and check it out!

1973, USA. D: PHILIP LEACOCK
AVAILABLE FROM WARNER ARCHIVE

Chloris Leachman gives a tour de force performance as a woman stuck in a small-town mystery in **DYING ROOM ONLY**

JESS FRANCO & SOLEDAD MIRANDA:

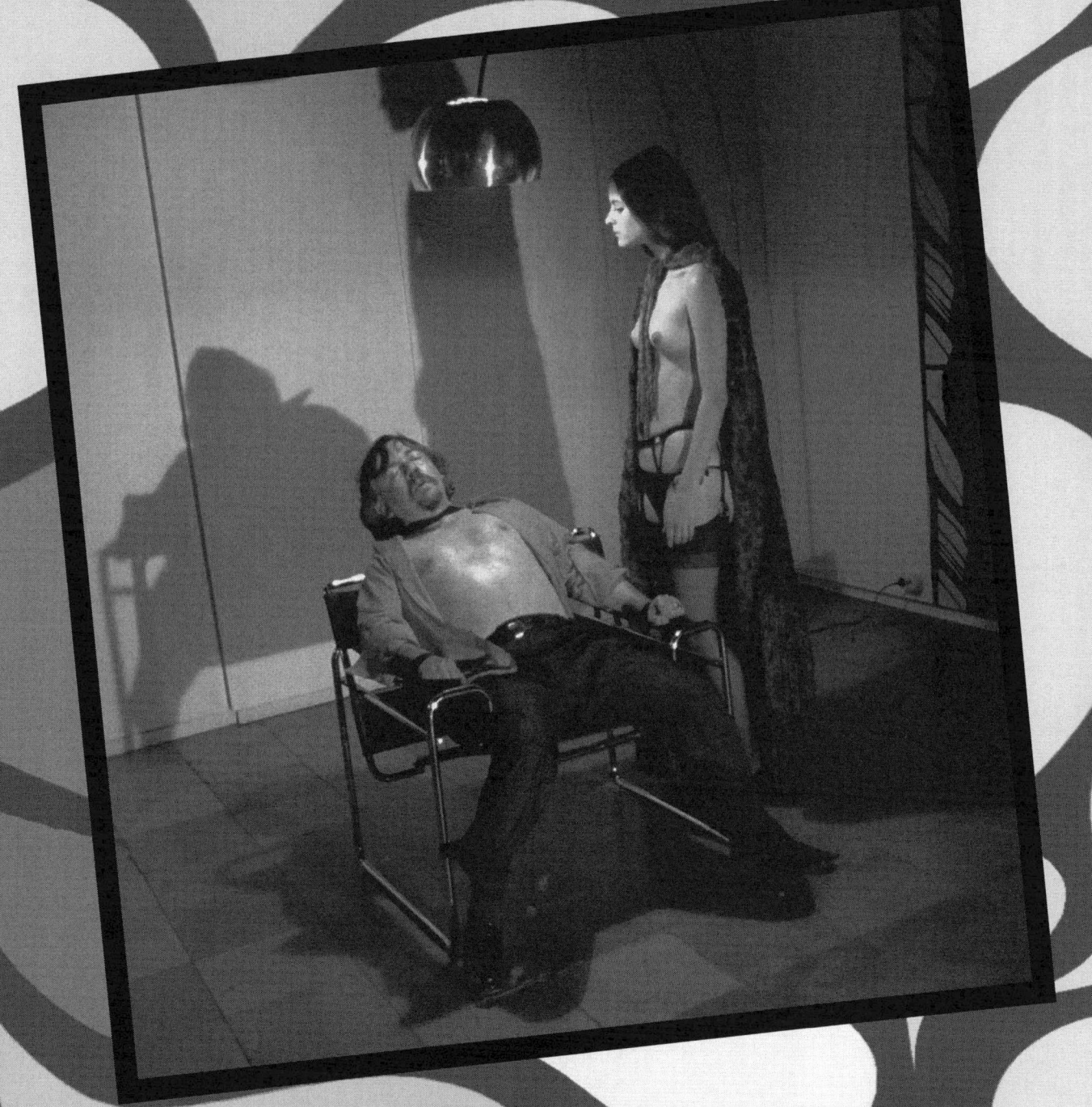

A MATCH MADE IN EURO-CULT HEAVEN

by Troy Howarth

There are certain pairings of actors and directors which seem to have been heaven-sent: just think of Martin Scorsese and Robert De Niro or Federico Fellini and Marcello Mastroianni or Billy Wilder and Jack Lemmon or, perhaps most appropriately in this context, Josef Von Sternberg and Marlene Dietrich. The chances are good that, unless you're an aficionado of what we converts call European Cult Cinema, the names Jess Franco and Soledad Miranda are not known to you. Fortunately, if you're reading this august publication, you are almost certainly very familiar with them and their works. And while it's quite possible you've never sat down and watched a Von Sternberg/Dietrich movie (though you really should!), well—I think it's safe to assume that you've seen at least one of the eight feature films "Uncle Jess" made with his tragically short-lived fetish actress, Soledad Miranda.

Miranda was born in Seville, Spain on July 9th, 1943. Her birth name was Soledad Rendón Bueno, and she came from a humble family background. She began to work as a flamenco dancer when she was just a child and eventually made her film debut while still in her teens. Adopting the pseudonym of Soledad Miranda, she worked her way up the ladder, recording some albums and providing grace and beauty to otherwise forgettable bit parts throughout the early part of the 1960s. She started netting larger, more challenging roles around 1963, in such films as **CUATRO BODAS Y PICO** (a.k.a **FOUR WEDDINGS AND A TIP**) and **LAS HIJAS DE HELENA** (a.k.a. **THE DAUGHTERS OF HELENA**). In 1964, she played a supporting role in the Spanish/American horror title **PYRO...THE THING WITHOUT A FACE** (*Fuego*), starring Barry Sullivan and Martha Hyer. Miranda does not appear until fairly late in the proceedings, but she certainly makes a strong impression as the angelic young girl who becomes smitten with Sullivan's scarred anti-hero. Miranda's next genre credit came the following a couple of years later, in the cheapjack **SOUND OF HORROR** (*El sonido de la muerte*, 1966). This is the notorious film which was so cheap that they couldn't even afford to build an actual monster—thus, the cast cowers in fear at an invisible dinosaur! Much better was Franco Giraldi's spaghetti western **SUGAR COLT** (1966), which features Miranda as a saloon singer who catches the eye of star Hunt Powers (a.k.a., Jack Betts). 1966 also saw Miranda embarking on an exciting phase of her personal life when she married actor and racecar driver José Manuel Simões. The young couple had a son named Antonio in 1967, and Miranda's presence on-screen became more and more infrequent. Still driven by a desire to attain stardom, she elected to go back to making films at the end of the decade, at which point she became a key presence in the films of Jess Franco... but more on that in a bit.

As for Jess Franco, he was born in Madrid on May 12th, 1930. His birth name was Jesús Franco Manera, but he would often be billed simply as Jess Franco, though he would accumulate a list of aliases as long as your arm. He showed musical talent from an early age and studied piano and composition, but his passion for films proved to be overwhelming. He broke into films as a composer and assistant director in the early 1950s and by the end of the decade, he made the transition to directing. Franco's early works show him to be a careful and stylish artisan capable of moving from genre to genre. He directed musicals, comedies, *noir* thrillers—but it was the release of **THE AWFUL DR. ORLOF** (*Gritos en la noche*, 1962) which established him as an icon among fans of the European horror film. The film's success prompted Franco to direct more and more horror films, but it was his collaboration with the great Orson Welles on **CHIMES AT MIDNIGHT** (*Campanadas a medianoche*, 1965) which proved to have the greatest impact on his personal and professional life. It would not be accurate to say that every step of his journey working with Welles—as second-unit director and general assistant—was all smiles and roses: Welles is notorious for his temper as well as for his capacity for attacking his colleagues with a pity insult, and Franco was not entirely immune to his attacks. Even so, Welles' credo to "live to film", as opposed to filming for a living, made a profound impact on the young director. Franco would gradually use this as his *modus operandi*, working tirelessly and even recklessly on numerous projects simultaneously. He scored some triumphs working for producers like Adrian Hoven (**SUCCUBUS** [*Necronomicon—Geträumte Sünden*, 1968]) and Harry Alan Towers (**VENUS IN FURS**, 1969), but in the early '70s, he started to become more of a maverick, often putting what little money he earned into projects that would seldom earn him much of a profit, if any.

The story of Franco's collaboration with Miranda reaches its peak and tragic climax in this time frame, but in truth it began much earlier. In 1960, Franco directed a fairly large-budget musical romance titled **LA REINA DEL TABARÍN** (a.k.a. **QUEEN OF THE TABARIN CLUB**). The story deals with a gigolo who chases various women before falling for a flamenco dancer. Almost lost amid the supporting cast is—you guessed it—Soledad Miranda, in her second screen role, no less. Miranda's appearance is minor at best; it's literally a blink-and-you'll-miss-it appearance as a young noblewoman who patronizes the club where much of the action takes place—but the fact that she crossed paths with Franco so early in her career is an interesting footnote. As it happens, **LA REINA** would prove to be the first of Miranda's films to get a theatrical release. As Amy Brown notes on her excellent website devoted to the actress, her first film—**LA BELLA MIMÍ** (a.k.a. **BEAUTIFUL MIMI**)—was not released until 1963, even though it had been filmed shortly before the Franco production. Like so many of Franco's early works, **LA REINA DEL TABARÍN** has never been released officially on home video in the U.S. and it remains unavailable with English subtitles, but it offers ample evidence of the director's ability to stage a larger production with plenty of extras, musical numbers and real production value. In terms of assessing and appreciating the director's use of Miranda's peculiar and ethereal screen presence, however, the film is at best a footnote: the role is virtually non-existent and Miranda does not have an opportunity to really register.

1969 would prove to be a pivotal year for both Franco and Miranda. During that year, Franco completed several films for producer Harry Alan Towers, including his masterpiece **VENUS IN FURS**. Knowing that his tenure with Towers was coming to an end, he began to put feelers out for other sympathetic producers. The precise chronology of what happened next is open to debate and discussion, but according to Franco scholar Alain Petit, the director began work on two very, very low-budget productions while on a

Jess Franco is tormented by his muse Soledad Miranda in a scene from his **SHE KILLED IN ECSTASY**

break from Towers in between the completion of **EUGENIE... THE STORY OF HER JOURNEY INTO PERVERSION** (1970) and the start of filming **COUNT DRACULA** (a.k.a. *El conde Drácula*, 1970). These films were **SEX CHARADE** (1970) and **NIGHTMARES COME AT NIGHT** (a.k.a. *Les cauchemars naissent la nuit*, 1970) —or rather, that is what they would eventually become. Franco was obliged to halt production on the two pictures when the time came to start filming **COUNT DRACULA** in October of 1969. Soledad Miranda, having made only a minor impression on Franco in 1960, became fixed in his gaze when she was cast to play the pivotal role of Lucy, who is destined to become the first "English" victim of Dracula (Christopher Lee).

COUNT DRACULA was conceived as an ambitious production by producer Harry Alan Towers. The producer secured the services of star Christopher Lee with the promise that this would be a film that would finally bring Bram Stoker's novel to the screen. There were rumors early on that the film would also star Vincent Price as Professor Van Helsing, but the casting went out the window when it became apparent that there was no room in the budget for him. Faded British matinee idol Dennis Price was briefly drafted in to replace him, but he had to bow out and he was ultimately replaced by Czech character actor Herbert Lom—not a bad piece of casting, as it worked out. Unfortunately, the best intentions of Towers did not result in the kind of budget which would allow for the scope and majesty of Stoker's book. Lee, already disillusioned by the waning quality of Hammer Films' various Dracula sequels—he would go on to appear in **TASTE THE BLOOD OF DRACULA** (1970) for the company immediately after wrapping up his work in the Franco film—was mortified when he realized that the production was not going to accommodate the original game plan. Towers, who penned the screenplay under his usual *nom de plume* of Peter Welbeck, compensated by editing out the more "epic" sections of the story. As the producer, he also allowed for some unusual casting accommodations: Klaus Kinski, cast in the role of Renfield, was assured that he was not appearing in a Dracula film (though why he should have cared is anybody's guess; he would go on to star as the Count in Werner Herzog's magnificent **NOSFERATU THE VAMPYRE** [*Nosferatu, Phantom der Nacht*, 1979]) and was kept separate from the main unit, while Herbert Lom appeared in his scenes opposite Lee without being in the same room—or indeed the same country!—as his co-star. The international co-production status called for some studio work in Germany, but much of it (including Lee's material) was filmed in Barcelona. The budget didn't allow for the best sets or special effects, so much of the film comes off looking vaguely impoverished. Even so, Franco's flair for creating atmosphere is evident in the early scenes depicting Jonathan Harker (Fred Williams)'s journey to Castle Dracula and his initial meetings with the Count. The film didn't allow for quite the scope

and quality that Lee had been hoping for, but Towers and Franco remained true to their word on one thing: the film would allow Lee to portray the Count (more-or-less) exactly as described by Stoker. Thus, the early scenes see Lee in a silver wig, with a bushy mustache and stooping ever-so-slightly with age. As he drinks more blood, however, his posture becomes straighter and his hair becomes darker and darker. No film prior to this had attempted this rejuvenation-by-blood effect, and it is indeed one of the picture's strong suits. Lee, for his part, is simply magnificent. Hammer's sequels often put the character on the sideline and gave the actor little to do, but here he has a chance to sink his teeth into some of Stoker's speeches, and he makes the most of it. The super-intense Kinski seems an ideal casting choice for Renfield, but he is given no dialogue—possibly to further conceal from him the true nature of the film he was participating in?—and relatively little screen time. Kinski's natural magnetism is evident, but it's ultimately just another "paycheck" gig for the actor. Lom makes a good impression as Van Helsing, but the need to film all of his scenes in Germany keeps him separate from the action where it really counts: the climax. Thus, the character is sidelined by a stroke late in the action, though he somehow rallies the strength to get up under his own power when confronted by Dracula. Sadly, their one and only showdown in the film

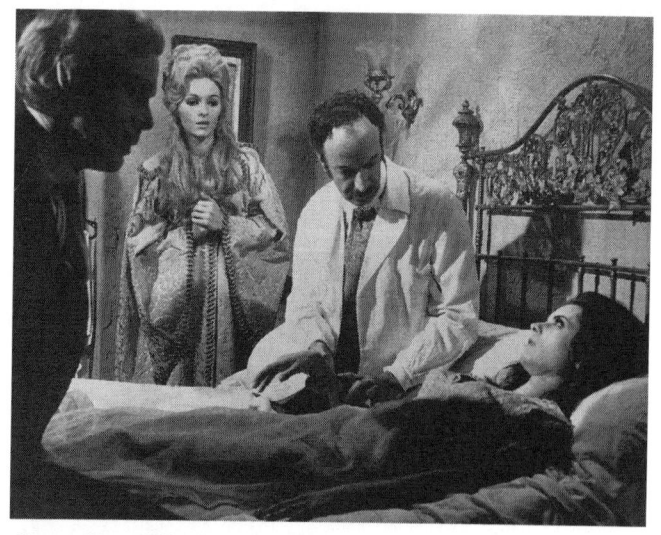

Doctor Seward (Paul Müller) wonders what the best salve is for Lucy's (Soledad Miranda) vampire bites in Franco's 1970 **COUNT DRACULA**

Weng's Chop 51

in such films as **99 WOMEN** (*99 Mujeres*, 1969), **EUGENIE... THE STORY OF HER JOURNEY INTO PERVERSION**, and especially **VENUS IN FURS**, but she is given little to do as the damsel-in-distress, Mina. The character of Lucy is far more interesting, and fortunately Franco found the right actress for the job: Soledad Miranda. It's been said that the normally hard-to-impress Christopher Lee was impressed with her talent and screen presence. Lucy starts off as another boring Victorian wallflower, but after she falls under Dracula's spell, she gets a chance to let her hair down. The transformation from prim and proper society woman to sexy but frightening vamp is every bit as compelling as Barbara Shelley's rightfully-praised turn in Terence Fisher's **DRACULA: PRINCE OF DARKNESS** (1966). Miranda shows tremendous range in the role and while her screen time is not luxurious, she manages to make a very powerful impression. Sadly, despite the best efforts of (most of) the cast, **COUNT DRACULA** is not one of Franco's better films. Part of the problem is Franco himself: he simply is not well-suited to this kind of drawing room horror story. He does a fine job early on, but as the film unfolds it becomes slacker and more careless. The pacing is all over the map. Some of the scenes are truly laughable: look no further than the bizarre sequence in which the heroes are terrorized by a room full of stuffed birds! The finale, normally a highlight to be relished, is thoughtless and rushed. It's a pity, really, since there is so much else to admire, from the sometimes-striking color play in Manuel Merino's cinematography to Bruno Nicolai's magnificently eerie soundtrack. When the film finally emerged in 1970—though it did not get theatrical play in the U.S. or the U.K. until 1973—it was seen as a major disappointment. It failed to make the kind of money Towers had been hoping for and it marked the end of the line with regards to his association with Franco. For Franco, it was a blessing in disguise: he had been champing at the bit, looking for greater creative freedom, so being freed from the confines of working for a producer who liked to keep tabs on him proved to be music to Franco's ears.

As a side note, one would be remiss not to make mention of the film **CUADECUC, VAMPIR** (1970), a sort of arty "making of" **COUNT DRACULA**, which was filmed by experimental filmmaker Pere Portabella. In this context, the term "making of" is misleading: Portabella was granted full access to the production, but sooner than make the usual PR puff piece, he elected to film assorted sights—including some now-treasured glimpses of Miranda behind the scenes—and then compile them into a sort of dreamlike tone poem. There are no interview segments or indeed any dialogue to speak of, save for a brief excerpt of Lee reading from Stoker's book at the end of the movie. Filmed in ethereal black and white **CUADECUC, VAMPIR** is as atmospheric and captivating as **COUNT DRACULA** should have been and it deserves to be more widely seen by fans of the *fantastique*.

One of the things Franco was hell-bent and determined to hold on to following his separation from Towers was Soledad Miranda. He had been massively impressed by her good nature, her willingness to work hard, and her seemingly effortless ability to make love to the camera. He would later recall that she was not a particularly intellectual performer, but she had great instincts—and he was prepared to exploit these instincts to their fullest. Franco was also quick to realize that she could be "inserted" quite easily into his two gestating projects, **SEX CHARADE** (1970) and **NIGHTMARES COME AT NIGHT**. He struck a deal with producer Karl Heinz Mannchen for completion funds on the understanding that he would showcase Miranda in three erotic features. Miranda was not frightened by the prospect of showing her body on-screen, but in the interests of not embarrassing her family, she made one stipulation: she would have to be billed under a pseudonym. Thus, the remaining films featuring Soledad Miranda bill her as Susann Korda. The precise order of the films that resulted is not always agreed upon, but it seems likely that he completed **SEX CHARADE** and **NIGHTMARES COME AT NIGHT** (in that order) by introducing new subplots involving Miranda, then got to work on one of his cheapest—and best—productions, **EUGÉNIE DE SADE** (a.k.a. **EUGENIE SEX HAPPENING**, 1974). All three films were finished by the early part of 1970, but their distribution would prove to be erratic. According to Franco, **SEX CHARADE** received its first—and as fate would have it, final—exposure at the 1970 Cannes Film Festival, which was held from May 2nd to May 16th. No doubt the film was shown out-of-competition in the hopes of attracting potential distributors, but nothing came of it. It has since disappeared completely into obscurity, which is a great pity: not only is if of interest for its place in the then-ongoing Franco/Miranda collaboration, but it also came about during a period of great artistic creativity for Franco. Whether the film is a lost gem or a dud can only be guessed at, but what we do know about the film is this: it deals with a girl named Anne (Miranda) who is kept hostage by an escaped lunatic; in order to keep the lunatic at bay, Anne tells

Chris Lee's **COUNT DRACULA** *knows a quality meal when he sees one!*

is rather perfunctory, precisely because of the unusual way in which it had to be filmed. Lee and Lom, both powerful presences, are hermetically sealed in their own frames and never really have a chance to interact. Swiss actor Paul Müller—who had already appeared for Franco in **EUGENIE... THE STORY OF HER JOURNEY INTO PERVERSION** and **VENUS IN FURS**—does a credible job as Dr. Seward, while Franco stalwarts Jack Taylor (**FEMALE VAMPIRE** [*La comtesse noire*, 1975]) and Fred Williams (**SHE KILLED IN ECSTASY**) do their best to inject some interest into their blandly written hero roles as Quincy Morris and Jonathan Harker, respectively. Maria Rohm—a.k.a. Mrs. Harry Alan Towers—had already given stellar performances for Franco

him some stories. In addition to Miranda, the cast includes a number of familiar faces: Maria Rohm, Jack Taylor, Paul Müller and Howard Vernon, all of whom were also featured in some of the features the director made for Towers during that timeframe. Rumor has it that picture elements for the film have been unearthed, but a soundtrack remains elusive; other sources insist that the film is completely lost, save for a plot synopsis and a few advertising materials. Franco later maintained that he had no idea whatever became of the picture, so it's possible that it was impounded by the producer when it failed to attract a potential buyer at Cannes. Why it should have proved to be such a difficult sell is difficult to fathom: it certainly has an intriguing premise, and the cast is excellent. Judging from the title and from Franco's willingness to explore sex and sexuality on film, it also seems a safe bet that it had plenty of exploitable material. Maybe it really wasn't very good, but then again, plenty of genuinely bad films by Franco and others have found an audience in the end. Hopefully the film will resurface at some point, but for now one can only guess at its qualities.

Right after (or slightly before—again, accounts vary, and it's unlikely that even Franco remembered after a certain point!) completing her scenes for **SEX CHARADE**, Miranda started work on her scenes for **NIGHTMARES COME AT NIGHT**. A dreamy and oneiric thriller, the film deals with a woman (Diana Lorys) whose vivid dreams of sex and violence begin to spill into reality. The original concept was not at all commercial, but Franco spices the film up with plenty of nudity and a plot twist. In order to secure the completion financing, he improvised a subplot which changed the overall tone and feel of the picture. In the subplot, the protagonist's no-good neighbors (Miranda and André Montchall) plot to rob the woman of some ill-gotten diamonds. Whether the plot device of a jewel heist was ever part of the original concept is open to speculation, but the end result is a striking if occasionally frustrating mishmash: on the one hand, the dream vs. reality plotline is slight but hypnotic, while the jewel subplot threatens to take the film into a more pedantic and routine direction. In truth, the reality is this: Franco was obliged to inject a bit of conventional plotting into a film that, while interesting, didn't stand a snowball's chance in hell of finding theatrical distribution. As such, the subplot involving Miranda was crucial in allowing the picture to be completed, let alone for it to see the light of day. It would seem that the picture received some scant theatrical exposure in the early 1970s, but it was pulled from circulation and remained unavailable until 2004, when it made a surprise debut on DVD in the U.S. thanks to Shriek Show. Fan reaction to the film was mixed: this is a slow, arty kind of a picture and it's not exactly the type of fare that most people would elect to unwind to, but those who were able to get past its imperfections found much to enjoy in it. The real star of the show is Paul Müller, who excels as the sardonic psychiatrist who may or may not know more about the jewel heist than he is letting on. Müller always made a strong impression, but he was particularly memorable in some of his Franco film appearances—ironically the actor would later complain that, while he liked Franco and thought he was a talented man, he didn't care for his very loose and improvisational nature of filming. Leading lady Diana Lorys, who had already played the damsel-in-distress in **THE AWFUL DR. ORLOF**, makes a strong impression as the exotic dancer who becomes a pawn in a robbery scheme. Lorys is a distinctive and beautiful presence and she handles the various facets of the character in a convincing fashion; we can never be entirely sure if she is a sinner or if she is being sinned against, and Lorys' performance is key to the mystery. Jack Taylor makes a brief but memorable appearance as one of Lorys' lovers in a "is it a dream or isn't it" set piece that really shows off Franco's particular strengths as a filmmaker. As for Miranda, she is somewhat cut off from the main thrust of the narrative, for obvious reasons, but she still comes off very well. The film was quite possibly the first to show her in the nude—it is not clear if her scenes in **SEX CHARADE** were "sexy" by nature, though it does not sound like they were—and she approaches the various nude and sexy scenes with gusto. Unlike Franco's later muse, Lina Romay, Miranda was never a particularly carnal or animalistic presence on screen: she had a lovely body and penetrating eyes, but her sex scenes were always tinged with melancholy. Romay had no problems grabbing the bull by the horns, if you'll pardon the expression, but with Miranda there was an underlining sense of mystery that made her linger in the mind. Her role in **NIGHTMARES** is not one of her darker ones for the director—truth be told, the role is basically that of a dim-witted trollop—but it stands out for that reason. Miranda has good chemistry with the somewhat wooden Montchall, who would go on to co-star with her in **EUGÉNIE** and **VAMPYROS LESBOS** (*Vampyros Lesbos: Die Erbin des Dracula*), as well. The overall effect is well complemented by an atonal and eerie soundtrack by Bruno Nicolai.

French/German bilingual poster for **NIGHTMARES COME AT NIGHT**

Following the completion of **NIGHTMARES**, Franco lunged into the filming of **EUGÉNIE DE SADE**. A very low-budget—even by Franco's standards—adaption of "Eugénie de Franval", written by the director's favorite author The Marquis de Sade. It deals with a naïve young woman (Miranda) who falls under the malefic influence of her sadistic and perverse step-father (Paul Müller)…or, is it the other way around? Franco keeps the psychology ambiguous as father and daughter unite for a veritable orgy of forbidden pleasures, including murder and incestuous sex. The film's frank but non-judgmental approach is perplexing for some viewers, especially those who are just inherently uncomfortable with the nature of the subject matter. Early on, Eugénie is presented as a doe-eyed innocent, but there is a sense that her psychopathology is a trifle askew right from the beginning. Her devotion to her step-father at the very least pegs her as co-dependent in the extreme: she does not appear to have anything resembling a private life, nor does she desire to attain one. It is sufficient for her to be available to her father's beck and call, and this culminates in disastrous consequences for them both. Franco prefers to maintain a clinical distance, neither condemning nor condoning the actions of his characters, and Miranda and Müller respond with career-best performances. The haughty and imperious Müller is ideally cast as the acerbic and condescending intellectual who presumes to lecture about the irrationality of morality, while Miranda is pitch-perfect as the adoring daughter-turned-crazed lover.

EUGÉNIE DE SADE is in many respects an ideal starting point for any viewer looking to familiarize themselves with Franco's aesthetic and approach. The film is clearly very low-budget: there are no sets, only standing locations. Eugénie's hospital room appears to have been a hastily converted hotel room, for example. The camerawork is hectic, sometimes going in and out of focus as it attempts to light upon little details in the décor or the actors' faces. Special effects work in the murder scenes is strictly from hunger, as well. And yet, none of this really matters. The underlining theme of voyeurism and depravity is so strong and so rigidly applied, one would think that Franco was working from a well-thought-out screenplay. Truth be told, however, it would seem that much of the film was improvised in a feverish manner; this propensity for improvisation irritated the disciplined and theatre-trained Müller, but it seemed to suit the more intuitive Miranda just fine. As such, the film solidified Franco's conviction that she was destined to be his ideal star performer.

Soledad Miranda and Paul Müller in Franco's **EUGÉNIE DE SADE**

Miranda has great chemistry with the icy Müller, and the sequences of the two of them feeding on the naiveté of their prospective victims are both darkly humorous and subtly chilling. Franco gives himself the key role of the writer Atilla Tanner, who acts as a sort of avenging conscience figure throughout the film. Franco often liked to take on quirky character roles, but he was a highly competent actor and he adds to the film's enjoyment value. Once again, Bruno Nicolai's music—mostly culled from his soundtrack for the Italian TV movie **GEMINUS** (1969)—sets the perfect mood, and Franco indulges in some of his usual extended, but oddly hypnotic jazz club sequences. The film is loaded with ample nudity and thus fulfilled Franco's promise to deliver "erotic" content, but this ties into another facet which marks this as a defining example of his work. It's unlikely that the seedy down-market theatres specializing in "adult" material proved to be the ideal home for this incisive and unsettling gem. The raincoat brigade no doubt looked at the film in askance, while the critics who may have best appreciated what Franco was aiming for would never have been caught dead reviewing material such as this. Now that the film is preserved on DVD—the Blue Underground edition is highly recommended—it is possible to assess the film fairly and to better appreciate what a key work it is in Franco's oeuvre. Sadly, it barely made a ripple upon its original release and was apparently only given a scant release in France in 1974 or 1975, if the notoriously unreliable IMDb is to be believed. In any event, it never played theatrically in America and only became officially available in the States when Wild East issued it on DVD in 2002; this version was eventually surpassed by a superior edition released by Blue Underground in 2008.

Following the completion of **EUGÉNIE**, Franco struck a deal with German producer Artur Brauner, of CCC Filmkunst/Telecine. It's possible that Franco created a show reel of Miranda highlights out of his recent trilogy of titles, given that none of the films in question ever managed to secure a theatrical screening in Germany, but in any event he managed to talk the producer into bankrolling a series of films starring the young actress. Franco recognized that if he played his cards right, he could make a major European—and maybe even international—star out of Miranda, so he carefully concocted a couple of vehicles which would serve as showcases for the actress. To get things off and running, he first turned to Bram Stoker for some inspiration. The disappointment of **COUNT DRACULA** was not that far in the rear view mirror, but Franco did not allow that to deter him: he would take elements from the book, as well as from the short story *Dracula's Guest*, which was in essence a deleted episode from the original book, published a couple of years after the Irish writer's death in 1912. Instead of allowing himself to be reined in by the material, however, Franco simply used it as a springboard for a psychedelic fantasmagoria which incorporates elements of horror, surrealism, and eroticism. If Count Dracula showed the director struggling to make his mark on an established classic of literature, then **VAMPYROS LESBOS** demonstrates the magic which could occur when he was given the freedom to riff and improvise on a theme. Franco's script—or outline, which seems more likely—deals with a beautiful real estate agent named Linda (Ewa Strömberg) who goes to a seaside resort town to close out a transaction with the mysterious Countess Nadine Carody (Miranda). When the heroine arrives at Carody's estate, she falls into a (literal) web of sex and the supernatural.

Make no mistake about it, **VAMPYROS LESBOS** is an unusual film. Franco's propensity for crash zooms is much in evidence, and one's tolerance for this device may dictate just how much you enjoy the end result. The director eschews convention and sets much of the action in the daylight. Indeed, as numerous critics have suggested, the film is best read as an inverted re-telling of *Dracula*, with female protagonists, a sunny beach house in place of a musty castle, and vampires who seem to thrive on the sunshine. Approached as a straight horror film, it may seem a little disappointing: it's not conventionally scary, after all. But that does not seem to have been Franco's intention, anyway. Instead, he thrives on playing with genre conventions and weaving a dreamy atmosphere which allows the film to coast through its running time with just the barest hint of a dramatic story arc. Story, character, logic…these things are secondary to the all-important mood and fortunately, Franco delivers quite handily on this front. Miranda makes an unforgettable impression as the vampire countess. Truth be told, the film does not present her with the same acting challenges as the vehicles which flank it, but it is for this film that she is best remembered. Franco introduces her right away, lounging about in the background as the credits unfold, her arms extended out towards the camera, the effect rendered surreal by the choice of camera lens—her eyes seem to burn the very screen itself. From there, Franco gives her a magnificent entrance proper as she performs in one of his best night club routine set-pieces—those who know Franco's work know that he loved such sequences, and this introductory number in **VAMPYROS LESBOS** is one of his very best. Miranda moves provocatively in a sensual—but never overtly smutty—fashion as she removes her clothing, piece by piece, then puts it on a shapely female "mannequin," which is in reality portrayed by a real actress; the routine concludes when the mannequin springs to life and embraces Miranda. From there, the film begins to follow a slightly more conventional narrative trajectory, but Miranda's presence literally dominates the entire proceedings. The pretty but bland Strömberg cannot hope to compete with her, though she makes for a credible heroine. The vampire savant figure this time is Dr. Seward, played here by Dennis Price, who narrowly missed out on playing Van Helsing in **COUNT DRACULA**. The great British actor appears older than his years (he would die three years later at the age of 58), but he still appears healthier and more robust than he would in Franco's 1972 duo **DRACULA, PRISONER OF FRANKENSTEIN** (*Drácula contra Frankenstein*) and **THE EROTIC RITES OF FRANKENSTEIN** (*La maldición de Frankenstein*). Instead of being a knight in shining armor, however, Seward, well… he's a bit of a shit. He uses Linda to get closer to the Countess and instead of seeking to eradicate her, he wishes to join her army of the undead! Speaking bluntly, Price deserved better than to be making such low-budget genre fare at this stage in the game, but he needed the money and despite major problems with gambling and alcohol off the set, he proved to be a perfect pro during filming and Franco was in awe of his talents; the director might have shown a little more concern for his on-going leg pain issue, however, and not staged a chase scene with the aging actor clearly hobbling in pain while supposedly running for his life at one point. Paul Müller is also on-hand to play Linda's psychiatrist; it's not a particularly large role, but he brings his usual polish to it. Franco also appears as the psychotic hotel porter in a subplot which seems curiously grafted on—not that I'd want to lose it for anything, of course. The production values are a bit more substantial than they had been in the last few films, and the ultra-mod décor and trappings are frequently eye-catching. However, the proverbial icing on the cake is presented in the form of the music score by Manfred Hübler and Siegfriend Schwab. In fact, the music was not composed for the film at all, but was taken from two 1969 albums by Hübler and Schwab, entitled *Sexedelic* and *Psychedelic Dance Party*. In fact, Hübler and Schwab signed the latter as The Vampires' Sound Corporation. Franco was given the albums to listen to while in production on **VAMPYROS LESBOS** and quickly recognized that it was ideally suited to the film he was currently working on; indeed, he liked the music so much, he even recycled it for his next two films for Brauner and starring Miranda, as well. When the time came to prepare a watered-down version of the film for his native Spain, however, Franco elected to compose a new soundtrack on his own; the alternate score is not without merit, but it simply does not hold a candle to Hübler and Schwab's inspired compositions. The Spanish edition, titled **LAS VAMPIRAS**, removes all of the nudity and substitutes some tamer footage where possible; it is the full strength German edit, however, which continues to attract new admirers. **VAMPYROS LESBOS** may not be the best of Miranda's films for Franco, but it is the one that has cemented her legacy; the combination of her smoldering beauty and Franco's playful variations on the vampire mythos make it essential viewing.

For his next Miranda vehicle, Franco switched gears somewhat. **VAMPYROS LESBOS** was loosely plotted and effervescent, but **SHE KILLED IN ECSTASY** (*Sie tötete in Ekstase*) would be more plot-driven and a whole hell of a lot darker. In fact, it is closer in tone to **EUGÉNIE DE SADE** than any of the other Franco/Miranda films, and it also offers the actress her best showcase, in terms of actual acting, beside that earlier gem. The story has definite connections to Franco's earlier "revenge" films, **THE DIABOLICAL DR. Z** (*Miss Muerte*, 1966) and **VENUS IN FURS**, but it also can be read as a sort of unofficial adaptation of Cornell Woolrich's *The Bride Wore Black*, which was originally published in 1940. Woolrich's story deals with a woman who sets about avenging the murder of her husband—struck dead by a group of five men on his wedding day. Woolrich's story was formally adapted in 1968 by director Francois Truffaut, but it proved to be an unhappy experience for the French *auteur* and he would later refer to it as one of the films he made which he liked the least. Franco, an avid reader of pulp fiction, almost certainly drew upon memories of the book when he and Jean-Claude Carrière were developing the screenplay for **THE DIABOLICAL DR. Z**. That earlier film took the plot even further into the realm of the fantastic by introducing such outré plot elements as mind control and poisoned fingernails, but for his new variation on the theme, **SHE KILLED IN ECSTASY**, it is more grounded in reality.

The story deals with the young and ambitious Dr. Johnson (Fred Williams), who is driven to suicide when his research (involving human embryos) is derided and discredited by four pompous and powerful colleagues (Howard Vernon, Ewa Strömberg, Paul Müller and Franco himself). Johnson's wife—identified only as Mrs. Johnson, and played by Miranda—takes it upon herself to avenge him by killing the doctors, one by one.

SHE KILLED IN ECSTASY is a denser, more plot-heavy film than **VAMPYROS LESBOS**—but it is also less successful on the whole. Part of the problem is the plotting itself: it almost feels as if there's too much going on during its relatively brief (less than 90 minutes) running time. Franco seems to have lost interest in the story early on, preferring instead to focus his obsessive gaze on his leading lady. Miranda never had a better showcase in many respects: she wears a number of eye-catching wigs and outfits and is frequently nude, as well. Franco stops the flow of the narrative at many points to dwell on her as she apparently improvises her way through little vignettes—staring at her husband's moldering corpse, tears filling up in her eyes, toying with her victims as she seduces and then murders them, and so forth. The actual progression of the narrative is a little unsteady and uncertain. Indeed, the actual order of the murder scenes appears to have been rethought in the editing room. At one point, it is alluded that Franco's character has been killed and that Müller's is still alive, but as it plays out in the narrative—the opposite is true! If indeed Franco elected to re-order the events in the editing, one can

An erotic nightclub scene helps set the tone for **VAMPYROS LESBOS**

and Schwab, and it presents Miranda in one of her very best performances. If the often-stilted dialogue and uneven pacing conspire against it being as successful a film as **EUGÉNIE** or **VAMPYROS**, it still offers more than enough points of interest to warrant a serious look.

It has often been written that **SHE KILLED IN ECSTASY** was the last of Miranda's films and that the car crash therefore has some eerie significance which spilled into her private life. While the fact that she would ultimately perish in just such a fashion is an interesting coincidence, it is nevertheless precisely that: a coincidence. In fact, following the completion of **SHE KILLED IN ECSTASY**, she went directly into Franco's next project, a chaotic and rather silly spy thriller titled **THE DEVIL CAME FROM AKASAVA** (*Der Teufel kam aus Akasava*, 1971).

The story is based—very loosely!—on "Keepers of the Stone," a segment in Edgar Wallace's popular adventure, *Sanders of the River*. As such, the film is part of the *krimi* series which Brauner had been producing to great commercial success since the late 1950s—but unusually for a film in the franchise, it is based not on one of the writer's detective thrillers, but rather on a vignette of a boys' own adventure saga. In order to shoehorn it more comfortably into the series, Franco injects a dash of Mickey Spillaine, by way of *Kiss Me Deadly*: in common with both stories is a mysterious substance (in this case, a stone), which all of the characters are anxious to get their mitts on; the stone reportedly has the ability to facilitate the turning of metals into gold, so it's easy to see why it should prove so desirable. The 1955 film version of Spillaine's tale concluded on an apocalyptic note as the case containing the unknown material is opened and causes death and destruction; Quentin Tarantino would quote the image of the light radiating from within the case for **PULP FICTION** (1994). In Franco's film, the destruction the stone causes isn't quite so widespread, but it does have the annoying habit of frying the characters to a crisp whenever they are exposed to its power. A Scotland Yard inspector (Fred Williams) and a Secret Intelligence Service agent (Miranda) compete to bring the bad guys to justice before the stone causes more destruction.

understand why. His own demise at the hands of Miranda is far and away the best-staged and most impressive of the four murder scenes. The director's shirt is torn open and he is tied to a chair as Miranda digs her nails into his chest and goes to town on him with a knife. It's a wonderfully staged and photographed vignette and it plays far better than the other, more recklessly staged revenge sequences. The lack of regard for the narrative is most evident in the extremely limp finale, in which a particularly underwhelming car chase ends with a whimper rather than a bang—as Miranda's vengeance-sated anti-hero dies in a less-than-impressive car crash. Franco's propensity for improvising and for flying by the seat of his pants often resulted in less-than-polished sequences such as this, but here the deficiencies are particularly disappointing. Ultimately, one doesn't wish to be too hard on the film, however. For all its faults, **SHE KILLED IN ECSTASY** makes inspired use of the music of Hübler

Franco's love of pulp scenarios often compelled him to undertake quirky little adventure thrillers such as this; in fact, next to lurid horror and sex melodramas, this was probably his favorite type of material to indulge in. Quite often, his chaotic approach to filmmaking resulted in thrillers which bordered on the incomprehensible. As had been the case with **SHE KILLED IN ECSTASY**, **THE DEVIL CAME FROM AKASAVA** suffers from an abundance of

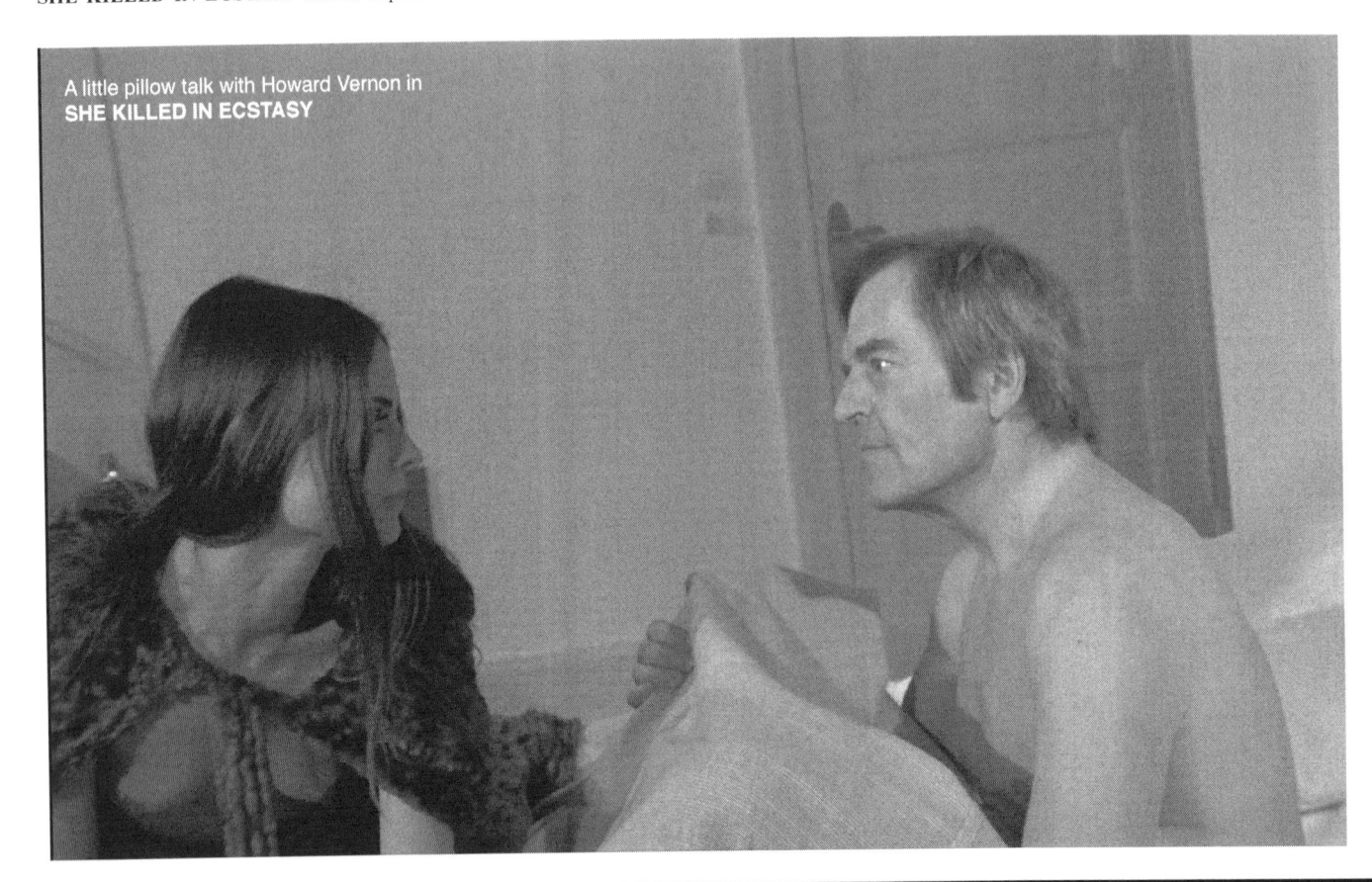

A little pillow talk with Howard Vernon in **SHE KILLED IN ECSTASY**

Modeling casual laboratory attire in **SHE KILLED IN ECSTASY**

plot—in this case, it's done in even further by the need to work in a fresh plot twist every 15 minutes or so. Franco's earlier pulp detective adventures like **KISS ME MONSTER** (*Küss mich, Monster*, 1969) and **TWO UNDERCOVER ANGELS** (*Rote Lippen, Sadisterotica*, a.k.a. **SADIST EROTICA**, 1969) were more successful at creating and sustaining an outrageous air of mystery and intrigue. By comparison, **THE DEVIL CAME FROM AKASAVA** only works in fits and spurts. The film moves at a decent clip, however, and contains quite a few Franco (and *krimi*) regulars getting in on the spirit of fun and frivolity. The use of Hübler and Schwab's music isn't quite as effective this time around and it occasionally seems to work against what we are seeing on screen, and not necessarily in a good way: consider the music used for Miranda's night club routines, which is far busier than her languid movements seem to suggest. As for Miranda, she is not given nearly so much to do here this time, but she brings charm and presence to a thinly written character. There's something disarmingly naïve about a secret intelligence agent working undercover as a stripper; plot elements such as this make it clear that this is going to be one of *those* movies. Miranda looks great (of course) and seems to be having a ball, but compared to **EUGÉNIE, VAMPYROS LESBOS** and **SHE KILLED IN ECSTASY**, the film feels like a bit of a step backwards for her. Fred Williams is okay as the horny Scotland Yard official, while Paul Müller, Alberto Dalbés (uncredited, but featured in a prominent role; he would go on to play central roles in such films as **THE EROTIC RITES OF FRANKENSTEIN** [1972] and **THE NIGHT OF THE SKULL** [*La noche de los asesinos*, 1974]); Howard Vernon and Franco himself are fun in their roles; Franco is particularly disarming as the funny Italian agent who has been assigned to help Williams. *Krimi* veterans Horst Tappert (best remembered for his role on German TV as *Derrick*, which ran for a staggering 25 years!) and Siegfried Schürenberg (reprising his long-running role as the stuffy Sir John of Scotland Yard from the more "authentic" Brauner productions) are an enjoyable addition to the ensemble, as well.

Technically speaking, **THE DEVIL CAME FROM AKASAVA** would become Soledad Miranda's final film appearance—but it was not intended to be that way. Indeed, during the production of **SHE KILLED IN ECSTASY**, Franco—who was prone to indulging in such subterfuge—"borrowed" the cast and crew to begin work on a project of his own, without the direct participation of Brauner as producer. JULIETTE was another De Sade-inspired thriller and it appears to have been very much in the vein of **EUGÉNIE DE SADE**, right down to the casting of Miranda and Paul Muller in the key roles.

The following plot synopsis gives one a taste of what might have been and has been borrowed from Amy Brown's "cyber-shrine" to Miranda, *soledadmiranda.com*: "Driven by an irresistible force that obliges her to do evil, Juliette attracts men and executes them after seducing them. Undermined by remorse, she then goes to a church, where she prays feverishly for redemption of her crimes. Her religious fervor and her frequent visits to the temple are noticed by a man who follows her and begins to live in her shadow. The man rents a room near that of Juliette and witnesses, through the keyhole of their doors, the bloody crimes of his neighbor. All at once fascinated and madly in love with the beautiful criminal, the man is silent and can take no more, eventually causing their meeting, a meeting which can be completed only in the death and blood…" The title JULIETTE seems to indicate a kinship to Franco's first (and by far, tamest) De Sade adaptation, **MARQUIS DE SADE: JUSTINE** (a.k.a. **DEADLY SANCTUARY**, 1969), but the particulars of the plot are very different. It seems likely that the positive experience of making **EUGÉNIE** with Miranda and Muller inspired the director to undertake another personalized De Sade subject, but sadly the film was never completed. Franco reportedly managed to get about 40 minutes of material in the can, but the interruption of filming **THE DEVIL CAME FROM AKASAVA** and the tragic events which unfolded in its wake put an end to the fantasy of coming back to complete the picture. As for the footage that was filmed, rumor has it that Franco had plans to make use of it later on—but he never did, and for all we know, it may well be lost to the mists of time.

Having completed the filming of three very different films in rapid succession, Franco knew he had something special on his hands. He decided to show his producer some footage from the films in the hopes of whetting his appetite for more. As it happens, Artur Brauner was thrilled with what he saw. He recognized Miranda's talent as well as her beauty and was seized with the notion that she could potentially become the next big sex symbol of the European film industry. Sooner than risk another producer coming along to make her a better offer, he put his cards on the table: he offered Franco a contract to make a series of films starring the actress; the films would grow in budget and ambition, depending on how they performed commercially. Franco was over the moon: in Miranda, he had found his ideal screen muse. She could be light and charming, as well as dark and despairing. She had the ability to convey innocence, but she also could convey a worldly and seductive quality. In short, she was the ideal Franco Fetish Actress, and he damn well knew it. Excited by the offer, he contacted Miranda, who was on a well-deserved vacation with her husband in Lisbon. Brauner was keen to have her sign the contract as soon as possible—all the better to avoid having some unscrupulous competitor get word of her exceptional beauty and steal her away from him. Franco explained the terms of the contract to Miranda by phone, and she was thrilled: finally, stardom was within her grasp. Franco took a flight to Lisbon and arranged to meet with her at his hotel on August the 18th, 1970. Franco eagerly prepared for the meeting but grew concerned when Miranda failed to show up. That afternoon, he received a phone call which would haunt him for the rest of his life: Soledad Miranda was dead. As it happens, the actress was being driven to the hotel by her husband—a race car driver, no less—when they were taken by surprise on a treacherous turn: a truck came barreling at their car, striking it with full force on the passenger side, which is where Miranda was seated. Miranda sustained fractures to her head and spine and she would die from her wounds a few hours later at the hospital; Miranda's husband only received minor injuries, though the loss of his beloved wife would prove to be a heavy burden to bear. Franco and Brauner were devastated to see their dreams of making movie magic with Miranda snatched away so suddenly and so cruelly. The director threw himself into a period of intense work, moving even more rapidly from project to project. Many of his films would take on a gloomy, fatalistic tone, notably his elegiac pet project **A VIRGIN AMONG THE LIVING DEAD** (*La nuit des étoiles filantes*, 1973). He would find another muse in the form of Lina Romay, a young Catalan actress who would become the centerpiece of his filmmaking—and of his personal life. Romay's talents and virtues were many, but she never quite captured that sense of melancholy and mystery which Miranda exuded so easily. Romay was an exhibitionist who enjoyed shocking people's susceptibilities; Miranda was much more ambiguous and is arguably much more haunting because of it.

And what of the films Miranda made with Jess Franco? Her three big star vehicles for Brauner were completed after her death. All three were released to Germany, albeit in a different order from which they were produced: **THE DEVIL CAME FROM AKASAVA** premiered in March of 1971, **VAMPYROS LESBOS** would follow in July of 1971, and **SHE KILLED IN ECSTASY** would bring up the rear in December of 1971. Miranda's homeland would only see two of the films released theatrically: **THE DEVIL CAME FROM AKASAVA** played with some cuts involving nudity in 1974, while the heavily reworked "soft" edition of **VAMPYROS LESBOS**, titled **LAS VAMPIRAS**, would emerge in 1973; the latter actually credited Miranda by name—not as Susann Korda—though whatever attention this attracted was too little, too late for the young actress. Reference sources list the Spanish title of **SHE KILLED IN ECSTASY** as **MRS. HYDE**, but I can find no confirmation of it ever having played in Spanish cinemas. None of the films were ever released theatrically in the United States, and they would only emerge on video, "officially" speaking, until many years after their release. **VAMPYROS LESBOS**—for many, *the* Jess Franco cult movie—became the first to rate a proper DVD release, from Synapse in 1999. This was followed by Synapse's release of **SHE KILLED IN ECSTASY** in 2000 and Image's release of **THE DEVIL CAME FROM AKASAVA** in 2003. In between the latter two, Wild East released **EUGÉNIE DE SADE** in 2002, while **NIGHTMARES COME AT NIGHT** followed (from Shriek Show) in 2004, and **COUNT DRACULA**—for years, the most accessible of the films in the U.S., thanks to VHS releases and the like—finally emerged in 2007 through Dark Sky. In the meantime, **VAMPYROS LESBOS** and **SHE KILLED IN ECSTASY** were re-issued in slightly improved (but inaccurately framed) DVD editions courtesy of Image, while **EUGÉNIE** finally got the release it deserved from Blue Underground in 2008. The Blu-ray boom of the 21st century has witnessed a surprising volume of Franco films getting high definition transfers, as well. For those of us who first discovered these films via grainy VHS bootlegs, sometimes without even the benefit of English subtitles, this is nothing short of miraculous. Thus far, only two of the Franco/Miranda films have been issued to Blu-ray, but hopefully more will follow in time. Happily, Severin Films have seen fit to give **VAMPYROS LESBOS** and **SHE KILLED IN ECSTASY** proper special edition Blu-ray releases. The quality on **VAMPYROS LESBOS** almost defies belief. I first saw this film on a bootleg VHS, in blurry quality and without English subs. Now it's possible to sit back and appreciate every detail in the cinematography and art direction—and believe me, there's plenty here to savor. The detail is superb, colors are bold and the film is completely uncut. Removable English subtitles are included on the feature itself, as well as the bonus presentation of **LAS VAMPIRAS**—yes, now you can even watch the watered-down Spanish version and take note of the many differences between the two versions! The quality on **LAS VAMPIRAS** is far inferior to that of **VAMPYROS LESBOS**, but that's okay—just having it as an extra is a great touch on Severin's part. Extras include an interview with Amy Brown about Soledad Miranda—just try not to choke up when she talks about the late actress and her tragic demise—as well as an interview with Franco scholar Stephen Thrower, author of the upcoming two-volume Franco study, *Murderous Passions: The Delirious Cinema of Jesús Franco*. Best of all is an interview segment with the late Jess Franco, apparently conducted during a much earlier interview with the anticipation of using it for a later release of these films. The director—who passed away in April of 2013—talks candidly about the film (which he claims to hate less than some of his other films) and its production; as always, he's a hoot. "Jess is Yoda" is a brief interview excerpt in which Franco, holding a figuring of Yoda—yes, the little green mystic of the *Star Wars* franchise!—and claiming that make-up artist Stuart Freeborn (who worked with Franco on his Fu Manchu films) told him that the character's look was based on Franco. It may well be another instance of "Uncle Jess" spinning BS, but it may well be true—and I sincerely hope that it is! The original German titles are included as a bonus—they appear in rough shape, but they are of interest for retaining a Heinrich Heine poem quote which is omitted from the French version. **SHE KILLED IN ECSTASY** is also given a robust looking transfer, but the elements on this title are more problematic. Previous home video versions omitted about three minutes of material, much of it of a sexually sadistic nature and included in the murder scenes, but the transgressive material is finally reinstated as the director intended. The cut scenes appear to have been sourced from an inferior source and there are some anomalies evident in the soundtrack, including some changes in the levels, but on the whole it's a very handsome-looking transfer, with much more detail than in any other video edition to date. English subs are also included here, as is a reprise of Amy Brown's interview, a different Stephen Thrower piece on the film at hand, and what may well prove to be the last "new" Jess Franco interview we will ever see. This was also obviously recorded at the same time as the **VAMPYROS LESBOS** interview, and Franco is as candid and witty as ever. Even in his declining years, the man was sharp as a tack—so enjoy! A bonus disc includes the original, uncut CD release of *Three Films By Jess Franco*, featuring the Manfred Hübler and Siegfried Schwab music used so memorably in **VAMPYROS LESBOS**, **SHE KILLED IN ECSTASY** and **THE DEVIL CAME FROM AKASAVA**. As noted above, the music was culled from two 1969 LP releases. The music was first compiled for the *Three Films By Jess Franco* CD release, but it went out of print and was replaced by the now-famous Crippled Dick/Lucertola release titled *Vampyros Lesbos Sexadellic Dance Party*. Sadly, that later release omitted some excellent cues—notably three versions of "Psycho Contact" and "Ghosts or Good and Bad Onions"—thus making the previous CD release a prime piece of real estate for CD collectors. Fortunately, the Severin release of **SHE KILLED IN ECSTASY** levels the playing field somewhat, making it unnecessary for Euro soundtrack enthusiasts to shell out crazy money for the complete soundtrack…if only they had done it in time to spare my pocket book a couple of years back!

In conclusion, it really does go without saying that Jess Franco is not everybody's cup of tea. Just about any of your reading this magazine already have your minds made up which side of the fence you occupy—flawed genius or no-talent hack—but if you're looking to get a sense of Franco at his best, you could do a lot worse than to arrange for a marathon of these films Franco made with Soledad Miranda.

Note: Sincere thanks are owed to Amy Brown, Soledad Miranda scholar extraordinaire, for the invaluable information she shared in the Soledad Miranda documentary included on the Severin Blu-ray releases of **VAMPYROS LESBOS** and **SHE KILLED IN ECSTASY** (both 1971). Make sure to visit Amy's website at: *http://www.soledad-miranda.com*. Special thanks are also due to Roberto Curti, whose knowledge of all-things Franco is both considerable and invaluable.

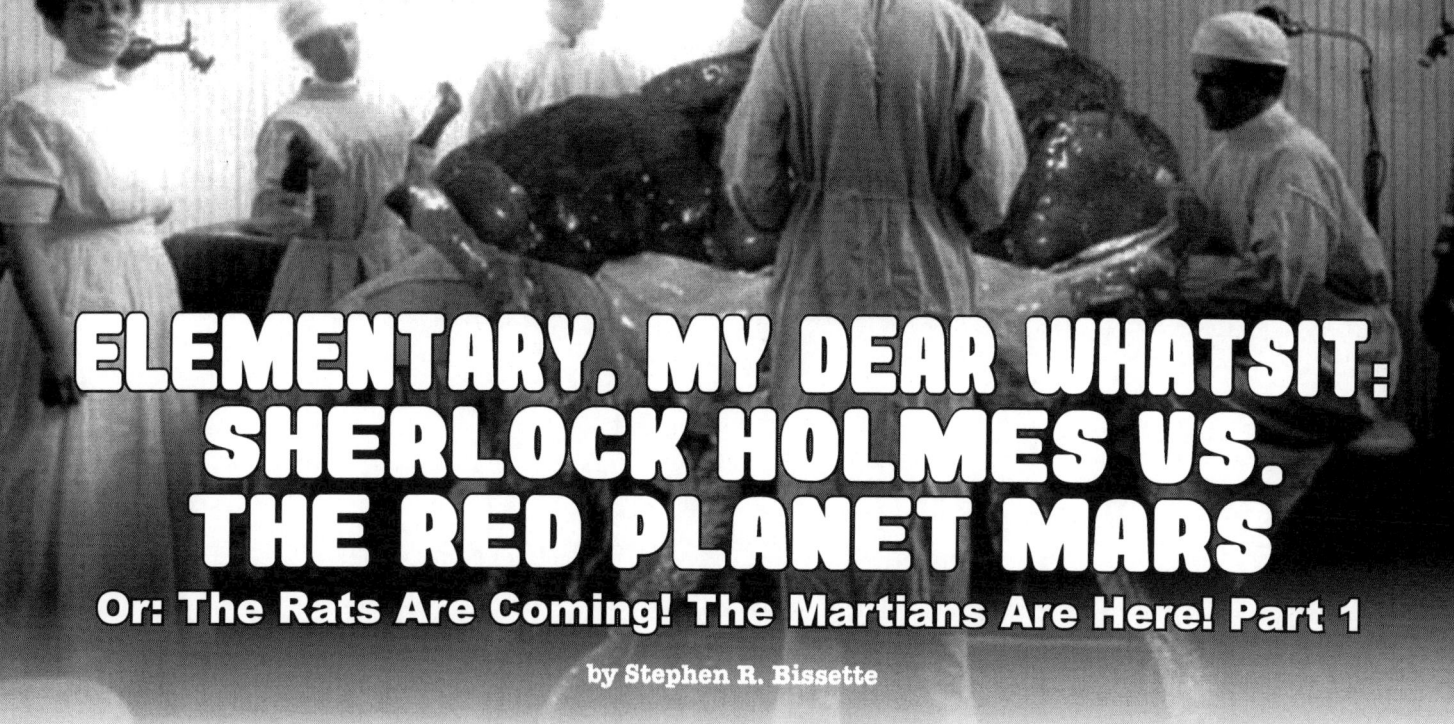

ELEMENTARY, MY DEAR WHATSIT: SHERLOCK HOLMES VS. THE RED PLANET MARS
Or: The Rats Are Coming! The Martians Are Here! Part 1

by Stephen R. Bissette

The Tripods rise; the Towers fall.

This begins with a great plunge, a falling; all-out war in response to cataclysmic invasions; death and destruction, followed by lofty discussion, and ends in the gutter. It opens with high-end science-fiction and tales of deduction, and winds up in the trash bin of paperback history—but stick with me, please.

There's a mad buzz from the latest spin on Herbert George Wells' venerable novel *War of the Worlds* (serialized in 1897, first published in book form in 1898), the BBC's **THE GREAT MARTIAN WAR: 1913-1917** (2013; US broadcast debut 2014). Wells' science-fiction classic had already gotten a lot of traction since the millennial shift, post-9/11. Echoing, conflating, reflecting, and anticipating the endless war between (religious) worlds fomented since the devastating mayhem of September 11, 2001 and the madness that has followed, H.G. Wells' Martians invade and invade and invade in ever-escalating cycles. As noted in **THE GREAT MARTIAN WAR** production notes, Wells forged the original "*War of the Worlds* pre-WW1 to express his deep and well-founded fears of what a great war would be like in the industrial age," and that creative amplification and transmutation has continued to use Wells' metaphoric Martian war to reflect contemporary 21st century dread: new wine, old bottle.

As if anticipating what was to come, Alan Moore and Kevin O'Neill's graphic novel *The League of Extraordinary Gentlemen Volume II* (2002-2003) posited a Martian alliance led by John Carter and Gullivar Jones booting from Mars invading extraterrestrial "Molluscs", driving these non-Martian invaders to wage war on Earth circa 1898. You see, everything Wells "knew"/wrote was wrong—and thus *The War of the Worlds* became the post-millennial-shift metaphor for the American post-9/11 invasion of Afghanistan and Iraq. It could be argued that Moore and O'Neill codified the new template (and you *know* all of Hollywood was reading their work), though there was already at least one film production in the works (Timothy Hines' adaptation for Pendragon Pictures, which actually stopped filming in September 2001 due to the 9/11 World Trade Center catastrophe).

The Steven Spielberg big-budget movie reboot/adaptation opened theatrically June 29, 2005, repositioning the Martian invasion to America, here and now, just as the George Pal/Byron Haskins **WAR OF THE WORLDS** had for 1953. Before the release of Spielberg's version, it had already spawned an explosion of direct-to-DVD *War of the Worlds*: Timothy Hines/Pendragon Pictures' **H.G. WELLS' THE WAR OF THE WORLDS** (June 14, 2005; also released in variant editions as **H.G. WELLS' THE WAR OF THE WORLDS: DIRECTOR'S CUT,** September 2005, and in what Hines declared the "definitive" version, **CLASSIC WAR OF THE WORLDS,** De-

TOP: Martian autopsy from Timothy Hines' **WAR OF THE WORLDS: THE TRUE STORY** (2012); **ABOVE:** Henrique Alvim Corrêa's depiction of the Martians for the 1906 limited edition of only 500 copies; the original artwork was recently auctioned off.

cember 2006), the first-ever feature film adaptation accurately set in Wells' 1898; David Michael Latt/The Asylum's adaptation **H.G. WELLS' WAR OF THE WORLDS** a.k.a. **INVASION** (June 28, 2005)—starring C. Thomas Howell as "George Herbert," a nod to Herbert George Wells, natch—followed by director/star C. Thomas Howell's sequel **WAR OF THE WORLDS 2: THE NEXT WAVE** (2008, Asylum). Between the two Asylum productions came **SCARY MOVIE 4** (2006), spoofing Spielberg's outing, and this run has been capped (at present) by another Pendragon mockumentary (and best of the lot), Timothy Hines' **WAR OF THE WORLDS: THE TRUE STORY** (2012). There was a plethora of contemporary Wellsian invasions that didn't bother to cite Wells as their catalytic agent, though the lineage was obvious: **SKYLINE** (2010), **BATTLE: LOS ANGELES** (2011), **THE DARKEST HOUR** (2011), **THE EDGE OF TOMORROW** (2014), etc. Even as it's part of the cycle, the recent BBC spin **THE GREAT MARTIAN WAR,** supplant-

Tripods OPEN FIRE! Cover art by Kevin O'Neill (*The League of Extraordinary Gentlemen, Volume 2*, #4, 2002), Lou Cameron (*Classics Illustrated* #124, January 1955), and Jack Gaughan (for the paperback original from DAW Books, 1976; more on this novel in the next *Weng's Chop*!).

ing World War 1 with Wells' imaginary extraterrestrial invasion, is revving up the revamp invasions all over again.

Welcome to futures past, and past futures, collapsing in on one another. Tripods rise, towers fall.

There's another aspect to all this, too: projecting worldly foes onto/into imaginary foes has been a venerable trope of propaganda. In the 20th century alone, print propaganda was ripe with visual demonization of cultural enemies: thus, during World War 2, the Allies depicted the Axis as subhuman, non-human, inhuman monsters, while Axis propaganda identically demonized the Allies. Currently, we are in a "politically correct" perpetual war media saturation that is desperately avoiding the specificity of past wars: outside of the realm of editorial cartooning, most mainstream corporate culture and media venues aren't permitting traditional modes of vicious caricature of "the enemy". The old models and modes and tropes are bad for global business. Propaganda has been, by and large, pre-sterilized; after all, via ISIS/ISIL "snuff" videos, "the enemy" has handily demonized itself without resorting to cartoon likenesses.

Thus, the Marvel Comics media empire is (for a multitude of reasons) erasing Germany and the real-world Axis from their 21st century—in effect, supplanting WW2 with an imaginary war, populated by wholly invented (and wholly corporate-owned) villains. Thus, the remake of **RED DAWN** (2012) was withheld from completion until all traces of China as the invading/occupying force were obliterated, supplanted with safer interlopers: North Koreans, off-market "safe" turf for screen villainy in a variety of films (**TEAM AMERICA: WORLD POLICE** [2004], **OLYMPUS HAS FALLEN** [2013], **THE INTERVIEW** [2014], etc.). Attentive media viewers and scholars could see the shift in the late 1990s, when mounting outrage over vicious caricatures of Middle Eastern villainy in films like James Cameron's **TRUE LIES** (1994) prompted the embrace of non-human foes. The brutally direct satire of jingoism, patriotism, fascism, and a militarized citizenry central to Edward Neumeier and Paul Verhoeven's adaptation of Robert E. Heinlein's **STARSHIP TROOPERS** (1997) was rendered palatable by the (accurate to the source novel) depiction of the "enemy" as extraterrestrial non-human super-arthropods. This makes the non-human Martians of *The War of the Worlds* ideal for post-9/11 exploration/exploitation/projection of the dreaded "Other", without demonizing/caricaturing any Middle Eastern or religious faction.

Better the enemy sport tentacles and look like invertebrates, lest we recognize ourselves in the pop cultural mirrors (after all, America and our few Allies were the invading forces in 2002 and after).

This ploy was identical to the very one Wells had consciously adopted in formulating *The War of the Worlds*. Comics scholar William B. Jones concisely outlined Wells' process, and his reasons for embracing a "scientific romance" metaphor (the term science-fiction had not, as yet, been conceived or coined):

> H.G. Wells's 1898 novel...had its origins in the author's response to three sets of circumstances that had come to the attention of the general public in late-Victorian England. The first was the increasing threat posed by rising German militarism to the balance of power secured by the 19th century Pax Brittanica... feeding on English fears—realised in 1914—of a future war with the Kaiser's Germany.
>
> A second occurrence that informed the writing of The War of the Worlds was the strikingly close positioning of Mars to Earth in 1894 and the subsequent attention devoted to the red planet... Finally, as the 19th century drew to a close, a number of Britons, including H.G. Wells, began questioning the morality of the colonial system that supported the Empire on which the sun never set... Wells himself pointed to a conversation he had with his brother Frank about the dispossession and extermination of the native Tasmanians as the ultimate spark for The War of the Worlds. He hoped that readers of his novel would draw ironic parallels between the self-satisfied British empire-builders and the technologically advanced Martian colonizers.[1]

Clearly, Alan Moore and Kevin O'Neill understood and riffed on such "ironic parallels" for *The League of Extraordinary Gentlemen Volume II*. Just as clearly, Spielberg and his creative partners did not (or, more to the point, *chose* not to).

Precious few Americans, post-9/11, want to recognize ourselves in and as the Martians. Most Americans only recognize themselves as *the invaded*, victims of the Martians as the "Other"—the invaders—and the destruction they spread an echo of the World Trade Center towers plunging into dust, rather than reverberations from the seemingly interminable wars we've since carried overseas.

In either case, *The War of the Worlds* continues to speak to us all.

The Twin Towers fall; the Tripods rise.

———

Among the 21st Century Wells *War of the Worlds* reboots, *The League of Extraordinary Gentlemen Volume II* and **THE GREAT MARTIAN WAR** are

---

[1] William B. Jones, quoted from *Classics Illustrated* #124, *The War of the Worlds* (First Classics, Inc. edition, 2005), inside front cover text introduction, with permission of the author.

of a peculiar genre—invented faux-history, specifically recombinant faux-history. It's something that's been done in comicbooks and graphic novels for decades now, with a real boom over the past 20 years thanks to key works by Alan Moore, Neil Gaiman, Grant Morrison and others—all of whom are following in the footsteps of masters and hackmeisters who preceded everyone.

It's a few of those predecessors I want to focus on herein.

Long before novelist Michael Chabon won a Pulitzer for *The Amazing Adventures of Kavalier and Klay* (2000), Tom De Haven was blazing the trail for Chabon with *Funny Papers* (1985) and what became the *Funny Papers* trilogy with *Derby Dugan's Depression Funnies* (1996) and *Dugan Under Ground* (2001). Long before Alan Moore and Kevin O'Neill's *The League of Extraordinary Gentlemen* graphic novel series, Philip José Farmer was fusing real-world people with characters from classic pop and pulp literature, primary among them Tarzan and Doc Savage—as themselves or in slightly mutated form, renamed "Lord Grandrith" and "Doc Caliban".

In the remarkable (then absolutely pornographic) *A Feast Unknown* (1969, Essex House, the North Hollywood publisher renowned for, in their own words, "the very finest in adult reading by the most provocative modern writers"), Farmer posited Lord Grandrith and Doc Caliban pitched into mortal combat with each other by a sect of ancient immortals called the Nine. Both were suffering from the manifestation of a genetic perversion which suddenly "equated the act of coitus with killing, the thrust of the penis with the thrust of the knife, orgasm with *the bliss of the knife*, as Nietzsche called it," their common father none other than Jack the Ripper.[2] Farmer was playing at a much more arresting mature level than any previous author dared—and than any successive author would, until Alan Moore rolled up his sleeves, truth to be told. Those currently making hay from the explicit sexual aspects of Moore's work, including the role of rape and sexual assault in his fiction, should be required to dive into *A Feast Unknown* before launching their attacks.

In this realm, context—specifically that which came before—is *everything*.

---
2   Philip Jose Farmer, *A Feast Unknown* (1969, Essex House 1st edition), pg. 260; the italicized Nietzsche reference is Farmer's.

For *The Adventure of the Peerless Peer* (1974), Farmer teamed up Tarzan and Sherlock Holmes; via his surrogate characters Lord Grandrith and Doc Caliban, Farmer radically experimented with Edgar Rice Burroughs and Kenneth Robeson (a.k.a. Lester Dent)'s most popular characters for the trilogy *A Feast Unknown* (1969), *Lord of the Trees* (1970) and *The Mad Goblin* (1970). He then scribed mock biographies of the "'real'" characters as *Tarzan Alive!* (1972) and *Doc Savage: His Apocalyptic Life* (1973). Farmer's conceit was that Burroughs and Robeson based their original pulp novels on the lives of *real people*, and he concocted an inventive genealogical tree linking Tarzan and Savage with a brace of other supposedly fictional characters to forge the *"Wold Newton family"*.

Whatever others are doing today, they owe a vast debt to Farmer, who wrote sequels to *Moby Dick* and *King Kong*, offered Jules Verne readers *The Other Log of Phileas Fogg* (1973), sent Samuel Clemens a.k.a. Mark Twain steamboating with Richard Burton, Hermann Göring and others in the afterlife of the Riverworld, and wrote *Venus on the Half-Shell* (1975) as *"Kilgore Trout"*, the woefully mistreated science fiction writer Kurt Vonnegut had created as a character in some of his novels. Vonnegut had given Farmer permission, which he soon regretted and withdrew, only adding to the mystique of Farmer's accomplishment (that duly noted, Farmer did have to cave to legal pressure from the Edgar Rice Burroughs estate and remove "Tarzan" as "Tarzan" from a number of his novels, including *The Adventures of the Peerless Peer*).

Farmer mixed and matched and essentially created the mold for what some now call the *"literary mashup"*, which has yielded everything from faux-Jane Austen sequels to the likes of *Pride and Prejudice and Zombies* ad infinitum. Hell, *I've* even played in Farmer's conceptual sandbox: Farmer's template was the one Alan Moore, Rick Veitch, and I (and our many collaborators) used for the Image Comics series *1963* (1993). We reckoned (rightly) if you can't write and draw for Marvel Comics and DC Comics in the early 1960s, write and draw as if your characters had been and *were* published by Marvel and DC in the early 1960s.

Toying with this kind of mindset and material taps my own avid teen- and college-year readings of some of my all-time favorite writers, and some less

Startling imagery from BBC's **THE GREAT MARTIAN WAR: 1913-1917** (2013; US broadcast debut 2014); at the time of this writing, this gem still remains unavailable legally on any home video format in any country.

Richard Corben's rendition of "Doc Caliban" (aka Doc Savage) getting himself aroused via carnage, from Philip José Farmer's classic *A Feast Unknown* (1969); Corben illustrated the 1975 limited edition (hardcover, 200 copies signed by Farmer; trade paperback limited to 800 copies, both from Fokker D-LXIX Press)

beloved but no less fascinating wordsmiths. I've been revisiting Kurt Vonnegut, Manly Wade Wellman, Philip José Farmer, George H. Smith, and others, and it's been a lot of fun—and productive, in that it's fed my waking hours and ongoing creative collaborative work on my own projects. Rereading a number of books that inspired my own thinking about this kind of invented history (including Borges, Lovecraft and Chambers, whose key works often involved the discovery of books that never existed in our world) prompted my revisiting two curious paperbacks I've held on to over the years because they meshed some of my favorite literary characters with one of the all-time great science fiction novels.

Both paperbacks were 1960s spins on H.G. Wells' classic *The War of the Worlds*; both were playing in Farmer's sandbox; both were anticipating today's *War of the Worlds* post-9/11 boom.

One of these was *The Second War of the Worlds* (1976, Daw Books) by George H. Smith, whom you'll be *completely* sick of after you read the second installment of this essay in the next issue of *Weng's Chop*—this I vow.

But far more interesting was and is the more significant speculative novel of the pair, Manly Wade Wellman and Wade Wellman's collaborative *Sherlock Holmes's War of the Worlds* (1975, Warner Books; reprinted by Titan Books in a new edition in 2009[3]). Wellman and Wellman's novel remains an imaginative and quite entertaining fusion of Wells and Sir Arthur Conan Doyle that not

[3] Still in print and available from http://www.amazon.com/Further-Adventures-Sherlock-Holmes-Worlds/dp/1848564910/ref=sr_1_1?s=books&ie=UTF8&qid=1417278481&sr=1-1&keywords=Sherlock+Holmes+War+of+the+Worlds

only brings Doyle's famed detective and his faithful friend Dr. Watson into the arena of the catastrophic Martian invasion, but finds Holmes actively joining forces with another of my all-time favorite imaginary adventurers, Professor Challenger.

We've a lot of preliminary ground to cover first, however.

Like most kids of my generation, my introduction to H.G. Wells' original *The War of the Worlds* wasn't the novel. I was introduced to it via the *Classics Illustrated* comicbook adaptation (#124, January 1955), adapted by writer Harry G. Miller and illustrated by the great Lou Cameron, who also painted the cover. As *Classics Illustrated* historian William B. Jones wrote, "Cameron's gripping visual narrative featured the definitive depiction of the deadly Martian tripods. A two-page splash portrayed the lethal effect of the Martians' attack in one of the most memorable drawings ever to appear in the series." It was the most popular of all the *Classics Illustrated* H. G. Wells adaptations, earning eleven printings (1955-1970) and "accorded almost totemic significance by young readers whose imaginations were fired... It was also highly regarded by the artist's peers in the comics realm." In multiple venues, Jones tells how artist Ken Steacy was approached to provide new artwork for a new adaptation for the First Comics revival of *Classics Illustrated*, and Steacy refused, deferring to the Miller/Cameron version.[4]

I later read the novel, a couple of years before I saw the George Pal/Byron Haskin 1953 movie version on NBC-TV (on the prime-time *Tuesday Night at the Movies*, February 21st, 1967), and I loved both. The Pal/Haskin *War of the Worlds* is one of the key films from that era I've since revisited every couple of years. As soon as there was an LP release of the Orson Welles October 1938 *Mercury Theater on the Air* broadcast (Murray Hill Records S44217, 1969), I snapped that up, too, and savored it; it was the very LP I loaned the local radio station in Brattleboro, VT when I convinced First Run Video owner Alan Goldstein that it was a great idea to build our video store Halloween promo around rerunning the broadcast around the time parents were driving their trick-or-treaters door to door, neighborhood to neighborhood (and we indeed got a lot of great feedback on that!). Once Howard Koch's paperback book *The Panic Broadcast: The Whole Story of Orson Welles' Legendary Radio Show Invasion From Mars* (Avon Books, 1970) hit the racks, I snagged that, too, and learned all that was then available about the infamous Orson Welles program that shocked and rattled a pre-WW2-jittery America.

But it was the Harry Miller-scripted, Lou Cameron-illustrated *Classics Illustrated* #124 issue that indelibly shaped my initiation into the *War of the Worlds* and my reading of all the Herbert George Wells I could lay my hands on. This was somehow appropriate, as the first edition of that comicbook debuted the same year I was born (1955), and it seems it was always in either my brother Rick's or my stacks of comics, or in the piles at our neighbors' houses. To this day, when I think of the Martian war machines, it's Cameron's majestic version of the tripods that instantly come to mind. I can't help it; it's how I'm hard-wired. Such is the power of comics!

Cameron's iconic imagery stands tripod-tall above all that followed in comics: Marvel Comics' *Amazing Adventures* #18-39 (1973-1976) Killraven series (despite the high points of Don McGregor's scripts and P. Craig Russell's art) and its sequels, Alex Nino's vivid artwork for the Vince Fago-produced Pendulum Now Age Classics paperback comics adaptation of the Wells novel (1974), Roy Thomas and Michael Lark's *Superman: War of the Worlds* (1999), Moore and O'Neill's *The League of Extraordinary Gentleman Volume II*, Ian Edginton and D'Israeli's adaptation for Dark Horse Comics (2006), and so on.

I read the original H.G. Wells *War of the Worlds* at a tender age—along with Jules Verne's *Journey to the Center of the Earth* and Robert Heinlein's *Have Spacesuit, Will Travel* (1958), it was among my initial extensive readings of science-fiction. Like Verne (Heinlein was streamlined for my generation), reading Wells was initially a tough slog for a tyke, but I got into it, and soon

[4] William B. Jones, quoted from *Classics Illustrated: A Cultural History* (McFarland & Company, Inc., 2002), pg. 147, and from *Classics Illustrated* #124, *The War of the Worlds* (First Classics, Inc. edition, 2005), inside front cover text introduction; both quoted with permission of the author. For more on this classic *Classics Illustrated* adaptation, see http://www.war-ofthe-worlds.co.uk/classics_illustrated.htm

was overwhelmed with the vivid pictures Wells' prose put in my head. I became an avid reader of any and all science fiction I could put my hands on, and luckily our local Waterbury Public Library had a great collection of Wells, Verne and a couple spinner-racks of more recent paperbacks, including a fair SF selection. I devoured them all, and later tracked down the Wells that had eluded me, including his short stories and my favorite of all his novels, *The Island of Dr. Moreau* (1896).

No need to detail more about Wells' *War of the Worlds* except where necessary as we move on. Suffice to say his novel was a masterpiece, a masterstroke of imagination that codified the entire "invasion" genre—from afar (aliens) and in terms of less imaginative xenophobic fantasies of localized invasions (think *Red Dawn*, 1984 and 2012). Despite the specificity of Wells' descriptions of the Martians and their war machines, the many illustrators who have illuminated various book editions over the past century+ (starting with those in its serialization, and for the original book-format revised novel) are delightful in their variety, and that's part of the novel's allure, too.[5]

If you doubt how immediately *War of the Worlds* forged the *definitive* template for its genre, consider how *promptly* other writers ripped off Wells. *The Fighters from Mars: The War of the World In and Near Boston* by an uncredited author was serialized in *The Boston Evening Post* beginning the very first week of January, 1898—Wells' novel had just completed serialization in 1897, and had yet to be published in novel form—and who could concoct a faster rip-off than that?[6]

This act of piracy reset Wells' London, England invasion in Boston, Massachusetts, so we were into *War of the Worlds* being the all-purpose, retrofit one-size-fits-all before the turn of the 20th Century. Copyright laws then weren't what they are today, and so popular was the *Boston Evening Post*'s rip-off that a *sequel* to the rip-off—the first "unofficial" sequel of many—of the *War of the Worlds* was serialized in the spring of 1898. This was Garrett P. Serviss' *Edison's Conquest of Mars*. Somewhat hilarious to contemplate today is the fact that the paper and author secured inventor Thomas A. Edison's permission to use his name and feature Edison as the protagonist; no such courtesy was extended to H.G. Wells for the wholesale theft of his original novel, premise or version of Mars, Martians or their invasion.[7]

So, before Philip José Farmer was even born, Thomas Edison was waging war on Wells' Martians!

When they started work on their *War of the Worlds* revamp in the late 1960s, Wade and Manly Wade, of course, asked permission of no one: not Herbert George (long dead) or Sir Arthur Conan Doyle (ditto), nor Holmes, Watson or Challenger.

—

Who is Manly Wade Wellman?

Among the pulp-era writers who reveled in weird fiction, Wellman was one of the best. I grew up reading Wellman, so it's tough to pick an entry point. Wellman wrote weird fiction, adult fiction, young adult novels, and he was a historian, journalist, folklorist, Civil War expert and more. He wrote comic books, too, including the first issue of *Captain Marvel Adventures*.

His work struck a chord for me (pun intended) when I stumbled on his Silver John stories, a.k.a. John the Balladeer, tales of a wandering minstrel with a silver-string guitar facing mountain monsters, backwoods witches, warlocks and forest spirits. Wellman's distinctive Appalachian-set Americana, steeped in genuine dread yet oddly folksy and comfortable thanks to Silver John's own laid-back personality, stoicism, candor and wit, had an incredible sense of place that *resonated* for me in ways no other writer's work ever did. Growing up in the backwoods of northern Vermont, I ached for something similar set in my home state; Wellman never set a story in my home state, but *damn* his mountain folk tales *sang*, and it did fire up the storyteller inside me.

The first unauthorized serialized "sequel" to H.G. Wells' *War of the Worlds* was *Edison's Conquest of Mars* (1898) by Garrett P. Serviss. **TOP:** This paperback edition (Powell Publications, Inc., August 1969) was edited and condensed by Forrest J. Ackerman ("...I removed some thousands of words of excess herbage which had overgrown and obscured the action...[and] tried to straighten out some of the tortuously tangled syntax...") with cover art by Bill Hughes. **ABOVE:** 1898 artwork (uncredited) for the first publication of Serviss's 'sequel.'

---

5   For an overview of the many illustrators who delineated the Martian invasion and war machines in the many editions of *The War of the Worlds*, go to http://drzeus.best.vwh.net/wotw/illus/interior.html

6   To read the first installment, go to http://www.war-ofthe-worlds.co.uk/fight_1.htm and for more information on this first-ever American *War of the Worlds* spinoff, see http://www.war-ofthe-worlds.co.uk/fighters_from_mars.htm

7   For more on the first-ever sequel to the first-ever *War of the Worlds* rip-off, see http://www.war-ofthe-worlds.co.uk/edisons_conquest_of_mars.htm

Already the old dream was reality, and the civilization I had known was slipping away—

Original illustration by William Elliott Dold, Jr. (1892-1967) a.k.a. "Dold" for Manly Wade Wellman's excellent short story "Pithecanthropus Rejectus" in *Astounding Stories* (Vol 20, No 5, January 1938); though uncredited, Wellman's story was clearly the inspiration for Rupert Wyatt/Rick Jaffa/Amanda Silver's **RISE OF THE PLANET OF THE APES** (2011) starring Andy Serkis as Caesar (via Weta Digital CGI effects)

These prompted me to scrounge for any and all Wellman fiction I could find. A frequent contributor to the pages of *Amazing Stories, Weird Tales, Startling Stories, Thrilling Wonder Stories* and peer of Henry Kuttner (whose own Hogben stories were snug fits in my skull with Wellman's backwoods mythos), A.E. Van Vogt, Robert E. Howard, H.P. Lovecraft, Robert Bloch, Arthur C. Clarke and Ray Bradbury, Wellman remains a top-shelf writer of his generation.

Given my proclivities for all things prehistoric, I also dug Wellman's tales of tribal leader Hok and his brutal struggle with antagonistic Neanderthals, all vying for survival in an unforgiving world; it also seemed to me during my underground comix reading days that George Metzger's marvelous proto-"Steampunk" *Moondog* SF comix owed a debt to Wellman's Patch Merrick.

The Silver John stories were initially collected into the Arkham House anthology *Who Fears the Devil?* (1963), opening with the first published John story *"O' Ugly Bird"* (*Weird Tales*, December 1951). These were eventually adapted by TV horror pioneer John Newland (*One Step Beyond*, **DON'T BE AFRAID OF THE DARK** [See *Monster!* digest #16, p.27], etc.) into the low-budget independent feature **THE LEGEND OF HILLBILLY JOHN** (1973).[8] I caught the movie at the drive-in when Jack Harris (producer of **THE BLOB** [1958], and distributor of similarly inventive low-budget gems like **EQUINOX** [1970] and **DARK STAR** [1974, See *Monster!* digest #14, pp.8-33]) was handling the movie; unfortunately, it never got much theatrical play and it's still tough to scratch up.

Some folks really loathe the movie, though I quite like it; Newland does all he can within his limited budget and means, it looks and feels fine, the music (especially a devilish tune by Hoyt Axton) works, it's got a *brilliant* final shot, and Gene Warren and Wah Chang provided some nifty stop-motion animation to breathe brief life into that "ugly bird". Still, it was a major disappointment, most of all for the painful lead performance by Hedges Capers as Silver John, who *looks* the part and had an affable manner and sings nicely. Capers does his utmost, but the boy just can't act a lick.

In 1979, as if to reclaim his territory, Wellman launched the John the Balladeer novels, all of which I highly recommend (*The Old Gods Waken, After the Dark, The Lost and the Lurking, The Hanging Stones*, and *The Voice of the Mountain*).

A few of Wellman's other stories were adapted to television over the years ("The Devil is Not Mocked" on *Night Gallery*, October 27, 1971; "Rouse Him Not" on *Monsters*, December 1988), but he's never really gotten his due in the larger pop culture.

The best of all Manly Wade Wellman movie "adaptations" (read: appropriations/thefts) of his work to date was **RISE OF THE PLANET OF THE APES** (2011), drawn from Manly Wade Wellman's excellent short story "Pithecanthropus Rejectus" in *Astounding Stories* (Vol 20, No 5, January 1938). I've got the original pulp edition of in my collection, but I originally read Wellman's story on a plane via the UK paperback *The Rivals of Frankenstein* (1977, Corgi), en route home from my first-ever UKAK in 1985.[9] Wellman's story was, in its day, a concise rethink of a number of already-chestnut SF novels, including H.G. Wells' *The Island of Dr. Moreau* (1896) and Gaston Leroux's now-forgotten *Balaoo* (1911, first published in *Le Matin*, October 9-December 18, 1911).

Balaoo was incredibly popular in its time, internationally renowned and widely imitated; Leroux, after all, was the author of *The Phantom of the Opera*. Leroux's seminal tale of a scientist hyper-evolving a primate via surgery was repeatedly filmed, starting with Victorin-Hippolyte Jasset's **BALAOO THE DEMON BABOON** (1913) and often "borrowed from". Official adaptations included **THE WIZARD** (1927) and **DR. RENAULT'S SECRET** (1942), but the rip-offs span from the Lon Chaney vehicle **A BLIND BARGAIN** (1922) and the Universal "Paula Dupree the ape woman" films (starring

---

8 See article on p.80.

9 Wellman's story has often been reprinted, making its access to the *Rise of the Planet of the Apes* authors exceedingly likely. The story has been reprinted in *Science Fiction of the Thirties* (both editions, 1976 and 1977), *The Rivals of Frankenstein: A Gallery of Monsters* (1977 and 1980), *The Best Animal Stories of Science Fiction and Fantasy* (1979), *The Mammoth Book of Frankenstein* (1994), etc. See http://www.isfdb.org/cgi-bin/title.cgi?43973

Acquanetta and/or Vicky Lane) of the early 1940s on through the Mexican man/ape transplant horror films like Chano Urueta's seminal **EL MONSTRUO RESUCITADO** (1953), Fernando Méndez's **LADRÓN DE CADÁVERES** (a.k.a. **THE BODY SNATCHER**, 1957), and René Cardona's **LAS LUCHADORAS CONTRA EL MEDICO ASESINO** (a.k.a. **DOCTOR OF DOOM**, 1963) and **LA HORRIPILANTE BESTIA HUMANA** (a.k.a. **NIGHT OF THE BLOODY APES**, 1969/1972, Monster! digest #20, p.13).

An aside: even 1990s comicbook megastar creator Todd McFarlane ripped on *Balaoo* (in *Spawn*), and didn't even know it (I *know* he didn't: in the one and only "want to work with me?" phone call I ever received from Todd, when he was asking me to take on a horror spinoff comic with or for him, and he told me it was the *Spawn* man/gorilla character he wanted me to work with, I mentioned Balaoo—he thought I was suddenly talking about the fucking *singing bear* from the Disney animated adaptation of *The Jungle Book*)!

The ol' "surgically evolve an ape and/or transplant a man's brain into a gorilla" shtick was and is just *everywhere*. But they all owed and still owe a debt to H.G. Wells and Gaston Leroux—and Manly Wade Wellman knew that.

In Wellman's tale, his put-upon narrator is an ape named Congo who has been surgically altered to increase his intelligence and allow him to speak. He details his life with the scientist and the scientist's kind, caring wife, and the fact that he matured more quickly than the couple's own son, Sidney, who remained *"a fat, blue-eyed baby that drooled and gurgled and barely crept upon the nursery linoleum, while I scurried easily hither and thither, scrambling up on tables and bedposts, and sometimes on the bureau."* Congo's account notes his own ability to speak and his unhappiness with the patience and affection showered on Sidney while the scientist *"acted grave—almost stern—where I was involved."* Congo is also painfully aware of the ongoing surgeries necessary to his own rapid development, and how this further sets him apart from Sidney.

Sounding familiar?

In fact, much of the first third of Wellman's "Pithecanthropus Rejectus" reads like a *template* for much of **RISE OF THE PLANET OF THE APES**, sometimes with uncanny fidelity. The overall theme and thrust is also in accord with **RISE OF THE PLANET OF THE APES**, in many striking ways—in fact, I'd argue that Wellman was due a credit or at least an onscreen "thanks to" acknowledgement.

The narratives diverge significantly, however, when the scientist sells Congo to subsidize his future experiments. Congo is essentially recruited into show biz (shades of **MIGHTY JOE YOUNG** [1949]!), but Wellman was a most literary man—and so, Congo is offered the part of Caliban in a production of William Shakespeare's *The Tempest* (and Congo himself is sharp enough to respond to the role, and recognize his affinity with Caliban's plight).

Eventually, though, Congo contrives to realize his personal dream—his (ahem) "return to Africa", where he is violently rejected by the natural tribal apes and forced to instead return to civilization, totally aware of his complete misfit status and utter singularity as a sentient being: the tragedy of Frankenstein's monster, just as Mary Shelley conceived her monster.

When Congo is reunited with his maker, the scientist informs Congo of his plan to surgically mass-produce *more* of man-ape hybrids:

> "...each a valuable property—each an advance in surgery and psychology over the last... In six or eight years there'll be a full hundred of you, or more advanced... I will lighten the labor of mankind..."

At which point, Congo—just as Caesar does in **RISE** (as articulated in screenwriter Paul Dehn's original imaginary arc of the first *Planet of the Apes* movie series)—objects, and...go, read "Pithecanthropus Rejectus", then revisit (or enjoy for the first time) **RISE OF THE PLANET OF THE APES**.

And tell me I'm wrong.

In any case, Manly Wade Wellman is, to many, an unknown quantity—to others, an acquired taste. To those of us who grew up on his work, we can only say, *"You don't know what you're missing, so you'd better start reading!"*

The Oregon Literary Review has an excellent website dedicated to Wellman and his work.[10] Daniel Alan Ross' "The Voice of the Mountains: Manly Wade

10 http://orelitrev.startlogic.com/v2n2/OLR-rickert.htm

Wellman" is an essential resource for anyone interested in finding out more, or for diehard devotees just trying to keep tabs on what's new regarding reprints, adaptations, and everything regarding Wellman's remarkable body of work.[11] Just make sure you don't *start* with media adaptations of Wellman's work—read the man's work. As I said, save for the sadly uncredited **RISE OF THE PLANET OF THE APES**, the movies and TV adaptations don't do him justice, and much as I have a soft spot in my skull for it, **THE LEGEND OF HILLBILLY JOHN** is no way to introduce anyone to Wellman—and that's not just me talking.[12]

While I don't need to introduce Sherlock Holmes and Dr. Watson, a few words about Sir Arthur Conan Doyle's Professor Challenger might be in order. Conan Doyle introduced the burly, no-nonsense egotistical scientist in *The Lost World* (1912), a book beloved to all dinosaur-loving lads like me (for whom, according to Conan Doyle's dedication, the book was written). I read this early in life, too, but after my first exposure to Verne and Wells, it was harder to find Conan Doyle's book, for some reason. I finally got to read it around age 10 or 11. Now, understand, devoted reader, that Sir Arthur Conan Doyle so *loved* Challenger that he once had himself made up as his protagonist and photographed.[13]

11 http://www.manlywadewellman.com
12 For instance, visit Tom Bagley's entry on the "7 Deadly Sinners" blog at http://7deadlysinners.typepad.com/sinners/2008/06/who-fears-the-devil.html to see Tom's own one-sheet poster to the movie version of *Who Fears the Devil?* Tom *wishes* existed instead of **THE LEGEND OF HILLBILLY JOHN**.
13 There were five Professor Challenger novels/novellas in all: *The Lost World* (1912), *The Poison Belt* (1913, borrowing much from and arguably Conan Doyle's retort to M.P. Shiel's *The Purple Cloud*, 1901), *The Land of Mist* (1926), *The Disintegration Machine* (1927), and *When the World Screamed* (1928). Though long out-of-print, The Complete Professor Challenger Stories (1952 and 1977 editions) can still be found at http://www.amazon.com/Complete-Professor-Challenger-Stories/dp/0719503604/ref=sr_1_2?s=books&ie=UTF8&qid=1417273067&sr=1-2&keywords=The+Complete+Professor+Challenger+Stories (on kindle at http://www.amazon.com/Complete-Professor-Challenger-Chronological-Contents-ebook/dp/B006MHG5CC/ref=sr_1_1?s=books&ie=UTF8&qid=1417273104&sr=1-1&keywords=The+Complete+Professor+Challenger+Stories) . For more on Conan Doyle's adventurer, see http://www.internationalhero.co.uk/c/challeng.htm

American movie trade journal ad art for Victorin-Hippolyte Jasset's **BALAOO THE DEMON BABOON** (1913)

Among a number of masterstrokes that inform Wellman and Wellman's collaboration on *Sherlock Holmes's War of the Worlds*, their decision to fold Challenger into the adventure is among the most obvious—and sharpest. Why, exactly, nobody ever thought to bring Holmes and Challenger together before, I don't know; it would seem to be a no-brainer, and they play off one another as characters beautifully.

The fact that Wellman and Wellman settled on setting their Holmes/Challenger/Wells mashup when they did—in the Year of Our Lord 1902 (more about that shortly)—makes *Sherlock Holmes's War of the Worlds* a *prequel* to *The Lost World* and Doyle's other Professor Challenger novels. It also makes the Martian invasion the Professor's first brush with world-destroying apocalyptic events, something he would become quite well-versed in later in his career.

So, what about this Holmes vs. Martians book?

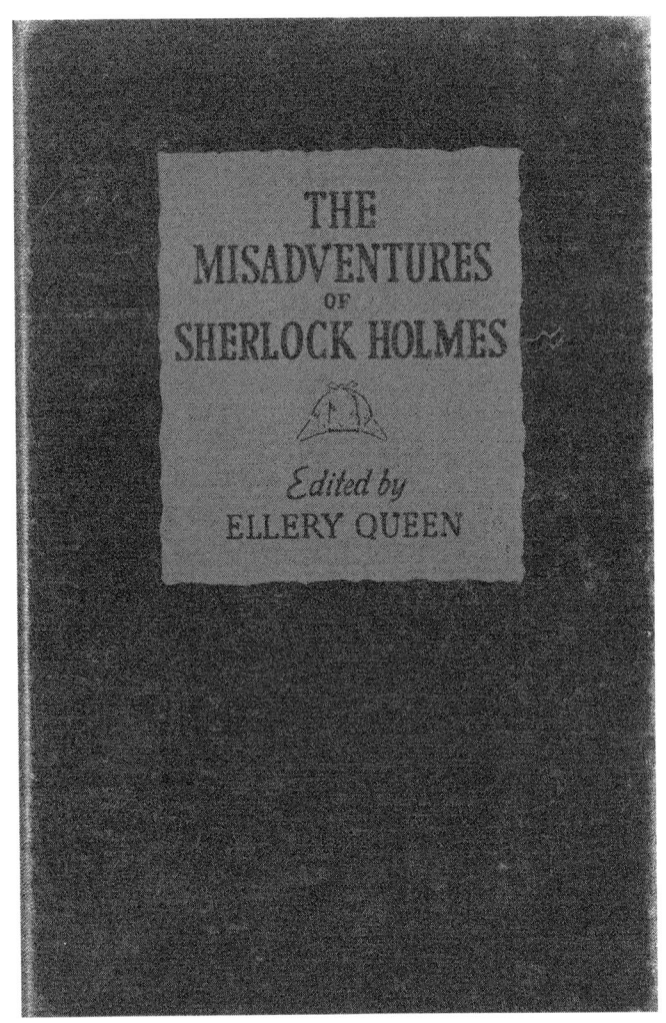

These days, revisionist Sherlock Holmes media is a booming industry. There are even contemporary competing adaptations and TV series, with no end in sight.

Consider, just to provide some context, the fact that literary science-fiction outings featuring Sherlock Holmes have been a tradition since at least the 1970s. Isaac Asimov, Martin Harry Greenberg, and Charles G. Waugh collected sufficient stories for *Sherlock Holmes Through Time and Space* (St. Martin's Press, 1986). Dame Jean Conan Doyle authorized Martin H. Greenberg editing another such collection, this time with Mike Resnick, for the 26-science-fiction-story anthology *Sherlock Holmes in Orbit* (DAW Books, 1995). This collection showcased more revisionist sf Sherlock Holmes stories, each with a twist: cloning (Gary Allen Ruse's "The Holmes Team Advantage"), time travel (Dean Wesley Smith's "Two Roads, No Choices"), computers (Byron Tetrick's "The Future Engine"), crop circles (Vonda N. McIntyre's "The Adventure of the Field Theorems"), and the virtually indescribable (Josepha Sherman's "The Case of the Purloined L'isitek").[14]

While such anthologies showcase a fine spectrum of speculative works spinning new adventures for Sir Arthur Conan Doyle's legendary detective and his erstwhile companion Dr. Watson, the fact is that missing from these collections were the earliest and still among the best of all extraterrestrial SF Holmesian extrapolations. Almost half-a-century ago, an inauspiciously designed paperback original popped up on the racks offering an imaginative conflation of not only Holmes and *The War of the Worlds*, but one of the finest rewoven narrative tapestries comprised of Conan Doyle's complete fictional universe to boot.

Co-authored by the father (Manly Wade) and son (Wade) Wellman team, the novel is in fact a revised and expanded compilation of *two* published short

---

[14] This has gone far beyond a cottage industry; for a list of authors of new Sherlock Holmes fiction, see http://en.wikipedia.org/wiki/List_of_authors_of_new_Sherlock_Holmes_stories

---

Hardcover (*sans* dust jacket) of the Ellery Queen-edited anthology *The Misadventures of Sherlock Holmes* (Little, Brown and Company, March 1944); in his introduction, Queen (the collaborative pen name of Daniel Nathan and his cousin Emanuel Benjamin Lepofsky a.k.a. Manfred Bennington Lee) wrote, "The publication of this anthology marks the first time the great parodies and pastiches of that 'Extraordinary Man,' as Mark Twain affectionately called him, have been collected in a single volume. Why no one thought of doing it before, we shall never understand..." Well, they soon would: this earliest and scarcest of all Holmes anthologies was reportedly suppressed shortly after publication by the Doyle estate, though there were at least three printings (the last dated October 1944) before it was pulled from the market. Rarest of all are the 125 copies of the first edition featuring a numbered presentation page signed by Ellery Queen "for presentation to friends and admirers of Sherlock Holmes at the Sherlock Holmes dinner held March 31, 1944, Murray Hill Hotel, New York City."

THE MAN WHO WAS NOT DEAD
by MANLY WADE WELLMAN

It is singularly fitting that the last story in our book, reprinted from "Argosy" magazine, August 9, 1941, should have as its underlying theme the most important issue in our lives—the winning of the war.

Mr. Sherlock Holmes, you'll remember, did his bit in World War I, but it was not, thank the Lord, His Last Bow.

Holmes will never die—he is unconquered and unconquerable. For Sherlock Holmes is England.

OUT OF the black sky plummeted Boling, toward the black earth. He knew nothing of the ground toward which he fell, save that it was five miles inland from the Sussex coast and, according to Dr. Goebbels's best information, sparsely settled.

The night air hummed in his parachute rigging, and he seemed to drop faster than ten feet a second, but to think of that was unworthy of a trusted agent of the German Intelligence. Though the pilot above had not dared drop him a light, Boling could land without much mishap. . . . Even as he told himself that, land he did. He struck heavily on hands and knees, and around him settled the limp folds of the parachute.

At once he threw off the harness, wadded the fabric and thrust it out of sight between a boulder and a bush. Standing up, he took stock of himself. The left leg of his trousers was torn, and the knee skinned—that was all. He remembered that William the Conquerer had also gone sprawling when he landed at Hastings, not so far from here. The omen was good. Boling stooped, like Duke William, and clutched a handful of pebbles.

"Thus do I seize the land!" he quoted aloud, for he was at heart theatrical.

Introductory page to Manly Wade Wellman's contribution to the Ellery Queen-edited anthology *The Misadventures of Sherlock Holmes* (Little, Brown and Company, March 1944), citing its original publication in *Argosy* (August 9, 1941).

Sir Arthur Conan Doyle's Professor Challenger character never enjoyed the instant and lasting fame of Holmes, but Doyle had great affection for the character, who "starred" in five novels/novellas: *The Lost World* (1912; originally serialized in *The Strand Magazine*, April-November 1912, first illustrated by Harry Rountree, **CENTER**), *The Poison Belt* (1913), *The Land of Mist* (1926, originally serialized in *The Strand Magazine*, July 1925-May 1926, **LEFT**), *The Disintegration Machine* (1927), and *When the World Screamed* (1928). **RIGHT:** The sole illustration in this article's author's copy of the Ellery Queen-edited anthology *The Misadventures of Sherlock Holmes* (Little, Brown and Company, March 1944); the artist was uncredited. Anyone have any ideas or evidence of who might have drawn this?

stories and carefully prepared additional material to flesh the whole out nicely to novelistic scope. But before the paperback edition of *Sherlock Holmes's War of the Worlds*, there was a single short story, published in a SF newsstand digest/pulp:

It all began with "The Adventure of the Martian Client" in *The Magazine of Fantasy and Science Fiction* (December, 1969; hereafter *F&SF*), presented as a memoir written (in the appropriate Sir Arthur Conan Doyle style) by John H. Watson, M.D.

The game was afoot!

Now, negotiating one's way around this terrain is a bit tricky. I'll do my best, but if you lose your footing, stick with it, please. You're sure to regain the path in due course, and I'll plant sufficient reminders to keep you on track.

First off, understand that the Wellmans were literary men, steeped in their shared love for and knowledge of writing and their favorite genres.

They were writing for a market operating with the presumption that its readership was *also* quite knowledgeable in the arcana of the genre and its traditions. They presumed—as I have to here, too—that their readers had not only an affection and working knowledge of the works of Sir Arthur Conan Doyle, but also a familiarity with Wells' *The War of the Worlds*.[15] If you lack that, dear reader, an extended session with the still-entertaining novel is highly recommended. So omnipresent and pervasive was the impact of Wells' novel, so readily available in its countless adaptations in various media, that it was even fair to presume in 1975 that those unlucky souls who had never read the novel were familiar, via pop cultural osmosis, with its iconography and details. It's a bit like the origins of Batman and Superman: even though precious few people have *actually read* the original comicbook stories themselves, *everyone* knows the origins of these characters. Our pop culture has inoculated us with them, seemingly from birth, via other media; in the 1960s and 1970s, that was true of Wells' *War of the Worlds*, too.

This gave the Wellmans a tremendous, shared imaginative scenario to play with and within.

The arcana of Holmes obsessed a readership at times feverishly devoted to its tiniest details; less well-known was that associated with Conan Doyle's Professor Challenger, whose first adventure (*The Lost World*, 1912) was and remains the best-known and most widely read. While H. G. Wells devotees were less obsessive or possessive than Holmes buffs, the fact that *The War of the Worlds* was such a fully-absorbed work presented ample opportunities to both adhere to its familiar elements and count upon the gaps in the most attentive reader's memory. While we all "knew" the narrative and imagery of *War of the Worlds*, how many of us had ever actually read it more than once—or only knew it from the *Classics Illustrated* adaptation, or Orson Welles's radio drama, or the George Pal film? If any details could be tweaked, revamped or fudged, those stemming from the Wells novel were the most malleable by far.

When the Wellmans wanted to maintain devotion to the Wells text, they could and would cite the Wells novel, even quote it verbatim; wherever the Wellmans wanted to fabricate some new twist, or simply deviate from the canonical text, they were free to do so with surprising elegance and ease.

Among the tricks up their collective sleeves was the fact that fewer readers still were familiar with Wells' own prequel to *The War of the Worlds*, the short story "The Crystal Egg" (1897). As Manly Wade Wellman noted in his portion of the book author's notes: *"All our labors would be plagiarism, did we not make positive and grateful acknowledgement to Wells's* The War of the Worlds *and his short story, 'The Crystal Egg,' which is a supplement to the novel..."*

The Wellmans wisely incorporate the key concept, prop and trappings of Wells' own introductory short story, "The Crystal Egg", into both their catalyst short story and the opening chapter of the novel proper. And oh, what a gift that was![16]

In Wells' short story, a dealer of unusual antiques gains possession of a mysterious crystal egg from another (deceased) dealer, and sees "things" within the object. It is a window of a kind, looking out on an alien world:

> *...But the use of an old velvet cloth, which he used as a background for a collection of minerals, occurred to him, and by doubling this, and*

---

15 For an overview of the countless editions of *The War of the Worlds* already in print before the Wellmans dove in, see http://drzeus.best.vwh.net/wotw/wotw.html

16 The complete original text to H.G. Wells' "The Crystal Egg" is online at http://www.online-literature.com/wellshg/2878/ —and those wishing to see a heavily-illustrated summary of the October 12, 1951 *Tales of Tomorrow* TV adaptation should visit http://monstermoviemusic.blogspot.com/2009/10/tales-of-tomorrow-crystal-egg-tv-1951.html

Ed Emsh (Ed Emshwiller) cover art (for Sonya Dorman's "Bye, Bye, Banana Bird") for *Fantasy and Science Fiction* December 1969 issue (Vol. 37, No. 6), which debuted what became a series of Sherlock Holmes/War of the Worlds stories by Manly Wade Wellman and son Wade Wellman with "The Adventure of the Martian Client."

putting it over his head and hands, he was able to get a sight of the luminous movement within the crystal even in the day-time. He was very cautious lest he should be thus discovered by his wife, and he practised this occupation only in the afternoons, while she was asleep upstairs, and then circumspectly in a hollow under the counter. And one day, turning the crystal about in his hands, he saw something. It came and went like a flash, but it gave him the impression that the object had for a moment opened to him the view of a wide and spacious and strange country...

The ingenious adoption of this device that Wells himself provided allowed the Wellmans the means *essential* to tapping the characteristics of both Conan Doyle heroes: Holmes's almost preternatural observational and deductive skills, and Challenger's unflagging curiosity and ferocious scientific acumen. With a literal window to Mars itself, and later to the invaders in their warships, we *believe* that Holmes and Challenger can both anticipate *and* have the means to spy on the invading force.

But I'm getting ahead of the narrative. Let's go back to the first Wellman and Wellman short story from the December 1969 *F&SF*, and the opening window on an as-yet-unformed revisionist world the Wellmans were creating.

Yes, they were working with familiar elements. But they were only beginning to manipulate and formulate where they were going with them, and where those actions might lead them—and the readers.

In the new context of the whole, "The Adventure of the Martian Client" became Chapter IV of the final novel *Sherlock Holmes's War of the Worlds* (pp. 147-172). In both incarnations, it begins:

Mr. H. G. Wells's popular book, The War of the Worlds, *is a frequently inaccurate chronicle of a known radical and atheist, a boon companion of Frank Harris, George Bernard Shaw, and worse. He exaggerates needlessly and pretends to a scientific knowledge which plainly he does not possess. Yet scientists and laymen alike read and applaud him, even while they scorn the brilliant deductions of Sherlock Holmes and Professor Edward Challenger.*

Wells refers in his book to the magnificent and almost complete specimen of an invader, preserved in spirits at the Natural History Museum, but he carelessly, or perhaps even deliberately, overlooks the history of its capture, examination, and presentation. And both scholarly journals and the popular press almost totally disregard Professor Challenger's striking rationalization that the invaders were not Martians at all. As for Holmes, he shows little concern over these injustices, but after consulting him, I have decided to put the true facts on record for posterity to judge...

—

So: "The Adventures of the Martian Client" in *F&SF* for December, 1969 (sporting an exquisite Ed Emshwiller cover); the catalyst for all that followed by the Wellmans involving Sherlock Holmes, Dr. Watson, Professor Challenger and *The War of the Worlds*. The novel that grew from this short story, *Sherlock Holmes's War of the Worlds*, is a fascinating precursor to Alan Moore and Kevin O'Neill's *League of Extraordinary Gentlemen Volume II*. In that epic graphic novel—as already noted—Alan and Kevin crafted their own revisionist take on *The War of the Worlds* and how a clutch of other then-contemporary fictional heroes and villains interacted with the Martian invasion—specifically, H. Rider Haggard's Allan Quatermain, Mina Murray *née* Harker (from Bram Stoker's *Dracula*), Jules Verne's Captain Nemo, Hawley Griffin (a.k.a. H.G. Wells' *The Invisible Man*) and Robert Louis Stevenson's *Dr. Jekyll/Mr. Hyde*, intermingling with Gullivar Jones from Edwin Lester Arnold's *Lieutenant Gullivar Jones: His Vacation* and John Carter from Edgar Rice Burroughs's celebrated pulp Barsoom novels. The latter two plot against the "Molluscs" from Wells' *The War of the Worlds*, which sends them fleeing to Earth where Griffin conspires with the Martians to ensure his having a cushy position with the planet's new overlords.

It's all very entertaining and clever and quite brilliantly done, but it does leave me wondering at times what Alan is complaining about when others (like DC Comics) start tooling around with his characters and concepts (which are often, in turn, derivative of previous characters and concepts). It's all a game, which Alan and Neil Gaiman and Grant Morrison and other contemporaries do play wonderfully, but which all began with predecessors like Manly Wade Wellman, Philip José Farmer and many others. And once you play the game with characters that once belonged to others, you should be prepared for others to follow suit with your various revamps, reboots and reinventions. It only seems fair.

Given all the justifiable attention paid to works like *The League of Extraordinary Gentlemen*, I think some attention needs to be paid to the Wellmans' novel: it is, to my mind, one of the key forgotten works in an entire genre of fiction, graphic novels, television and movies our pop culture is consumed with of late. This includes everything from the appalling **VAN HELSING** (2004) movie to Seth Grahame-Smith's best-seller *Pride and Prejudice and Zombies*, from Alan Moore and Melinda Gebbie's *Lost Girls* to—well, much of today's pop culture in all media.

Why did the Wellmans tackle their venture? The answer demonstrates how and why these games are played by creators, and their rollover debt to the works of others before them. In "A Postscript by the Junior Collaborator" (Manly's son Wade Wellman), all was explained.

It started with an *earlier* confection pitting Sherlock Holmes against a real-life legendary murderer, a historical figure that *should* be very familiar to Alan Moore fans:

This story was ultimately the result of a thought which kept recurring to me when I saw the Sherlock Holmes movie, A Study in Terror, *in Dubuque, Iowa last year. The film—easily the best Holmes movie I have ever seen—involved Holmes and Watson pitted against Jack the Ripper; the indicated time was about 1890. All through the film I kept wondering how a man like Holmes might have reacted to the Martian invasion about ten years later. H.G. Wells had imagined this event as taking place when*

Holmes, according to Doyle, was still actively solving cases in London, which meant that he would have been participant in the catastrophic flight described in the chapter entitled "The Exodus from London." The question of what Holmes and Watson were doing when the Martians landed kept plaguing me throughout the cinema. I passed it on subsequently to my father, and out of this developed the collaboration on the story which may be read here.[17]

A STUDY IN TERROR (1965, debuted in the US in the late summer of 1966) is an essentially forgotten film today, known primarily to hardcore Holmes fans and Ripperologists and a handful of those fascinated by the films of producer Herman Cohen, who executive produced this, one of his best films.

It's amazing that Wellman lucked into a theatrical showing of the film at all, as it was hardly a success in the US (it must have been in its second or final run by that time, dumped into remote rural theaters most likely at the bottom of a double-bill or as a matinee). Since that time, the movie has been out of circulation in the US, rarely screened or broadcast. It wasn't available via 16mm venues when that was the primary means of distribution to schools and colleges. It had a single VHS release stateside (from RCA/Columbia Pictures Home Video) a quarter century ago in an edition typical of 1980s VHS transfers (lackluster color, pan & scan full-screen), and even then it barely circulated in rental stores. It only recently was issued on DVD—in Australia in 2004 (via Umbrella Entertainment)—and can still be found via some venues in the UK and elsewhere in Europe, though it didn't attract much attention. It has only recently been released on DVD in the US via Sony Pictures Home Entertainment studio DVD-R (March 2011) and in the UK on Blu-Ray.

In its day, **A STUDY IN TERROR** enjoyed modest boxoffice success in the UK and most international markets, where the combo of Sherlock Holmes, Jack the Ripper and its splashy, sexualized murders (circa 1965) carried sufficient allure. In Britain, the producer/distributor Compton Films handled the movie as a proper Sherlock Holmes outing spiced with horror elements, in the style of Hammer Films' earlier **THE HOUND OF THE BASKERVILLES** (1959). However, in the US the one-sheet poster and ad campaign proved American distributor Columbia Pictures didn't know what to do with the film. The *Batman* TV show was a hit in 1966 and James Bond and spymania was rampant, so Columbia stupidly went for ballyhooing **A STUDY IN TERROR** as a campy lark in that mode, which was completely inappropriate to the film and sure to disappoint any audiences expecting *Batman* or Bondian antics.

Still, there's evidence of some attempt to promote the movie, including an Ellery Queen paperback tie-in adaptation (ghosted, at least in part, by Paul W. Fairman) and the LP soundtrack album (my only exposure to the movie prior to catching it on TV in 1971 or so) featuring John Scott's score, some of which has dated badly and may rankle 21st Century viewers (lots o' bongos, baby, *bongos!*), though collectors should note it has been reissued on CD.

The Ellery Queen paperback novelization juxtaposed the Holmes vs. Ripper narrative with a framing device in which detective Ellery Queen reads a long-lost document detailing the case. The novel deviates from the theatrical movie in a number of ways. According to those more knowledgeable than I, Queen actually wrote the framing sequences, interwoven with the Paul Fairman-scribed movie novelization which (much to my consternation as a lad) had a *completely different ending* than the movie, with a different solution to the Ripper murders. I'm also told that the novel was *not* penned by another writer using the "Ellery Queen" house name. To further confuse matters, the novel was reissued as *Ellery Queen vs. Jack the Ripper: A Study in Terror* (Gollancz, 1967), without a mention of the movie as its wellspring—which gives you some idea how promptly the movie faded from popular view. Note, too, that Ellery Queen was the pseudonym for two crime-fiction writing cousins, Daniel Nathan (a.k.a. Frederic Dannay) and Manford Emanuel Lepofsky (a.k.a. Manfred Bennington Lee). Among their incredible body of collaborative works spanning decades (!) was editing the rare anthology *The Misadventures of Sherlock Holmes* (1944), which included a story entitled "The Man Who Was Not Dead" (1941) by—Manly Wade Wellman.

What made the lame American promotional antics so unfortunate was that **A STUDY IN TERROR** was such an unpretentious, straightforward entertainment: briskly-paced, atmospheric (Desmond Dickinson's cinematography and Alex Vetchinsky's production design make the most of what was undoubtedly a modest budget), at times genuinely horrific and still blessed with plot twists that work. It was never a great movie, but it was and is a *good* movie.

[17] *F&SF*, December 1969, pg. 71

The American ad campaign Columbia Pictures mounted for **A STUDY IN TERROR** (1965, US release 1966) tried to play the Holmes vs. Jack the Ripper shocker off as a romp or camp confection, misappropriating comic book sound effects graphics to evoke the American TV smash-hit *Batman* (1966)

The fiery finale *still* packs a punch, and the final Ripper murder was shot in part from the Ripper's point-of-view—making this a stylistic "missing link" between the killer's POV shots central to Robert Siodmak's **THE SPIRAL STAIRCASE** (1945), David Greene's **THE SHUTTERED ROOM** (1967), and John Carpenter's **HALLOWEEN** (1978), a device which later became a slasher movie staple.

A STUDY IN TERROR stood out among all Ripper films to date in that it made an effort to adhere to the facts of the crimes themselves to what was then an unusual degree, including quoting the text of one of the Ripper notes sent to the newspapers and suppressed by police. The film's initial depictions of the Ripper's crimes were cliché and inaccurate. We saw overtures from prostitutes cut short by the flick of a blade, presented in more gruesome detail than previous Ripper films (and in color)—a vivid knife through the throat, a vicious stabbing in a water trough, etc. The fact is, *no* Ripper film until the 1980s dared go into the appalling anatomical particulars of the genuine Ripper murders, though some of the morgue dialogue references herein were mighty close (*"careful there, the head is almost entirely detached"*).

Nonetheless, the women presented as Jack's victims were properly cited using their real names, and murdered in the order of their real-life deaths; they were, however, cast as much younger and more attractive belles than their real-life counterparts, and hardly register as characters. **A STUDY IN TERROR** was also the first Ripper movie (and perhaps the first pop cultural work, period) to align the notorious murders with the British aristocracy, almost a decade before Joseph Sickert's theory was shared and popularized (the theory which informed the subsequent Holmes/Ripper feature film **MURDER BY DECREE** [1979], and that Alan Moore and Eddie Campbell embraced for *From Hell*).

A STUDY IN TERROR still looks, feels and sounds like the Robert S. Baker and Monty Berman productions of the late 1950s and early '60s, which were essentially Hammer Films rip-offs (including **BLOOD OF THE VAMPIRE** [1958], **THE FLESH AND THE FIENDS** [a.k.a. **THE FIENDISH GHOULS**, 1960], **THE HELLFIRE CLUB** [1961], and their biggest box-office hit, their own **JACK THE RIPPER** [1959]). That's not a negative, mind you; this was and remains a pretty effective and in its way quite original cinematic incarnation of Sir Arthur Conan Doyle's most popular creation.

The cast remains the film's anchor and greatest attraction. John Neville was and remains simply terrific as Holmes; he looks, sounds and moves to the specs of Conan Doyle's original texts, and plays marvelously off both Donald Houston as Dr. Watson and the rest of the sterling cast. John Neville is a familiar face to many Americans now—known to most 21st Century viewers for having played Terry Gilliam's Baron Munchausen (in **THE ADVENTURES OF BARON MUNCHAUSEN** [1988]) and "The Well-Manicured Man" in *The X-Files* (1995-98)—but in 1965, he was landing his first major lead playing Holmes. His primary work prior to this was on stage and television; his first film role was playing Lord Alfred Douglas to Robert Morley's **OSCAR WILDE** (1960). In the 1960s, diehard American genre fans like me only knew Neville as the scientist with an alien wife in the obscure John Krish SF sleeper **UNEARTHLY STRANGER** (1963), which really was a gem (and another film worthy of resurrection). Neville is an excellent Holmes, bolstered by a top-notch supporting cast including Frank Finley as Inspector Lestrade—which happened to be the same role Finley played *again* in Bob Clark's fine Holmes-vs-the Ripper feature **MURDER BY DECREE** (1979), which I most highly recommend, particularly to fans of *From Hell*.

The cast also boasts veterans like Robert Morley (as Mycroft Holmes), *Carry On* series players Edina Ronay and Barbara Windsor (as Annie Chapman), and a *very* young Dame Judi Dench as the niece of always-fine Anthony Quayle (who *also* appeared in **MURDER BY DECREE**) in a red-herring role. Morley graces two of the film's best sequences; the first unreels 50 minutes into the movie, the second (Mycroft's angry intrusion on brother Sherlock's "recital") 59 minutes in. Aside from Holmes arcana and a few anachronisms most casual viewers would miss completely (for instance, the songs sung in the pub are all from the wrong period, actually scribed and sung a decade or more after the period the film is set), there's interesting bits of trivia to share. Curiously, co-star John Fraser—who played young Lord Carfax in **A STUDY IN TERROR**—also played Lord Alfred Douglas in **THE TRIALS OF OSCAR WILDE** (1960), the same role Neville played the same year in **OSCAR WILDE**!

For vampire movie fans, it's worth noting Adrienne Corri's appearance here (as the acid-scarred Angela Osborne) and that of Terry Downes (as hunk slaughterhouse worker "Chunky", who declines even a freebie with one of the Ripper's prostitute victims aching for a safe bed for the night). Corri spiced Hammer Films like **THE VIKING QUEEN** (1967) and **MOON ZERO TWO** (1969) before indelibly marking the genre as the blood-drinking gypsy in Robert Young's terrific **VAMPIRE CIRCUS** (1972, *Weng's Chop* #7, p.60, and Monster! digest #14, p.81), while Downes was unforgettable as the vampire's lackey Koukol in Roman Polanski's **DANCE OF THE VAMPIRES** (a.k.a. **THE FEARLESS VAMPIRE KILLERS, OR: PARDON ME, BUT YOUR TEETH ARE IN MY NECK**, 1967). And if you think being done in by Jack the Ripper is some claim to screen fame, Corri was also the ill-fated Mrs. Alexander—playing the wife of the character played by Patrick Magee—the rape victim brutalized and murdered by Alex and his droogs in the core set-piece of Stanley Kubrick's **A CLOCKWORK ORANGE** (1971).

Director James Hill had made a dozen films in the UK prior to **A STUDY IN TERROR**, working throughout the 1950s and '60s and dabbling with television (including episodes of *The Saint*) before hitting paydirt with the international hit **BORN FREE** (1966), adapted from Joy Adamson's 1960 best-selling novel. That blockbuster is still Hill's greatest claim to fame; though he worked in many genres, subsequent projects like **THE LIONS ARE FREE** (1969), **AN ELEPHANT CALLED SLOWLY** (1970), **BLACK BEAUTY** (1971) and **THE WILD AND THE FREE** (a 1980 TV movie) kept him rooting in the "family animal movie" stables. My personal favorites of his films remains **A STUDY IN TERROR** and the MGM oddity **CAPTAIN NEMO AND THE UNDERWATER CITY** (1969), featuring Robert Ryan as Captain Nemo going head-to-head with a monstrous manta ray. Hill was, at best, a skillful craftsman and effective storyteller, *sans* any noticeable personal style or flashy cinematic fingerprints. He always got the job done, and done well.

Screenwriters Derek and Donald Ford were responsible for the quite ingenious story and screenplay, so they must be cited for their catalytic role in the whole revisionist "literary mash-up" genre. The brothers later coscripted the brutal, bizarre Peter Cushing horror movie **CORRUPTION** (1968) and the even odder **VENOM** (a.k.a. **THE LEGEND OF SPIDER FOREST**, 1971), which was Donald's last film credit (he lived until 1991, but never scripted another movie after becoming a London magistrate). Brother Derek kept his hand in the game, scripting and often directing adult films (**I AM A GROUPIE**, **THE SWAPPER**, both 1970; **SUBURBAN WIVES**, 1971; **COMMUTER HUSBANDS**, 1973; **WHAT'S UP NURSE!**, 1977; **WHAT'S UP SUPERDOC!**, 1978; etc.) and scripting the occasional horror film, including **THE HOUSE THAT VANISHED** (1974) and **DON'T OPEN TILL CHRISTMAS** (1984, in which he also appeared as the Santa Claus in the circus).

Though American exploitation mogul Herman Cohen was the executive producer, **A STUDY IN TERROR** was hardly typical of Cohen's output. Beginning with his associate producer work on **BELA LUGOSI MEETS A BROOKLYN GORILLA** (1952), Cohen produced and co-scripted some of the most lurid and successful genre films of the '50s sporting some of the most memorable titles of the decade: **TARGET EARTH** (1954), **I WAS A TEENAGE WEREWOLF, I WAS A TEENAGE FRANKENSTEIN, BLOOD OF DRACULA** (all 1957), **HOW TO MAKE A MONSTER** (1958), and **HORRORS OF THE BLACK MUSEUM** (1959). By the '60s and early '70s, with the notable exception of **A STUDY IN TERROR**, Cohen's films were becoming harder for even genre fans to love: **KONGA** (1961) and **BLACK ZOO** (1963) have their fans, but his Joan Crawford vehicles **BERSERK** (1967, See *Weng's Chop* #4, p.115) and the caveman-on-the-loose atrocity **TROG** (1970) were hardly class acts, and Cohen's final two films (**CRAZE** [1974, See *Weng's Chop* #6.5, p.21], with Jack Palance, and the despicable **WATCH ME WHEN I KILL** [1977]) are among the worst of their decade, which is saying something.

Since the 1944 Ellery Queen anthology, there have been other collections, such as this one edited by Marvin Kaye (1994, St. Martin's Press)

A STUDY IN TERROR stands out amid Cohen's filmography as his absolute best effort, which leaves one wondering how much he might have actually had to do with the production. Given how hands-on Cohen usually was as a producer, and how unapologetically he reveled in the worst possible taste (which is why many of us *love* his films!), it's still somewhat astonishing he had a hand in the film at all. By all accounts (see below for one of them), Cohen fulfilled his obligations on the Holmes/Ripper film with aplomb.

The production company was Compton Films, the British outfit behind the horror curio **THE BLACK TORMENT** (1964, scripted by Derek and Donald Ford), producer Richard Gordon's **THE PROJECTED MAN** (1966), Peter Collinson's scathing "forced entry" shocker **THE PENTHOUSE** (1967, a too-long-neglected precursor to **FUNNY GAMES** [1997; remade in 2007], **THE STRANGERS** [2008] and many similar films), the genuinely bizarre "swinging London" artifact **WONDERWALL** (1968), and best of all Roman Polanski and Gérard Brach's one-two suckerpunch of **REPULSION** (1965) and **CUL-DE-SAC** (1966; Brach also scripted **WONDERWALL**, which must be why it was made at all). Compton returned to Conan Doyle turf with Billy Wilder's delightful, sorrowfully underrated **THE PRIVATE LIFE OF SHERLOCK HOLMES** (1970), which was and is far superior to **A STUDY IN TERROR** but proved to be a compromised work and utter boxoffice disaster, bringing a close to Compton's existence.

Compton partner and producer Michael Klinger (who was a strip club manager before entering the film industry, which explains some of **A STUDY IN TERROR**'s *milieu* and leering flavor) continued bankrolling interesting movies, though, including the crime film classics **GET CARTER** (1971) and **PULP** (1972).

Klinger's Compton partner Tony Tenser founded Tigon British Film Productions in 1966 after amicably parting ways with Klinger. Tigon was the wellspring of Michael Reeves's **THE SORCERERS** (1967) and his masterpiece **WITCHFINDER GENERAL** (US title: **THE CONQUEROR WORM**, 1968), Piers Haggard's gem **THE BLOOD ON SATAN'S CLAW** (1971), Freddie Francis's curio **THE CREEPING FLESH** (1973) and more, including the Raquel Welch western **HANNIE CAULDER** and James Hill's version of the venerable **BLACK BEAUTY** (both 1971).

Interviewer John W. Hamilton talked to co-producer Tony Tenser in the late 1990s, providing the most comprehensive chronology to date on the making of **A STUDY IN TERROR**:

> *DS: While* Repulsion *was shooting you started on the Sherlock Holmes movie,* A Study in Terror. *Herman Cohen takes all the credit for that one. What's the definitive story on how the film came about?*
>
> *TT: Herman Cohen was a co-partner in the film. He had the western hemisphere, the same deal as we had later with AIP [American-International Pictures]. We had the eastern hemisphere, which gave us just enough money to make a bigger film next time. He shouldn't take all the credit, he should take his due credit; he did a lot in the film and was a lot of help to us. I had a wonderful relationship with him and he is a great guy, I like him very much. During the making of* Repulsion, *Gene Gutowksi brought in another mid-European-American type, a fellow called Henry Lester, who had the responsibility of the Arthur Conan Doyle Estate. He said he wanted to make another Sherlock Holmes film, and would I like to do it? So I said "Great." I called in the Ford brothers and told them we had got the okay to make a Sherlock Holmes film. The fictitious Sherlock Holmes was set in the same period as the genuine Jack the Ripper, and in the same area, the East End, so my idea was that we should have Sherlock Holmes discovering who Jack the Ripper was. The Fords did an outline, which we liked, and then they did the script. Now, to make it sound like a Sherlock Holmes film, I took a little bit of poetic license with one of the books, which is called* A Study in Scarlet, *and we called it* A Study in Terror. *All these titles, with the exception of a couple, were really my own. They come too me quite easily.*
>
> *We wanted it directed by someone who was accustomed to making big money films, and Jimmy Hill was available at the time. His agent had come into the office and said "Jimmy's looking for a project," and I showed him the script and he said he thought Jimmy would do this. I phoned up Herman Cohen, who was spending a lot of time in London then, and he agreed to come in for half the budget, which to his standards*

Amicus totally ignored the associative link with Sherlock Holmes (via the character of Mr. Mycroft, a retired gentleman and beekeeper) in the bestselling 1941 source novel, *A Taste for Honey* by H.F. Heard, when they turned it into the botched **THE DEADLY BEES** (1966). Robert Bloch had retained the Holmes association in his original screenplay for the film, but subsequent revisions by other hands removed Mycroft completely.

was reasonable but to our standards was a little bit more than we wanted to pay. I think it was £160,000, a bit more than Repulsion! *We were getting into the big league by then. The film was very well made, excellently well made. Some of the press slated it but they slated it because of the company that made it.*[18]

All of which is to say, **A STUDY IN TERROR** holds a curious position in the legacy of 1960s British horror films.

On its own terms, it's among the best of all Sherlock Holmes films, and one well worth your tracking down. That the film also inspired Wade Wellman to distraction, so much so that he convinced his father to collaborate with him on a fine short story that grew into a novel, only adds to its considerable merits.

—

It must be understood that the Wellmans undertook the writing of *Sherlock Holmes's War of the Worlds* as more than just a fancy or a lark. They were earnest in their efforts, which were grounded in their deep regard, respect and reverence for Wells' original novel, and their belief that it was much, much more than just a classic science-fiction novel.

Continuing Wade Wellman's postscript to the original publication of "The Adventures of the Martian Client" in *F&SF* for December, 1969 (note that I have preserved Wellman's own punctuation here):

---

[18] Quoted from John W. Hamilton's interview with Tony Tenser, "Tigon Tales of Terror" in *The Dark Side (The Magazine of the Macabre and Fantastic)* #78 (April-May 1998)

H.G. Wells's The War of the Worlds, *first published in 1897, has even more relevance to our time than to the 1890s—as shown by the grotesque failure of the 1953 movie by the same title, which tried to update the conception to the 1950's, and ruined it completely. The story needs no updating. It is not really a science fiction novel but an extremely profound and magnificently conveyed philosophical conception. Man knows his relationship to lower animals on the earth; what is his relationship to higher animals on other worlds? Wells's narrator, with stunningly effective concision, describes the Martian reaction to efforts made to signal them: "The Martians took as much notice of such advances as we would of the lowing of a cow." The conception which underlies the novel is timeless and can never become obsolete. In one respect, however, we were forced to deviate sharply from Wells's fictional structure: native intelligence on Mars nowadays seems so unlikely that it was necessary to make this alteration in the Wells canon.*

The depth and magnitude of Wells's idea is increasingly relevant as the years go by. It seems to me that the UFO's may well represent a technology as far above human civilization as we are above the communities of jungle animals. Their observations of the earth might be likened to a zoological team observing zebras in the jungle. Again, a human being watching a UFO hover in the air may be in the position of a baboon watching a hovering helicopter. I strongly suspect that this is the case. But, whatever the reality behind the UFO's may be, I feel that our emergence into space must inevitably, at some time, bring us into contact with "minds that are to our minds as ours are to those of the beasts that perish," to quote again from Wells's own text. We must not refuse this challenge, but even so I am disturbed by the efforts now being made to signal other worlds. Years ago an unnamed space scientist was quoted as saying that, to certain alien races, we might be "the finest beef animals." He knew his H.G. Wells, and that his warning was unheeded is a reproach to the poor alertness of his colleagues.

In any case, the conquest of space and the UFO surveillance are the beginning of events which will broaden our horizons tremendously, whatever their final outcome. It is for this reason that every thinking person should study Wells's original idea and apply its significance and implications to our own time.[19]

This isn't a flippant afterword; it is Wade Wellman lending gravity to their enterprise.

Six years later, when the story had borne the fruit of the completed novel *Sherlock Holmes's War of the Worlds* (all page numbers that follow reference the original 1975 Warner Books paperback edition), "The Adventures of the Martian Client" was folded into the novel as its fourth (its penultimate) chapter. As such, it reinforces the philosophical imperative the Wellmans were proffering, and what may have seemed like needlessly graphic extrapolations on the Wells original were in fact the gruesome centerpieces of their arguments.

The story itself remains a lively read, attuned to its characters and neatly utilizing the unique properties of "the crystal egg" from Wells' 1897 short story. Not only did the "egg" give Challenger, Holmes and Watson privileged insights as to what the invaders were up to, but it was *so* unique—a singular crystal *able to communicate planet-to-planet*, per Wells' original story, and hence of great importance to the invaders as they began to succumb to terrestrial infections—that Holmes's famed apartment became a target: *the invaders need the "egg".*

As soon became obvious, this was integral to Challenger's and Holmes's plan, the goal of which was to *capture a live invader.*

This they accomplish utilizing something quite specific to each Conan Doyle character: Challenger's size and brute strength, and Holmes' former addiction (thus his instant access to a syringe and the infamous "seven percent solution", which he plunges into the invader, *"into the heaving body, just behind the face"*).

In the final paragraphs of this first story, Challenger argued the Martian wasn't even a Martian, proposing the most radical of all the Wellman and Wellman conceits:

> ...*the creature's lungs show Mars was not his native planet... For this great mass of flesh—I estimate it at four hundred pounds—they are not particularly big. They would be fatally inadequate in a Martian atmosphere... No, they came to Mars and existed there temporarily, with respirators of some sort, until they could accomplish the attack upon Earth.*

Again, this anticipates Moore and O'Neill's *The League of Extraordinary Gentlemen Volume II*; Moore and O'Neill adopted this conceit as their own and ran with it.

The Wellmans cannily enhanced Challenger's theory with the fact that the famed "canals" of Mars weren't seen until 1894-96, *"evidence of gigantic artificial construction on Mars."* (*F&SF*, Dec. 1969, pp. 70-71; novel pg. 170)

For a self-standing short tale, this was smart, succinct and inventive revisionist fiction, and the fidelity to Conan Doyle (at the expense of Wells, taken so irrevocably to task by Watson in the story's opening paragraph) was a delight.

Another aspect of the Wellmans's revamp of the original *War of the Worlds* that bears immediate mention is their decision to confront that which Wells himself was tastefully reticent about: Wells never described what, precisely, the Martians *did* with their human prey.

In the novel's second movement, "Book Two: The Earth Under the Martians", while scavenging for food the narrator and the Curate see a Martian fighting-machine seizing human beings and dropping them into "a great metallic carrier which projected behind him, much as a workman's basket hangs over his shoulder," most likely for "a purpose other than destruction." Wells also leads the reader to believe the unconscious Curate later suffers the same fate—transfusion of his blood to feed the Martians—but this, too, is only inferred, not seen or shown. Another passage is more explicit: watching through a hole in a wall from his hiding place, Wells' protagonist only notes he saw some-

---
[19] *F&SF*, December 1969, pp. 71-72

The Wellmans (father and son) were back with another dose of Holmes, Watson, Professor Challenger, and the Martians in "Venus, Mars, and Baker Street" in *Fantasy and Science Fiction March* 1972 (Vol. 42, No. 3). Cover art by Chesley Bonestell "depicts a globular star cluster about 500 light-years distant from an airless planet that is illuminated by a sun on the right outside of the picture. In the sky are two satellites of the planet..." (pg. 67). Just in case you were wondering.

thing terrible, sans specifics:

> *It was on the third day, if my memory serves me right, that I saw the lad killed. It was the only occasion on which I actually saw the Martians feed. After that experience, I avoided the hole in the wall for the better part of a day.*

That's it—amid the many horrors in Wells' novel, this is among the most understated.

Wellman and Wellman aren't so coy (**KILLER KLOWNS FROM OUTER SPACE** [1988] fans, take note). In their first short story, they allowed Professor Challenger to spill the beans:

> *"I have watched, on three occasions, what happens to human captives,"* Challenger went on. *"They are held down by the tentacles of smaller machines – I saw their mouths gape open to scream – while Martians gather and pierce their veins with metal pipettes. The living blood is drawn directly into Martian bodies."*

The revised text of this chapter in the novel adds, *"much as we drink with a straw. Probably it goes into their circulatory systems."*

Even more chilling was the cold pragmatism of Challenger's suggested methodology for dealing with the Martians via their dietary needs:

> *"As for horror, how would an intelligent pig view our relish for his species? Their feeding methods, together with their obvious unacquaintance with many terrestrial factors, suggests a possible plan of campaign against them... Give them diseased victims, to infect them,"* replied Challenger...[20]

In their revised and expanded novel, Wellman and Wellman detailed the feeding process Challenger witnessed:

> *...the man... had been shoved into the pit and captured. The fellow strove helplessly against a myriad of metal tentacles that cross-latched upon his body. He was naked, and his mouth gaped wide open as though he screamed in terror. One invader hunched above him. Challenger saw a wink of light on metal, something like a long slender pipestem. A steel tentacle drove this down into the struggling victim. The bladder-bulk stooped close above it, making contact at the free end of the pipe.*
>
> *Challenger forced himself to watch the process through. Now he knew how the invading monsters fed.*
>
> *"A drawing of living blood,"* he muttered. *"Living blood, from a living victim. Holmes is right. We are lower animals, and to them we mean food."*[21]

Thus, Wellman and Wellman tipped Wells' not-from-Mars-really Martians into the "space vampire" turf arguably initiated by Wells and expanded incrementally in bizarre stories like Everil Worrell's "The Bird of Space" (*Weird Tales*, September 1926), its sequel "Cattle of Furos" (*Weird Tales*, October 1926), and arguably Wilford Allen's "Night Thing" (*Weird Tales*, July 1929). The "space vampire" concept was popularized via theatrical and especially late-night TV showings of the Howard Hawks/Christian Nyby **THE THING FROM ANOTHER WORLD** (1951), Roger Corman's sleeper **NOT OF THIS EARTH** (1957) and Curtis Harrington's **QUEEN OF BLOOD** (1966, syndicated to TV as **PLANET OF BLOOD**).

What might strike some (particularly Holmes aficionados) as simply unnecessary grue was in fact another ingenious fleshing out of the original Wells conception: the "Martians" succumbed quickly to terrestrial diseases because they had been *directly ingesting* human blood brimming with bacteria and microbes fatal to their systems.

The rapidity with which the infection spread into the invaders was hammered home vividly: Watson said, *"'To judge from the odor, it rots, even as it lives...,'* to which Challenger adds, *'They came among us, breathing, feeding, drinking, and took death into themselves.'"* (*F&SF* Dec. 1969, pg. 70; novel pp. 169-170).

This was and is smart stuff, and deliciously horrific for its time.

[20] *F&SF* Dec. 1969, p. 66; book p. 159
[21] Novel, pg. 102

TOP: *Amazing Stories* (May 1926) cover art illustrating a reprint of H.G. Wells' "The Crystal Egg," artwork by the great Frank R. Paul.
ABOVE: Blood-drinking Martians from the Monsterwax limited edition trading card series War of the Worlds, artwork by Ricardo Garijo (see http://www.monsterwax.com/waroftheworlds.html)

The Wellmans' more explicitly stated feeding habits of the Martians, and their succumbing to infection-by-blood, has since become a standard plot element of adaptations and spinoffs, including Eric Forsberg's script for the C. Thomas Howell **THE WAR OF THE WORLDS 2: THE NEXT WAVE**, etc.[22]

[22] Later adaptations and spin-offs have expanded on the Martian harvesting of human blood and tissue as a story point, but for other purposes. Cannibalism was introduced in the ongoing "Killraven" *War of the Worlds* saga in the Marvel Comics title *Amazing Adventures* (1973-1976): female humans were cultivated as "breeders" by our Martian overlords, who fed on newborn infants as a delicacy. Human bodies were used as "hosts"—"possessed" by aliens—for the invaders in the American/Canadian TV series *War of the Worlds* (1988-1990). Humans were harvested in David Michael Latt/Carlos De Los Rios' **H.G. WELLS' THE WAR OF THE WORLDS** (a.k.a. **INVASION**, 2005), with human blood protected by

1908 illustration by William Julian-Damazy for "Le Horla" (1887) by Guy de Maupassant

As already noted, Manly Wade Wellman was one of the pioneers of 20th Century genre literary "mashup" fiction. I'm not well grounded enough as a reader to say with any certainty he was the first or even among the first. But I know enough about Wellman's body of work—and the context of the weird, horror, fantasy and SF pulps and (post-1950) the SF digests his work debuted in—to confidently say he was among those writers who first played such games with his short fiction.

I earlier mentioned the Ellery Queen-edited uber-rare anthology *The Misadventures of Sherlock Holmes* (1944, reportedly suppressed by the Sir Arthur Conan Doyle Estate immediately after publication) included a Wellman Sherlock Holmes story entitled "The Man Who Was Not Dead" (1941), so Wellman was already dabbling in Conan Doyle's turf prior to America entering World War 2, over three decades before *Sherlock Holmes's War of the Worlds* was published.

In the pages of the justly celebrated fantasy pulp *Unknown*, Wellman had earlier crafted a tale involving Edgar Allan Poe himself entitled "When It Was Moonlight" (February 1940), and pitted Bram Stoker's Dracula against the invading Third Reich in "The Devil Is Not Mocked" (the June 1943 issue)—before the end of WW2, mind you. The latter was later adapted into a *Night Gallery* episode (first broadcast on October 27, 1971, featuring the 1958 **THE RETURN OF DRACULA**'s Francis Lederer as the Count) and Wellman's story is a precursor to F. Paul Wilson's classic novel *The Keep* (1981, and far superior to Michael Mann's misbegotten 1983 film adaptation[23]).

I could go on, but you get the idea: Wellman was an old hand at this game before 1950. He was clearly a man of letters; in this, too, Wellman is a significant predecessor to Alan Moore, Neil Gaiman, Grant Morrison, *et al* who have carved significant careers from similar constructs. He seemed to retain everything he'd read, and deftly reference it as subtly or overtly as he felt the need to, story by story. I have no idea how much of that was passed on to his son Wade Wellman, but judging by the book at hand, they were kindred souls in more than blood.

One component of *Sherlock Holmes's War of the Worlds*, the novel, that is *unique* to the novel (in that it did not appear in either of the two short stories/novel chapters originally published in *F&SF*), bore further evidence of the Wellman's insightful knowledge of genre literature.

The context for this reference isn't as obvious as the Wellmans' adoption and appropriation of H. G. Wells' "The Crystal Egg", though that very story is the springboard for this other literary aside. This arises (bear with me, I'll soon define what *"this"* is), somewhat obliquely. It is presented *before* the events of Wells' *The War of the Worlds* intrudes upon Holmes' London; after Holmes' purchase of the crystal egg, and the beginning of Holmes and Professor Challenger's observations of Mars and the "Martians" via the viewing device of the crystal egg. This arises as Holmes, Watson and Challenger are pondering precisely *why* Holmes was drawn to a certain antique shop to purchase a certain crystal egg—the action that opens the novel expanding upon the two previously published *Fantasy and Science Fiction* stories.

It is Holmes who places the egg in Professor Challenger's hands and initiates the study of the object, which leads directly to Challenger establishing (via the "egg") direct observation of and communication with the invading force on Mars, prior to the launch of said invasion.

The ever-self-analytical mind of Holmes is clearly concerned with the *"why"* of that purchase. *Why* was he drawn to purchase the egg, and do so with such urgency? (He snaps it up seconds before the scoundrel Morse Hudson was intending to do so, instantly setting up another subplot I won't get into in this essay.)

Later in the same chapter, when Holmes and Challenger are face-to-face with a "Martian" via the "viewscreen" of the egg, Holmes says,

> *"What if I acted under some sort of direction in buying the crystal and giving it to you* [Challenger] *for joint scrutiny? What if this Martian is trying to say that? Perhaps thought waves come through the crystal; perhaps they came to me in the shop."*

What Holmes ponders initially here, and again later in the novel, is whether the "Martians" are capable of mind control, and whether he and Challenger are susceptible to it.

This speculation was set into motion by an apparent *non sequitur* while Holmes and Watson were alone in their Baker Street apartment. Holmes was reading something he commented upon, which Watson naturally asked about. This passage also played upon the particularly extreme loathing the British have for the French. In this case, Dr. Watson articulated that quite eloquently even as Holmes did his utmost to prompt the good doctor to transcend that national revulsion and just *listen*:

> *"What is your book?" asked Watson, stirring sugar into his coffee.*
>
> *"A collection of the writings of Guy de Maupassant. The section I am reading is a chronicle – it is almost like nonfiction – in the form of diary entries."*
>
> *Watson's mouth drew thin under his moustache. "Maupassant was a man of dissipated life," he remarked austerely. "I have always thought that he preached immorality in his stories."*
>
> *"I fear I must disagree with you," said Holmes. "Maupassant, as I think, has always striven for objectivity. In any case, much of what we consider immoral is merely pathological. Oscar Wilde, for instance, was imprisoned under our English laws for a morbid aberration. He would have been shown more mercy in France."*
>
> *"But what is this particular chronicle you are reading?" asked Watson. "It is entitled 'Le Horla,' fully laying bare the soul of the diarist. It tells*

---

rabies vaccine the contagion that may have infected the Martians, implying blood consumption, but this was unclear in the film. In the Josh Friedman/David Koepp screenplay for Steven Spielberg's **THE WAR OF THE WORLDS** (2005), human blood and tissue was used essentially as fertilizer for a quick-rooting "red weed" the Martians were terraforming Earth with as part of their colonization schemes; the "red weed" was introduced in the original Wells novel.

23 See Dawn Dabell's analysis in *Monster!* digest #16, p.17.

how he came under the power of some unknown, invisible being. Apparently the power departed, for the writer in the last entry is threatening suicide in despair, yet there is no evidence that the threat was carried out."

Watson bit into a buttered crumpet. "Maupassant died a hopeless madman. I've read that Horla story you mention. It struck me as complete proof that he was losing his mind as he wrote it."

"No, Watson, it is too well organized for that. Even if we choose to read the story as fiction, as a highly imaginative tale, I must argue that only a clear, sane mind could have conceived it so artistically, written it so vividly..."[24]

Here's the de Maupassant passage Holmes references:

There was no moon, but the stars darted out their rays in the dark heavens. Who inhabits those worlds? What forms, what living beings, what animals are there yonder? What do those who are thinkers in those distant worlds know more than we do? What can they do more than we can? What do they see which we do not know? Will not one of them, some day or other, traversing space, appear on our earth to conquer it, just as the Norsemen formerly crossed the sea in order to subjugate nations more feeble than themselves?

That is all Holmes (and the Wellmans) cites—but here is how the complete passage in "The Horla" ends:

We are so weak, so unarmed, so ignorant, so small, we who live on this particle of mud which turns round in a drop of water.

This is indeed evocative of the opening lines of H. G. Wells' *The War of The Worlds*, and many other passages in that classic novel:

No one would have believed in the last years of the nineteenth century that this world was being watched keenly and closely by intelligences greater than man's and yet as mortal as his own; that as men busied themselves about their various concerns they were scrutinised and studied, perhaps almost as narrowly as a man with a microscope might scrutinise the transient creatures that swarm and multiply in a drop of water...

It is historically true that many speculate de Maupassant was perhaps succumbing to mental illness brought on by syphilis at this point in his life; de Maupassant suffered from syphilis to his dying day. He tried to cut his own throat in January of 1892, and was thereafter committed to an asylum, where he died on July 6, 1893.

H.P. Lovecraft cited "The Horla" as a key work, writing that it related *"...the advent in France of an invisible being who lives on water and milk, sways the minds of others, and seems to be the vanguard of a horde of extra-terrestrial organisms arrived on earth to subjugate and overwhelm mankind, this tense narrative is perhaps without peer in its particular department..."* (Lovecraft, *Supernatural Horror in Literature*, 1927, revised 1934). It was this interpretation of "The Horla" the Wellmans obviously shared and were voicing via Holmes.[25]

After reading the cited passage aloud, Holmes concludes,

"Confess, Watson, is that not a fairly sane and rational proposition?"

"If it is fiction, I consider it high-flown, fanciful writing," said Watson stubbornly. "I remember, incidentally, that the diarist burns his house at the end of the account. Wasn't Maupassant's house burned?"

"It was burned, as a matter of fact, but Maupassant never admitted to setting the fire, unless in this account," said Holmes. "If he is confessing that act, we may take the whole as offered for fact."

"Suppose it is factual and sane," said Watson. "If beings such as the Horla did actually exist, do you think that you could be subjugated by one of them, like Maupassant or his fictional diarist?"

---

24 Quoted from the novel, pp. 38-39
25 You can read the complete English translation of de Maupassant's "Le Horla" online at http://www.online-literature.com/maupassant/2988/

"Perhaps not," said Holmes. "A man of sufficient intellect and will might resist such subjugation, or find a way of defeating it."

Key to the characterizations of Holmes and Challenger in the Wellmans' novel is the ways in which Challenger's egotism impacts the partnership of these two great intellects, and how Holmes manages to deftly negotiate that potential minefield. It is Challenger's enormous egotism that makes him susceptible to the "Martian" influence (though that is subtly drawn)—and these "The Horla" references that establish the possibility of the coming invasion, man's place in the cosmic food chain, and Holmes's acute perception of his own vulnerabilities.

The momentary discussion of the fiery end of the story—and its association with de Maupassant's own tragic final years—serves the multilevel purpose of elucidating de Maupassant's true story, sketching the conclusion of "The Horla", and chillingly foreshadowing the smoldering ruins of London that Holmes, Challenger and Watson will soon be crawling in and around to evade the invaders.

Again, this is brilliant writing, by any measure, and very sharp associative adoption of the Wellmans' literary precursors.

In the "Two Authors' Notes" introduction to the novel, Wade Wellman writes:

...it seems evident that Wells's The War of the Worlds *was to some extent influenced by Guy de Maupassant's "The Horla," though the influence has never, to my knowledge, been observed by a critic.*

The Wellmans revised and expanded their trilogy of *Fantasy and Science Fiction* stories for publication as a stand-alone Warner Books paperback novel edition, *Sherlock Holmes's War of the Worlds* (September 1975), sporting cover art by F. Accanero. It proved instantly popular enough to spawn a second printing (October 1975)

Though it was an adaptation of "Le Horla" (1887) by Guy de Maupassant, the title for the 1963 movie **DIARY OF A MADMAN** was appropriated from the English language title for Nikolai Gogol's classic 1835 short story "Записки сумасшедшего" and sold to audiences as a new Vincent Price vehicle amidst the ongoing success of the Price/Roger Corman/American-International Pictures Edgar Allan Poe films.

Nor has it ever since been noted anywhere that I've noticed, making the Wellmans' observation still quite unique.

I hasten to mention, too, that Manly Wade Wellman wrote a sort-of sequel to "The Horla", the supremely creepy "The Theater Upstairs" (1936), involving—get this—an actor who stumbles upon a tiny theater showing what appears to be an adaptation of "The Horla" in which he recognizes an actress he once knew and spurned, prompting her suicide. Alone with a friend, the only two people in the audience, the actor becomes even *more* disturbed as the film unreels and he recognizes other deceased actors in the movie—who seem to be paying unwelcome attention to the lone pair watching the movie…

I wonder, is this one of the first "haunted movie" tales? I leave that to wiser genre scholars than I to ascertain. It's a *great* story, though; I've never forgotten it.

Just as the Holmes-vs.-Jack the Ripper movie **A STUDY IN TERROR** was the springboard for the initial father-and-son collaboration, Wade Wellman cites another forgotten 1960s low-budget horror movie at this point in his introductory note to the novel:

> *Readers of this saga should take notice of an excellent moving picture based on de Maupassant's tale,* Diary of a Madman. *The bad title has damaged the film's reputation, but the title character, superbly played by Vincent Price, is a man who outwits and destroys a superior being in a fashion well worthy of Holmes. Two motion pictures, then, have played their parts in the various inspirations for these five tales.*

I won't go into **DIARY OF A MADMAN** (1963) with the same intensity I brought to **A STUDY IN TERROR**, but it does merit some attention. Like **A STUDY IN TERROR**, it's a completely forgotten film that only recently became available legally in the US on DVD, as an MGM studio DVD-R (released January 2011). It was released legally twice on VHS—once by Wood Knapp Video/UA, and again by MGM back in 1998, both with completely nondescript box art—but it was hard to come by even then. I first caught it on a late-night TV broadcast in the dead of winter around 1968-69 (when I was 12 or 13 years old), and it made quite an impression on me.

It's among the first non-alien "possession" movies I recall seeing—though the Wellmans might argue that point with me, as they clearly are proposing (via Holmes's dialogue) that de Maupassant's protagonist may have indeed been possessed by an extraterrestrial being.

Historically, **DER DIBUK** (a.k.a. **THE DYBBUK**, 1937)—and silent precursors like **ONE GLORIOUS DAY** [1922] and the *Dybbuk* comedy *A Vil-*

na Legend (*Tkies khaf*, 1924)—definitely predated the "demonic possession" films so prevalent later in the 1960s and throughout the 1970s. I wasn't aware of these films at the time I first caught **DIARY OF A MADMAN**; that may have been why it so impressed me as a teen, though I still find much to enjoy in the movie.

DIARY OF A MADMAN has the feel of most of the Vincent Price gothics from this period. That was calculated. The film's art director was Daniel Haller—fresh from the American-International Pictures (AIP) Edgar Allan Poe movies Roger Corman directed Price in—per usual milking all the period atmosphere possible from a meager budget. Producer/screenwriter Robert E. Kent and coproducer Edward Small carefully cultivated that association, as they had with two of their other Admiral Pictures efforts (the moniker for Robert E. Kent Productions after 1962): Edward L. Cahn's lycanthropy take on **BEAUTY AND THE BEAST** (1962, with a very *Wolfman*-like "Beast" makeup on Mark Damon designed and applied by Jack Pierce, creator of the classic Universal monster makeups) and the Vincent Price vehicle **TWICE-TOLD TALES** (1963). The latter film was even closer to the Corman/AIP/Price/Poe films, adapting three of Nathaniel Hawthorne's genre stories. Of the three Kent horror films, **DIARY OF A MADMAN** is the best.

In de Maupassant's story, the act of waving at a mysterious passing ship (a *"superb three-master"*) inexplicably initiated the possession, inviting the demonic presence into the first-person narrator's life. In **DIARY OF A MADMAN**, Price starred as magistrate Simon Cordier, whose prison visit to the condemned Louis Girot (Harvey Stephens) leaves him open to possession by the "demon" that drove Girot to murder—the Horla (voiced by an uncredited Joseph Ruskin, who appeared in and/or voiced almost 150 films and TV episodes, and had then most recently appeared on the tube as Louis "Lepke" Buchalter on *The Untouchables*). The Horla forces Girot to try and kill Cordier; when Cordier kills Girot in self-defense, the Horla in turn plagues Cordier. As the Horla nibbles away at Cordier's life and sanity, the magistrate's amateur sculpting efforts culminates in the film's most effective shock, which I won't give away here.

It's not a particularly faithful rendition of de Maupassant's story—the movie title is lifted from Nikolai Gogol's classic 1835 short story (*Записки сумасшедшего*), the morality play completely antithetical to de Maupassant but very much typical of early '60s mainstream gothics. Nevertheless, Reginald Le Borg's workmanlike direction is solid, Ellis Carter's cinematography is effective (my favorite of all Carter's efforts remains his work on **THE INCREDIBLE SHRINKING MAN** and **THE MONOLITH MONSTERS** [both 1957, *Monster!* digest #14, p.68]), and Price is quite good here, ably supported by Nancy Kovack (Medea of Ray Harryhausen's 1963 classic **JASON AND THE ARGONAUTS**) and character actor Ian Wolfe.

FYI, Le Borg directed a lot of westerns (movies and TV), and had helmed a couple of the 1940s Universal *Inner Sanctum* movies, along with **JUNGLE WOMAN** and **THE MUMMY'S GHOST** (both 1944) and a string of comic-strip adaptations (at least seven *Joe Palooka* movies and *Little Iodine* [1946]) before the rather dreadful-but-fun **THE BLACK SLEEP** (1956) and **VOODOO ISLAND** (1957). This was his last decent horror film, and arguably his last decent movie, period. It's frankly a little amazing how much Wade Wellman professed liking this movie; given his curt dismissal of Byron Haskin and George Pal's superior **THE WAR OF THE WORLDS** (1953), one can imagine some readers might take Wellman's recommendation of **DIARY OF A MADMAN** with a grain of salt. But I quite agree with Wellman on this one: **DIARY OF A MADMAN** is well worth tracking down and spending an evening with, particularly if you're a fan of 1960s horror films.

It's also a rather important little movie, given how vital "possession" themes became in subsequent years. Let's forget, for the moment, about William Peter Blatty's *The Exorcist* and all that followed. Along with Robert Bloch's "demon Ripper" stories (his 1943 *Weird Tales* classic "Yours Truly, Jack the Ripper", the December 22, 1967 *Star Trek* episode "Wolf in the Fold", etc.), "The Horla" and **DIARY OF A MADMAN** were the precursors to what became a subgenre in and of itself in the 1980s and '90s, in which various versions (demonic, alien, etc.) of "evil incarnate" leapfrogged from person to person as if from vessel to vessel: **THE HIDDEN** (1987), **SHOCKER** (1989), **THE EXORCIST III** (1990; based on writer/director William Peter Blatty's own 1983 novel *Legion*), **FALLEN** (1998), etc.

Back to the Wellmans' *Sherlock Holmes's War of the Worlds*: The *"five tales"* Wellman referred to were the chapters of the novel, which may indeed have been written as five separate short stories, three of which were previously published: "The Adventure of the Crystal Egg" (*"by Edward Dunn Malone,"* pp. 9-50), "Sherlock Holmes Versus Mars" (also credited to Malone, pp. 51-93; original version published in *F&SF* for May 1975), "George E. Challenger Versus Mars" (Malone again, pp. 95-143, original to the novel), and as chapters IV and V, the two slightly revised *Fantasy and Science Fiction* stories wrap up the novel, "The Adventures of the Martian Client" (credited, as in the original publication, to *"John H. Watson, M.D.,"* pp. 147-172) and "Venus, Mars and Baker Street" (also credited to Watson, pp. 175-201), followed by "Appendix: A Letter from Dr. Watson" (pp. 205-208; original to the novel).

"Venus, Mars and Baker Street" was effectively a sequel and coda to the original *The War of the Worlds*, which was how it read to those who first lucked into the tale in the pages of *F&SF* for March, 1972.

I apologize that much of the arcane information to follow may matter and/or be fully decipherable only to the most devout Holmes fanatics, but that's the juncture we've arrived at, faithful reader, and so we must proceed.

F&SF was reportedly a revelation in science fiction publishing when it hit in 1950. It began life as *The Magazine of Fantasy* with its maiden voyage, cover dated Winter 1949, and became *The Magazine of Fantasy and Science Fiction* with its second issue, Winter-Spring 1950. Along with *Galaxy, F&SF* upped the whole genre's game for the coming decade+, and definitively marked the end of the true pulp era. For what it's worth, *F&SF* was among the few SF digests I picked up from time and time throughout the 1960s and early '70s (and held on to some copies of for my permanent collection).

In Manly Wade Wellman's career, *F&SF* was pretty important, too: his celebrated "Silver John" stories began in their pages with the debut of "O Ugly Bird!" (*F&SF*, December 1951).

> ...*First out I saw it was dark, heavy-winged, bigger than a buzzard. Then I saw the shiny gray-black of the body, like wet slate, and how it seemed to have feathers only on its wide wings. Then I made out the thing snaky neck, the bulgy head and long stork beak, the eyes set in front of its head—man-fashion in front, not to each other...*

Even as the Sherlock Holmes/Mars stories were appearing in *F&SF*, Wellman Sr. was launching a new phase of his South Appalachia-set stories in the same magazine, beginning with the October 1973 issue's publication of "Dead Man's Chair":

> ...*Some 25 years ago, I began wandering the Southern Appalachians, looking for old songs & old tales, making friends with the mountain people, finally building a cabin among them where I spend what time I can spare...*

(Wellman fanatics should note that the fourth of the 1970s *F&SF* Appalachian tales, "Where the Woodbine Twineth" in the October 1976 *F&SF*, has inexplicably never been collected.)

Thus, the catalyst and gestation *F&SF* provided for *Sherlock Holmes's War of the Worlds* was of a piece with the role the magazine had played in many other phases of Wellman's creative life.

One of the advantages of nurturing larger works—in this case, a novel—via publication of shorter, initially self-contained works is the opportunity provided for reader feedback. And that, above all, is what I'd like to discuss in this final phase of this essay.

On the distant heels of "The Adventures of the Martian Client" (*F&SF* December 1969) and "Venus, Mars and Baker Street" (*F&SF* March 1972), reader feedback was indeed forthcoming on "Sherlock Holmes Versus Mars" (*F&SF* May 1975). I'm forever indebted to my friend Joe Citro for bringing this to my attention, and Rick (Roderick) Bates for promptly following up and steering me directly to the issue his own letter appeared in, from which I was able to track the Wellman reply (again, thanks to an alert from Joe that the reply existed).

As to "Sherlock Holmes Versus Mars", the online *F&SF* index notes:

The most famous of all cinematic Professor Challengers remains the first: Wallace Beery in **THE LOST WORLD** (1925, **TOP**), who galvanized the screen as powerfully as did Willis O'Brien's stop-motion animated dinosaurs and Bull Montana's savage troglodyte (**ABOVE**)

3rd & last story in their Sherlock Holmes/War of the Worlds *series; Wellman Jr as ps. John H. Watson MD has Holmes novels* S. H. vs Dracula *(1979),* Dr. Jekyll and Mr. Holmes *(1979),* S. H. and the Golden Bird *(1985),* S. H. and the Red Demon *(1996), etc.*[26]

More on those other sequels at a later time.

Whether the following exchange played any part in how the father-and-son Wellman team expanded their narrative to create the novel, I will leave to you to surmise.

Now, on to the letters...

In the September 1975 issues of *F&SF* (*"Letters,"* pp. 159-160), two letters were published commenting on "Sherlock Holmes Versus Mars", and specifically its conceit that Sherlock Holmes and Mrs. Hudson were romantically involved with one another to the point that Holmes spirited her from London before the arrival of the invaders from Mars, and ensured her safety before returning to London to join forces with Professor Challenger against the extraterrestrials invasion. They read complete as follows:

Romance and Holmes

> *I am troubled by the short story "Sherlock Holmes Versus Mars," which appeared in the May 1975 issue of your magazine. The authors, Manly and Wade Wellman, have evidently researched their subject well – the 17 steps up to 221 B Baker Street, a note to Watson transfixed upon the mantle, references to Colonel Moran and Reichenbach Falls, the interesting suggestion that Morse Hudson, the Kensington road shopkeeper, was husband to Holmes' housekeeper and son of the vile Hudson who drove*

[26] Quoted from the Fantasy & Science Fiction index site; see entry for May 1975 issue at https://www.sfsite.com/fsf/bibliography/fsfstorieswhen197502.htm

James Armitage to his death – these and other touches amply demonstrate a deep knowledge of the affairs of Mr. Holmes.

By what error of judgement, then, can the authors suggest an affair between Mr. Holmes and his housekeeper? The authors say of Mr. Holmes and Mrs. Hudson, "they kissed, holding each other close, her rich curves pressed to his sinewy leanness." Further, they purport to quote Mr. Holmes as saying to Mrs. Hudson, "You never embarrass me, because I love you."

What an outrage it is to suggest that Mr. Holmes would do or say such things. I refer to the writings. In "The Adventures of the Dying Detective," it is said of Mr. Holmes regarding women, "he disliked and distrusted the sex." Holmes himself states in "The Adventure of the Devil's Foot," "I have never loved, Watson." But it is in "A Scandal in Bohemia" that all doubt is laid to rest. Watson writes, of Holmes, "all emotions, and that one (love) particularly, were abhorrent to his cold, precise but admirably balanced mind."

I am troubled that the authors could at the same time write so interesting and so bad a story. To mention the Persian slippers in the same story as "rich curves" and "sinewy leanness" is in the poorest possible taste.

I can think of no more fitting punishment than that Mr. Holmes should leave his bees in Eastbourne, journey a second time across the Atlantic, and souse both Wellmans with a gasogene.

- Roderick G. Bates[27]

[27] Quoted with permission of Roderick Bates. If I could have secured Mycroft's permission, I would have.

That caustic gem was followed with this even more curious letter, which claimed to be from the hand of the gentleman cited in the dubious signature:

I must say I was rather disturbed to see your recent account of my brother's activities during the so-called "War of the Worlds" (May). Whoever wrote the story (certainly not the more-or-less truthful Dr. Watson), although accurate in many respects, was guilty of a romanticism far worse than anything Watson has written.

I have spoken to Sherlock on the matter, but since his retirement he has taken little interest in the published accounts of his cases, real or otherwise. Indeed, it is difficult these days to get him interested in anything but his bees. "After all," said he, "it is a fiction magazine; as long as they call it fiction they may say anything they like about me."

Nevertheless, I would like to set the record straight. At no time, contrary to your story and others, has Sherlock been in love with anyone, let alone his landlady, Mrs. Hudson. Naturally a certain fondness existed, but certainly not to the degree shown in your story. In any case, Sherlock says he has never met the Wellmans, and idly wonders how they could possibly know what went on in Mrs. Hudson's private apartment.

Moreover, Mrs. Hudson's first name was not Martha. Martha was the woman Sherlock hired from 1917 to 1929 to keep house for him in Sussex. To imply that his landlady of many years would later work as a menial is irresponsible.

- Mycroft Holmes, London

The final installment of the collaborative Wellman father-and-son Conan Doyle/H.G. Wells mashup was "Sherlock Holmes Versus Mars" in *Fantasy and Science Fiction* May 1975 (Vol. 48, No. 4), cover art by Dario Campanile (for Harlan Ellison's "Croatoan"). The same issue's back cover ballyhoo (at right) brought special attention to Manly Wade Wellman as a frequent contributor to the magazine.

In short order (*F&SF*, January 1976, "Letters", pg. 157), Manly Wade Wellman himself replied to this dismissive duo—and did so as the man of letters he undoubtably was:

> *My son Wade and I feel obliged to comment on two letters in* F&SF *for September, which challenge our argument in "Sherlock Holmes Versus Mars" (*F&SF*, May) that Holmes and his lovely landlady, Martha Hudson, were lovers.*
>
> *To Roderick G. Bates, we respectfully point out that only the excellent but unperceptive Watson argues that Holmes never loved. True, he told Watson as much, and was only courteous to many a lovely lady – because he had the best of love with the best of sweethearts.*
>
> *Why was Holmes so anxious to lodge with Mrs. Hudson that he accepted a haphazard stranger to share the rent? Why, on returning from his 5-year absence after Reichenbach Falls, did he have a reunion with his landlady before seeing his brother Mycroft or his dear friend Watson? We can give numerous telling references in the Sacred Writings and cheerfully will do so on request.*
>
> *As to the letter signed Mycroft Holmes, we are naturally dazzled by such distinguished interest. Yet we diffidently suggest, Brother Mycroft is now somewhere past 120 years old, and must be fixed more than ever in his favorite chair at the Diogenes Club. And even his brilliant mind could be foiled by the circumspect Sherlock. I hope it is not the advance of years that makes him bobble when he denies that Mrs. Hudson's name was Martha, that Martha was another retainer "Sherlock hired from 1917 to 1929" to keep house for him in Sussex. Martha, we know from "His Last Bow" was helping Holmes usefully in thwarting Von Bork. And we hold that it is significant that Holmes made a date to meet her at a London hotel.*
>
> *We are honored to hear from Mycroft that Holmes noticed us. If, as Mr. Bates recommends, he comes visiting us armed with gasogene, we will welcome him with a flowing tantalus.*
>
> *In conclusion, both of us wish Holmes and Martha every joy of a romantic relationship which, we feel, does both of them credit.*
>
> *- Manly Wade Wellman (Holder of the Baker Street Irregulars investiture, The Dying Detective)*

Alas, Rick Bates has outlived Manly Wade Wellman, and is a friend of mine. Manly Wade Wellman died in 1986, and as best I can tell, there was no evidence of gasogene involved in his passing.

So Rick gets one more lick in, 35 years later:

> *"Some may think it unfortunate that Sherlock Holmes himself did not respond, but I can only assume that when he saw that not only had his smarter brother, Mycroft, spoken up for him, but so had Roderick Bates, he felt it quite unnecessary to add his faint voice to the choir."*[28]

You've had the final word after all, Roderick Bates![29]

---

28 Quoted from a personal email to the author, July 26, 2010; quoted with permission.
29 Well, *almost* the last word. Here's a relevant PS, in the grand spirit of Philip José Farmer and directly referencing more of Manly Wade Wellman's pioneer work, from a gentleman named Stu Shiffman (comment to the original *Myrant* posting of the final installment of the original serialized incarnation of this essay, dated September 11, 2010):

"Great stuff! *Sherlock Holmes's War of the Worlds* is a great favorite of mine and I am delighted to see it reprinted after so long. As a Sherlockian, I took issue with the relationship with Mrs. Hudson, but the whole is enough fun to ignore it! It was Manly Wade Wellman, best known as biographer of such occult investigators as Judge Pursuivant, John Thunstone and John the Balladeer (and numerous other works), who approached this issue in a critical work: 'The Great Man's Great Son: An Inquiry into the Most Private Life of Mr. Sherlock Holmes', in the *Baker Street Journal* (*Baker Street Journal* [OS], 1, No. 3 (July 1946), 326-336). In this work, Wellman contends that neither Lord Peter Death Bredon Wimsey nor Police Inspector Stanley Hopkins was the son of Sherlock Holmes. He then presents an elaborate argument to show that the offspring of the great detective was none other than Bertie Wooster's valet Jeeves, born to the Master and his landlady in 1891.

The author drew upon his own theory when editing his collection of short essays published under the title of *Sherlock Holmes's War of the Worlds* (1975). While a fresh look at those events, with its portrayal of a deeper emotional and physical relationship with Mrs. Hudson, this cannot be accepted as supplemental evidence to his theory. While I accept William Baring-Gould's theories of the Holmes parentage of the detective Nero Wolfe as set out in his works, I cannot agree with Wellman's conclusion, and further do not agree with the details of the parents of Reginald Jeeves as set out by C. Northcote Parkinson.

Compton Films, the British outfit that produced **A STUDY IN TERROR** (1965/66), returned to Sir Arthur Conan Doyle "speculative further fiction" turf with Billy Wilder's delightful, sorrowfully underrated **THE PRIVATE LIFE OF SHERLOCK HOLMES** (1970), which proved to be a compromised work (shorn of over 20 minutes, which were only partially restored for the film's laserdisc and DVD releases) and a boxoffice disaster, ending Compton's existence.

[TO BE CONTINUED IN ISSUE #8.5]

©2010, 2012, 2015 Stephen R. Bissette, all rights reserved.

Revised & expanded from the *Myrant* essay "Going Ape! Redux; More on Planet of the Apes Predecessors: Balaoo, DeCamp, Miller, Wellman," July 2, 2012, *http://srbissette.com/?p=15042* and the serialized *Myrant* essays archived at:

"Holmes vs. Red Planet Mars, Part 1; Or; Making Martians & Pining for Pulp Amid the Debris of 19th to 20th Century Pop Culture," June 29, 2010, *http://srbissette.com/?p=9324*

"Part 2," July 4, 2010, *http://srbissette.com/?p=9354*

"Part 3; Or; How Jack the Ripper Brokered the Martian Invasion of London, Continued," July 12, 2010, *http://srbissette.com/?p=9419*

"Part 4; Or; "What Shall We Do With a Drunken Martian?", July 15, 2010, *http://srbissette.com/?p=9444*

"Part 5; Or; Is That A Horla In Your Pocket, Or Are You Just Happy to See Me?" July 22, 2010, *http://srbissette.com/?p=9485*

"Part 6; Or; Who Shall Have the Final Word, Mr. Holmes?" July 27, 2010, *http://srbissette.com/?p=9519*

"Holmes vs. Red Planet Mars Redux, Or; Who is George H. Smith, and Why is He Manhandling Mr. H and Dr. W?" September 17, 2010, *http://srbissette.com/?p=9617*

Rather, in my own research, it has become increasingly clear that Jeeves must have been the son of the Great Detective and the housemaid Agatha, to whom he became engaged in the course of the case of Charles Augustus Milverton , 'king of all the blackmailers'."

THE TRANSFORMATION OF THE LEGEND OF JOHN: FROM SILVER BALLADEER TO HILLBILLY HIPPIE

by Tony Strauss

He don't have the answers and if he did he'd lie.
The Devil is a joker and he don't want you alive.
- "The Devil (Song of the Defy)" by Hoyt Axton

Most folks who do much reading in the sci-fi, mystery, horror and supernatural genres of 20th century literature have probably at one point or another at least run across the name of Manly Wade Wellman (1903-1986), the prolific American author who from the late '20s through the mid-'80 published some 500 short stories, essays, comics and novels, and has influenced countless other authors for three generations and counting. He wrote history-inspired tales of Native American mythology, stories treading the waters of Lovecraft's Cthulhu mythos, youth fiction, occult detective mysteries, Sherlock Holmes adventures[1], galaxy-spanning sci-fi...he pretty much ran the gamut of weird and wild genres of fiction in his productive 60-year career.

But what Wellman was and is probably best-known for are his Appalachian folk tales—backwood stories of horrific wonderments inspired by legends and superstitions he learned through his lifelong study of the mountain cultures of North Carolina, his adopted home state—specifically those starring his most famous creation, the wandering balladeer known in the stories simply as John, but culturally dubbed "Silver John" or "John the Balladeer". Introduced in the December, 1951 issue of *The Magazine of Fantasy and Science Fiction*, John was a lone hero archetype who travelled the Appalachian hills with his silver-stringed guitar slung across his back, and through his ever-increasing knowledge and understanding of the occult—frequently with the help of his guitar strings made of pure, evil-repelling silver—battled darkness in defense of the righteous and brought those of evil intent to swift backwoods justice of the supernatural variety. An immensely popular character, Silver John would continue his literary adventures with regularity—in both short story and novel form—throughout Wellman's career, with the last Balladeer novel seeing publication in 1984.[2]

As popular and influential as the character was and continues to be—and despite the fact that a few of Wellman's stories had already been adapted for television by the likes of *Lights Out*, *The Twilight Zone* and *Night Gallery*—it is rather surprising that only one successful (depending on your point of view) attempt has ever been made to bring the Balladeer to the big screen: the rarely seen, low-budget 1974 oddity known as **THE LEGEND OF HILLBILLY JOHN**, directed by John Newland (best known for helming the 1973 TV horror classic **DON'T BE AFRAID OF THE DARK**) from a script by Melvin Levy (who also helped make some historic television in 1973 by penning **THE SIX MILLION DOLLAR MAN**, the TV movie that launched the hit series), and produced by Barney Rosenzweig (a mostly TV-based producer responsible for many a *Charlie's Angels* and *Cagney & Lacy* adventure, who managed to acquire himself the "A Film by" credit in the present film's opening titles). The little independent production came and went without much notice, and has more or less wandered off into obscurity, seemingly only ever to be brought up when someone wants to complain about the lack of Wellman adaptations (a valid complaint), and beat the film up mercilessly for having the "lone wolf" honor and not being amazing (understandable, but hardly fair). As is often the case with hard-to-find genre films, the public consensus tends to get written by the loudest of those few who've managed to see the movie, and as we all know, the loudest tend to be the most inflammatory. Sad as it is, that's just the way the world works...but that means said "public consensus" is frequently pretty far away from any kind of informed verdict.

---
[1] See Stephen Bissette's "Holmes vs. Mars" article on p.59.
[2] Wellman had announced another forthcoming Silver John novel, but passed away before the novel was written.

I would posit that's pretty well the case with **THE LEGEND OF HILLBILLY JOHN**. So few have actually seen it and even fewer have bothered to make their opinions of it public that primarily only the disappointed dissenters have bothered to go on record by writing about it. Understand that I'm not trying to make a case that it's some great lost masterpiece of indie cinema—because it certainly isn't—but I do feel the film has unfairly gotten a pretty bum rap, and is actually a pretty fun and unique little slice of folksy fantasy, when given its fair shakes and not expected to bear the weight of its position as the only Silver John movie, a mutually exclusive disappointment which occurred through no fault of its own.

Though faults of its own the film certainly does have. The most prominent of its shortcomings is probably the (mis-)casting of its title character with the alarmingly uncharismatic and aggressively milquetoast presence of one Hedges "Hedge" Capers, a now-forgotten seeker of '70s folk-crooning stardom[3]... and clearly *not* an actor. Of any sort. Not any.

The other big setback with this film is its common-for-the-times bid for/pandering to the counterculture market, the result of which is an uneven presentation at best, with not infrequent bursts of field-strolling and love-gazing montages overlaid with the soft strummings of the Hedgester's hippie melodies. Fortunately for us all, these Flower Child assaults never occur within any of the adventures proper, but within the framing segments, yet they still pack a double-barrel saccharine punch that brings the proceedings to a grinding halt when they arrive. Damn hippies.

Combine these two rather unfortunate intrusions and the confident, wise and honorable balladeer hero of Wellman's beloved tales becomes transformed into...well, I guess a sort of nature-boy "innocent, pure of soul" archetype was what they were going for, but we really end up with a neutered hippie simpleton for our hero, one who escapes supernatural peril and conquers darkness more often through dumb luck than wisdom of any kind. I guess that's fine for what it is—and the "nature-boy/innocent" is definitely a common archetype of that era—but as an adaptation of a great literary character that seems ripe for the cinematic plucking, it's a definite letdown. And this is the film's curse, because as an example of backwoods fantasy-folktale horror, it's not a bad little film, and one that could be readily enjoyed by the kinds of people who enjoy Wellman's style of genre storytelling; however, those same people are probably pretty much the *only* audience that would seek a film like this out, and due to the film being such a direct adaptation of such classic and familiar stories, there's no hope for these viewers to be able to fully separate the film

Severn Darden as Mr. Marduke, our Greek Chorus and John's sometime spiritual guide

from its source material, so they won't be able to help but judge it as an annoying (and unnecessary) distortion of a beloved character. So in a way, it is understandable why this movie gets so much criticism, even though it's not at all a terrible film in and of itself.

Purported by the opening credits to be "Based on the book by Manly Wade Wellman"[4], the movie is actually an adaptation of just Wellman's first two Silver John stories, padded out by material unique to the film. It's a mixed bag, to be sure, but judged on its own merits (as much as is possible, anyhow), it's an interesting slice of '70s cinema, and a fun little entry into a woefully underpopulated subgenre. So let's put our preconceptions and literature-loyal nitpicks aside, and take a look at **THE LEGEND OF HILLBILLY JOHN** for what it brings to the table on its own.

—

After a rousing, burly opening credits folk song belted out through the husky pipes of Hoyt Axton, we are informed, in a Greek Chorus-style introduction, that the Devil is everywhere in many forms, from the simple transgressions of men to the eight-lane superhighways cutting through nature's untamed landscape. Deep in the Appalachian backwood hills of North Carolina, a young,

---

3   Along with singer Donna Carson, Hedges was known with some small amount of popularity as one half of the folksy-country "power" duo, Hedge and Donna, who released a handful of albums between 1968 and 1973.

4   We can safely assume, since there's no book bearing the same title as this film, they mean it was based on *Who Fears the Devil?*, an anthology of previously-published Silver John short stories, which had its first printing in 1963 and has since been reprinted myriad times under both its original title as well as *John the Balladeer*.

Who Fears the Devil (**left**) original art by Lee Brown Coye for the 1963 Arkham House limited edition, and (**right**) Grandpappy John sings the Defy at the Devil himself

good-hearted man named John once conquered fears he never knew he had and defied the Devil himself, going on to become a legend in our lifetime. And this is the tale of how it all started…

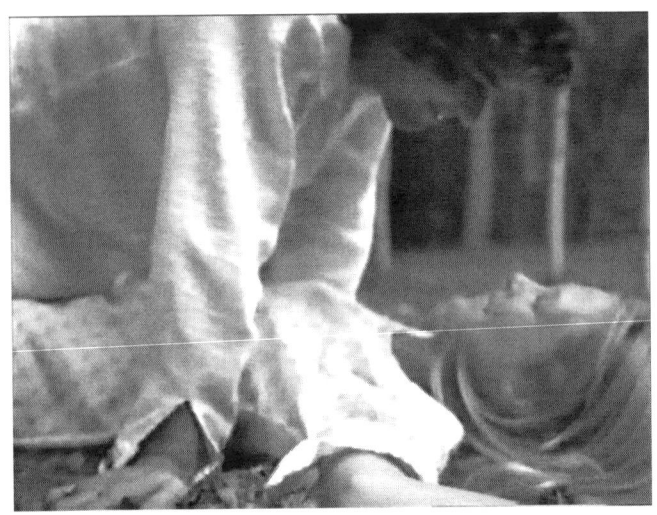

One morning after a night of outdoor lovin' with his gal Lily (Sharon Henesy, looking happily tranquilized), sweet, naïve young John (Hedges Capers) returns home to find that his Grandpappy John (Denver "Uncle Jesse" Pyle) has sworn by his own name to "sing the Defy" to the Devil himself on this very day, intending to put pay to Old Nick once and for all and drive evil out of the land. Grandpappy has saved up and melted down five shiny new half-dollars into guitar strings with which to battle the Dark Lord through his mighty musical assault. You see, "true silver" is a well-known repellant of evil, and will surely give the ornery coot the extra power he needs to defy Ol' Scratch. Young John stands proudly beside his Grandpappy that night as the old man courageously sings the Defy to summon and battle Beelzebub…

Unfortunately, nobody told ol' Grandpappy that the damn government cut back the quality of their coin-makin', and the shiny new coins used to make his guitar strings were far from "true silver". Alas, things don't go so well for Grandpappy…in fact, things go so poorly that they nearly destroy the very film we're watching, as the Devil's might snaps the celluloid from its sprockets right before our ever-lovin' eyes! (A rather creative and effective visual gag that serves as a clever alternative to depicting an epic supernatural showdown that would've been leagues beyond this film's chicken-scratch budgetary reaches.)

At Grandpappy's funeral, young John vows to continue the old man's work, and find a way to defy that mean ol' Devil his own self, regardless of what temptations and damnations might lay ahead. Thanks to the helpful divining powers of his mysterious and sage-like old friend, Mr. Marduke (our "Greek Chorus" from the film's intro, genre mainstay Severn Darden), John unearths three buried Spanish pieces of eight, and uses them to fashion himself a set of *true* silver guitar strings with which to arm himself against evil. Marduke hints to John that there's a great deal more treasure buried there if they only take the time to unearth it, but John remains resolute in his mission and resists this temptation, much to the impressed Mr. Marduke's satisfaction. Then, with his trusty canine companion Honor Hound (as himself) by his side, John leaves home and sets off into the world to do his defyin'. What follows is a trio of supernatural adventures in which John must use his honor, wits, and silver-strung songs to do battle with the dark forces that operate within the hidden hills of Appalachia.

John's first adventure in his defyin' quest is (rather freely) adapted from Wellman's second Silver John short story, "The Desrick on Yandro" (1952), in which John unwittingly plays a key role in fulfilling a 75-year-old curse by merely playing a song. Though maintaining the same basic structure and characters, the film takes great license with the details and presentation; understandable, since the original story involves a variety of actual monsters that would have been well beyond this meager production's reach. Still, Newland's film manages to capture the essence of the source material fairly well, considering, and kicks the adventure off promisingly. While attending a hoedown in a small valley settlement, John is enlisted by party-crashing, buzz-killing codger/undertaker Zebulon Yandro (ubiquitous character actor Harris Yulin, from **SCARFACE** [1983]…and pretty much every other movie and TV show ever made)—a miserly landowner who uses his wealth and generally shitty personality to bully the local populace—to help find the location of a treasure trove of gold supposedly hidden on Yandro's inherited land. John, heeding the legend that the gold is cursed by a witch spurned three quarters of a century ago by Yandro's grandfather, refuses the offer of a share in the treasure, but leads the greedy would-be heir into the haunted mountains to claim his rightful inheritance. Unfortunately for Yandro, the jilted witch (Susan Strasburg, "mother" of **THE MANITOU** [1978]) has been guarding over the treasure for generations, and now, on the 75th anniversary of her curse, is more than willing to hold Yandro accountable for his grandfather's transgressions. Before leading the doomed Zebulon to his grody fate (a fairly jokey, juvenile gag played so over-the-top horrifically that you can't help but grin and enjoy it), the lovely witch foretells to John a hint of what lies ahead of him: an "Ugly-Bird", which, if he survives the encounter, the witch informs him, "you will know the truth of your silver."

Top to bottom: John and Lily enjoy a little outdoor romance. Harris Yulin as the menacing and miserly mortician Zebulon Yandro. Susan Strasberg as the witch Polly Wiltse. John croons a freewheelin' hippie tune.

This leads us directly into the wandering hero's next adventure, based on the very first Silver John tale, "O Ugly Bird!" (1951), which follows Wellman's original story much more closely than the Yandro installment (aside from the movie's segues into and out of the tale), although the adaptation broad-strokes some of the more interesting, Wellman-esque aspects of the story, and in doing so makes the story a bit muddy and confusing.

After hearing the witch's prophecy, John sets off immediately to find this mysterious "Ugly-Bird". Deep in the hills, he discovers a trail leading to foreboding Hark Mountain, a trail on which not even Honor Dog will follow him. Leaving his faithful companion to cower behind, John sets off alone up the mountain. He finds a strip-mine with signage indicating ownership by one O.J. Onselm...and the petrified body of a woman buried near the sign! Then, he is suddenly attacked by a hideous giant beast that swoops down upon him from the sky—the dreaded Ugly-Bird! He escapes by deflecting its attack with his silver guitar strings—which, to his surprise, seem to hurt the beast—and makes his escape. John soon happens upon the mountain home of a man who is in the process of being accosted and verbally abused by a crazed man in a tattered suit—none other than O.J. Onselm himself (played by Alfred Ryder with an impressively twitchy, birdlike manner)—who is demanding the man prematurely slaughter his cow so that Onselm may take the meat. John scares the raving bully away, and the grateful man tells John that Onselm has a way of getting what he wants from anyone around, and that the Ugly-Bird attacks anyone who can resist Onselm's seemingly hypnotic power-of-will. John suspects that Onselm and the Ugly-Bird share a supernatural connection related to tales he's heard of witches and their beasts[5], and when Onselm and the Ugly-Bird return for a renewed assault, John once again uses the power of his silver strings to put pay to the double-menace, but it costs him something dear.

The third and final of John's adventures (in this particular presentation, anyhow) follows another important encounter with/lesson from Mr. Marduke, who helps John a second time on his road to defyin' before once again going their separate ways, after which John is reunited with Lilly and Honor Dog, and Lilly "tempts" John with the idea of settling down together in a little house in the woods. But John is made of more ramblin' material, and sticks to the path he's chosen as a defier of evil. Perhaps to prove that he's not completely emotionally unavailable, he allows Lilly to join him in his wandering, and they montage-walk down many a country road singing many a tree-hugging folk song.

The happy couple travels along the dusty ol' road a good long spell before encountering a great wooden gate out in the middle of nowhere, which opens itself just as John reaches out to touch it. On the other side, the sky changes color (via cheap filtering) and they find themselves on a great cotton plantation, whereupon the sharecroppers are being mentally enslaved (and financially cheated) by the landowner through the assistance of a voodoo priest named Captain Lojoie H. Desplain IV (played by the ubiquitous Percy Rodrigues), who has stolen the wooden idol of the African workers' god and is using it to keep them in a supernatural submissive stupor. John witnesses this heinous exploitation and faces down with Capt. Desplain, once again using his silver strings to save the day and free the poor workers from their enslavement. What follows is probably the most racially condescending (yet well-intended, in an almost charmingly ignorant way) hippie victory song these old ears have ever encountered. Seriously, you will not freakin' believe this one.

This final adventure is a story original to the film, not based on any story from the Wellman book...and it shows. While still somewhat interesting and in keeping with the general supernatural theme, this is the weakest of the tales, arbitrarily removing our hero from his Appalachian setting and running him through a rushed-feeling tale that felt kind of like a stage play (probably primarily due to the fact that it almost all takes place on a single set) that is over as soon as it really begins. I can only imagine this was crafted as more counterculture-bait, intended to add a relevant political "message" to the film (essentially: Don't be mean to black folks, y'all!), be it ever so ham-fisted and unwittingly racially offensive in a really naïve and stoned-out sort of way...and

---

5 Though we assume in the film that John is referring to the concept of a witch's familiar, an animal enchanted by a witch as a companion/minion, in Wellman's short story it is suggested that Onselm is a hoodoo man who "creates" the Ugly Bird with ectoplasm secreted from his own body...which is pretty fucking cool.

Top to bottom: John finds a petrified body buried in a strip-mine... before being attacked by the horrifying and deadly (and cheaply-animated) Ugly Bird! Alfred Ryder plays O.J. Onselm, the mean ol' coot who seems to control the Ugly Bird.

therefore: pretty fucking hilarious. While this segment is the weakest of the bunch, it might be the most memorable just for its heavy-handed soap-boxing.

After freeing the sharecroppers and reuniting them with their sacred idol, John sets off again, leaving Lilly behind to wonder why he never settles down for long. Mr. Marduke shows up to console her, and, after revealing to her that he is actually the Mesopotamian god Marduk, patron deity of Babylon (a reveal that will seem arbitrary to viewers unaware of the deity's historic association with judgment and magic), explains that people like John never settle down anywhere for very long, but will always go wherever they are needed most.

Cut to: scenic shot of John, his guitar slung across his back, walkin' towards Capitol Hill in Washington, DC. Far out, man...heavy.

———

While far from a satisfying adaptation of Wellman's iconic character and his stories, and far from any kind of undiscovered cinematic masterpiece, **THE LEGEND OF HILLBILLY JOHN** is full of its own brand of charm—warts and all—and is definitely undeserving of the dismissal and invective with which it's been treated. Aside from the production's unfortunate glaring missteps in casting and translating the central character, the supporting cast is populated with many familiar faces giving quality performances (Henesy's Lilly being a non-intrusive exception), it features great authentic Appalachian locations that really cement the proceedings in the region where they're meant to be occurring, and in the process delivers some quirky and fun folk tales told with a decent amount of cinematic ambition, given the restrictive budgetary conditions everyone was obviously working under. Despite its historic status as a disappointment to Silver John fans, it's certainly not a film that deserves to be shuffled away in the ever-growing pile of "lost" genre films. While grey-market VHS rips of it can still be tracked down with only minimal effort[6], it deserves to be remastered, presented and preserved in a respectable digital format. Hopefully, one of those awesome specialty labels out there like Code Red or Twilight Time will pick up this endearingly oddball little pic and make it more widely available to genre fans, even if only in a limited release.

———

THE LEGEND OF HILLBILLY JOHN
1974, USA. D: JOHN NEWLAND

[6] It can be obtained from most decent online sources of grey-market media; I got my copy from *iOffer.com* for about eight bucks, and it's a completely watchable transfer, suffering only from the usual image softness (and squareness, given its pan-scan source) characteristic of all digital transfers of OOP VHS releases.

Baen paperback edition from 1988, cover art by Steve Hickman

Left, top to bottom: John resists Lily's temptation to settle down in favor of his quest to defy. Percy Rodrigues as the evil Captain Lojoie H. Desplain IV. John sings a well-meant but culturally condescending victory tune...before heading off to where he's needed most.

Why do I *continue* making movies? Making movies is **better** than cleaning toilets.

2016

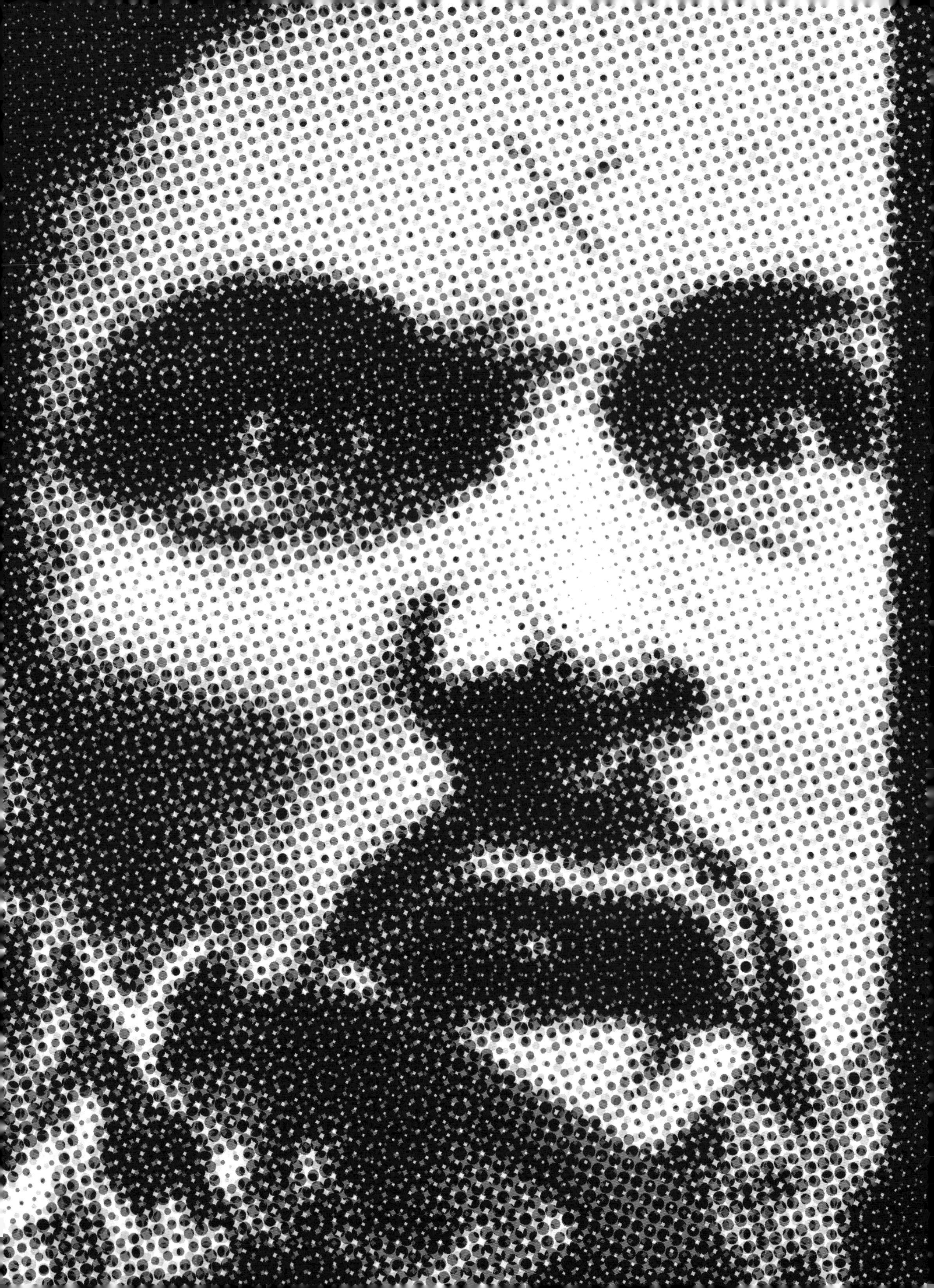

THE OTHER SIDE OF MADNESS:
A Creepy-Crawl through the Cinema of Charles Manson

by John Harrison

Closing in on nearly fifty years after the event, the dark enigma of Charles Manson and the horror that was the Tate-LaBianca murders continue to fascinate and haunt us in a way that very few crimes before or since have. Over the nights of August the 8th and 9th, 1969, Manson managed to reach out and terrify the world by sending a selection of his acid-fueled young (and mostly female) followers on a murderous rampage through Los Angeles, a spree that would ultimately leave seven people dead, including a pregnant Sharon Tate, the 26-year-old actress wife of film director Roman Polanski (who may very well have ended up among the victims, had he not been over in the UK at the time). Of course, the combined death toll attributed to Manson and his "Family" was much higher than seven, and included musician Gary Hinman, lawyer Ronald Hughes, Spahn Movie Ranch hand and Hollywood stuntman Donald "Shorty" Shea, and possibly many others.

I have long held a strange fascination with the Manson case, as I also have with the November 22, 1963 assassination of President John F. Kennedy in Dallas, two crimes which bookended the decade of the pop-'Sixties, a contradictory one played up as a time of "peace and love", yet seeing record increases in racial violence, psychopathy and random acts of senseless killing. Not to mention a pointless war in South East Asia that was being played out nightly on television sets across American living rooms. The Tate-LaBianca killings, along with the stabbing murder of black concertgoer Meredith Hunter by the Hell's Angels at the Altamont rock festival in San Francisco on December 6, 1969, brought the decade to a screaming halt.

While the case itself was horrific enough on its own to send shockwaves reverberating around the world, the Manson mythos was certainly enhanced by Vincent Bugliosi, the Deputy District Attorney of Los Angeles County who successfully prosecuted Manson and his co-accused in a sensational trial that galvanized the public almost as much as the murders themselves. It was Bugliosi who latched onto and propagated the theory of "Helter Skelter", the belief that Manson was inspired by the Beatles' famous "White Album" (the unofficial name given to their self-titled double-LP from 1968) to instigate a race war between the blacks and the whites of America, a war which Manson believed the blacks would win. However, Manson also believed that the blacks would not be able to govern the world properly after their victory, and would call on him and his followers to emerge from their Death Valley caverns to be their new leaders. Manson himself always dismissed Helter Skelter as pure fantasy dreamed-up by Bugliosi, but it was reiterated and confirmed by a number of Manson followers (not to mention the daubing of the phrase "Healter Skelter" [sic] in human blood on the door of the LaBianca's fridge).

After the death sentence was handed down on the all the accused (later commuted to life in prison after California revoked the death penalty in 1972), Bugliosi would turn his high-profile triumph into the book *Helter Skelter*, a detailed account of the case and trial which became a huge best-seller when it was published by W. W. Norton & Company in 1974. Co-written with Curt Gentry, the book won a 1975 Edgar Award and, while it may not have started the true crime book genre, it was certainly instrumental in popularizing it, especially when it was reprinted in mass-market paperback form.

With the recent passing of Bugliosi at the age of 80 (dying somewhat ironically before the man he sent to death row way back in 1971), I felt the time was right to take a look back at the many filmic interpretations of Manson which have appeared over the years, not just the official dramatized tellings of the story, but also some of the many documentaries on the subject, as well as the exploitation films of the 'Seventies which were clearly inspired by the case, either thematically or aesthetically. Virtually every element of the Manson case had a cinematic quality to it. Not just the Hollywood Hills setting and the high-profile celebrity victims, but the perpetrators and the bizarre alternative lifestyle they led, the Beatles (and Beach Boys) associations, the Spahn Movie Ranch location where the Family made camp for a while, the rumors of snuff movies filmed by the Family—it all seemed like a strange, LSD-drenched exploitation film that was being violently played-out in real life.

For Manson, who had spent most of his adult life in prison before he was released out into the free world for the last time at the age of 32 in 1967, "Helter Skelter" had been fermenting in his strange psyche for some time. For the outside world, it started when Winifred Chapman, the maid at the Tate-Polanski residence, turned up for work on that morning of August 9th, 1969, and came running down Cielo Drive moments later, screaming bloody murder.

Movie Manson

My own first exposure to Manson was, appropriately enough, a cinematic one. I was only five years old at the time the events took place, so while I may have heard his name being mentioned on the news or by older family members, my first conscious introduction to Charles Manson was the screening of the two-part telemovie **HELTER SKELTER** (1976), which I first saw at the age of thirteen, probably the perfect age for the film and its story to have maximum impact on my impressionable mind. In the lead-up to the broadcast, I started learning a few things about Manson and the murders, from TV reports and newspaper articles hyping the mini-series, as well as from exaggerated and misinformed schoolyard chatter. But you didn't need to exaggerate anything in this case—the crime and the facts surrounding it, not to mention the news footage and images of Manson and his perpetrators, spoke for themselves. So by the time **HELTER SKELTER** aired in Australia, I was primed and already terrified out of my wits. After the first part of the telemovie had aired, I slept with the bedroom door opened and the hallway light turned on, for the first time in years. Of course, I also couldn't wait for the second part to air the following night.

Directed by Tom Gries and adapted from the Bugliosi/Gentry book from J. P. Miller, **HELTER SKELTER** is told primarily through Bugliosi's eyes, so it's a one-sided though at-times effectively harrowing re-enactment of the Manson story from the prosecutor's point of view, and boasts a compelling performance by Steve Railsback as Charlie, who plays the character with a refreshing degree of subtlety, rather than opting for an over-the-top display. Though Railsback's voice doesn't have the same degree of menace or madness to it as Manson's, where he comes alive is in the craziness lurking in his eyes and the facade of his welcoming smile. What makes Railsback's performance even more of an achievement is that it was accomplished at a time when Manson himself was still keeping himself mostly hidden away behind bars, and there wasn't the abundance of videotapes of subsequent parole hearings and television interviews to reference and draw upon, which actors who have played the role since have had at their disposal.

Railsback's performance is the obvious lynchpin which **HELTER SKELTER** hangs on, but he is almost matched by George DiCenzo, who puts in a much more restrained but no less authoritative turn as Vincent Bugliosi, though his voice is unusually dubbed in a few scenes, making his on-screen dialogue sound more like voice-over narration. Fans of **THE TEXAS CHAIN SAW MASSACRE** (1974) will also enjoy seeing Marilyn Burns (who played Sally Hardesty in Tobe Hooper's terror classic) as Linda Kasabian, the Manson girl who later turned state witness, while Nancy Wolfe as Susan Atkins has some moments when she conveys a genuine sense of psychopathic menace, particularly in the scenes where she confesses her crimes to cellmate Ronnie Howard (Sondra Blake). The film has a slightly grimier look to it than many other American telemovies at the time, including the use of the "N-word", and it's one of the most authentic-looking of all the commercial Manson movies, if only by design of it being made so close to when the events occurred, so many of the fashions, cars and interior designs still have that late-'Sixties hangover to them.

Unable to secure permission to use The Beatles' original music in **HELTER SKELTER**, a jobbing LA band called Silverspoon (whose members included the son of director Gries) was brought in to record four cover tunes: "Helter Skelter", "Piggies", "Revolution 1" and "Long, Long, Long". It's a pity the original recordings weren't able to be used to preserve some authenticity, but the covers serve their purpose well enough (though Silverspoon's take on "Piggies", played over a sequence where County Sheriff authorities raid Spahn Ranch, is pretty awful). The remainder of the music in **HELTER SKELTER** was composed by Billy Goldenberg, whose prolific television career included scoring episodes of *Ironside*, *Kojack* and *Columbo*, as well as Paul Wendkos 1973 TV movie **TERROR ON THE BEACH**, which in itself had some Manson-esque elements, being about an average American family being terrorized by a bunch of hippies whilst on vacation.

After its initial American television broadcast, **HELTER SKELTER** was subsequently edited down (and spiced up with some additional nudity and violence) for overseas theatrical release. The complete 184-minute version was released as a bare-bones DVD in the USA on the Warner label in 2004. The shorter theatrical cut has also surfaced on video in several countries (such as Australia in 1984 on the CBS/Fox label, as well as in America under the title **MASSACRE IN HOLLYWOOD**), but has yet to see an official DVD or Blu-ray release.

HELTER SKELTER wasn't the first film to tell the Manson story, however. That honor belongs to Frank Howard's low-budget wonder **THE OTHER SIDE OF MADNESS** (1971), which is perhaps better known under its 1976 re-release title of **THE HELTER SKELTER MURDERS**. While many people are quick to dismiss Howard's film, I've always found it incredibly fascinating. The seedy black-and-white photography, so at odds with its late-'Six-

Above: (left) Vincent Blugliosi (George DiCenzo) tries to stare down Charlie (Steve Railsback) in an Australian lobby card for the theatrical release of the 1976 **HELTER SKELTER** telemovie, while **(right)** Brian Klinknett plays Manson as the strong, silent type in **THE OTHER SIDE OF MADNESS** (1971, a.k.a. **THE HELTER SKELTER MURDERS**)

ties setting, gives it a surreal *cinéma vérité* feeling, and the long passages devoid of any dialogue or music also seem quite experimental in nature (as does the inclusion of a brief color sequence, depicting the Sharon Tate character on the set of one of her films). The film plays around with some of the facts, but the murders which took place on Cielo Drive are depicted rather accurately and quite harrowingly, and Manson himself is portrayed as a very ethereal and almost supernatural character, saying little and communicating primarily though hypnotic eyes (much like he was being portrayed in the press at the time). A spiel before the end credits seems to place the entire blame for the tragic events on the easy availability of illicit drugs. The mystique of **THE OTHER SIDE OF MADNESS** is compounded by the fact that the director and virtually the entire cast seem to have dropped off the face of the earth after its release. The soundtrack features an effective mix of fuzz guitar rock, cheesy lounge music and even an original Charles Manson recording ("Mechanical Man"). A great piece of grimy exploitation cinema and an important documentation of an early take on the Manson mythos, when it was all still so fresh in everybody's minds. Produced by Wade Williams, the film went into production not long after the murders had occurred, and was completed while Manson and his co-accused were still on trial, resulting in none of the perpetrators being named (though the leader is referred to as Charlie, and actor Brian Klinknett bears a strong physical resemblance to Manson; the characters are listed in credit on as "The Killers" and "Their Victims"). The opening scroll of the film also avoids any specific names, simply stating: "In the late summer of 1969 an unknown band of hippie-styled characters committed the most bizarre crimes in history."

One of the rarest of the exploitation films produced to exploit the Manson killings, Kentucky Jones' **THE CULT** (a.k.a. **HOUSE OF BONDAGE**, a.k.a. **TOGETHER GIRLS**, 1971) had long been considered a lost film, with endless searches through dusty old film vaults always failing to locate a print. Later re-released as **THE MANSON MASSACRE**, the sense of mystery and intrigue surrounding the film was such that even the director's name caused debate—it is thought that Kentucky Jones was a pseudonym thought up by the director, who feared that his life might be in danger from Manson loyalists (although another rumour suggests that the film was actually funded by peripheral Manson Family members, and the director changed his name to avoid potential backlash from police or outraged relatives of the victims). Amazingly, just when it looked like **THE CULT / THE MANSON MASSACRE** may have been lost forever, a print turned up in 2001 in the most unlikely location—on a German DVD released on the low-budget Astro label, bearing the title **DIE TOCHTER DES SATANS** ("*The Daughter of Satan*"). Unfortunately, the print has been dubbed into German language and does not contain any English subtitles, but the quality of the transfer is fantastic, and even includes the original German theatrical trailer.

Despite the lack of subtitles, the film is easy to follow for anyone at all familiar with the Manson story, and is a quintessential piece of early-'70s scuzz, dripping with sleaze and jam-packed with topless hippie chicks and psychedelia-drenched violence. The film does seem to take great liberties with the facts behind the case, but does contain an interesting structure, with frequent black-and-white flashbacks filling us in on the background of Manson's girls, along with their first meeting with the Messiah (one of the girls falls for Charlie when he helps her steal a vibrator her horrified father refuses to buy for her!). Other flashbacks depict Manson killing the husband of a woman he has been sleeping with (played by the lovely and buxom Russ Meyer starlet Uschi Digart—surely someone worth killing for) and being gang-raped in the showers by a group of fellow inmates during his subsequent prison sentence. Until an English-language (or at least subtitled) print of this gem comes along, this German cut of **THE MANSON MASSACRE** is required viewing for all those with a fascination for Mansonsploitation cinema.

The later part of the 'Seventies surprisingly saw Manson fade from cinema and television screens. This was, after all, before the true crime genre—both as a book and a film/documentary form—really started to expand in the 1980s, and to middle-class America, the *Helter Skelter* book and telemovie told pretty much all there was to tell. The Manson case was still worthy of news headlines at this time, but perhaps the sobering reality was the proliferation of serial and spree killers who had emerged across America in the late 'Seventies and 'Eighties had stolen a lot of the attention away from the Tate-LaBianca bloodbath. With Charlie and much of his hardcore followers behind bars, there were people still out there on the wrong side of jail for the public to worry about and the media to exploit—The Hillside Stranglers in Los Angeles, the Son of Sam in New York, John Wayne Gacy in Chicago,

Top: Manson (Steve Railsback) grins maniacally despite being in chains after a Sheriff's raid on the Family in **HELTER SKELTER** (1976). **Above:** "Any similarity to persons living or dead is purely coincidental", claims this great lurid poster for **THE CULT** (1971, a.k.a .**THE MANSON MASSACRE**). I don't think any viewers were convinced by the disclaimer.

and Ted Bundy pretty much all over the country. Not to mention the enforced "mass suicide" of over 900 American followers of the paranoid and delusional Rev. Jim Jones in Guyana in 1978. All of which fed the public's fear and kept providing exploitation filmmakers with new angles to play up in their product (the Jonestown mass suicide itself would inspire two movies in quick succession—René Cardona Jr.'s seedy **GUYANA: CULT OF THE DAMNED** [a.k.a. **GUYANA: CRIME OF THE CENTURY**, 1979] and the telemovie **GUYANA TRAGEDY: THE STORY OF JIM JONES** [1980]).

son myth, and its continued influence on certain disassociated elements of modern society.

With many people convinced that **CHARLIE'S FAMILY** was a masterpiece in the making, Creation Books in the UK made the rather audacious move of publishing Van Bebber's entire screenplay in book form in 1998, amply illustrated with stills from the film (some in color), original production storyboards, an introduction by Jack Sargeant, and an illustrated essay on Manson-related films, written by Jim Morton. It would take another five years before **CHARLIE'S FAMILY** would finally be completed and see limited theatrical screenings and a subsequent home video release. Given the rather uninspired (but more publicly recognizable) retitle of **THE MANSON FAMILY** (2003), it ultimately failed to live up to years of expectation, and was considered something of a letdown after **DEADBEAT AT DAWN** and some of the shorts he directed in-between (such as his 1994 short films, *Roadkill: The Last Days of John Martin* and *My Sweet Satan*).

Though it's uneven, there is still a lot to admire about **THE MANSON FAMILY**. Some of the photography, by Mike King, really captures the sense of a late-1960s 8mm home movie, and utilizes a lot of the camera tricks that filmmakers were using at the time when trying to capture the counterculture life, such as fish-eye lenses. There's a lot about the film that is impressively experimental, but unfortunately it is just so often contrived and hokey. The sequence of Manson in a recording studio almost looks and plays like a bad television comedy skit, and the segments which take place in the present are mostly unnecessary, bogging the film down and seemingly there only as a means to allow Van Bebber to wrap the whole thing up, while trying to "say" something about Manson's lingering influence. Perhaps the biggest fault with the film is in its casting, with Marcelo Games looking the part of Manson, but having no real menace or charisma, coming across as little more than a mumbling stoner. The brief flashes of Manson as a bloodied devil are pretty striking, however, and the staging of the various murder set-pieces are very visceral and splattery.

While Van Bebber's film was finally seeing the light of day, the 35th anniversary of the crimes saw Bugliosi's *Helter Skelter* adapted as yet another made-for-television project, with writer/director John Gray at the helm and Bugliosi himself on board as producer. Where Bugliosi's novel and the original **HELTER SKELTER** telemovie focused primarily on the police investigation and subsequent murder trial, Gray's take on **HELTER SKELTER** (2004) chooses the viewpoint of Linda Kasabian (played by Clea DuVall), depicting her introduction to Manson (Jeremy Davies) and seduction into his Family, her part in the Tate murders (she drove the car but didn't enter the house or participate in the killings), and her subsequent convincing to turn state witness against Manson, saving her own skin and giving Bugliosi probably his biggest advantage in winning the case.

Clea DuVall is fine as Kasabian, though once again the focus is naturally on the actor wearing Charlie's beard. Jeremy Davies, perhaps best known previously for his roles in the indie hit **SPANKING THE MONKEY** (1994) and Steven Spielberg's violent D-Day epic **SAVING PRIVATE RYAN** (1998) certainly pulls out all the stops in trying to deliver a *tour de force* performance. Ultimately, the major drawback of Davies' performance becomes almost opposite to what made Steven Railsback's turn so effective in the 1976 original, in that Davies seems to have had *so much* reference material at his disposal that he comes across at times looking like someone who is trying just a bit too hard to replicate Manson's unique physical movements. It also feels at times like he is playing Manson as he was in the 1990s, not 1969. Still, there is no denying that Davies completely immerses himself in the character (the USA DVD release from Warner Brothers features some of his early test rehearsal footage as a special feature), and this is a decent and engrossing enough retelling of the story, particularly for those coming in unfamiliar with the events or previous cinematic interpretations.

One curious project which surfaced in the mid-'Eighties was **MANSON FAMILY MOVIES** (a.k.a. **MANSON HOME MOVIES**, 1984), a film by noted Manson historian and collector John Aes-Nihil inspired by stories that the Manson Family filmed much of their activity and even crimes (a myth that had its origins within the pages of Ed Sander's notorious 1971 book *The Family*). The film was shot without sound on 8mm between 1974 and 1979, on many of the actual locations where the events occurred, with music and sound effects added in post-production, and crude title cards to describe some basic plot elements and characters (being filmed sporadically over five years, different people often play the same character throughout the movie). Coming off like a disturbed pantomime production, **MANSON FAMILY MOVIES** is certainly one of the most interesting and offbeat tellings of the Manson story, though anyone who is fooled into thinking they are genuine home movies filmed at the time (as some have claimed) have either never actually seen it or must suffer from extreme astigmatism.

By the mid-1980s, Manson had started gaining a newfound infamy, becoming almost something of a cult hero to certain factions of the pre-grunge youth culture—many of whom had not even been born when the crimes were committed—and saw in Manson some misguided sense of rebellion or injustice. Notorious Hollywood glam rockers Mötley Crüe played up their public fascination with the dark side of Los Angeles by recording a cover of *Helter Skelter* for their *Shout at the Devil* LP in 1983. "Charlie Don't Surf" t-shirts became a controversial piece of fashion wear[1], and Guns N' Roses attracted criticism for recording a version of Manson's "Look At Your Game, Girl" for their 1993 covers album, *The Spaghetti Incident?*. Combined with the increasing number of new documentaries on the subject that were cropping up on cable television networks, it seemed like the time was right for another cinematic take on Manson, one that wouldn't be restricted by the limits imposed by television. After the underground film festival and fanzine acclaim which accompanied the release of Ohio-born filmmaker Jim Van Bebber's low-tech, urban gang drama **DEADBEAT AT DAWN** (1988), many people eagerly awaited his follow-up feature, **CHARLIE'S FAMILY**, the young auter's take on the Man-

Kasabian's viewpoint was once again chosen as the narrative focus for another television movie, Neil Rawles' **MANSON** (a.k.a. **MANSON 40 YEARS LATER**, 2009). For this project, executive producer Nick Godwin actually went out of his way to track down the reclusive Kasabian, eventually finding her living in a trailer park in near-poverty, and spent the next few months trying to convince her to become involved and tell her story in her own words. Kasabian finally agreed, and **MANSON** was constructed in the docudrama format, with Kasabian narrating and appearing onscreen in shadowed silhouettes, juxtaposed with re-enactments, vintage newsreel footage and interviews

---

[1] A famous line of dialogue from Coppolla's **APOCALYPSE NOW** (1979) with "Charlie" originally referring to the Viet Kong, the phrase "Charlie Don't Surf" was appropriated for a popular t-shirt design depicting Manson's face. —ed.

with Bugliosi, Sharon Tate's sister Debra, and one-time Family member Catherine Share (a.k.a. "Gypsy").

Although the look of **MANSON** suffers at times from its jumble of narrative and visual styles (washed out and modern one moment, the next presented as *faux* 8mm home movie footage), the film as a whole is reasonably effective, even if the exclusive access to Kasabian didn't reveal a whole lot more than what was already known. The depiction of the Cielo Drive murder is particularly well-constructed and tense, narrated by Kasabian as the events are played out primarily via screams and as violent silhouettes in the windows (the only point of view which Kasabian claims to have had of the murders, apart from those of Abigail Folger and Wojtek Frykowski, both of whom managed to stumble out into the backyard before Tex Watson and Patricia Krenwinkel emerged to resume their frenzied stabbing attacks on them). Tamara Hope plays Kasabian in the re-enactments, while Charlie is portrayed by Adam Wilson, who looks pretty decent in the part, though plays it a little too low-key to be genuinely menacing—he's more the laid-back wannabe rock star than a psychotic, pent-up ball of anger and paranoia (though Wilson does bring that side of the character to the fore as the film progresses).

Documenting Helter Skelter

There have probably been more documentaries produced about Charles Manson than any other modern true crime event, save for September 11th and JFK's assassination. Nominated for an Oscar in the Best Documentary category (it lost out to the evangelical exposé **MARJOE** [1972]), and banned from screening in California for many years, **MANSON** (a.k.a. **MANSON AND SQUEAKY FROMME**, 1973) provides a chilling insight into the mindset of Charles Manson and—more particularly—his followers, most of whom were still in the grip of a fierce loyalty towards their leader.

Co-directed by Robert Hendrickson and Laurence Merrick, and filmed when Manson and the convicted Tate-LaBlanca slayers were still languishing on death row, **MANSON** captures the climate of the times, when the killings were still fresh in the public's mind, and Manson himself was already being looked upon by many as a counterculture antihero. The highlight of the film is no doubt the footage of Manson girls Sandra Goode and Lynette "Squeaky" Fromme holed-up in a shack, brandishing firearms and threatening to kill anybody who gets in their way. While Laurence Merrick was murdered in Hollywood in 1977, in an unsolved case which some theorists have tied to vengeful Manson extremists, Robert Hendrickson still fiercely protects his documentary, chasing down anyone who tries to sell unauthorized copies. The film was released on VHS in 1984 by United Home Video, and on DVD in 2000 by Telefilms International, but is currently only available from Hendrickson himself, at pretty high prices but with some additional footage not included in its original release, through his Exclusive Films company.

An infamous "mondo" documentary, **THE KILLING OF AMERICA** (a.k.a. **VIOLENCE U.S.A.**, 1981) was produced primarily for the Japanese market, and was co-written and co-directed by Leonard Schrader, the late older brother of **TAXI DRIVER** (1976) screenwriter Paul. While the film only received some brief screenings in America at the time (at The Public Theatre in New York City), it became a poplar and controversial early VHS release in some countries, including the UK and Australia (where it was issued on the notorious Palace Explosive label). A look at the rise in violent and senseless crime in the United States, **THE KILLING OF AMERICA** is an unflinching and frequently brutal film that starts with the killing of President Kennedy and ends with the assassination of Beatle John Lennon, and includes lots of authentic and disturbing newsreel footage. Naturally, a segment on the Manson killings is included in the film. Bolstered by the great use of the song "Homicide" by English punk band 999, **THE KILLING OF AMERICA** still makes for confronting viewing, and shows that not a lot has changed in the thirty-odd years since its release.

Written, produced and directed by Nikolas Schreck, **CHARLES MANSON SUPERSTAR** (1989) is a somewhat revisionist documentary that is widely considered to be the definitive dissemination of the Manson myth, and how it has been sensationalized, abused and manipulated by the media in the years since 1969. Even if you disagree with Schreck's overtly pro-Manson approach to the subject, the extended interview footage is never less than fascinating and engaging, and quite often insightful and uncomfortably hilarious. Interspersed with the interview footage (during which Manson verbally savages the two guards in the room, and tries to turn them against each other) are various archival clips and still photographs, as well as the use of some original Manson music on the soundtrack.

From the Ed Wood school of filmmaking, Michael Gonzales' *Forgiven: The Charles "Tex" Watson Story* (1993), is an hilariously inept Christian docu-drama short, produced by the students at California's Biola University and designed to uplift us with the story of Charles "Tex" Watson's miraculous

Above: (**Left**) Classic early 'Eighties Australian VHS release of **THE HELTER SKELTER MURDERS** (1971, aka **THE OTHER SIDE OF MADNESS**) on the Video Classics label. (**Right**) Charlie's Angels look like they are ready for violence and hate, rather than peace and love, in this publicity still for **THE MANSON MASSACRE** (1971, a.k.a. **THE CULT**).

salvation, from Charles Manson's most savage deputy to redeemed (albeit still incarcerated) church minister within ten short years. As Watson, Paul McGinty at times resembles a young Keanu Reeves (and looks farcical as he sits in prison wearing an obvious wig and moustache that looks to have been made out of cardboard, staring stoney-faced as he answers questions put to him by a young lady dressed as an Amy Grant wannabe). Mark Caso plays a well-fed Charles Manson in this cheesy yet wholly enjoyable exercise in spiritual recruitment. Some prints of **FORGIVEN** have the prison interview scenes replaced with actual interviews snippets with Watson, which helps to give it more of a serious, darkened tone (it would come as no surprise to learn that this re-edited version was put together because even enlightened viewers couldn't help but snicker at the grade-school-play quality of the re-enactments). This re-edited print was released on VHS by Jeremiah Films, a distributor specializing in Christian-based films and documentaries.

Produced for cable television, the *Biography* episode "Charles Manson: Journey Into Evil" (originally aired Sept. 11, 1995) provides a fairly concise (though predictably one-sided) overview of the Manson mythos. While sticking to the widely-accepted versions of events, the documentary does a commendable job of tracing Manson's life from birth through current day, concentrating naturally on the murders and the hypnotic power and influence which he wielded over his Family. Includes then-current interviews with Manson and Lynette "Squeaky" Fromme (jailed for the attempted 1975 assassination of President Gerald Ford and still completely devoted to the cause), along with interviews with convicted killers Patricia Krenwinkel and Leslie Van Houten, who describe their role in the killings in horrific yet almost eloquent detail, and express their remorse over their involvement (along with chastising their former leader for not accepting his share of responsibility for the crimes).[2]

Assembled by the late Sverre H. Kristensen[3], *Charles Manson: No Sense Makes Sense* (1994/Denmark) presents a barrage of rapid-fire, senses-assaulting Manson media clips, interspersed with interviews with Manson aficionados such as Nikolas Schreck, Boyd Rice and JR Bruun. Highlights of this 21-minute short include Schreck inciting audience anger on *The Wally George Show* by claiming Charles Manson to be one of the great philosophers of the 20th Century, and Rice sparring off with Doris Tate (mother of slain actress Sharon) on a 1990 talk-back radio show.

Manson Grindhouse

Fear sells, and the Manson case contained elements more lurid than what any exploitation filmmaker could dream up. Low-budget filmmakers, always keen to play on the anxieties of the public, were quick to cash-in on the hysteria which the Tate-LaBianca murders left in their wake. Of course, some of the films which we have already covered here are considered exploitation or grindhouse movies (such as **THE OTHER SIDE OF MADNESS / THE HELTER SKELTER MURDERS** and **THE CULT / THE MANSON**

Japanese poster for **DRACULA A.D. 1972**

[2] "Charles Manson: Journey Into Evil" was released on video and DVD in the US by A&E Home Video (like all their releases, it comes in a generic A&E sleeve). Also released on VHS in Australia on Volume 2 of *Serial Killers: Profiling The Criminal Mind* (paired with the 1996 A&E documentary *John Wayne Gacy: Buried Secrets*). The expansion of cable television, including the emergence of dedicated true crime channels, saw the production of many documentaries that were similar to "Journey Into Evil". Among them: *Rivals: Chalres Manson vs. Vincent Bugliosi* (1995) and the *Biography* episode "The Manson Women: An American Nightmare" (July 16, 2002). Manson was also featured in episodes of *Deranged* (2008-) and the *Born To Kill?* episode "The Manson Family" (Oct. 2, 2012).

[3] Sverre H. Kristensen was a Danish artist best known for his works as a cartoonist, having had a huge number of drawings and comics published in a wide variety of comic books, magazines, fanzines and book anthologies. He also edited the notorious fanzine *Sewer Cunt* in 1994, and put out two spoken-word compilations and a compilation of phone pranks. His other short film works include *Pray to the Virus*, *Anus Presley*, *Mondo Sicko* and *Severed Finger Feels All*. Kristensen died in 1997.

MASSACRE), but other genre filmmakers from this period also used Manson as either a direct or obvious influence, or merely as an indefinable but definite background buzz, a feel that informs and permeates a film.

Russ Meyer's **BEYOND THE VALLEY OF THE DOLLS** (1970) climaxed with a drug-fuelled orgy of madness and murder taking place inside the Hollywood home of a famous music producer (Meyer and co-screenwriter Roger Ebert admitted the film was partly their take on the Tate-LaBianca hysteria, though the film was made before Manson had been connected to the crimes), while in Boris Sagal's adaptation of Richard Matheson's *I Am Legend*, **THE OMEGA MAN** (1971), the nocturnal people who walk the streets, mutated survivors of bacterial warfare, address themselves as "The Family", and their leader, Matthias (Anthony Zerbe) has something of a resemblance to Manson, with his long stringy hair and hypnotic influence over his followers. And in the Hammer Horror film **DRACULA A.D. 1972** (1972), a group of young English hippies decide to partake in a blood ritual for kicks, only to have the sacrifice turn out to be all too real (later, a Scotland Yard detective investigating the female body left behind opines that it "Could be a cult murder. Had a spate of them in the States some time back.").

The early 'Seventies certainly saw a grimier, harder edge develop to a lot of exploitation films, which even if they didn't reflect the events of August, 1969, certainly had a strange tone which seemed to suggest they were influenced or informed by them, or some aspect of them. Wes Craven's **LAST HOUSE ON THE LEFT** (1972) and Tobe Hooper's **THE TEXAS CHAIN SAW MASSACRE** (1974) reflected a new level of viciousness that mirrored the rise of violence in America at the time, while Craven's later **THE HILLS HAVE EYES** (1977) had a family of killers hiding out in the desert, picking off middle-class American holiday makers who dare venture into their domain. Don Siegel's classic cop drama **DIRTY HARRY** (1971) may have been inspired narratively by the (still officially unsolved) Zodiac killings then terrorizing the San Francisco area, but the film's psychotic killer, Scorpio (a classic turn by Andrew Robinson) has a Manson-esque vibe about him, with his shock of wild unkempt hair, crazed eyes and large peace symbol belt-buckle to give the character a touch of irony. **BLUE SUNSHINE** (1978), Jeff Lieberman's follow-up to his low-budget Southern horror gem **SQUIRM** (1976), has a group of young adults losing their hair and becoming psychotic killers, the delayed effect of a bad batch of LSD which they had taken in college a decade earlier. The image of the bald killers has a clear visual connection to the Manson Family, after they had all shaved their heads (in emulation of Charlie) during the trial.

Some exploitation and horror films from this period, however, certainly had more overt Manson-esque elements to them. In 1971, the appropriately named Jerry Gross foisted a memorable double-bill onto unsuspecting grindhouse and drive-in patrons, the charmingly titled **I EAT YOUR SKIN** and **I DRINK YOUR BLOOD**. While **I EAT YOUR SKIN** was an old 1964 Del Tenny film (**VOODOO ISLAND BLOODBATH**, a.k.a. **ZOMBIES**) that Gross had bought and re-titled, **I DRINK YOUR BLOOD** (1970) was a new film that he had produced alongside director/screenwriter David Durston. An incredibly seedy piece of work, **I DRINK YOUR BLOOD** casts muscular Indian actor and dancer Bhaskar (a.k.a. Bhaskar Roy Chowhury) as Horace Bones, a clearly Manson-esque guru to a group of satanic hippies calling themselves SADOS (the Sons and Daughters of Satan). When their van breaks down on the outskirts of a small town, they decide to amuse themselves by tormenting some of the locals, including a teenage girl and her grandfather (whom they force-feed LSD, sending poor grandpa on a wild senior's trip). Angered by their behavior, the girl's bratty kid brother decides to get even by selling the hippie cult a tray of meat pies which he has injected with blood from a rabid dog that he has shot dead out in the woods. The Sons and Daughters of Satan soon begin to foam at the mouth and turn on each other, committing a ritualistic killing and dismemberment of one of their own, while turned-on hippie chick Sylvia (Iris Brooks) spreads her favors, along with her infection, to a group of rowdy construction workers at a nearby quarry. It all climaxes in an orgy of violence, as both hippies and quarry workers run riot over the countryside, brutally killing and chopping up anyone who gets in their way, while one of his own followers thrusts a sword up Horace's back until it protrudes out of his mouth, effectively bringing an end to the cult of SADOS (though the rabid carnage continues for a while longer).

Filmed in Sharon Springs, NY (a once-popular summer spa town that had fallen on hard times and was virtually deserted by 1970), **I DRINK YOUR BLOOD** certainly has a sparse desolation to it, which helps add to its uneasy atmosphere. While David Durston's direction is rather flat, he definitely knows how to exploit a headline and turn a stomach—the way he lingers on close-up shots of the hippies noisily slurping down their infected meat pies is sure to spoil your appetite. Of the film's cast, Bhaskar is certainly the standout as Horace; with his black vest and long locks falling down over his strong, toned frame, he brings a lot of charisma to his role, spouting classic lines of quotable dialogue, including this gem from the film's opening satanic ritual sequence: "Let it be known, brothers and sisters, that Satan was an acid-head. Drink from his cup. Pledge yourselves, and together we'll all freak out!"

Released the same year as **I DRINK YOUR BLOOD**, Bob Roberts' **SWEET SAVIOR** (a.k.a. **THE LOVE THRILL MURDERS**, 1971) is a thinly-veiled attempt at telling the Manson story, brilliantly casting former teen heartthrob Troy Donahue as a cycle-riding hippie cult leader known as Moon, who flies his followers with drugs while plotting the murder of a Tate-like actress named Sandra (Renay Granville) and her friends, who are indulging in a swinging Hollywood party when the invasion and killings occur (unlike Manson, Moon is actually present in the house when the massacre goes down).

While promoting **SWEET SAVIOR**, star Donahue had this to say to Rex Reed in the August 8th, 1971 edition of the *Chicago Tribune*, regarding the film and its Manson-esque elements:

> *"I play Moon, a religious creep who murders a lot of people, a real heavy trip. But I don't want anyone to think I'm playing it in some phony exploitation flick that takes advantage of the Manson case to make a fast buck. I don't like many things, man, but I dig this picture… We're trying to show both sides of the problem. The Hollywood glamor society is as guilty as the depraved hippy cults. They pick up people on the Sunset Boulevard and tease them. When they made fun of Manson they picked on the wrong guy. I was up at the Tate house. It was a freaky scene. Sure, I met Manson at the beach playing volleyball."*

In the same article, director Roberts explains part of his own motivations for making the movie and the cautionary tale he wanted to tell:

> *"I had the idea not to make the Mason story per se but to inform people the Sharon Tate thing was not just an isolated incident. Many other cults are murdering people. They're just not as publicized. There are a lot of so-called families like Mason's with one dictatorial leader who controls his group through drugs, pills, sex, LSD and many other ways. These people are a threat to the fabric of society because they commit murder without conscience."*

When Lloyd Kaufman, who worked as production manager and (uncredited) actor on **SWEET SAVIOR**, went on to establish Troma Films a few years later, he picked up the movie for redistribution in 1978 through his new company, giving it the less original, but far more blatant, title of **THE LOVE THRILL MURDERS**, the title it is perhaps best known under, having been issued on VHS under that moniker by Vestron Video. In France, the film was released under the rather odd title of **FRENETIC PARTY** (!). Sadly, while Troma has an extensive and thriving home entertainment division, the company has so far failed to give **SWEET SAVIOR / THE LOVE THRILL MURDERS** any kind of love in terms of a DVD release.

In Ray Danton's **DEATHMASTER** (1972), Robert Quarry, riding on his genre success as the title character in the two *Count Yorga* films—not to mention **DR. PHIBES RISES AGAIN** (1972)—was cast as Khorda, a charismatic vampire who becomes a guru to a group of soul-searching hippies hanging out in Topanga Canyon. Spouting greeting-card philosophy while plucking petals from a flower, the group are easily sucked-in by Khorda, who soon has his followers joining the ranks of the groovy undead, dispatching those who fail to see the light. With some biker action thrown in for good measure, and a pretty terrific finale (with a bowl of leeches providing a handy makeshift weapon), **DEATHMASTER** is a great low-budget horror film from its period. Quarry himself both co-produced and help finance the movie, and the main inspiration behind his character, and the drive and tone of the film itself, is obvious, with Quarry's long hair, goatee and flowing kaftans making him appear every bit the undead Manson. Quarry himself later confirmed where the idea for **DEATHMASTER** came from on the audio commentary track included on the 2002 Retromedia DVD release:

> *"At the time, the Charles Manson thing was kind of heavy, so my idea was to do a film about a vampire who was really kind of based on Charles Manson and the Manson Family."*

When **DEATHMASTER** was released on home video in Australia in 1990 (on the CBS Fox label under their 'Midnight Marquee' line), the back cover exclaimed: *"HELTER SKELETON! IT'S THE CHARLES MANSON OF THE VAMPIRE SET!"*

One of the most notorious exploitation films of the 'Seventies, **SNUFF** (a.k.a. **AMERICAN CANNIBALE**, 1975) began its life in 1971, when the infamous New York-based sexploitation filmmakers Roberta and Michael Findlay decided to try and make their own (highly fictionalized) riff on the Manson killings. Flying down to Argentina, the pair filmed the ultra low-budget **THE SLAUGHTER** (1971). Shot without sound and with local (and low-paid) actors, the resultant film was hated by the Findlays so much that it sat unreleased for five years, before low-budget distributor/producer Allan Shackleton picked it up and used it to cash-in on recent reports and newspaper articles debating the existence of snuff movies (a film in which a person is actually—and deliberately—murdered in front of the camera). Shackleton retitled the film **SNUFF** and brought in a director by the name of Horacio Fredriksson to film a new end sequence to the movie, in which a young woman is seemingly murdered and mutilated by one of the film crew members on the set, all while the cameraman catches the gory act, the film fading out just as the crew member lifts up the woman's entrails in victory, as we hear a crew member exclaim, "Shit, Shit! We ran out of film!" while another asks "Did you get it all?".

Anyone who actually sat through **SNUFF** (even on a grainy bootleg VHS tape, which is how I first saw it) could see that this tacked-on ending was clearly fake, and the work of some pretty enthusiastic but not very accomplished special effects make-up artists. But that didn't stop protest groups jumping all over the film, calling for its banning because they were convinced it depicted actual murder. Though the film didn't initiate the myth of the snuff movie, it was certainly instrumental in propagating it. Shackleton, in true exploitation spirit, helped the controversy along by dreaming up a classic advertising campaign, where the posters, newspaper admats and trailers all contained the memorable tag-line: *"The film that could only be made in South America... where life is CHEAP!"*

Even though it's the film's title and tacked-on footage which **SNUFF** has become most known for, the original **SLAUGHTER** film is a very strange viewing experience in itself, and to me much more interesting and effective than the footage which Shackleton added to it. Opening to a blast of raucous early-'70s guitar rock, the film follows a group of hopped-up hippie chicks who ride bikes, torture and terrorize each other (especially if they discover any of them holding back the "good stuff"—i.e. heroin—from them), and pledge their allegiance to Satan (Enrique Larratelli), the Manson wannabe who orders the girls to stalk and kill a pregnant American actress named Terry London (Mirtha Massa), who has flown in to South America with her scuzzy manager to make a movie. Filled with stock footage and dripping with sleaze, the echo-ey, dubbed voices really add a dream-like ambience to the film—I love how the girls pronounce "Satan" as "*Say-Tarn*".

In mid-2015, the very media-shy Roberta Findlay gave a terrific interview about her career on the Rialto Report podcast, in which she has this to say about **SLAUGHTER/SNUFF**: "It's about the Charles Manson gang. Now

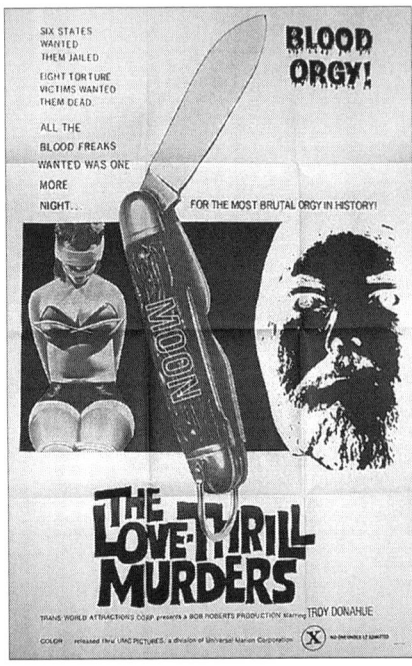

I think of it, it was really morally questionable. So he [Michael Findlay] took that [the Manson story] and duplicated all the events. I shot it. It was all dubbed."

The Modern Mechanical Man

In 2015, public interest in all things Manson remains high, another indication of the lasting impact which the man and the murders had on the psyche. At age 80, Manson himself continues to make news from behind bars—most recently, for his engagement to a 26-year-old "supporter" named Afton Elaine "Star" Burton (the pending wedding was eventually called off after it was revealed that Burton was planning to use Manson's corpse as a travelling tourist attraction after his death!).

Likewise, new filmic interpretations of the Manson killings continue to be examined, both in true crime documentaries as well as cinematic and television docu-dramas. In 2015, the John McNamara-created crime television drama *Aquarius* debuted on the NBC network. Set in 1967 Los Angeles and combining actual events and people with fictional characters and story arcs, the series stars David Duchovny as an LAPD detective who is investigating the disappearance of a teenage girl, who turns out to have hooked up with Manson and the Family. Planned as a hopeful six season series, there was also a short prequel series titled *The Summer Of Love*, which was produced as four short webisodes and looks at some of the events prior to the start of season one, and looks at how Charlie started recruiting his Family and establishing his ability to wield both psychological and physical control. Unfortunately, while the premise of *Aquarius* is an intriguing one, and the show is fairly entertaining and well-acted, it suffers in the casting of the short-haired Gethin Anthony as Manson, who looks more a handsome GQ cover model than a freaked-out psychedelic shaman.

Also recently completed or on the horizon, but unseen by this writer at the present time, are Brandon Slagle's **HOUSE OF MANSON** (2014), which is due for home video release at the end of 2015, while Susanna Lo's **MANSON GIRLS** is currently in pre-production, as is a film adaptation of Ed Saunder's *The Family,* along with several other projects that will no doubt gather steam and attention as the 50th anniversary of the crimes approaches.

The terror of "Helter Skelter", it seems, will linger and reverberate long after Manson and his one-time Family follow their victims into the deep, dark beyond.

—

EXPLOITATION MOVIES FILMED AT SPAHN RANCH:

Famously used as the place where Manson and the Family lived for much of 1968-69, the Spahn Movie Ranch was a 500-acre piece of mountainous and desolate terrain in Los Angeles County. Purchased by dairy farmer George Spahn in 1948, Spahn Ranch was used as the filming location for a multitude of western movies and television shows throughout the 1940s and '50s, as well as the low-budget horror/sci-fi film **THE CREEPING TERROR** (a.k.a. **THE CRAWLING MONSTER**, 1964). Aged 80 and virtually blind, Spahn allowed Manson and his followers to live at the ranch, rent-free, in exchange for helping out around the place with labor, cooking, and, it has been said, female companionship from some of Charlie's angels.

During the Family's stay at Spahn, a number of low-budget exploitation and softcore sex movies were partly filmed at the ranch, including Al Adamson's **THE FEMALE BUNCH** (a.k.a. **A TIME TO RUN**, 1971), the David Friedman-produced roughie **THE RAMRODDER** (a.k.a. **CATTLE RIGGERS**, a.k.a. **SAVAGE PASSION**, 1969), and Herschell Gordon Lewis' nudie western **LINDA AND ABILENE** (1969). Before he was arrested for the murder of Gary Hinman, Manson associate Bobby Beausoleil landed the role of an Indian brave in **THE RAMRODDER**, which also featured an appearance from Family member Catherine Share (Beausoleil also appeared in Kenneth Anger's influential short underground film *Lucifer Rising*, which was shot over several years starting in the mid-1960s, before finally being completed in 1972).

Most of the film sets and buildings at Spahn Ranch were destroyed in 1970, while George Spahn died four years later. The site now forms part of the Santa Susana Pass State Historic Park. When he was interviewed for *Psychotronic Video* magazine #19 (Winter 1994), the late Al Adamson shared some recollections of filming **THE FEMALE BUNCH**:

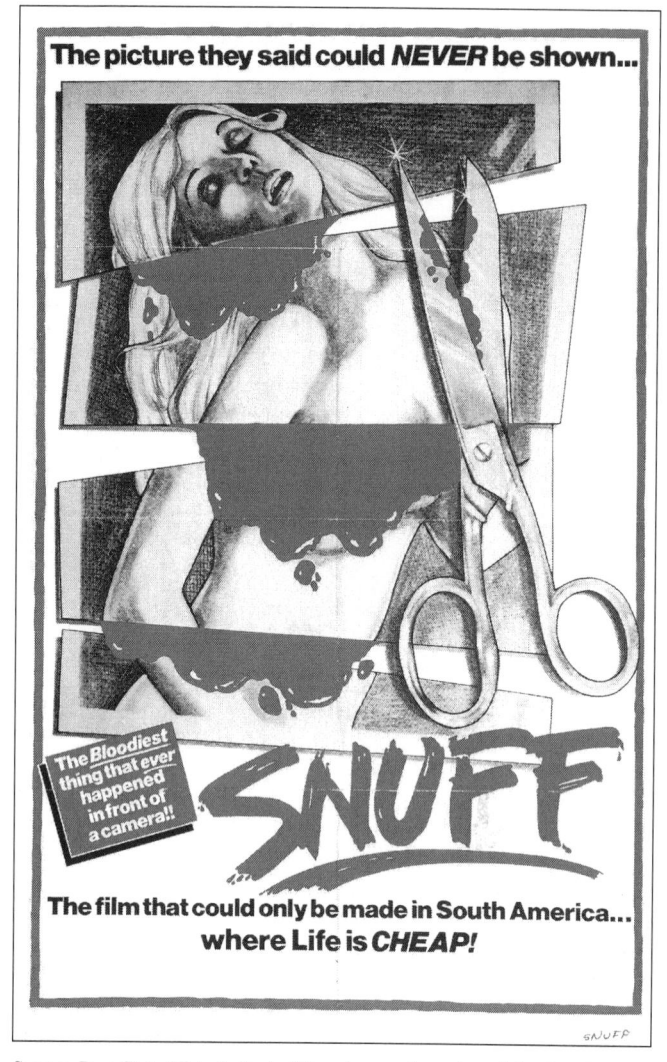

"We were shooting **THE FEMALE BUNCH** *up in Utah in 1969 when they broke the case, when they found out who'd done the murders and one of the members of the Manson gang or at least one of the people that was hanging around the commune had signed on with us to be a grip. But the reason he did it was to get out of town because he knew something was going to come down. When we got back from our shoot there, we saw him on television. He was being interviewed and actually had to be a witness in the trials. So I thought that was interesting."*

FURTHER READING:

Killing For Culture
by David Kerekes & David Slater
(1994, Creation Books, UK)
A groundbreaking and classic study of the mondo movie genre and snuff film mythos. Includes chapters on **SNUFF** and **MANSON FAMILY MOVIES**. A revised and updated edition was published by Creation Books in 1995, while a new and further updated edition is due soon from Headpress.

Charlie's Family: An Illustrated Screenplay to the Film
by Jim Van Bebber
(1998, Creation Books, UK)

Rue Morgue #43
(Jan-Feb 2005, USA)
Cover feature on Jim Van Bebber's **THE MANSON FAMILY**

Weng's Chop

Nightmare USA: The Untold Story of the Exploitation Independents
by Stephen Thrower
(2007, FAB Press, UK)
A huge cement block of a book, Thrower's 528-page volume provides a remarkable look at independent American exploitation filmmakers operating between 1970 and 1985. Includes a chapter on David Durston discussing **I DRINK YOUR BLOOD**.

HELTER SKELTER
1976, USA. D: TOM GRIES
AVAILABLE FROM WARNER

THE HELTER SKELTER MURDERS
1971, USA. D: FRANK HOWARD
AVAILABLE FROM IMAGE

THE CULT (a.k.a. **THE MANSON MASSACRE**)
1971, USA. D: KENTUCKY JONES

MANSON FAMILY MOVIES
1984, USA. D: JOHN AES-NIHIL
AVAILABLE FROM CULT EPICS

THE MANSON FAMILY
2003, USA. D: JIM VAN BEBBER
AVAILABLE FROM SEVERIN

HELTER SKELTER
2004, USA. D: JOHN GRAY
AVAILABLE FROM WARNER

MANSON 40 YEARS LATER
2009, CANADA/USA/UK. D: NEIL RAWLES
AVAILABLE FROM A&E

MANSON (a.k.a. **MANSON AND SQUEAKY FROMME**)
1973, USA. D: ROBERT HENDRICKSON, LAURENCE MERRICK
AVAILABLE FROM EXCLUSIVE FILMS

THE KILLING OF AMERICA
1981, USA/JAPAN. D: SHELDON RENAN, LEONARD SCHRADER

CHARLES MANSON SUPERSTAR
1989, USA. D: NIKOLAS SCHRECK
AVAILABLE FROM SCREEN EDGE

Forgiven: The Charles "Tex" Watson Story
1993, USA. D: MICHAEL GONZALES

Biography: "Charles Manson: Journey Into Evil"
1995, USA. Wr/Pr: ALAN GOLDBERG

Charles Manson: No Sense Makes Sense
1994, DENMARK. D: SVERRE H. KRISTENSEN

I DRINK YOUR BLOOD
1970, USA. D: DAVID E. DURSTON
AVAILABLE FROM GRINDHOUSE RELEASING

SWEET SAVIOR (a.k.a. **THE LOVE THRILL MURDERS**)
1971, USA. D: BOB ROBERTS

DEATHMASTER
1972, USA. D: RAY DANTON
AVAILABLE FROM RETRO MEDIA [OOP]

SNUFF
1975, ARGENTINA/USA/CANADA. D: MICHAEL FINDLAY, HORACIO FREDRIKSSON, SIMON NUCHTERN
AVAILABLE FROM BLUE UNDERGROUND

A BODY-SLAMMING LOOK AT THE HORRIFIC RELATIONSHIP BETWEEN WRESTLING AND HORROR

by Adam Carl Parker-Edmondston

At first glance you would think the above title is slightly strange. What the heck would a bunch of sports entertainers in skin-tight shorts have anything to do with the likes of Jason, Freddy or Michael? On closer inspection however it seems there is quite a lot. Both genres of entertainment have a loyal and diverse fan base, one which is sometimes looked down upon by other less-educated souls. They also involve a certain degree of abandonment. In horror you have to forgive the teenagers on screen for their stupidity in going into the abandoned building (forest, street, etc.) at night without help, because otherwise you would be inclined to kick the telly in. While with wrestling you have to turn a blind eye to the fact that wrestlers make the worst storyline decisions ever and still seem surprised when they are screwed over by the big bad boss. If we look beyond these similarities, though, we find even more parallels, showing that the line drawn between both is quite often crossed and, in some cases, blurred altogether.

Wrestlers appearing in movies is quite commonplace nowadays. Former wrestlers like "Stone Cold" Steve Austin and Dwayne "The Rock" Johnson can be seen in big Hollywood productions, while the wrestling legend that is "Hulk Hogan" (real name: Terry Gene Bollea) is constantly appearing in direct-to-DVD nonsense. Hogan was the biggest ambassador for wrestling up until Dwayne took his mantle, so most people associate him with being one of the first wrestling stars to hit the silver screen. But in fact this relationship goes even further back—to 1955 in fact—where we see a certain Tor Johansson ply his trade. Tor, under the name of "Tor Johnson", started out as a wrestler. By 1934 he had started to appear in uncredited cameo roles, but in 1955 he appeared in the horror movie **BRIDE OF THE MONSTER**, mostly because of his friendship with Ed Wood, the director who gave us some of the worst and most beloved movies in the history. In **BRIDE**, Tor plays Lobo, a mute giant who works for Bela Lugosi's mad scientist-type Dr. Eric Vornoff. Eric is trying to create a race of super-soldiers and also has a pet octopus that decides to go on the rampage. It was the '50s…I guess this kind of thing happened all the time! From here Tor enjoyed a consistent run of bad movie roles, including starring in another Ed Wood movie in 1959 called **PLAN 9 FROM OUTER SPACE** (a.k.a. **GRAVE ROBBERS FROM OUTER SPACE**), a now-cult classic which had Tor playing Inspector Dan Clay, who is soon dispatched by a zombie and a vampire and brought back to life himself as one of the undead. The aliens involved have decided the best way to stop humanity from creating a world-destroying doomsday bomb is to bring the dead back to life. It is hard to top this performance, but Tor certainly had a go with roles in **THE UNEARTHLY** (1957) and **NIGHT OF THE GHOULS** (1959), where he reprised his character of Lobo. His final horror film was **THE BEAST OF YUCCA FLATS** (1961), which had Tor playing a Soviet scientist who defects, gets mutated by radiation, and goes on a rampage. For connoisseurs of bad movies, a double-bill of **PLAN 9 FROM OUTER SPACE** and **THE BEAST OF YUCCA FLATS** is a winner. An interesting side note to this

Relaxing in the company canteen: Tor Johnson, flanked by Lon Chaney Jr. **(left)** and Bela Lugosi **(right)** during **THE BLACK SLEEP**

Rowdy Roddy Piper has come to chew bubblegum and kick ass in **THEY LIVE**

is that in Tim Burton's 1994 homage to director Ed Wood (called, funnily enough, **ED WOOD**), Tor Johnson is played by former WWE (World Wrestling Entertainment) star George "The Animal" Steele.

Each country tends to favor a certain wrestling style. For example, in the U.K the emphasis is on technical moves, rather than the more powerhouse approach taken by a lot of the wrestling federations in the states. In Mexico they use a style called *lucha libre*. Here the wrestlers are famously known for their masked wrestling attire, which hides their true identity and is very rarely removed during the wrestler's career. *lucha libre* is a very athletic style and involves numerous jumps, acrobatics and aerial assaults. In the US the most famous wrestler using this style is the WWE Rey Mysterio Jr., but before he started out you had guys like "El Santo" (Rodolfo Guzman) and "Blue Devil" (Alejandro Munoz Moreno) entertaining the Mexican wrestling masses. It would not be too long before they entertained the world. They starred in a series of movies called *luchador* films. Most of the *luchador* movies came out during the '60s and '70s and mixed the psychedelic mindset of the time with their own brand of Mexican flavor. It is a genre of film that would require an entire article to do it justice. El Santo himself had over 40 features to his name, while Blue Devil was just lagging behind with 25. It is a genre of film I wish I was better versed in, and with its focus on vampires, witches and even Frankenstein's daughter as well as some wrestling maneuvers thrown in for good measure, it will certainly appeal to a lot of film fans out there, too. This carefree and crazy atmosphere would soon disappear when wrestlers returned to movies in the '80s and '90s. They would not be as playful as their Mexican counterparts.

Wrestlers had slowly started to appear in more action-oriented movies in this time. Professor Toru Tanaka's face will be recognizable to film fans having starred in the Chuck Norris/Christopher Lee flick **AN EYE FOR AN EYE** (1981), as well as fighting Arnie in **THE RUNNING MAN** (1987). But he also had a part to play in the 1991 movie **ALLIGATOR II: THE MUTATION**. "The Madman from the Sudan, Abdullah the Butcher" (Lawrence Robert Shreve), had a role in the 1982 kung fu action flick **ROARING FIRE** (*Hoero tekken*). Jesse "The Body" Ventura, another '80s wrestler popped up in sci-fi classics (or not so classic) like **ABRAXAS, GUARDIAN OF THE UNIVERSE** (1990), **PREDATOR** (1987) and **DEMOLITION MAN** (1993); the huge powerhouse "Vader" (Leon Allen White) used his menacing posture to great effect in the 1995 **FIST OF THE NORTH STAR** live-action adaption; and who could forget "André the Giant's" (André René Roussimoff) appearance in the fantasy action movie **THE PRINCESS BRIDE** in 1987? But it was Hulk Hogan who really paved the way for wrestlers to cross over into movies. One such crossover was Hogan's storyline nemesis in the WWE at the time, "Rowdy" Roddy Piper. He starred in two sci-fi/action/horror mashups (as well as many, many action parts in his filmic career). **THEY LIVE** (1988) is his most famous movie, with Roddy finding a pair of sunglasses that reveal to him aliens that have infiltrated our society without us knowing about them.

But he also made a movie called **HELL COMES TO FROGTOWN** (1988), a ridiculously fun schlockfest of a movie which has Piper playing the lead role of Hell, the only fertile man in a post-apocalyptic future. If the prospect of Rowdy fighting mutant frogmen and rescuing fertile women does not win you over, then what about if I tell you he has to do it all while having a bomb strapped to his nether regions? The viewer's enjoyment of the film will all depend on how much cinematic cheese you can tolerate. Personally, I loved it!

Finally, we get to the '90s and '00s, where, thankfully, we see a little more horror action coming our way. The WWE is one of the biggest wrestling federations on the planet, and seeing the potential of growth for their industry and expanding into other avenues of business, they made their first wrestling-based film in 1989. Staring Hulk Hogan, **NO HOLDS BARRED** is considered one of the worst films about wrestling ever made (again, *I* loved it!). This did not deter them, and years later they decided to go even further and make their own production company. Each of their films would have the biggest WWE star at the time headlining it, sometimes with mixed results. To be fair, "mixed results" is being kind, as most of their output is terrible. But they do span the genres, even making a Scooby Doo wrestling animated feature last year! They have also created two horror movies. **SEE NO EVIL** (2006) has the big red machine known as "Kane" (wrestler Glenn Jacobs) taking on the role of a bonkers slasher, Jacob Goodnight, in a kind of *Friday The 13th/The Hills Have Eyes* hybrid. You know the drill: stupid teenagers break into a deserted hotel and get offed one-by-one by the psycho who lives there. It is nothing incredibly special, but does have its moments, especially as Kane's character collects eyeballs. The sequel arrived in 2014 and was even more generic, and not as much fun. They somehow managed to make the cast members come off as even more annoying than the first film. This time the action is set inside the morgue and has Jacob coming back to life, having flashbacks of his mother treating him bad and hacking up some teens along the way. They have also finished work on a reboot of the Warwick Davis series *Leprechaun*. Called **LEPRECHAUN: ORIGINS** (2014), it stars the vertically challenged wrestler Dylan Postl, also known as "Hornswoggle". It goes for a more serious tone than the majority of the films in the franchise (aside from the first), but actually loses some of its entertainment value because of that choice.

Other notable entries (in no particular order) include: Bill Goldberg takes he role of a ticked off Santa in **SANTA'S SLAY** (2005)—a pure horror slapstick piece, it has Saint Nick actually being a defeated demon, who, after losing a bet with an angel, is forced to be a jolly old soul for 1,000 years. When the deal expires, Santa goes bonkers and goes on a killing spree using various Christmas-related items along the way. If you hate Christmas but love comedy, this could be the perfect film for you. **GALLOWWALKERS** (2012) is a mind-numbingly dull movie which has Wesley Snipes in a cowboy environment killing off intelligent zombies. This movie has a small cameo by "Diamond" Dallas Page. This is not his first cameo, having performed in movies like **THE DEVIL'S REJECTS** (2005), **DRIFTWOOD** (2006) and **HOOD**

OF HORROR (2006). Al Snow turns up as a hitman who has to fight his way through, among other things, zombies, to get to his son's birthday party in OVERTIME (2011). "Triple H" (Hunter Hurst Helmsley) plays a vampire in the below-average BLADE: TRINITY (2004) movie, which also has the added bonus of having one of the worst Count Draculas seen on-screen. Tyler Maine also had the chance to let horror fans down when he starred in Rob Zombie's unnecessary remake of HALLOWEEN (2007), while in DOOM (2005) we see Dwayne Johnson loss his cool while fighting mutated monsters in this video game conversion, and "Tommy Dreamer" (Thomas James Laughlin) fights zombies in ARMY OF THE DAMNED (2013). Maybe he should have teamed up with Al Snow there? Former WWE wrestler "Brodus Clay" (George Murdoch) had a part in NO ONE LIVES (2012). By far the worst of the bunch has to be RIVER OF DARKNESS (2011) which has the combined talents of Kurt Angle, Kevin Nash and "Psycho Sid" (Sidney Raymond Eudy) all vying for the role of worst professional wrestling actor. The film is incredibly painful to watch and has Angle playing a small-time sheriff investigating some brutal murders which seem to have been committed by people that are already dead. I have watched this twice now and although I remember the terrible acting, I can remember little else. I think that my brain is trying to protect me from the trauma of it all. Angle has a small cameo part in SHARKNADO 2: THE SECOND ONE (2014), but heck so did pretty much everyone else!

Films that focus just on wrestling and horror are a lot harder to find. THE CALAMARI WRESTLER (2004) sounds like it might have promise, but alas, it is just a *Rocky* movie if Rocky was a giant squid. It is fantastic fun but not horror. Aside from the above-mentioned '60s Luchadore movies (WRESTLING WOMEN VS. THE AZTEC MUMMY [*Las luchadoras contra la momia*, 1964] is a great example) and ARENA (1989), which plays out again like a *Rocky* movie only this time in space, having the only human combatant in an outer space fighting tournament, there was nothing till the '00s. WRESTLEMANIAC (a.k.a. EL MASCARADO MASSACRE, 2006), however, does exactly what it says on the tin and has a crazed Mexican wrestler killing of a bunch of porn star filmmakers who were daft enough to cross his path. PRO WRESTLERS VS ZOMBIES (2014) has a wrestler dying in the ring and his brother using necromancy to bring the dead back to life to avenge his death. It has a boat-load of wrestling talent involved, including "The Franchise" Shane Douglas, "Rowdy" Roddy Piper, Matt Hardy, Kurt Angle and "Hacksaw" Jim Duggan. But the film that sums up both genres superbly has to be MONSTER BRAWL (2011), which is just that: monsters smacking seven bells out of each other. With Kevin Nash appearing as a zombie soldier, commentators calling the monster smashing action and wrestling manager "The Mouth of the South" Jimmy Hart also in attendance, it adds up to a special little movie. Utterly daft, but if you like monsters and wrestling, there really is no reason not to watch this film.

So, the relationship between the two forms of entertainment in the movies seems clear. But what about the in ring performers themselves? How has the wrestling industry been influenced by the horror genre itself? Well, in some cases quite discreetly, in others blatantly copied! It all started with the release of Pay-Per-View events, where people paid their cable networks so they could get the exclusive event. Obviously, these needed to be a bit more Hollywood to get people interested an in the WWEs *Wrestlemania* 2; horror host Elvira made an appearance, while on the smaller screen on WCW *Nitro*, Scott Steiner came

Superstar Dwayne "The Rock" Johnson in **DOOM**

face-to-face with the killer doll Chucky from the *Child's Play* movies. WCW in fact devoted an entire yearly PPV event to the spookiest month of the year: October. Called *Halloween Havoc*, it used Halloween-styled ring setups, but one year it had a truly horrific (in more ways than one) match. The event had a giant cage around the ring with an electric chair in the center. The only way to win the match was to strap someone in said chair and pull the switch, essentially electrocuting them. This is where the suspension of disbelief comes in! This is also the company that had Hulk Hogan wrestle a mummy (oddly called a Yeti), and Robocop rescuing "Sting" from a cage, so I suppose anything goes. In an odd turn of events, this year in his match against Triple H at *Wrestlemania* 31, Sting got to see the other side of a robotic encounter when Hunter Hurst Helmsley come out in a modified Terminator-style costume carrying the remains of numerous other Terminators, while a group of other Terminators all appear in the background. Moving away from the big federations, we have the independent companies like The Florida Supercon which hosts regular wrestling events with fandom characters wrestling established pro wrestling talent. In 2014 they even had the Toxic Avenger turn up for a match, brought to the ring by his creator, Lloyd Kaufman. Then we have The Horror Wrestling Federation, which has actual wrestlers dressing as horror characters (like Michael Myers and Jason Voorhees) and has them battling it out. This would be slightly more shocking if it had not already been done before.

Left: Bill Goldberg in **SANTA'S SLAY**–"Who's Next?!" **Right:** "Hacksaw" Jim Duggan enjoys a quick snack in **PRO WRESTLERS VS ZOMBIES**

Weng's Chop 99

In Japan, wrestling is a beloved entity which is treated with a great deal of respect. So it is surprising to find some horrendous breaches of copyright law with some of their wrestlers' gimmicks. Doug Gilbert wrestled under the name "Nightmare Freddy" and was a blatant copy of Freddy from **A NIGHTMARE ON ELM STREET** (1984). He was not alone, either. Eddie Gilbert (brother to Doug) took up his own horror-based gimmick of "The Boogeyman", who looked very similar to a certain Michael Myers from **HALLOWEEN** (1978). Michael Kirchner decided Leatherface was a good idea for a wrestling gimmick, as did Rick Patterson, leading to what must have been a truly epic match of Leatherface vs. Leatherface! Japan was not the only country guilty of this, either. Over in Mexico you had "El Monstruo", which was based on Frankenstein's monster, in Canada we had "Jason the Terrible", who looked like an all-white Jason Voorhees. There were even wrestlers who dressed up as the Wolfman, and, of all things, The Crypt Keeper, but alas, I could find little information on who they were or where they wrestled.

So where does this leave us? Well, it leaves us with a whole heap of wrestlers inspired by the horror genre in general. Voodoo was a popular gimmick at one point, with the WWE having not one, but *three* magical-based beings. "Papa Shango" (Charles Wright) looked like Baron Samedi from **LIVE AND LET DIE** (1973), with a career highlight being when he made the Ultimate Warrior throw up! Then we have "Damian Demento" (Phillip Thies), who came from "The Outer Reaches of Your Mind" but did little else, and finally we have "The Boogeyman" (not related to Eddie Gilbert's character, but instead played by Martin Wright) who looked like a bulked-up tribal Darth Maul, sung the nursery rhyme from **A NIGHTMARE ON ELM STREET**, had a big clock and ate worms. Speaking of tribal, the '80s gave us "Kamala" (James Harris), a native tribal warrior who was believed to be a cannibal. Then we have numerous wrestlers who focused on the dark side of life. "The Undertaker" (Mark Calaway) and his brother Kane (mentioned above) wreaked havoc in the WWE in the '90s to the present day. With their manager Paul Bearer in tow, The Undertaker was originally an unstoppable monster who got his power from an urn; he soon turned into a demonic cult figure who amassed a Ministry of Darkness which among its members had a vampire, "Gangrel" (David Heath). He was not the only vampire-style character, as "Kevin Thorn" (Kevin Matthew Fertig) also played a character that was very similar. If you thought the wrestling mummy was a step to far, how about "The Giant Gonzales" (Jorge Gonzalez), who appeared in the '90s and was meant to be a wild, yeti-based monster?!

Other wrestling companies have jumped on the supernatural bandwagon. The rappers Insane Clown Posse set up their own wrestling federation called Juggalo Championship Wrestling. In it their champion was none other than a zombie who needed constant help getting in the ring, but somehow managed to keep his belt. "The Sinister Minister" (James Mitchell) was an ECW (Extreme Championship Wrestling) manager modelled on Robert De Nero's Louis Cyphre in *Angel Heart*, while World Championship Wrestling franchised one of the band Kiss characters and created "The Demon" (Dale Torborg), who was basically Gene Simmons as a wrestler, but he had some supernatural overtones.

People who are slightly twisted seem to turn up a lot in wrestling. "Mankind" (Mick Foley) was a disturbed madman who wore a Hannibal Lector-style mask (which also inspired another insane giant, the wrestler "Abyss"), who was partial to taking massive bumps off of steel cages and getting hit constantly with chairs. We have "Waylon Mercy" (Dan Spivey) who played a **CAPE FEAR** (1991)-styled villain, while "The Wyatt Family" mixed redneck craziness with a dash of **THE EXORCIST** (1973). "Bray Wyatt", especially is slightly freaky. He distorts his body in the ring, doing a walk last seen in films like **THE LAST EXORCISM** (2010) or in the "spider-walk" stair scene in **THE EXORCIST**. Sting over in WCW and TNA has used not only Eric Draven from *The Crow* as a character design; he has also modelled himself on a crazy man with face paint very similar to the Batman villain, the Joker. Kamala would have had a pal in "The Mad Man from the Sudan, Abdulla the Butcher" (Lawrence Robert "Larry" Shreve). He was an imposing figure and with his massively scarred forehead looked like he had stepped right out of a foreign version of **THE HILLS HAVE EYES** (1977).

Now, there are bound to be wrestlers I have missed off this list, but hopefully it will give you an idea of how deeply rooted the horror genre is within professional wrestling. With wrestlers like The Wyatt Family taking the lead from the pioneers before them, it makes this an interesting time to be a fan of both wrestling and horror. Who knows what the future will bring? Knowing professional wrestling as I do it will no doubt be bonkers, but a whole lot of fun!

HORROR ON THE AIRWAVES: DOOMED DISC JOCKEYS

by Matthew St. Cyr

I've been an EMT for almost a decade now, and I've seen some seriously messed-up stuff. You think you've seen some sick stuff in horror movies? You'd be shocked by just how truly grisly real life can be. I've seen horribly decayed dead bodies that have sat rotting for weeks and I've seen freshly mangled bodies that were in horrific traffic accidents. Sure, it's shocking at first, and some of the things I've seen will stay with me for the rest of my life, however, some of the most chilling calls I've been involved with have been on the other side of the radio.

See, I've been off the road for awhile and now work the graveyard shift as a communications specialist for a major metropolitan hospital. I take 911 calls, dispatch ambulances as well as an air medical helicopter. Now that I'm "behind the scenes", so to speak, I am involved in far more of the emergencies that occur in the city. Instead of handling one call at a time, I'm handing multiple. Instead of seeing everything first hand, I sit in a (usually) darkened room and listen and interact with the paramedics through radio. I'm here to tell you that some of the most horrifying things I've encountered have been while listening to and interacting with an ambulance response as it plays out on the radio and sometimes via phone.

On the flipside of things, when the crews are out in a sticky situation, my voice is their reassurance that I'm there watching out for them. When a crew goes up in a helicopter in the middle of the night, the only contact they have in the great lonely expanse of darkness is my voice. It reassures them that that I am there and tracking them, and that makes them feel a bit safer knowing that if (God forbid) something happens, I am there and know exactly where they are and what's going on. It's a relationship based completely on trust and at times it's terrifying when for any various reason communications fail and you're left in the dark, hoping and praying that those who count on you are okay.

So what does this have to do with horror films? Well, I got thinking about my job and my role on the radio. There are some nights that a chill runs down my spine when something horrifying happens. It got me thinking about other people who work with or on radios. It just so happens that a few nights later I was listening to *Coast to Coast AM* with George Noory. For those of you who are not in the know, *Coast to Coast AM* is a late-night talk show that deals with (mostly) the paranormal, conspiracy theories and UFO-related stuff.

I've been listening to it since back in the day when Art Bell was the host and I started to think about a call that Art took from a caller who claimed that he was a former employee at Area 51. The caller was frantic and said that "THEY" were going to triangulate on his position and that the government was working with extraterrestrials to exterminate the bulk of the populace so that the rest of us would be easier to control…then the radio transmission was mysteriously cut. After about 20 seconds of brutal silence, everything came back online. Art was at a loss to explain what happened. The alleged Area 51 employee was gone. A chill ran through me that I have rarely experienced.

This got me thinking about horror movies that deal with radio DJs. The idea of listening to something horrific happening as it happens live is something that is not explored very often in horror, and even then when it is, is not always explored very well. I have compiled here a list of horror films (with the addition of a few anthology horror television show episodes) that deal with exactly that premise. Some are absolutely chilling and serious in their exploration of the subject, while others are strictly tongue-in-cheek. I think it's going to be an interesting excursion into a sub-subgenre that I'd like to see more of in the future. Let's get listening!

Swedish poster for **WHO DONE IT?**

The first film I'm dialing up is a bit of an exception to the rule, but I feel it's also important because it's one of the earliest examples of foul deeds being aired on a radio broadcast. To make it an even more bizarre entry in this list: It's a comedy! That's right, first up is **WHO DONE IT?** (1942), starring comedy duo extraordinaire, Abbott and Costello. Bud and Lou star as a pair of friends who work as soda jerks at the food counter of a radio station…but their true ambition in life is to be writers for the radio mystery show *Murder* *at Midnight*. On the night that they attend a live broadcast of the show, the station's manager is mysteriously electrocuted. Bud and Lou decide that they are going to impersonate detectives to get to the bottom of the mystery, apprehend the murderer and get their dream jobs writing for the show. Naturally, being an A&C vehicle, the boys bumble their way through the investigation while much slapstick and many shenanigans ensue.

It's totally tongue-in-cheek, but the murder of the station manager is handled with a sinister touch; the show is being broadcast in front of a live audience and the studio is dimly lit with gothic shadows for theatrical effect. When the station manager goes to make an announcement before the show starts, he is electrocuted by his microphone. The live audience is quickly herded out the doors as the narrator announces to the listening public that the show is being held up by circumstances out of their control and they would be entertained by alternate programming. As I said before, this entry does not exactly fit in with the rest of the films, but I think it's still important to view it for its historical context. While this may not be the first film to depict a murder during a live radio broadcast, it's certainly one of the most memorable, and for that reason I have decided to include it on the list. From here on out we're going to be in radio DJ territory.

The first film that significantly dealt with a DJ being terrorized is a classic that doesn't get enough attention. **PLAY MISTY FOR ME** (1971) is Clint Eastwood's directorial debut and is a taut little thriller. Eastwood also stars as Dave Garver, a radio DJ who has a nightly jazz radio show. Sometimes he'll recant a bit of poetry during his program, as well. One night he encounters a woman at his favorite bar named Evelyn Draper (Jessica Walter). After taking her home, she admits that she heard him mention the bar during his show and sought him out. It turns out she is a recurring caller that constantly requests that Dave play the old jazz standard *Misty* for her.

Dave begins a casual sexual relationship with Evelyn, but before long she beings to show her true colors…showing up at his home and his work uninvited and generally stalking him day and night. She demands more and more of his attention, demanding that he spend every waking minute with her. After having enough of *that* craziness, Dave tries to cut the relationship off, which leads to Evelyn attempting suicide by slashing her wrists at his house. After recovering from her wounds, she begins to pursue him once again, only to be rejected again. This is all it takes for Evelyn to go off the deep end, breaking into his house while he's not home and stabbing his housekeeper with a knife. Finally she is committed to a mental hospital, giving Dave some respite from her attacks. While Evelyn is away, Dave rekindles his relationship with an old girlfriend and all is well and good for a few months until one night Evelyn calls Dave at the radio station requesting him to play *Misty*…and this is where stuff starts getting creepy…she quotes a line from Edgar Allen Poe's "Annabel Lee": *"Because this maiden she lived with no other thought than to love and be loved by you."* The poem factors into the rest of the film, but I am certainly not going to spoil the ending here. While the film doesn't exclusively take place at the radio station, I think that its creepiest moments do. By the time Evelyn calls and recites the poem, we know how mentally unhinged she is, and there's something about a well-read psychopath that is truly unnerving.

Radio horror could also be found on the small screen in 1971 on *Night Gallery* (1969-1973). In a segment titled "The Flip Side of Satan", which aired September 29, 1971 (Season 2, Episode 3), Arte Johnson plays J.J. Wilson, a DJ with a career in a downward spiral. After a fifteen-year stint in New York City, J.J. has been banished to tiny radio station in a small podunk town on the other side of the country. When he arrives, he is dismayed to find that the station is less than optimal and calls his agent, Sid to complain. J.J. may have been having an affair with Sid's wife, who has since committed suicide, causing J.J. to suspect that Sid may have sent him off to the middle of nowhere as punishment.

There are instructions for J.J. to play the preprogrammed records provided and that he is not allowed to deviate at anytime from the programming. The records have white labels with nothing more than a number on each one (1, 2, 3, etc.). When he plays record 1, it plays some creepy, gothic sounding organ music. Record number 2 isn't much better and contains some rather sinister sounding electronic "music". Record #3 contains satanic incantations and we (as well as J.J.) realize that he is not meant to ever leave the station.

"The Flip Side of Satan" is a bit cheesy and campy, but it also has an underlying creep factor. Arte Johnson carries the entire short for the approximately 13-minute run time. There are absolutely no other actors, which really helps to sell the desolate loneliness and isolation. Even when J.J. is on the phone, we never hear the person on the other end. Even the voice reciting the satanic incantations on the record is Johnson's. It's not utterly terrifying, but it absolutely deserves a look.

John Carpenter gave us an interesting take on the sub-subgenre in 1980 with his leprous zombie/ghost pirate masterpiece, **THE FOG** (1980). Adrienne Barbeau plays late-night DJ Stevie Wayne, who broadcasts on KAB from on top of a lighthouse in Antonio Bay, CA. This film just oozes creepiness and there is a palpable sense of dread that permeates throughout. What I find interesting about this particular film (I don't think there's any reason to bring up the '05 remake) is that it changes the dynamic of Stevie's situation throughout the film. As I'm sure you're aware, the film is about the ghosts of a bunch of lepers who were betrayed by the founders of Antonio Bay…and the gold they were carrying used to found the town.

When the film begins, she plays more of a guardian role, warning a trawler named *The Seagrass* about the mysterious fog bank that appears to be moving against the wind. Unfortunately things don't work out so well for the lads about *The Seagrass*. Stevie's son, Andy gives her a piece of driftwood that he found. The word *Dane* is scrawled on the driftwood—which is of course a piece of the *Elizabeth Dane*, the ship that carried the doomed lepers. Stevie takes it with her to the radio station and it causes a tape player to mysteriously malfunction as a creepy voice swears to wreak vengeance. The words "*Six Must Die*" appears on the piece of wood before everything (for a moment, anyway) returns to normal.

That night, the town's centennial celebration is to take place, which is naturally when the ghosts in the fog will launch their final assault. Dan O'Bannon (named for the now-late writer/director) is a meteorologist that provides Stevie with her weather updates. He calls the station to let her know that there is another fog bank approaching. As they're talking, the fog gathers outside the weather station and Stevie is forced to listen in horror as he is slaughtered by

"This is Stevie Wayne, on top of the world tonight and I'll be here right up until about one o'clock"

the ghosts, and her role begins to shift from guardian to victim, though she will continue to fill dual roles.

As the fog encroaches on the town, it cuts off the phone lines and electricity. Stevie is able to continue broadcasting thanks to a back-up generator that she has. She sends out a plea to anyone listening to check on her son, who is home with a babysitter. Luckily (but unknown to her), the film's main protagonist, Nick Castle (played by the inimitable Tom Atkins), arrives just in time to save little Andy from becoming ghost fodder. It's hard to imagine the feeling of isolation, hopelessness and terror that Stevie must feel as she sits in the lighthouse, watching the deadly fog spread across her town and threaten those that she loves. Her only viable action is to continue broadcasting and pray that someone is listening to her.

As she continues to broadcast she warns anyone in town to avoid the fog at all costs and continues to send out warnings until she is besieged by the vengeful ghosts as the fog envelopes the lighthouse. Stevie's harrowing experiences on that night as she broadcasts alone from high atop her lighthouse perch run through a wide spectrum, as does her role as the film progresses. It is interesting to note that even though she becomes a victim herself as the fog envelopes the town, she always maintains the role of a sentinel, trying to warn and protect the people of Antonio Bay from a horrific doom.

Going back to the small screen and jumping forward five years, we come to an interesting episode of *Tales From The Darkside* titled "The Devil's Advocate". Airing on November 10, 1985, the George A. Romero-penned 7th episode of season 2 finds a late-night talk/call-in radio host (played by Jerry Stiller!) who calls himself Mandrake, The Devil's Advocate. Mandrake is an angry, bitter husk of a man who blames all of the world's problems on society at large.

Whether it's verbally attacking a woman whose husband just lost his job or belittling a night watchman for his choice of profession, Mandrake manages to twist everything to fit his own cynical and angry agenda. As various people call in to be verbally abused by him, things start to get strange as people begin to call in from different time periods. As the evening progresses and Mandrake because more and more angry and frustrated with the callers ("I GIVE UP!" he constantly yells), he begins to physically change into a demon, until his misguided rage turns him quite literally into The Devil's Advocate!

I suppose I could be stretching things a bit to include this episode here. It's not as though Mandrake or his listeners know that anything is askew until the final twist at the end of the story. However, I think it still merits a look and it still is an example of the paranormal and the horrific befalling DJs and radio personalities. Not only that, but Jerry Stiller carries the entire episode almost completely by himself. The only other person to appear on screen is his engineer,

and he is only relegated to a couple of lines at the beginning of the episode, at that. The rest of the time, it's strictly Stiller conversing with faceless voices.

A year later, the silver screen unleashed **THE TEXAS CHAINSAW MASSACRE 2** (1986) on the world, twelve years after the original cult classic, and it has been criticized for being such a departure from the original film. The sequel opens with a couple of yuppie morons headed out for a weekend of debauchery in Dallas. As they drive along a long and lonely Texas highway, they decide to prank-call DJ "Stretch" Brock (Caroline Williams) at W-OKLA. The two act like complete buffoons while harassing Stretch and essentially holding the phone line hostage by refusing to hang up.

THE TEXAS CHAINSAW MASSACRE 2: Chop Top wants to request a song (**top**), but Stretch (**bottom**) has some reservations about his tastes...

Weng's Chop 103

While still live on the air, the two encounter a mysterious pickup truck on the road. It begins to drive up alongside them, and Leatherface (Bill Johnson) appears from the bed of the truck wielding his trusty chainsaw. The boys try to flee, but end up meeting the business end of the saw, while Stretch is left to listen in horror. This would be enough to mess up anyone but good, however Stretch has the sense to make a recording of the attack on a cassette tape. After reading a small newspaper article about Lieutenant "Lefty" Enright (uncle of Sally and Franklin Hardesty from the first film) and his quest to bring the clan of killers to justice, she tracks him down and has him listen to her recording.

Lefty (Dennis Hopper) asks her to play the recording of the attack on the air so that local officials will start to take the matter more seriously. That night, Stretch plays the recording on her show, the screams and buzz of the chainsaw filling the airwaves with shock and horror. Leatherface and his brother Chop Top (Bill Moseley) appear at the radio station to silence her. She barricades herself in a storage closet until Leatherface makes short work of the wall with his trusty saw. Thanks to some fast talking, Stretch is able to able to convince the simpleminded slasher to leave her be. The rest of the film takes place outside the radio station and thus will not be discussed.

Again we get a couple of different terror situations for our DJ hero. The opening scene in which the two yuppies are massacred live on the air is still quite effective and chilling. As the audience, we are able to witness the actual event as it happens, but one can only imagine the shock and terror of Stretch as she sits helplessly by, not entirely certain of what she is listening to…and most likely not understanding the full magnitude of what transpired until the following day when reading it in the paper or seeing it on the news. The radio station assault by Chop Top and Leatherface is equally unnerving. Stretch first encounters Chop Top in the station's lobby as she's getting ready to leave. He is sitting in the dark and begins requesting songs for her to play as he burns the end of a wire hanger and scratches his metal plated scalp with it. Stretch attempts to get rid of him, and that's when Leatherface appears, forcing her to barricade herself inside a storage closet in the station.

In addition to that, there is the fact that Stretch plays the recorded bloodbath on the air. It's not shown in the film, but I can't help but imagine the people who happened to be listening in at that point. I could easily see a young couple driving home from their date when suddenly aurally accosted by the sinister sounds. Or perhaps the patrons of an all-night diner, sitting around eating pastrami sandwiches and drinking coffee, nearly choking on their fries when the soothing music is suddenly replaced with the horrific recording. You get the idea.

Changing things up a little bit, let's take a look at **PSYCHO IV: THE BEGINNING** (1990), which serves as a sequel and a prequel! Here we find Norman Bates (Anthony Perkins) calling in to a talk radio show to discuss his mother. The radio show's subject is matricide and Norman (having been released from the mental institution and deemed "rehabilitated") feels that discussing his mother on the show may give him closure. He is also now married to a nurse and expecting a baby, and he is afraid that his child will take after him.

When Norman calls the show he uses the alias "Ed". However one of his former psychiatrists, Dr. Richmond (Warren Frost) is a guest on the show and recognizes that "Ed" is in fact Norman. I've included this film in the list because while host Fran Ambrose (CCH Pounder) and Dr. Richmond are in no danger while they are on the air, there is an air of creepiness as Norman discusses his childhood and states that he is afraid that he will kill again…possibly his wife to prevent to birth of his child (or as he puts it, "a monster").

Again, this one works (for me, at least) on a more expanded level. You must put yourself in the shoes of Fran and understand the unease she must feel when she realizes who she is speaking with…especially as Norman becomes more and more upset. Also, much like we did with **THE TEXAS CHAINSAW MASSACRE 2**, just try to imagine the audience listening in. Perhaps a night watchman sitting alone in his office, listening to a deranged man's confessional. After listening to some of his horrific deeds, I'm sure that watchman's next rounds are going to be extra intense. Or what if a friend of Norman's wife was listening and recognized his voice. Imagine the horror they felt when they realized who their friend was married to! Sure it may be a bit of a stretch, but it's still worth a look. Plus it's a surprisingly good considering it's the third sequel in the series!

I'm going to jump one final time to the realm of television to discuss an episode of *Monsters* titled "A Face for Radio" (season 3, episode 19), which is an interesting take on the subject. Morton Downey Jr. plays "shock jock" Ray Bright on a late-night talk radio show. His character is not all that dissimilar from Jerry Stiller's Mandrake character in *Tales from the Darkside*. Ray hosts a paranormal talk show and spends most of his time ridiculing his guests.

Ray's first guest is a psychic who tries to warn him that he is in grave danger; she says that she sees him in a dark room unable to escape. Of course, he scoffs at this and sends her packing. His next guest is a woman named Amanda (Laura Branigan), who claims that she has captured a small creature (after being abducted by aliens) and has it in a box that she's brought with her. Because she's young and sexy, naturally Ray is all ears and lays on the greasy, sleazy charm…though he still doesn't believe her.

Turns out the creature feeds on hate and anger, which Ray (much like Mandrake in *Darkside*) has in spades. Even when Amanda reveals the strange critter to him, he still dismisses it, claiming that his niece could make a better looking "puppet" and accusing Amanda of being a ventriloquist. The critter begs Ray to believe and to "save himself" claiming it's not too late.

Without spoiling the episode, let's just say that it *is* too late for Ray (you didn't think otherwise, did you?).

As I mentioned before, this episode is a spiritual sibling to "The Devil's Advocate". Both revolve around hate- and rage-filled "shock jocks" who thrive on other people's misery. Both take place exclusively inside radio studios, and in both stories these despicable men get their comeuppance. Neither of these is particularly frightening, but they both have a bit of a creepy vibe. I can't help but imagine something like this happening on an episode of *Coast to Coast AM* in some alternate universe.

Staying with the "aliens in the studio" theme, let's take a look at the silliest of the entries in the list: **BAD CHANNELS** (1992). Written by Charles Band and released by Full Moon Entertainment, you *know* that stuff's gonna get funky with this one! The film revolves around Super Station 66…a radio station that is about to switch formats from Polka to Rock 'n' Roll. Manning the helm for the switch is former morning radio host Dangerous Dan O'Dare (Paul Hipp), who was suspended for six months and then reassigned from his cushy morning radio position after taking the traffic reporter's wife to Pleasure Town live on the air.

Covering the event is reporter Lisa Cummings (MTV's Martha Quinn!), who dislikes Dan and his publicity gimmick—he's chained himself to the console with a polka record on repeat and cannot change it until someone calls in and guesses the right combination on the padlock holding his chains...the winner also scoring a shiny new car. News anchorman Flip Humble (Roumel Reaux) gives it a shot while on air and suspiciously gets the combination right. Lisa smells a fixed contest and bails.

After leaving the studio in a huff, Lisa spots a UFO landing nearby and goes off to investigate. An alien—with a head that looks like a pile of crap with a porthole—which apparently arrived in said UFO, takes over the radio station, trapping Dan and station engineer Corky (Michael Huddleson) inside. From here on out, it's a wacky kind of take on Orson Welles' 1938 broadcast of *War of the Worlds*. Dan continues to broadcast desperately calling out for anyone to help him. The alien (and his little robot sidekick) take over the airwaves from time to time, playing rock music (supplied by Blue Öyster Cult!) that hypnotizes women and then sucks them through the airwaves back into the radio station, where they are miniaturized and put into little glass bottles to be kept as pets!

While there is absolutely *nothing* frightening about this one, it's got a fun and goofy kinda spookshow vibe to it. Not only do we spend a lot of time with Dan in the studio as he observes the creature and continues his marathon broadcast (which everyone thinks is a joke/stunt), but we also see various people listening in to the broadcast—especially when the alien is targeting a nubile young victim. Dan does his best to convince people to turn off their radios, but to no avail. Everything thinks it's a hilarious prank...until of course when a girl vanishes right in front of them. Dan even goes so far as to release a string of expletives, hoping the FCC will shut them down, but the alien has full control of the station's power. Worse yet, a strange mold has formed around the door, sealing Dan and Corky in with the extraterrestrials.

Taking another large leap forward in time, **PONTYPOOL** (2008) is a very effective and quite a different film; once again taking place solely inside a radio station. Taking its cue from zombie flicks, we follow "shock jock"-turned-morning-radio-host Grant Mazzy (Stephen McHattie), as one morning during a blizzard, traffic-man Ken calls in and informs Mazzy that there appears to be a riot outside of a doctor's office. Ken describes a grisly scene that has resulted in multiple deaths before his transmission is cut.

When Ken calls back, he states that he has found the son of a well-known citizen in town; he says that the child is mumbling to himself. Before we can hear what he's saying the transmission is cut again, this time replaced with a message in French. I should mention at this point that the film takes place in Pontypool, Ontario. The message is in fact instructions to remain indoors, avoid terms of endearment (like cutsie-pie phrases, not the movie...though I'm not really a fan of the movie, either) and to also avoid speaking English!

As a large group of infected people begin to gather outside the radio station, a member of Grant's crew apparently becomes infected and she starts to mumble and repeat the word "missing" over and over again. Grant and the remaining crew lock themselves inside the recording studio. The infected girl starts to bash herself against the studio window before chewing her own lip, spewing out gore and viscera and falling to the floor, dead. Going with the theory that somehow a virus has found its way into human language—particularly the English language—Grant goes on the air after finding a way to reverse the effects of the virus...to no avail. Parallels could be drawn in a way between the character of Grant and Steve Wayne in **THE FOG**. Both fill protective roles, trying to help the people listening to their voices over the airwaves and save as many lives as possible.

Something that **PONTYPOOL** does better than perhaps any other film on this list is emulate a disaster—or in this case, catastrophic viral outbreak—in a realistic way. From Ken's initial report to the French transmission that is essentially the Canadian version of the Emergency Broadcast System (you know: the annoying tests they run that never fail to interrupt you in the middle of the season finale of your favorite show!), you really get the sense that this is something that could happen.

Also much like the best films on this list, you never get to see anyone outside the studio. You feel as closed off and isolated as the characters do, and you're left to imagine the horrors that are occurring outside. There's a certain sense of claustrophobia and hopelessness that sets in as the film progresses that is really quite affecting.

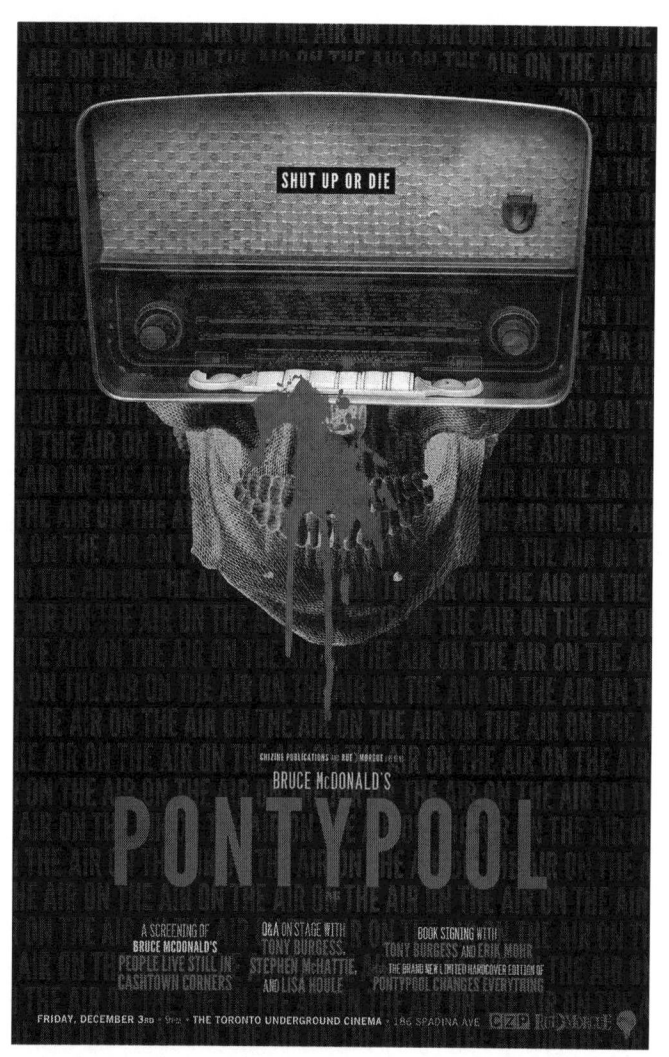

Serving as a sister film is **DEAD AIR** (2009), which also deals with people becoming infected. This time instead of language becoming infected with a virus, people are turned into rage-crazed maniacs by a toxic bomb set off by terrorists in Los Angeles. Radio host Logan Burnhardt (Bill Moseley) is the voice behind the mic this time. As his usual morning show starts, he soon starts receiving phone calls alerting him to the situation.

The film starts out much the same as **PONTYPOOL**, but makes the fatal flaw of cutting away repeatedly, destroying the palpable sense of dread that was built up so beautifully in the former film. Instead we repeatedly cut away, which completely undermines the tension that they are trying to build.

There are a few moments that are rather effective in helping to create some moments of dread—one phone call in particular, in which a man (voiced by Larry Drake) meets his demise while Burnhardt and co. listen in. The film becomes a siege flick at about the mid-point and starts to feel more like **DIE HARD** (1988) than a taught thriller.

Completely switching gears from zombies (or more accurately, infected people) to witchcraft, we come to the final title in our collection of DJs in peril. Of course I am referring to **THE LORDS OF SALEM** (2012). This particular film is near and dear to me for a couple of reasons. First of all, I am an unashamed fan of Rob Zombie's films. Secondly, **TLOS** takes place in nearby Salem, Massachusetts.

The film centers on late-night DJ Heidi Hawthorne (Sheri Moon Zombie) who is part of the power trio "The Big H"; the trio also includes the two Hermans: Herman "Whitey" Salvador (Jeffrey Daniel Phillips) and Herman Jackson (Ken Foree). One day a mysterious wooden package appears at the radio station addressed to Heidi. It has a bizarre symbol on it and it contains a record ('cause vinyl just *sounds* better, damnit!) sent by "The Lords".

Heidi assumes that it's a local band looking to get some airplay, and one night she and Whitey listen to the record at her apartment. Heidi goes into a sort of trance as the record starts to play backwards. They decide to play the record on the air, which spreads the trance-inducing music to the masses. Soon women everywhere are falling into homicidal trances and The Lords send another package announcing that they will by playing a gig in Salem, supplying a cache of tickets to give away to listeners.

While most of the film takes place outside of the radio station, the scenes that take place inside are still quite effective. There is a chemistry that works well among the three DJs. What makes this especially interesting is that this is the only film in the bunch where (as opposed to the other films such as **THE FOG** or **PONTYPOOL** where the DJ's act as a guardian or sentinel of sorts) Heidi and The Big H are directly—though unknowingly—responsible for the doom that befalls the denizens of Salem.

I'm sure there are many more examples of horror films that either take place in a radio station or feature a radio station and/or DJs and radio hosts in danger, but for our purposes, I think these twelve films and television episodes exemplify the subject best. Whether it's a hostile alien takeover or leprous ghost pirates coming to claim their gold, catastrophic viral infections or a chainsaw massacre caught live on the air, the ultra-obscure and possibly overlooked sub-subgenre of radio station terror is one that deserves to be explored.

WHO DONE IT?
1942, USA. D: ERLE C. KENTON
AVAILABLE FROM UNIVERSAL

PLAY MISTY FOR ME
1971, USA. D: CLINT EASTWOOD
AVAILABLE FROM UNIVERSAL

Night Gallery: "The Flip Side of Satan" (s2e3)
1971, USA. D: JERROLD FREEDMAN
AVAILABLE FROM UNIVERSAL

THE FOG
1980, USA. D: JOHN CARPENTER
AVAILABLE FROM MGM and SHOUT! FACTORY

Tales from the Darkside: "The Devil's Advocate" (s2e7)
1985, USA. D: MICHAEL GORNICK
AVAILABLE FROM PARAMOUNT

THE TEXAS CHAINSAW MASSACRE 2
1986, USA. D: TOBE HOOPER
AVAILABLE FROM MGM

PSYCHO IV: THE BEGINNING
1990, USA. D: MICK GARRIS
AVAILABLE FROM UNIVERSAL

Monsters: "A Face for Radio" (s3e19)
1991, USA. D: BRUCE FEIRSTEIN
AVAILABLE FROM ENTERTAINMENT ONE

BAD CHANNELS
1992, USA. D: TED NICOLAOU
AVAILABLE FROM FULL MOON

PONTYPOOL
2008, CANADA. D: BRUCE McDONALD
AVAILABLE FROM MPI

DEAD AIR
2009, USA. D: CORBIN BERNSEN
AVAILABLE FROM ANTHEM PICTURES

THE LORDS OF SALEM
2012, UK/CANADA/USA. D: ROB ZOMBIE
AVAILABLE FROM ANCHOR BAY

*Stephen McHattie as shock jock Grant Mazzy in **PONTYPOOL** advises everyone to shut up*

RELEASE SPOTLIGHT: LAST EXIT ENTERTAINMENT

by Brian Harris

Every now and then I'd like to take a page or so and spotlight a fun release label with some noteworthy films on their way to DVD/BD. It's always good to know when you're looking for new stuff to add to your collection. So for the first RELEASE SPOTLIGHT, I'm hooking up our good friend Jason Meredith ["The Pink Beyond: The Iconography of Hisayasu Sato", Weng's Cop #0] and his business partner Tomas Sandquist and their new cinephile endeavor over in Sweden, Last Exit Entertainment.

*With a nice lineup of new films coming, including improved releases of Andrei Iskanov's art-house horror films, two films everybody is talking about right now stand out as highly recommended, **DER SAMURAI** and **HORSEHEAD** (both 2014). Check out the press release info below as well as my own thoughts on each film!*

DER SAMURAI

THE SYNOPSIS:
"A wolf prowls around the edge of a small, desolate village. By feeding it young policeman Jakob tries to keep it away. A more peaceful solution than his chief desires. One day a package from an unknown sender is delivered to Jacob. Soon, the phone rings and a voice on the other end asks Jacob to deliver it to a house on the outskirts of the village. There he meets a man wearing a dress and makeup who pulls out a samurai sword from the package. The strange man jumps out of the window and starts a massacre of the village and its inhabitants. Jacob starts an intensive search of the samurai, but before the night is over, he will realize that it is something else than a confused maniac he is hunting."

THE LOWDOWN:
Call it what you like, "queer horror", "gay fantasy", or just plain weird and cool art-house cinema; **DER SAMURAI** is a gorgeous, odd and startlingly violent film that focuses on a cat-and-mouse relationship between a savage killer toting a samurai sword and the police officer drawn to him. This was truly an interesting production that I had all sorts of theories about as the final credits scrolled; it really had me thinking. If you're the kind of horror fan convinced there's nothing new, beautiful or worthwhile being made, you'd be wrong and I would highly recommend checking out **DER SAMURAI**.

THE SPECS:
Director: Till Kleinert
Country: Germany
Year: 2014
Genre: Horror/Thriller
Runtime: 79 min
Image: 1:78:1 [OAR] Anamorphic Widescreen
Audio: German, Dolby Digital 5.1
Subtitles: Swedish (No English Subtitles)
Street Date: 01-26-2015

THE SPECIAL FEATURES:
Personal introduction by Kleinert (Unique to this release)
Audio Commentary with Till Kleinert & Producer Linus de Paoli
Interview with Till Kleinert
Q&A from FFF Lund 2014
Featurette
Trailer

THE LINK: lastexitentertainment.typepad.com/my-blog/shop.html

HORSEHEAD

THE SYNOPSIS:
"Since childhood, Jessica has been plagued by mysterious nightmares. When her grandmother passes away, she reluctantly returns to her childhood home. The chilly relationship with her mother Catelyn (Catriona MacColl), and her grandmother's dead body lying in the next room does not make it better.

"During a dream encounter, Jessica's grandmother pleads for help and it turns out that she was obsessed with the same tower that Jessica has seen in her dreams. To go deeper into her dreams and subconscious, Jessica uses chloroform to reach the tower and uncover its secrets. But the path is guarded by The Cardinal, a fearsome and relentless figure with a horse head."

THE LOWDOWN:
HORSEHEAD is a real trip, seriously. A chloroform-fueled, fever-induced, nightmarish trip. The colors, visuals and special effects all lead up to a powerhouse finale. While I can't say for certain as I've not read any interviews with the director, but **HORSEHEAD** looks to have been inspired by the Italian cinema of Dario Argento and Lucio Fulci. The tension is sky-high, colors bright and beautiful and the villain ("The Cardinal") is truly iconic. As **DER SAMURAI** above, **HORSEHEAD** falls more in line with art-house horror, but labels be damned, check it out.

THE SPECS:
Director: Romain Basset
Country: France
Year: 2014
Genre: Fantasy/Horror
Runtime: 92 min
Image: 2.35:1 [OAR] Anamorphic Widescreen
Audio: English, Dolby Digital 5.1
Subtitles: Swedish
Street Date: 05-25-2015

THE SPECIAL FEATURES:
Making of Horsehead
Complete Soundtrack with Photo Gallery
Bloody Current Exchange (short)
Light Drowning (short)
Trailer

THE LINK:
lastexitentertainment.typepad.com/my-blog/shop.html

We are LAST EXIT ENTERTAINMENT, enthusiasts, creators and connoisseurs, dedicated to releasing movies in the Horror and Cult genre. Our goal and ambition is to bring mind-expanding, intriguing, original independent horror and genre films to a wider audience. From artistic Russian mind fuckers, to German nihilistic gore-fests, we will pursue only the strangest and finest of alternative genre cinema for your viewing pleasure.

We look forward to entertaining you and showing you sights unlike any you have seen before.

If you have a film and you think we might be interested in it, please send screeners to:

Last Exit Entertainment
att: Tomas Sandquist
Rosenlundsgatan 48a
118 63 STOCKHOLM
SWEDEN

Or digitally, to our mail address:
lastexit@telia.com

TAKE IT TO THE LIMIT

Karate Warrior, Larry Ludman and 'Eighties Italian Trash Cinema

by George Pacheco and David Zuzelo

*Diehard devotees of Italian trash cinema will likely recognize Fabrizio De Angelis as a noted producer of such certified horror classics as Lucio Fulci's **ZOMBIE** (Zombi 2, 1979) and **THE BEYOND** (...E tu vivrai nel terrore! L'aldilà, 1981), released under his Fulvia Films imprint. It was in the mid-'Eighties, however, when De Angelis—perhaps reading the writing on the wall in terms of Italian horror's gradual decline throughout the latter part of that decade—decided to take film making art into his own hands, switching things up as a director for an astonishing twenty-one films in just over a decade's time.*

*What's even more amazing is that six of these films belonged to De Angelis' Karate Warrior franchise, a series of films initially designed to take advantage of the Stateside success of **THE KARATE KID** (1984), yet—for better or worse, depending on your take—gradually grew into their own, strange microcosm of low-budget trash cinema at its most unapologetically repetitive yet hypnotically entertaining.*

In order to properly analyze the *Karate Warrior* series, we first need to understand a couple of things about De Angelis as a filmmaker. Fabrizio comes from a producer's background, one naturally concerned with the bottom budgetary line at all times. As a result, most of De Angelis' films run fast and cheap, with little time wasted for multiple takes, needless character development or expansive sets or effects. Instead, the films of De Angelis often feel as if they're flying by the seat of their creative pants…because they are!

Given what we know about De Angelis in this respect, it also makes sense that he would favor the action genre, a style designed to yield quick and easy financial returns without as much attention placed on acquiring Oscar-caliber actors, expert screenwriters, or expensive, elaborate sets. This isn't to say, of course, that the action films of Fabrizio De Angelis—at least his early work—didn't feature some bang-up actors, delivering some primo work. Indeed, cinematic bad-asses Fred Williamson, Bo Svenson and Christopher Connelly all made pictures for De Angelis at one point, starring in such Italian action highlights as **DEADLY IMPACT** (*Impatto mortale*, 1984), **THE MANHUNT** (*Cane arrabbiato*, a.k.a. **MAD DOG**, 1984), and 1986's **OPERATION NAM** (a.k.a. **COBRA MISSION**), by far the most cohesive and full production helmed by De Angelis.

However, as the 'Eighties drew on and the production money began to dry up, the film output of De Angelis began to showcase the strain, with the director often choosing to cast inexperienced or local actors for his pictures. Oddly enough, however, De Angelis would favor American locations for many of his later films, similar to Joe D'Amato's latter-day productions for his own Filmirage imprint. Still, late-period De Angelis pictures—usually credited under his pseudonym of "Larry Ludman"—almost always delivered the goods when it came to entertainment value…even if said entertainment wasn't always due to the "quality" of what was on the screen, but rather the awkwardness with which Ludman's neo-thespians and local non-actors handled the increasingly trashy material.

Nowhere is this better evidenced than in the *Karate Warrior* franchise, a series of films which begins on a "what the fuck?" high note, yet ends on an equally "what the fuck?" series of head-scratches. It's a fun cinematic ride full of high kicks and hijinks, so let's dive on in, shall we? ~*GP*

KARATE WARRIOR
(*Il ragazzo dal kimono d'oro*)
1987

Reviewed by George Pacheco

This 1987 inaugural installment for Fabrizio De Angelis' *Karate Warrior* franchise is probably the easiest to find here in the States—having received a couple of VHS releases from such companies as First Look—as well as the most well made picture of the series, having at least a modest budget behind its sub-**KARATE KID** aspirations.

Indeed, De Angelis (directing as Larry Ludman) makes no apologies here for his heisted story of a young, bullied boy named Anthony (Kim Rossi Stuart), who takes to studying under a mysterious and mystical monk (Ken Watanabe) after upsetting the local karate champion (Enrico Tollalba). It's all in good fun, of course, and Stuart is certainly likable enough in his role as Anthony, his performance made even more enjoyable thanks to the awkward dub track which so often made an appearance here in late-period Italian cinema.

Elsewhere, **AENIGMA** (1987) and **NEW GLADIATORS** (*I guerrieri dell'anno 2072* / "*Warriors of the Year 2027*", a.k.a. **FIGHTING CENTURIONS**, 1984) star Jared Martin takes a break from his work with Lucio Fulci to appear here for Ludman as Anthony's father Paul, while the lovely Janet Agren—who herself was no stranger to trashy Italian flicks, having appeared in way too many cornball comedies alongside Alvaro Vitali and Lino Banfi—also phones in a quick performance as Paul's estranged wife Julia. The *Karate Warrior* series would see a noticeable dip in star power after this initial flick, with many of the future installments utilizing a revolving cast of nobodies and locals, albeit with the occasional big name co-star, such as David Warbeck.

difference being that, when Anthony attacks, his punches come packaged with a magical blue glow! Of course, this magic is never really explained within the plot, but it looks like this was where most of the effects budget was spent!

True, the acting is basic, the dubbing awkward and the story derivative, but **KARATE WARRIOR** is still a fun time. It's a cash-in which never takes itself too seriously, and as a result can be enjoyed by just about anyone with a high tolerance for Italian cheese. Speaking of said glorious gouda, Stefano Mainetti's synthesizer score sets up the perfect '80s action montage atmosphere for a movie with the title **KARATE WARRIOR**, a collection of electronic themes and sappy vocal ballads which would be replicated a year later for the first **KW** sequel…but methinks my *Weng's Chop* colleague Davey Z can cover that one quite nicely, right David?

KARATE WARRIOR 2
(*Il ragazzo dal kimono d'oro 2*)
1988

Reviewed by David Zuzelo

"You will use the secret stroke…*THE STROKE OF THE DRAGON!*"

Karate Warrior Anthony Scott returns only to be played for the last time by Kim Rossi Stuart in an adventure that is wackier than the first! "Larry Ludman" pulls out all the stops, as Tony returns from defeating the villainous Quito from the Philippines as producer De Angelis settles in to what would be one of his favorite cheap spots to film in the late '80s: Florida. We quickly recap that Tony has sworn to his master that he would not misuse his gift of Karate Warriorism, but as with all good (and even not-so-good) martial arts films, it doesn't take long until he is sorely tempted to put the "*YAAAA!*" in saying "Hi" to the new cast of characters (and even one alligator) around him. Worry not, gentle viewer, Tony stays in shape by pounding heavy bags on a boat. Yet while his fists are strong, his promise to not battle is stronger. Or is it?

Tony is headed to college, and after a surprise birthday present of perhaps the worst gift-wrapped car I've ever encountered, it doesn't take a few minutes for the local gang of Karate Toughs, The Tigers, to mark their tuff turf and cause him to wreck his gift into a small body of water. Tony just wants to talk to the thuggish high-kickers and get his money for the repairs. This brings him to the big dick behind it all, the appropriately named Dick, played with malefic glee by Christopher Alan. Dick doesn't want to pay up, and Tony doesn't want to beat the small sum out of him, but as expected, Dick keeps pushing hard at Tony's resolve. Some new pals join the cast, with the most interesting of the batch being Luke (David Haynes), a rich kid who obviously hates his parents and drinks himself silly and throws his glass into the family fireplace in rebellious anger, and Patty (Howard Stern show regular Amy Lynn), who starts off as Dick's girl but sees the light and slides on over to the side of The Karate Warrior. This chafes Dick so much he breaks up with Patty by threatening her with *gang rape*. Dick, you are a dick. Seriously.

After a bit of hemming and hawing and spaghetti western-style beating of the hero while he resists the urge to pummel his foes is mixed with less-than-stylish John Woo-ing of the lady, Tony forces Dick into a sanctioned match and they square off in front of an *epic* gold curtain. Why? Because it matches the golden kimono of **KARATE WARRIOR** as referenced in the original Italian title! Also, a guy in a chicken suit appears to cheer on Dick. Why? Because *Ludman!*

After the two realize they are evenly matched and blows are traded, Tony snaps and uses his super power-stroke on Dick and the villain is rendered flaccid! But Dick isn't going down on himself like that. No…he hires a special just-out-of-jail Karate Villain to seek vengeance!

But that villain isn't just anyone, it's trash cinema legend David Prior of the nudie/weirdie Fred Olen Ray classic, **POSSESSED BY THE NIGHT** (1994), and ultimate smash action hit **DEADLY PREY** (1987)! Prior plays a controversial drug-abusing Karate Champ with all the chomping-of-scenery you could hope for and brings the movie to a new level when he busts up Tony and then almost twists Luke's head off! Luckily, Patty saves the day and they decide to settle it in the ring. KW needs help, so he calls in his master once more and we get *training scenes galore*. In Florida. All good fun, and it leads

This doesn't matter, really, as the main stars of the **KARATE WARRIOR** show are the awkwardly staged fight sequences and the training montage footage between Anthony and Watanabe's Master Kimura, culminating in Anthony's acquisition of the iconic yellow kimono, which would become the character's trademark garb throughout the rest of the series. It's also here where Anthony learns the "Dragon Blow," a final finishing maneuver which is the **KARATE WARRIOR**'s take on Daniel-San's crane kick, the one main

to a final showdown where not only Prior brings the FuckFace Fu to a maximum level, but the old master even punches a few guys in the throat to send us home.

KARATE WARRIOR 2 is probably the last typical entry in the series, because after this they slip more into ensemble comedy and action. But De Angelis as Ludman never makes things boring, even when it is typical. Using the simple plot, he pulls a few fun performances out of Stuart, Prior, and especially Alan, and uses his locations—which include a **JAWS** (1975) tribute raw bar—to their maximum. It's hard to call it much of an action picture, or martial arts film, but it's definitely a fine bit of schlocky fun that can't decide whether to be family fish or kick to the balls foul. While the plot and story are as simple as any PG family movie about a boy using his martial arts training to overcome bullies, the dubbing is *loaded* with profanity that has all the earmarks of the best of action one-liners. Look for the scene where Tony and Luke escalate from calling each other minuscule to monolithic (!) assholes. And the jarring scene that has a scorned boyfriend "jokingly" sending his buddies to gangbang his now ex-girlfriend mirrors another gangbang subplot! I can't make it up; this comes straight out of De Angelis and Dardano Sacchetti's screenplay…Karate Warrior does *not* support all of this gangbanging at all.

And speaking of Sacchetti, a master of the Eurotrash quill, this production includes several of Fulvia's best behind-the-scenes with a great and partially recycled score by Stefano Mainetti and editing from Vincenzo Tomassi. De Angelis really had the A Team of the golden '80s of exploitation, and even on the tiny budget here, they still manage to keep it interesting in the visuals and sound department. Actor and stunt coordinator Jeff Moldovan is also credited with choreographing the fights. The Prior one isn't half-bad at all and can stand with all other Italian martial arts epics of the late '80s. All…well, all *Karate Warrior* of them.

So many more battles ahead, but for a great night's fun, I can't recommend a double-shot of Karate Warrior original action more than this. The series continues, but will the direction remain the same? George, take it away…

KARATE WARRIOR 3
(*Il ragazzo dal kimono d'oro 3*)
1991

Reviewed by George Pacheco

KARATE WARRIOR 3 takes place immediately after the second installment in the series, recapping the story up to this point by recycling the final battle between Anthony Scott (Kim Rossi-Stewart) and bully baddy Joe Carson, played by Christopher Alan, one of the few actors to be a semi-constant in the series as a main nemesis for the "Karate Warrior", a.k.a. "The Man With the Yellow Kimono".

Rossi-Stewart wouldn't return for this third episode of the *Karate Warrior* saga, his character instead being replaced by actor Ron Williams as "Larry Jones", a nondescript nebbish blond whose reputation as a karate badass is severely hampered throughout most of this film. The effect as a whole is similar almost to that of "The Two Darrens" on television's *Bewitched*, a surreal swap-out which is made all the more bizarre given that Ludman opened this film with a recycled scene of his old actor!

Then again, given that my review copy of this film was in Italian with Greek subs, it's entirely possible that Williams' "Larry Jones" character—together with his even nerdier sidekick—are friends or relatives of the original Karate Warrior, as there are still posters from the first two films hanging on the walls of the sidekick's home. It's in this setting where Christopher Alan (returning here in yet another villain role) and his crew of flunkies show up, kick ass and steal Jones' yellow kimono and parade it to the local nightclub, asserting their assholish supremacy to an intimidated local crowd of youths.

Right away, it's clear that **KARATE WARRIOR 3** isn't cut from the same cloth as Ludman's first two installments. There's a drastic change in style and tone, even if the plot is still unabashedly stealing from **THE KARATE KID** territory. The film overall boasts brighter cinematography (and colors… seriously, almost every character here is wearing day-glo as bright as the sun), yet is saddled with what is clearly an even cheaper budget, Ludman resorting to a cast of mostly amateur unknowns mugging against some really dated early 'Nineties Italian synth music from Stefano Macrino and Francesco Capogrossi.

The whole thing is indicative of the sad state of affairs in which the Italian genre film industry was mired at this time. Although it's admirable that De Angelis was even able to find funding for this series in 1991, the fact that only the first two installments possessed a widespread English dub track is proof positive that even the producer himself probably had doubts that this series had legs anywhere but maybe Asia or at home in Italy.

This isn't to say, of course, that true connoisseurs of ridiculous trash can't find something to hang on to here, despite the awkward acting and ill-placed comic relief characters amongst the ancillary cast. There are unrelated romantic subplots which contain no karate, an overweight friend working for a fried chicken stand subplot which contains no karate…and a number of other sequences which—surprise!—contain no karate! Ludman at least made sure to include some part-time Fashion Bug models to appear on his beach scenes and on the arms of his evil karate gang, even if the film itself never really rises above a PG-level of violence or sexual situations. Amy Lynn Baxter, come back, we beg you!

Yup, there's just very little actual karate to be had here with this installment of *Karate Warrior*, a notion which would unfortunately be a calling card for many of the series' latter efforts. Instead, the script here, from Italian genre legend Dardano Sacchetti—written under the ashamed pseudonym of David Parker, Jr.—is bare-bones and basic to the extreme, limping along to the inevitable conclusion where (*SPOILER ALERT!*) the Karate Warrior trains through a montage, kicks the villain's ass and recovers the yellow kimono to the side of good.

….but you probably already figured that out, right?

KARATE WARRIOR 4
(*Il ragazzo dal kimono d'oro 4*)
1992

Reviewed by David Zuzelo

The Karate Warrior Era (or should I say "*error*") of Ron Williams continues as the fourth film plays very much like the third, with De Angelis and crew bringing back much of the same cast to carry on some wacky hijinx and a little karate action to satisfy the title requirement and keep the *Golden GI* alive for his fan—okay, George and I make fan*s*! Without an English-language version to watch, the film becomes even *more* entertaining for this die-hard trash cinema nut, as I have to just roll with the situations and imagine all that lovely profanity the dubbers could have brought to the table. After the final battle of part 3 is recapped through a long credits scene, it turns out that the result of said fisticuffs to restore the honor of our Golden God of Fu just happened to put his opponent in a wheelchair. And then the former tough bad guy is *mocked* until his crew can stand no more. So, in comes a new opponent for Larry Jones, and he is Japanese. *Oh shit, it's on!* But really, he just sort of seems like a decent enough guy stuck with some bad friends, which doesn't mean they won't collide in a final battle after the Japanese kid assaults some plates in a favorite restaurant. I had a momentary flashback to the infamous **A BETTER TOMORROW II** (*Ying hung boon sik II*, 1987) Chow Yun-Fat moment of "*Apologize to the rice*" here, and that made the entire film entertaining for me. But wait, this is a Larry Ludman movie, so it's got weird things going on all over the place. I mean, totally weird. Like, fat-dudes-getting-beat-up-at-urinal weird.

Larry's chubby pal is selling *diet pills*, and the dummy actually ends up getting Larry *poisoned* by their dangerous nature before the final showdown. He hawks diet pills at school, and most entertainingly, during a volleyball game at the beach. Perfect spot for some early '90s fad pills! And let us not forget that David Warbeck must have had a contractual obligation or enjoyed free money, because he pops up again, spending a lot of time in a bathrobe in a Veteran's hospital where everyone wears fatigues, because *that* won't cause any PTSD issues or anything. It's like an oddball "WHAT IF **THE LAST HUNTER** (*L'ultimo cacciatore*, 1987) SPAWNED A **KARATE WARRIOR**" vortex of Eurotrash glory. Now, I assure you there is a final battle, and it's actually pretty entertaining, even though it's in a top-floor dojo in a strip mall and probably the tiniest battle space I've seen in the series. It makes the *giant golden curtain* you'll see later seem like a lush extravaganza of Ludman-like proportions. But perhaps the most exciting (well, relatively) scene is a long motocross race between the rival Karate Warriors/Diet Pill Salesman you are likely to see. And just when it can't get odder? *Ron Jeremy shows up!* The icon of schlong is uncredited and simply appears to fire a starting gun and hand out a trophy, so it's more *free money* from Larry Ludman, I guess. I swear, my spirit animal must be a hedgehog to have bumped into this cameo!

Is this an exercise in cinemasochism or an entertaining little side street of trash cinema? I'd say both. **KARATE WARRIOR 4** is fun to look at, and I must admit that I was taken by just how much the series changed after Stuart relinquished the role of Karate Warrior. It feels like De Angelis was using the shotgun approach to making these entries by mixing the promised action—which the final battle does deliver—and channels the Israeli series of *Lemon Popsicle* films into making silly comedies. Minus any sex appeal.

As with part 3, the clothes and lipstick and bathing suits and décor is bright like a *Miami Vice* pop-shot in the eye with Ron Jeremy smiling at you when it's over. Fun enough, but I'm ready for more. I need action! Does it deliver in part 5? Let's see...

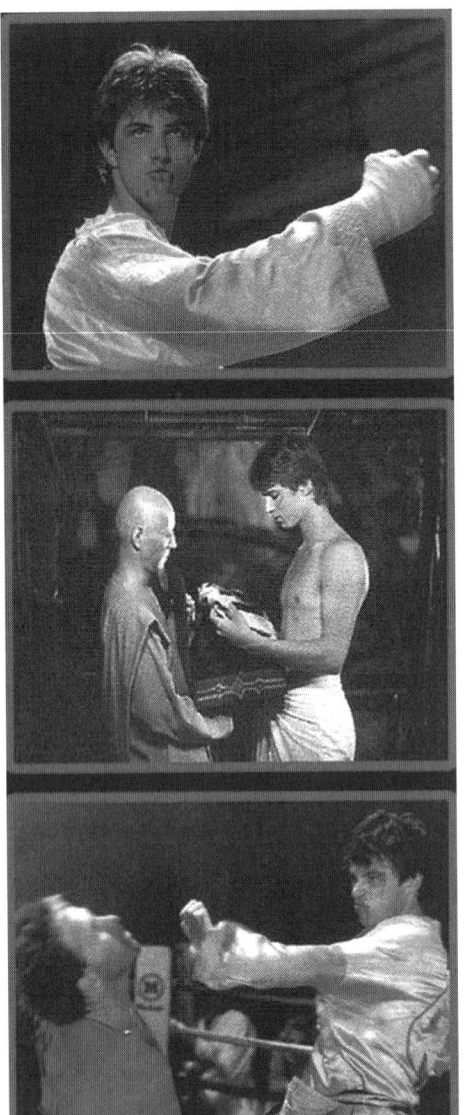

KARATE WARRIOR 5
(*Il ragazzo dal kimono d'oro 5*)
1992

Reviewed by George Pacheco

KARATE WARRIOR 5 was one of two *Karate Warrior* films released in 1992, and it once again takes place immediately following the events of its predecessor. Fans such as David and myself are probably welcoming all of the absurdity at this point, as director Fabrizio De Angelis/Larry Ludman feels no shame at recycling entire sequences and storylines from previous installments in the film, almost as if he figured, "Fuck it, no one's watching these things anyway. Who's gonna bother pulling my card that I'm filming the same movie five times in a row!?"

Larry Jones should actually be called the "BMX Warrior" at this point, for the character—once again played by Ron Williams—spends more time in this series riding on two wheels than he does setting off spin kicks or dragon blows. Christopher Alan returns once again as a villain here (although he apparently avoids any serious jail time after being arrested at the end of **KARATE WARRIOR 4**), but his purpose is more behind-the-scenes, in line with the plan of Martin Kove's "Kreese" from **THE KARATE KID III** (1989), as Alan decides to set up the Karate Warrior up against his own personal killing machine, the devastating "Alabama Bull".

Again, there are numerous tedious sub-plots which mainly concern themselves with the supporting cast, such as Jones' girlfriend being kidnapped, the overweight comic relief couple heading to an "Extra Large Group of America" meeting at some hotel. It's not funny, and it has nothing to do with karate, but this is where Ludman decides to pad his movie rather than spending any money on special effects or fight choreography. Perhaps, if my review copy was in English the comedy would translate...but somehow I still have my doubts.

The musical score from Capogrossi and Macrino is more of the same beep-boop synthesizer and muzak which constituted earlier films in the series, while most of the characters are all still wearing the same gaudy colored Panama Jack beach gear left over from **KARATE WARRIOR 3** and **4**. David Warbeck does show up for a quick paycheck as Larry's estranged father, and Ron Williams at least seems comfortable in his role of Jones at this point, yet his titular character of the "Karate Warrior" receives so little screen time compared to his compadres, that his fight against Alabama Bull almost seems like an afterthought.

Still, there's a masochistic part of me which simply can't stop watching these movies, no matter how deep Ludman and his crew dig to cobble the *Karate Warrior* series together. The absurdity of it all is a real hoot, and it's almost as if I'm in disbelief that these movies actually exist. None of the films in the *Karate Warrior* series have any users reviews on IMDb after the first, and you'd be hard pressed to find much information about them on the Internet, either. It's almost as if Davey Z and I are the only ones who have braved this branch of the wilderness of Italian genre cinema in the early 'Nineties, in order to come back from the fringe and report just how strapped the country was for entertainment and ideas during this time.

KARATE WARRIOR 6
(*Il ragazzo dal kimono d'oro 6*)
1993

Reviewed by David Zuzelo

"*Look, here's your mermaid, you damn jerks!*"
"*She's a man...a damn man!!!*"

A six-year odyssey. Six films. **KARATE WARRIOR 6** is actually available in an English dub, so it's nice to see how things came to a raging conclusion with a little closure on what exactly happens. However, this film is possibly the silliest of the batch and manages to squeak in just a little martial arts mayhem at the end, mostly involving Karate Warrior's master rubbing his head and giving him strength. Dorian Field shows up once again as Larry's girlfriend and it would have been much more interesting if our pal, just like the *Lemon Popsicle* crew, were actually trying to get laid or something more than what he aspires to. But I can say this, just as part 1 took Original Styled Karate Warrior to the Philippines, the series finale takes place in Greece! Turns out that diet pill seller extraordinaire is actually called *Tubby* (Leo in the English dub), and he has a big stroke of semi-luck in not being killed after a king's limo hits him as he rides his bike. Seriously. He ends up with ten thousand dollars in his grubby hands (and the boys even rip up some of the *one dollar bills* he holds, thinking it's a joke) and decides to do up summer vacation right. And hey, Larry's best gal is going away, so he is a free man to get a new semi-romantic thing going, which crashes and burns as his appeal is about zero to anyone but this one lady. First, they get some "class" on a shopping trip. To *JC Penney*! The Larry Ludman era of style continues, though this film tones down the now passé pastels and just looks drab and touristy.

Once they land in Greece it's a game of Roundabout the Ruins, and they see the sights until Tubby is targeted by a devious man with a violin. This man promises him a chance to buy a license (uh-oh) to photograph the mysterious "Mermaid of Hydra". (WHAT??) Of course, Tubby can't resist and away go the intrepid Karate Warrior Crew until the skeptics of the group de-tail the mermaid and mock Tubby. Not only is it a *man* pretending to be a mermaid, but the violin guy has made off with all their money!

Now, first I wondered where the Golden Gi of Italian Action Kung Fu-lery could be. What if it was stolen? An epic is in the making. Or not. Instead, the boys meet a pretty island girl who happens to know the epic **TUFF TURF** (1985)-styled crew of the island. They want to fight of course, but let us just recap the fact that Larry Ludman stands for recycling the same stories over and over when things get *Karate Warrior*'d, so we have a *motocross* battle through the streets! It's cool, I like these scenes, though sadly Peter North doesn't show up in this one to waggle the North Pole at the start line. No free Ludman cash for him! Ron Jeremy got off easy. Of course Larry rules the motocross portion of our program and agrees to fight the toughest of the tough. The boys strap on pillows and let Karate Warrior punch them, but it becomes obvious he is out of shape. Badly. And "that guy is a monster!" A quick call brings the master, the girlfriend and even *David Warbeck* to a vacation to watch their pal/Kid get smacked around some more until he unleashes the one-legged crane variation of doom from **THE KARATE KID**! The circle is complete. The series is over. And it all ends with a wacky bit of Tubby getting slapped around by some guys as his friends laugh at him.

KARATE WARRIOR 6 creeps over the finish line, but it's actually an excellent look at the wobbly state of affairs in Italian genre film. Even the action genre had sort of burnt out at that point; there was probably not a lot of interest in this kind of comedy and trying to push the hybrid styles to a global market just wasn't working. I'm grateful that it did find its way to being dubbed, simply because it is exactly the kind of movie I enjoy watching flounder around in a variety of attempts to be marketable while succeeding in…well, none of them. But honestly, I'll take a scattershot experience of all-over-the-blood-stained-gi of *Karate Warrior* over bland and boring one-genre comedies or Franco and Ciccio nonsense.

Into the halls of legend strides Karate Warrior…with one last slap to a chubby pal's face. I'm glad we met you, Larry…but you are no original-flavored Tony Scott. I'll always remember him!

And is it me, or was De Angelis paying tribute to his own character when the *set designer* is listed as Anthony Scott?

So, now that we have chopped, punched, taken diet pills, devoured chicken, never once got laid and traveled around the globe with *Karate Warrior*, what have we learned? I think George and I have realized that within these films there are hours of entertainment, sometimes despite themselves, though also honestly fun and bizarre given their oddball sensibilities. While none of these are at the high end of the Larry Ludman output, they are a marker in the production career of Fabrizio De Angelis. With a career spanning two decades, the man was involved in the very highest points of the Lucio Fulci filmography, was responsible for several classics in both the '70s crime genre and the '80s Italian apocalypse films, and produced one of the most "grindhouse"-styled splatter films with **ZOMBIE HOLOCAUST** (1980—rampaging around America as **DR. BUTCHER, M.D.**). As times changed, he produced and took directorial credits on what I've always thought of as The Italian Action Explosion of the '80s, with 'Namsploitation, big scale adventure films and Rambo-inspired series that includes the *Thunder* films that you couldn't escape on VHS if you were perusing the shelves in the '80s. As **KARATE WARRIOR** provided some laughs and promises half-delivered as being action movies, the series appears to have sold fairly well globally, if only partially in the English language market. Heck, he even knocked-off his own series with **KARATE ROCK** (*Il ragazzo delle mani d'acciaio*, 1990), a film that could be a part of the series, but seems to actually up the star power by casting Antonio Sabato, Jr. in what feels like a remake of the highlights of the series to date, even including Dorian Field as the girlfriend once more! David Warbeck reprises his role as "Dad" but has a very different take on his son's adventures. Honestly, it's as good as any of the *Karate Warrior* films and deserves the time any of you may take to watch these if you have been inspired to put the Ludman Fist into action after reading this.

It is hard to believe that as Larry Ludman, during a time when he was shooting fat guy humor in Miami, he would also be carving out classics of as yet to be truly discovered merit such as **THE LAST MATCH** (*L'ultima meta*, 1991) and two great "EuroMonsters on the Loose" films in the *Killer Crocodile* series. **KARATE WARRIOR 6** is listed as his final production, and that stands as a sign of the commercial times as cinema moved to television in Italy. But fear not, the legacy of Ludman stands as tall as Kim Rossi-Stuart at the finale of the first **KARATE WARRRIOR**, and these little quickies stand the test of time and provide endless entertainment for the Trash Celluloid Archaeologists.

Take it to the limit, Ludman! We will always remember the times when evil was defeated by **IL RAGAZZO DAL KIMONO D'ORO**! *All SIX TIMES!* ~*DZ*

KARATE WARRIOR 1-6
1987-1993, ITALY. D: "LARRY LUDMAN" (FABRIZIO DE ANGELIS)
AVAILABLE FROM CDE/AVO FILM [R2]

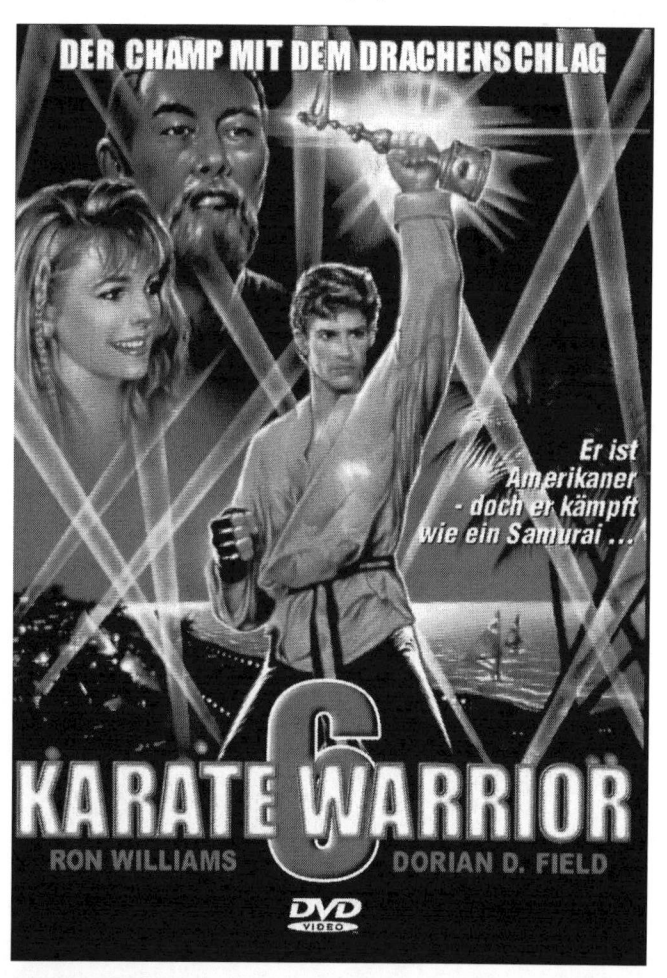

MONSTER!

$5.95 each

Each and every monthly issue of MONSTER! is chock-full of reviews and articles on rare, unusual, and classic creature features from all over this wide and wild world!

WENGSCHOPSTORE.COM

Home of Wildside/Kronos Publications

The Stupendous Cinema of SyFy:
THE MANEATER FILM SERIES

by Brian Harris & Christos Mouroukis

Love it or hate it, the SyFy Channel has always been a great platform through which many independent producers have—and still do—showcase their low-budget, CGI-filled monster movie efforts. The films this network broadcast are usually formulaic—what's not made for profit in cinema, especially on television, nowadays—and chock-full of third-rate Hollywood wash-outs. That's their charm; they're dependably cheesy and usually pretty bad, like generic macaroni and cheese. It's still comforting to know there's still a home and fanbase for B-movies though; without SyFy the made-for-TV market would sorely lack a horror and sci-fi presence.

Legendary filmmaker/producer Roger Corman has made great use of the channel, giving us the ultra-successful Sharktopus *franchise, and production house The Asylum made history as millions upon millions have consistently tuned in for their* Sharknado *trilogy (2013-2015). Lesser production company Sonar Entertainment, Inc., previously RHI Entertainment,[1] has also left their mark on SyFy Channel viewers with their popular* Maneater *films (2007-15).*

The Maneater *series isn't an easy viewing experience. With more bad than good, one can lose interest quickly and before you know it, wander off in search of better cinema. However there are some really exciting, entertaining films in the series that horror and sci-fi fans would be well-advised to check out. Whether your thing is rampaging tigers, flesh-eating ants, zombie-making wasps or mythical beasts, Sonar's* Maneater *series has something for everyone. So here, long-suffering cinema junkies, in all of its cheesy glory, is the* Maneater *series, spanning from 2007 to present (2015). We hope you find one or two films to your liking!*

BLOOD MONKEY

Reviewed by Brian Harris

I know, you're wondering if this is the one that stars F. Murray Abraham (**SCARFACE**, 1983)—*The* F. Murray Abraham—and it is. I cannot say for certain whether he was "slumming it" for a paycheck or this was the lowest point in his career. After seeing him in Wes Anderson's **THE GRAND BUDAPEST HOTEL** (2014) though, I'd guess it was a bit of both. Hey, whatever buys the Italian Ice and Newport 100's, right? So anyhow, yeah, he is in it but not even he can save this offal from setting a questionable standard for future installments.

A group of anthropology students flies out to a remote jungle to meet up with their mentor, Professor Hamilton (Abraham), and join him in his field research. Once safely at camp, Hamilton and his strong-arm *femme*-thug Chenne (Prapimporn Karnchanda) reveal that this will be no ordinary outing; he's discovered a species of primate, possibly prehistoric, and intends to be the first to document the creatures. Initially the group is asked to remain with the professor voluntarily but they quickly realize they're being held as prisoners and used as bait to draw the creatures out…which is exactly what their presence does. Lunch is served and it's anthropology students on the menu.

As one might expect from a film called **BLOOD MONKEY** (2007), there are apes on display but only occasional glimpses here and there—and even those look more like gorillas than a species of undiscovered primate. Instead of suits, appliances, or even hand puppets, the creatures are nothing more than poorly composited CGI. It's ugly, cartoonish work and I couldn't help but wonder why they would flip for Abraham and then settle for this level of trash.

The acting from Abraham, a pre-*Constantine* Matt Ryan and Amy Manson was enough to keep the production on track and most of the attention diverted from Freishia Bomanbehram's grating performance, but the end result was still a major disappointment. If ever there was a candidate for a credit removal, one would think **VAMPIRE CIRCUS** (1972)[2] helmer Robert Young would have had his immediately stripped from this jalopy, but nope. Do everything in your power to not see or own this. Or, check it out for yourself! Hell, we've all got our dirty little kinks!

2007, THAILAND. D: ROBERT YOUNG
AVAILABLE FROM RHI ENTERTAINMENT

---

[1] Said company was also known at one time as Cabin Fever Entertainment, and at another time as Hallmark Entertainment.
[2] See review in *WC#7*, p.60.

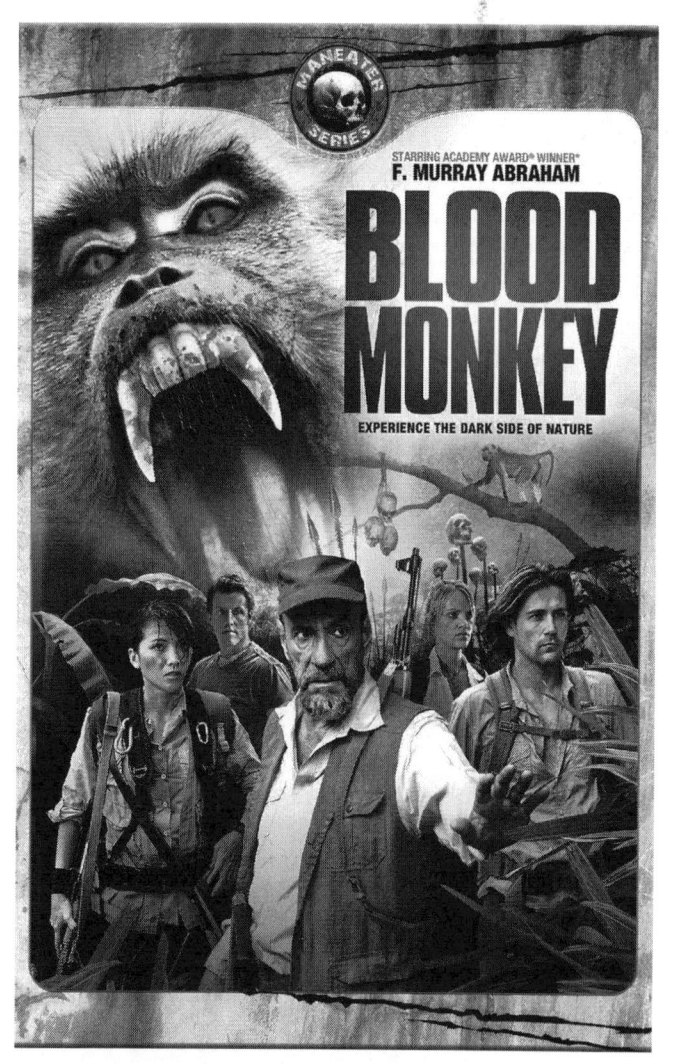

The **BLOOD MONKEY** is out for…uh… BLOOD!

IN THE SPIDER'S WEB

Reviewed by Brian Harris

A group of friends backpacking through the wilds of India are sidetracked when one of them is bitten by a venomous spider. Being too far from civilization for medical treatment, her only chance of survival lies in the hands of a reclusive doctor by the name of Lecorpus (Lance Henriksen), residing in a remote village not too far from their camp. Agreeing to split up, one group heads off to seek help, while the others accompany the victim to the village.

While coming off a tad unfriendly and more than a touch sinister, Lecorpus agrees to treat the young woman, though he offers no promises concerning her recovery. The particular spider that bit her was a rare and deadly species. A few decide to hike up to a well-known cave temple in the area for some sightseeing, giving their traveling companion time to regain her strength, but what they find may be the death of them all. Dr. Lecorpus, his hideously deformed, hooded brother and a cult of spider-worshipers from the village are seeking sacrifices, and only the freshest of victims will do!

You know, no matter how corny and cartoonish CGI may be, these low-budget spider movies never cease to make me shudder in disgust. Sure, sure, I know that shit is fake, but tell that to my world-class arachnophobia! The wee beasties in this heap would barely pass as spiders in today's cinema, as they were just animated black blobs with legs made to resemble spiders, but that didn't keep me from scratching and slapping at my arms, legs and neck throughout. Don't take that to mean this film was "scary" or anything, because it was far from it; **IN THE SPIDER'S WEB** (2007) is nothing more than **TURISTAS** (2006)-meets-**KINGDOM OF THE SPIDERS** (1977) with no story-driven tension or thrills...or the great Shatner. We do, however, get the next best thing to The Shat, which is Lance Henriksen!

Recently somebody mentioned to me that Henriksen must have fallen on awful hard times to have stooped to such drivel, but the truth is, he's been stooping to similar drivel since '99. The man works, consistently, and whether he's doing a low B or a high Z, he brings his A. Meaning, he brings his *ASS* to the set and phones it all in with intensity that can only be matched by weapons-grade lasers. Fault the man all you want for paying his bills with crap films, but you cannot hate on The Lance's technique, which is usually a grumble delivered with a stone-faced, hollowed-eye glare and the emotional range of an Egyptian mummy. Intense is Lance Henriksen's middle name. He eats intensity for breakfast. He shits it, too...in movies like this.

Terry Winsor's **IN THE SPIDER'S WEB**, written by Gary Dauberman (**ANNABELLE** [2014]), looked relatively nice, but it didn't taste all that great. This is where I'd normally insert a vagina joke but this is 2015 and being crude is so '14. I speak the truth, though; this "Scooby-Doo in The Jungle" mess featured atrocious CGI even for 2007, quite a bit of uneven acting and a head-slappingly stupid finale. If you're expecting a monster, think again. There are no government experiment spiders, extraterrestrial spiders or spiders gone amok. There are just a lot of them, everywhere, and many of them were real. Gross. The highlights of this film include the aforementioned Henriksen, a hulking hooded thug with a hideous face and...hmm...yeah, that's pretty much about it. Oh, it also co-stars Michael Smiley, co-star of Ben Wheatley's **KILL LIST** (2011), though he doesn't get much screen time.

So, yeah. Seriously, I didn't regret my viewing experience, but I have no intention of ever watching **IN THE SPIDER'S WEB** again if I can help myself. Definitely not amongst my favorites from the *Maneater* series.

Your Spidey sense should be tingling! Emma Catherwood, Lisa Livingstone, Sohrab Ardeshir in the spider cavern (**top**) from **IN THE SPIDER'S WEB**. And organ harvesting with Lance Henriksen (**above**)

2007, USA. D: TERRY WINSOR
AVAILABLE FROM RHI ENTERTAINMENT

MANEATER

Reviewed by Brian Harris

While illegally transporting a deadly tiger to a black market buyer, the driver crashes the truck avoiding a sleepwalking boy in the road. On the prowl and hungry as hell, this man-eating beast stakes its territory and begins hunting the locals of the nearby town of Stonewall. Sheriff Grady Barnes (Gary Busey) does his best to keep the town's Corn & Apple Fest on track, but soon it becomes all too obvious that nobody is safe from the tiger. Now Barnes, the national guard and a professional tiger hunter from India must track it, and the key to that may lie with the sleepwalking boy.

Swap out the shark for a tiger and Roy Scheider for Gary Busey (**SILVER BULLET**, 1985), and you've basically got **MANEATER**. Sure, there are a few original bits here and there, but you've got a prime example of "Jaws with Paws" films. Strangely enough, it's not unwatchable; Busey is rather tame and the visual FX and editing used to create the illusion that the tiger was in the same shots with actors was convincing. In fact, I found this to look a bit more realistic than Carlos Brooks's 2010 tiger-on-the-loose film, **BURNING BRIGHT**. Throw in an affable British big game hunter (Ian D. Clark), police and national guardsmen playing meat for the beast and a nutty subplot involving a Christian woman and her son living in seclusion in the woods. **MANEATER** is not a good film; there wasn't a ton of tension, really, but it was entertaining in its own way and Busey's presence reminds us that, at one time, he was quite the actor. Is it worth the $2 or $3 you might find it for at a used DVD shop? That depends on your tolerance for B-movie cheese.

2007, USA/CANADA. D: GARY YATES
AVAILABLE FROM RHI ENTERTAINMENT

SOMETHING BENEATH

Reviewed by Brian Harris

Remember back in the day when Kevin Sorbo (*Hercules* [1995-1999]) was the kind of high-powered celebrity that offered thought-provoking insight that could only come from somebody with a deep passion for his fellow man and a dedication to the environment? Hmm…yeah me neither. I actually hear he's a pretty philanthropic dude. Good for him. He also appears to be your typical whiny (Hollywood Liberals are blacklisting me!), prejudiced (Jews killed Jesus!), science-denying (There's no climate change!) religious yahoo. All of that makes this film that much more comical, as he plays an Episcopalian Priest heading up an ecological summit. Outstanding.

Despite grave warnings from biologist Walter Connolly (Brendan Beiser) about the toxicity of the Cedar Gate Conference Center construction site, corporate tycoon Lowell Kent (Frank Adamson)—curiously working out of a warehouse instead of a posh office—decides to bury the reports and move forward with the project. Bad move.

Months later, the Cedar Gate Conference Center is open for business and social crusader Father Douglas Middleton (Sorbo) has brought together a group of oddball personalities for the first annual Clean Planet Conference. With the help of event coordinator Khali Spence (Natalie Brown), Middleton is able to cater to them as best as possible, but accidents begin occurring around the conference center and bodies soon pile up. With guests dropping like flies, the conference center's security, headed by ex-dirty cop Jackson Deadmarsh (Peter MacNeill), is called in to investigate further. Without much more to go on though, outside of a death by natural cause and a suicide, security can only sit on the bodies and wait.

When a pair of janitors go missing while rooting around in the sewers beneath the center, Deadmarsh and his assistant head underground to find answers. Meanwhile Doctor Connolly reaches out to Father Middleton and Khali with information regarding an entirely new, unidentified biological entity living beneath the grounds of the center! Can Father Middleton, Khali, Connolly and Deadmarsh stop the entity before it rages out of control?

The answer is: you won't care.

Most would probably slam Sorbo for being a "just okay" B-movie actor who only seems capable of playing "Kevin Sorbo" in different outfits, but the truth is he lent this production a bit of class. I would say "star power" but… uh…well…come on. Don't get me wrong, the supporting cast members were no slouches, there wasn't a ton of bad acting on display, but many low-budget films—especially those premiering on SyFy—need that extra *oomph* to draw in viewers. These days that oomph is achieved by casting actors with one-time household names on the ass-end of their careers. There's no denying that during the mid-'Nineties, damn near everybody knew who Hercules was. So yeah, expect some iffy performances here and there, but it's nothing too off-putting.

The biological entity mentioned above starts out as a convincingly oozy and gooey beast; a gross oversized skull/skeleton mash. But things go south fast, and before you know it you're watching a cartoony, CGI Sarlacc. It is what it is, and what it is is a bit lame. I didn't expect much from **SOMETHING BENEATH** (2007) so I wasn't too disappointed, but that's not to say it was an entertaining film. I watched it, it happened, I don't intend to revisit.

2007, CANADA. D: DAVID WINNING
AVAILABLE FROM GENIUS PRODUCTS (TVN),
ALLIANCE (UNIVERSAL) [BOTH OOP], AND SONAR [VOD]

CROC

Reviewed by Brian Harris

Small-time business owner and Thailand tourist trap entrepreneur Jack Mc-Quaid (Peter Tuinstra) runs afoul of a big-time criminal enterprise fronting as a construction company when he refuses to vacate the land they need to expand their empire. Not that the group to take "no" lightly; they call in the services of animal welfare worker Evelyn Namawong (Sherry Phungprasert, a.k.a. Sherry Edwards), hoping she'll find enough violations to get the attraction closed down. She does indeed find a few violations but nothing that would warrant closure. Defeated but still determined, the slimeballs sneak into his place and let some crocs loose, hoping the press and city will blame him for some recent croc attacks. Though their plan works like a charm, Jack and Evelyn know the croc attacks weren't perpetrated by his animals.

There's something hunting the waters, something far bigger and hungrier than anything he owns, and the arrival of grizzled hunter Croc Hawkins (Michael Madsen) confirms their suspicions. Can Croc, Jack and Evelyn locate this massive monster before he moves on for new hunting grounds?

What do you get when you throw Michael Madsen (**SPECIES** [1995], **HELL RIDE** [2008]) into a film about a killer croc? Answer: "Michael Madsen in a film about something or other, we forget." Yeah, it's like that. Admit it, the guy is a beast; he's an acting gangster. Madsen can take any damn B-movie role and make it instantly legit. He's that good, folks.

Seriously, who cares about a killer **CROC** when you have Sherry Phungprasert running around in the film?

"But Brian, what about the film itself?"

CROC is silly garbage, total Sunday afternoon blow-off cinema. The titular creature doesn't look bad; he even eats a kid (*cool!*), but the star…well…I think it's clear who the real attraction is in this heap. I had a hard time connecting with lead actor Tuinstra, but, as far as lead actors go he did his job well. The lead actress (Phungpraserat), total stone-cold stunner, delivered pretty much the same flat character as Tuinstra's. But seriously, did you come for award-winning acting in a film about a killer croc? Probably not, because if you did…the Thai "real estate villains" will have you slapping forehead so hard you may end up with a concussion. Think "'80s valley girls with braces". The croc does its thing; Madsen—in a reversed 2Pac-style bandana—hunts it and the world is a better place…kinda. **CROC** is crappy, though watchable. I wouldn't own it.

2007, USA. D: STEWART RAFFILL
AVAILABLE FROM RHI ENTERTAINMENT

EYE OF THE BEAST

Reviewed by Brian Harris

When the waters surrounding Fells Island appear entirely fished out, tempers flare and Native and non-Native fishermen seek to blame one another for the loss in revenue. Instead of welcoming marine biologist Dan Leland (James Van Der Beek) and his investigation to find out what happened—backed by oceanographic institute NORA—the locals eye him with distrust. The last time NORA was out to Fells Island searching for answers about the marine life levels, they closed the only fishery on the island, forcing families to leave. Though Leland makes no promises, he's determined to find out where the fish are going, even if that means thinking outside the box. Can it be a coincidence that dead bodies begin showing up around the island with signs of attack by an impossible aquatic animal—the gigantic squid?

Can you tolerate racial tension? Can you tolerate a hot chick that never gets naked? How about James Van Der Beek? If you can handle all that, well, that's pretty much **EYE OF THE BEAST** (2007). There's also a killer squid and we even get a glimpse of it but none of that will matter. The film is a single view, at best; nothing too entertaining or offensive. I suppose "mediocre" is accurate. I can't even hate on it; there's nothing to hate *per se*, but there's nothing to love either. It's all so ho-hum.

2007, CANADA. D: GARY YATES
AVAILABLE FROM RHI ENTERTAINMENT

GRIZZLY RAGE

Reviewed by Brian Harris

"*You take the good, you take the bad,
You take them both and there you have
GRIZZLY RAGE, GRIZZLY RAGE!*"

Okay, so that's not quite the theme song from **GRIZZLY RAGE**, but to be fair the film was no good either, so…yeah. I can't hate on David DeCoteau and what he does; the guy is a goddamn hustler, a thoroughbred production pimp that few on his level can compete with. Hell, he's literally kicked the establishment's door in and made himself at home with his *1313* series, films some might call "Queer Horror" but I've given the trendier "Q-Horror" label to. While his camera may linger on shirtless man-meat a bit longer than the average straight male horror film fan is accustomed to, he still gets the B-movie job done. That, however, did not happen here. Job not at all accomplished.

A group of twenty-somethings…er, teens…out for a weekend of camping and partying—in a grotto closed to the public—accidentally hit and kill a bear cub. With no cell signals and the SUV damaged, there's no way to call for help or leave, unless they can find water for their cracked radiator. Oh, and there's a pissed-off mother bear looking for them.

While **GRIZZLY RAGE** had all the right ingredients for an entertaining B-movie, it missed its mark entirely. Setting aside the stereotypical "horrible camping trip" trope that kicks things off to a lukewarm start, the bland acting by the four pretty faces on display and the cheap, crap rock score did this film no favors. Throw in shots of radioactive waste barrels and toxic water that hint at a wildlife mutation we don't get, and the unwise decision to keep Kate Todd—the only female on display—relatively clothed while slathering on the mimbod, and you've got yourself a film filled with wasted potential. To be fair to David though, the terrible script that I assume most of this was spawned from was written by Arne Wilson, the monster responsible for the *Maneater* misfire, **HYBRID** (2007; reviewed below).

On the flipside, the gore and occasional appearances by the bear were well done enough that I stuck it out. I kept hoping the radioactive angle was going to come to fruition before it all ended but that was unexplored, as I mentioned above. Of course, neither gore nor bear shots will convince you that this was worth your time and money. It just wasn't. I'd recommend skipping it but if you're on a quest to complete the series and you must see this, drink lots of beer.

2007, CANADA. D: DAVID DECOTEAU
AVAILABLE FROM VIVENDI ENTERTAINMENT

THE HIVE

Reviewed by Brian Harris

The high-tech extermination company THORAX is called in when a small island in Southeast Asia is overrun with an aggressive ant swarm. Just when the team succeeds in pushing the swarm back, they encounter behavior inconsistent with ants. Not only are they acting intelligently, but they make strategic strikes working with several species of ants! This unlikely and highly unnatural cooperation leads THORAX and a leading entomologist to suspect the evolution may allow some form of communication to be established between man and ant, which turns out to be correct. The ants have a simple demand: they want half the island to call home. No humans.

Now the island's leadership and THORAX must decide whether to give in to the demands or find a way to eradicate them, once and for all.

Let's get something out of the way before I move on to the review because it "bugged" the shit out of me as I watched this film. A collection of ants is not referred to as a "hive," that's typically reserved for bees, wasps and hornets; the correct word is for a collection of ants is "colony". Sure, I'm being a nerdy stickler but it's one of those things that just nagged me. Moving on.

Not really a ton of star power here—unless you consider Tom Wopat's (*The Dukes of Hazzard*, 1979-1985) minor celebrity status to be something of a draw—but **THE HIVE** (2008) has something else going for it that works surprisingly well, despite a few bumps along the way: it has a story. And a cool one at that. I really liked **THE HIVE**; it reminded me quite a bit of another super fun "intelligent ants" film, **PHASE IV** (1977).

Instead of pulling leading man duty, Wopat plays second fiddle to Kal Weber, but both do a decent job. Elizabeth Healey (**CROC**, 2007) returns to another SyFy outing, this time as a love interest—every movie has gotta have 'em! Due to the fact that it was filmed in Thailand, a few familiar Thai actors show up, as well. Some of the "sorta" notables include Pisek Intrakanchit (**BANGKOK DANGEROUS** [2000]), Chalad Na Songkhla (**GARUDA** [*Paksa wayu*, 2004], **THE SISTERS** [*Pee chong air*, 2004]) and Kittiphit Tamrongweenijchai (**THE MEAT GRINDER** [*Cheuuat gaawn chim*, 2009]).

As I mentioned earlier, this is pretty similar to **PHASE IV**, though it's nowhere near as deep, or as trippy. This is a straight-forward B-movie with an interesting concept featuring just enough action, gooey gore, and CGI to carry the film forward from scene to scene. Hell, even the score by Charles Olins and Mark Ryder—neither strangers to composing for sci-fi and SyFy—was notably good. Not everything worked, of course; I'm still not at all sure what the subplot—if you can even call it that—involving Wopat and an ant deep in his head was all about. It (the ant) seems to have been at odds with the goals of the colony, which makes less sense once you reach the finale. Another issue was the limp romance angle; totally ineffective. I just wasn't feeling the chemistry between Healey and Weber's characters. Again, not a great film but it was more than I'd expected and it even managed to deliver some effective jabs, including a swarm swallowing an infant. I don't think you'll be too disappointed if you happen to score this in a SyFy films DVD set.

2008, USA. D: PETER MANUS
AVAILABLE FROM RHI ENTERTAINMENT

BLACK SWARM

Reviewed by Brian Harris

Having left her hometown of Black Stone, New York after the tragic death of her husband, Jane Kozik (Sarah Allen) returns years later with her young daughter Kelsey (Rebecca Windheim) to fill the deputy sheriff position. Just in time, too, as the whole town is wandering about like zombies, and it's up to her, her late husband's twin brother (Sebastien Roberts), Kelsey, and town eccentric Eli Giles (Robert Englund) to discover why. Could it have something to do with the genetically altered wasps nesting under Eli's trailer?

Freddy Krueger and mutant wasps?! The only thing that could make this better would be Jayne Heitmeyer's (*Earth: Final Conflict*) smoking hot body…

MANEATER TRIPLE FEATURE DVD – THE WORST TRIPLE FEATURE EVER!

which we get! No nudity, though. But seriously, **BLACK SWARM** (2007) is predictable as hell but it was an entertaining little poop glob. It'll never be mistaken for a good film, but certainly passable is fair. It's exactly what you'd expect for a made-for-TV film that would air on SyFy. You get your good guys, bad guys, mad scientist, inquisitive kid, a cantankerous coot, killer insects and some romance. Sebastien Roberts even plays twin characters, *a la* some cheapo '80s/'90s film (*LAME!*). It's all in good fun, though don't expect much comedy, even with Englund on hand. He plays it straight—though he never seems to shake the Freddy.

The acting was present, some not all that good, and the CGI looks decent. Some of the kills and infested humans are gross. So, yeah, there's that. I can't say I hated it…it was better than I'd expected, though.

2007, CANADA. D: DAVID WINNING
AVAILABLE FROM RHI ENTERTAINMENT

HYBRID

Reviewed by Brian Harris

The Olaris Company, a medical research group, has developed a breakthrough procedure that would allow them to transplant any organ from one species to the next with little to no side effects or rejection. Naturally, the military is keen to see just what their funding has gone to and how they can utilize this for warfare. The opportunity to observe the procedure in action presents itself when the perfect test subject (Cory Monteith[3], **KRAKEN: TENTACLES OF THE DEEP** [2006]) is brought in with irreparable blindness due to an industrial explosion. The young man receives donor eyes from a wounded wolf and, at

---

3 Died in 2013, at only 31 years old.

first, everything appears to work perfectly but soon he's experiencing strange visions and displaying heightened senses, elevated strength and aggressive tendencies. Unwilling to be the military's permanent prisoner and Olaris's lab rat, he escapes from the facility with the help of a young Native woman (Tinsel Korey, **WYVERN** [2009], **BLACK FOREST** [2012]).

On the run with no place to go, can the instincts of the wolf guide him to safety before Olaris catches up with him?

Ah, Christ! This was so insanely annoying I wanted to give it a wedgie. Somebody get me some aspirin! Granted, most of the films in the *Maneater* series aren't by any stretch of the imagination great, but this is among the worst entries. It was absolute crap, in my opinion, and had no place in this series. No beast, no animals run amok, nothing. Just a dude in contact lenses and his half-breed, though highly-attuned-to-nature, Native American companion. The acting ranged from decent to "just okay"; nothing outstanding. Justine Bateman (*Family Ties*) delivered the only real stand-out performance.

HYBRID (2007) consistently beats viewers over the head with flashbacks to sequences of wolves feeding, frolicking, and fighting, all set to shitty "Alternative Hip Hop" (Sketch Williams) and "Norwegian Yoik" (Mari Boine). For somebody so principled, Boine really sold out on this one. It's your stereotypical "New Age, Quasi-Native, Nature Lovefest vs. Super-Evil Big Pharma/Military Industrial Complex" canned ham. "Ah, but Brian," you ask, "what would fluff viewing be without a totally unconvincing lovemaking scene in which the woman never seems to lose her bra?" No worries, it's in there. Perhaps if I'd held up a dreamcatcher to the TV it would have changed how it saw this film—who knows. What I do know is it's not worth breaking out your crystals, wolf posters or Mystic Incense for. The premise was "*meh*", action sequences redundant and the finale was just goofy. I suspect SyFy received some incredibly low ratings on this premiere and I can't imagine the DVD selling all that well either. Avoid.

2007, USA/CANADA. D: YELENA LANSKAYA
AVAILABLE FROM RHI ENTERTAINMENT

SHARK SWARM

Reviewed by Christos Mouroukis

A bunch of jerks throw toxic sludge into the sea (even though they are aware of the damage they do) and the sharks in it consume the polluted goods, thus becoming mutated fish. These scenes are part of the title sequence, so you suspect you're in for some true entertainment; but unfortunately that won't be the case.

These sharks attack and kill random people (they couldn't possibly choose or discriminate), but they would do that even if they weren't mutated, so I'm not sure why this minor plot point was even considered during the screenplay writing stage. We don't see much of the sharks slaughtering people (which would be entertaining)[4] so our focal point is Hamilton Lux, an evil businessman who has sinister "development" plans; he is played by Armand Assante (**JUDGE DREDD** [1995]), but I presume he doesn't mention this title on his professional résumé.

Another focal point is the relationship which is formed between Chris (Shane Van Dyke from **PARANORMAL ENTITY** [2009]) and Kim (Mimi Michaels from **BOOGEYMAN 3** [2008]), but even this sub-story is more interesting because Kim's mom (played by Daryl Hannah) is hot. All the girls in the film are gorgeous (especially TV actress Heather McComb), but this is neither explored nor exploited at all, even though this is a film set by the beach.

2008, USA. D: JAMES A. CONTNER
AVAILABLE FROM RHI ENTERTAINMENT

VIPERS

Reviewed by Brian Harris

Hey, killer snakes? Right on. Oh shit, they eat flesh?! Hell yeah! Man, that CGI sucks…but they're eating flesh, so that's cool!

The small population of Eden Cove Island is under siege when genetically-enhanced, flesh-eating vipers escape from a nearby Universal Bio-Tech laboratory seeking food. Now nursery owner Nicky Swift (Tara Reid) and the island's new doc Cal Taylor (Jonathan Scarfe) must find a way to keep survivors alive long enough for Universal Bio-Tech Corporation's crack team of experts to arrange an island-wide evacuation and viper extermination.

To my surprise, **VIPERS** (2008) wasn't all that bad a film. I suppose casting Tara Reid (**SHARKNADO** [2013]) for this flick was a great move on producers' part—she certainly pulled her weight when it came to overacting—but the real draw is the flesh-eating vipers. Though the CGI is totally unconvincing, the vipers are just realistic enough to make the bloody, gory mayhem entertaining. Director Bill Corcoran (**RISE OF THE GARGOYLES** [2009], reviewed below by Christos), working from a "*meh*" script by Brian Katkin (**MASK OF THE NINJA** [2008]), puts Scarfe and his "aw shucks" charm to good use, never focusing too hard on the vipers until an up-close and personal encounter is required. It works. Corbin Bernsen (**RAPTOR** [2001]) also stars as a corporate villain, a role he plays exceptionally well, and Don S. Davis (**WYVERN** [2009]) as the retiring island doc. Both are a pleasure to see and perform like champs.

---

[4] There is even a big-ass whale that was presumably killed by the sharks, yet we see none of that. And that would be interesting not only visually but story-wise too, since we'd see how menacing these mutated sharks really are.

As the film rolled into its final quarter, I found myself rooting for the survivors as they made their last stand! Any film with CGI this silly that still manages to put a smile on my face deserves its props. I may even grab the DVD.

2008, USA/CANADA. D: BILL CORCORAN
AVAILABLE FROM RHI ENTERTAINMENT

YETI: CURSE OF THE SNOW DEMON

Reviewed by Brian Harris

Have you ever watched the 1993 film **ALIVE**, starring Ethan Hawke, based on the 1972 Andes flight disaster and thought to yourself, "Damn, what a terrible tragedy, really depressing shit. This would *totally* kick ass if a flesh-eating Yeti were hunting them!" If so, you're a monster…and B-movie workhorse Paul Ziller (**BLOODFIST IV: DIE TRYING** [1992], **SHOOTFIGHTER II** [1996]) has a treat for you!

A plane *en route* to Japan, carrying an American college football team, crashes in the deadly cold mountains of the Himalayas. Stranded, freezing and running out of options, the survivors begin eyeing the dead as a possible food source, but they're not the only ones interested in survival. Something in the mountains waits until nightfall to snatch corpses one-by-one and it's only a matter of time before the corpses are gone and it seeks fresh meat.

YETI: CURSE OF THE SNOW DEMON (2008) is a bad film, no question, but it's also fun…really fun, actually. We've got a terrible tragedy, ragtag group of survivors led by a square-jawed, All-American hero straight out of the '50s, his trusting arm candy, a selfish cad, the moral dilemma (cannibalism) and, of course, the titular Yeti. The tension between guy and gal, guy and cad, cad and group, and eventually group and Yeti definitely kept things moving. It also becomes a bit annoying and a little clichéd at times, as well. Still, a few of the cool things about this production were the authentic setting—it looked cold as fuck out there in Vancouver—and the Yeti, which filmmaker Ryan Nicholson had a hand in bringing to life, looked great. It was nice to see a creature done with practical effects work.

Now, the not-so-good of **YETI: CURSE OF THE SNOW DEMON**. Instead of creating a little tension by showing the creature creeping, leaping and spring up from the snow, some genius decided to show it making ridiculous 50-foot leaps, and of course to do so meant using CGI. One moment we get a man-in-a-suit monster trailing behind a victim, the next he's "cartooning out" and taking to the air like Superman; it was all very stupid-looking and the CGI is awful.

In the end, this gruesome, poopy production satisfied. Director Ziller, who also did **THE SEA BEAST** (2008) reviewed by Christos in this article, wasn't creating a masterpiece, nor should anybody settling in to a film called **YETI: CURSE OF THE SNOW DEMON**, expect one. Oh yeah, one of the DeLuise brothers also stars in this, alongside the radiation-hot Ona Grauer (**HOUSE OF THE DEAD** [2003]) and Ed Marino of *Hill Street Blues*. Their presence certainly didn't hurt this production.

2008, USA/CANADA. D: PAUL ZILLER
AVAILABLE FROM RHI ENTERTAINMENT

SWAMP DEVIL

Reviewed by Christos Mouroukis

Jimmy Fuller (Nicolas Wright from Roland Emmerich's **WHITE HOUSE DOWN** [2013]) is calling Melanie Blaime (Cindy Sampson from Jon Knautz's **THE SHRINE** [2010]) to tell her that her father (Bruce Dern, whom kids know from Tarantino's **DJANGO UNCHAINED** [2012], but my generation knows him from masterpieces such as *blah, blah, blah…*) is dying, and she needs to immediately come to her hometown of Gibbington, Vermont. She wasn't on good terms with her father and they hadn't spoken in ages, but she takes the trip because that's how family works, right?

Once there, Jimmy tells Melanie that her father isn't dying, but that actually he stands accused of the murder of a 17-year-old girl. He told her this story because otherwise she would probably not bother to visit. This boy Jimmy is a bit weird, though; he doesn't want to go outside the county, and his hands always seem to be dirty from the titular swamp's mud. Also, he appears and disappears so much that even the Sheriff (James Kidnie from Guillermo del Toro's **MIMIC** [1997]) never saw him or heard about him before, even though he says he knows everybody that lives in this small town.

Guess what? Jimmy boy is the title monster!

No, these were not spoilers. You actually figure this out very early on, unless you're as dumb as a bag of rocks or you've never seen a genre picture before, which I'm sure is not the case. The father is accused of the murder because nobody has seen the swamp monster, but this "mystery" is solved very early in the film; so again, I didn't spoil anything, alright?

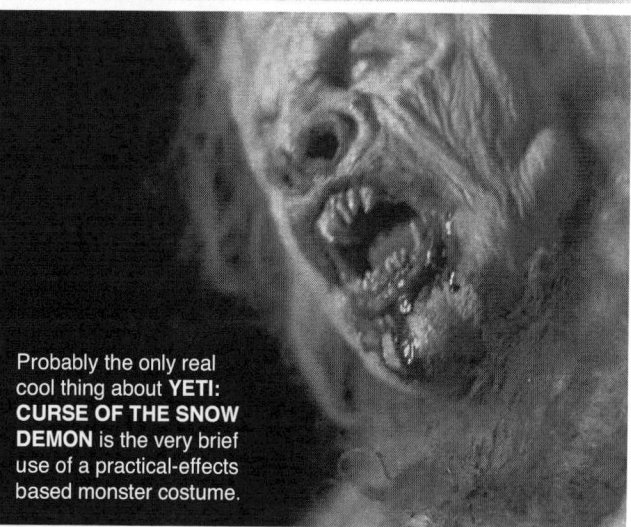

Probably the only real cool thing about **YETI: CURSE OF THE SNOW DEMON** is the very brief use of a practical-effects based monster costume.

The creature itself is quite interesting; it's obviously very much like DC's Swamp Thing, but it can also transform (now, try to think something between **SWAMP THING** [1982] and **TRANSFORMERS** [2007], only much less spectacular), and even stretch-out like Mr. Fantastic (okay, don't try to think **FANTASTIC FOUR** [2005], but think, if you will, **THE FANTASTIC FOUR** [1994]).

Creature aside, most of the story (by Gary Dauberman, who went on to write **ANNABELLE** [2014]) works as a slasher film (the killer monster even has a Voorhees-like mother), and the opening scene is quite terrifying. The same applies for the last scene too, but everything in the middle is just so-so.

All would be forgiven had the few murders at least been gruesome, but unfortunately, even when the monster drags his victims into the swamp this seems like merely a studio-made pool (which was probably the case); but then again, this is not the '70s, so I don't expect actors of the caliber mentioned above to wallow around in the mud.

SWAMP DEVIL premiered at the 2008 Houston Film Festival and was released on disc in 2009. With a budget of around $2,000,000, this should have been so much better, but it's so cheap to own on DVD that you probably won't complain much.

2008, CANADA. D: DAVID WINNING
AVAILABLE FROM RHI ENTERTAINMENT

THE SEA BEAST
(a.k.a. TROGLODYTE)

Reviewed by Christos Mouroukis

A ship is going through a storm, and one of the crew members dies under suspicious circumstances—but don't worry, it'll get blamed on alcohol!—in what has to be this film series' *worst* CGI sequence (and that says a lot), but if you manage to get through the opening credits you will be rewarded handsomely, as this is truly the most entertaining movie in the short-lived (but prolific) franchise.

It will later be revealed that the incident was caused by a creature, but more on that later. The majority of the attacks take place on land instead of the **SEA**, so the title and the box art are a bit misleading, but the creature did in fact came from the sea so you can't say you've been cheated. Plus, you don't get only a **BEAST**, but *beasts*! (Yes, in the plural.) You see, this monstrous marine creature produces eggs and carries its little beastlings on its back…and they are a very evil and murderous breed indeed.

These semi-transparent sea beasts have the ability to appear and disappear at will (John McTiernan's oft-imitated **PREDATOR** [1987] comes to mind, but these things here are way more cool), and when they are about to attack they spit a green slime which paralyzes the victim, after which they lick the subject a bit with their Gene Simmons-like tongues before murdering them in gruesome fashion. What would Freud say about all that?

The kills in this film are utterly fun (more than you should be allowed to have from a TV movie) and the ending has to be seen to be believed; I won't tell you more about it because I wouldn't like to spoil your good time. *Enjoy!*

2008, USA. D: PAUL ZILLER
AVAILABLE FROM RHI ENTERTAINMENT

WYVERN

Reviewed by Brian Harris

The *Maneater* series is probably more miss than hit, but that doesn't mean the hits aren't worth checking out. **WYVERN** (2009) is one I would definitely count amongst the better films the series has to offer. With unique characters backed by solid acting, a cool creature and surprising amounts of gore, it'll no doubt take some viewers by surprise. Steven R. Monroe—known to most horror fans as the director of **I SPIT ON YOUR GRAVE** (2010) and **I SPIT ON YOUR GRAVE 2** (2013)[5]—is no stranger to the SyFy horror film, having directed such films as **OGRE** (2008), **MONGOLIAN DEATH WORM** (2010), **JABBERWOCK** (2011) and **GRAVE HALLOWEEN** (2013)[6]. He gets in, gives the fans what they want and gets out, all the marks of a B-movie filmmaker that knows his way around schlock.

Things really warm up for the small town of Beaver Mills, Alaska, when a melting glacier—thanks to climate change—unleashes a long-dormant monster. Though most of the townsfolk (pop. 300) have left before the winter solstice's scant daylight hours, those remaining plan to celebrate at the Solstice Festival with family, friends and good food. Unfortunately, the legendary winged dragon has different plans for them, which include tearing everyone to pieces. The only hope for Beaver Mills may lie with a tormented ice road trucker (Nick Chinlund, **LETHAL WEAPON 3** [1992], **HALLOWED GROUND** [2007]), a diner owner, radio disc jockey (Tinsel Korey, **HYBRID** [2007]), and a few locals.

I have to say, I like Nick Chinlund as an actor; he has quite a bit of talent, but he's far more memorable in roles in which he's required to play the heavy. While he was convincing enough as an ice road trucker tormented by the death of his brother, there's just something about his style that's hard to connect with. He comes alive with maniacal glee when he's the "bad guy." No such enthusiasm here, but he still made the "good guy" worth rooting for. Co-stars Erin Karpluk, Tinsel Korey and veteran actors Don S. Davis (*Stargate SG-1*, 1997-2007) and Barry Corbin (*Dallas*, 1979-1984) round out the cast and keep things moving. Writer Jason Bourque mixes the occasional comedy—sometimes of the black variety—into the script, as well as a healthy dose of action, so the film never sits too long, wearing out its welcome.

The best thing about **WYVERN** (pronounced "WHY-VERN") was the creature, which didn't really match its medieval counterpart, but that's neither here nor there. It looked great! It swoops, claws and chomps away with abandon and the CGI, while not being super high-quality, did indeed make this production pretty damn enjoyable. Was it good enough to own? For a geek like me, that's a yes. Be sure to check it out.

2009, CANADA/USA. D: STEVEN R. MONROE
AVAILABLE FROM RHI ENTERTAINMENT

---

5 See review in *WC#5*, p.155.
6 See review in *WC#4.5*, p.105.

MALIBU SHARK ATTACK

Reviewed by Brian Harris

Let's be honest, actress Peta Wilson (*La Femme Nikita*, 1997-2001) was a drop-dead knockout back in the day, but the minute she opened her mouth to speak it was like listening to Paul Robeson singing "Ol' Man River". Some call it smoky; others husky…it was pretty much erection repellent for me. Don't no man fantasize about a gorgeous woman whispering sweet nothings into his ear sounding like James Earl Jones. Did I also mention she's got the enthusiasm of a turtle baking in the summer sun? Yeah, moving on…

A killer tsunami, generated by underwater quakes, slams into Malibu, forcing a handful of lifeguards and civilians to seek shelter in a guard house. Unfortunately help is far from on its way, and they're completely surrounded by water…and a school of ultra-rare, super-hungry goblin sharks. Their only hope for safety may be a construction site a short distance away, but with people injured and the goblin sharks close behind, it just might become their watery graves.

MALIBU SHARK ATTACK (2009), like pretty much every other shark film out there, will never be considered great—which it isn't anyhow—because like every other shark film out there…it isn't **JAWS** (1975). Harsh, I know, but true. No matter how hard a director tries, no matter how good the script is, no film will ever attain the status **JAWS** holds. **DEEP BLUE SEA** (1999) is good, but it's no **JAWS**. **SHARKNADO** (2013) is all 100% "*F-YOU JAWS! WE'RE LOCO!*" and it's still no **JAWS**. The same can pretty much be said for every demonic possession film never being able to measure up to **THE EXORCIST** (1973). It just isn't gonna happen. So, the question is…can a film that will never be great still entertain? The answer is a resounding, "Hell yeah!" This film, for me, was actually entertaining. Despite the grotesque goblin sharks being ugly as sin (they're supposed to be) and the CGI a bit sketchy, this was relatively fun. Wilson's acting was a total flop, but with a supporting cast of adequate actors and some fun shark attack sequences, what we get is something watchable. The finale was a wild, bloody little ride indeed as the survivors play cat-and-mouse with a shark in a flood house. Good for a single viewing.

2009, AUSTRALIA/CANADA. D: DAVID LISTER
AVAILABLE FROM ARC ENTERTAINMENT

SAND SERPENTS

Reviewed by Brian Harris

A small detachment of US soldiers are ordered to investigate a possible sapphire mining operation run by the Taliban in the Badghis province of northwest Afghanistan. No sooner do they arrive than the Taliban ambush them, taking the survivors hostage. While blindfolded and awaiting possible execution, the captives hear gunfire. Assuming a rescue or some kind may be underway, they use the distraction to escape their bonds but discover the Taliban gone and no evidence of a rescue. Instead they find themselves at the mercy of massive worms living beneath the rocky terrain. The slightest noise brings them to the surface, which is going to make escaping fairly difficult. Caught between armed Taliban and ravenous sand worms, someone is bound to lose, and Lt. Richard Stanley (Jason Gedrick) will do everything in his power to make sure it's not his men.

Sure, yeah, this film is bound to be compared to **TREMORS** (1990), and for good reason, but that doesn't actually make it a bad film. On the contrary, **SAND SERPENTS** (2009) is actually pretty good, and in my opinion better than the 2nd *Tremors* sequel and prequel. The worms are sort of an amalgamation of graboids from **TREMORS**, the Arrakis sandworms from **DUNE** (1984) and the goofy sandworms from **BEETLEJUICE** (1988). Though obviously CGI, the "sand serpents" don't look as cartoony as one might expect from this budget. For me, if they can't look good, they should at least provide me with some cheesy entertainment value. Thankfully they were convincing enough to keep the film moving, along with some fun action sequences, decent production design and a jaw-dropping finale.

Some may find the acting in **SAND SERPENTS** to be uneven (and occasionally it is), but this is a B-movie so some concessions have to be made. I didn't find it off-putting enough to ruin the film for me, but it may not work for others. Though not as good as some of the better films in the *Maneater* series, it's still a decent low-budget monster movie—one I'd probably see again.

2009, CANADA. D: JEFF RENFROE
AVAILABLE FROM RHI ENTERTAINMENT

RISE OF THE GARGOYLES

Reviewed by Christos Mouroukis

Do you fancy your monster movie set in Paris, with most of the actors having heavy French accents (aside from a British person and an American)? I know this sounds like the beginning of a joke, but unfortunately there is no punchline to be found in this flick, unless your sense of humor can go beyond the bottom of the barrel.

Okay, the American actor Eric Balfour (from **THE TEXAS CHAINSAW MASSACRE** [2003]) is "portraying" the weird professor at some university (oh, how *terribly* he is miscast!). This professor is weird because he wrote a book about how in ancient times there really were a species of animals that people now call gargoyles. He actually delivers the most unconvincing performance this side of **THE DA VINCI CODE** (2006).[7]

Pre-credits we witnessed two proletarians die in a church (this event is later described as "*just* an industrial accident"[8]). We don't really see what killed them, but this is how the game works, and, because we are monster movie fans, we know that the titular creatures are responsible. These creatures are

---

7 I'm not a fan of **THE DA VINCI CODE** (2006, USA/Malta/France/UK), but I'm pretty sure it somehow inspired the film under review.
8 Yes, I wanted to "accidentally" murder the person who said this.

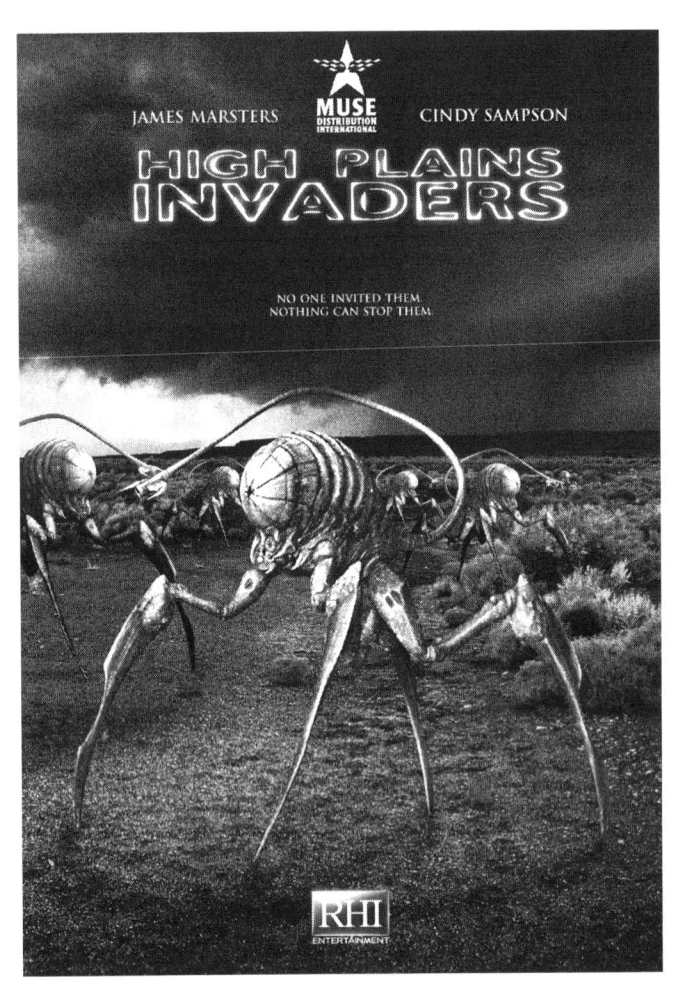

now after the professor's girlfriend, played by MILF Tanya Clarke (from **A BEAUTIFUL MIND** [2001]); she is hunted down in her apartment, and—after we get some glimpses of her cleavage and ass cheeks—she is beheaded.

The film's creature, a big gargoyle lady, only wants to protect her eggs, but to do so she is murdering people, and that sparks the interest of a blonde reporter, played by Caroline Néron (from **ETERNAL** [2004]), and her cameraman is the aforementioned one with the British accent (played by Justin Salinger from **VELVET GOLDMINE** [1998]).

Speaking of cameras, the movie was seemingly shot on video, and this frankly doesn't compliment it at all (it also didn't help the fact that the copy I watched was in the full-screen 4:3 aspect ratio). It is sometimes so amateurish that for a moment I thought I was watching a "found footage film". But, believe it or not, the monster does look fantastic (which is probably all that matters)! I don't know how the CGI department managed to do such great work only to composite it into such crappy material, but they actually did!

But, back to the acting: even the film's *dog* doesn't put in a decent performance; I guess the $2,000,000 budget wasn't enough for a better-trained pet. On the other hand, the red-haired girl that walks the dog is stunning, for those brief moments that she appears before getting gruesomely slaughtered. Yes, another plus is that there is some really cool gore to be seen here.

Last but not least, I should mention the church's priest, played by Nick Mancuso (from **UNDER SIEGE** [1992]); this poor actor seems so ashamed to be part of this that if you didn't know who he is you'd believe that the producers hired an actual madman to pretend he is a preacher who is nuts...but then probably there is no other kind anyway. He is suicidal (he blabs something about how sacrificing his and others' lives is not important compared to the greater whatever) and homicidal (he targets workers at the church site with his rifle).

2009, CANADA. D: BILL CORCORAN
AVAILABLE FROM RHI ENTERTAINMENT

HIGH PLAINS INVADERS
(a.k.a. ALIEN WESTERN)
Reviewed by Christos Mouroukis

Ah, the great American westerns...! *Erm*, no, to be honest I don't like these much; I'm more of a spaghetti western fan, because, you know, John Wayne's acting can't compare to Sergio Leone's creations, or even the other Italian films that ripped these off. Then, allow me to say...Ah, the great American horror/western hybrids! Yes, there are not many of them, but when they are done right the results are pure cinematic gold; take for example Earl E. Smith's **THE SHADOW OF CHIKARA** (a.k.a. **DIAMOND MOUNTAIN**, a.k.a. **SHADOW MOUNTAIN**, 1977).[9]

Yes, **HIGH PLAINS INVADERS** (2009)[10]: this is a horror western—or, more appropriately, I should say "sci-fi western" (which actually predates Jon Favreau's **COWBOYS VS. ALIENS** [2011])—and it starts awesomely when, in a small dusty town, a man is murdered by something we don't see.

We later of course see what this something was. Yes, those titular creatures! And—*oh boy!*—do we *ever* see 'em! They are just plain (pun intended) awesome. Controlled by a spaceship (yes, we see that, too), they are giant mechanized alien robots of advanced technology that resemble four-legged spiders, can actually shoot bullets and dig holes in the ground in order to back-up and organize their attacks. Can it possibly get any better than that?!

Yes, it actually *can*...and does. The whole affair seems to have been shot on film (I can't stress enough how good everything looks), which was a wise decision, because it wouldn't be fair to spend so much time on western costumes and set design only to then have your film shot on some cheap video format.[11]

Other than this, the performances are very good too, with the one which most stands out being that of Sanny van Heteren, who plays a "Clint Eastwood"-type of female bounty hunter. The CGI looks great, too. By all means, run out and purchase this thing! Or, you know, just use your favorite online retailer and do the same.

2009, CANADA/ROMANIA. D: KRISTOFFER TABORI
AVAILABLE FROM RHI ENTERTAINMENT

HELLHOUNDS
Reviewed by Brian Harris

A mighty warrior named Kleitos (Scott Elrod) must enter Tartarus—and defy the will of Hades himself—to rescue his murdered bride from its infernal depths. Before he can do that though, he and his band of fellow warriors must face-off with the minions of Hades: ferocious hellhounds tasked with fulfilling the wishes of their dark master. Though Kleitos risks being barred from the Elysian Fields for eternity, he'll stop at nothing to retrieve his bride...*nothing*—not Hades, his hellhounds or the traitor in his midst.

I like Andrew Howard (**THE DEVIL'S CHAIR** [2007], **I SPIT ON YOUR GRAVE** [2010])—I don't know many genre fans that don't like him. However, Howard cannot handle this kind of bad, especially with an accent that's guaranteed to make your butt hair curl. Unfortunately for viewers, Howard is the only actor of any worth in this production. The lead (Elrod) looks like a wax mannequin of Henry Cavill's Superman, and his acting was just as stiff. There was also a girl, a dude and some other guy. Oh, and some CGI "monster dogs" that chase our hero around.

So, look, **HELLHOUNDS** (2009) wasn't so bad that I was regretting my viewing experience; at times it was even decent. I watched it from beginning to end and it was exactly what you'd expect from a low budget B-movie set in a mythical Greek setting. The costumes and props all appeared to be left-overs from *Hercules: The Legendary Journeys* and the sets from an off-season haunted house. When characters weren't walking and walking, they were

---

9 I will soon review this for my "Greek VHS Mayhem" column in *Weng's Chop*, so stay tuned!
10 Kristoffer Tabori's film was shot in 2008 on location in Romania, premiered on TV in 2009, and got released on disc in 2010.
11 Nothing wrong with video, it just doesn't work well with period pieces, and proof of that is Michael Mann's multi-million-dollar **PUBLIC ENEMIES** (2009).

talking and talking. Without much action or tension, things got a bit stale, but a few loose intestines during a torture sequence gave it little boost. Watch it or don't, but whatever you decide, do not look Indra Ové directly in the eyes.

I can't say I hated it, but I won't watch it again…and you can't make me. Did Rick Schroder—*THE Ricky Schroder*—really direct this?

2009, CANADA. D: RICK SCHRODER
AVAILABLE FROM VIVENDI ENTERTAINMENT

CARNY

Reviewed by Christos Mouroukis

Two carnies make an under-the-table deal: some merchandise (i.e. a devilish monster) changes hands, and then it spreads havoc. And then we read the titles, which are actually nicely stylized and classy. So is the set design; the entire film revolves around a small town and the visiting sideshow, so this was a perfect opportunity for all the creative departments to showcase their work.

Now, the monster looks great and the CGI is good, even when it comes to the grotesque wings that allow the beast to fly around and bring mayhem down upon unsuspecting townsfolk. Apparently the Sheriff (Lou Diamond Phillips from **COURAGE UNDER FIRE** [1996]) has a difficult job, because aside from catching the creature, some of the carnies have a lot to hide, and there is also a pastor (Vlasta Vrana from **SECRET WINDOW** [2004]) who is so out of his mind that he becomes an obstacle, and, later on, incites a riot.

This film is really not about the creature. It is more about the establishment going after the carnies. But because you read this review in *Weng's Chop*, you should root for the misfits. After all, the crucial influence the tent shows had on early US exploitation films is well-documented. Thank you, Mr. Friedman!

2009, CANADA. D: SHELDON WILSON
AVAILABLE FROM RHI ENTERTAINMENT

BEHEMOTH

Reviewed by Christos Mouroukis

This one has William B. Davis playing a professor who is trying to warn everybody about things the Mayans predicted, which is pretty much the same thing he was doing on *The X-Files* show, where he played my favourite character, the Cigarette-Smoking Man. Sometimes I wonder how a movie that cost less than $1,500,000 is able to get a star of his caliber, but then everyone has a rent to pay, right?

This film works pretty much like an old Roger Corman movie, in the sense that tension is built along with our anticipation for the monster to show. And man, does a monster *ever* show. This thing is nothing less than spectacular: a huge—no, I mean *really* fuckin' *HUGE*!—dragon with tentacles!

The only thing that disappointed me about this movie was that it really is more of an earthquake/disaster flick. You see, this massive monster is causing the land to move, and that in turn causes the camera to shake and quake…you get the idea. The whole scenario of people running around trying to escape what they think is nature's revenge may be a bit unique for this franchise, but it doesn't work too well. It's probably also because the actors seem to have difficulty even climbing up a ladder or a seemingly harmless hill; there's really nothing for them to struggle against here, yet they unconvincingly pretend that they are.

Also, my favorite kind of monster movies are those in which the creature spreads terror by killing the cast members one by one (or even in small groups), pretty much like a serial killer would do. Man, I do so like body counts! But this is not the case here. Some people die, but this happens very early on, and apart from one case, none of the main characters has to face any genuine danger, so it's difficult to keep your attention focused on what's going on.

2011, USA/CANADA. D: W.D. HOGAN
AVAILABLE FROM RHI ENTERTAINMENT

FEROCIOUS PLANET

Reviewed by Brian Harris

When a small Senate committee, a few scientists, and a security detail are accidentally transported to a parallel dimension during a cold fusion generator demonstration, they must locate a source of water to refill the generator in order to get back home. The only thing stopping them is that dimension's occupants: deadly, rampaging dinosaur-like creatures with healthy appetites. The group's only hope for survival rests in the hands of Col. Sam Synn (Joe Flanigan), a damn good soldier left out to dry by the country he served faithfully.

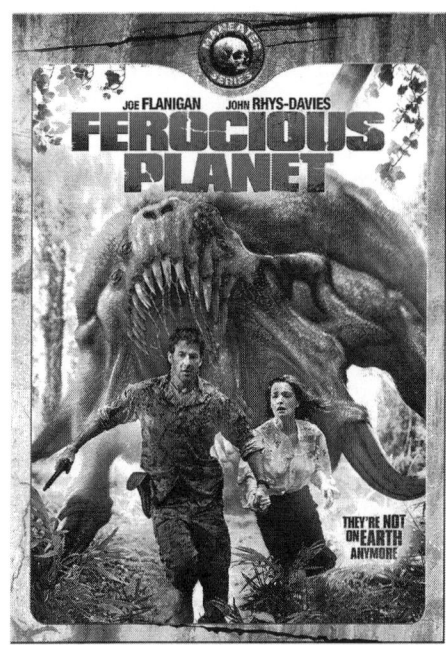

FEROCIOUS PLANET (2011) is a pretty straightforward film; there are no major surprises to be had. One by one, humans bite the dust and it all falls on the lone hero to save the remainder not only from the monsters, but themselves. We've seen it before and, to be honest, I've seen far worse. I liked this film quite a bit. Actor Joe Flanigan, of *Stargate: Atlantis* fame, is a solid lead; everybody loves the "walk soft, carry a big stick"-type of brooding hero and it certainly helped, as very few in the case seemed charismatic enough to carry the production themselves. Sure, John Rhys-Davies (**RAIDERS OF THE LOST ARK** [1981]) makes an appearance, and he's more than a capable actor, but his role was brief and Flanigan looks better dashing about, shooting monsters.

Concerning the beasties in this flick, they were an odd cross between spiders and T-Rexes. They looked cool, but, as expected, they were CGI and came off pretty cartoony as well. Actor interaction with them was decent though, and the action was fast-paced and relatively entertaining. If I didn't know better, I could have sworn **FEROCIOUS PLANET** was a pilot for a series, sort of like **THE LOST WORLD** (1999).

2011, USA. D: BILLY O'BRIEN
AVAILABLE FROM RHI ENTERTAINMENT

ROADKILL

Reviewed by Brian Harris

A group of Americans driving through Ireland run afoul of a clan of small-town hillbillies, leading to a chase that's cut tragically short when they accidentally hit and kill a gypsy witch with their mobile home. Before taking her last breath, she drops a terrible curse, making them all the target of a winged creature known as the Roc.[12] Of course the viewer already knew that was coming as the opening scene, and even the DVD/poster art, pretty much spells it out for us that terror will indeed be coming from the sky.

Anyhow, turns out the very item the entire affair started over—a fancy pendant—is the key to evading the Roc, as it somehow magically cloaks the wearer. As you can guess, the hillbilly clan is less-than-enthusiastic to be losing this talisman, as it protected them from the Roc as well.

With the Roc hot on their tails, the travelers must also fight the clan for their lives. Winner takes all, the losers…well, they're meat for the Roc.

ROADKILL (2011) is one hell of an entertaining romp by genre filmmaker Johannes Roberts, perhaps one of his best. Horror fans may not immediately recognize Roberts' name but he's made quite a few decent horror entries including **F** (a.k.a.**THE EXPELLED**, 2010) and **STORAGE 24** (2012). No doubt some will steer clear of this, recognizing it as a made-for-TV SyFy premiere, but they'd be missing out on really fun little film.

Both the gore and monster look pretty good, mixing practical with CGI in places. The Roc occasionally looked like claymation, which took me back to the *Sinbad* films, and some of the gore was surprisingly gruesome considering it was played on TV. I was blown away by one particular sequence about 31 minutes in that left one of the characters nearly faceless. This monster works, and that's what you want in a good B-movie; a relentless killing machine with lots of cardboard characters for the offing.

I will say, none of the lead characters are likable—the good guys, not the villains—so no worries about losing somebody you love, because it's doubtful you'll find yourself attached to any of them. The lead actress (Kacey Barnfield, **I SPIT ON YOUR GRAVE 2** [2013][13]) can act, but her character stood out only a bit from the rest. The real prize was the lead of the Irish family, a sleazy, lowdown scoundrel by the name of Luca, played by Ned Dennehy. He's the human monster in this monster movie and he doesn't disappoint. You've likely seem him in films like **REIGN OF FIRE** (2002), **DEAD MEAT** (2004) and **GRABBERS** (2012), good actor that plays well to his "sinister" look. The great Stephen Rea also makes an appearance.

This is one of my favorites in the *Maneater* series and, in my opinion, another well worth owning. There aren't many in this series that I can say that about, so enjoy.

2011, USA. D: JOHANNES ROBERTS
AVAILABLE FROM RHI ENTERTAINMENT

---

12 The Roc, a Persian creature, is mistakenly referred to in this film as a "Samruk", which isn't Persian at all but a mythical creature hailing from Turkey. *Like you care.*
13 Again, see review in *WC#5*, p.155.

Despite its title, Sheldon Wilson's budgetless thriller **SCARECROW** is in no way related to William Wesley's excellent supernatural monster film **SCARECROWS** (1988). Whereas in Wilson's film fate traps the lovely Lacey Chabert and her family smack dab in the middle of some Canadian farming community with a killer scarecrow, Wesley's characters are a group of hardened criminals on the lame with three million in cash and some innocent hostages. They hijack a plan and have the unfortunate luck of landing to refuel near a haunted farm house surrounded by spooky scarecrows. Both films may sound dumb (as do the best supernatural thrillers), but it is Welsey's film which excels in its slick production, great cinematography, cool monsters and the luck of being made before CG became the go-to for low-budget filmmaking. **SCARECROWS** is available on DVD from MGM Home Video

SCARECROW

Reviewed by Brian Harris

A group of high-schoolers on detention are bussed by teacher Aaron (Robin Dunne, *Sanctuary* [2007-2011]) to a small farm on the outskirts of town in order to disassemble a scarecrow there and bring it back to town for the 100th Annual Scarecrow Festival. The group meets up with the current owner of the farm, Aaron's old love interest Kristen (Lacey Chabert, *American Dad* [1999-2012]), and old high school rival Eddie, but the love/hate reunion is cut short when a cruel joke goes bad. There's more than pranksters in the corn field, something is stalking the teens and picking them off one by one.

As the group dwindles, the local legends of an evil scarecrow and its vendetta with Kristen's family are revealed to be true. Can Aaron and Kristen stop the diabolical creature before it kills all of the kids and sets its sights on the townsfolk at the Scarecrow Festival?

SCARECROW (2013) is a surprisingly gruesome flick filled with action, numerous locations and a few recognizable faces (Robin Dunne and Nicole Muñoz) from SyFy Channel programming. Sounds good, right? Well, it also lacks what I felt was some necessary back-story, like where the creature came from, why it had a grudge against Kristin's family, what role the town played in its defeat and why burying it is the only effective method of defeating it. Any why in hell did we not get to hear the entire legend, or rhyme associated with it? Unfortunately, it was missing more than just exposition, I felt it also lacked scares. There was just no tension here at all. I know, it's a B-movie so I shouldn't expect much, but we never truly feel any threat, the scarecrow looks menacing enough—like burned, twisted vines and roots—but it never managed to get my heart pumping. A few well-placed, effective jump-scares wouldn't have hurt.

The film basically uses a formula in which the scarecrow pops up, kills somebody, the survivors run, on to the next location, replay formula. It works but quickly becomes redundant. I suppose one might say this was predictable, but I find many B-movies to be predictable, and that doesn't stop me from enjoying them. And, believe it or not, I enjoyed this despite lacking necessary horror film ingredients. Not good enough to own—at all—but I've seen it twice. Director Sheldon Wilson (**SHALLOW GROUND** [2004], **SCREAMERS: THE HUNTING** [2009]) tends to deliver mildly entertaining, though highly forgettable, fare and if you've got a high tolerance for blow-off cinema, you may find this one watchable.

2013, USA / CANADA. D: SHELDON WILSON
AVAILABLE FROM SONAR ENTERTAINMENT

SHARK KILLER

Reviewed by Brian Harris

A renowned shark killer, Chase Walker (Derek Theler), is hired by a beautiful lawyer on behalf of a mysterious employer to kill a shark (natch!), to which he agrees. He accompanies her to Cape Town, South Africa only to discover the employer is none other than his sleazy brother Jake (Paul du Toit), a lowdown crook and conman. Turns out, the shark he's been hired to dispatch has a priceless diamond in its belly—thanks to a heist mishap—and his job is to locate this distinctive, black-finned shark and retrieve the diamond.

As if the job weren't hard enough, a local crime lord by the name of Nix (Arnold Vosloo, **THE MUMMY** [1999]) notifies Ace that the diamond actually belongs to him and was lost after Jake double-crossed him. He's ordered to hand over the diamond directly to Nix instead of Jake…or else. What's a womanizing, shark-killing, ass-kicking good guy to do?

You know, if I had caught this on SyFy or Netflix, I may have been able to overlook the fact that it missed its mark but it ended up on Hulu a week after I paid $3.99 on Amazon, so I'm understandably a bit bitter. Still, even after paying for a film I don't think worked all that well, it managed to hold my attention. The biggest issue for me was a film called **SHARK KILLER** (2015) should have…well, shark killing, and this had very little. Two off-screen shark kills and one past kill implied; I just wasn't believing this badass who hated the ocean was an infamous shark killer the title promised us. So, yeah that didn't work for me, but the film itself was slightly entertaining. Lead actor Derek Theler was a charming mimbo with a goofy grin, the lead actress (Erica Cerra) a weak-willed hottie, Vosloo plays a blood-thirsty psychopath, and du Toit's Jake is the film's comedy relief.

SHARK KILLER is more of an action/crime flick with elements of comedy, and it's predictable as hell. Expect more gunplay than sharks and some

Lacey Chabert keeps an eye out for the **SCARECROW**

cheesy slapsticky hijinks between brothers and you won't find yourself as disappointed as I initially did. Screenwriter Richard Beattie is listed alongside director Sheldon Wilson as a co-writer, and considering some of Beattie's recent work—three Seagal films—I see now where the action/crime elements came from.

2015, CANADA / SOUTH AFRICA. D: SHELDON WILSON
AVAILABLE FROM SONAR ENTERTAINMENT

—

Now, we know what you're thinking, "Most of those films sound terrible! Why in hell would I want to watch them?" Why indeed? You all are hopeless cinematic sadists on an unholy mission to subject your eyes and brains to the kind of sludge-foolery that only SyFy can hurl at you. Your DNA yearns for it, and though you proclaim your undying love for practical FX, you harbor an unexplainable passion for cartoony, unconvincing dreck. It's not one of those ironic hipster things, either—you genuinely love to turn off your brains and watch these films just as much as the next cult cinema addict. Don't hide from it, embrace it.

We can't guarantee you all of these films will leave you feel satisfied, but many will leave you entertained. They're B-movies through and through, and if they claim to be about snakes, you'll get snakes. If they promise you killer insects, you'll get those as well. You won't always get competent scripting or quality acting, but we don't always need those to successfully lose ourselves in a fantasy world. So, purchase a set or two of some of these *Maneater* films, grab yourself a good beer and prepare to smile, laugh and do a whole lotta head-slapping. *~BH*

—

I used to see the ads for the *Maneater* DVDs in *Fangoria*, and their box covers always looked intriguing. Nobody's showing those films on TV here in my homeland Greece, so every time I hear about something interesting on SyFy, I have to wait for a disc release. That's fine though, as they are usually not expensive to buy.

The thing with the *Maneater* TV movies is that, although they seem to have been particularly profitable, not many fans have reviewed them online, let alone film critics. So, they proved to be an excellent opportunity for me to study them as an (almost) virgin territory. *~CM*

One night in 1989, four teenage boys went out to an abandoned sewer facility in the woods in search of marijuana plants.

The night ended in murder.

Read the new true-crime eBook by *Weng's Chop* staff writer
Scott Wachtler

Available at amazon.com

A FEW EARLY FILMS BY UMBERTO LENZI

by Anthony Thorne

*Although Umberto Lenzi has been retired since 1992, his career appears to be going through something of a re-evaluation as younger fans and filmmakers celebrate and reassess his output. Lenzi's gory trash classic **CANNIBAL FEROX** (1981) is about to get a deluxe Blu-ray release through Grindhouse Releasing, and his fun 1980 Hugo Stiglitz zombie flick **NIGHTMARE CITY** (Incubo sulla città contaminata)—itself scheduled for a special edition from Arrow later this year—is potentially (I'll believe it when I see it!) being prepped for a remake, with Tom Savini as director. I've always found it interesting to check out the earliest works of Eurocult directors that I admire, so I decided to do the same thing with Lenzi. Here are some observations about his earliest films.*

AN ITALIAN IN GREECE
(*Mia italida stin Ellada*)
1958, Greece. D: Umberto Lenzi

Vandiza Vavtzi (Wandisa Guida), a young Italian student, travels to Greece after winning a television competition on the subject of Greek history. In Athens, she meets and eventually falls in love with Niko (Andreas Barkoulis), a poor local artist. The duo enjoys a romantic interlude until Vandiza discovers that Niko has hidden his privileged and wealthy background from her. Vandiza breaks off the relationship and leaves town, while Niko, still in love with the young beauty, pursues her across the Greek countryside in the hope of regaining her affections.

Umberto Lenzi's first film, an easygoing romantic comedy, lacks any particularly exploitative elements but is likeable and pleasant to watch throughout its running time. Guida (seen two years earlier in Riccardo Freda's **LUST OF THE VAMPIRE** [*I vampiri*, 1956]) is easy on the eyes and gives Lenzi several excuses to display her in a series of figure-hugging outfits. (A floral dress shows off Guida's curvy frame and typically voluptuous Italian butt when she walks into a bar early on in the movie, and Lenzi lingers on her behind when she attempts to push-start a car later in the film). Shot in black-and-white (with infrequent camera movement beyond a few low key dolly shots), **AN ITALIAN IN GREECE** is professionally made throughout and likely utilizes widescreen framing to a greater extent than the currently available cropped copy can display. (Some travelogue scenes of the two leads exploring the scenic hills, with wide shots of the city spread out below, would have more pictorial impact in a correctly framed version). With numerous scenes throughout of slick male characters helping well-dressed Italian women in and out of long, open-topped cars, and plenty of scenic footage of the Greek countryside, the film remains enjoyable as a record of the faces, sights, sounds and culture of a Europe now more than a half-century in the past. It also—even in the un-subtitled copy located for review—amuses with some wry moments of comedy. The narrative briefly features some English-language dialogue when two gormless travellers ask Guida to help them hitch a ride from the road during their travels. In the next scene, a middle-aged male driver who stops and allows the svelte Guida inside his car floors the accelerator when the two travellers stumble hopefully out of the bushes. When Guida goes out for a long drink with her driver, the film cuts back to the same two guys still fruitlessly trying to hail down traffic. A peppy orchestral score by Kostas Kapnisis features lyrical female vocals suggestive of romance and travel over the opening credits, light jazzy guitar during various outdoor scenes, and accompanies a sequence of young lovers frantically boogying in a club with an upbeat swing version of Bill Haley's "Rock Around the Clock". The circular narrative sees the heroine arrive alone on an airplane at film's beginning, and depart in a somewhat happier state at film's end.

Guida would appear in various peplum pictures throughout the 1960s before working with Lenzi again on **THREE SERGEANTS OF BENGAL** (*I tre sergenti del Bengala*, 1964), and reappeared decades later in Sergio Martino's made-for-TV horror flick **THE SCORPION WITH TWO TAILS** (*Assassinio al cimitero etrusco*, 1982). **AN ITALIAN IN GREECE** has been released as a Greek budget DVD, but at the time of writing was also viewable for free online.

Nikos (Andreas Barkoulis, right) and Giorgos (Stavros Xenidis) knock back drinks in a juke-joint in **MIA ITALIDA STIN ELLADA**

It's unclear to me what Lenzi did in the few years between this movie and his next, and I don't currently have my copy of *Spaghetti Nightmares* handy to glean tidbits from the English-language interview that Lenzi did for that book many years ago. (*SIDE NOTE:* I actually contacted Lenzi on Facebook during the writing of these reviews and asked him if I could ask a couple of questions. Lenzi politely declined and noted that the various interviews available by him elsewhere online should be enough. I don't disagree, but the question of what Lenzi was up to in the late 1950s hereafter became a lot less urgent.). He's listed as an extra in Alessandro Blasetti's **LOVE AND CHATTER** (*Amore e chiacchiere (Salviamo il panorama)*, 1958), so I presume he was still working in the film industry in some capacity. Lenzi's next production was of a bigger scope, and had a greater impact.

QUEEN OF THE SEAS
(*Le avventure di Mary Read*)
1963, Italy/France. D: Umberto Lenzi

Mary Read (Lisa Gastoni), a notorious thief and adventuress, disguises herself as a young man to steal jewels from the aristocratic women of 17th Century England. When her thievery is discovered, she is captured and sent to a castle prison where she meets Peter (Jerome Courtland), a fellow criminal. Mary develops affection for her cellmate and, once each of them escapes captivity, journeys to visit Peter at his home. Upon her arrival, Mary is angered to discover that Peter is a womanising, wealthy son of a Lord, and she immediately departs to undertake a life of piracy on the high seas. When Peter is made commander of a British man-of-war, his efforts to stop the pirates will lead him to confront Mary in circumstances more dangerous than their earlier encounters.

QUEEN OF THE SEAS shares with Lenzi's previous film **AN ITALIAN IN GREECE** (*Mia italida stin Ellada*, 1958) the storyline of a supporting male character hiding his background of wealth and privilege from the film's female lead, then pursuing and attempting to woo her back after the discovery of his real situation causes her to flee. As enjoyable as that first film was, though—

The lovely Lisa Gastoni as swashbuckling adventuress Mary Read, **QUEEN OF THE SEAS**

and acknowledging the pictorial deficiencies **AN ITALIAN IN GREECE** likely suffers due to the substandard nature of its available print—**QUEEN OF THE SEAS** is a step upwards in scope and ambition, possibly as a result of Lenzi impressing the producers of the day with his earlier professionalism. Lenzi's first colour feature is a splendid, comparatively big-budget (for the country and era), audience-friendly matinee epic that shows him to be a proficient director of large-scale action, crowd scenes, widescreen framing, comedy and romance. The Italian director makes the most of his resources with numerous extras, detailed sets, colourful costumes and extensive period detail, all of which help recreate the period atmosphere of old England in engaging fashion.

Gastoni is quite lively as the title pirate, giving a feisty, credibly athletic performance that features multiple costume changes, a dance scene, several fights and a sequence of accomplished sword-fighting during the final moments.

(The attractive actress doesn't particularly convince when going undercover in male drag to steal jewellery in the opening scenes. "You're different from the other men here," says Courtland, slower than the audience in noticing the obvious). As Gastoni's repeated romantic foil, Courtland plays stock hero and seductive rake effectively. Later, when Mary Read takes to the sea, she rebuffs the attention of the awkwardly named, larger-than-life Captain Poof (Walter Barnes), who nonetheless warms to the unexpected presence on his ship. Mooning over Gastoni's scantily clad presence in his quarters and bellowing at his men, Barnes remains amusing to watch until his character exits the story during battle, allowing Gastoni to take command of the crew. The substantial budget and the availability of striking period locations and large sets allow Lenzi to stage visual moments that would be impossible on a smaller budget. Scenes where Gastoni scales a mast to lower the ship's sail, or joins her fellow pirates in confronting dozens of Spanish soldiers as they attempt to board during an attack, are poetically thrilling images that Lenzi depicts with the same amount of verisimilitude as any American film from the period. Augusto Tiezzi's 'scope photography is stylish, with an opening jail cell lit with a blue gel and rays of colour at left of frame to indicate sunlight through a barred window. Elsewhere, Lenzi lets the distracted Barnes spy on Gastoni as she undresses within his cabin, her naked silhouette seen in profile through the curtained cabin window. Late in the film, a throwaway, magic hour shot of the Captain's ship waiting off shoreline, a mountainous background just viewable through distant fog, and beach foliage decorating the left of frame, evokes greater visual pleasures than its brief time onscreen would seem to allow.

QUEEN OF THE SEAS' consistent pictorial craft is impressive. When Captain Goodwin meets Mary Read again and attempts to seduce her (before recognising who she is), Lenzi and Tierri stage one of their most elegant and seductive camera set-ups. Gastoni and Courtland enter a garden away from the castle's revelry, and the trees behind them are decorated with multi-coloured flowers. The leaves shine green in the evening light, and in the far background at left, the distant castle is illuminated in solid blue, highlighted by burning torches flickering in the foreground. With both characters dressed in period finery and Gino Filippini's lush orchestral music providing gentle accompaniment, it's perhaps Lenzi's most effective, understated demonstration of how the golden age of Italian cinema can match the visual pleasures of its American equivalent. The film lives up to its poster's promise of large-scale romantic adventure, and—to refute an accusation occasionally heard in relation to the director's later work—in its entertainment value, technical proficiency and overall slickness, it is nowhere near the work of a hack.

Online reviews of **QUEEN OF THE SEAS** (under both this English title and **HELL BELOW DECK**) show with accompanying screenshots just how pan-and-scan prints of the movie remove a great deal of its visual appeal. The remastered copy viewed here, a beautiful fan-subbed version taken from M6 Vidéo's French DVD release, makes me wish that every peplum, western and horror film from the period could be made available in similarly attractive and satisfying editions. Gastoni continued acting throughout the '60s and '70s, appearing in Lenzi's later **MESSALINA VS. THE SON OF HERCULES** (*L'ultimo gladiatore*, 1964), Lucio Fulci's episodic Barbara Steele comedy **I MANIACI** (a.k.a. **THE MANIACS**, 1964), and Roberto Mauri's 1965 *giallo* **NIGHT OF VIOLENCE** (*Le notti della violenza*), then returned to roles in Italian film and television as recently as 2011. Courtland starred in a few more films before working for Disney, and then went behind the cameras to direct numerous episodes of mainstream TV soap for Aaron Spelling. Barnes appeared in westerns both European (the *Winnetou* series, Sergio Sollima's **THE BIG GUNDOWN** [*La resa dei conti*, 1966], Gian Rocco's **GARTER COLT** [*Giarrettiera Colt*, 1968]) and American (**HIGH PLAINS DRIFTER** [1973]) until his retirement in the '90s.

Lenzi's third film was the western **DUELLO NELLA SILA** (a.k.a. **DUEL OF FIRE**, 1962), which is currently available only as a poor-quality VHS rip without subs. It certainly appears of interest, but I've avoided reviewing it in any sort of depth (or at all) until a print turns up that can offer some guidance as to what the heck might be going on. Lenzi followed that production with another adventure movie.

IL TRIONFO DI ROBIN HOOD
(a.k.a. **THE TRIUMPH OF ROBIN HOOD**)
1962, Italy/Yugoslavia. D: Umberto Lenzi

England, 1194. Following the Third Crusade, King Richard the Lionhearted is captured and imprisoned by German forces. Loyal subjects, led by Robin Hood (Don Burnett), attempt to raise money for the King's ransom. Their efforts to save the monarch are soon targeted by Baron Elwin, the Sheriff of Nottingham (Arturo Dominici). Amid the lush environs of Sherwood Forest, Robin's men find themselves fighting against forces determined to wipe out King Richard's loyalists and cement German rule.

As with the earlier **QUEEN OF THE SEAS** (*Le avventure di Mary Read*, 1963), Lenzi's fourth film is a skilfully crafted, efficiently directed matinee constructed and shot to highlight scenes of action and spectacle. The burgeoning film industry of the period, gifted with a substantial audience, allowed numerous Italian filmmakers to reappropriate storylines from outside their local culture, and **IL TRIONFO DI ROBIN HOOD** unselfconsciously embraces the English tale of the title character with the same confidence Lenzi's countrymen would use to repeatedly portray tales of the American wild west. Giancarlo Romitelli's script follows the traditional Robin Hood story with little obvious variation, and the pertinent characters—Maid Marion, Friar Tuck, Little John, and Robin Hood himself—all appear at appropriate points throughout. Robin's merry men suffer casualties and intermittent setbacks until their final confrontation with King Richard's army, a clash that allows the survivors among them to settle old scores on the battlefield. **IL TRIONFO DI ROBIN HOOD** punctuates the quest of Robin and his men with intermittent scenes of slapstick and violence, the latter sometimes pushing a step beyond the film's family-friendly tone. The humour of the movie occasionally drifts towards the surreal, as when Friar Tuck clobbers one character into unconsciousness with a wooden staff, passes the fellow a basket of vegetables, and then leads him by the arm for a goofy march off into the woods. Elsewhere, the fate of the Sheriff of Nottingham during the final battle may prove more brutal than some younger viewers might anticipate. (Tonal shifts like this are worth noting in a film that could otherwise appeal to younger viewers...but it is perhaps absurd to post a content warning in an article about the man who is better known for later directing **CANNIBAL FEROX**).

While it largely succeeds as a fast-paced adventure, **IL TRIONFO DI ROBIN HOOD** merits additional attention as an example of the director's overall technical proficiency at this early stage of his career. Lenzi shows himself to be an able craftsman, and though his directorial manner throughout this period lacks the more distinctive stylistic flourishes visible in work by directors such as Enzo Castellari and Mario Bava, it still impresses through a dogged reliance on overall technical professionalism. Lenzi—on what appears to be a just above-average budget—choreographs fights and attacks that propel the film forward with fast-paced action, and stages them for maximum impact in front of exemplary sets and carefully chosen locales. The film's efficient combination of costuming, background detail and artful location shooting frequently captures a storybook verisimilitude that would likely flourish if seen in a better version than the one under review. (As a guide to the deficiencies of the current print, the cropped titles during the film's opening narration, along with an evident reduction in the width of some onscreen compositions, suggest that a new telecine would offer room for improvement). Though **IL TRIONFO DI ROBIN HOOD** features a different cinematographer than **QUEEN OF THE SEAS**, the similar shooting style and reliance on widescreen framing suggest that it could be just as visually effective if seen in a more polished edition. The film also uses colour in a painterly manner. The opening scene, where Robin's band of men talk among themselves inside a castle, features thematically appropriate shades of green in the costuming, décor and—in the version under review—the cast of the film print itself. (The latter, of course, could be due to a fading print or emulsion damage rather than any particular directorial intent). Pictorial subtleties of this sort inevitably benefit from upgraded home video transfers, and also suggest why the critical reputation of some Italian cult directors remains intertwined with the availability, or otherwise, of their films in suitably restored versions. Spanish director Jess Franco's stylish and erotic **EUGENIE...THE STORY OF HER JOURNEY INTO PERVERSION** (a.k.a. **DE SADE 70**, 1970) was relegated to being a footnote in reference books until Blue Underground released their widescreen DVD of the film in 2002, and Franco's later, similarly titled **EUGÉNIE DE SADE** (a.k.a. **EUGENIE SEX HAPPENING**, 1974) was obtainable for years only in a horrible bootleg edition, until various DVD editions (culminating in a 2008 release, again from Blue Underground) revealed it to be one of that director's most impressive and affecting productions. The situation continues to improve, but it's evident that the early work of cult directors like Lenzi cannot be satisfactorily assessed until the films are made available in versions that do the films justice.

Lenzi's directorial emphasis during certain scenes is studied but impressive, as in the sequence depicting the attempted hanging of William Cantwell (Vincenzo Musolino). Lenzi creates an atmosphere of escalating tension through sound and framing alone. Crowds of townspeople stand in front of a panorama of brick buildings and castle architecture, watching a parade of royalty take their seats at the top of a castle wall. Soldiers in black, with a drummer marching in front, are shown leading Musolino to his execution. In a wider shot we see the royal party at far left, the crowd in the foreground, and more soldiers on horseback at frame right, all watching Musolino being led to the gallows. The camera lingers on the wide shot, letting the viewer absorb the details and texture of the crowd, and the drum continues its steady beat. When Lenzi cuts to a closer shot of Musolino being read his sentence, with attendant royalty nearby watching events unfold, a horizontal line of soldiers standing with pikes can be seen positioned in the far background across the castle wall, covering the width of the frame in an orderly array from left to right. The sequence maintains a continual, understated tension until Musolino greets his hangman—an old acquaintance who has a surprise or two in store for the gathered crowd.

Lenzi concludes the film with a final battle that (as with the other action scenes that appear throughout the movie) looks like it would have been fun to shoot. Larger-than-life peplum star Samson Burke appears in the supporting cast as one of Robin's merry men. (During one key fight, he picks up an attacking guard with both hands and throws him off-screen like a rag doll). Burnett is serviceably dashing as Robin Hood, but seems to disappear for much of the film's final third. When he reappeared at film's end to be knighted the Duke of Nottingham, I'd forgotten he was in the movie, and was more pleased to see that his co-star Burke had survived the final battle to lead the chorus of cheers in the film's last shot.

IL TRIONFO DI ROBIN HOOD was Burnett's final movie. Burke played the title character a year earlier in Luigi Capuano's **THE VENGEANCE OF URSUS** (*La vendetta di Ursus*, 1961), and later appeared in disparate genre entries such as Rudolf Zehetgruber's **KOMMISSAR X - DREI GRÜNE HUNDE** (a.k.a. **DEATH TRIP**, 1967), and the second entry in the Sartana western series, Giuliano Carnimeo's outstanding **SARTANA THE GRAVE-DIGGER** (*Sono Sartana, il vostro becchino*, 1969). A budget, full-screen DVD of **IL TRIONFO DI ROBIN HOOD** was released in Greece, and was followed by a widescreen Italian edition in 2008.

—

Umberto Lenzi would continue making adventure films after this for a few more years, before diverting into spy films (**KRIMINAL** [1966]), war movies (**DESERT COMMANDOS** [*Attentato ai tre grandi*, 1967], spaghetti westerns (**PISTOL FOR A HUNDRED COFFINS** [*Una pistola per cento bare*, 1968]), *giallos* (**SO SWEET... SO PERVERSE** [*Così dolce... così perverse*, 1969), and a run of highly regarded *poliziotteschi*/Eurocrime productions. His entire career is worth investigating, and I expect a closer look at the rest of his oeuvre would reveal as many treasures as the above viewings did for me. Thank you for your work, Mr Lenzi.

STEVE'S VIDEO STORE:
LOST-IN-THE-SHUFFLE DVD ERA EDITION

by Steven Ronquillo

When I say "lost in the shuffle", I don't mean "unknown", because a lot of these films were loved when they first hit but have been forgotten about in the glut of easy-to-digest fanboy pandering that gets mentioned in a good or bad way. It is sadly way too easy to get lost in the streaming era because of the easy access to titles.

Yes, the DVD era is over; most of the non-hardcore audience has moved on to streaming and only we hardcore collectors remain, even we aren't buying like we used to. But during DVD's heyday the complaints from my fellow fans were insane and stupid, with complaints like "no insert, no sale" and "I won't buy this if it doesn't have extras".

We were like the Romans at the fall of Rome: spoiled, bloated, lazy, demanding pigs who thought the whole world revolved around our whims and desires. And we sat around wondering why the small boutique labels went under or just said, "The hell with this," after dealing with the whining masses we call our fellow fan base. And that led to a lot of good titles getting caught in the glut as the fans bought the same DVDs over and over again, blind buying so many titles and getting burnt by the mid-range-budgeted piece of crap or the J-Horror blandness of the week; it was a glorious and a shitty time to be a DVD junkie.

But with the amazing outpour of titles that came out during the DVD era's prime, it's not shocking that a lot of titles washed under the bridge, and that's the subject of this issue's column. I plan to discuss a lot of great and underrated titles that hit DVD and were missed, passed over, or just ignored for some reason. So here we go!

DEAD END

This is a very creepy little *Twilight Zone*-esque movie about a family who takes a shortcut for the first time in 20 years to get to the family Christmas gathering. During the trip they find themselves being followed by a black car and seeing a lady in white. This is a real old-school slow-burner that lets the creepiness develop before it gets to work. Ray Wise knocks it out of the park, as usual. My biggest issue about movies with twist endings is: does the movie cheat? By "cheat", I mean having stuff happen off-screen or just lying to the audience so when you go back to it a second time you go, "Oh, *horseshit!*" This one does not cheat the second time you see it; it develops more and more and is just a creepy joy to watch. This can be bought on Amazon for $5 or less, so if you like it creepy, buy it!

Next are two films from a Canadian director I worship: Maurice Devereuax. He has done only four films but all are amazing! **BLOOD SYMBOL** (1992) and **LADY OF THE LAKE** (1998) are his first two and here are his last two, which I love to death. For some reason after his 4th film he stopped making movies, but I still will trumpet he and his movies until the cows come home and go out again!

LAHER$
(a.k.a. SLASHERS)

laher$ is the most popular game show in Japan, and tonight is its first all-American special! Six red, white and blue-blooded American contestants fight for prizes and glory if they survive all two hours! So join the sexiest

There's one rule with this ghoul: When you're out of the game your out of your life! Preacherman is just one of many perils awaiting the contestants of LAHER$

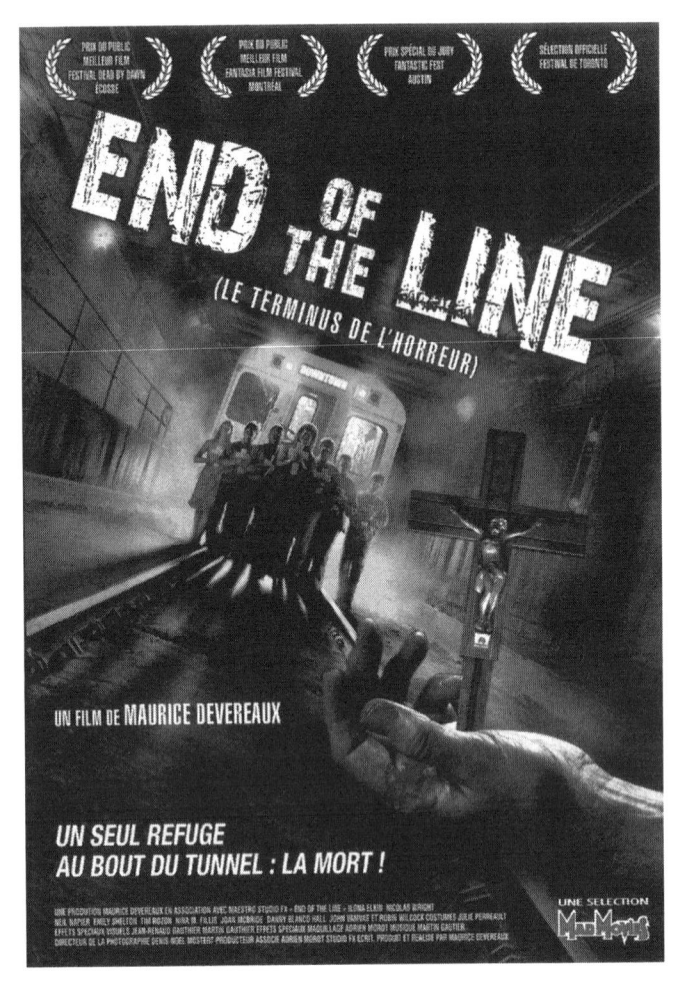

host ever, Miho (Claudine Shiraishi), and the always-great DJ Slash (Shigeru Fugita), as we over here in the US enjoy our first taste of the most violent game show ever! But why is the show named laher$? Because of the three very big and nasty slashers who stalk, kill and motivate our six victims! This episode's slashers are the inbred redneck from hell, Chainsaw Charlie (Neil Napier), and the second is a newcomer named Preacher Man (also played by Napier). Not much is known about him but you can tell he's a first-timer by his lack of a gimmick weapon. Last, but not least is the returning all-time killing champion, back by popular demand, Doctor Ripper (Christopher Piggins)! So watch and see as laher$ meets Americans!

That is the setup for Maurice Devereuax's film, and gotdamn if it isn't a blast. Shot with no budget and with some stilted acting, this is definitely what you get when you watch a reality show. This movie is scarily prophetic of how a serial killer reality show would play out. It features good performances from Piggins as Doctor Ripper, and Tony Curtis Blondell and Sarah Joslyn Crowder as two of the contestants, but the standout was Napier as Chainsaw Charlie and Preacher Man. How in the hell he did it is a mystery to me since one is a small scrawny guy in a preacher costume and one is a big buff muscular motherfucker. A certain scene between he and one of the contestants made me drop my jaw and say "hell-fucking-yes!" It's a classic and must be seen!

Yes, the effects are low-budget, but who cares—it gets everything else pitch-perfect, especially the camera work which is filmed by Hideo, a cameraman following them. And I can say it's almost all seamless, and I say it is a must-see! This also has an amazing soundtrack that fits the visuals perfectly. It's awesome how the movie characters talk about it since it is part of the show. In short, this is an underrated and unique movie, so go see it now!

END OF THE LINE

This is one of the creepiest slashers I've seen, about a cult who, on the word of their leader, tries to kill all the passengers in a subway during a citywide blackout where all the info they are receiving makes it seem like the end of the world is going down. This movie is as intense as hell and it hits the ground running as soon as it starts, with an Asian patient having flashbacks which cause her to jump in front of a train.

This is an excellent movie about blind faith, for the cultists believe they are saving their victims' souls by killing them, repeating "God loves you" over and over as they stab. Their belief is that everyone they don't kill will get dragged away to hell by the coming of demons. Yes, this movie does tell you what might be going on, but it's hidden, and it will take you noticing certain moments to suss it out.

I can't talk enough about how awesome this movie is and how most of my fellow fans haven't seen it. Give it a chance. The music is awesome and the cult's theme is one of the creepiest tunes I've ever heard. So go see this and remember…God loves you!

DEAD BIRDS

A group of rogue Confederate soldiers rob a bank before setting off for a hideout a friend told them about, but they find a beast running at them as soon as they get near the house, and things get weirder as they get closer. This may be the best damn haunted house movie of this decade (next to the one I'm writing about right after this).

This is not a movie you can see once because there is a lot of shit hidden in the background or in places you wouldn't notice. My ex-wife paused it to go to the bathroom I looked up at a place on the frozen screen and *holy shit*! I jumped out of my skin! So any film that can do that deserves as much love as it can get!

Everyone in this movie is amazing, so there are no single standout performances…because they all are great. So see this. Probably the most well-known film on this list, and for good reason!

COOKERS

"I know drug-real from real-real."
- Beef from **PHANTOM OF THE PARADISE** (1974)

Hector (Brad Hunt), Dorena (Cyia Batten), and Merle (Patrick McGaw) have just ripped-off a bunch of bikers for enough material to make a huge meth batch and retire on the profits. But they are degenerate tweakers and do as much meth as they cook. And to boot, the house they are hiding in is a locally rumored haunted house, so when you get three junkie crooks with meth paranoia and possibly ghosts, the shit will really hit the fan!

This film keeps you on your toes by crossing "real-real and drug-real", so you don't know what is really menacing them or are they tripping their asses off. That is the thing that makes this movie unique and probably why it was so hard to market. Hell, I had to buy a crappy double-DVD set with one of the most godawful slashers I have ever seen.

This movie really gets into how nasty meth addiction is, so if you're expecting your normal run-of-the-mill horror movie you will be disappointed to say the least. But if you are looking for a creepy-ass little movie that's a little different you will be hella satisfied. I recommend this with all my heart!

BLOOD AND BONE

Isaiah Bone (Michael Jai White) is an ex-con just out of prison, and his goal is to fulfill a promise he made to a friend on the inside. This prison's highlights include trying to not get raped by Kimbo Slice, which Bone avoids because he is an ass-kicking machine, which helps when he goes into the underground fighting scene that is featured in all these movies. You wouldn't expect this movie to be as damn amazing as it is, but good god, is this one of the best martial arts movies I've ever seen. Every fight scene in this movie is amazing because they use a lot of MMA fighters as the bodies for Michael Jai White to mangle.

With a good villain played by Eamonn Walker, and Julian Sands in full rich junkie mode, this is an amazing little movie and one of the best DTV action movies ever!

This part of my column is a love note to Isaac Florentine and Scott Adkins. You two are the best pair in the DTV realm right now.

My love for them started with **UNDISPUTED 2: LAST MAN STANDING** (2006), a follow-up to the crappy 2002 boxing movie from Walter Hill, Wesley Snipes and Ving Rhames about a champ who is sent to prison and ends up in a prison boxing match with another champ. Well, **PENITENTIARY 2** (1982)—D'oh! I mean **UNDISPUTED** (2002)—hit like a wet fart, so why a follow up? But we got one anyway, and this one has Michel Jai White so I was very interested. Then I seen the main villain in the movie, played by a fighter named Yuri Boyka, and good god, was I blown away. This guy was a force to be reckoned with, and every scene with him in it was a glorious opera of ass-kicking.

But fast-forward three years later and **UNDISPUTED 3: REDEMPTION** (2010) was out, and again…wow! This one picks up with Boyka in a shit-hole because of his injuries from the last movie, and to the movie's credit he is still the same mean unlikable bastard he was in the previous film, but damn it, he is *our* mean and unlikable bastard, and he never goes all cuddly…and that is to the movies credit, and my joy. I loved everything about this movie and it goes into the DTV hall of fame in my eyes.

And the next one I saw was (yes, I know there are other films, but this is my column damn it, so hush) **NINJA: SHADOW OF A TEAR** (a.k.a. **NINJA II**, 2013), and good god, is this an amazing-ass little movie!

It's your basic "ninja gets his wife killed so he kills the hell out of everyone in his way 'til he finds the ones responsible and kills them as well" story. With Shane Kosugi as his backup he kills his way to the surprise climax. The only thing I feel sad about is that the guy who played Chang (Vithaya Pansringarm) in **ONLY GOD FORGIVES** (2013) is in it, but he never fights because Adkins broke his ankle in one of the fights. But otherwise this is pure action bliss and I enjoyed every moment.

To sum it up, there are a staggering amount of DTV gems out there that a lot of you probably haven't seen. So comb your used video store or eBay to find them, and like always…

Always keep looking. There are always new titles to find.

Be nice to the new fans. Because you were once a wet-behind-the-ears fan yourself.

Embrace the past. But don't drown it in nostalgia.

…And always remember: it's our love that keeps these movies alive more than anything else, so keep scanning the shelves!

DEAD END
2003, FRANCE/USA. D: JEAN-BAPTISTE ANDREA, FABRICE CANEPA
AVAILABLE FROM LIONSGATE

LAHER$
2001, CANADA. D: MAURICE DEVEREAUX
AVAILABLE FROM KINO LORBER

END OF THE LINE
2007, CANADA. D: MAURICE DEVEREAUX
AVAILABLE FROM CRITICAL MASS

DEAD BIRDS
2004, USA. D: ALEX TURNER
AVAILABLE FROM SONY PICTURES

COOKERS
2001, USA. D: DAN MINTZ
AVAILABLE FROM ALLUMINATION

BLOOD AND BONE
2009, USA. D: BEN RAMSEY
AVAILABLE FROM SONY PICTURES

UNDISPUTED 2: LAST MAN STANDING
2006, USA. D: ISAAC FLORENTINE
AVAILABLE FROM NEW LINE

UNDISPUTED 3: REDEMPTION
2010, USA. D: ISAAC FLORENTINE
AVAILABLE FROM NEW LINE

NINJA: SHADOW OF A TEAR
2013, THAILAND/USA. D: ISAAC FLORENTINE
AVAILABLE FROM MILLENNIUM

Next time from
STEVE'S VIDEO STORE:
R.I.P. 2015: An Irreverently Loving Tribute to Some of Those We Lost This Year

Michael Jai White chest-kicks some poor unlucky sap into orbit in **BLOOD AND BONE**

GREEK VHS MAYHEM 5: TROMA

by Christos Mouroukis

As promised in the previous Weng's Chop *issue, the 5th installment of the Greek VHS Mayhem column is dedicated to Troma. I've been a Troma fan since I was a teenager; I always found Lloyd Kaufman to be hilarious and intelligent at the same time.*

TromaDance Detroit, TromaFling Edinburgh, and Tromanale Berlin have all screened my films in the past, and in the latter I got to meet Uncle Lloyd[1], who was very friendly. I then ran into him once in London, and once again in Berlin, at Berlinale International Film Festival's Market, of all places. Oh, I forgot—he was the president of the US IFTA.[2] He was even kind enough to introduce me to the EU IFTA chair-person. But I digress…

As you'll see in the text that you are about to read, there were plenty of Troma movies (either in-house productions or simply films picked up for distribution) released on VHS in Greece back in the day. I think I tracked down all of them, but please, correct me if I'm wrong. What was unique about those releases was that the Troma logo almost always appeared on the box cover, which made it easy for me to spot the flicks.

CRY UNCLE is truly one of cinema's **AMERICAN ODDBALLS**!

THE BATTLE OF THE LAST PANZER
(*La battaglia dell'ultimo panzer*)
1969, Spain/Italy. D: José Luis Merino

José Luis Merino ranks among my favourite Spanish film directors. *Weng's Chop* readers should be aware of his zombie flick **TERROR OF THE LIVING DEAD** (*La orgía de los muertos*, a.k.a. **BEYOND THE LIVING DEAD**, a.k.a. **THE HANGING WOMAN**, 1973), which is his best work in my opinion. Senior Merino is also capable outside the horror genre, and a good example of that is his war picture, **HELL COMMANDOS** (*Comando al infierno*, 1969).[3] So my expectations when I bought this tape were really high.

Needless to say, I was disappointed…big time; mainly because the story is a mess and hence difficult to follow. You know your war film is problematic when the most interesting thing about it is a plot that involves the love story of a French girl and German soldier, especially if your backdrop is WWII. Maybe you'll watch it anyway because the cast is quite interesting (Stelvio Rosi, Guy Madison, and Antonio Mayans).

shot with a wide lens and a red filter was added in post-production. Said red filter is also used along with a blue one in a split-screen end-credits scene. The cinematographer (Emanuele Di Cola, **BLOOD CASTLE** [1970]) is using depth in his shots and many scenes are beautifully staged, giving the whole thing an overall pulp comic book feel, but other than that it's hard to recommend anything more about this minor Spanish/Italian co-production.

CRY UNCLE
(a.k.a. **AMERICAN ODDBALLS**)
1971, USA. D: John G. Avildsen

The beginning titles and the song that accompanies them make the film seem like a James Bond affair, but in reality what you will see is Detective Jake Masters' (Allen Garfield from **THE NINTH GATE** [1999]) mission, who is a sex maniac and will not hesitate to molest even a corpse.

The jokes in this comedy are unfunny at best, and not even the many nude scenes can save this disaster. For example, the male lead throws a cup of coffee to a woman, and then he's arrested by two cops (one of whom is played by Paul Sorvino)…both of these inane occurrences are played as "humor", but it all just falls flat in its attempts.

It currently has a good rating on IMDb (5.5 stars for a nearly unknown film that was shot for $250,000 is not bad at all), but unless you have a time capsule to go back to the early '70s with, the jokes simply don't work. The film's history has become a little bit of a conversation piece because it was banned in a couple of Scandinavian countries, but otherwise there's not much to speak of here.

DEMENTED DEATH FARM MASSACRE…THE MOVIE
(a.k.a. **HONEY BRITCHES**, a.k.a. **DEATH FARM**)
1971, USA. D: Donn Davison, Fred Olen Ray

This tape kicks off with trailers: one for a movie that I could not identify, one for Troma's **STORY OF A JUNKIE** (a.k.a. **GRINGO**, 1985; see below)—both without subtitles—plus a very '80s commercial for a furniture store in Athens (I didn't check if it is still there). The Greek video distributor was called New Line, but obviously there was never any relation to the American mini-major studio.

Philip (Jim Peck from **PET SEMATARY II** [1992]) is the leader of a small gang (the other members are played by Trudy Moore, Mike Coolik, and Pepper Thurston) who robbed some jewels in New York and now are on the run in the middle of nowhere. The criminal quartet seeks shelter in the title's farm, where they find the owner's young and sexy wife (Ashley Brooks). When her husband (George Ellis) returns home with the gang's abandoned Jeep, the real troubles begin.

---

1   There's a photo of myself being shot by Lloyd Kaufman on page 10 of his *Produce Your Own Damn Movie* book. That stands among the very few proud moments of my miserable life.
2   Independent Film and Television Alliance
3   To be reviewed in future *Weng's Chop* issue.

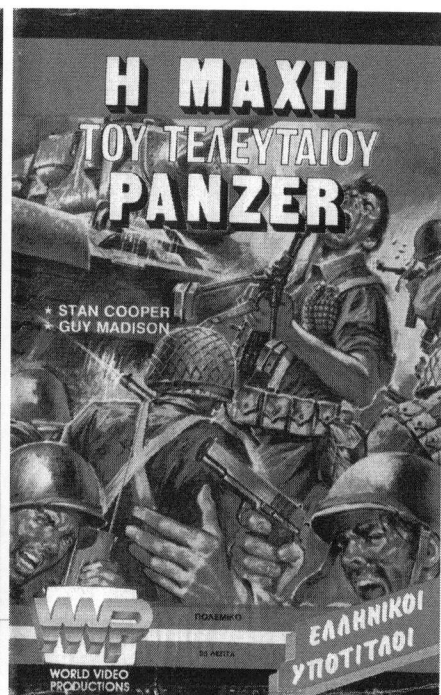

It's all Greek to me: (left to right) 'TIS PITY SHE'S A WHORE, THE CHILDREN, and THE BATTLE OF THE LAST PANZER

Fred Olen Ray ranks among my favourite directors (I own all of his films in some format or other), but this looks more like Troma than Ray (if you can feel the distinction you'll understand what I'm talking about, or simply focus on the acting), but this is because the auteur shot only a little bit of John Carradine footage (more on that bellow) and the rest of the film was directed beforehand by Donn Davison. It is quite funny at times, and even attempts to offer a spectacular ending with an endless chase, but the framing is so bad that it will most likely put you off.

John Carradine appears for mere seconds as the narrator, but his shots (a static shot does *not* a scene make) are padded throughout the movie, but nobody is fooled: he clearly worked for only one day and got star billing. Was this one shot the "marquee value" reason that made Troma buy the flick?

G.I. EXECUTIONER
(a.k.a. WIT'S END, a.k.a. DRAGON LADY)
1971, USA. D: Joel M. Reed

This VHS starts with trailers for **PARENTS** (1989) and **FAR FROM HOME** (1989). And the box cover tells us that the present movie was released on home video in Greece in May of 1990. I have two copies of it, and they are presented with two different covers, one of them is the one presented here, and the other one looks cooler but is misleading and most likely utilized art from another unrelated movie.

Anyway, this Troma movie kicks off with credits that look like those of TV series of the period, and we are informed that the thing was shot entirely on location in Singapore. The film itself is about Americans talking on said location. Well, there's something going on about C.I.A., money, prostitution, and numerous gay jokes, but it doesn't really matter as you'll fall asleep pretty quickly. A couple of chases (on foot, on boat, etc.) and copious amounts of uninteresting nudity won't keep you awake.

Of course, half a decade later, director Joel M. Reed made **BLOODSUCKING FREAKS** (a.k.a. **THE INCREDIBLE TORTURE SHOW**, 1976), which is one of my favourite grindhouse movies of all time, but the action flick reviewed here just doesn't work. I'm anxious to read the upcoming book on his films, though.

'TIS PITY SHE'S A WHORE
(Addio fratello crudele)
1971, Italy. D: Giuseppe Patroni Griffi

Set in Italy in the 16th Century, the male lead (Oliver Tobias from **ARABIAN ADVENTURE** [1979]) sees his sister (the amazing Charlotte Rampling) after a very long time. She has now become a very attractive woman, so they fall in love and the two of them develop an incestuous relationship. In case the incest sequences are not enough for your perverted eyes, there is a scene in which two horses have sex with each other…which I guess will appeal to randy *National Geographic* fans.

Jokes aside, this is the sole art-house flick in this article, and I wonder what Troma saw in this and under what criteria they picked it up for distribution. Probably Lloyd saw the nudity in it and thought he'd sell the film with a cleverly edited naughty trailer? Or maybe the word "whore" in the title was enough for them? Okay, it was most likely due to the generous amounts of gore in the blood-splattered finale, which is full of one-shots and stage-like acting. Certainly it wasn't because of the poetic dialogue.

Troma is known for picking up Italian movies for distribution, such as Dario Argento's **THE STENDHAL SYNDROME** (*La sindrome di Stendhal*, 1996), and fans of Italian exploitation cinema should enjoy **'TIS PITY** because Fabio Testi (**WHAT HAVE YOU DONE TO SOLANGE?** [*Cosa avete fatto a Solange?*, 1972]) is in it, and the music was written by Ennio Morricone and conducted by Bruno Nicolai.

In Greece this was released on VHS by Sunrise Video, known to cult movie fans from their various Jean Rollin tapes. The copy is dubbed in English and the image is cropped to shit standards (and totally destroying Vittorio Storaro's occasionally inspirational cinematography), but there are so many other options available for you to view this film, so don't lose any sleep.

THE CHILDREN
(a.k.a. THE CHILDREN OF RAVENSBACK)
1980, USA. D: Max Kalmanowicz

There's a nuclear factory in Ravensback (the flick is actually shot in Massachusetts)…and before long a school bus full of children disappears in a fog that had no place to be in such a road. The sheriff (Gil Rogers) and the locals are looking for the lost kids, but when one of them (Nathanael Albright) appears, his nails are black and he kills a couple of adults (fittingly, in a cemetery).

Well, more kids come back to terrorize the adults of Ravensback (one touch from them is enough to roast someone alive), and once more the question is: Who can kill a child? You'll be better off finding the answer in the superior **WHO CAN KILL A CHILD?** (*¿Quién puede matar a un niño?*, 1976).

Some people tend to call this a zombie movie, but there's nothing to suggest that the evil kids are living dead of any sort. It is implied that they may be infected by the radiation, but this doesn't make them walking corpses. It makes them

Weng's Chop 137

somehow possessed. And this possession gave them this power of killing with only a touch from those hands.

This concept would work better in a film from, say, the 1930s, but the whole affair is very atmospheric in its presentation, hence its creepiness is timeless. Harry Manfredini's score from **FRIDAY THE 13th** (1980) is a reworking of the one used here, and as you already know it occasionally becomes too similar to the soundtrack from **PSYCHO** (1960). Julie Carrier provides some welcome nudity, and it's a shame that she has never been in anything else.

MOTHER'S DAY
1980, USA. D: Charles Kaufman

A pre-credits sequence shows us two brothers beheading a boy, and viciously punching his girlfriend, before their mother strangles the poor girl. From the first few minutes you estimate that you are about to see a mean film…and you won't be let down. From then on the boys brutalize various young people, who they kidnap and torture. Their mother (Beatrice Pons) is training them for destruction and mayhem. Other than cruelty, the brothers have interests such as music. One is a punk rocker while the other is into disco, which seems to be a reason for them to argue. (Isn't if funny how, only three decades ago, people would fight over music genres, while today everybody seems to be "into everything"?)

Many have accused this film as misogynist (it was rejected outright by the BBFC in the UK), but to its defence it must be said that the humiliation on-screen is aimed at both men and women, and also the nudity comes equally from both male and female actors. There are the occasional comments about race in it too, but they are too brief to generate analysis. The wordplays in it are funny though, and it's a pity that they are lost in the translation of the Greek subtitles; the translator just couldn't get them straight.

Charles Kaufman (brother of Lloyd) was a very capable director, and many shots reveal loads of inspiration, and so does the lighting (Joseph Mangine was the cinematographer, and a couple of years later he went on to shoot Jack Sholder's **ALONE IN THE DARK** [1982], which is brilliant). The finale is a bit anticlimactic, but I won't reveal why, as I wouldn't like to spoil it for those who have not seen it. Other than that, this is a true Tromasterpiece.[4]

Back when I was a kid, I used to see this tape on my local video store's shelf and the back cover used to scare the shit out of me, because it had a picture of

---
[4] Darren Lynn Bousman remade/reimagined **MOTHER'S DAY** (from a script by Scott Milam) under the same title in 2010, starring Rebecca De Mornay as the sadistic mother, an oft-overlooked remake that packs an intense punch and is highly recommended, as well… the two actually make a great double-feature! –ed.

the electric kitchen knife used in the film, full of blood, and I was wondering: could a film be *this* violent? When I finally found the guts to rent it for the first time, I wasn't as shocked as I hoped I would be, but still this is a very enjoyable movie. When I watched it again for the purpose of the present article, my VCR was making some weird noises; so weird that I couldn't tell if I was listening to the film's original score or the old machine's noises.

GRADUATION DAY
1981, USA. D: Herb Freed

I was recently seeing all sorts of reviews for the Blu-ray release of this film appearing on my newsfeed on Facebook. I'm glad people enjoy it in High-Definition, but I don't understand how such a film will look any better at 1080p. I'm probably wrong, and that's why I'm stuck with this lame-ass videotape.

George Michaels (Christopher George from **THE EXTERMINATOR** [1980]) is the coach of the high school track team, and he's pushing Laura Ramstead (Ruth Ann Llorens) a bit too hard in order to win a race and break a record. As a result, she gets a heart attack and dies.

From then on, there's a killer on the loose, slaughtering students on campus while counting their last moments with a stopwatch. He also has a picture of the track team, crossing off with a red lipstick whoever gets murdered. The kills—while not spectacular—are very entertaining. My favourite is the one in which a guy lands in a bed of nails. The first kill is fun too, especially considering that after the fact we get to see a close-up of the poor dead girl's ass. Yes, it's awkward.

But it's not just the kills that are great about this film. It is the **PSYCHO**-like surprise that audiences witness a couple of scenes before the finale; this scene is genuinely scary. The ending comes appropriately with a Final Girl practicing some martial arts against the recently identified serial killer.

Speaking of **PSYCHO** (1960), it must be said that Arthur Kempel's music is very similar to the classic score by Bernard Herrmann. Surprisingly, the songs are really good, too, as they occasionally bring to mind popular tunes by Motörhead and Iggy Pop.

There are sexual moments to be enjoyed here, as well. A truck driver offers some sexy comments about lesbians and makes a pass at a young student, but she kicks his ass. And yes, Linnea Quigley appears topless several times. Michael Pataki is in it too, but luckily he doesn't get naked.[5]

---
[5] Also see Phillip Escott's coverage of **GRADUATION DAY**—which includes an interview with star Patch Mackenzie—in *Weng's Chop* #7, p.125. –ed.

THE TOXIC AVENGER
1984, USA. D: Lloyd Kaufman (as "Samuel Weil"), Michael Herz

When I was young I saw Toxic Avenger toys in the super-market, but I can't remember why I didn't purchase one as they looked so cool. Years later I found out what the buzz was about: the first super-hero from New Jersey, albeit one holding a mop.

Melvin (Mark Torgl) is a sloppy nerd, who is constantly bullied at the gym where he works, and at some point he is pushed out of the window and into a barrel of toxic waste. This changes him into The Toxic Avenger (Mitch Cohen), a monster with a good heart (in the Roger Corman tradition) that will become a hero and fight the rampant crime of Tromaville. In the meanwhile, he will fall in love with blind hottie Sara (Andree Maranda).

Producers/directors Michael Herz and Lloyd Kaufman show a lot of sensibility with a variety of subjects, and give us a solid exploitation film, which has now become a cult classic. It was released on VHS in Greece by two different distributors with two slightly different box covers. (I provided scans for both—how exciting is that?)

Oh, and just around the time I was about to re-watch this classic, I happened to be on a flight from Alexandroupoli to Athens. It so happened I had a VCR in my luggage. You should have seen the security people's reaction to the device, looking with amazement and trying to understand what this ancient piece of history is. A video cassette player! Doesn't that sound like a terrorist bomb? This story has nothing to do with the rest of the article, but it is too awesome not to share it with you tape lovers.

COMBAT SHOCK
(a.k.a. AMERICAN NIGHTMARE)
1984, USA. D: Buddy Giovinazzo

The credits sequence and the font style are edited in a very Tromatic way (even the film's logo explodes in-sync with an actual explosion), bringing to mind the company's comedies, which doesn't properly prepare the audience for the film they are about to see. This is also a clue that tells us that this is one of the many butchered copies of **COMBAT SHOCK** that were floating in the international VHS market back in the day. Don't be afraid—all the cruelty is intact, but you're better off purchasing one of the many special editions released on disc.

Frankie (played by Rick Giovinazzo, who also scored the picture, and some years later went on to become one of the top Hollywood composers) is a Vietnam Veteran, who cannot help going back to the battle memories. He's wondering why he is hated in the battlefield, and struggles to pull the trigger, but nevertheless he's killing an unarmed Vietnamese girl.

Now he's back in Mama America, in New York, where he's stuck in a seedy apartment with his white trash wife (Veronica Stork, whose only other film credit is Troma's **CLASS OF NUKE 'EM HIGH PART II: SUBHUMANOID MELTDOWN** [1991]) and their monstrous baby. Poverty is all over the neighbourhood (the suburban setting seems like it was bombarded and is now on its post-nuke phase), and it got ahold of their apartment, too, which is swallowed in misery. The sets alone are enough to create the ultimate feeling of disorientation and desperation.

Frankie has been unemployed for the past four months, and he sees only a dead end at the unemployment office (which by the way has a **DAWN OF THE DEAD** [1978] poster on one of its walls). The baby was born a monster because the army used chemicals in the war that his father fought. I've read so much about the "Chemical Warfare" theories of this particular war, but I've never before seen such a clever commentary about the issue.

Frankie sees a stray dog eating, but he himself has no access to food. Frankie owes money to the local gangster (Mitch Maglio) who says that if he doesn't get his dough back he'll either sell Frankie's kid, or turn his wife into a prostitute (although I'm not sure who would pay to sleep with her). Frankie befriends a junkie (Michael Tierno, who has produced a string of short films the last few years), and even sinks so low as to call his racist father to ask for money. All this is part of a bigger picture; a picture from suburban madness where the most important asset of a poverty-stricken household is the television set.

This was produced by 2000 A.D. Productions (no relation to the British comic book company). Director Buddy Giovinazzo went on to direct a few minutes of the sequel to **MANIAC** (1980), which was never finalized; he is still active.

DREAMS COME TRUE
1984, USA. D: Max Kalmanowicz

In a pre-credits sequence we learn all we need to know about this film: there's a couple having space and time travels, only to have passionate sex (in some sort of supernatural way). Actually the whole film is an excuse to wrap something around scenes of attractive people making love. I guess an interesting trailer was made out of these.

The protagonists confuse reality with fantasy and so some dates go wrong (and life becomes a mess). The visual effects are more than decent for a low-budget film of its time, but the back and forth in time that the leads are experiencing is way too convenient for the screenwriter to be believable.

This is essentially a love story disguised as a Sci-fi flick, and the most interesting thing about it is the scene in which the protagonists are at the theatre watching **THE CHILDREN** (1980)—this was made by the same director and extended scenes from the earlier flick are used here, and the kids with the black nails even get to enter the reality of the dreamers. Overall, nothing special, though.

THE DARK SIDE OF MIDNIGHT
(a.k.a. THE CREEPER)
1984, USA. D: Wes Olsen

The Creeper (Dan Myers) may be looking ridiculously funny, but he is this film's serial killer. He commits several brutal murders, but we only know that because the protagonists describe them; we rarely get to see any gore, as this would cost money to the production. Also, the lead characters don't think of the mayhem too much, and don't seem to care about the investigation too much either, as all they do is discuss local political influences, police hierarchy, and the press. And oh, man, do they discuss! There's endless talking here, so much that it will remind you of the worst moments from Herschell Gordon Lewis' film career.

The whole thing seems less like a slasher film and more like a boring drama, but it has its charm, although for all the wrong reasons. For example, you'll find yourself noticing a young police officer's moustache appearing and disappearing all in the same scene! The song title that plays over the credits and shares the film's title is the only thing that really stands out.

The tape wraps with a trailer for another Troma movie, **ZOMBIE ISLAND MASSACRE** (1984). This is strange for a couple of reasons: first it is rare for a Greek VHS tape to have the trailer/s in the end, and second I don't think that the film advertised here was ever released in Greece; if I am wrong then we are talking about a personal Holy Grail. The box cover that you see is from the North Home Video Hellas release (which was a distribution company from Thessaloniki, Northern Greece), but the same version was also released (with an equally awesome cover) by Video Tower (which was another distribution company from Thessaloniki).

THAT'S MY BABY!
1984, Canada. D: John Bradshaw, Edie Yolles

This tape kicks off with lengthy trailers for Jess Franco's **DARK MISSION: EVIL FLOWERS** (a.k.a. **DARK MISSION: FLOWERS OF EVIL**, 1988)[6] and an action film called **THUNDER III** (a.k.a. **THUNDER WARRIOR III**, 1988)[7]. These two trailers are so badly cut that I'd bet that they were quickly put together by the Greek distributor's staff.[8] The copyright on the box art is registered as 1987, but we all know that this film was first released in 1984. All these clues tell us that it took the flick a few years in order to find distribution in Greece. But, does anyone really care?

The credits (both at the beginning and in the end) are edited over a song in a way that the whole thing looks more like a TV show. The Greek subtitles throughout the entire running time are hilarious, as they were probably done by somebody who couldn't understand English very well, because they are so wrongly translated that they change the point of the dialogue completely.

---

[6] I reviewed this film in *Greek VHS Mayhem*'s Jess Franco Special back in *Weng's Chop* #6, p.162.
[7] I have not seen this film.
[8] I mean, trailers just don't look like this; they were never supposed to.

Don't let the misleading box art fool you; this is not a situational comedy about a baby; it is a talk-fest about a guy (Timothy Webber) who is a failure but wants to have a kid, and his girlfriend (Sonja Smits from **VIDEODROME** [1983]) who is successful but does not want a kid (she prefers to focus on her career as a TV producer). But because nobody would want to see that, Troma sold the picture with promises of big laughs. "He wants a baby... She wants a career" reads the tagline; and "They hit the jack pot". Also, the Greek title literally translates as "He, She, and the Baby".

Nothing is funny about this film; not even the male lead's flirt encounters that include one with a suicidal housewife played by Kate Trotter from the *Friday The 13th* TV Series. There is brief nudity to be seen (both male and female) but that still doesn't make things any better. Imagine that the "Call to Action" happens in the last few minutes, when the baby gets to crawl and gets lost for a few seconds, and this is the most interesting thing in the entire length of the film.

SPLATTER UNIVERSITY
(a.k.a. **CAMPUS KILLINGS**)
1984, USA. D: Richard W. Haines

Time goes back and forth in this slasher film which revolves around a series of killings that take place at the St. Trinian's College. Obviously you shouldn't expect this to live up to the awesome box cover, but surprisingly the whole affair is very generous with the blood spilt before your eyes.

The film has plenty of religious overtones: the university chairman is a catholic priest (who happens to decorate his office not only with Catholic crosses, but also with Orthodox paraphernalia); there are endless pointless discussions about the ethics of abortion; and if all that wasn't enough a Greek book (*Τα Θαύματα του Χριστού*) about Christ's miracles makes a brief appearance.

When I re-watched this for the purposes of this review my VCR was acting weird and for a few minutes it screened the bottom half of the picture at the top and the top half of the picture at the bottom. Every time you watch a film on VHS it could well be an original experience!

BLOOD SONG
(a.k.a. **DREAM SLAYER**)
1984, USA. D: Alan J. Levi

In 1955 in Portland, a guy sees his wife with her lover in their marital bed; he kills them both and then commits suicide. His underage son is witness to all that…and, he plays his flute!

It is now 1982 and the boy has grown up (now played by Frankie Avalon) and is still obsessed with his flute. However, he is locked in a mental institution where he's not allowed to play his favourite instrument. So he kills a guard and escapes. Sounds like **HALLOWEEN** (1978), right?

Then the killer is picked up by a van driver (who also doesn't like his flute music) and I thought this made more sense than **HALLOWEEN** in which The Shape drives a car, despite never having been in one before in his life. But I was wrong; the killer puts an axe in the driver's face and takes the vehicle!

Marion (Donna Wilkes from **ANGEL** [1984]) is a young girl who, thanks to her drunken father, injured her leg in a car accident and is now handicapped. She has these nightmares, seeing the murders that the serial killer commits. And guess what, this happens because at some point she had blood transfused from the maniac!

There is some welcome nudity in this (apparently the killer is successful with a cute girl, but then strangles her anyhow), the splatter is more than decent, and the whole thing is overall well-shot (by cinematographer Steve Posey, known for **FRIDAY THE 13th: A NEW BEGINNING** [1985]), but you can't possibly take it seriously no matter how hard you try, because when the story involves a flute-playing murderer, many things become hilarious. Watch out for the ending though, where two scenes have quite high production values, and there are some interesting subversive elements.

STAR WORMS II: ATTACK OF THE PLEASURE PODS
1985, USA. D: Lin Sten

This tape presents us with trailers for **ONE MAN FORCE** (1989) with Charles Napier, **MOONTRAP** (1989) with Bruce Campbell, and a Greek comedy (of the worst kind) called **O FAKIRIS** (1989) with Kostas Tsakonas. This tells us that it took this Troma release five years to see the light of the video market in Greece.

Despite what the title may have you believe, this is not a sequel. And despite what the awesome box cover art will have you believe, this movie doesn't deliver. Some of the FX are good, but most of the film is shot around a small river, which makes things difficult if you want to defend it as a sci-fi picture. It is also much too lengthy (89 minutes long) for its own good, and the matte paintings are outrageous.

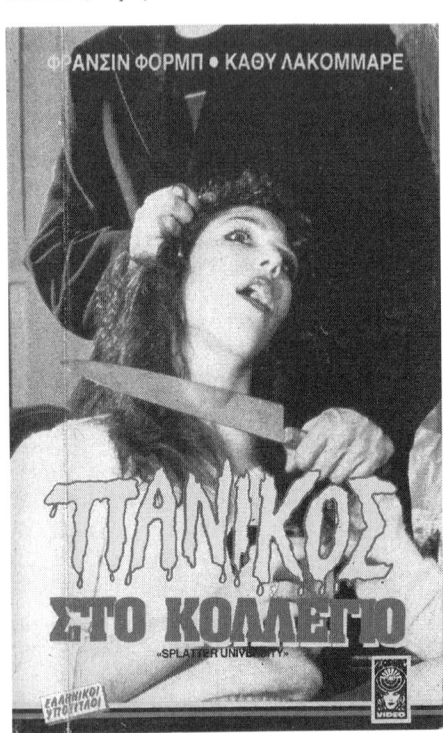

The Cover Tells the Tale: (left to right): SPLATTER UNIVERSITY, STAR WORMS II: ATTACK OF THE PLEASURE PODS, and **THAT'S MY BABY**

WHEN NATURE CALLS
(a.k.a. **THE OUTDOORSTERS**)
1985, USA. D: Charles Kaufman

As you see, the title on the box cover is **WHEN NATURE CALLS**, but the one printed on the tape is **THE OUTDOORSTERS**. But that's not much of a discovery, as I don't think this film went through any cuts.

The movie under review is a comedy about a family man who's fed up with his shit job in the city and makes the huge decision of moving with his wife and their kids into "The Wilderness", where they'll get to live several adventures, surrealist situations, and slapstick absurdities.

This is hands-down the funniest film I have ever seen, but the problem with reviewing it is that you don't know what to write about it as there are so many jokes in it that you don't know where to begin. Bottom line is that this is the kind of movies that Troma should've been making today. In general, Lloyd Kaufman's recent films are the best thing to ever come out of New York's leading independent production company, but none is as good as this masterpiece by his brother, director Charles Kaufman. It is so post-modern that you could say that it was way ahead of its time.

What I also love about my copy is that it is still in excellent condition. It almost looks like a Blu-ray. Okay, not quite, but you get the point…

I WAS A TEENAGE TV TERRORIST
1985, USA. D: Stanford Singer

This one offers two badly cut trailers; one of them is for a horrible-looking animated and badly drown imitation of **THE JUNGLE BOOK** (1967), which I could not identify.

The film itself is about a young couple. The boy (Adam Nathan) is pushed by his divorced mother to go to New York to work at the TV station of his father (John MacKay), and so his ambitious actress girlfriend (Juliet Hanlon) follows thorough.

They start working at the TV station's basement, but soon they start the bombing attacks to such establishments (we don't actually see any of that). I'm getting pretty desperate here; if this is the idea the filmmakers had of mid-'80s "terrorists" then I give up. This is the worst kind of puritanical propaganda a conservative film from that era could do. People don't just become radical because their parents want them to learn "the value of a buck". The old are always right; the youth is lazy, etc. But, why am I even getting into this? This is pure crap and none in their right minds should even start debating about that.

Films like that make me think that the hunger for content was so huge back then that the appetite of the audience was fed with every kind of gutter shit imaginable! I mean, what is there to like about a film with the agenda this one has? As of this writing it has an above average rating on IMDb, so there you go. Hey, this doesn't make the film any better; even if you don't mind the horrible politics behind it, then the badly framed shots will reveal that this is not even on-par with shit TV movies from the era.

ROCKIN' ROAD TRIP
1985, USA. D: William Olsen

When I first watched this film something like 15 years ago, I liked it so much that I borrowed the title to name one of my band's instrumental songs. Now that I've watched it again for the purpose of this article…I found it pretty boring. That is because the back cover promised me several known bands and their hit songs, but all I got was an act called Cherry Suicide (fronted by one Margaret Currie). But that's exploitation, so what was I expecting?

The band's vocalist has a sister (one Katherine Harrison) that meets a boy (Garth McLean)…and that's all, basically. A plain love story. There is some humour involving a blind guy (Steve Boles from **TRICK OR TREAT** [1986]), and there is a knife-wielding maniac punk (Graham Smith from **SILVER BULLET** [1985]), and then there are endless supposedly funny fight scenes, but nothing really works.

Now, as you see from the box cover, this was released in Greece by Τσάρλυ ("*Charlie*") Film Productions (and they got their company name from Charles Chaplin, not Charles Manson), but the actual distributor listed before the credits is Iris Home Video, which makes me think that this title could have well seen another release previously, and what I hold in my hands is a re-packaging; but since I cannot confirm this hypothesis yet, the investigation should be considered ongoing.

IGOR AND THE LUNATICS
1985, USA. D: W.J. Parolini

This tape kicks off with trailers for two Italian genre films, **THE KISS OF THE COBRA** (*Meglio baciare un cobra*, 1986) and **WARTIME** (*Tempi di guerra*, 1987). That tells us that it took at least a couple of years before this particular Troma title found distribution in Greece.

The title makes you think that you may get lucky and watch a movie about thousands of lunatics[9], but all you get is Ygor (Joe Niola) and two "lunatics". These guys were part of a larger drug-using cult group of heretics (Charles Manson style; there are a few such references to be found here). They were jailed for a while, but they are now free again to spread mayhem, and to look for a child which is supposedly theirs. This story idea is great!

People say this is terribly bad, but I actually enjoy it very much. I mean, the nudity and the violence are here, so what's not to like? Lloyd Kaufman and Michael Herz were actually creatively involved in the process of the making of this film (as executive producers), so the entire thing is very close to what a movie directed by the duo looks like (usually the films produced by Troma are very different from those only distributed by Troma, but such is not the case here). So, since all these exploitative elements are here, why this is not as famous as other similar titles? I've also heard people saying this film is misogynist, mainly because there is a scene in which a woman is cut in half, starting from her vagina, but if you look more carefully, you'll see that the violence in this movie is targeted at both females and males.

---

9 Not unlike Herschell Gordon Lewis' **TWO THOUSAND MANIACS!** (1964).

STORY OF A JUNKIE
(a.k.a. GRINGO)
1985, USA. D: Lech Kowalski

This tape starts with a trailer for **GEMINI - THE TWIN STARS** (1988)[10], which is a clue that tells us that it took at least four years for **STORY OF A JUNKIE** to find its way from the US screens to Greek home entertainment.

Master documentary filmmaker Lech Kowalksi follows the story of heroin addict John Spaceley, in the seedy streets of New York. You know, how he's cleaning used needles to shoot poison in his system, and other everyday routines that go along with enslaving your body to drugs.

We see people making drug deals through holes in the wall, and we see interviews with a variety of lowlifes. We are talking about brave filmmaking here, if you only think how they managed to go to the streets they went to and come up with the priceless footage that ended in this film.

Some shots seem a little bit too "good" to be true (although they are still not too conventional), but fear not dear reader, as this is the real deal. In documentaries certain shots are staged too, and that doesn't make them any less real.

This is not as good as people told you; it's actually way *better*. I have seen tons and tons of Troma movies and this is hands-down the best they ever dared to distribute, and I'm taking my hat off because they had the balls to do so. Oh, and the title card at the beginning stinks so much of '80s New York that it is beautiful.

CLASS OF NUKE 'EM HIGH
1986, USA. D: Richard W. Haines, Lloyd Kaufman

We first get the theatrical trailer of this movie, *sans* subtitles. This is one of the first Troma movies that I watched when I was a kid, and I liked it a lot. A few years later I watched **CLASS OF NUKE 'EM HIGH PART II: SUBHUMANOID MELTDOWN** (1991) and all I liked about it was the theme song, so I never bothered with **CLASS OF NUKE 'EM HIGH PART 3: THE GOOD, THE BAD AND THE SUBHUMANOID** (1994). **RETURN TO NUKE 'EM HIGH VOLUME 1** (2013) is director Lloyd Kaufman's most polished movie (especially when it comes to cinematography), so you should check it out.[11]

CLASS OF NUKE 'EM HIGH, the original, is about the High School of Tromaville (notice how even back then Troma was trying to make a brand out of itself by using the company name for everything?), which is located only

---
10 A film that was apparently partly shot in Greece; I have never seen it before and this badly cut promo material did not generate much appetite.
11 And check out Brian Harris' review of it back in *Monster!* Digest #1, p.29 –ed.

one mile away from a factory that is producing nuclear waste (Lloyd Kaufman was always interested in the subject of pollution and he even made a short film about it called *Radiation March* which you can find as bonus supplement in many a Troma disc). Now, the school's bullies, a gang calling themselves The Cretins (one of them bears a Hitler-like moustache), are buying a radiated kind of weed from a corrupt factory doctor (grown in the establishment's facilities), and selling it to kids, who in turn become chemically mutated monsters with superpowers and bad temper…that old story. A classic you're probably well familiar with by now.

BLOOD HOOK
1986, USA. D: Jim Mallon

This release features a trailer for Umberto Lenzi's **WARTIME** (*Tempi di guerra*, 1987), which is a clue that tells us that the film was most likely released in Greece when it was still new. I found this tape in a video store in the middle of nowhere in Northern Greece more than a decade ago, and it is the only copy I've ever seen (and unfortunately, it is in really bad condition), so my guess is that it is a pretty rare item; not much of this matters though as you can easily score a cheap DVD from a variety of online retailers.

Now, the film is about a 21-year-old guy who (along with his teenage friends) goes to visit the lake in which his grandfather was murdered or disappeared 17 years ago. Yes, they meet the old guy who warns them about the lake. And guess what, the murders begin! **FRIDAY THE 13TH** (1980), all the way…

But the above is not really what is problematic about this film. It is a weak flick mainly because it is essentially a movie about fishing (yes, you read that right), with some murders thrown in to wrap it up and present it as a horror movie. Also, the absence of nudity doesn't help things in this sort of genre. And, there is blood, but not enough to justify the **BLOOD HOOK** title, but I must stop complaining because this is an exploitation film. After all, the original title was **MUSKIE MADNESS**, but Troma changed it when they picked it up for distribution. The only thing that is somewhat recommendable about it is a dream sequence in which sound and images are used fairly creatively.

GIRLS SCHOOL SCREAMERS
1986, USA. D: John P. Finnegan

This film's pre-credits sequence shows us a bunch of kids daring a boy to go to a supposedly haunted house, where he sees a ghost. The young man ends up in the hospital, in shock.

Left to right: I WAS A TEENAGE TERRORIST, IGOR AND THE LUNATICS, and STORY OF A JUNKIE

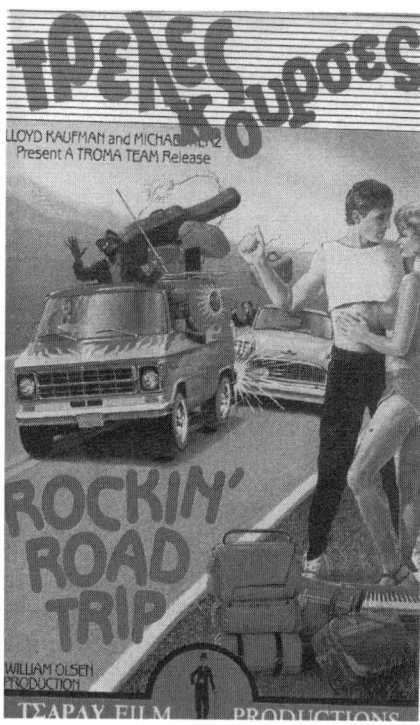

Left to right: SURF NAZIS MUST DIE, NIGHTMARE WEEKEND, and ROCKIN' ROAD TRIP (bonus VHS cover)

Fast-forward a little bit and we are now at the Trinity School for Girls, where a string of strange events take place (such as séances and murders), but **SUSPIRIA** (1977) this is not.

The thing is, the kills are quite well-shot, and there are even some creepy moments towards the end, and you'd think those would be more than enough in order to make a good slasher film, but unfortunately this is not the case here; the flick simply doesn't work.

This tape was released by North Home Video Hellas. They must have made a good deal with Troma, because they distributed quite a few of the New York Company's titles.

NIGHTMARE WEEKEND
1986, UK/USA/France. D: Henri Sala

Look, there's so much going on with this box cover that even if it was used for packaging a Michael Bay film, it still wouldn't live up to it. I mean, I see a sexy girl wearing only her bra, I see a biker (nowhere to be seen in the film), I see a skull (also nowhere to be seen in the film), and I even see an angry dog!

Misleading cover aside, this film is excellent and it kicks off with a pre-credits sequence in which a guy is mysteriously killed by a computer. We then learn that a good scientist has developed some sort of technology that allows him to control guinea pigs through his computer. Even his daughter is using the software in order to crash vehicles! But, the scientist's arrogant assistant wants to use the program on human beings as well. Somehow, from then on, all we see is softcore sex scenes, and believe me; most of them are incredibly sexy.

Things get especially creepy towards the end, but not only then, as every murder that we see is an opportunity for some more-than-decent practical special effects. There is even the casual rape scene in which the rapist gets what he deserves, in spectacular fashion.

The whole thing may look a bit S-O-V, but the combination of sexiness and creepiness that it delivers it makes it look like a Jean Rollin film shot in the States. Okay, now that I've said that I must expect the lynch mob at my doorstep… The director was French! Stop slapping me, dammit!

SURF NAZIS MUST DIE
1987, USA. D: Peter George

Do you remember a time, ages ago, when Napster was the most popular website for downloading music off the Internet? Do you remember how some bands went after it, especially Metallica? Well, Lloyd Kaufman wrote (as part of one of his *Lloyd's Roids*[12]) an article entitled *Rock Nazis Must Die*, in which he attacked such musicians, and praised the public who acquired media through this new outlet. He even went as far as making available some of Troma's theme songs on the company's website for free. In various interviews he has stated that piracy has helped Troma to become more popular, and that he'd rather have his films downloaded for free rather than make a humiliating deal with another distributor. He stuck to his word and now many of Troma's classics are available on YouTube for free, on the company's official channel. The thing is, the debate about piracy nowadays is completely irrelevant, as the Internet is more and more dictated by media fascists who want to stop the freedom it provided since the beginning. This monopoly of opinion, taste, and share of information, should become again illegal, because what the majority simply wants is freedom.

So, the *Rock Nazis Must Die* article was named after the film under review, which is about a bunch of punks who terrorize the local beach community somewhere in the near future, when crime has risen dramatically. They are such a mixed bag of characters that you could hardly call them Nazis, were they not painting swastikas with every given opportunity. But, Nazism and Anarchism are two terms used very often in this movie in ways that reveal that the filmmakers had no clue about what these two mean and probably used them because they thought they were exploitable.

Other than that, the film is going nowhere with its lack of story (it seems that the filmmakers didn't even knew if they wanted to make a comedy, an action picture, or what), and the only interesting thing about it is the ending, in which a big black mama (Gail Neely) is kicking plenty of Nazi ass. But when your box cover mentions **MAD MAX** (1979) and **A CLOCKWORK ORANGE** (1971), then no matter what you do, your product will look like shit in comparison to these two classics.

LUST FOR FREEDOM
1987, USA. D: Eric Louzil

Gillian Kaites (Melanie Coll) is an undercover cop, and while on a set-up that goes wrong her partner (and future husband) Ron Peterson (John Benjamin Martin from **WISHMASTER 4: THE PROPHECY FULFILLED** [2002]) is killed.

Not that it has to do much with the introduction mentioned above, but the female lead will then find herself confined in some sort of rural all-female prison in

---
[12] Those were a series of articles by Troma's president in which he expressed his opinions about a variety of subjects. Most were well-written and you should find them online and read them, if only to see that the self-proclaimed lunatic is in reality a very intelligent person.

which the dodgy guards blackmail and torture the inmates and sell them to either pimps who turn them into prostitution, or dirty old men who force them into becoming snuff movie actresses.

This is W.I.P. the Troma way (complete with political commentary; for example, authority figures planting drugs in order to frame innocent people—which is not very far from real life)…but, you ask, is it any good? Well, it is light on many things such as tits, explosions, fights, gunshots, gore etc., but it does contain all these, so I guess it qualifies for good exploitation watching material. Bear in mind that all these elements here are in quantities just enough to make a good trailer out of.

The truth is that this is one of the better films in this list, and if you like your entertainment to be accompanied by heavy metal music (by what has to be the same band) then you'll enjoy it very much.

This was directed by Eric Louzil, whose career with Troma lasted a few years, as he also helmed **FORTRESS OF AMERIKKKA** (1989) which is reviewed bellow, and two *Nuke 'Em High* sequels (**CLASS OF NUKE 'EM HIGH PART II: SUBHUMANOID MELTDOWN** [1991] and **CLASS OF NUKE 'EM HIGH PART 3: THE GOOD, THE BAD AND THE SUBHUMANOID** [1994]).

DEATH TO THE PEE WEE SQUAD
1988, USA. D: Neal Adams

This tape kicks off with a badly cut full-screen trailer for **WARBIRDS** (1989), which was most likely put together by a staff member of the Greek distribution company; it is actually so bad that I couldn't help thinking who in their right mind would want to rent this flick. Then what follows is the widescreen theatrical trailer for **FURY** (1988). These two clues tell us that the Troma movie under review was released on tape in Greece when it was still brand new.

The movie itself is about two kids who learn a secret, and then a variety of baddies are after them. But I wouldn't know if I hadn't read the synopsis on the back, because this is a talk-fest of the kind that tries really hard to hypnotize you. Oh, and there's something going on with a devil doll, but I can assure you that "Talky Tina" this is not.

The only good thing I can write about this movie is the titles…those look actually cool. And there is a scene in which a gang member is using his wig's blades to bitch-slap a guy. Could you possibly understand how desperate I'm getting here? This is a good contender for the "Worst Troma Movie" award, and that says a lot.

The good news is that my copy is in excellent condition, and I feel somehow privileged, because to my knowledge this film was never issued on DVD. As of this writing it doesn't have a rating on IMDb, as it seems that not five people have seen it. And I couldn't find any reviews online or in any of my reference books. So, how's that for Tromatic rarity?

THE NEWLYDEADS
1988, USA. D: Joseph Merhi

Jackie (Scott Kaske) is a transvestite, and she goes on to rent an expensive suite at a hotel for newlyweds (the room is your basic shit-hole). The hotel's owner (Jimmy Williams from **THE EXECUTIONER** [1978]) offers her a glass of wine and the two of them start making out. That is until the transvestite's wig goes off and the owner starts mumbling about how he doesn't like men. Brief awkward conversation ensues (with typical late-'80s anti-gay remarks) and the hotel guy grabs an ice-cutter and with it he kills Jackie.

It is now 15 years later and the transvestite's ghost not only appears in order to attack the hotel owner and every one of his clients that will stand in its way, but also to somehow possess some of the tenants and turn them violent too. Andy Milligan and Eddie Wood would be proud, right?

This is actually a pretty nasty little film, offering gratuitous violence and unnecessary nudity…so what's not to like? Okay, those practical make-up effects would actually look creepy if the coverage wasn't so bad, and if we weren't distracted by the camera shadows being visible on the actors that receive close-ups, but you can't have everything, right?

DEATH BY DIALOGUE
1988, USA. D: Thomas Dewier

My copy of this is in terrible condition, with the picture going on and off, but the box art is in excellent condition, so what do I care? In fact, the quality is so shit that I had thoughts of illegally downloading the film for the purpose of this review, but I resisted and remained away from the evil torrents. I don't know if this was a good choice, and maybe Uncle Lloyd would encourage me to cheat my way around it, as the on-and-off business in the screen may have negatively coloured my view; it certainly made my eyes bleed.

Well, with a title like that, what do you expect? For one thing, you get honesty. I mean, there is a lot of dialogue here. Amidst people talking this is about a demon of some sorts, who cursed a script. And there is a hair metal band playing their asses off.

Luckily, midway through, the image on the screen became clearer and things got more interesting as I could now see the occasional tit that was on offer. Mind you, there are some quality boobs here, which is all that really matters. Oh, and there are plenty of beheadings, as well.

Aside from the anticlimactic ending (I'm dying to reveal it so I can poke fun at it, but I won't, in case you'd like to proceed and watch this). There was a lot of potential here; for example, the cinematography by Vojislav Mikulic (**FUTURE ZONE** [1990]) is very good in most places, and had director Thomas Dewier (a veteran stuntman) played this straight it would be able to stand out in this list.

The tape wraps with the film's extended trailer, which curiously was not subtitled.

DEAD OF NIGHT
(a.k.a. **MIRROR OF DEATH**)
1988, USA. D: Deryn Warren

Bobby (John Reno from **BLACK MAGIC WOMAN** [1991]) beats up Sara (Julie Merrill from **THE MONSTER SQUAD** [1987]), who then does some witchcraft ceremony that takes away the bruises and fixes her haircut. Then she gets dressed, she goes into a bar, plays pool, does some dancing, and begins killing people. Nothing amazing here.

NOTE: The above short review was originally published on a Greek website and is not online anymore. It is presented here for the first time in English and edited. I was planning to re-watch this film in order to write a lengthier review but the tape broke down my VCR (sparks coming out of it and all, but luckily it did not catch fire), and then I brought in my back-up VCR and it broke down that, too. I then went back to my first VCR and fixed it and realized it was the stupid tape's fault in the first place. I did not want to buy the film again on DVD because I am not very fond of it, and I did not want to download it either because I stay away from the torrents. So please excuse this small exception in this otherwise lengthy Troma article.

TROMA'S WAR
(a.k.a. **1,000 WAYS TO DIE**)
1988, USA. D: Michael Herz, Lloyd Kaufman

This tape offers up trailers for **EPIKINDYNOS EROTAS** (1989), **DEATH SPA** (a.k.a. **WITCH BITCH**, 1989)[13], and **POIOS PANTREVETE TI GINEKA MOU** (1989), which appears to be a trash Greek comedy that even IMDb has no listing for (I had to cross-reference its existence elsewhere). These elements reveal that the Troma movie under review was released in Greece just after it played theatres (if it ever did). Hooray!

On to the movie: A Tromaville airplane is flying around the Caribbean when it suddenly crashes. A motley crew of survivors (you know, the usual Tromatic exaggerated rough stereotypes, such as the feminist that is called "dyke" on at least one occasion, the vegetarian who must have been something back then, a singing priest, and the rockers that only care about their broken guitars) will then encounter a bunch of commandos[14] (here we go again, with a German leader that is presumably a Nazi, a Native American, a black man, a Spanish man, and even Joe Fleishaker in what was his first appearance in a Troma film) and all hell

---
13 I plan to review this slasher flick in a future installment of the present column.
14 Eh…they wear some weird gas masks that they obviously won't need—at least not in this film—and the set-up takes place on two sides of an island, and what appears to be a jungle.

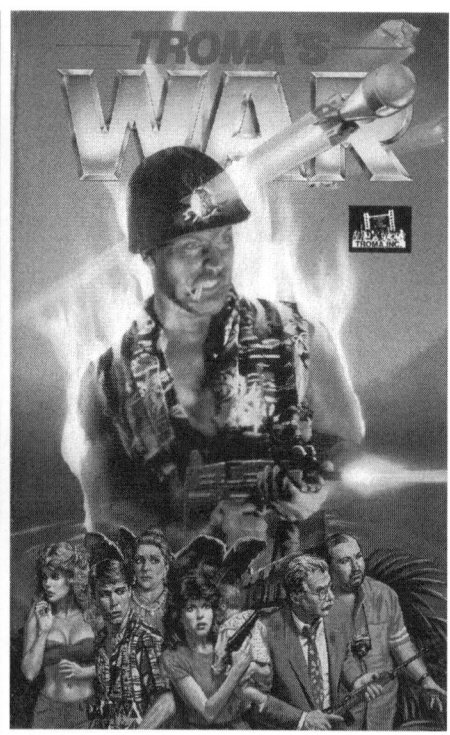

Left to right: LUST FOR FREEDOM, THE NEWLYDEADS, and TROMA'S WAR

breaks loose. From then on the film is an extended battle sequence that becomes a parody of war film clichés. Isn't it funny how war films (or even anti-war films) work as porn for soldiers?

What did I learn from this film? It told me that communists and fascists are the same. Such opinions are spread like shit-storm by people who have never read the theories behind either of these standings (or any political science books, for that matter) and they are so generic and stupid that I can't even get angry anymore.

It cost Troma $3,000,000 to make, which is the most money they ever spend on a single film (note the success of some of the films reviewed above)…and it was a flop. In theory this was because of the heavy cuts that were imposed by the MPAA, but we should also note that this era was dying. Troma, for better or worse, continued to make more or less the same kind of parodies up to the present time, which allowed them to have a steady fan base. I could only find two of their films released on tape in Greece in the next year (these are reviewed bellow), and none after that. It took a few more years for VHS to die, but the evil major studios had apparently done their job against the independents.

BLADES
1989, USA. D: Thomas R. Rondinella

This tape kicks off with trailers for **SLUMBER PARTY MASSACRE II** (1987) and **THE 13th FLOOR** (1988), and these work as elements that prove that the film under review was released on tape in Greece while it was still new.

Something (we see only its point of view at the beginning) is killing people one-by-one (mutilating them to pieces—gore fans will be pleased) in a golf venue. There are the voices in the community that want the event to be shut down until they find what is tearing their fellow citizens apart, but the businessmen want to continue making the monies because the tournament is scheduled to be broadcast on television.

Yes, this is **JAWS** (1975) with a lawnmower instead of a shark.[15] I wouldn't reveal who the killer is, but the advertising department already killed any potential of suspense thanks to the tell-all title and indiscreet poster. But I guess that if the title was more abstract then people wouldn't go to see this in the Times Square theatre that it played.

Director Thomas Rondinella was the A.D. in **GIRLS SCHOOL SCREAMERS** (1986), which is reviewed above, and he is still active today.

---
15 And the similarities don't end there; for example, check out the soundtrack.

FORTRESS OF AMERIKKKA
(a.k.a. **FORTRESS OF AMERIKKKA: THE MERCENARIES**)
1989, USA. D: Eric Louzil

This release launches with trailers for: **O PIRATIS KAI I FILIPINEZA** (1990), which is an obscure trash Greek comedy that looks like it's not on IMDb but there is a YouTube upload for those who hate themselves; **O PROTARIS BATSOS KAI I TROTEZA** (1989), which is another trash Greek comedy crap; and **RAGE OF VENGEANCE** (1993), which is the element that tells us that the film under review was released in Greece something like four years after it was made, unless this was an alternative title for some earlier film that I could not identify because my copy is in really bad condition.

This film by producers Michael Herz and Lloyd Kaufman is about John Whitecloud (Gene Lebrock from **METAMORPHOSIS** [1990])[16], who will find himself in the midst of a war between corrupt authorities and the titular eastern syndicate at the Troma city. Other than that it is business as usual with gunshots, explosions, and girls of every hair colour (mainly blond) and every breast size (ranging from small natural ones to gigantic silicone ones)[17], including those of the insanely gorgeous Leslie (Karen Michaels from **DEATH SPA** [a.k.a. **WITCH BITCH**, 1989]).

THE BATTLE OF THE LAST PANZER
1969, SPAIN/ITALY. D: JOSÉ LUIS MERINO

CRY UNCLE
1971, USA. D: JOHN G. AVILDSEN
AVAILABLE FROM TROMA

DEMENTED DEATH FARM MASSACRE…THE MOVIE
1971, USA. D: DONN DAVISON, FRED OLEN RAY
AVAILABLE FROM TROMA

G.I. EXECUTIONER
1971, USA. D: JOEL M. REED
AVAILABLE FROM TROMA

---
16 I plan to review this George Eastman flick in a future installment of the present column.
17 They are taking their clothes off from the very first scene, so you should be satisfied. And even when they are wearing clothes, these are usually a white tank top and jean shorts. Also note how in the box cover the girl's nipples are visible through the tight shirt. Okay, enough, you Peeping Toms!

'TIS PITY SHE'S A WHORE
1971, ITALY. D: GIUSEPPE PATRONI GRIFFI
AVAILABLE FROM TELEVISTA

THE CHILDREN
1980, USA. D: MAX KALMANOWICZ
AVAILABLE FROM TROMA

MOTHER'S DAY
1980, USA. D: CHARLES KAUFMAN
AVAILABLE FROM ANCHOR BAY/TROMA RETRO

GRADUATION DAY
1981, USA. D: HERB FREED
AVAILABLE FROM TROMA AND VINEGAR SYNDROME

THE TOXIC AVENGER
1984, USA. D: LLOYD KAUFMAN, MICHAEL HERZ
AVAILABLE FROM TROMA

COMBAT SHOCK
1984, USA. D: BUDDY GIOVINAZZO
AVAILABLE FROM TROMA

DREAMS COME TRUE
1984, USA. D: MAX KALMANOWICZ

THE DARK SIDE OF MIDNIGHT
1984, USA. D: WES OLSEN
AVAILABLE FROM BCI/ECLIPSE

THAT'S MY BABY!
1984, CANADA. D: JOHN BRADSHAW, EDIE YOLLES

SPLATTER UNIVERSITY
1984, USA. D: RICHARD W. HAINES
AVAILABLE FROM FILMRISE

BLOOD SONG
1984, USA. D: ALAN J. LEVI
AVAILABLE FROM NAVARRE

BONUS cover!

STAR WORMS II: ATTACK OF THE PLEASURE PODS
1985, USA. D: LIN STEN
AVAILABLE FROM TROMA [VOD]

WHEN NATURE CALLS
1985, USA. D: CHARLES KAUFMAN
AVAILABLE FROM TROMA

I WAS A TEENAGE TV TERRORIST
1985, USA. D: STANFORD SINGER
AVAILABLE FROM TROMA

ROCKIN' ROAD TRIP
1985, USA. D: WILLIAM OLSEN
AVAILABLE FROM VCI

IGOR AND THE LUNATICS
1985, USA. D: W.J. PAROLINI
AVAILABLE FROM TROMA

STORY OF A JUNKIE
1985, USA. D: LECH KOWALSKI
AVAILABLE FROM TROMA

CLASS OF NUKE 'EM HIGH
1986, USA. D: RICHARD W. HAINES, LLOYD KAUFMAN
AVAILABLE FROM TROMA

BLOOD HOOK
1986, USA. D: JIM MALLON
AVAILABLE FROM TROMA

GIRLS SCHOOL SCREAMERS
1986, USA. D: JOHN P. FINNEGAN
AVAILABLE FROM TROMA

NIGHTMARE WEEKEND
1986, UK/USA/FRANCE. D: HENRI SALA
AVAILABLE FROM TROMA

SURF NAZIS MUST DIE
1987, USA. D: PETER GEORGE
AVAILABLE FROM TROMA

LUST FOR FREEDOM
1987, USA. D: ERIC LOUZIL
AVAILABLE FROM VINEGAR SYNDROME

DEATH TO THE PEE WEE SQUAD
1988, USA. D: NEAL ADAMS

THE NEWLYDEADS
1988, USA. D: JOSEPH MERHI
AVAILABLE FROM TROMA

DEATH BY DIALOGUE
1988, USA. D: THOMAS DEWIER
AVAILABLE FROM TROMA

DEAD OF NIGHT
1988, USA. D: DERYN WARREN
AVAILABLE FROM TROMA [AS MIRROR OF DEATH]

TROMA'S WAR
1988, USA. D: MICHAEL HERZ, LLOYD KAUFMAN
AVAILABLE FROM TROMA

BLADES
1989, USA. D: THOMAS R. RONDINELLA
AVAILABLE FROM TROMA [VOD]

FORTRESS OF AMERIKKKA
1989, USA. D: ERIC LOUZIL
AVAILABLE FROM TROMA

PIMPING GODFREY HO

by Jeff Goodhartz

Godfrey Ho Jeung-Keung is perhaps the most reviled "auteur" in all of Hong Kong cinema. Serious Hong Kong film buffs rarely have a kind word to say about the man's work, and that's understandable. His cut-and-paste epics are not only terrible Grade-Z filmmaking, but in most cases were created merely to earn a cheap buck among unsuspecting U.S. video renters and buyers throughout the '80s and early '90s. So why devote a regular column to the man? I do it because as someone who enjoys a "bad" movie almost as much as a "good" one, I find his work to be an irresistible brain-draining experience.

*At their very best (**MAJESTIC THUNDERBOLT** [1985], **NINJA TERMINATOR** [1985], **PLATOON WARRIORS** [1988]) Ho (along with cronies Tomas Tang and Joseph Lai) takes an already wonderfully over-the-top film and actually improves upon it (arguably) through his warped inserts, resulting in some of the best psychotronic movie viewing experiences imaginable. Even at their worst (most of the "great" man's '90s output), they can give off the vibe that one is being privy to entering and watching someone else's irrational dream.*

In addition to being entertaining (hopefully), this column is also intended to be educational. One of the pitfalls of choosing Godfrey Ho movies as a topic is trying to identify the "borrowed footage" (or "host film", if you will). While I will do my best to put a name to the many films that Ho, Lai and Tang secretly borrowed (cough!) and used, there will be times where said epic will prove to be unidentifiable. I'll certainly do my best here, but this is an ongoing learning experience, for myself as well as you fine folk who have chosen to read this column...you are *reading this, right?*

MISSION THUNDERBOLT
(雷霆出擊)

This particular entry represents an historic moment in the career of director supremo Godfrey Ho, as well as great overlord Joseph Lai and his storied IFD Films and Arts company, as it is the very first of their many…many… cut-and-paste ventures. That's right, friends: for those who have been viewing these two-in-one epics with wide-eyed wonder and were anxious to discover where the genesis of such a cinematic movement came from, look no further. It begins right here with the seminal **MISSION THUNDERBOLT**.

For this inaugural combo effort, Lai chooses to utilize the 1982 revenge pic, **DON'T TRUST A STRANGER** (別愛陌生人). Directed by actor-turned-director Dong Jan-woo (a.k.a. Chin Hu Tung, who has helmed some pretty good '70s kung fu movies such as **SNUFF-BOTTLE CONNECTION** [神腿鐵扇功 / *Shen tui tie shan gong*, 1977], **THE INSTANT KUNG FU MAN** [霎眼功夫 / *Zhen jia gong fu*, 1977], **A MASSACRE SURVIVOR** [人在江湖 / *Ren zai jiang hu*, 1979] and **BUDDHA ASSASSINATOR** [佛掌皇爺 / *Fo Zhang huang di*, 1980]), this turned out to be a particularly strong and involving "host" film. The story revolves around Allison (Lu Yi-Chan of **QUEEN BEE** [女王蜂 / *Nu wang feng*, 1981] fame), who witnesses her friend Rosie being stabbed to death by an unknown gang. Attempting to put herself in a position of power, Allison goes to work as hostess for femme gangster Phoenix (Chu Mei Yam). Gaining Phoenix's trust and proving herself physically able, Allison begins going on assignment swhile taking the opportunity to go sleuthing and ultimately discovering Rosie's

Lu-I Chan from **MISSION THUNDERBOLT**

killer to be none other than Phoenix's right hand man, Panther (Shut Chung-Tin). Michael Chan Wai Man plays the formidable (and formidably named) Hercules, leader of rival gang, The Serpents. Rosie was his girl and was murdered by Panther as retribution (I think). When Allison gets too close to the truth, Panther has her and Hercules set up to be taken down by the police (led by Chen Kuan Tai, who until the finale does little more than sit behind a desk). Allison and Hercules learn too late of Panther's maneuverings, and must team-up for survival.

Dong Jan-woo makes a compelling picture here, and much of that has to do with star Lu Yi-Chan. An intense actress with a totally believable look of hatred and bloodlust in her eyes, she has carried many an '80s Taiwan revenge pic seemingly on sheer force of will. Director Dong gives her ample opportunity to unleash her rage in several notable killings as well as a match against the very formidable Michael Chan whom she fends off quite believably (no mean feat, there). In fact, other than the underuse of venerable Chen Kwan Tai, there is nary a false step taken in the material. So strong is it that for once I actually found myself wishing that it wouldn't cut away to the IFD footage (which is more often than not, the part of these films I prefer watching), but it does…

Godfrey Ho's new material starts off remarkably similarly to the earlier **JAGUAR FORCE THUNDERBOLT** (飛豹行動 / *Fei bao xing dong*, 1981)—a Taiwan actioner that was presented complete and un-spliced-into by IFD films the same year. A series of worldwide assassinations are being carried out by a pair of murderers, one male (Jeet Kune Do exponent John Ladalski) and the other a female black widow-type (played by a beautiful unnamed blonde actress). On the case is an Interpol agent (Steve Daw) who after dispensing with the murderous pair, ultimately tracks down the leader (the ever-present Phillip Kao Fei, who seems to be dress-rehearsing for his far more over-the-top role in **MAJESTIC THUNDERBOLT** [霹靂智多星 / *Lei ting chu chuan*, 1985] made the following year) who, by the way, is also somehow responsible for the inter-gang fighting in the other film (we learn this as usual by ever-reliable phone conversation gag which attempts to connect the two disparate films, but never really does).

Though perhaps not some of the Ho-ster's strongest ever footage, there is enough on display here to make for a good time. Steve Daw takes the lead for the lone occasion and makes the most of it. He's no Richard Harrison (who had yet to make his debut for IFD), but he's sturdy enough and a decent fighter. In fact, there is quite a bit of hand-to-hand combat to be found, which is fine with me; I love gunfights, but love the empty-handed stuff even more. The unidentified actress playing the black widow killer scores points for her unusual killing techniques (including slicing a man's neck with a blade hidden in her mouth and puncturing another poor slob's cranium with long fingernail/blades), which are always done while in the throes of making whoopee. She makes for mucho coolness and it made me wish that Ho had revisited this type of character in later ventures.

MISSION THUNDERBOLT is, all in all, a fine debut in IFD's cut-and-paste universe. The IFD footage, though good, would get even wilder and more outrageous as the series progressed (see my reviews for **MAJESTIC THUNDERBOLT** [*Lei ting chu chuan*, 1985][1] and **SCORPION THUNDERBOLT** [1984][2] in previous issues for the pinnacle of this group) while the borrowed footage from **DON'T TRUST A STRANGER** is strong enough to warrant its own untampered-with release.

1982/1983, HONG KONG. D: DONG JAN-WOO (CHIN HU TUNG)/GODFREY HO

---
1 Reviewed in *WC* #5, p.177
2 Reviewed in *WC* #6, p.190

Promotional slick for **NINJA OPERATION: KNIGHT & WARRIOR**

NINJA THUNDERBOLT
(Zhi zun shen tou)

Firstly, allow me in my great shame to apologize to you good readers. In my very first review for this column several issues ago, I made the erroneous (and incredibly naive) statement that the film which I reviewed, **NINJA IN THE KILLING FIELDS** (野戰忍者, 1984)[3] was the first of Godfrey Ho's (and IFD's) cut-and-paste pics. Not only was that not the case (that credit would go to **MISSION THUNDERBOLT** [雷霆出擊, 1983]—see above), but it wasn't even the first to feature the ever-popular fad of the 1980s, the ninja. For that, we have this seminal 1984 entry, **NINJA THUNDERBOLT**, which helped mark the end of the superior, more professional and noticeably more enthusiastic *Thunderbolt* series and usher in the most financially successful (and exploitive) of IFD's ventures, those featuring the ever-popular shadow warriors.

The success (or lack thereof) of these Frankenfilms from IFD and Filmark has always depended in large part on the "host" film they choose (seeing as their loopy original footage is almost always fun). Here, Ho selects a rather spunky and silly little Taiwanese action caper from 1984 called **TO CATCH A THIEF** (至尊神偷, a.k.a. **TO CATCH A NINJA**, 1984). As originally scripted, ninja Richard Ling (Yasuaki Kurata) is hired by shady businessman, Cedric Chan to steal a valuable jade horse so that he may collect on the insurance money. Dogging both of our villains' trails is detective Don (Don Wong Tao) who loses his wife for his snooping. He is in turn joined by a super tough female insurance agent (Yin Su Li).

Director Tommy Lee was an accomplished choreographer throughout the second half of the '70s with the occasional on-screen baddie role (he was the Vicious in the cult kung fu film, **THE HOT, THE COOL AND THE VICIOUS** [南拳北腿沾閻王 / *Nan quan bei tui zhan yan wang*, 1977]) before turning toward directing in the early '80s. His most noteworthy project in the director's chair was the fun *femme fatale* actioner, **IMPOSSIBLE WOMAN** (飛簷走壁 / *Fei yan zou bi*, 1982), starring Elsa Yeung. Here he offers up a project that, while hardly a well-made film, does score points when it counts. Beginning with a very long and uninvolving heist sequence, it builds slowly (too slowly) as we are witness to some similarly uninvolving sleuthing among our heroes. Spicing things up a bit are some soft-core sex sequences, at least one of which gets quite randy. Just when things appear to be getting nowhere, the action suddenly kicks in during the final third, and this is where Lee pulls out all the stops. We have crazy (laughably so) car stunts, ninja on roller skates, ninja on skis and a rather dangerous-looking fire stunt. It's a constant stream of carnage leading up to the finale where Wong and Yin catch up with Kurata for a fittingly hard-hitting smackdown. So fast and furious—and at times goofy—is this footage that I can forgive the near hour of general tedium leading up to it.

In the new footage, Richard Harrison plays a ninja cop. He is not only Wong Tao's (renamed Harry) superior, but also Kurata's (renamed Chima) disciple. Seriously questioning the ideals of Master Chima's "Ninja Empire" (who, according to their creed, will kill God, the dead and family…and stuff), he sends Harry out to help get to the bottom of things.

For their first cut-and-paste ninja pic, Ho and Joseph Lai used a remarkable amount of care and surprising restraint (for them, anyway). The new footage is quite sparse and extra care was taken to integrate it into the original footage. Richard Harrison really does at times seem to be in the same film with Wong and Kurata. In particular, there's a meeting sequence from the original that contains maybe the most professionally shot intercutting in IFD's lengthy history, as Harrison and Wong really do seem to be interacting. It is apparent that the background of the interior set in the original was studied closely and there was a decent amount of effort to merge the new Harrison footage with an identical set. Such care and attention to detail would quickly evaporate as these films progressed. Also of note is the subtlety of the ninja outfits themselves at this early juncture. The multicolored uniforms that we grew to know and…love…is nowhere to be found here. Simple black uniform and (*gasp!*) no sign saying "Ninja" on the headband! Could it be Ho and Lai were actually attempting to Frankenfilm a serious ninja pic here? The mind boggles…

If nothing else, **NINJA THUNDERBOLT** proved that this kind of cut-and-paste filmmaking could be done professionally and convincingly. It's easily the most subtle of the IFD "Ninjer" splice epics (comparatively speaking) but oddly due to the new footage's said subtlety, perhaps not the most fun.

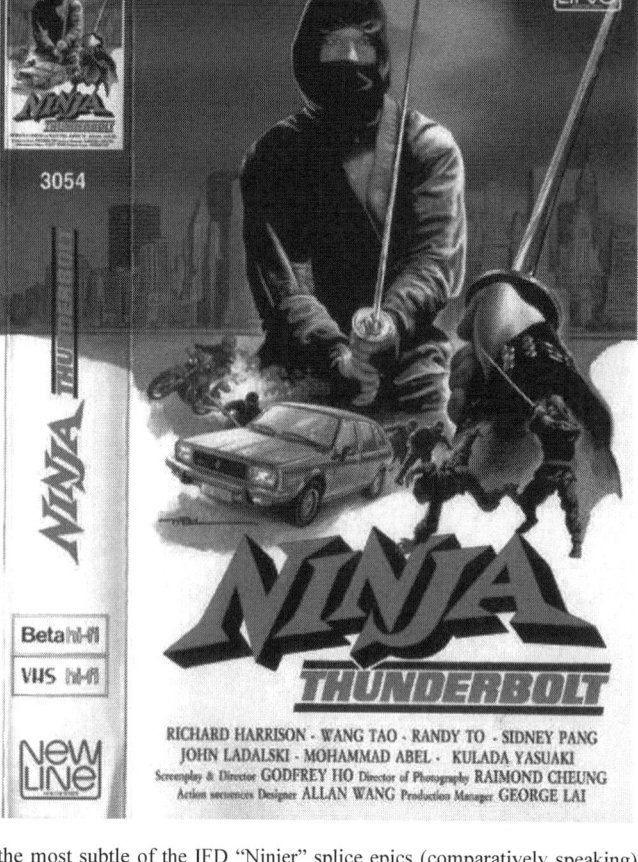

1984, HONG KONG. D: TOMMY LEE/GODFREY HO
AVAILABLE FROM BCI/ECLIPSE AND EASTWEST

NINJA OPERATION: KNIGHT & WARRIOR
(忍者太保之武士行, a.k.a. **NINJA: SILENT ASSASSIN**, a.k.a. **BLACK NINJA**)

No matter which of its monikers it chooses to go by, **NINJA OPERATION: KNIGHT AND WARRIOR** is flat-out one of the most entertaining ninja cut-and-paste adventures that IFD has ever put out, and it's fairly simple to understand why; unlike nearly every other Frankenfilm experiment (ninjers or no ninjers) in which 25 to 30 minutes of brand spanking new footage (if even that sometimes) was shot, on this occasion, Godfrey Ho and the gang have oh-so-generously presented more than half a film's worth of zany, over-the-top Shadow Warrior action and intrigue. This not only gives the film greater continuity, but for once this extended footage can now qualify as the "host" film with the "borrowed" footage being just that: merely extra footage used to fatten the running length as opposed to having to carry the damn thing on its secretive shoulders.

After being the lone actor featured over the credit sequence, Richard Harrison is then uncharacteristically given the next 30 minutes off (as if to say, "But that's not who our story's *really* about!") as we are introduced to Alvin (Alphonse Beni). Alvin's a narcotics officer and secret ninja (naturally) who arrests a suspect during a drug deal gone bad (is there any other way for it to go in one of these films?), but not before flat-out riffing Dirty Harry ("Did I fire six shots or only five?"). Promising he and his family money and protection in exchange for testimony against his boss, Paris-based drug overlord (and ninja) Rudolph (played with sufficient over-the-top menace by none other than Stuart Smith of **NINJA IN THE KILLING FIELDS** [野戰忍者, 1984][4] fame), the suspect-turned-rat is almost immediately cut down by the latter and

---

3 Reviewed in *WC* #4, p.125

4 In case you missed it earlier: Reviewed in *WC* #4, p.125

Weng's Chop   149

his underlings. Alvin also loses his wife at the hands of the international creep supreme. Grief-stricken, Alvin is told by his superior to take some paid leave. Learning that Rudolph has relocated to Hong Kong, Alvin instead teams-up with international agent (and ninja), Gordon (Harrison) and his group (which includes veteran actor John Cheung). When Gordon is in turn suspended, he and Alvin decide to go rogue. Slicing and dicing through the ranks, our heroes finally square off with Rudolph and his main associate (who's also a ninja) in a two-on-two duel to the death.

It would appear that Ho and producer Joseph Lai were intent on doing things a little differently right off the bat as we are treated to a whopping twenty-plus minutes of original IFD footage before there is even a glimpse of the "borrowed" film. This allows for more dialogue than usual in these scenes, which, though as incompetent as ever, does at least give viewer ample time to get used to these characters before the inevitable cutting away to the unrelated stuff that we've come to know and…love. The "stitches", because they are apparent only after a considerable amount of spent time, become somewhat less intrusive and therefore make for a smoother watch. Some might complain that the early scenes are slower than usual (which they are) as more buildup is allowed, but if we are going to watch dialogue scenes anyway, I'd much rather watch them come from new IFD footage, personally. After all, that's what originally drew us to these films in the first place, right? When the action does arrive, it is the standard "ninjer" stuff. What makes these scenes work is the scenery-chewing presence of the increasingly agitated Stuart Smith and the surprisingly understated performance of Alphonse Beni (which may have been even better than advertised here if it weren't for the patented goofy re-dubbing of his voice). Though top-billed, Richard Harrison doesn't have much to say or do in this one, but that's okay as his mere presence in the film is enough. He also seemed perhaps a little less embarrassed this time around for whatever reason.

The "borrowed" footage in question this time comes from a particularly spunky 1984 actioner from Taiwan called **A GIRL ROGUE** (女太保 / *Nu tai bao*, 1983). Directed Chiu Chan-Kwok (a.k.a. Chao Chen-Kuo, who helmed a dozen or so films including **LUCKY SEVEN** [七擒七縱七色狼 / *7 xiao fu*, 1986] and **LUCKY SEVEN 2** [7小福 2 / *Qi xiao fu zai chu ji*, a.k.a. **MAGNIFICENT 7 KUNG-FU KIDS**, 1989]—a pair of films that feature a group of kid heroes; the second of which has no less than Yukari Ôshima as the lead villainess). It's hard to gauge this film as most of the plot and character buildup was removed. In this re-dubbed version, star Li Hui-Fang (whom I could not find another acting credit for)[5] plays a delinquent teenager who will have charges dropped from her record in exchange for helping our heroes locally (or something close to that). Though as disparate as any pilfered by Lai, **A GIRL ROGUE** does feature some fantastic fights as well as stunt work that would make Jackie Chan proud (most of which is supplied by co-star Yau Ming Yin [a.k.a. Chiu Ming-Hsien] of **MATCHING ESCORT** [金粉遊龍 / *Jin fen you long*, a.k.a. **WOLF-DEVIL WOMAN 2**, 1983] fame). One stunt in particular that features Yau crashing through the back of a moving bus and landing flat on his back on the pavement (all in one long slow motion shot) looks particularly dangerous and has "rewind" written all over it. Hard to say for certain if the rest of the unseen film lives up to the plentiful acrobatic action and back-breaking stunts, but suffice it to say, it has now jumped to the top of my need-to-find list.

It's too bad that **NINJA OPERATION: KNIGHT AND WARRIOR** was (as far as I know at this point) the lone IFD effort to utilize so much of its own footage as I personally think this is the way it usually should have gone (some may disagree). The only other instances I can think of off the top of my head where as much or more originally shot footage was incorporated into these cut-and-paste thingies were in Filmark's **CLASH OF THE NINJAS** (1986)[6] and **ROBO VAMPIRE** (1988)[7] and those two films certainly benefited from an extra 10 to 15 original minutes in the can.

1986/1984, HONG KONG. D: GODFREY HO / CHIU CHAN-KWOK

ZOMBIE VS. NINJA
(魔幻狂迷, a.k.a. GRAVEDIGGER)

Ha! I'm finally reviewing an IFD cut-and-paste epic featuring the legend that is Pierre Kirby. Kirby, whose main job was reportedly delivering yachts to different parts of Asia, was discovered by IFD head honcho Joseph Lai while looking for extra work on the side. Handsome, charismatic and a natural martial artist who can actually act, Lai struck gold and cast his prize find in at least nine films from 1987-88. Then (and adding to his legend), Pierre mysteriously vanished at sea while delivering a yacht full of goods. Rumors spread (for those few in the know, at any rate), some saying that he merely retired and dropped quietly out of site while others suggesting anything from dying at the hands of pirates to his checkered past (?) catching up with him. Some closure to the saga was found by number one Kirby fan, Brad Jones a.k.a. The Cinema Snob (go look him up on the 'net, the guy's a riot); after doing some considerable digging around, Jones was contacted by Kirby's sister who confirmed that our international man of mystery did indeed die out at sea around 1990.

This 1989 film, **ZOMBIE VS. NINJA** (which has a whole host of aliases, including **ZOMBIE RIVALS** and **ZODIAC AMERICA: THE SUPER MASTER**, and was released on home video as part of the "Wu-tang Clan Presents" collection as **GRAVEDIGGER**) appears to have been his debut (though the way these things are filmed, it's impossible to tell). The "host film" chosen for this one was a 1983 South Korean kung fu feature called **THE UNDERTAKER IN SOHWA PROVINCE** (少和省葬儀師, 1983). Directed by Kin Jung Young, it stars the stupendously named Elton Chong as Ethan, who is forced to watch while his father is slain at the hands of a group of thieves. After wandering the land, Ethan comes across a kindly, bucktoothed undertaker (Kim Yong Wan) who offers to train him in new fighting techniques which is essentially combating re-animated corpses (sure, why not?). Going undercover, he tracks down the nasty do-badders and gets his revenge.

As a standalone, **THE UNDERTAKER IN SOHWA PROVINCE** is a decent concoction for genre fans. Elton Chong (there is no way that I don't grin when I say that name) gives an energetic performance as he usually does

---

5   IMDb has her only other film work listed as handling continuity for the 1984 HK actioner **NEW YOUNG HERO OF SHAOLIN** (*Xin fang shi yu*).
6   Reviewed in *WC #5*, p.178
7   Reviewed in *WC #4*, p.104

(**INVINCIBLE OBSESSED FIGHTER** [乞食通師 / *Qi shi tong shi*, 1983] and **DEADLY SHAOLIN LONGFIST** [廚房長, 1983] are also pretty good showcases for his skills). Kim Jung-Yong is given a pretty whacky script that he admittedly doesn't seem to make full use of, but at least he keeps things moving at a good clip. The "comedy" here is largely unwelcome; this includes a mid-film fight that's deliberately sped up, *Benny Hill*-style. It nearly made me give up on the picture. Fortunately, it is an isolated incident and the last third builds nicely with improved fight scenes, leading to a finale that is definitely rewindable.

Back at IFD, director Charles Lee frames it with ninja footage that never comes close to looking like it comes from the same film (as per the usual at this stage of the cut-and-paste game). It's merely a running battle between good and bad ninja. Sure, the attempt is made to appear as if good ninja Pierre Kirby is giving advice to the Undertaker, but when you have backgrounds that don't even come close to matching, it's obvious the attempt is a halfhearted one at best. To be honest, the original footage is entertaining enough that these new scenes aren't needed and don't really enhance the project. And to that I say, who gives a shit?! We have Pierre Kirby kicking all kinds of ninja ass and that's all *any* action film requires! Dressed in one of the cooler costumes I've seen in a while, Kirby comes on like gangbusters, making each and every other ninja his personal bitch! Go Pierre, go!

Okay, so ultimately **ZOMBIE VS. NINJA** adds up to a sum that is less than its entertaining parts, but what the heck, I'll take it over a lot of other things I can think of.

"The Dragon's fire burns hot." Yes it does, Pierre. Yes it does.

1983/1989, HONG KONG. D: KIN JUNG YOUNG/"CHARLES LEE" (GODFREY HO)
AVAILABLE FROM GROUND ZERO

RINGS UNTOUCHABLE
(突攻神探, a.k.a. **ROBO-KICKBOXER – POWER OF JUSTICE**)

As the 1980s drew to a close, IFD studios came to realize that their greatest money making machine, the ever-present ninja, were starting to fade in popularity. That they also lost golden boy Godfrey Ho at this same juncture caused producer Thomas Tang and little-discussed crony Betty Chan (whose production credits date all the way back to the early '70s) to shift their cut-and-paste focus away from the Shadow Warriors and toward that new fad that was sweeping the planet: the kickboxer craze. For this particular entry, **RINGS UNTOUCHABLE** (which incidentally, carries *both* titles on the credits of the dupe I viewed), the decision was to combine the newfound fad with the luminous robo-cop character which had previously reaped rewards in rival Filmark studio's **ROBO VAMPIRE** (1988)[8]. But there's a catch…

The opening sequence is one of the most off-kilter in the entire IFD canon: Kickboxer Jack (Nick Brandon) waits impatiently in a ring for his surprise opponent. Smoke fills the entrance and out of the mist emerges an awesome (*cough!*) robo-fighter. Jack understandably looks on befuddled as his nemesis enters the ring. After several furious moments of ring combat (handled pretty well, actually), the robo-fighter sticks two fingers through Jack's abdomen. Jack screams and falls, apparently dead…or not. He immediately jumps to his feet. Not only are his fatal wounds gone, but so is his opponent. Turns out it was all a drug-induced hallucination (!). Jack was injected with a heavy-duty serum that is supposed to bring out his greatest strength, but unfortunately likewise reveals his darkest fears. He refuses to take any more of it. He then finds himself out of a career as his seedy manager decides he has no use for him. Desperate for money, Jack, at the behest of his friend and fellow kickboxer Kevin (Steve Brettingham), agrees to be a go-between in a drug deal. It goes wrong (naturally), and after a knock-down, drag-out fist fight, Jack shoots the contact dead (our hero, ladies and gentlemen). The contact's partner Axel attempts to get away with the cash. Jack gives chase, but both men are arrested and thrown in jail. Jack plots to get out along with his newfound friend (in a white guy/black guy mismatched couples sort of way; **THE DEFIANT ONES** [1958] this isn't). While in the slammer, we discover that Jack was double-crossed by Kevin. During an uprising, Jack and Axel escape. Jack swears revenge on Kevin (though he was not privy to Kevin's intentions, but

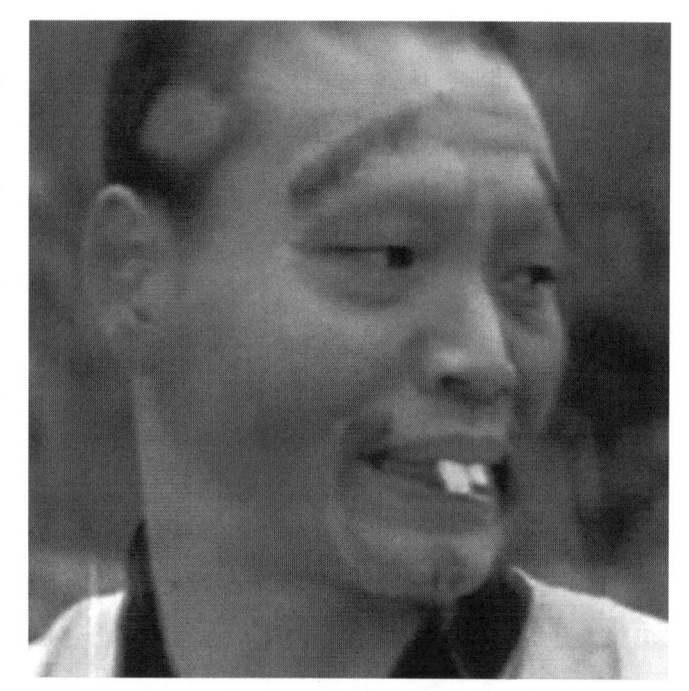

ZOMBIE VS. NINJA: Enter the bucktoothed undertaker (Kim Yong Wan) who teaches his young student the mysterious Three Zombie Strike, Frozen Mantis and other Gravedigger-style kung fu.

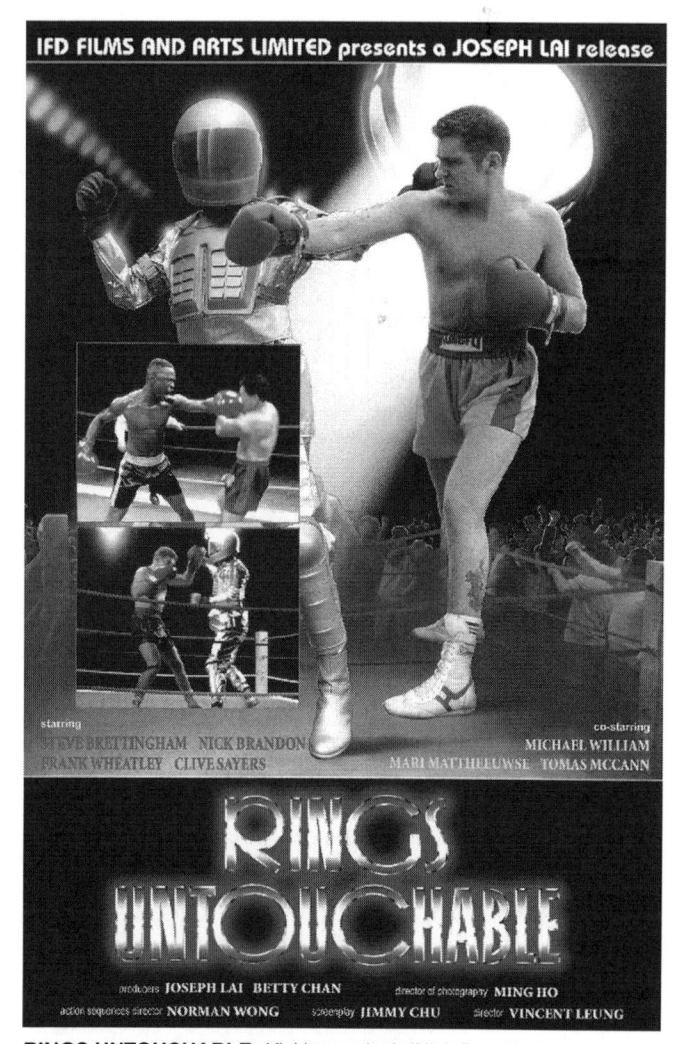

RINGS UNTOUCHABLE: Kickboxer Jack (Nick Brandon) must battle with his inner demons in the form of a **ROBO-KICKFIGHTER** in quite possibly the oddest IFD title to date!

---
8 Again, reviewed in *WC* #4, p.104

RINGS UNTOUCHABLE: It's [*cough*] non-stop thrills and action galore when Jack, a down and out has-been, must enter the ring with... Oh, no!

no matter). Jack decides to look up an old contact, big time boxing promoter Parker. Parker, as it turns out, is still mad at Jack for not working for him several years earlier, but after Jack defeats Parker's top protégé, a deal is begrudgingly reached. Jack will now get his revenge against Kevin in a match sponsored by Parker (who's forcing Kevin's hand in the matter by withholding drugs that are rightfully his). The match initially does not go well for Jack, as it becomes clear that Kevin is a far superior fighter. That is until Jack unwittingly ingests more of the performance-enhancing serum (at the behest of Parker, the ring doctor replaced Jack's water with it). Jack wins, but also begins hallucinating again. One moment he's fighting Kevin, the next, it's robo-fighter (this part was surprisingly well-staged and -edited).

I'll admit that my disappointment in learning that the robo-fighter wasn't actually real prevented me from initially enjoying what turned out to be a really loopy time, even as these things go. As simplistically crappy as the robo-suit (little more than a biker uniform) was, it was shot and edited well. The acting is the usual over-the-top goofiness (though for his part, the actor who played Parker was competent) with the anticipated ridiculous IFD voices nonsensically subbing for the already English-speaking...er, thesps. Okay, it's far from IFD's most accomplished footage, but (conceptually, at least) it's definitely among the wackiest. For the "host" film, IFD picked up the moody 1980 Filipino action/drama, **PUGA**, starring popular local Rudy Fernandez (a great big thanks goes out to Tim Chmielewski, who through Andrew Leavold, director of **THE SEARCH FOR WENG WENG** [2013][9] identified this rare title just as I was starting the review). **PUGA** begins with Wilfredo (Fernandez) killing Ralph (I personally think Ralph should be a go-to name with Filipino actors, no?) because Ralph beat and raped Wilfredo's sister, Cindy. Wilfredo is arrested and sentenced to life in prison (for the next fifteen minutes or so, this is where the two films link, as both sets of characters are simultaneously in the pokey). There's a prison riot and mass escape (brought about by the old fake sick prisoner routine). Many of the prisoners are gunned down by the guards but several escape, Wilfredo among them. Meanwhile, gangster Henry learns of the jailbreak and fears Wilfredo may be gunning for him (since Ralph worked for Henry...that still doesn't make a ton of sense, does it?). Henry is also concerned about Jack's escape. Seems the drug deal that went wrong in the IFD footage was orchestrated by Henry, and Henry sends one of his men to alert Kevin about it (really convoluted stuff here, but you have to give props to IFD for at least attempting to connect the two films). Wilfredo meanwhile finds himself unwittingly involved with two of the ex-cons, Ramon and Alfredo, and is forced to be their getaway driver, this while fighting and dodging Henry's goons. In the middle of this, Wilfredo even finds time to romance a love-struck girl named Anna whose family nursed him back to health. Too bad Anna's parents don't approve (there's a shocker). Nor does the gang when told by Wilfredo that he wishes to quit them and settle down with his new squeeze. Holding her at gunpoint, Wilfredo begrudgingly goes on one more heist. This one goes horribly wrong and Ramon is killed. Wilfredo makes plans to flee with Anna, but while talking to her in a phone booth, he is dramatically gunned down by another of Henry's thugs. At least, I think that's who did the deed. It was tough to tell as it became obvious that much of the footage that would have explained these late scenes was edited from this print.

It's something of an accomplishment in and of itself that IFD went to the lengths they did to attempt to make two such disparaging films made over a decade apart behave as a cohesive whole (never mind that they failed, regardless). Directors Jun Gallardo (**PUGA** footage) and Vincent Leung (IFD footage) each offered some impressive moments, with the aforementioned opening boxing scene as well as several of the later robbery and standoff sequences in Gallardo's original being standouts. Unfortunately, it does still add up to a whole that is less than the sum of its parts (as seems to be the norm in most of the later IFD output), but in this case, at least the parts can be somewhat entertaining on an individual basis. Sort of...

HONG KONG, 1980/1992. D: JUN GALLARDO/VINCENT LEUNG

---

[9] See Leavold's shooting diary for the film in *WC #4*, p.24.

...In Which a Brief Discussion Is Had with Stephen Biro Regarding the Violent Nature of the American Guinea Pig

Interviewed by Scott MacDonald

Stephen Biro is the man responsible for bringing legitimate Guinea Pig *DVD releases to American shores in the early 2000s, through his company Unearthed Films. Aside from that achievement Unearthed has been releasing a blend of new and disturbing horror with the occasionally classic mixed in. In 2013, Stephen announced that he would be directing a new* Guinea Pig *chapter entitled* **AMERICAN GUINEA PIG: BOUQUET OF GUTS AND GORE**. *The film had its world premiere at the 2014 Housecore Horror Film Festival, and I had the pleasure of speaking to him moments after the premiere let out.*

Congratulations on the premiere; what do you think of the response so far?

It was good…only 13-14 people walked out, and you can tell it was a bunch of couples, and you can expect that. The promoter, the guy who went over all the technical aspects of the movie, his girlfriend walked out at the end, which we can't tell you what [the scene] is—no spoilers—so we knew we had something. Crowd reaction was great.

You released the Guinea Pig *series on DVD through your company Unearthed Films over a decade ago. What made you want to continue it?*

I was trying to get the rights back when I got the rights to release them (on DVD), but there was a lot of problems in Japan with the rights, and the government banning them, and the child serial killer, [Tsutomu] Miyazaki. So they didn't want to have a new *Guinea Pig* series come, because they didn't want to sell it to us in the first place. There are a lot of people who acted in the first series who are quite famous in Japan, and it brings them great shame.

How did you come to work with Jim Van Bebber on this film?

Don't ask me why, but Jim ended up moving about 20 minutes from where I am in Crystal River, Florida. Crystal River, Florida is a Podunk town, and Jim moved 20 minutes from me. I get a call that a filmmaker moved right by me. [I ask,] "Who?" and they say "Jim Van Bebber." "Oh cool, let me talk to him."

And he just got involved?

Well, I helped him with the *Gator Green* [2013] short, and I'm helping him with the **GATOR GREEN** full-length feature, and in the meantime **GUINEA PIG** fell into my lap, the budget fell into my lap, so I said let's do this.

So on the subject of Van Bebber's GATOR GREEN feature, how is that coming along?

It's good. He's in talk with a bunch of financiers, so that will blossom, and it blossoms.

AMERICAN GUINEA PIG: BOUQUET OF GUTS AND GORE seems like an excellent jumping-off point for a second Guinea Pig *series; is that the intention?*

It's the beginning of a new series. I am working with a bunch of film directors worldwide, because they want to be a part of *Guinea Pig*. It has a historical weird horror vibe that people have always talked about, but it's not mainstream, but [it's] for real gorehounds that have to see everything, and those are the people I'm talking about.

You worked with Marcus Koch, one of the best practical FX artists currently in the business, on this. Did you work together on planning the violence in this film beforehand? Was any of it improvised?

It was all pre-planned; it was all in the screenplay. The one thing, the skinning of the legs—we were on-set, and Marcus said if we did it this way (makes a motion indicating a cut lengthwise) where it splits open, and I said, "Yeah, that's better."

Outside of film, you are also known as a writer. Your book Hellucination *was optioned for film recently. What state is that project in?*

The people actually got afraid of the movie, the book. They were hardcore Christians, [and said things like,] "There are things here that could be taken differently." It's supposed to. It was going to be a $15 million budget. Right now we're shopping around **AMERICAN GUINEA PIG**; I've already sold it to a number of territories, that's going to grow. Meanwhile, me stepping into the limelight is going to help the books to grow.

So I know we're at the world premiere, and right now you're focusing on getting the film shown theatrically, but is there a DVD release planned in the near future?

Yeah, we're debating doing an Indiegogo. Because we want to do limited signed editions, offer screenplays with limited, unlimited; we have tons of props, knives, stuff that was on the table of death with Indiegogo I can put one of each, and we're probably going to do that, and due to the feedback that's going to do real well. We'll do the special limited; the retail will probably have the making of by then.

Is there anything else you want to exit with?

We [Unearthed Films] just released *Necrophile Passion* [2013] which makes **NEKROMANTIK** [1987] look like a walk in the park. We have Ryan Nicholson's **COLLAR** [2014] coming out in November; we have a limited edition nude version of the cover with the CD soundtrack in January. We have **MORRIS COUNTY** [2009] coming out in December, and then we have **REVENGE IS HER MIDDLE NAME** [2011] coming up.

KNOXVILLE 7 HORROR FILM FEST

presented by
REGAL ENTERTAINMENT GROUP · Scruffy City Hall · 90.3 The Rock

CELEBRATING SEVEN DEADLY YEARS
WITH HOURS OF STARTLING SHORTS AND 7 FEATURE PRESENTATIONS

TALES OF HALLOWEEN | DEATHGASM | SUN CHOKE | INTERIOR | TURBO KID
THE TEXAS CHAIN SAW MASSACRE | DEATH SPA | PLUS THE GRINDHOUSE GRIND-OUT FILMMAKING CONTEST

FRIDAY & SATURDAY AT REGAL DOWNTOWN WEST 8
SUNDAY AT SCRUFFY CITY HALL — INCLUDING TCM BBQ DINNER & 80s HORROR COSTUME PARTY

WEEKEND PASSES ONLY 60 BUCKS
KNOXVILLEHORRORFEST.COM

OCTOBER 23-25

Reviews

A MIGHTY COLOR SPECTACLE -
RODAN!
MORE STARTLING THAN JULES VERNE!

print by TECHNICOLOR   THE KING BROTHERS

SIN CITY: A DAME TO KILL FOR

Reviewed by L. Thomas Tripp

At the end of last year, I decided to catch **SIN CITY: A DAME TO KILL FOR** (2014) before it departed theatres, but it was already unavailable in Las Vegas. What was an upstanding film-lover to do? Well, I found the nearest listing—which was in St. George, Utah, a two-hour drive from Vegas—prepaid for the most unimaginably mediocre room available, hijacked my girlfriend's jalopy, and away we went.

The original **SIN CITY** (2005), directed by Robert Rodriguez and Frank Miller, was always my favorite Rodriguez film, and I never forgot the experience when I saw it on the big screen. At that time, the special effects were incredibly unique, which made the movie a true manifestation of the comic book it evolved from, and it preserved that old fashioned feel through semi-colorless scenes and well-used hard-boiled *noir* dialog. For the most part, the sequel is similar to the original, especially the graphic quality created by the green-screen effects.

Although the sequel is presented differently than the 2005 original, the story is still essentially fragmented, spinning three different dark tales. All three stories are intricately intertwined by recurring characters, and the story is not divided into chapters here like its predecessor. Ultimately, this makes for a refreshing sequel, one that offers a slightly different presentation.

The story begins with the marvelous Marv, played by Mickey Rourke, as he flies through the windshield of a car. Confused and seemingly uninjured, Marv quickly finds some trouble with a bunch of over-privileged frat boys, and pursues them to the projects where the situation escalates fast. Keep in mind: that's just the pre-credit introduction.

Johnny (Joseph Gordon-Levitt), a gambler with unbelievably good luck, strolls into one of the clubs and begins gambling, seeming unable to lose. With a woman in tow that he just met, Johnny finds some serious action when he decides to play poker with the infamous Senator Roark (once again played by Powers Boothe). Unfortunately, Johnny beats the senator while Nancy (Jessica Alba) spies on them in utter disgust from another room, for her hatred of the senator growing worse by the day, while the ghost of Hartigan (Bruce Willis) lingers unnoticed around her. As Johnny collects his winnings, Senator Roark warns him… and sure enough, soon after leaving, Johnny is captured by the senator's henchmen, tortured badly, and dumped in the street like garbage.

From there, the story reintroduces the character of Dwight, now played by Josh Brolin (replacing Clive Owen from the original film), who did wonderfully under the circumstances. Dwight is working as a private investigator, which involves a case with a crazed businessman named Joey (Ray Liotta, who does a great job in his cameo performance). Before long, Dwight gets summoned by Ava (Eva Green), a gorgeous harpy and former lover of his. She tells Dwight she needs help, insinuating that her husband is dangerous, and eventually ensnared Dwight into her diabolical plan that centers around a large fortune.

Dwight realizes he needs help, so he recruits Marv. A battle royal ensues after Dwight and Marv storm Ava's mansion in search of her husband, and Dwight is nearly killed after part of his face is badly damaged in the ruckus. Betrayed by Ava, Dwight recovers in "Old Town" with the help of Gail (Rosario Dawson), and later returns to the mansion to settle the score with Ava, resulting in a bloody battle between the girls of old town and Ava's guards.

Meanwhile, Johnny finds a junkie doctor, played by Christopher Lloyd, who laughably administers medical aid to him. Johnny quickly finds his girlfriend dead, is harassed by the Senator once more, and decides to challenge Roark again. Even after all the punishment, Johnny beats the senator at another game of poker. Having achieved victory, Johnny incites the rage of Roark, and the situation gets ugly.

The story comes back to a maddened Nacny, whose life is spiraling out of control. She wants to kill Senator Roark because he set up her lover, Hartigan. After a self-mutilating craze, Nancy gets Marv to help her go after Roark, but the matter is only settled with the help of a certain ghost. Has justice really infiltrated Sin City?

Just like the original, the sequel was directed by Robert Rodriguez and Frank Miller, from a script by Frank Miller that nicely reflects the comic book he created. Comically, the film had almost as many executive producers as cast members, but the Weinstein brothers remain as the most popular members of that group. The cast includes people like Jeremy Piven, Christopher Meloni, and Stacy Keach, which keeps things interesting.

This was a movie that got better with the second viewing. If you have ever enjoyed old-fashioned cinematography and dialog, then this picture was built for you. Largely, the film runs the genre gamut of action, crime drama, and suspense, yet it also delivers numerous deliberately comical moments. Inevitably, the sequel was not the super-success that Troublemaker Studios wanted, but it was successful with diehard independent and action film fanatics, and that made it a winner.

2014, USA. D: ROBERT RODRIGUEZ, FRANK MILLER
AVAILABLE FROM ANCHOR BAY

SAVIOUR OF THE SOUL
(*Gau yat: San diu hap lui*)

Reviewed by Eric Messina

This wacky Hong Kong film opens with a dude that sports an '80s Asian Fantastic Sam's sweeping male model-type hairdo. When he dons a black cloak, though, watch the fuck out, as he flies through the air spinning like a whirling dervish that deflects bullets. There's enough neck-piercing swords and firepower to sustain about 20 minutes before it peters out into some other kind of Hong Kong action flick, but knowing Andy Lau and the genre as a whole, I think it'll work out. The film is loosely based on Tsukasa Hojo's *City Hunter* (1985-1991), a manga series which was later adapted into another film by Jing Wong, **CITY HUNTER** (*Sing si lip yan*, 1993), starring Jackie Chan (who apparently thinks it kind of sucks).

Our floppy haired superhero (played by Aaron Kwok Fu-Sing) is called Silver Fox; he's on a mission to avenge his master Old Eagle (Henry Fong Ping), who was blinded by a wicked bitch. I like how he asks his student to quickly kill him as he leaps into the air and gets obliterated like a human piñata before Silver Fox prepares a grave. None of this is featured in the comic, by the way, and they just invented everything for the film.

There's some sweet-ass creative weaponry, like suffocating bullets and dagger bombs. There's lots of slicing and dicing but no splatter—but don't let that discourage your viewing, because it doesn't hinder the action like it does in **THE HEROIC TRIO** (*Dong fang san xia*, 1993), a film that many love but I felt was too watered down and confusing. As I predicted, the action is waiting at bay to be recharged and the slim character development and hammy comedy takes over.

The kick-ass magic action then resumes in a neon-lit rainy bathroom brawl that includes a brutal wood stabbing sequence between Silver Fox and Siu Chuen (Kenny Bee). There are yuppie glass tiles everywhere in the background as Fox catches a sharp blade in his eye socket—*yowch!*

City Hunter's baseball hat-wearing girlfriend Wai Heung (the adorable Gloria Yip) becomes his assistant as they train for battle in separate locations. When Ching (Andy Lau), the main character, uses a wobbly sword, the noises it makes reminded me of the javelin Lamar (Larry B. Scott), the gay nerd character from **REVENGE OF THE NERDS** (1984) hurls in the frat competition. Ching flips around in the sunset and then we see a "Zoltar"-type Eastern fortuneteller nearby.

This film was adapted by Independent Asian film darling Wong Kar-Wai and Jeffery Lau, who also wrote **THE HAUNTED COPSHOP** (*Meng gui chai guan*, a.k.a. **THE HAUNTED COP SHOP OF HORRORS**, 1987) and **THE HAUNTED COP SHOP OF HORRORS 2** (*Meng gui xue tang*, 1988).

The characters keep talking about a Madam that eventually shows up...are Wayland Flowers and his elderly puppet going to appear? There are all these dudes in tuxedos hoping that Madam Pet (Carina Lau Ka-Ling) will grant them longevity. All the women in her crew dress in white and wear veils over their mouths; after one girl takes hers off, Ching smacks her in the face—it's played for laughs, but violence in that fashion is not very funny. He's on a mission to marry his childhood sweetheart May (Anita Mui) who's beneath one of those white cloaks, but first he must beat the piss out of those standing in the way.

Ching's fighting style is pretty strange; he uses that wobbly sword again and gives people *Three Stooges*-style eye gouges. I imagine Mr. Miyagi trained at the same dojo as Moe, Larry and Curly!

The storyline is pretty clumsy and if you're a fan of the manga, skip it all together because unlike **RIKI-OH: THE STORY OF RICKY** (*Lik Wong*, 1991), which follows its comic book source material, this one just makes it up as it goes along.

The goofy relationship elements overpower the supernatural and fantasy ones. Ching uses primitive Facebook technology to spy on May and bugs her phone, then Silver Fox makes another special appearance...and this time brings bombs. The two characters gratuitously fly around and more mellow drama ensues.

This supposed "City Hunter" never makes it out of the guarded palace and makes me want to check out the comic instead; the film sort of fizzles out before the end and just ends up going through the motions. Ching and May get all lovey-dovey—it's a tad nauseating—but then Silver Fox shows up again to battle to the death, cracking vials of smoke and doing choreographed kung fu flapping moves. The ending with him getting trapped in a mirror making smoochy faces is monumentally retarded! This one is not bad, but it's not that good either; it comes off like an extremely bizarre Asian melodrama with superhero elements...it's definitely out there and original. This title was in the infamous Deep Red catalog along with the sequel, and is currently available to stream on Fandor.

1991, HONG KONG. D: COREY YUEN KWAI, DAVID LAI DAI-WAI
AVAILABLE FROM TAI SENG

THE HUMAN CENTIPEDE 3 (FINAL SEQUENCE)

Reviewed by Tim Merrill

In 2009, independent filmmaker Tom Six slapped on his lab coat and introduced the world to his cinematic biological monstrosity, **THE HUMAN CENTIPEDE (FIRST SEQUENCE)**. Within no time the film became notorious for its disgusting reputation, and for Six's unique way of bringing strangers closer together. To be fair, the original *Human Centipede* film was nothing more than a modern abstract re-telling of the standard mad scientist trope of trying to save Hitler's brain, or to create a two-headed monstrosity.

Not to rest on his laurels, Six returned in 2011 with the second "sequence" in the trilogy, **THE HUMAN CENTIPEDE II (FULL SEQUENCE)**. This time, we were introduced to Laurence Harvey as the slimy Martin, who set out to duplicate the atrocities of the first film. In terms of repulsiveness the sequel pushed the limits far beyond expectations, and many were not only surprised, but also put-off their feed for a good long while. With the two films under his belt, Six promised a new extended centipede of epic proportions, and one could only wonder what he had up his sleeve for the finale.

Well, the wait is finally over, and the spiraling trail of centipede horror has finally reached its filthy conclusion. Those expecting to be surprised by the tail end of this trilogy will be, but not for the obvious reasons. This time Tom Six decided to make an abstruse statement about Western corporal punishment, and the seemingly American obsession with torture and violence.

Centipede regulars Dieter Laser and Laurence Harvey play the leads in the finale in very differing roles. Where Laser played the cold, clinical Dr. Heiter in the first film, he plays the insane, frothing warden Bill Boss in the third installment. It seems like no coincidence that Klaus Kinski happens to be Tom Six's favorite actor. Dieter Laser plays the sadistic warden with such an overblown manic fervor, he's like Kinski on a crack binge. What might be seen as a tribute to Kinski is nothing more than a mockery. The problem is that he spends so much of the film in this catatonic state chewing on dried clitorises (don't ask) and pointing guns at people that he forgets to even breathe. After watching five minutes of this shtick, you wish that Laser would be put out of his misery toot suite. There's chewing on scenery, and then there's just the point of unbearable beyond tolerance.

Laurence Harvey, on the other hand, plays it mild this time as the bookkeeping toady of the warden, who once again looks to the original film as an inspiration to creating a monstrosity. He spends a large part of the film trying to convince Laser that the only solution to inmate violence and overcrowding is to stitch up fifty-plus convicts, ass-to-mouth, and let nature take care of the rest.

A few notable faces show up as inmates including Tiny "Zeus" Lister and Robert LaSardo, plus Eric Roberts makes an embarrassing appearance as the state Governor Hughes. The lengths that some people will go to in order to cash checks knows no bounds in Hollywood, or so it seems.

In a nod to the "Warhol's" **FLESH FOR FRANKENSTEIN** (1973; D: Paul Morrissey, Antonio Margheriti) gall bladder quote, Six attempts to disgust his audience by having an inmate use a gaping knife wound to screw the warden in his kidneys. It doesn't matter how hard the director tries to top the limits of his previous films, it's all for naught.

Anyone who is going to sit down with this should know that the film rolls on for a good hour before any semblance of the new "centipede" is shown. Six promised that the conclusion to his trilogy would be his crowning achievement, to his "Magnum Orifice". Instead of ending on a high note in a blast of filth and bodily fluids, the third sequence ends as a dry popcorn fart, as loud as a mouse pissing on cotton. Tom Six spends the duration of two films setting up a joke with no punch-line in the end.

In all fairness one must give a nod to Tom Six for brewing up such an original concept from the start, but it was a creation that could only crawl so far. It used to be that Uwe Boll was the modern whipping boy when it came to talentless hacks, but Uwe has continued to show a surprisingly wide breadth of creativity and skill in his career. It seems that Tom Six, on the other hand, might soon be donning the crap crown as Uwe Boll has vacated the throne.

2015, USA. D: TOM SIX
AVAILABLE FROM IFC MIDNIGHT [VOD]

DJANGO KILL... IF YOU LIVE, SHOOT!

(*Se sei vivo spara*)

Reviewed by Scott Wachtler

Blue Underground's recent Blu-ray release of Giulio Questi's notorious gothic psychedelic spaghetti western **DJANGO KILL... IF YOU LIVE, SHOOT!** (1967) restores the infamous graphic mutilations to all their oversaturated, bloody glory.

In less-able hands this movie could easily have been an over-the-top mess, but Questi, with help from editor and co-writer Franco Arcalli, elevate this into one of the more coherent psychedelic trips through the off-kilter spaghetti western landscape (ahem...**EL TOPO** [1970]).

Arcalli's editing is really brilliant here. His use of flash-cuts never seems schlocky, and only adds to the surreal images and storyline. Arcalli worked with many of the greats of Italian cinema, including Bernardo Bertollucci, with whom he wrote and edited **LAST TANGO IN PARIS** (*Ultimo tango a Parigi*, 1972). He was also one of the many to lend a hand in writing Sergio Leone's semi-masterpiece **ONCE UPON A TIME IN AMERICA** (1984).

According to the interview with Questi included as a special feature, this was Questi's first feature film. Prior to this he had made documentaries, where, he said, he learned how to use the camera. Watching **DJANGO KILL... IF YOU LIVE, SHOOT!** (a title forced upon Questi by the distributors to cash in on Sergio Corbucci's **DJANGO** [1966]), it's hard to believe that this is his first time shooting a feature. Although it's deeply soaked in the hot sandy mud and grime of other spaghetti westerns, the movie certainly has its own feel and captures a late-'60s gothic psychedelic vibe—think Hammer Horror set in a spaghetti western-style desert shanty-town.

The movie really does have everything you expect and want from an Italian western. A good soundtrack, sweaty close-ups, double- and triple-crosses, questionable heroes, great shootouts, women being "Gaslighted" and kept locked up by their greedy preacher husband, Italians acting as Native Americans, gay henchmen...*wait, what?* Yep, the town's main bad guy has a posse of gay henchmen. Their sexuality is only hinted at in the beginning—mostly by how neat and pressed their

THE HUMAN CENTIPEDE 3 (FINAL SEQUENCE)...Get in line!

Tomas Milian as "The Stranger" shares words with the lovely Lori (Marilù Tolo) in DJANGO KILL...IF YOU LIVE, SHOOT!

all black outfits are—but it becomes more obvious in the middle of the movie when it's used as a plot point. The "Native Americans" in the movie forward the mystical element of the story and seem to be the forefathers of the Nobody character in Jim Jarmusch's underrated **DEAD MAN** (1995).

Tomas Milian's star power really shows throughout this movie, and there's no doubt that he's the star of this Unlike his co-starring roles in **COMPAÑEREOS** (*Vamos a matar, compañeros*, 1970)[1] and **THE BIG GUNDOWN** (*La resa dei conti*, 1966)[2], where he shared the spotlight with scene-stealers like Franco Nero, Jack Palance and Lee VanCleef, Milian dials it back here and gives a more nuanced performance, wherein you can tell he's tortured by what he's been through. Maybe it's the way the character is written, but it does seem that Milian had more to do with that than the writers. In the special feature interviews, Milian talks about what a "pain in the ass" he was to work with when he was younger, and how he would argue with Questi about his character's motivations and style. Whoever it is who created his Stranger character here, it works. Unfortunately, what doesn't work is that Milian's voice is dubbed. Not as badly as Franco Nero's voice in **DJANGO**, but it is a little distracting and does take a little away from his performance.

Milian's character is called "The Stranger"—*never* Django—and the movie opens with his outstretched hand reaching out from a shallow grave, and some nice plucky guitar plays over this in the background. In the dark of night, the bandana'd stranger crawls up from the grave while the credits roll and some very Italian-looking Native American Indians find him, give him water, and revive him with what looks like rabbit tails and just old-time Indian know-how. This segues into flash-cut fever-dream flashbacks that at first resemble the washed-out acid flashbacks popular in '60s cinema, but slowly become more lucid and explain the double-cross that led to The Stranger's shallow grave. Naturally, it all had to do with gold; his Mexican partners swindled him out of

1   See my review in *Weng's Chop* #5, p.216.
2   I reviewed this one in issue #6, p.216. (Apparently page 216 is Wacthler's domain! Be warned! –*ed*.)

his full share, shot him, and left him buried in the desert.

The "Indians" find some of the gold, melt it down and make it into gold bullets for him to use on his enemies. It's unclear whether they see him as reborn and back from the dead as an avenging angel, or as a Christ figure, since both tropes are used in the movie, and, for the most part, they work. The Indians tell The Stranger that the bandits have probably gone to the nearby town called "The Unhappy Place". It's here where the film earns its creepy gothic vibe that makes it famous. The town certainly has that lived-in, ramshackle look common to Italian westerns, but as The Stranger's double-crossers make their way down the streets of The Unhappy Place, they're met with some wonderfully surreal images. One of the first is a bare-assed kid peeing into the street. The slow pan of the creeped-out bandits walking through the street reveals a young girl torturing a boy by holding his head back and telling him to "give up!" A drunk is shown dry-heaving into a barrel, while a man sitting on a box pins a girl under his foot while she pleads "Please uncle, Max." It's a scene out of a demented *Twilight Zone*, or better yet, *Night Gallery*. The soundtrack ratchets up the tension with a tick-tock motif reminiscent of the scene in Leone's **A FISTFUL OF DOLLARS** (*Per un pugno di dollari*, 1964) where Eastwood's Stranger first arrives to the town and sees the possibly dead guy on the horse leaving town with an "Adios Amigos" sign on his back. That scene itself was an attempt to replicate the creepiness of the scene in **YOJIMBO** (*Yôjinbô*, 1961) where Toshiro Mifune encounters a dog with a human hand in its mouth as he makes his way into town. Questi ups the ante on these two scenes considerably, and it works really well.

There's a shootout with The Stranger and his old gang where he exacts justice with his gold bullets. Check out the scene where he hunts the main bandit in the general store, eventually shooting him. It's so well-done that you feel enclosed in a well-stocked store where bullets ricochet off pots and pans while the two gunslingers square off among hats, bottles and heaping strands of drying red peppers hanging from the ceiling. The Stranger ends up shooting his adversary full of gold bullets, and when the creepy townsfolk—who would give the townsfolk in **TWO THOUSAND MANIACS!** (1964) a run for the money—find out there's gold in that bandit, they quiet literally tear him apart to get it, which is also where the movie had been cut. Blue Underground restores those bits of gore for your viewing pleasure.

DJANGO KILL... IF YOU LIVE SHOOT! is a fun movie, and worthy of its high regard in the pantheon of spaghetti westerns. Blue Underground does a great job with the restoration and with the extras. The interviews with Milian, Questi and Ray Lovelock are funny and interesting. Make sure to watch the trailer, which couldn't be a more direct copy of **THE GOOD, THE BAD AND THE UGLY** (*Il buono, il brutto, il cattivo*, 1966) if it tried.

1967, ITALY/SPAIN. D: GIULIO QUESTI
AVAILABLE FROM BLUE UNDERGROUND

RODAN
(*Sora no daikaijû Radon*)

Reviewed By L. Thomas Tripp

Directed by Inoshiro Honda, **RODAN** (1956) was always my favorite of the old monster movies that depicted colossal creatures of a prehistoric nature, though **GODZILLA** (*Gojira*, 1954) was a close second. As a kid—thanks to Turner Broadcasting—I hardly ever missed an opportunity to watch those B-movie classics, which I enjoyed immensely; however, the intensity of **RODAN** left an impression on me I never forgot. Never before had I seen a *Godzilla* film that "looked" better than **RODAN**, and I had digested many *kaiju* movies by that point, which included **GODZILLA, GODZILLA RAIDS AGAIN** (*Gojira no gyakushû*, 1955), and nearly every other film in the *Godzilla* franchise that led to **TERROR OF MECHAGODZILLA** (*Mekagojira no gyakushu*, 1975). Many of those movies had bizarre story lines, strange characters, and abrupt (yet humorous) plot twists, but not **RODAN**; it had a serious tone that some of the other "giant monster" movies lacked.

The film begins by showing the U.S. military as it tests the infamous hydrogen bomb. As the introduction progresses, the narrative is clear: What furious response does nature have planned for human civilization? The story quickly focuses on a mining village in Japan; a breathtaking view of Kyushu and Mount Aso are revealed, as are the lives of the local population, which relies on the coal mine for economic support. This is all neatly folded into the introductory narrative.

Shigeru (Kenji Sawara) works in the mine with his fiancée's brother, Goro (Rinsaku Ogata). All the workers know that tensions are high on the job, especially since they're digging deeper into the mountain, yet a sense of *real* foreboding overcomes the men as disaster strikes: Goro and some of the workers are fatally attacked by *something*… which turns out to be a large insect. Shigeru and a band of armed guards return to the mine shaft in search of answers, but they encounter another giant insect, and gunfire erupts. Unfortunately, Shigeru is caught in a cave-in resulting from the firefight, and is later found unconscious at the base of the mountain.

Meanwhile, a UFO Is spotted and intercepted by Japanese jet fighters, but the object is moving fast and difficult to follow. Outmatched, one of the fighters is quickly destroyed during the skirmish, which leaves the Japanese military baffled; however, Shigeru, in the hospital, has a flashback, and soon provides an answer for everyone. He remembered being trapped in the mine as he watched the awful sight of the newly hatched Rodan gorging on giant insects, so a team is sent in to investigate, and a small piece of shell is recovered.

At this point in the story, Professor Kashiwagi (Akihiko Hirata) is introduced, voiced by George Takei in an uncredited performance (having no choice in the matter, I watched the U.S. dubbed version…and consumed it like a hungry child). The professor figures out what hatched from the egg, and he describes Rodan as a colossal prehistoric bird that was ultimately disturbed by atomic testing and underground mining, which led to the perfect environmental conditions needed for proper incubation and development of an old, extremely well-preserved egg. *Bam!* Human folly just went into overdrive.

In an unparalleled act of foolishness, the Japanese military launches an attack on Mount Aso, but they only infuriate Rodan. The monster pops out of the volcanic mountain and takes flight, only to be pursued by fighters. The planes are no match for the colossal creature that flies at supersonic speeds, and several fighters are destroyed in mid-air. Meanwhile, a second Rodan escapes the mountain and flies away.

In a disastrous display of power, Rodan lands in a nearby city. While people panic, the monstrous bird flaps its wings wildly, and cyclonic winds tear through the city. The military launches a violent assault on the creature using a combination of fighter planes and tanks. An unimaginable battle between nature and military might ensue. Panicked screams, cannon fire, and roaring rip through the air as debris flies in every direction…and suddenly, the second Rodan appears over the battle zone! Will the military be able to stop this double-menace from destroying everything in sight?

For a film made and released in the late '50s, it packs a punch like no other monster movie made around that period. Epic scenes of violent destruction are littered throughout the film, but the last twenty minutes are nearly all action. Overall, the story is well-crafted and -executed. The plot is fairly simple, not outrageous, and that's part of the charm—along with stunning special effects that minimize ridiculousness throughout the film.

RODAN was a great success for Toho Studios, and the film was popular with Japanese and American audiences alike, which was the reason Rodan returned in movies like **INVASION OF ASTRO-MONSTER** (*Kaijû daisensô*, a.k.a. **GODZILLA VS. MONSTER ZERO**, 1965) and the like. Notably enough, **RODAN** was one of Toho Studios first color films, produced by Tomoyuki Tanaka; the story was originally written by Takashi Kuronuma and later adapted by David Duncan for American audiences. Frank King and Maurice King produced the U.S.-release version of the film…and a classic was born.

The film works well within the genres of adventure, drama, *kaiju*, horror, and science fiction, which made for a versatile and fantastically fashionable film. As a monster movie fanatic, this is a film I've advocated for years, and nothing has changed. Bravo!

1956, JAPAN. D: INOSHIRO HONDA
AVAILABLE FROM CLASSIC MEDIA

DAUGHTERS OF DARKNESS
(*Les lèvres rouges*)

Reviewed by Tony Strauss

"You don't love me, I don't love you—apparently we were made for each other." So says Stefan (John Karlen) to his new bride, Valerie (Danielle

Ouimet), following their passionate lovemaking session which opens director Harry Kümel's colorful 1971 contribution to the lesbian vampire genre, **DAUGHTERS OF DARKNESS** (1971). Far more than just another '70s vampire booby movie, it is a subtly chilling depiction of the human tendency to express our sexual and emotional roles through apathy and cruelty, even though all anyone really wants is someone to love.

Beautifully photographed against a breathtaking Belgian countryside, the drama unfolds thusly...

When their train is forced to make an unscheduled stop in Ostend, newlyweds Stefan and Valerie decide to spend the night in town before continuing on to England to announce their marriage to Stefan's mother—something Stefan seems in no great hurry to do. They take residence in a beautiful seaside hotel, where the frail and insecure Valerie, fearing that Stefan is deliberately delaying their voyage out of fear of his mother—or worse, shame of his bride—immediately insists he telephone his mum. Stefan asks Pierre (Paul Esser), the nervous concierge, to do so, but slips him a note to say there's no reply.

That night, two more guests arrive at the hotel: the lovely Countess Elizabeth Bathori (Delphine Seyrig)—whom Pierre recognizes as a hotel guest from 40 years earlier, looking not a day older than she did then—and her beautiful "secretary", Ilona (the stunningly sensual Andrea Rau). The Countess spies Stefan and Valerie in the dining room, and becomes immediately captivated with them, much to Ilona's dismay.

The next day in Bruges, the newlyweds come upon the scene of a murder, apparently the fourth in a series of brutal slayings of young local women, all completely drained of blood. Stefan is so morbidly fixated on glimpsing the corpse that he unconsciously backhands Valerie when she tries to pull him away. It's a shocking, foreboding moment, but Valerie lets it go, frail and submissively desperate as she is.

Back at the hotel, the couple learns from the Countess that she had an ancestor, known as the Scarlet Countess, who bled hundreds of virgins to death. Valerie is horrified when Stefan and the Countess reach a heightened state of arousal while recalling the graphic details of the Scarlet Countess' M.O., and she flees to her room, where she discovers a naked Ilona prowling outside her window! What the hell?! (And: *hubba-hubba!*)

Naturally, Valerie wishes to leave immediately, cornering Stefan into calling "Mother", who is no mother at all, but a *male* ex-lover (*gasp!*). Despite his obvious disapproval, "Mother" (Fons Rademakers) gives his blessing to the both of them. Obviously conflicted, Stefan hangs up the phone and turns on Valerie, giving her a brutal goodnight belt-whipping! Apparently his earlier eruption of violence was just a preview of coming attractions with regard to his misplaced anger with his own identity, and of course it will probably just get worse from here. Early the next morning, Valerie takes flight from Stefan, but is swiftly apprehended by the Countess, who has her own wicked plans for the newlyweds...

Without giving away the (admittedly predictable) climax, I'll just tell you that, before the film ends,

you will witness one snooping ex-detective, no less than two sex scenes, three bloody (albeit highly implausible) deaths, moonlit body-disposals, and a big damn explosion, just for good measure.

If history has taught us anything, it's that the world needs lesbian vampire movies, and plenty of 'em. Deliberately paced and heavy in mood, this is arguably in the upper echelon of lesbian bloodsucker flicks, being more than just another card in the genre's deck. With emphasis on cerebral rather than mere physical titillation, it delivers eroticism aplenty without having to rely on gratuitous T&A (though genre dictates that it must also deliver at least some beautiful nekkid people, which it does). The relationships between the central characters are cruelly fascinating, since most of them are so out of touch with their true emotions that they lack the ability to express themselves with any degree of sincerity. Most of the acting is fine, particularly the edgy-eyed Esser, and Seyrig's Dietrichesque portrayal of the Countess (Dietrich is cited in the commentary as one of Kümel's big influences), though Danielle Ouimet has a tendency to look as though she just wandered into the wrong restroom by mistake (but this actually works in her character's favor, as Valerie is clearly a frail little flower who's way out of her element in this relationship). Despite the somewhat simplistic plotline, Kümel's imaginative presentation of the material manages to keep things engaging through to the finale, showing a deft hand at handling the more subtle nuances and duality of his characters, their inner turmoil and their complex relationships.

This is a film less interested in salacious sensationalism than it is in subtlety and atmosphere. Though it was made smack-dab in the heyday of sexy vampire films, when more permissive censorship laws prompted more overt titillation within genre films, **DAUGHTERS OF DARKNESS** is more about people than it is about bloodsuckers; indeed, the vampire element is almost presented as a wistful, depressing longing for "life" than it is a lust for blood. One gets the feeling that the Countess at this point pursues immortality merely because it is the only option left to her in her meandering existence, rather than a genuine desire for blood or eternal life. There is a sense of aimlessness and dissatisfaction that casts a pall over all the central characters, nicely adding to the overall feeling of loneliness and dread within the film.

Thanks to our friends at Blue Underground, this film is given the treatment it really deserves. The transfer presents the film in its originally-intended length (we are reminded of this by the subheading "director's cut" superimposed in cheap white video lettering onto the title card), and its proper 1.66:1 aspect ratio. The image is crisp and vibrant (lending proper emphasis to Kümel's use of color—particularly red), and intrusions of speckling or video noise are almost nonexistent.

In addition to director Kümel's incredibly engaging and informative commentary, which nicely covers all aspects of the production (though memory fails him once or twice on some details, he impresses with the amount he does remember from a four-decades-old production), also included on the fully-loaded Blu-ray is a second audio commentary featuring star John Karlen interviewed by stalwart film historian David del Valle. Now, my first thought when I encounter a commentary in which the only participant is one single actor is, "Why bother?"—but I was pleasantly surprised by this one. Del Valle does an excellent job of prompting Karlen (at the very few points where he needs prompting—he's a pretty good talker), and the actor proves to be an entertaining and informative commentator (though one wishes he would be a bit more candid, and elaborate on a few of the scandalous behind-the-scenes anecdotes at which he frequently hints, cheeky bastard). Also included are interviews with Danielle Ouimet, Andrea Rau, Harry Kümel and producer Pierre Drouot, a theatrical trailer and a handful of radio spots…plus, as a super-duper bonus, an entire 2nd feature film: Vincente Aranda's **THE BLOOD SPATTERED BRIDE** (*La novia ensangrentada*, 1972)! Sure, it's a standard-def presentation, but still: *thanks!* My advice? If you're a fan of rich, character-driven genre suspense heavy with atmosphere and nuance, pick this one up…you won't be disappointed.

1971, BELGIUM/FRANCE/WEST GERMANY.
D: HARRY KÜMEL
AVAILABLE FROM BLUE UNDERGROUND

HOW TO SAVE US

Reviewed by Brian Harris

Jason Trost, one half of the Trost Bros. (the other is Brandon), the filmmaking team responsible for the outrageously entertaining film **THE FP** (2011), has been hard at work since 2011 steadily crafting genres films such as **ALL SUPERHEROES MUST DIE** (2011) and **WET AND RECKLESS** (2013). Having tackled sci-fi, comedy, action and fantasy, it was only a matter of time before horror fans could expect to see something from him.

I must say, I'm a huge fan of **THE FP**. If you haven't seen it, you should check it out. It's this insane sci-fi/comedy about the dystopian town of Frazier Park and the two gangs that battle for supremacy by playing a game called "Beat-Beat Revelation" (think: Dance Dance Revolution). Imagine the hilariously stereotypical gangbangers from **DEATH WISH 3** (1985) filtered through '80s fashion, '90s gamer culture and a touch of **8 MILE** (2002) Hip-Hop and you're close to the nuttiness that is **THE FP**. It feels like a gangstafied, post-nuke **ZOOLANDER** (2001). Most would probably shy away from calling it "visionary", but I'm not most.

Enter **HOW TO SAVE US** (2014), written and directed by Jason, an "about average" sci-fi/horror production about a desperate brother who enters a quarantined Tasmania to locate his missing sibling. There, instead of a plague, he discovers the evacuated island "infected" by supernatural entities passing through a portal into our realm. With the help of a journal sent by his younger brother, he's effectively able to evade the entities, but what lies at the end of his journey may require more than he's got.

HOW TO SAVE US is a well-made film with an interesting, yet slightly familiar, premise—it reminded me at times of Soisson's **PULSE 2** (2008) and **PULSE 3** (2008). I wasn't at all disappointed with my viewing experience, despite budgetary constraints—no joke this was made for around $20k. The director and crew were able to shoot some breathtaking sequences in impressive locations. I have nothing but praise for the look and sound of this film.

The acting, from Trost himself and co-star Coy Jandreau, was admirable, though I found Trost to be emotionally uneven at times in his portrayal. I don't want to give too much away but in one particular sequence his unconvincing attempt to resuscitate an unresponsive person by chest-thumping their propped-up body had me chuckling. Still, he delivered just enough when needed to keep the film moving. His character was obviously (to me) supposed to be a bit emotionally detached, due to the trauma he'd experienced as a child, but there were times that it needed to be pulled back in a bit, perhaps. My biggest criticism concerning the acting though would have to be leveled at the voiceover actors (other than Trost and Jandreau): very disappointing work. Certainly not enough to derail the production, but notably stiff and awkward nonetheless.

I have to say, I quite liked the entities and the rules created by Trost; there was enough mythology to give viewers a sense of these entities and their abilities and limitations. Knowing more about them and how to repel/evade them helped build some realism as well as necessary tension. Because, as we all know, you can protect yourself all you like but eventually the supernatural has a way of waiting you out. One "character" that was simply flawless was the film's sound. From the radio playing to the wind blowing, it had me on edge, bracing myself for a glimpse of one of them or an all-out attack. Tori Letzler's score was exceptional as well, appropriately moody and just memorable enough to stand out without overshadowing the film itself.

HOW TO SAVE US isn't a game-changer—but that shouldn't deter you if you're a true genre film fan. It's a sound entry that I'd recommend showing

Perhaps this spiffy gamer glove will show everyone **HOW TO SAVE US**

support to and checking out. I admit, there were a few bumps and bruises here, as one might expect from a low-budget film, such as mail being picked up from an evacuated city and delivered. At its heart though, **HOW TO SAVE US** is a film about a dysfunctional family torn apart by alcoholism and domestic abuse and the journey one of them is willing to undertake in order to put the broken pieces back together again for all of them. It's the kind of story that will resonate with many viewers.

Jason Trost's **HOW TO SAVE US** is already hitting theaters and will no doubt go VOD soon enough. When you can, take some time out and kick back with this one.

2014, USA/AUSTRALIA. D: JASON TROST
AVAILABLE FROM PARADE DECK FILMS

THE DISCO EXORCIST

Reviewed by Tony Strauss

Seriously, how do you refuse a movie with a title like this?! Well, I guess if you're a fucking asshole, it'd be pretty easy…but for the rest of us weird-cinema junkies, a title like this is gold-plated catnip. The film was already on my distant radar as something to check out based on title alone, but I hadn't yet prioritized it as a must-see film until last October, when I saw Richard Griffin's **FUTURE JUSTICE** (2014) at the 2014 Telluride Horror Show.[3] I completely fell for that film's throwback vibe and '80s low-budget sci-fi spirit, and immediately decided that I must see more of Griffin's films. Looking through his insanely prolific list of films (seriously, I think the guy is some kind of undead monster that never sleeps, and just keeps making more and more movies), I decided that the next film I watched by this audacious auteur should be **THE DISCO EXORCIST** (2011), because…well, because it's fucking called **THE DISCO EXORCIST**! C'mon, that's a no-brainer, right there!

A modern production made to look like it was filmed in the late '70s (via outstanding production design, stylistic lighting and digital print-aging), the film tells the story of disco super-stud Rex Romanski (Michael Reed), a womanizing regular at all the best disco clubs, who never goes home alone and always leaves a stream of hungry-for-more women in his wake. His lifestyle pretty much consists of drinks, drugs, dancing and dames, and that's the way (uh-huh, uh-huh) he likes it (uh-huh, uh-huh). One night out at his favorite disco, he spots the lovely Rita Marie (Ruth Sullivan), and is instantly drawn to her. After whisking her out to the dance floor for some flirtatious footwork, the two make no delays in getting back to Rex's bachelor pad for some hot '70s-style montage sex that leaves them both spent and satisfied. For Rex, this is just another night out on the prowl, but Rita seems to want something more substantial. The next night out at the club, while dancing with this newest gal-for-now, Rex spots his favorite porn star, Amoreena Jones (Sarah Nicklin), at the bar and boogies on over to her to make his move, leaving Rita alone on the dance floor…not the classiest of moves, to be sure, but that's just how Rex Romanski plays it, Baby.

He and Amoreena hit it off immediately, and start busting their sexy disco moves to the bouncin' beat, when they are angrily interrupted by a seething-with-jealousy Rita, who makes her position very clear on the matter: Rex is going to regret this. Rex and Amoreena brush her off and head back for some steamy and soulful montage nookie, and all seems just peachy. Better than peachy, in fact…Rex really feels something more than simple lothario lust for this bangin' babe, and just might actually possibly consider the remote hypothetical potential of seeing himself getting marginally serious with this one…maybe.

Unfortunately for our new libidinous lovers, it turns out that the spurned Rita intends to make good on her threat, which is made all the more dire when it is revealed that she's not only psychotically jealous, but well-schooled in the craft of *voodoo*! (Wouldn't you just know it!) She sets out on a spiteful mission to not only ruin but to *end* the lives of Rex and his new love interest by employing voodoo dolls, demonic possession and bloody murder. Will our horny hero be able to save his own skin and thwart her evil plans to ensure that the music—and the fucking—never stop? After all, there are still so many orgies to attend and dance floors to dominate!

I sincerely hope I don't need to tell you that this whimsically perverted film doesn't take itself the least bit seriously, because…well, because it's fucking called **THE DISCO EXORCIST**! What I *do* need to tell you is that the movie is a giant econo-sized tub o' wicked fun that succeeds on pretty much every level. Aside from a couple of very minor hand-tips (such as the briefly-glimpsed back of a "modern" credit card cutting up cocaine), the flick really feels like an authentic 1979 genre entry, from the color palette to the costume and hair design to the overall lighting and image texture. Really, by this point I've seen an alarming number of attempts at the "retro" look in modern indie films—an affected effect that I tend to find tedious and distracting in most cases—but, with the possible exception of Astron 6's **THE EDITOR** (2014)[4], this is about the most authentic-feeling artificial print-aging that I've yet seen. The effect fools the eye nicely without ever being too intrusive about it (except when it's done for a deliberate joke, which I won't spoil here), and the film allows you to just settle in and enjoy it like you've just unearthed it from the dismal depths of a long-forgotten VHS clearance bin.

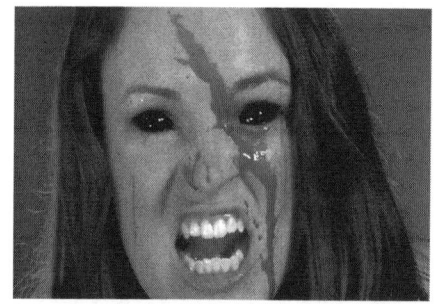

Ruth Sullivan takes the "woman scorned" adage to terrifying new levels in **THE DISCO EXORCIST**

Across the board, the cast is up to the task and in full understanding of what they're attempting here, and they pull it off with flying colors, really making the most of the solid material the script provides (case in point: genre mainstay Babette Bombshell's hilarious non-drag turn as porn director Bernie Munghat, which is almost worth the price of admission alone). The jokes are genuinely funny, the sex scenes appropriately sexy and "hard-R" smutty without ever becoming belabored or feeling like time-filler (a common problem within the retro/grindhouse subgenre), the gore is properly over-the-top, and the pacing is perfect for the story. Honestly, if this film had been done any better it probably would've ruined the magic. Boogie out and watch it; you'll be a better person for it—and you might just learn some hot new dance moves in the process!

2011, USA. D: RICHARD GRIFFIN
AVAILABLE FROM WILD EYE RELEASING

[3] See full festival coverage in *WC #7*, p.27 (**FUTURE JUSTICE** reviewed on p.33 of that same issue).

[4] See reviews in *WC #7*, on p.41 and p.88.

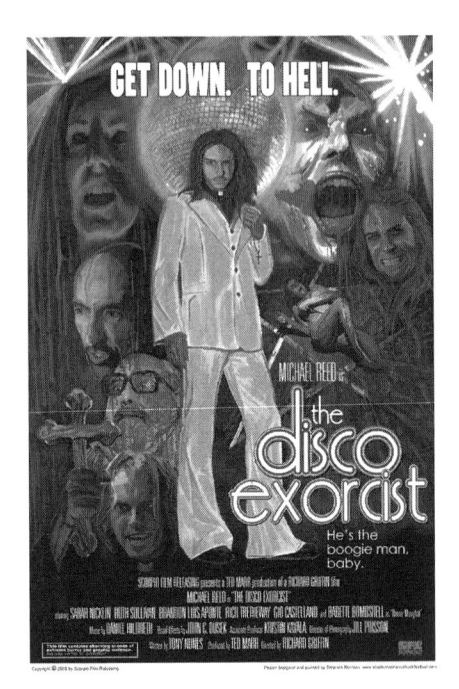

CONTROL FACTOR

Reviewed by Christos Mouroukis

Ad-lines: "*When your thoughts are not your own*", "*Free thought is about to become deadly*".

Seriously, conspiracy theories make me laugh so hard, especially when they are expressed by conservatives who turn their anger against whatever suppressed minority they feel like. Conspiracy theories are usually so dumb that they are enough to explain the fact that the person supporting them has nothing better to argue about. However, yes, capitalism's corrupted governments and corporations do control your life, but this is a film magazine so let's not focus on that. Evil "powers that be" are interesting in film and television. And they came to an all-time high of greatness with *The X-Files* (1993-2002), popular culture's sci-fi phenomenon. In literature, the most serious example is George Orwell's *1984* novel, which was first published in 1949. This book has an actual basis and its metaphorical power is stronger than ever in post-9/11 western civilization's hysteria with terrorism. And then there are tons of crap in both film (fiction and documentaries) and novels (fiction and non-fiction).[5] So, where does this piece of **THEY LIVE** (1988) cinema stand?

Trevor Constantine (Peter Spence from Michael McGowan's **ONE WEEK** [2008]) is hearing voices that force him to grab a gun, go ape-shit bananas, and kill a few people inside an insurance company's building, until he is gunned-down by a trigger-happy security guard (as if police shooting right and left is not enough). Before he dies he delivers the message to Lance Bishop (Adam Baldwin from **PREDATOR 2** [1990]) that people are sheep (as if we didn't know) and that there are horrors to be seen.

He is indeed right, as it appears that a mega-conglomerate is hypnotizing people with Special Forces' extraordinary guns, and then injects microchips in their brains which control every thought and emotion they have, and so on. We learn that the project started in order to fight terrorism (eh, the holy war, right?), but the men in the suits enjoyed it so much that they decided to become god. Their objective is to see the day that people will no longer have the will to be free. I say science-fiction my ass, as it is pretty common these days for us people to sit on our couches to watch the revolution unfolding by our eyes on television instead of joining it. Oh yeah, we have excuses, such as a family and a job…it is depressing how pathetic we are and it is sad to see the evolution of the totalitarian nanny states.

Everything in Lance's life is a set-up, even his wife Karen (Elizabeth Berkley from **SHOWGIRLS** [1995]) is an agent with the code-name "Medusa", and she is trying to perform an experiment on him: to see if he will be able to kill her. Luckily he finds a comrade (Tony Todd, who around the same time he was also in **FINAL DESTINATION 2** [2003]) who managed to trick the system and together (along with a group rebels they will assemble) will fight the only good war, the one for their freedom.

This may be a Sci-Fi Channel original film (before they became SyFy), but believe me when I say it is absolutely one of their best, and possibly their most serious one. The screenplay by John Dombrow (his debut) is quite excellent and the direction by Nelson McCormick (**THE STEPFATHER** [2009]), although occasionally over-stylized (in a modern pretentious way), is flawless most of the time. The finale is a bit anticlimactic but it matches perfectly with the dark tone of the film.

Such a picture could not have been handled if the performances were not top-notch[6], so here's honorary mention to the supporting cast members: Conrad Dunn (**ALIEN NATION** [1988]), John Neville (**SPIDER** [2002]), Ann Marin (**HENDRIX** [2000]), Susan Potvin (**LOVE AND BETRAYAL: THE MIA FARROW STORY** [1995]), and David Ferry (**MAN OF THE YEAR** [2006]).

2003, USA/CANADA. D: NELSON McCORMICK
AVAILABLE FROM UNIVERSAL

---

5 I could go on and on about this subject, but this review is not the time. I may return to the subject in the future, here and there.

6 The special effects are not that great as you can imagine, but this is irrelevant in this film.

DISASTER ZONE: VOLCANO IN NEW YORK

Reviewed by Christos Mouroukis

Elsewhere in this issue I review **CONTROL FACTOR** (2003)[7], which was a co-production between the USA and Canada. Equally randomly I offer you another one for the reviews section, and I hope you enjoy. The film in question is **DISASTER ZONE: VOLCANO IN NEW YORK** (2006), which if nothing else bears a title that makes pretty clear the intentions of the people who made it: what we have here is a disaster movie that tried to jump on the panic bandwagon of 9/11 New York. But is it any good? Let's see…

Michael Ironside (yes, *that* Michael Ironside, from **TOTAL RECALL** [1990]) is playing a pill-popping doctor who works on a very important project. Pills should not be demonized and the fact that the film's scientist is "crazy" (as in so many similar films) is a bit annoying. He is under a lot of pressure from the people who finance his research and he wants to take every caution, but in the end he does not because he gets bitten by the bug of grandeur and puts New York into danger. What kind of danger? Well, a volcano from the core of the earth is about to be unleashed.

The titular danger makes its first steps by killing dozens of homeless people in Central Park, which is an interesting message on how the poor die first in any sort of crisis. The film is low on political commentary and when it has something to say it is usually cliché at best, or stupid at worst.

The soundtrack by Michael Richard Plowman (**A LONELY PLACE TO DIE**, 2011) reminded me of the score from Roger Corman's *Black Scorpion* TV Series. The CGI is bad beyond belief (stones falling slowly in shots that are not supposed to be in slow motion; fires and lava are usually incredibly bad too, etc), and the editors (Bethany Handfield and Trevor Mirosh) did their best to save the situation by utilizing quick cuts, but this did not help because no matter how quick you cut, if all you have to cut from and to is badly rendered footage, then you still get nothing.

The only thing I liked about this film is Robert Lee's direction. It is really interesting, as he is employing handheld camerawork most of the time and some zooms, and it really makes the film watchable. He usually works as an assistant director in big-budget films such as **FREDDY VS. JASON** (2003), but he occasionally directs. Aside from the film under review he also helmed another TV movie in 2005, **ABSOLUTE ZERO**, which I have not seen.

CORE: BOILING POINT (this was the working title) was written *sans* passion by Sarah Watson (at that point she had written one feature, **RACHEL'S ROOM** [2001], and since then she only does TV work, including scripting the aforementioned **ABSOLUTE ZERO**), and it was produced by Robert Lee (with an estimate budget of $1,000,000).

---

7 On this *very* page!

Many familiar faces parade on the screen and these include, Costas Mandylor (**THE DOORS** [1991]), Alexandra Paul (**CHRISTINE** [1983]), Eric Breker (a character bit-part actor who pops-up in major studio films such as **X-MEN ORIGINS: WOLVERINE** [2009]), Ron Selmour (**SUCKER PUNCH** [2011]), Pascale Hutton (**GINGER SNAPS 2: UNLEASHED** [2004]), Zak Santiago (**BATTLESTAR GALACTICA: BLOOD & CHROME** [2012]), Robert Moloney (**MAN OF STEEL** [2013]), Kaj-Erik Eriksen (**SEE NO EVIL 2** [2014]), Matthew Bennett (**BATTLESTAR GALACTICA: RAZOR** [2007]), Andrew Kavadas (**UNDERWORLD: EVOLUTION** [2006]), Michael Boisvert (**DEADLY SKIES** [2006]), Kevin McNulty (**FANTASTIC FOUR** [2005] and **FANTASTIC 4: RISE OF THE SILVER SURFER** [2007]), William MacDonald (**SLITHER** [2006]), and William Taylor (**WILLARD** [2003]).

2006, USA/CANADA. D: ROBERT LEE
AVAILABLE FROM ECHO BRIDGE

YEAR OF THE DRAGON

Reviewed by Christos Mourourkis

Before we begin, check out the credits this movie has: it stars Mickey Rourke—a little before he did a masterpiece called **ANGEL HEART** [1987]), it was produced by Dino De Laurentiis (who the same year also made the amazing **SILVER BULLET** [1985]), it was scored by David Mansfield (**DESPERATE HOURS** [1990]), and it was directed by Michael Cimino (back when he was making things such as my favourite three-hour-long film, **THE DEER HUNTER** [1978]) who also co-wrote it with Oliver Stone (who the next year went on to make my personal favourite, **SALVADOR** [1986]). Can anything go wrong with such personnel? Not too many things.

The film is about Stanley White (Mickey Rourke), a tough cop who is a little bit of a sexist and a racist, and while neglecting his wife (Caroline Kava from **BORN ON THE FOURTH OF JULY** [1989]) he has a goal: to take down the underworld that rules New York's Chinatown and bring order and justice.

Said underworld is led by Triad boss Joey Tai (John Lone from **THE LAST EMPEROR** [1987]), who is responsible for many extortion and protection businesses and other criminal activities, but the shit really hits the fan once problems start to get solved with a series of mafia-like executions.

Stanley White, being white, can't penetrate Chinatown, although he finds the time to penetrate a very sexy Chinese reporter (Ariane from **KING OF NEW YORK** [1990]). Whilst becoming his girlfriend she also helps him with the investigation, but most of the work is done by an undercover Chinese cop (Joey Chin from **CHINA GIRL** [1987]).

To be honest with you, I watched this film because I knew it was supposed to be full of stereotypes (and indeed it is—as you'd expect from a neo-*noir*—so if you're easily offended skip on to the next review) of a mainly racial nature, and since I knew that the two leads (the white cop and Asian reporter) would eventually become a couple, I was hoping for a sex scene to include in my *Interracial Sex Havoc* column that I maintain over at Cinema Head Cheese. Well, there are a couple of occasions that a sex scene is implied, but the audience sees nothing more than a kiss. To level this disappointment, the film gets even and becomes awesome in the nudity department, as the female lead bears all for your eyes only, you filthy perverts.

The film may have opened in the 5th position at the box office, and although that may sound as a decent success for an independent film today, it should be taken into consideration that because it cost $24 million to make and it grossed only $18 million, it was heralded as one of the biggest flops from the mid-'80s. This may be due to the numerous protests against it that were held by Chinese communities that proclaimed that the film discriminates them.

But, is it any good? Well, I am glad I watched it, because it is a time capsule, and it is really interesting to back in time in such a particularly interesting area and see how such Cimino envisioned many things, however exaggerated they may seem. It is certainly a good film, no question about that, but it is also a bit dated, and you should either proceed if you know what you're getting yourself into, or be cautious.

The real diamonds on this piece of celluloid though are the stars, and other than the performers mentioned above, you will also see many familiar faces from the '80s such as Leonard Termo (**ED WOOD** [1994]), Ray Barry (**BORN ON THE FOURTH OF JULY** [1989]), Eddie Jones (**THE TERMINAL** [2004]), and Victor Wong (**BIG TROUBLE IN LITTLE CHINA** [1986]).

1985, USA/FRANCE. D: MICHAEL CIMINO
AVAILABLE FROM WARNER

NIGHT WARNING
(a.k.a. **BUTCHER, BAKER, NIGHTMARE MAKER**)

Reviewed by Tim Merrill

Poor Billy. After the gruesome death of his parents at a young age, the boy is left to the care of his dear Aunt Cheryl (played by Susan Tyrell). Before

YEAR OF THE DRAGON

Jimmy McNichol (brother of 'Seventies teen idol Kristy McNichol) plays Billy, a simple teenage boy who just wants to play high school basketball, earn his scholarship, and take off with his girl. If only it were that easy. Someone must have told aunt Cheryl that next of kin is best of skin, because she's got it hard for her nephew, and will do anything to keep him by her side. With all her longing glances, and suggestive innuendos, Susan Tyrell plays Aunt Cheryl like Kay Parker, and lays it on more twisted than Opedius at a family reunion. Tyrell really goes out of her way to try to fit into Joan Crawford's high heels in this one. Both are eerily comparable when you consider Crawford's roles in such films as **WHATEVER HAPPENED TO BABY JANE?**, **JOHNNY GUITAR** (1954), and **STRAIT-JACKET** (1964). Throughout the film Tyrell plays it sweet on the surface as the doting aunt, but also instantly turns on the psychotic rage when she is pushed to her limits. Make no mistake, Tyrell serves up the crazy in this film like a 25lb turkey stuffed with PCP. She's a whirling dervish of insanity in this, channeling both Crawford and Cesar Romero's joker, and is a *tour de force*.

Aunt Cheryl tries to find lovin' wherever she can get it, and tries to fire up a TV repair man making a house call for a little afternoon delight. When the poor schmuck turns her down for a little slice of strange, Tyrell kills him, just as her darling nephew comes home to her aid. Billy is talked into telling the police that he defended his aunt from a sexual assault and killed the man, but detective Joe Carlson (Bo Svenson) has other ideas.

We've all seen our fair share of portrayals of crooked cops and sadistic law enforcement, and Bo Svenson earns his name in the books. For some unexplainable reason detective Carlson is a raging homophobe, thinking anyone in the area who is a man—aside from himself—is up to some locker room hanky-panky. There's a strong undercurrent of homophobia that sticks out in this film from various angles. Bill Paxton shows up in one of his earliest roles as a fellow teammate of Billy's who is forever accusing him of sucking up to the coach for "extra credit". Svenson also thinks Billy is involved in a tryst with his coach, despite the fact that Billy has a girl, Julie (Julia Duffy). The whole gay angle is pushed so aggressively by Svenson's character that he comes across like a homophobic Reggie Nalder in **MARK OF THE DEVIL** (1970). Nobody's going to tell him that there isn't any grab-ass going on in his town right under his own nose. Meanwhile, Aunt Cheryl becomes increasingly wound tighter than a tourniquet, seeing anyone close to Billy as a potential threat to her bond with her nephew. Once she gets rolling, Tyrell chomps through scenery like a full-throttle lawnmower.

It is interesting to note that **NIGHT WARNING** was released in the slasher era, and while there are elements of gore and violence in the film, it stands out as a breath of fresh air in a period that mass-produced masked killers. Despite what some might tell you, there were a fair number of original horror-based films to come out of the '80s, like **FADE TO BLACK** (1980) and **MOTEL HELL** (1980). Definitely worth a look as a unique nugget from the bygone era. Those curious about the film will be happy to know that Code Red has just recently released a deluxe remastered DVD with a commentary by the late Susan Tyrell, as well.

long, Billy becomes a strapping young man, and begins to set out on his own to finally get out from under the thumb of his domineering aunt. While Billy is ready to split the scene and claim his independence, dear Aunt Cheryl has other devious plans in mind for her nephew.

Released by Royal American Pictures in 1982 (also under the title **BUTCHER, BAKER, NIGHTMARE MAKER**), **NIGHT WARNING** is a sleazy little grease stain of a film that seems more apt to have been released alongside the typical drive-in fare of the 'Sixties and 'Seventies. If anything stands out initially with this film it is its puzzling title that really doesn't have a thing to do with the picture at all. The alternate name seems more applicable to the nature of the film, as it plays out as a skewed domestic gothic that is very reminiscent of such films as **WHATEVER HAPPENED TO BABY JANE?** (1962) and **THE BABY** (1973), mixed with aspects of **PSYCHO** (1960).

While you're at it, pay your respects to the lady with a watch of **FORBIDDEN ZONE** (1980).

1982, USA. D: WILLIAM ASHER
AVAILABLE FROM CODE RED

RAIDERS OF THE LIVING DEAD

Reviewed by Eric Messina

What has Scotty Schwartz, the kid who famously got his tongue frozen to a flagpole, been up to lately? If you said "He wound up in porn," then give yourself a gold star because you are (partially) correct! He was also in this cheesy zombie flick that opens with one of the most amazing fake Foreigner title songs ever written by Tim Ferrante. That rockin' tune really gets you amped-up for some Canadian zombie hijinks.

Sam Sherman, Al Adamson's partner-in-grime directed this non-stop thrill-ride (that starts off strong, then takes a nose-dive into toilet town). Sherman is no stranger to B-movies and I actually like some of his work with Al Adamson; you just have to suspend your disbelief and expect a crummy time. Apparently, Sherman explains all the bumps and hiccups in the commentary of the Image Entertainment special edition DVD—for more info check out Chris Poggiali's excellent 'blog, *Temple of Schlock*.

The library Driver's Ed. stock music attempts to enthrall the viewer as cars chase other cars—slow down, movie, we've got an hour and a half!

Terrorists are holding the nuclear safety inspector hostage (Wait a minute, wasn't that the plotline of a Simpsons episode? Man, they've done everything)! I love the vacant human-fish-looking people in this film who gawk as exhilarating stock music plays over them. Something exciting could happen at any minute, so stick around!

People silently walk down hallways, but at least we're in the power plant, so things are about to heat up! I feel as if I need the cliff notes for this film because there's no dialogue for long stretches; I guess I really needed that commentary to explain things. Suddenly a nameless guy in blue jeans gets electrocuted, and then Scotty Schwartz shows up—hooray, a celebrity will get this thing going right?

He likes to rock out when he does homework, his grandpa needs to get his VCR repaired—this is some crucial dialogue that will pad the storyline later (but probably not).

Schwartz smirks a lot; his face muscles must be killing him from overexertion. He snips high voltage wires and has a hamster named Felix; man, can this movie be any more exciting?

All that fumbling worked out, because somehow he invents a laser! Next, zombies mysteriously show up…well, you knew they were coming. I'd just expected a slight reason as to why they're here, but okay, I'll take it! A guy in a leather jacket immediately sets one grey rotting corpse on fire.

He tries to flee, but his car won't start and then makes his way over to a gun store where he complains about bleeding-heart liberals—man, I hate when those pinkos try to stop us from murdering innocent people and zombies!

Next, a woman talks on the phone like it's a real conversation…I mean she really sells it. People at a theater watch a famous clip of *The Three Stooges* for no apparent reason. Immediately after, Scott fuses all the laserdiscs, beta tapes and treasures the video pirates from **AMAZON WOMEN ON THE MOON** (1987) would drool over and creates a laser gun.

The woman who really sells her phone-talking skills goes to look for the leather jacket guy as saxophone-heavy Muzak plays, which kind of sounds like "Hello it's Me" by Todd Rundgren (1972). There's a mildly entertaining zombie dream sequence with a bunch of ghouls that look like the Arthur Grimsdyke makeup from **TALES FROM THE CRYPT** (1972).

As nonsensical and annoying as I found **NIGHTMARE CITY** (*Incubo sulla città contaminata*, 1980) to be, I take back all the rotten things I said about it after watching this brainless mess. This miserable zombie flick makes that one look like a masterpiece. If you're looking for cool zombies, then whatever you do, don't bother with this film. The worst part is that it just keeps trying and has no idea what makes an entertaining film; it even fails as an unintentionally funny one. We're supposed to like the characters (whose names and back stories are never established), but they're so uninteresting. IMDb would try to convince you that there are character names, but to me they were inaudible. If you have the stomach for a dopey zombie movie that shambles on aimlessly, maybe that was the point, to turn the viewer into a zombie, then by all means checks this one out!

Zombies have risen from their graves by all sorts of methods before, like sonic waves, radiation and acid rain, this movie doesn't even attempt to explain or offer any reason for the plague; all **RAIDERS** has going for it is a catchy theme song.

1986, USA. D: SAMUEL M. SHERMAN
AVAILABLE FROM IMAGE ENTERTAINMENT

THE LIVING SKELETON
(*Kyûketsu dokuro-sen*)

Reviewed by Richard Glenn Schmidt

Tagline: *"The mummy's hand will devour you, never to be separated again! The ocean's depths send forth a procession of trembling ghosts!"*[8]

If you can think of a Japanese horror movie of the 1960s that is more underrated than Hiroshi Matsuno's **THE LIVING SKELETON** (1968)[9] then tell me what it is and I'll watch it! My first thought when I picked up Criterion's *When Horror Came to Shochiku* box set was "Oh, **THE LIVING SKELETON**, where have you been all my life?" This vengeful female ghost meets ghost ship meets mad science mash-up is a gem that must be seen to be believed.

The film opens with a hostage situation going very wrong on a ship named the Dragon King, somewhere in the middle of the ocean. A pirate with a hideously scarred face leads a group of mutinying sailors to steal a shipment of gold and leave no survivors. With the crew and passengers chained together in a manner that is eerily reminiscent of a slave ship, the pirates shoot anyone who defies them. After terrorizing a young woman named Yuriko (the lovely Kikko Matsuoka) in front of her husband, this monster orders his goons to machine-gun everyone down.

Years later, Saeko (Matsuoka again), Yuriko's sister, spends her carefree days working with Father Akashi (Masumi Okada) at the church and canoodling with her fiancée Mochizuki (Yasunori Irikawa) on his boat. But these happy times are tinged with melancholy, as Yuriko is still missing along with her husband, Dr. Nishizato (Kô Nishimura), the ship's doctor. The official story is that the ship sunk during a typhoon, but Saeko knows her sister is still out there…somewhere.

One fateful day, while Mochizuki and Saeko are scuba diving, they encounter a ghastly sight: skeletons wrapped in chains floating ominously towards them! That night, a fog bank rolls in, and the missing ship appears just offshore. Saeko flips out and makes Mochizuki pilot his boat out to it. A wave capsizes the boat and Mochizuki barely survives the ordeal. Saeko manages to climb up onto the ghost ship where she discovers the truth of what happened to everyone on board.

Now possessed by the spirit of Yuriko, Saeko returns to get revenge on the men who have been living off the stolen gold for years. One by one, these scumbags get what's coming to them, but their leader, the mysterious Tanuma, still has some tricks up his sleeve. All of this climaxes in the bowels of the Dragon King where the spirit of Yuriko runs rampant and her devoted husband, the now mad and very undead Dr. Nishizato, can finally have his revenge using a chemical compound that he's had all these years to perfect!

The comic book horror atmosphere of **THE LIVING SKELETON**, combined with its expertly crafted gothic melodrama, otherworldly charm, and wild turns in the plot, make it an instant favorite for me and something that I will be returning to again and again. This film would make a great double-feature with the unfortu-

---

8 My wife LeEtta spent an hour translating this from the top of the poster.
9 The original Japanese very roughly title translates to "Vampire Skull Ship".

Spanish-language poster for **THE LIVING SKELETON**

Gaze into the eyes (well, sunglasses, anyway) of horror in **THE LIVING SKELETON**!

nately out-of-print J-horror classic, **MATANGO:** (a.k.a. **MATANGO: ATTACK OF THE MUSHROOM PEOPLE**, 1963), or, on the Italian side of things, **NIGHTMARE CASTLE** (*Amanti d'oltretomba*, a.k.a. **THE FACELESS MONSTER**, 1965), starring Barbara Steele.

Director Hiroshi Matsuno really should have done more horror movies because **THE LIVING SKELETON** leaves me hungry for more in a bad way. The black-and-white cinematography by Masayuki Katô is pretty much perfect—dig that monochrome gore!—as even the nighttime scenes are easy on the eyes. Composer Noboru Nishiyama straight-up nails it to the wall with his score that is spy movie smooth, scary in all the right places, and filled with those old tape-driven echoed guitars that make my ears detach from my head and dance around on the floor.

My only criticism of the film lies with the underwater skeletons, which are hilariously and embarrassingly fake. They are shackled with chains and are floating around while the stingers in the soundtrack blare, scaring no one. Oh shit, I just remembered the ubiquitous rubber bats that no horror film from this era would dare not prominently feature. I was trying to repress the memory of them in the dark corners of my mind. Rubber bats: lowering the standards of horror movie fans for generations! And I guess I have to mention the hokey model ship used to show the Dragon King floating out in the swimming pool that's a stand-in for the ocean. But in all seriousness, this whole paragraph describes a bunch of quaint details that just make me love this movie even more.

Some reviewers are saying that this film inspired John Carpenter's **THE FOG** (1981). While it's true that there are some similar plot points (revenge, a priest, stolen gold) and some imagery (a ghostly ship, fog), it honestly never occurred to me that **THE LIVING SKELETON** may have had a hand in **THE FOG**'s genesis while I was watching it. Other than an old Japanese VHS and recent appearances on DVD, this film seems to have slipped into unseen obscurity for a number of years. I can only guess that there was a limited British or American release thanks to a capsule review in Phil Hardy's *The Overlook Film Encyclopedia: Horror* and a publicity still in Denis Gifford's *A Pictorial History of Horror Movies*, released in 1973. I did find a gorgeous Mexican lobby card for **THE LIVING SKELETON** that leads me to believe that the film got around to some other parts of the world, as well.

I can't recommend **THE LIVING SKELETON** enough. If its foreboding vibe, utter weirdness, and spooky fun don't do it for you then you need to get in touch with your inner long-haired lady ghost. In fact, I suggest you scoop up that *When Horror Came to Shochiku* box set ASAP, as it features two other fine Japanese films, the bizarre Kaiju entry, **THE X FROM OUTER SPACE** (*Uchû daikaijû Girara*, 1967) and the essential horror oddity **GOKE, BODY SNATCHER FROM HELL** (*Kyuketsuki Gokemidoro*, 1968). The only dud out of the four is **GENOCIDE** (*Konchû daisensô*, 1968), but it's such a baffling flick that it's at least worth a look.

1968, JAPAN. D: HIROSHI MATSUNO
AVAILABLE FROM CRITERION

Japanese poster art for **THE LIVING SKELETON**

AVENGED
(a.k.a. **SAVAGED**)

Reviewed by Steven Ronquillo

Zoe (Amanda Adrienne) is a deaf-mute at a high point in her life. She has a great fiancé and she's moving to live with him by driving across the USA in the classic car her dad left her. But all of that crashes to a halt when she runs headlong into a group of rednecks killing a couple of Indians in a feud that's spanned generations.

From here on it gets into an **I SPIT ON YOUR GRAVE** (1978)-type situation with them leaving her dead in the desert…but this is where the movie gets interesting, as an Indian shaman finds her near-dead body and attempts to resurrect her. He succeeds, but she gets to share her body with an ancient Indian chief…and it's right to Carnage City!

I didn't expect much from this after its turbulent history and title change from **SAVAGED** to **AVENGED**; the prognosis of this was cloudy but in the end I was surprised. This may be the best damn sequel to **THE CROW** (1994) we never got. This is a violent, brutal little film with a decent amount of practical effects, careful use of CGI and hellified stunts once she starts kicking ass.

One of the things I love about this movie is how when she gets possessed she falls apart in a very nasty and gooey way because two spirits cannot inhabit a single body. This leads to some nasty body repair scenes that take this from the average **CROW** rip-off into a weird world of its own.

And the gender politics of this movie are interesting as well, since in most of these types of films the female is the one tied up and needing to be saved. In this, it's her boyfriend yelling, "You kill them! You kill them all, Baby!" They're also an interracial couple and that isn't a big plot point because they never bring up the fact that he is black, which is a nice turn. And there is a whole back-story about the bad guy's family and the Indian tribe, which is a nice little addition you rarely get in a movie like this.

This may be the best B-movies of the year. I know **SHARKNDADO 3** (2015) will probably get more love, but this is a brainless DTV classic and I highly recommend it if you're looking for a "woman kicking ass" film to fill the void after **MAD MAX: FURY ROAD** (2015). So get it, watch it, and enjoy it!

2013, USA. D: MICHAEL S. OJEDA
AVAILABLE FROM UNCORK'D ENTERTAINMENT

ROAR

Reviewed by Tim Merrill

Once in a while in the realms of cinema, certain film projects surface that inevitably wind up being a once-in-a-lifetime experience. Whether it's a Jerry Lewis clown holocaust film, or the **TWILIGHT ZONE: THE MOVIE** (1983) tragedy, there are some things that come down the pipe that should and can never be repeated.

Since the early 'Seventies, actress Tippi Hedren (**THE BIRDS** [1963]) made it a personal crusade to travel the globe protecting exotic jungle cats from illegal ownership and breeding. Hedren did all she could to make the public aware of the cruel and criminal actions taken towards these felines.

In 1981, producer Noel Marshall came together with his wife, Hedren, and their daughter Melanie Griffith to bring to the screen one of the most feral and life-threatening films ever made. At an estimated budget of over $15 million, **ROAR** took audiences on a real wildlife safari that comes across like an episode of *Wild Kingdom* on skanky meth. Good old Marlin Perkins would have shit a gold brick if he had been witness to this.

W.C. Fields once said the he would never work with children or animals, and for good reason. It's one thing to have to deal with one temperamental 1,200lb feline, but to surround yourself with over 60 wild lions, tigers, and pumas that could instantly shred you like wet tissue paper is sheer madness. Every moment brings about a feeling of claustrophobic tension that leaves a lump in your throat. Seeing male lions fight each other within a paw swipe of their human co-stars makes the whole experience feel absolutely unhinged, and ready to go wrong at any moment. It is simply insane to believe that anyone would put themselves within such close proximity with these ferocious animals. This goes far beyond unsafe work conditions, and makes the Siegfried and Roy shit seem like playtime with a kitten and string.

While none of the animals were allegedly harmed during the shooting, the same could not be said for the cast and crew. As a matter of fact, the film's trailer seems to proudly revel in the fact that most people involved in the project came away maimed, scarred, and/or permanently fucked-up. It's nothing short of a goddamn miracle that no one bit the dirt, or wound up as steak tartar in the belly of one of the cats. There's no **FACES OF DEATH** (1978) faked shenanigans in the film, and all the cat attacks captured on film were absolutely legit. Tippi Hedren herself received 38 stitches to her head after having a lion gnaw on her skull. Her daughter Melanie Griffith wound up in need of facial reconstructive surgery as a result of being mauled during shooting. Director of photography Jan de Bont (**LETHAL WEAPON** [1987], **BASIC INSTINCT** [1992]) was literally scalped by a lion during the filming, and had his wig re-attached before returning to complete the project. It seems unlikely that there was any kind of insurance coverage on this film, with all the levels of injuries that ensued.

Both Marshall and Hedren had envisioned the story of the unfettered feline insanity long before they were able to set it to film. Marshall plays a crazed naturalist, who puts all at risk by developing a free sanctuary in the middle of the African jungle to create a bridge between man and the great beasts. When all the social idealism is put aside, he comes off like a crazy cat lady in charge of 50 or 60 feral man-eaters. Before you can say, "Lions and Tigers and Bears, oh my!", his family soon lands in Africa to meet him. After a miscommunication, Hedren and her offspring finds themselves at the mercy of the rogue lion Togar, determined to cram them all down his gullet. The family is soon left with no alternative but to barricade themselves in the sanctuary quarters to wait while "Dr Doolittle" returns to the rescue. In all honesty, you find out that **ROAR** is actually a siege film at its core, and Tippi Hedren

*Nothing will stop Amanda Adrienne from being **AVENGED**!*

is no stranger to being besieged by animals, be it bird or beast. In terms of cinematography, Jan de Bont pulls off the impossible, capturing gorgeous shots of running giraffes alongside motorcycles, not to mention the lion-on-lion fights, and rampages. What's funny about the film is that it also comes off being comedic in spots, reminding one of the Spencer/Hill comedic westerns, and the *Gods Must Be Crazy* series. One can only guess that the comedic spots were included to break the ass-puckering tension that runs roughshod through the whole film. In the end, **ROAR** stands as a testament not only to the beauty of the majestic wild felines, but to the absolute perseverance and obsessive nature of batshit insane filmmakers. After the film was finally completed, Hedren swore there would never be a sequel, and she was absolutely right. There's no way in hell a film like this could ever be put together again, not only due to animal regulation laws, but also due to the inability to find anyone crazy enough to sign onto a project like this ever again.

I openly challenge anyone to sit down and watch this without involuntarily cringing or sweating profusely. Screw the Discovery Channel—you've never seen anything like this before.

1981, USA. D: NOEL MARSHALL
AVAILABLE FROM OLIVE FILMS

Ratline

Reviewed by Tony Strauss

Half-sisters Crystal (Emily Haack) and Kim (Alex Del Monacco), on the lam after pulling a big-money double-cross that left them responsible for two deaths, decide to lay low and rent a room from a woman they met online: cute, vivacious and naïve Penny Webb (Sarah Swofford). Penny is a City employee working on a project to move the town cemetery to a new location, and she's decided to take in tenants to help make her life a bit less financially stressful, hopefully thereby to become less of a burden on her kindly grandfather, Miles (Joseph R. Engel), who is the City Administrator. Miles would rather help her out with money than have her take in two strangers, but Penny assures him that they seem like very nice women. (You can *always* trust strangers you meet on the Internet, is what I've always said.)

Meanwhile, a group of young Satanists, after a bloody ritual in the woods in which they sacrifice a poor, cute doggy (don't worry, it's off-screen, but still...*assholes!*), decide that they need to up the ante in order to please the Dark Lord: they need to sacrifice a human life. Using the old roadside "Help! There's been an accident!" shtick, they lure some hapless Samaritan into pulling over to offer help. They kidnap him at gunpoint and take him to an old abandoned school building to perform their ritual. The man begs for his life, but they show no signs of mercy...so he calmly and effortlessly snaps the duct tape binding his wrists and proceeds to slaughter them all with seemingly superhuman strength. Take that, ya lousy puppy-killers!

The next day while working down at the cemetery, Penny meets a man standing over a crumbling, faded grave—yup, it's the Satanist-slaughtering supercreep! He introduces himself as Frank Logan (Jason Christ), and claims to not know whose grave it is when she inquires...but we get the distinct feeling that he's hiding something sinister (like, even more than being a crazy-strong murderer). Our suspicions are soon confirmed when Frank shows up at Miles' office and demands a certain

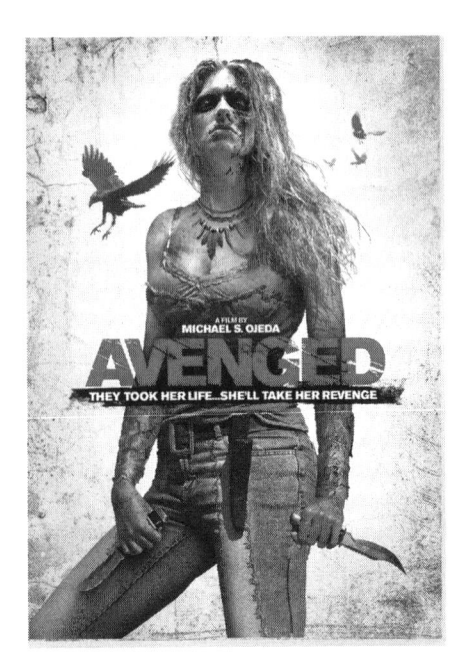

Webb family heirloom…one that no living person other than Miles could possibly know about!

Who is this scary super-goon named Frank Logan, and what is this secret heirloom he's after? And why is he so damned tough and unstoppable? Well, I'm sure as shit not going to tell you, so back the hell off, ya pushy weirdo! Anyway, that would spoil all the fun…and this movie is shitloads of fun.

As a fan of microbudget indie films, *this* is the kind of gem you hold out for while you're mining your way through all the mountains of mediocre muck[10]—the kind of ambitious and original film that makes sitting through all the myriad found-footage slasher/ghost clones worth it (well…almost). Sure, like most movies in this tax bracket, you have some uneven acting and the occasional sound recording imperfections, but that's just part and parcel for this category of filmmaking, and if you're put off by those kinds of issues

---
10 That is by no means a slight against microbudget indie films; when you get right down to it, *most* movies are mediocre (at best), no matter what their budget or genre. But that's part of the fun of being a cinema junky, isn't it—mining for the gems!

you probably wouldn't consider this film (or this magazine, really) in the first place. And anyway, it's never really a point of distraction, because the story and characters are so intriguing and the film is so well-paced and fun that those kinds of quibbles become negligible.

In both a storytelling and filmmaking sense, this movie delivers big in the genre satisfaction department: in addition to the aforementioned Satanists and superhuman dude, you get a lesbian love story, dirty double-crossings, lotsa vicious and brutal killings, freaky familial secrets, full-frontal nudity (of both sexes!), declassified military footage… and even *more* crazy awesomeness that I can't even bring up because it's too much fun to find out as it's revealed by the plot, and I don't want to spoil it for you.

Look, the point is that you should see this damned movie.

The demented ringleader behind all this mayhem is underground favorite Eric Stanze, director of such indie oddities as **CHINA WHITE SERPENTINE** (2003)[11], **THE CAPTIVES** (a.k.a. **I SPIT ON YOUR CORPSE I PISS ON YOUR GRAVE**, 2001)[12], **SAVAGE HARVEST** (1994) and **DEADWOOD PARK** (2007). If you're a fan of underground cinema, you've probably seen at least one of his movies. If you haven't, you should. There's a reason PollyGrind Film Festival named him "King of Underground Cinema"—granted, a hyperbolic title for anyone to hold, but not a ridiculous claim at all in Stanze's case, because this guy's got mad skills.

As any indie cinema fan knows, the most effective antidote against budgetary restrictions and all the handicaps they bring is creativity, and Stanze delivers that in spades; he's never afraid of swinging for the fences, budget be damned. Even when they're not as successful attempts as **RATLINE** (2011) is, Stanze's films are always worth seeing…ambitious in concept and creative in execution. He's really one of the most interesting underground filmmakers out there right now;

---
11 See my review in *Weng's Chop* #5, p.62
12 See Brian Harris' roundtable review in *WC* #5, p.158

one of the fine folks actively breathing life into the low-budget arena. Here wearing the trifecta of hats as director, cinematographer and editor (as well as co-writer, along with Jason Christ), Stanze demonstrates an adept filmmaking hand capable of delivering such an ambitious, idea-crammed story within the necessity of smaller-scale confines, and still manages to make it all feel larger than life— something that you rarely see even attempted in underground cinema, much less pulled off. The use of good, well-picked soundtrack music is spot-on throughout, as well, adding just the right punch and setting the right tones for the proceedings.

But above all, it's still primarily the story that really pushes **RATLINE** apart from the rest of the crowd. To say that this movie is unpredictable would be a pretty big understatement…it mashes multiple genres and insane B-movie plot twists together into something new and fresh, and wholly satisfying. I know I'm being fairly vague with the details, but that's for your benefit, trust me. Just suffice it to say that this one is a winner…and if you're the kind of nutjob who reads this magazine, this one is totally worth seeking out.

2011, USA. D: ERIC STANZE
AVAILABLE FROM WICKED PIXEL CINEMA

madman

Reviewed by Matthew E. Banks

1982 should have seen the birth of a new serial killer franchise to rival that of **HALLOWEEN** (1978) and **FRIDAY THE 13TH** (1980). **MADMAN** (1982) introduced us to Madman Marz (played by Paul Ehlers); with his distorted face and ingenious ways of killing those who call out his name in vain, he should have rivalled his contemporaries. His star shone bright until fading into near-obscurity, but word-of-mouth led the film into cult status. Phil Hardy, when describing **MADMAN**, states that "the film is nonetheless an unoriginal, derivative carbon copy of *Friday the 13th*."[13] This is hardly a fair statement, as by the time that **MADMAN** came out there had been three *Friday the 13th* films (1980, 1981, and 1982) and a *Halloween* sequel in 1981, as well as an imitation in **THE BURNING** (1981), which followed the *Friday the 13th* formula of kids at a summer camp getting slaughtered. As Stephen Thrower points out: "There are subdivisions in slasherdom, as elsewhere in the horror genre. Besides the 'Special Occasion Slashers' (*Bloody Birthday, Happy Birthday To Me, My Bloody Valentine, April Fool's Day, Halloween, Silent Night, Deadly Night, Christmas Evil, New Year's Evil*) there were the 'Summer Camp Slaughterthons' (*Friday the 13th, The Burning, Madman, Sleepaway Camp*) […]"[14] Logically then, the film follows what has already been laid out in at least two other films, so to throw it aside as though it is worthless really is not a fair statement. If anything, both **THE BURNING** and **MADMAN** owe a huge debt to **FRIDAY THE 13TH** parts 1 and 2 and John Carpenter's **THE FOG** (1980). Whilst the former two films set up the campsite scenario where the "action" is to take place, it is with **THE FOG** that the fireside telling

---
13 Hardy, Phil/Milne, Tom. *The Encyclopedia of Horror Movies*. Harper & Row, 1986, p.379
14 Thrower, Stephen. *Nightmare USA: The Untold Story of the Exploitation Independents*, FAB Press Publishers, 2007, p.26.

Marinading dinner in **ROAR**

of the legend setting up the back-story at the beginning of the film is introduced—both **FRIDAY THE 13TH PART 2** (1981) and **THE BURNING** have similar scenes, though neither are at the beginning of the film, with the former coming in about 25 minutes into the film and the latter coming in at around 40 minutes. The biggest difference between these two examples is that the pre-title sequence for **FRIDAY THE 13TH PART 2** is structured to continue on from the first film whilst reminding viewers of what went before, whereas **THE BURNING** is just reiterating the start of the film. **MADMAN** takes its stance from **THE FOG** and utilizes this idea for the beginning of the film, thus setting up the back-story in its opening scenes.

It is interesting to note that Marz's motivations for killing are never fully explored, and in that respect **MADMAN** follows in the footsteps of **HALLOWEEN**. We know that it was grief that drove Mrs. Voorhees (Betsy Palmer) to kill in **FRIDAY THE 13TH**, and we know that Jason's seeing his mother decapitated sends him on a killing spree in part 2. It would therefore appear that death or some other form of tragedy seems to set these serial killers off. Yet both Michael Myers and Marz do not fall into this category in any way, shape or form. As James Oliver points out: "While most slasher films simply lined up a killer and then supplied some cock-and-bull reason for him/her to go on the rampage, Carpenter was somewhat smarter. Although the killer in Halloween has a name and backstory, Carpenter treats him as something more mythical, almost as an incarnation of childhood fear. Madman Marz is cut very much from the same cloth, stripped of a precise motivation and painted as—essentially—a mythological figure."[15]

MADMAN was the brainchild of the late Joe Giannone and Gary Sales, two young filmmakers who had met whilst studying at Richmond College. Heavily influenced by John Carpenter's **HALLOWEEN**, they realised that there was potential in the bogyman concept; with Sales remembering a childhood campsite tale of the Cropsey maniac. After lengthy discussions over this they started to develop a storyline based on this urban legend and realised that the best way to shoot the film would be to use as few locations as possible, as had both **HALLOWEEN** and **FRIDAY THE 13TH** previously. Soon Giannone had developed a script, MADMAN – THE LEGEND LIVES, whilst Sales balanced his day job with the quest of finding an investor. Eventually they attracted the attention of Sam Marion and secured enough financing to begin production. It was at this time that they came across a major stumbling block as they found out that Bob and Harvey Weinstein's production of **THE BURNING** had a central character called Cropsey and was loosely based on a variant of that legend. Understanding that the two productions would, to an audience, resemble each other too much, Giannone re-wrote the script, dropping the character of Cropsey and creating the character of Madman Marz, a farmer who had murdered his family and was later lynched by a mob for his crimes, only to have disappeared the following morning. Filming commenced in November 1980 at Fish Cove in Southampton, Long Island, after a previous location fell through. Fish Cove would prove to be the ideal location, as not only did it have a large house to film in, it had twenty-five cabins where the cast and crew could stay. The film was meant to be set in the summer, but as production had begun in the fall when the leaves were turning brown, to give the appearance of summer the leaves were painted green.

Sales and Giannone brought in another friend, Paul Ehlers, to help with designing posters and artwork for the film. It was during a meeting where Ehlers was physically describing how he envisioned the artwork that Sales and Giannone realised that they had their central character of Madman Marz. It also helped that Ehlers was martial arts-trained and was physically strong enough to carry out the rigors of the role.

As the film was shot at night, when several members of the cast and crew spotted a strange figure watching them in the woods, they grew a little anxious. Sales asked Ehlers if he would take a look around, as he was in full costume. Ehlers was unable to find the mysterious watcher, much to his disappointment, and after his look around the figure was never seen again. Sales also gave Ehlers a beeper as his wife was expecting their first child and the hospital could contact him as soon as she went into labour. One night whilst filming a scene in his full costume and covered in blood, the beeper went off and by the time that he got to the hospital, Ehlers had got his mask off, but otherwise was still in full costume. The nurse on duty took one look at him and believing that he had been in an accident, tried to persuade him to go to ER. Fortunately it was resolved and Ehlers' son was born on November 15th 1980.

The only accident that happened on-set was to Sales himself. He spent his spare time on-set taking production pictures for press releases and promotion but in the scene where Betsy shoots her friend Ellie through a window, Sales had been above the camera taking photographs, when a piece of the breakaway glass fired out and landed between his eyes. As the glass was only synthetic and did not penetrate too deeply into his forehead, he escaped relatively unharmed. Giannone was forced to re-think the

---

15 Oliver, James. "Campfire Stories Telling Tales About Madman". Arrow video (FCD1131), 2015, pp.8-11.

shooting schedule when the prosthetics for Marz were late arriving to the set and actor Tony Fish was given one night to memorise the song that he sings to frighten his fellow counsellors around the campfire in the opening scene. For the effect of Marz crushing his wife's skull with the axe the make-up artists filled a condom with fake blood and placed a wig over it so as when the axe blade came down it would explode.

The production team originally wanted horror legend Vincent Price for the role of Max, the head counsellor, but two things went against this. Firstly, the film was a non-union production, thus giving young actors the chance to star in a film, and secondly, Price's fee would have been $12,000 for three days' shooting. Whether Price would have been right for the role is debatable considering his over-the-top roles in both **HOUSE OF THE LONG SHADOWS** (1983) and his last British film, **BLOODBATH AT THE HOUSE OF DEATH** (1984). Although he had been a dramatic actor early in his career, his later horror roles would see more tongue-in-cheek performances; this may have detracted from the authenticity that the filmmakers were looking for. Fortunately for the production, Tony Fish was able to ask his friend Fred Neumann to take on the role, though he is credited as Carl Fredericks. Neumann brings a brooding intensity to the role that echoes John Houseman's character of Mr. Machen in Carpenter's **THE FOG** when retelling the legend of Madman Marz around the campfire. The rest of the cast were made up of young actors and actresses looking for their big break, with the exception of Gaylen Ross (under the pseudonym of Alexis Dubin), who had portrayed the central role of Francine in George A. Romero's **DAWN OF THE DEAD** (1978). The slasher trope of, "death to all teenagers who fuck", as set out in these films has never been more apt than in this production. As for his first and only film as director, Giannone changed the rules of the slasher film by having his lead characters die and the main protagonist, Richie (Tom Candela under the pseudonym Jimmy Steele), survive; and with cinematographer James Lemmo filmed some excellent night photography and "blue-toned lighting that evoked the foreboding in these woods".[16]

16 Normanton, P. The Mammoth Book of Slasher Movies. Constable & Robinson Ltd, 2012, p.301.

The film was released in January 1982 and became a sleeper hit thanks to word of mouth in the drive-in circuit. It quickly gained a cult following. Around late 1982/83 the slasher film craze had peaked and many films including **MADMAN** found new life on the home video market on VHS tape. That would change in 1984 when in the UK the government introduced The Video Recordings Act and effectively banned many films that had once been widely available, including **THE BURNING**, which was classed (along with 74 other titles) as a "video nasty". Although **MADMAN** was seized by the police, it was never classed as a video nasty or banned. Despite its cult status, the film fell into obscurity, only to be revived when formats changed and it became available once again as a DVD in 2001, then again in 2010, and has finally received its Blu-ray release from Arrow in the UK and Vinegar Syndrome in the States.

REFERENCES
Normanton, P. *The Mammoth Book of Slasher Movies*. Constable & Robinson Ltd., 2012.
Sellers, Christian. The Making of Madman (1982). *http://retroslashers.net/the-making-of-madman-1982/*

1982, USA. D: JOE GIANNONE
AVAILABLE FROM VINEGAR SYNDROME,
CODE RED and [ZONE B] ARROW

CHILLERAMA

Reviewed by Michael Elvidge

Ad-line: *"The Ultimate Midnight Movie!"*

While I was at the local grocery store—which has a rack of new and used DVDs and Blu-rays for sale—one of the DVDs' cover art really appealed to me with its impressive painted appearance by Phil Roberts, who has created a massive amount of movie posters . So I added it to my grocery cart and proceed to check-out and purchased **CHILLERAMA** (2011)…

CHILLERAMA is an anthology feature in the tradition of **TWILIGHT ZONE: THE MOVIE** (1983) and **CREEPSHOW** (1982). A computerized intro leads us into the film, where a grave-robber exhumes the body of his ex-wife, saying "Time for a bit of dead head!" Just then the corpse's eyes open and it chomps off his testicle. He escapes the zombie and then gets a call on his cell phone that he is late for work, which happens to be at a drive-in theater showing a horror all-nighter. We learn the owner of the theater is Cecil B. Kaufman (Richard Riehle), and he is in possession of several rare prints of lost horror films. As carloads of theater-goers arrive, Cecil complains of VOD (Video On Demand) and DVD ruining his drive-in, but he is excited about the horror film lineup that he has scheduled for the venue's last night. The grave-robber finally makes it to the drive-in and enters Cecil's office, now with a zombie-ish appearance and blue fluid covering the crotch of his pants. Cecil tells him, "Clean yourself up!", then Kaufman begins the horror movie marathon with the film *Wadzilla* (D: Adam Rifkin).

Plot of the film-within-a-film goes like this: Dr. Weems (Ray Wise, famous for his role in David Lynch's *Twin Peaks*), is concerned with a patient, Miles (director Adam Rifkin), who has a low sperm count. The doctor suggests he try a new drug, Spermoprame, so the following day at breakfast Miles takes the new drug. On the train to work, a beautiful woman sits next to him; he lights her cigarette and experiences a shooting pain in his testicles. He starts making a scene so the woman will move to another seat.

Miles works for Blump Co. (a recurring fictitious mega-corporation in Rifkin's work); he attends a board meeting for the company and an attractive female co-worker is introduced. Miles looks at her ass and experiences crotch pain again. He returns to the doctor about the pain, so Dr. Weems asks him to masturbate to a porno mag to get a new sperm sample. We hear Miles scream and the doctor and nurses rush into the room—in the sample cup is one giant-sized sperm (!), which falls on the floor and Dr. Weems stomps it. Dr. Weems thinks the cause of this is the medication he prescribed, but tells Miles to continue taking it and to masturbate whenever he feels that pain.

Miles goes on a blind date that his friend Larry (Owen Benjamin) set up. As soon as Miles sees Louise (Sarah Mutch), he gets the pain and requests to use her washroom…and stumbles his way there to do his duty. Miles unleashes a monster-sized sperm in Louise's washroom; it hits the wall and splats on the ground…and slithers away! Miles tries to capture the renegade sperm, destroying Louise's washroom in the process. Attempts to flush the monstrosity down the toilet are to no avail, as it clogs it up. Louise opens the washroom door and sees the destruction firsthand…then the toothy, basketball-sized sperm sticks its head out of the bowl then chases Louise and Miles down the hallway before lodging itself between Louise's legs. Miles grabs it by the tail and throws it out a window, where it escapes into the night.

The newly-ejaculated "Wadzilla" goes on a bloody murderous rampage, killing several unsuspecting citizens (and one dog) that night. By this point Wadzilla has increased in mass and is completely animated with old-school stop-motion effects combined with CGI—nice! It grows so big that the military gets called in for a *kaiju*-style confrontation…but will they be tough enough to spermicide this raging spooge?

Next, **CHILLERAMA** returns focus to the drive-in wraparound segment—titled *Zom-B-Movie* (D: Joe Lynch)—where young friends Ryan (Brendan McCreary), Tobe (Corey Jones), and Mayna (Kali Thorne) enthusiastically respond to their viewing of *Wadzilla*. Ryan runs to get snacks at the intermission; he has his sights set on an attractive snack bar attendant. She runs out of butter for the popcorn and rushes off to get more…but little does she know that the butter has been contaminated by the masturbating, grave-robbing, now-zombified employee! She serves up the butter to the drive-in crowd. Cecil announces the next flick: *I Was a Teenage Werebear* (D: Tim Sullivan), and Ryan gives his older brother the polluted popcorn and returns to the car with his friends.

The *Werebear* segment starts with a young couple making out in a van, but Ricky (Sean Paul Lockhart) seems to be more attracted to men than his beautiful girlfriend Peggy Lou (Gabby West)… leading into a **GREASE** (1978)-style musical number about their relationship with a song titled

"Don't Look Away". But then Peggy Lou gets hit by a truck driven by Butch (Adam Robitel), who hates Ricky. Ricky is pulled out of the truck's path by a greaser character named Talon (actor Anton Troy) and his two friends Dan (John F. McCormick) and Den (Ward Edmondson). Ricky takes Peggy Lou to a beachside hospital where a gypsy woman works as a nurse. Talon and his pals appear and Ricky has a sexy fantasy about Talon…only to have the gypsy curse Talon and his friends!

During a Malibu High beachside wrestling match, Talon turns into a fanged, glowing-eyed creature and bites Ricky on the ass…which naturally breaks out into a musical number. In the locker room, Ricky explains to Coach Tuffman (director Sullivan) that he's gay; the coach is thrilled to hear it, being gay himself, and the two are about to get down when Ricky, now infected from Talon's bite, crushes Coach's head between his thighs! Ricky, Dan and Den arrive to help dispose of the body, and Talon admits that he infected Ricky. Ricky is now a "werebear", a murderous sex monster like the three of them, hilariously depicted as wolf-faced "leather men" (a.k.a. "bears"…get it?). There will follow much slaughter, butt-sex and musical numbers…but where will this grisly, throbbing gypsy curse all end? Rest assured, before you find out, you will learn to "Do the Werebear", so you've got that going for you!

Back at the wraparound drive-in "Zom-B-Movie", Tobe makes his way to the concession stand…as Cecil introduces the next film, *The Diary of Anne Frankenstein* (D: Adam Green).

Diary is presented in black and white, and almost entirely in German dialog with English subtitles. Hitler (Joel David Moore) bursts into a family's house to steal a book, the Frankenstein diary, written by the family's ancestors; the nasty Nazi kills the family and makes off with the diary. *Der Führer* intends to use it to unlock the mysteries of creating life, and orders his men to bring him dead bodies for his experiments; his zany wife Eva (Kristina Klebe) is there to help, as well. Then it seems as if a scene—a musical number with Hitler singing!—has been cut out of the film, as if it's been censored. The "monster" creation is finally unveiled: a Jewish rabbi with Popeye arms (played by horror film star and stuntman Kane Hodder, who played Jason Vorhees in three of the original *Friday the 13th* franchise entries[17])—complete with yarmulke and curls—all sewn up like the Universal Frankenstein creature, brought to hideous life by means of Hanukkah candles, Jewish prayer and electricity. Hitler and Eva decide to name the swastika-sporting monster Meshugannah…but will they be able to control it? (Don't bet on it!)

Back at the *Zom-B-Movie*, we see that the ticket-taker is now infected by the contaminated popcorn, as are the other drive-in customers, all turned into sex-crazed zombies that ooze blue glowing fluids!

The next film is *Deathication*, with a bad intro by director Fernado Phagabeefy (Joe Lynch) featuring the hazards that might be caused by viewing the film: horrible washroom visits. The film starts—it's a montage of gross humor crapping scenes—when suddenly the film stops projecting correctly. Cecil is attacked in the projection booth by the zombie employee from the beginning of the film as Tobe and Mayna enter. More undead mayhem ensues before the "big reveal", which you'll have to find out for yourself. As the credits roll, some outtakes from the film are shown…including the Hitler musical segment missing or censored from the *Anne Frankenstein* section.

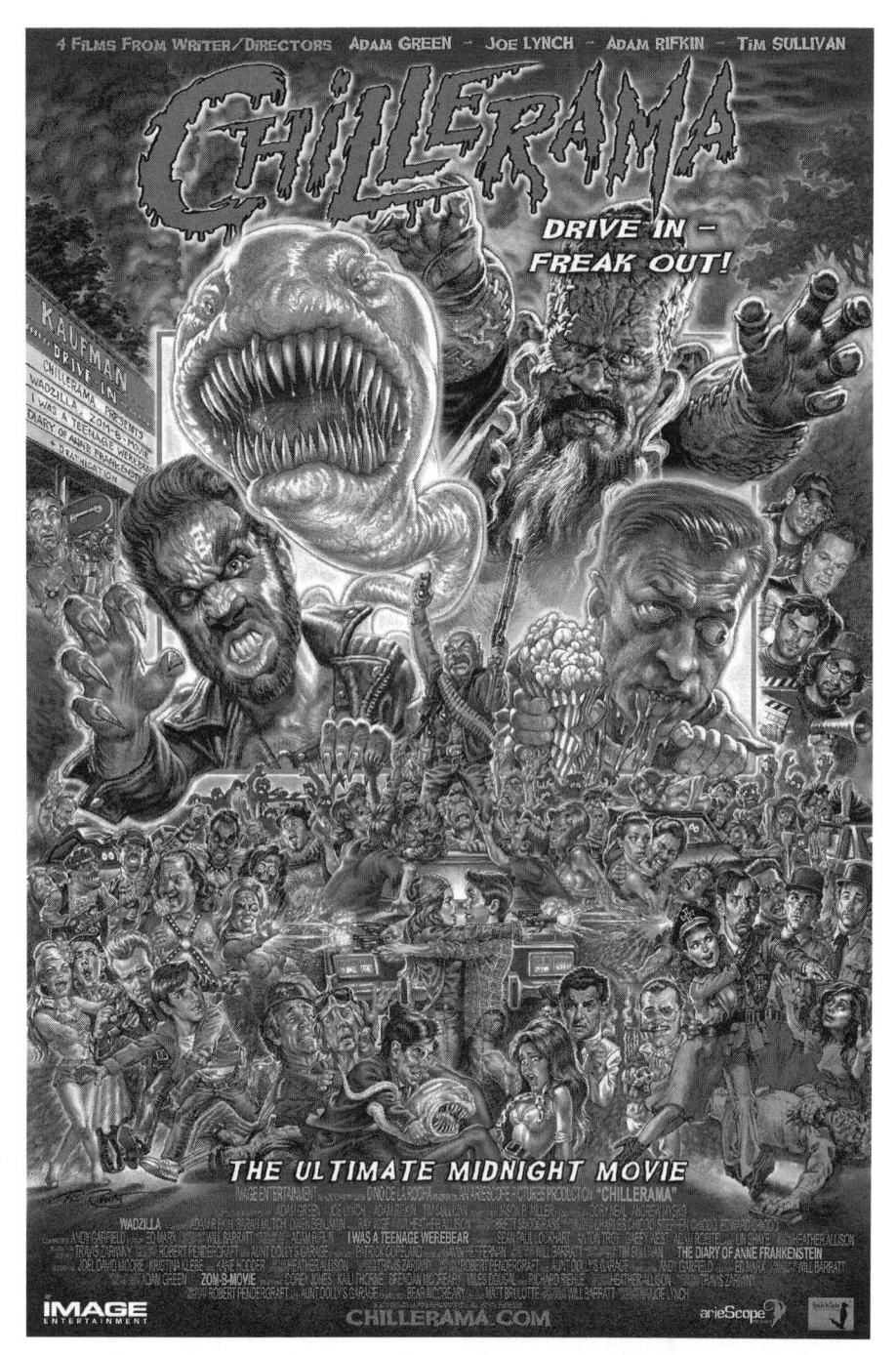

CHILLERAMA was released on October 14, 2011 in the USA. Due to the fact the film is an anthology-style movie I found there is an immense cast and crew—four times the amount for a regular feature film. The directors include Adam Rifkin, who helmed such films as **NEVER ON TUESDAYS** (1988), **THE DARK BACKWARD** (1993) and **PSYCHO COP** (1993). He directed and wrote *Wadzilla*, which is an homage to giant monster movies of the 1950s. *I Was a Teenage Werebear* was directed and written by Tim Sullivan, who also directed **2001 MANIACS** (2005) and **DRIFTWOOD** (2006). *Werebear* pays tribute to James Dean, **GREASE**, and werewolf films. *The Diary of Anne Frankenstein* satires both **FRANKENSTEIN** (1931) and *The Diary Of Anne Frank* (1947). Adam Green directed and wrote *Anne Frankenstein* and is known for films like **COFFEE AND DONUTS** (2000), **HATCHET** (2006) and **HATCHET 2** (2010). Joe Lynch is the writer/director of the *Zom-B-Movie* wraparound segment that spoofs zombie movies. Joe's directorial output includes **WRONG TURN 2: DEAD END** (2007). While viewing **CHILLERAMA**, it brought to mind a couple of other films, **MATINEE** (1993) and **POPCORN** (1991), as both films are set in theaters with horror film marathons. **CHILLERAMA** falls heavily towards comedy—this isn't a Dario Argento horror film. It owes a lot to Troma films, particularly **POLTRYGEIST: NIGHT**

---

17 **FRIDAY THE 13TH PART VII: THE NEW BLOOD** (1988), **FRIDAY THE 13TH PART VIII: JASON TAKES MANHATTAN** (1989), and **JASON GOES TO HELL: THE FINAL FRIDAY** (1993).

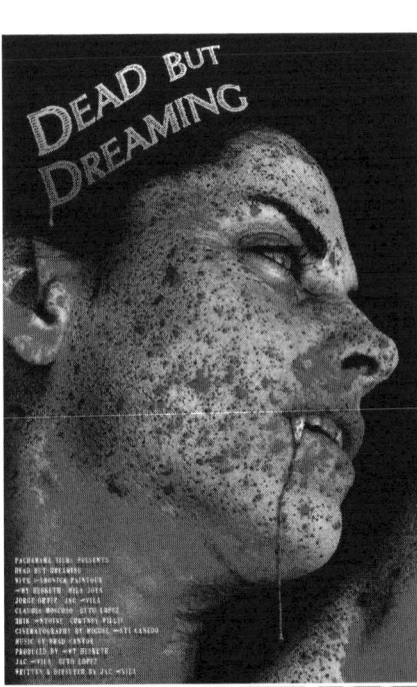

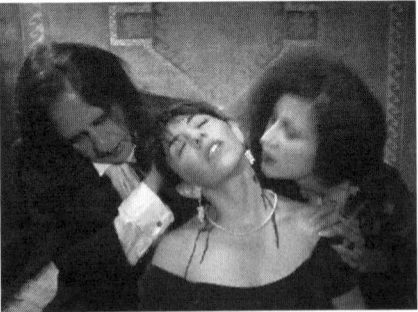

stream than **POLTRYGEIST**, as Troma goes for more of a sleaze factor. There's also a boatload of horror in-jokes in **CHILLERAMA**—for instance, a character is named Tobe, as in Tobe Hooper the horror film director. A masterfully fun anthology, chock full of goodies and film references—check out **CHILLERAMA**!!!

2011, USA. D: ADAM RIFKIN, TIM SULLIVAN, ADAM GREEN, JOE LYNCH
AVAILABLE FROM IMAGE

Dead But Dreaming

Reviewed by Tony Strauss

In 1805 in the Bolivian city of Nuestra Señora de La Paz, the populace lives in constant fear of an attack from the indigenous people outside the city walls, while inside, an underground rebellion is forming in hopes of rising up against Spanish rule. To make tense matters even more volatile, a series of grisly nighttime murders is plaguing the city, with bodies being found in the streets with their throats ripped out. Nobody feels safe anywhere, and the superstitious citizens suspect supernatural stirrings.

One night on a deserted street, a young Irish spy named Moira (Amy Hesketh), on a mission for the rebellion, witnesses a cloaked woman biting out the throat of a townsman. The mysterious masticator flees, and the spy rushes over to help the victim. Just then, a few locals come upon the scene, and, assuming her to be the murderer, capture the spy and throw her into a jail cell to await the carrying-out of her death sentence.

Meanwhile, a vampire lord named Asar (writer/director Jac Avila) continues his relentlessly obsessive quest to find the being that initially turned him centuries ago. With the help of his devoted companion Aphhrodesia (Mila Joya), he searches for an immortal named Nahara (Veronica Paintoux) in hopes of discovering the secret behind her power in an effort to become the most powerful being in existence.

But things take a complicated turn when Nahara, the very monster that has been sucking the town dry, pays a visit to the imprisoned Moira, and turns her into an immortal bloodsucker on the eve of her intended execution!

A local Franciscan priest (Jorge Ortiz), sensing the impending gathering of evil, beseeches a novice nun (Claudia Moscoso), struggling with her faith and wanting to join the rebellion, to stay on the holy path, for he fears a rampant evil coming to power within the city...there is indeed a revolution brewing, but it is perhaps of a less political—and far more supernatural—nature than initially suspected!

A mere synopsis can't properly convey the richness of the story told by **DEAD BUT DREAMING** (2013), a historically lush and mysteriously sexy vampire tale that literally spans centuries in its telling. It's hard to believe that such an ambitious project was accomplished so successfully on a shoestring budget, but here it is. Every once in awhile an indie filmmaker really shows us all what can be done with creativity and talent kicked into full-gear when big budgets are not obtainable, and Bolivian filmmaker Jac Avila has presented such a demonstration here...a very welcome one, at that. Most indie filmmakers would balk at such an expansive story idea, but Avila handles the scope of the storytelling with confidence and skill rarely seen in the microbudget arena. His ability to effectively convey the material by zeroing in on the individual characters involved in the greater intrigue does a fantastic job of large-scale storytelling through vignette and microcosm...it is truly impressive, and you never feel like you're watching a "compromised" version of the story. That's a pretty damned good trick, if you ask me.

Jac Avila first came onto the scene in 1988 with his critically-acclaimed documentary **KRIK? KRAK! TALES OF A NIGHTMARE**, a hallucinatory look at the brutality of life under Haiti's Duvalier regime. His first narrative feature was **MARTYR OR THE DEATH OF SAINT EULALIA** (2005), a sadomasochistic tale of a modern woman experiencing a 3rd century virgin martyr's passion which really established his auteurist style and his reputation as a maker of wickedly sexy tales based in historic times, all told with a BDSM slant. He soon formed Pachamama films with like-minded visionary Amy Hesketh[18], and the power duo and their ever-expanding team of talents have been producing an impressively steady flow of wicked and naughty narratives ever since.

This is Avila's third (fiction) feature film, and by far his most accomplished work to date. Sure, you still encounter some of the issues that arise when working on a restrictive budget—occasional uneven acting, sound mix problems, etc.—but they are few and far between, and hardly a significant distraction; certainly not enough to detract from the enjoyment of this terrific story. As implied earlier, the synopsis above only hints at the scope of this film—for instance, I haven't even mentioned the story segments that take place in ancient times! (See, I told you it was century-spanning!) Plus, the photography, editing and use of locations are just spot-on throughout.

Look, the bottom line is that we fans of weird and offbeat movies have to slog through a lot of dreck and must regularly make many a compromise with regard to production value in our endless quest for the cinematically different and unique. Every so often we are fortunate enough to come across an indie film that allows us to completely put aside our forgiving nature and just sit back and be swept away by a really good movie. This is one of those rare times where we get to do that, so don't deny yourself the opportunity—seek this one out!

2013, BOLIVIA. D: JAC AVILA
AVAILABLE FROM PACHAMAMA FILMS

Foxbat
(*Woo Fook*)

Reviewed by Jeff Goodhartz

In 1976, first time director Leung Po Chi (with help from actress turned part-time director, Josephine Siao) created a sensation in Hong Kong with the

---
Top to bottom: Poster for **DEAD BUT DREAMING**. Director Jac Avila as the obsessed vampire Asar. Sharing a succulent snack. Have you hugged your vampire today?

OF THE CHICKEN DEAD (2006), directed by Lloyd Kaufman (part of the name-tribute in character Cecil B. Kaufman). The comparison between the two films includes raunchy R-rated comedy, purposely corny gory effects, musical numbers and horror. **CHILLERAMA** is slightly more main-

---
18 See my feature article on Amy's films on p.8.

release of **JUMPING ASH** (*Tiaohui*, 1976). Arguably the single most original, unique, innovative and purely entertaining action film to have come out of that country to date (and would remain so for quite some time thereafter), the local audience responded to it by making it the highest grosser that year. So popular and profitable was this little picture that Leung's follow-up, **FOXBAT**, saw both the budget and stakes raised considerably.

FOXBAT stars Henry Silva (who somehow found time to do this in between appearances in a multitude of Eurocrime features in Italy) as US Special Agent Mike Saxon, who must leave his special lady friend behind when called into immediate action. The mission; to locate Foxbat, a Soviet military jet that has unexpectedly landed in Japan. Turns out the pilot wishes to defect and Saxon is to get the plans for this special plane out of the country. Using his artificial eye (with a camera inside it, no less), Saxon is able to obtain what he needs, but not before having to deal with a nasty Sumo wrestler whom he manages to kill by sticking a toothbrush into the big man's ear (!). Escaping to Hong Kong, Saxon finds his trail dogged by all manner of colorful characters, including local agent Cheung (James Yi Lui), the menacing Dr. Vod (Roy Chiao, supplying a most welcomed familiar face and presence)—who seems to have a nearly endless supply of assassins at his beck and call—and, perhaps the most mysterious of all, New York fashion designer, Toni Hill (Vonetta McGee) who gets into a terrific final-reel brawl with Saxon; one of the best man vs. woman smackdowns I've ever seen.

First, the bad: **FOXBAT** bombed locally and could not even get a theatrical release overseas, where it was sold directly to TV. In a way, it's easy to understand why. Unlike **JUMPING ASH**, which was tight and grabbed you from the first moment, **FOXBAT** is a rambling, shambling mess of a movie; really the very antithesis of the film it followed. The opening scenes in particular are pretty dodgy, and one can easily lose interest early on. Now the good: stick with it and you're in for quite a wild ride. Yes, the film is a mess, but it's a damn fun mess. This is bizarre and unique action cinema that doesn't seem to follow the rules of such things (in this one respect, it does bear a kinship to its predecessor). Indeed, the entire film has a cockeyed feel to it that's hard to define. The plot lurches, never really finding its footing (not that it necessarily was looking for it) and the characters often act bizarrely. For instance, the aforementioned Sumo wrestler's attack on Saxon…it just plays out like some cartoonist's bad hallucination. This could be a case of director Leung's apparent penchant for the eccentric (which was to a degree kept in check in his debut) being allowed to run with reckless abandon this time around. Even the very structure of the film is odd. Once Cheung accidentally swallows the microfilm which contained the all-important special Foxbat plans, things really come to life as the entire second half becomes essentially one long chase sequence; going from hide-and-seek in various alleyways to a high-octane car chase (culminating in an amazing van/bus collision; arguably the film's money shot…as it were), and finally on a dock at night where all interested parties make their last-ditch move. And even then, this is one of those films that ain't over 'til it's over. For those who love a good "dummy" death, the finale of this film contains one of the all-time great ones. Overall, **FOXBAT** is a film full of nutty charms that, once you've accustomed your cranium to them, you will find yourself well rewarded. It's also a film that improves on multiple viewings (as I can attest to, having watched it three times in four days just to get the right feel for this review).

It's always fun to watch Henry Silva in action, especially when playing the main protagonist. One of the great tough guys of '70s cinema, Silva somehow managed to play hero and villain nearly equally throughout his career while never making it feel that way. It's funny how the very same hissable sneer and cold smile he displays so effectively as a baddie can in turn, make the viewer decidedly very comfortable when his character is on "our" side.

A big thank you has to go out to Code Red, who rescued this film from virtual obscurity and presents the grateful viewer with a very nice, widescreen print, complete with some fine extras including a running commentary with the director and approximately five minutes of removed scenes that popped up on the Japanese release.

1977, HONG KONG. D: LEUNG PO CHI,
TERENCE YOUNG
AVAILABLE FROM CODE RED

GAMBLING CITY
(*La città gioca d'azzardo*, a.k.a. **THE CHEATERS**)

Reviewed by Steve Fenton

Luc Merenda talks tough as Luca: *"Don't try anything, or I'll plaster that pea-sized brain of yours all over the* wall*!"*

This film's American theatrical distributor, the prolific Joseph Brenner Associates, admirably made absolutely no attempt to conceal its distinct Italian origins (*bravo!*)… A stylish title sequence ends with Sergio Martino's director credit superimposed over an ace of diamonds concealed up a card sharp's sleeve. Typical for the period, Luciano Michelini's score is strongly derivative of that to George Roy Hill's US smash-hit conman caper classic **THE STING** (1973), while the plot, amongst other things, incorporates some trace elements of Robert Rossen's classic drama **THE HUSTLER** (1961), starring Paul Newman as a pool-shark whose overconfidence sometimes gets the better of him.

During an economic recession in the city of Milan, Luca Antieri (Merenda), a Venetian, earns his living by playing cards ("It's about the *only* game I'm *good* at"). While sitting-in on a high stakes poker game, Luca play-acts like a greenhorn to fool his opponents, then wins an easy 10 million lire. When he thereafter admits to having cheated, Luca is roughed-up then taken before Club 72's owner, a crippled tycoon known as "The President" (Eurocrime icon Enrico Maria Salerno, who starred in many keystones of the genre, including the film that was in large part instrumental in kick-starting it, "Steno"/Stefano Vanzina's **EXECUTION SQUAD** [*La polizia ringrazia*, 1972]). In the present film, having been impressed by Luca the cocksure cheater's nimble fingers, the President hires him on as a house player, at 10% commission on all his winnings. An unfortunate on-the-job hazard of this cushy gig is getting beaten bloody by disgruntled losers upon occasion.

While gainfully employed at the casino, Luca becomes attracted to Maria Luisa (Dayle Haddon, from Charles Matton's **SPERMULA** [1976], wherein she played the sexy extraterrestrial title character [a semen vampiress, of all things!]), who is the kept woman of the President's conniving son, Corrado (Corrado Pani). Their flirtation quickly develops into an all-out affair, which is discovered by Corrado ("So, you gave up your mink to get *balled*?!"), who treats Maria Luisa—pet name MéMé—as little more than his personal possession. As punishment for her infidelity, Corrado commands his henchman, Lysander (Giovanni Iavarone), to tear off her clothes and rape her right in front of him ("Go on, ball 'er!"). Upon hearing of Maria Luisa's violation, Luca engages Corrado in a fistfight that trashes his father's casino. In the aftermath, the two men challenge one another to an unfriendly round of cards. Prior to their prearranged game however, Luca is kidnapped by Corrado's goons, who beat him horribly and cripple his card-slinging hands (a situation highly reminiscent of Franco Nero's painful punishment in Sergio Corbucci's prototypical spaghetti western, DJANGO [1966][19]).

Despite the beating, Luca nonetheless keeps his prearranged "date" with Corrado. After Luca again trounces him at poker, Corrado threatens to castrate him, only to be interrupted by the arrival of his father. The President must then choose between killing Luca—for whom he feels displaced paternal affection—or his own son, whom he tolerates yet despises as a weak parasite. When the President chooses in Corrado's favor—blood *is* thicker than water, after all—Luca goes on the run. Because his former employer doesn't want him defecting to the competition and becoming a liability, he grudgingly decides he must eliminate Luca. Instead of having him killed however, the President settles for a more lenient solution: he makes Luca and Maria Luisa a gift of 20 million lire and tells them to get out of town for keeps. Complicating matters still further, having since received medical treatment for his wounds, Luca now decides he wants revenge against Corrado.

Meanwhile, Corrado has long had his beady eyes set on his hated father's empire, and in a treacherous power-play assumes control of the organization by murdering the President. He dispatches Lysander to abduct Maria Luisa and force her to lead them to Luca; but they manage to elude Lysander and light-out for Nice, France. Maria Luisa soon becomes pregnant, while Luca's compulsive gambling degenerates into a debilitating addiction, and he fritters away their entire recent windfall. An old friend of Luca's makes him a proposition: a game of cards with Mr. Logan, a Texas millionaire. Luca promises Maria Luisa just one more game, then he'll quit for good. In a bitter turn of events, they realize the game is a set-up staged by Corrado, whose men come after Luca and Maria Luisa. On the side, the contemptible Corrado also smuggles heroin, discreetly hidden inside tailor's mannequins. A gangster (regular genre baddie and reputed ex-altar boy Carlo Gaddi) representing the Hamburg connection approaches Corrado concerning a major dope-running deal. Club 72 is subsequently raided by police, and Inspector Quattroni demands a 3-million-lire monthly "protection" fee from Corrado. To solve this problem, Corrado has Quattroni murdered. Because he has jeopardized their impending major dope deal by killing Quattroni, Corrado is later abandoned as a bad risk by the Hamburg syndicate.

Mostly accenting talkative drama over physical action, **THE CHEATERS** (1975) nonetheless makes for very solid entertainment indeed, with at least two highly memorable sequences (and that's not even including the scrumptious Haddon's obligatory nude scenes!). The first highpoint comes when machine-gunners burst into Corrado's hideout to spray mobsters and drug-stuffed mannequins with hot lead, resulting in some picturesque shattering plaster faces (images straight out of one of Martino's *gialli*). All the film's slower spots are wiped away with a truly insane cat-and-mouse chase involving a carful of Corrado's killers and Luca and Maria Luisa on a motorbike.

You could do much worse than give this flick a spin.

Martino and Merenda would collaborate again on the majorly kick-arse **THE VIOLENT PROFESSIONALS** (*Milano trema: La polizia vuole giustizia*, 1973).

1975, ITALY. D: SERGIO MARTINO
AVAILABLE FROM NOSHAME FILMS [OOP]

JOHN THE BASTARD

(*John il bastardo*, a.k.a. **HIS NAME WAS JOHNNY**)

Reviewed by Steve Fenton

Furio Meniconi as Papa Buck: *"You're a bastard! That's why you do whut you do."*

John Richardson as John: *"Makin' love is one of Nature's commandments. There's nothing better than a pretty girl."*

A pretty girl, regarding Johnny: *"Look at him. He's so handsome. He's an angel!"*

I'm not going to go into too much—if any—synopsis detail this time out, so suffice to say that **JOHN THE BASTARD** (1967) is primarily a modified retelling of a Spanish folk legend about sword-swinging ladies' man Juan Tenorio (a.k.a. Giovanni Tenerico in Italy), as transplanted/updated to a western setting, complete with all the spaghetti type's duality of morality and other standard spaghettiisms. Don Juan's tale had first been told by 17th-Century dramatist Tirso di Molina in his work entitled *El burlador de Sevilla* ("*The Trickster of Seville*"). The character's exploits were also the subjects of both an (unfinished) 1819 epic poem by Lord Byron and Mozart's opera *Don Giovanni* (1787). Here the character gets put through the figurative wringer by cowriter-director Armando Crispino and his pen-partner Lucio Manlio Battistrada (the original story was written by seasoned Italo genre cinema scribe Sauro Scavolini). Interestingly enough, in the interests of irony, no less than openly homosexual filmmaker Pier Paolo Pasolini was cast as a clerical character named Don Juan in Carlo Lizzani's memorable spaghetti western **KILL AND PRAY** (*Requiescant*, 1967).[20]

Don Juan here becomes "John Donald", a gunslinging ladies' man. Before the titles begin, a Mexican soldier sings a song *en Español* glorifying Tenorio's exploits. As with George Hilton in Nando Cicero's similarly-themed **LAST OF THE BADMEN** (*Il tempo degli avvoltoi*, 1967), whom Richardson often resembles here, and who was apparently dubbed by the same voice actor, John the Bastard is as universally adored by Woman as he is abhorred by Man. In keeping with John's favorite pastime—doing the "horizontal tango"—when the credits roll they do so over a montage of the film's pulchritudinous female love interest, accompanied by Nico Fidenco's fully-orchestrated reprise of the soloist soldier's song. The bulk of the film is presented in one extended flashback, as imagined by Glauco Onorato's sidekick character.

Post-credits, star Richardson ("A bastard. A solid gold *bastard*!" – "I'm John the Bastard, and that's the truth!") grudgingly plays groom at a sixgun wedding presided over by blushing bride Gia Sandri's shamed father (played by frequent spagwest genre character player Furio Meniconi). With only a flash of his tarnished ivory smile and bedroom baby blues, a woman becomes pretty putty in Johnny's hands ("Pretty eyes like yours are not made for cryin', but for smilin'…for smilin' at a man," he flatters emptily). Only after he has murdered the entire male side of Nadia Scarpitta's onscreen family does she see John for what he truly is just a fraction of a millimetre below his pretty skin, but nonetheless, she still can't resist his silver forked tongue ("I *like* the idea of bein' a woman!"). The Bastard's philosophy is strictly "wham-bam, thank you, Ma'am"—sometimes without even the thank you. As soon as a woman (even his own platonic mother) has outlived her usefulness to him, John—a pathological liar and conman as well as a cold-hearted killer—simply moves on to the next. He views women as little more than livestock, to be kept by the herd ("Thoroughbred women are like mustangs—no price can tame them").

For the prologue—which seems to bode something along the lines of Questi's **DJANGO KILL… IF YOU LIVE, SHOOT!** (*Se sei vivo spara*, 1967)[21] or Lizzani's aforementioned **KILL AND PRAY**—it seemed as though above-average director Armando Crispino was bent on instilling certain "unsavory" sexual subtexts, involving for instance homosexuality and even bestiality. For example, a leering bandit embraces a bleating white lamb. When two other men begin wrestling, they are initially framed in such a way that they appear to be kissing one another on the lips. Elsewhere, other eroticism—being key to the storyline—creeps in. The almost fetishistic, depraved undertone of the prologue is soon dispelled by the more whimsical mood which takes over directly following the opening titles. However, this lightweight tone is apparently only a smokescreen as bogus as Johnny's honey-dripping affected persona, one which dissipates without notice once it has fulfilled its function; as when Richardson's conceited façade vanishes the instant when Meniconi dares to make

---
19 See *WC#2*, p.56
20 See *Weng's Chop #7*, p.154
21 See review on p.140

mockery of the Bastard's illegitimacy. Violence is seldom weakened by more humorous elements. After one of the O'Connells is shot in the eyes and blinded by Onorato, Richardson kills the man's older brother (Meniconi) with a thrown knife to the heart…not coincidentally right where the Bastard's wanton womanizing ways have *also* wounded him most.

As the alluring *doña* Antonia Tenorio, costar Martine Beswick—Richardson's then off-screen wife—doesn't first show her face for almost half an hour (the soon-to-be couple had recently co-starred in Hammer's **ONE MILLION YEARS B.C.** [1966]). The same scene also first introduces Beswick's onscreen husband, the always-interesting Claudio Camaso (Gian Maria Volontè's ill-fated ne'er-do-well kid brother, here sporting large, razor-sharp sideburns and a well-pruned moustache). During his dashing stagecoach rescue, Richardson first shoots a peephole into the vehicle through which to ogle Beswick, presumably to assess whether she's worth the time and effort to save. Using the same hole, he then puts another bullet between her captor's eyes (right in his one-track mind). John subsequently castrates a cactus at a full gallop.

On King Vidor's so-called "sex western" **DUEL IN THE SUN** (1946), for the first time in the history of the genre the self-conscious overuse of phallic symbolism was carried to almost delirious, parodic extremes; for instance, pistols, rifles, artillery pieces, cacti, guitars, cigars, trains, bulls and stallions. A semi-"erect" cannon accompanied the frenzied gyrations of star Jennifer Jones' ill-fated onscreen mother, while a cigar-sucking cuckold ogled her with lustful intent. Within its symbolically stylized milieu, the film's swaggeringly cocksure capital-A alpha male Gregory Peck(er) character becomes a virtual ambulatory penis. Indeed, so many objects are intended to be interpreted as surrogate penises that it is difficult in this context not to read virtually any other vaguely penile object as such! (Then again, maybe it's just *us*…) Informally tagged "LUST IN THE DUST" (a title consciously reappropriated decades later for Paul Bartel's lowbrow 1985 western parody of the same name starring Divine and Tab Hunter), this dated if fascinating antique stands as a milestone of suggestion—as prominent as its Squaw's Head Rock setting—from a post-war era notorious for its sexual repression rather than its open expression.

Similar such knowing symbolism later became a vital component of Samuel Fuller's eccentric Hollywood western **FORTY GUNS** (1957), whose carefully contrived stylization incorporated some unbelievably picturesque dialogue, often veiled in the form of sexually suggestive innuendo and double *entendre*. In that film—which both critically and commercially was generally unfavorably received on its home turf but became influential over on the Continent—costar Gene Barry was seen to sensuously caress his gunstock ("good *wood*") and suggestively ogled gunsmith's daughter Eve Brent through the detached cylinder of a rifle barrel ("Any *recoil*?"), as though sizing her up for a coffin rather than his bed. In another daring scene, ballsy cattle baroness Jessica Drummond (Barbara Stanwyck) was seen making rather blatant sexual overtures to lawman hero Barry Sullivan's hard, shiny Colt .45 ("It might go off in your *face*!" he cautions her). Even Fuller's very first directo-

Italian poster for **HIS NAME WAS JOHNNY** (art by Rodolfo Gasparri)

rial feature **I SHOT JESSE JAMES** (1949) had contained its share of intentional gun-as-penis imagery, this time of a more openly homoerotic kind, especially in a scene showing co-stars John Ireland and Preston Foster carefully cleaning their firearms with almost masturbatory obsessiveness while in each other's intimate company. The fact that Ireland's weapon (a six-shooter) is of a much smaller caliber than Foster's (a double-barreled shotgun, albeit sawed-off) symbolically indicates that the latter—a law enforcer rather than a lawbreaker—is considerably more of a man than the former—a lowdown, dirty back-shooter—is. All that said, Considering our propensity for potentially over-analyzing the symbolic content of movie imagery, we won't even get into discussing that scene in George Stevens' **SHANE** (1953) wherein preteen pee-wee Brandon De Wilde, holding an unloaded rifle, asks Alan Ladd as the title hero, "Will you teach me to *shoot*?" (You're on your own with *that* one…!)

Even more so than in another major "Johnny" film from the same season (i.e., Romolo Guerrieri's **JOHNNY YUMA** [1966]), **JOHN THE BASTARD** also knowingly and gleefully overdoses on phallic symbolism (i.e., the sixgun as sex pistol). Whereas Mark Damon as Johnny Yuma had doubted his shaky gunhand and manhood (i.e., sexual orientation), here Richardson—a veritable masculine nymphomaniac—maintains a firm grip on both. While on the verge of seducing Beswick, he must first whip out his *other* pistol to lay out a skulking assassin.

"The highest possible honor—that of loving" (one of the few sentiments he gets *right*): While John the Bastard—a nominal corruption of John the Baptist?—would certainly prefer to fuck than fight, he is also equally as adept at war (the *penis*…mightier than the sword?). "It's a strange war, friend," remarks Richardson to co-star Gordon Mitchell, who portrays a member of the secret Danite sect ("If it's a *secret*, I can't tell you, can I?!"). Properly known

Weng's Chop 177

Soundtrack cover for
HIS NAME WAS JOHNNY

as "The Sons of Dan" (a name taken from one of Israel's twelve tribes; one of whose members was Samson, the Biblical strongman), the Danites were a secret sect founded in 1838 by a newly-converted Mormon named Dr. Samson Avard. Members vowed violent vengeance upon any and all opponents of Mormonism. Historical evidence however points to the secret society never having actually pursued its avowed militant course, as Dr. Avard was subsequently excommunicated from his faith and the Danites disbanded. (Incidentally, Danites would also figure in John Guillermin's spaghetti-influenced American cable TV vendetta western, **THE TRACKER** [1988]). In the present film, while defending his (quote) "Mormon friends" from unfair persecution by the US military, Mitchell ("May God's angels of Zion watch over you, until the end of time") carries two massive silver six-shooters. If John's weapon does indeed represent his manhood, the well-hung Danite is more than *twice* his equal…and a lot less impotent, too. Mitchell looks strikingly impressive as this Man in Black, who is ironically both persecuted and a persecuter himself ("A hunter…*and* the hunted"). "What a face!" Onorato remarks regarding Mitchell's one-of-a-kind mug.

Richardson is most impressed by the Mormon credo ("They can marry as many women as they want. Doesn't seem like much of a *crime* to me"). Rather than from any genuine religious conviction, John uses Mormon polygamy as merely another convenient loophole for satisfying his dysfunctionally gluttonous libido; for which Mitchell's granite Danite descends like an avenging angel to make the bastard pay dearly for his dalliances. (*SPOILER ALERT!*) Climactic scene of Mitchell toppling a large stone statue atop Richardson might have originated in the former's sword-and-sandal period, and carries almost mythic resonances here. Seen elsewhere earlier, blockage of the tracks to waylay a train inevitably recalls Beswick's former SW hit, Damiano Damiani's exceptional **A BULLET FOR THE GENERAL** (*Quién sabe?*, 1966)[22], co-starring Camaso's bro, Gian Maria Volontè.

The bastardly John's ersatz Sancho Panza ("My guardian *angel*!") is Morenillo, a slow-witted but dog-loyal strongman played by Glauco Onorato. Having long condescended to this sidekick—who still calls him "master" even while his so-called

[22] See WC#7, p.149

master (read: mistreater) calls him Fathead—John welcomes the archaic feudal system perpetuated by the Tenorio clan with open arms. Camaso compares his peons to African-American slaves ("Serve me," John orders a black footman). He kicks Fermina, a stumbled servant girl, who immediately recognizes—and respects—his natural-born "leadership" abilities. His and Beswick's despise-and-desire relationship is steeped in volcanically fermenting S/M overtones ("I don't want to *touch* you. Undress by yourself").

For the most part the literate English dubbing job adequately conveys the script's sometimes subtle undercurrents of social and sensual decadence, and music *maestro* Nico Fidenco's beautifully evocative, multi-nuanced score adds immensely to the effectiveness and overall classiness of the production. Definitely *not* made by yer usual bozos, **JOHN THE BASTARD** is one original bastard indeed, and it's an absolute must-see for anybody interested in seeing just how good spaghetti westerns can be outside the canons of "The Three Sergios" (Leone, Corbucci and Sollima).

NOTES: Despite the more informal usage of his name in the film under its alternate Anglo title **HIS NAME WAS JOHNNY**, Richardson's character is always heard referred to more formally only as John on the English dubbing track Spanish-language prints were identical to the English-dubbed export print (formerly available on VHS/Beta tape with Greek subtitles from Key Video of Greece). It was filmed at De Laurentiis Studios western village and Ischia Film Studio, on the Italian island of Ischia (in the Gulf of Naples). Master-at-arms on the production was prolific stunt-actor Remo de Angelis. See also "Anthony Ascott"/Giuliano Carnimeo's westernesque swashbuckler parody **GOD HELP US! HERE COMES THE PASSATORE** (*Fuori uno…sotto un altro, arriva il Passatore*, 1973), whose title character was based on a different literary ladies' man of Continental descent, as played by SW genre icon George Hilton, one of whose amorous conquests in the film was his frequent *giallo* costar Edwige Fenech.

1967, ITALY. D: ARMANDO CRISPINO

MR. NO LEGS
(a.k.a. **THE AMAZING MR. NO LEGS**)

Reviewed by Michael Hauss

The Amazing Mr. Ted Vollrath…The True Crippled Master.

I used to buy off the gray market years ago, silently searching the back of magazines and 'zines to find dealers of the hard stuff. You know the stuff, right man? The shit, man…the shit to fuck you up.

Wait, hold on a minute—where is your mind heading? When I talk of the hard stuff, it's about obscure video releases…*of course* that's what you were thinking, right?

I amassed a nice collection at the time of obscure releases taped onto VHS and sent in mailers with only the name of the movie written on the VHS label. One movie I found on the gray market in the USA was **THE AMAZING MR. NO LEGS** (1979). I knew virtually nothing about this movie when I purchased it, thinking it more related to a kung fu flick, with maybe the Venoms or something from the great Shaw Brothers studios. Remember, in the early and mid-'Eighties without the Internet and not a lot of books or magazines devoted to exploitation films, the tree of exploitation knowledge when it came to these films was virtually bare for the consumer of the wild side of cinema. So I walked into the garden and plucked this forbidden fruit and I began to understand the good and the bad when it came to exploitation film. The film is a classic '70s exploitation flick with the super-badass idea to make the mafia hit-man in this flick a handicapped person. **THE AMAZING MR. NO LEGS**, as far as I can tell, has never had any type of proper release here in the United States.

Mr. No Legs (Ted Vollrath) is a wheelchair-bound henchman for Mr. D'Angelo (Lloyd Bochner), a mob boss. Mr. No Legs rolls into the flick right after the opening credits, and judging by his hardened facial qualities, this dude is badass. A couple of dock-working mob underlings try to pocket a bit of the drugs being transported until Mr. No Legs (or Lou, as he is called) rolls up and hits a switch and two double-barreled shotguns pop out of his armrests and blow these lowlifes away. The film then rolls on to show the undercover cops working on the case trying to break up the drug empire of Mr. D'Angelo.

Back to Mr. No Legs for a minute: Ted Vollrath was truly handicapped, having lost both of his legs while serving in the Korean War. That did not deter Ted from studying martial arts; he became the first person training out of a wheelchair to earn a black belt in Karate.

Now back to our movie. The cast does include a couple of known faces, including Richard Jaeckel, Rance Howard, John Agar and future wrestling heel Ron Slinker. The movie has the feel of not being completed, as if maybe the funds ran out and they cobbled together as much as they could to get a finished product. Some scenes end abruptly without completion, with fadeouts that kill an obviously unrealized scene duration. One thing that continues to be an issue regarding the film is who played Mr. No Legs, some reviews have Ron Slinker erroneously listed in the part but the actor who played Mr. No Legs was Ted Vollrath.

The drugs Mr. D'Angelo is peddling are sent in stalks of tobacco—bags full of the white stuff—which are then placed into capsules and rolled into cigars for distribution. Ken Wilson (Luke Halpin), a drug dealer, is living with Tina (Joan Murphy), who, after finding out that Ken is dealing decides to leave; a fight ensues and Ken pushes Tina, who falls back and hits her head on a television—death by television! Ken calls Lou's sidekick (Rance Howard), who runs the drug warehouse, and he brings Mr. No Legs to help tidy up the scene. Ken tells the duo that Tina's brother is a cop, and they decide to dispose of her body, first injecting her with dope so it looks like a drug-related accident. After disposing of her corpse, Mr. No Legs shoots Ken in the gut. The girl is the sister of Andy (Ron Slinker), a detective in the drug division who, after finding out about the death of his sister, goes to the local bar where the cheese superior band Mercy is performing their hit song "I still Remember Love". Andy's girlfriend works at the bar and takes him home; the interior of her house must be seen to be believed, with the floor littered with mass amounts of animal furs—pure '70s excess!

Our story rolls on to a party at the estate of suave mob Don, Mr. D'Angelo. Things are tense between Mr. No Legs and D'Angelo at the party because of the news regarding the Wilson boy and Tina. Eventually we hear that Mr. No Legs had some kind of a dock accident, which I would guess accounts for the loss of his legs. Cut to Andy and Chuck (Richard Jaeckel) in the parking lot of a dive bar called the 7 Seas; Andy has come here to meet an informant. Inside the bar a fight breaks out between a white trash chick and a black girl, which escalates into a bad fight scene with plenty of broken bottles over the heads of the bar patrons; throw in a cross-dresser, a midget, a choking scene involving a phone cord and some great '70s fashion and you have a basic blueprint to the 1970s.

The white chick stabs the black chick to death with a broken bottle, and as she is trying to exit Mr. No Legs stabs the white chick, who we find out is an informant. Andy walks in after this, and another badly choreographed fight scene breaks out. Andy kicks some slow-motion ass and Chuck comes in after the melee. So the mob guys decide to get the body of Ken Wilson from the morgue, and again with the police arriving and foiling the stiff removal. Chuck delivers the best line of the film when he says, "This is the liveliest morgue, I've ever seen."

Mr. No Legs decides to kill our hero Andy off; he makes an informant give Andy a call in the middle of the night to meet someone with info at the 7 Seas bar. Lou's sidekick (nameless in the film) waits for Andy when he shows up at the 7 Seas, and tries to strangle him. Andy breaks loose, Mr. No Legs flips the switch and out pop the two shotguns, and the sidekick gets killed in the ensuing blast. Andy escapes, but not before being chased outside by a sword-wielding killer, and another bad fight scene ensues. Again Chuck arrives late as always to the fight, being notified by Andy's girl about the mysterious phone call. After this failure by Mr. No Legs and the botched stiff removal, Mr. D'Angelo decides to eliminate Mr. No Legs.

A group of thugs attack Lou at D'Angelo's house by his pool, but he kicks their asses, even employing the use of a couple of ninja stars located on his wheelchair. To me, the pool scene is the highlight of the movie, and even out of the chair Mr. No Legs is a badass dude, even administering some kicks using his torso. I don't want to give too much away about the pool scene, as it really needs to be seen to be thoroughly enjoyed.

Well, Andy and Chuck realize that Mr. No Legs works for Mr. D'Angelo and stake his place out, and within the first few minutes see the Chief of police (played by Agar) exit the house. Agar's character had been introduced earlier in the film, but his scenes were painful to watch and my mind became mesmerized by his '70s suit and I flashed back to my own awkward '70s clothing choices. So now Mr. No Legs knows that Mr. D'Angelo had hired the hit on him and plots his revenge. He calls both the Chief and Mr. D'Angelo, telling them the other wants to meet at the drug warehouse. Andy and Chuck also arrive at the warehouse, as does Mr. No Legs, all converging together, setting up a showdown. No Legs rolls in and kills Mr. D'Angelo with a shotgun blast, Chief unloads a few pistol blasts into Mr. No Legs, Andy and Chuck arrive and exchange gunfire, a chase ensues. The chase goes on and on and on, cuts to a dispatcher a zillion times, back to the chase, and on it goes. Finally after ten mind-numbing minutes the chase ends and the chief is in the car dying; his last words are "I had nothing to do with Tina's death," and then some mumbo-jumbo about a book he kept with everything that happened. Cut to the cheese ending as we see Andy walking away and that '70s super-group Mercy's other big hit, "Killers Die Hard", plays. Roll final credits.

A few other cheese nuggets regarding this film: it was directed by Ricou Browning, who is best known as the Gill Man (uncredited) in the underwater shots in **CREATURE FROM THE BLACK LAGOON** (1954) and two of its sequels. Browning was also involved in the *Flipper* television series in different capacities. The actor Luke Halpin, who appears as Ken Wilson, the drug dealer working his way through college, is best known for his association with the television series *Flipper* and as Keith in the horror flick **SHOCK WAVES** (1977). The film was shot in the Tampa, Florida area.

This film, while far from being great, is a product of its times, but never reaches it true potential because of the issues with bad direction, bad acting, and badly choreographed fight scenes. But those things in my mind are pluses when it comes to cheesy movies, and this one is just about as cheesy as it gets—today's action films don't have a leg to stand on in comparison to this zany '70s classic. While finishing up my review it was brought to my attention that Massacre Video is preparing an upcoming release of **THE AMAZING MR. NO LEGS** on DVD with an eye towards an eventual limited edition VHS release and possibly a Blu-ray release. The exploitation gods are smiling down on the world today, and the tree of exploitation films has offered up another piece of golden fruit from its branches.

1979, USA. D: RICOU BROWNING

no room to die

(*Un lunga fila di croci* / "*A Long Row of Crosses*", a.k.a. **HANGING FOR DJANGO**)

Reviewed by Steve Fenton

Amedeo Timpani as a sheriff states the obvious: *"Dead men can't speak".*

William Berger as Father Murdock seconds the opinion: *"No...they can't talk much."*

Claudio Ruffini, in a rare goodie role as Sheriff Stone, regarding Berger's paid-to-kill Padre: *"Bountyhunter? To* Hell *with 'im!"*

Here's a quick synopsis (those wishing to avoid potential spoilers might want to jump down to the

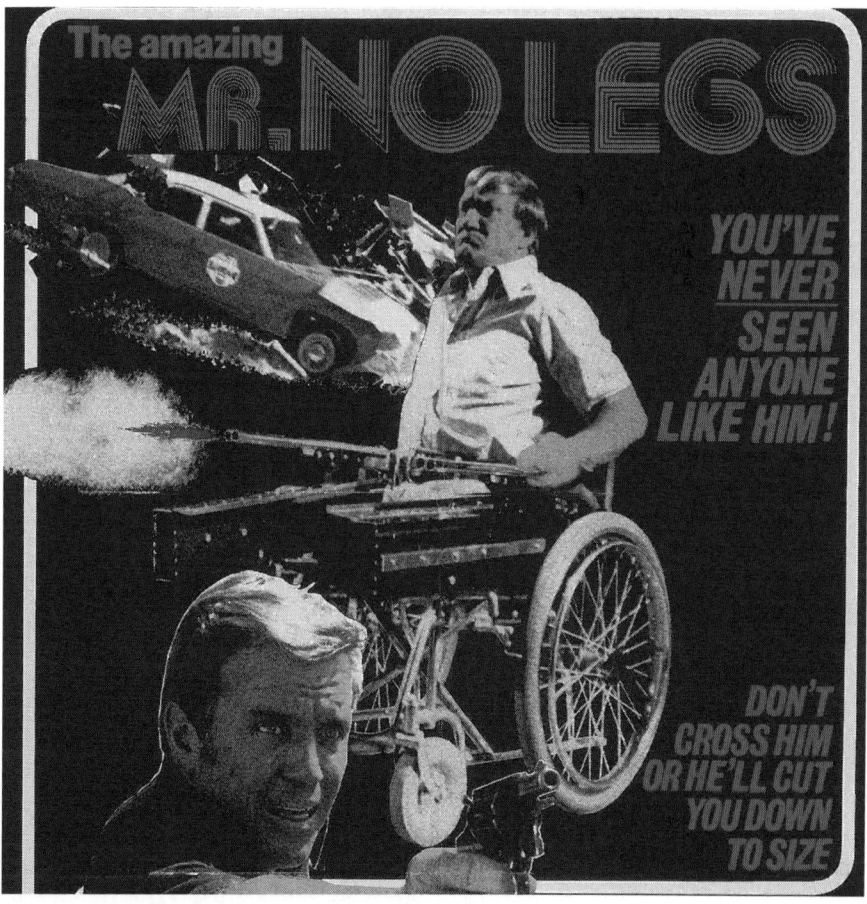

VHS box detail

Big Bill Berger, comin' at ya in widescreen...which means there's plenty of room to die in **NO ROOM TO DIE**

next paragraph): Following the War of Secession and abolition of slavery, white slave traders have been smuggling Mexicans across the border for $100 apiece to work as cheap field labour for wealthy Americans. When approaching US soldiers threaten to uncover their scheme, the slavers dispose of their latest human cargo by pushing their covered wagon into a canyon. Johnny Brandon, a gunman (Anthony Steffen), arrives looking for a *bandido* named Santana (Franco Ukmar) who has been working with the slavers. After killing Santana, Brandon forms an uneasy alliance with *Padre* Evert Murdock (William Berger), a preacher-*cum*-bountyhunter, and they set their sights on the $20,000 worth of wanted men in the slavers' employ at Nogales. US Cavalry Captain Stone vows to stamp out illegal slavery in the area. It is soon revealed that Mr. Fargo, a local banker (Riccardo Garrone), is the kingpin in the slave trade. During another attempt to transport Mexicans, Fargo and his thugs massacre a cavalry troop commanded by Captain Stone (Claudio Ruffini). Fargo then tries to bribe both Brandon and Murdock by doubling their expected net reward for his men. Brandon hightails it with the cash, but it is retrieved by Murdock. Brandon is forced to dig his own grave by Fargo's boys and Murdock is cornered at a forest cabin, where it is soon exposed that Fargo and the unorthodox priest are operating in cahoots in order to collect the bounty on the slavers. Brandon virtually returns from the grave to confront and punish Fargo and Murdock…

Albeit uneven in spots, here we have one enjoyable, midrange shot-in-Italy western; the larger chunk of whose budget was spent on hiring its four upscale principal players. Anthony Steffen appears sufficiently gristled in the lead, making for one of the more convincing Eastwood impersonators, even if his actual physical likeness is only exceedingly slight at best (if at *all*, most of the time). Contrary to the motivations of most spaghetti antiheroes, his seasoned bountyman is actually more concerned with aiding the course of justice rather than merely collecting his rightful monetary reward for a job well-done. As in Leopoldo Savona's **KILLER KID** (1967), Steffen once more represents the righteously "superior" incoming *gringo* protector of the down-trodden *méxicanos* (physically, Steffen literally *towers* over the pint-sized peons!). In appearance here he brings to mind a rougher, tougher, more thick-featured version of George Hilton, though minus the latter's built-in sense of humor (the usually stone-faced Steffen showcased his own lighter side in "William Hawkins"/Mario Caiano's **A TRAIN FOR DURANGO** [*Un treno per Durango*, 1967], but he was generally not known for poking fun at his own image, unlike Hilton, who frequently ribbed himself, especially in his later genre outings during the '70s, via such spoofish characters as "Tricky Dicky", etc.). As was so often the case in a Steffen SW vehicle, several scenes here are faithfully—if much more economically, natch—recreated from Clint's Leone *Dollars* series (their patented multiple-man gundown sequence is used not just once, but twice).

More fullness of characterization graces this serviceable quickie, which often glances upon the prejudices and motives behind criminal behavior, and such absolutes as "Good" and "Evil" are far from cut-and-dried or black-and-white (a standard trope of the spaghetti form which, in spite of the heavy stylization and unbelievability of many spaghettis, rang far truer to real life than many an old school Hollywood oat opus shot in the real America did). Soldiers despise bountyhunters. Sour grapes Texan businessmen complain about the lack of available labor following the abolition of slavery ("Since the war, ain't a black who'll do a decent day's work"). Mexican slavers mistreat their own countrymen (illustrating that man's inhumanity to his fellow man respects neither national boundaries nor skin color, the slavers also include an Asian and a black man among their ranks). Mexican peons voluntarily sell themselves into servitude like cattle in order to provide for their families. Even the unfeeling leader of the slave traders, Fargo—himself a Mexican—has a past which seeks to justify his cynical outlook on life (surreal B&W flashbacks symbolically intercut with a cockfight show how he was abused by racist bullies as a young man and had to fight tooth and nail to survive).

As the Bible-packin', bullet-pumpin' killing machine ("Start *prayin'*, preacher man!"), William Berger often outshines Steffen, and can depopulate a crowded *cantina* faster than an Ethel Merman karaoke medley. Offsetting his more violent vocation, Berger drinks milk instead of alcohol and is constantly shown leafing through his ever-present Good Book, which he obviously finds a real page-turner. In look and quiet demeanour, his character is seemingly modelled after Brett Halsey's glum, grim non-clergyman in Tonino Cervi's **TODAY WE KILL, TOMORROW WE DIE!** (*Oggi a me…domani a te!*, 1968), a film also co-starring Bill Berger. In the present title, Berger's pugnacious preacher-*cum*-bounty hunter gladly murders and fornicates, but becomes visibly upset when the Commandment "Thou shalt not steal" is violated (especially against *himself*). While not averse to quoting the Lord's will when it suits him, Berger prefers to underline his sermons with hot lead rather than the heated words of a fire-and-brimstone, pulpit-pounding evangelist. He is seemingly invincible, keeps wanted posters folded up inside his King James pocket edition and carries a howitzer-sized shotgun with no less than *seven* barrels—presumably one for each Deadly Sin. Possibly due to divine intervention, Berger's six-shooter is once heard to discharge upwards of ten bullets, while his blustering cluster-barreled scattergun fires close to *twenty* (!) without a reload. The big bass sound of latter portable artillery piece adds considerable punch to battle scenes, even if the sheer wholesale slaughter at times endangers the film's believability, threatening to nudge it over into all-out parody through simple overkill. These excesses in the munitions department satirically reflected the ever-escalating firepower of modern warfare; while simultaneously contributing to the late-'Sixties' audience expectations of exotic 007-esque gunnery (several Eurospy-influenced "gadget" SWs were produced during the mid/late '60s, including "Anthony Dawson"/Antonio Margheriti's **DYNAMITE JOE** [*Joe l'implacabile*, 1967] and Alfonso Balcázar's similarly-titled **DYNAMITE JIM** [*Dinamite Jim*, 1966]). And, when it came to weaponry, bigger invariably meant better in spaghetti westerns, much like in the real world.

Italian locandina for **NO ROOM TO DIE**

The cinematography of **NO ROOM TO DIE** (1969) is pliant, organic; at one juncture from a dying man's point-of-view, the camera does a 180-degree headstand as if emulating Giulio Questi's **DJANGO KILL...IF YOU LIVE, SHOOT!** (*Se sei vivo, spara*, 1967)[23]. Other shots squint in obsessive closeup through the trigger guard of a Winchester repeater, or up from knee-level at Steffen's crotch with pistol drawn at hip (I promise I'll refrain from making another "phallic symbol" reference this time!). With her unflusterable aura of distaff disdain upkept even under pressure, leading lady Nicoletta Machiavelli as usual provides a welcome islet of gracious femininity in this red sea of mindless machismo. A shootout between Berger and baddies in sandy wasteland was redone virtually verbatim in "Miles Deem"/Demofilo Fidani's downscale **DOWN WITH YOUR HANDS...YOU SCUM!** (*Giù la mani...carogna! (Django Story)*, 1971).

Consistently eloquent, given added clout by its succession of charismatic faces and decent dubbing, **NO ROOM TO DIE** is a lowercase "b"-grade Spaghetti Western of the highest order. One to watch again. (And again...)

<u>NOTES:</u> If you look very closely, an incidental reward poster reads "LUCA KLIMOVSKI", a clear tip-of-the-hat to Steffen's western mentor León Klimovsky, who had guided the actor through his paces on **FEW DOLLARS FOR DJANGO** (*Pocchi dollari per Django*, a.k.a. **DRANGO: A BULLET FOR YOU**, 1966). Director Garrone would recycle the main character names Johnny and Murdock for his next fine western, **THE STRANGER'S GUNDOWN** (*Django il bastardo*, a.k.a. **DJANGO THE BASTARD**, 1969), which also top-lined Steffen.

1969, ITALY. D: SERGIO GARRONE
AVAILABLE FROM RARO VIDEO [OOP]

Love Angels

(*Prostituzione*, a.k.a. **RED LIGHT GIRLS**)

Reviewed by Steve Fenton

Export trade ad: *"White Slavery, Murder, Gunfights: Behind the Scenes of the World's Oldest Profession."*

Private Screenings video-box blurb: *"Risky business in the world's hottest red-light district!"*

Aldo Giuffrè as the Inspector, upon cornering and collaring a suspect: *"You're finished... There were only six bullets. And you used two to kill one of my men. Y'know, I feel like doing the same thing to you, right now. But the* Law *will deal with you!"* [Slaps on 'cuffs.]

Gutter-level *giallo-poliziesco*—incorporating some ingredients from the previous year's superior Massimo Dallamano thriller **WHAT HAVE THEY DONE TO YOUR DAUGHTERS?** (*La polizia chiede aiuto*, a.k.a. **THE COED MURDERS**, 1974)—directed by the man arguably most notorious for making the sleazed-out sex horror **WEREWOLF WOMAN** (*La lupa man-*

23 See review on p.158

nara, a.k.a. **THE LEGEND OF THE WOLF WOMAN**, 1977).

After a young hooker named Giselle Rossi is found fatally strangled and stabbed, the Homicide Squad under a nameless Inspector (Giuffrè) and his off-the-ball assistant, Brigadiere Variale ("If I knew all the answers, I'd be the Inspector here!" [played by Andrea Scotti]) begin questioning local prostitutes for leads. One of their key witnesses is a seasoned older pro, Primavera (Maria Fiore, a talented actress whose central performance is far better than the lowly material warrants; despite much histrionic weeping and wailing, at least she was shrewd enough to keep her clothes on for the duration, unlike most of the other actresses seen herein).

One of Primavera's colleagues on the game is played by ill-fated sexploitation starlet Krista Nell (who died shortly after this film was completed; her English lines here were dubbed by a voice actress doing a bad Betty Boop impression), whose john spies on her through the bathroom keyhole as she squats over the bidet at her ablutions. When another hooker named Benedetta (Orchidea de Santis) expresses her concerns about using the proper contraception, her customer promptly spins her around for some impromptu anal intercourse instead ("Hahahaha! There's more than one way to do things, didn't you know?!"). Benedetta is subsequently gang-raped to death by the john and several of his buddies. Rather than wait for the police to catch her killer, the big underworld pimps form a four-man (quote) "special squad" on dirt-bikes to track down the psycho who's been messing up their girls. The vigilantes chase down the sleazebag who sodomized poor Benedetta, whereupon they brutally beat him and subject him to retributory anal rape with a wine bottle (this act is implied, but not graphically shown; the erstwhile Private Screenings VHS videocassette reviewed here [released in 1988] evidently having been struck from a cut print).

Typecast sleazebag Luciano Rossi is right in his element as a smut photographer ("What thighs, what legs…!") who uses compromising snapshots to blackmail a prominent businessman moonlighting as a voyeur along hooker row. The Inspector collars this businessman as prime suspect in the whore murders. The rather unimaginative resolution reveals that Giselle—dissatisfied with her earnings "on the game"—had been killed in a fit of pique by her slick "fiancé" (i.e., pimp), Michele Esposito (Elio Zamuto), who's also been banging the gullible Mrs. North (Magda Konopka). Latter's trendy fashion boutique fronts for a high-class call-girl ring, but proves to be only another red herring.

Much of the narrative takes great pains to humanize its cast of "working girls" via sundry scenes of catty female gossiping and squabbling in the interests of character development. On-the-job hazards include getting buzzed—or even gangbanged to death—by motorcycle punks looking for sick kicks. Pretty damn tolerant for a crimeslime genre police inspector from 1975, Giuffrè's character politely cautions a transvestite ("Have you ever heard about Article 773 of Public Order, which states that it is an offence for a man dressed as a woman to appear in public places?"). Rather

Italian newspaper ad (from La Gazzetta del Mezzogiorno, *5/75)*

than give him/her a friendly verbal warning, Maurizio Merli on the other hand would likely have punched this drag-hag's teeth down "his" throat at the slightest provocation.

Lesser-known composers Marcello Ramoino's and Roberto Fogu's decidedly diverse score switches fluently from fuzztone acid guitar with tremolo to gentle acoustic strumming, Jew's harp and weeping Neapolitan-style mandolins, circus oompah, *mariachi* or even jovial Parisian accordion; hence, quite the grab-bag of musical stylings for sure! (On strength of their eclectic work heard here, presumably they managed to score some more reputable gigs as a result?) Some decent spurts of action include the vigilante squad putting their bikes through their paces on some dirt-hill terrain, an exploding Fiat, and an extended pursuit/shootout at the same deserted rural-industrial location seen in at least one Umberto Lenzi *poliziesco*.

Add to all this a battalion of shapely Italo starlets dressed (or not) in hot-pants, miniskirts, black stockings and teetering platform shoes, and you've

Italian locandina for **LOVE ANGELS** a.k.a. **RED LIGHT GIRLS**

got a rather strange blend of subgenres that seems a little uncertain as to whether it's a softcore sexpo, a low-grade *giallo*, an overwrought kitchen-sink/social drama or a straight-ahead scuzz 'n' spuzz crime actioner. You be the judge…

Angry Film and director Rino di Silvestro also made another murky cross-genre hybrid, **WOMEN IN CELL BLOCK 7** (*Diario segreto da un carcere femminile*, 1973), which has generally been derided by WIP genre fans as too tame over the years, but has its moments if taken as more of a crime film than a sexploitative women-in-prison potboiler.

1974, ITALY. D: RINO DI SILVESTRO

HOW TO KILL A JUDGE
(*Perché si uccide un magistrato*)

Reviewed by Steve Fenton

Marco Guglielmi, as Judge Traini: "You must learn to pace yourself when meting out Justice… We magistrates are a breed of soldiers who nurture no love for war."

Franco Nero, as filmmaker Solaris: "A *film* won't stop a judge."

Italian filmmakers like Carlo Lizzani (1922-2013) and the present film's director Damiano Damiani (1922-2013) were sometimes criticized for opportunistically exploiting topical real-life news headlines as a basis for their crime movie scenarios. Hence, considering its premise, **HOW TO KILL A JUDGE** (1975) undoubtedly contains autobiographical aspects of Damiani's own directorial career. Damiani also appears in an uncredited minor acting part here, and had recently been more prominently seen in Florestano Vancini's acclaimed historical/political drama, **THE ASSASSINATION OF MATTEOTTI** (*Il delitto Matteotti*, 1973), a film also starring Nero in the title role of outspoken parliamentarian Giacomo Matteotti, who in June 1924 was abducted and subsequently murdered by *fascisti* under future "il Duce" Benito Mussolini.

HOW TO KILL A JUDGE is another sociopolitially aware drama from Damiani, who had previously directed Nero in **CONFESSIONS OF A POLICE CAPTAIN** (*Confessione di un commissario di polizia al procuratore della repubblica*, 1971), which was likewise co-written by the present title's co-scribe, Fulvio Gicca Palli. Nero here plays Giacomo Solaris ("He *doesn't* shoot westerns!"), a tenacious Sicilian movie producer/screenwriter with anti-Mafia sentiments whose (quote) "slanderous" latest hit, "INCHIESTA AL PALAZZO DI GIUSTIZIA" (*"Investigation Into the Halls of Justice"*) is threatened with seizure by government officials who consider it a barely disguised defamation of State Prosecutor-General Alberto Traini (Marco Guglielmi). The Solaris film ("…naturally, the names have all been changed…") alleges that Judge Traini is a fraternizer with mob-affiliated politicians and is also guilty of numerous "wrongdoings" committed during the unscrupulous furtherance of his career (so what else is new!?). Traini's on-screen equivalent had shown favoritism in the trial of known racketeer Carmelo Bellolampo, thus drastically truncating his prison sentence. The hypothetical end of Solaris's filmic "fiction"—which quickly becomes a domestic box office sensation—shows the surrogate State Prosecutor being gunned-down by the Mafia.

Real life begins imitating art when Judge Traini actually *is* murdered with a .22 caliber by person or persons unknown. Police and press suspect the real Bellolampo ("I don't belong to *any* political party!"), who is subsequently murdered while undergoing treatment on a kidney dialysis machine. Sensing involvement of both the *palermitani* (Palermo) mob and corrupt State factions connected to one Senator de Rasi, Solaris digs ever deeper only to ultimately learn the highly ironic truth behind the magistrate's murder…

Damiani's brief film-within-a-film sequences are as heavily stylized as any self-consciously arty arthouse epic. Each firmly believing the ends justify the means, neither the lawmaker nor the filmmaker are averse to pulling unethical strings in realization of their goals. Nero's character ("The film was purely fiction") openly confesses to using his own Mafia connections to acquire certain under-the-table shooting permits during production. His screen subject's dutiful wife Antonia (Françoise Fabian) makes no bones about her contempt for Solaris: "Your work is worse than any scandal-sheet. You hide, take refuge behind moral pretensions, half-truths… You feed them cheap, crude thrills, you stimulate, foment, you impel the simple mind to acts of *violence*!" Solaris's friend/information source is easygoing gangster Vincenzo Terrasini (seasoned Eurocrime genre character player Renzo Palmer), who freely admits their mutual debts to organized crime ("Without the Mafia, what would *you* have done?"). In a joking exchange that expresses both characters' innate moral duality, one accuses the other: "*You're* the crook!"; "No, *you're* the crook!" For playing both sides, Terrasini winds up a crimson-streaked carcass on a mortuary slab after being gunned-down in the street by two hired punks on a Kawasaki.

Luciano Catenacci, another seasoned Eurocrime genre character actor best-known for appearing in several archetypal '70s *polizieschi* by Umberto Lenzi, appears as the late Traini's attorney Meloria, who straddles the ethical twilight zone between the Mob and the Man and gets publicly bitch-slapped by Palmer's character for being such an insufferably smarmy bastard. Guglielmi's wily if short-lived character believes in keeping his enemies even closer than his friends—as with professional rival Senator Sallimi (Elio Zamuto), "Palermo's rising political star", who is pressured to resign after he becomes suspected of involvement in Traini's murder. Another prime suspect is Barra (Sicilian-born-and-bred sometime-director and frequent character actor Gaetano "Tano" Cimarosa), an elderly parking lot attendant and fan of Solaris' film. Then there's the blond, well-groomed Dr. Valgardini (Giorgio Cerioni)… Indeed, the list of potential perps and red herrings seems to be almost endless.

But in the final reel the true culprit—as per one of the oldest tricks in the whodunit how-to book—proves to be the very least likely suspect and absolute biggest hypocrite of them all; as Nero notes, "You exploited the film to cover a killing…and *I'm* your accomplice." Perhaps most surprisingly of all, the Mafia functions here mainly as a convenient scapegoat. But I do believe that somewhere therein lies Damiani's ultimate moral message: how perhaps too often organized crime is blamed for causing society's ills, when in actuality the reverse might sometimes be the case. That may well be an over-analysis, but thought-provoking movies such as this tend to provoke that kind of thinking.

As for the critics of the day, *Variety* ("Hawk.", 10/75) wrote: "Damiani sets his plot against a backdrop of social criticism where Mafia-Establishment is once again the equation, but this time lets his backdrop barbs get the upper hand over action, which slows down as a consequence."

In short, **HOW TO KILL A JUDGE** is a crime drama well worth your time.

1975, ITALY. D: DAMIANO DAMIANI
AVAILABLE FROM BLUE UNDERGROUND

JOHNNY YUMA

Reviewed by Steve Fenton

Ad-lines for Atlantic's US theatrical release: *"Call Him Johnny Yuma… Johnny Yuma's Gun Shoots Its Own Brand of Excitement!"*

Theme song lyrics: *"Johnny Yuma, don't go! / Johnny Yuma, stay here! / What do you think you'll find beyond the mountains? / Wherever* there's a road, he'll ride / Let him ride / Maybe he will return / He will return…"

Mark Damon as Johnny: *"Bury them!"* Fedele Gentile as Chorito: *"How can you bury $370?"* Damon: *"Just dig a* hole*!"*

For once I shall skip delving into this movie's synopsis—if you watch it, all will be made clear to you—and instead I'll dive right into my review proper…

Ignoring Damon's instructions in favour of some fast money, Gentile, proudly posing as a big tough bounty hunter, later rides into town dragging the three corpses—minus their valuable boots (representing their manhood)—behind his horse. He cashes-in the Smithers (not *Smothers*!) Brothers at the local telegraph office, which is busier than the New York Stock Exchange doling out bounty booty to all comers. Here, incoming baddies' bodies are cashed-in like beer bottles for the deposit. An incidental bounty hunter mosies up to the wicket, where he requests the going rate on another outlaw fraternity, the Gibson Brothers. "Only $500," replies the clerk, "unless they pull another bank robbery soon." The clerk subsequently complains about the number of fake bounty claims: "In the cemetery there are *seven* 'Jesse James,' *three* 'Ringos' and *three* 'Billy the Kids'…" When the clerk then asks him to make a donation towards funerals for "his" kills (eight bucks for coffins; "burial sacks" only a buck a pop), Gentile promptly slaps down one dollar onto the counter-top for a body-bag. When Gentile (who somehow succeeds in resembling both Franco *and* Ciccio simultaneously) asks his name, Damon calls back over his shoulder: "Johnny…but people call me 'Yuma.'"

A prologue one-eyed *bandido* named Emil—who has to squint extra-close to count his pocket change—is jokingly referred to as "Cyclops" before being dropped by Damon's character. At the Triana saloon, Damon causes a bar brawl after he catches gambler Nando Poggi with an ace up his sleeve. Ever on the scavenge for easy money, Gentile stuffs dollar bills inside his peasant shirt and follows Damon around like a mongrel scrounging for table scraps (i.e., stray dollars). At every opportunity the *gringo* mistreats the *Mexicano* (who calls him "boss"), but ultimately feels condescending affection for his persistent hanger-on (albeit more like a master for his dog rather than as his human equal). In a twist retake of the famous Baxter Corral sequence from Sergio Leone's **A FISTFUL OF DOLLARS** (*Per un pugno di dollari*, 1964), Damon comes to the aid of a bullied *chico* whose apples are stolen by swaggering toughs. The three older bullies laugh uproariously after cooling the boy off in a horse-trough, causing water to splash on Damon as he rides by. Dismounting quietly, rather than killing all three as expected, Damon instead much more peaceably merely puts the boots to the ringleader and disarms his two toadies with two well-placed bullets. Later letting his more violent side show, however, Damon drills a bushwhacker an extra eye-socket from a range of thirty yards.

Playing the treacherously duplicitous Samantha Felton, Rosalba Neri—who, as in other roles, here read her lines in English—was no stranger

Mexican lobbycard for **HOW TO KILL A JUDGE**

to *femme fatale* parts by this point, but 1966's **JOHNNY YUMA** (which was released under that title in most markets, its country of origin included) puts forth one of her most prominent and memorably vicious examples. We quickly learn that her on-screen husband—played by Leslie Daniel—is symbolically somewhat "less" than a man (i.e., possesses at least one game leg, possibly his *middle* one). Judging by Neri's sly look, we immediately suspect she's soon going to try getting into Johnny's jeans. When hubby Daniel misses the bull's-eye one time out of ten during pistol practice ("I usually miss *none*…"), we just know she'll soon be looking for a younger gun with a firmer grip on his—and her—butt. Not only that, but her old man uses an antiquated—albeit large-bore—flintlock pistol, which means a lengthy reload after each shot. Rosalba's cold, cold heart goes all a-flutter at sight of hubby's killer cocking the murder weapon, the other target pistol from a matching set. As morning mourning bells toll for her unmourned Dearly Departed, Neri ("You can't be happy *and* poor…") "grieves" by slipping into a respectfully black slinky silk negligee. This is applied after sex by a lover—none other than the very man she subsequently frames for her husband's murder—played by Franco Lantieri, who gives her one last kiss in time for the final peal of the bell. When Neri later seeks to shoot Damon using hubby's own flintlock, the weapon—all sound and fury, if nothing else—impotently discharges a load of gunpowder smoke and fire; but its intended target reveals that, as a preliminary precautionary measure, he had removed its balls (all *three* of them, made of lead). When Neri kills an infatuated admirer named Carradine (Lawrence "Larry" Dobkin) with her dainty lady-size pistol, she takes intense pleasure in shooting him right over the heart.

Before that, the hired gun played by Dobkin—who's obviously never heard of the old adage, "Don't shoot the messenger"—blows Neri's pawn to Kingdom Gone, but at least offers cash up front for his funeral ("Here's a *dollar* for the casket" [better make that a *sack*…]). With twin sinew lines down his cheeks as clearly-defined and perfectly parallel as railroad tracks, Larry Dobkin is offbeat but believable as the well-groomed, granite-faced Carradine, as adept at chess as he is at poker and pistols. He always tears his paper killing money in two to clinch a deal ("Half now, half later…as usual"); leaving one to idly ponder how in the hell he'd ever stick it back together again in the days before clear Scotch tape was invented.

As Pedro, in general look and unhinged temperament, "Louis Vanner"/Luigi Vannucchi often evokes American actor Robert Dix (of such US westerns as Sam Fuller's **FORTY GUNS** [1957], Al Adamson's **FIVE BLOODY GRAVES**

US pressbook

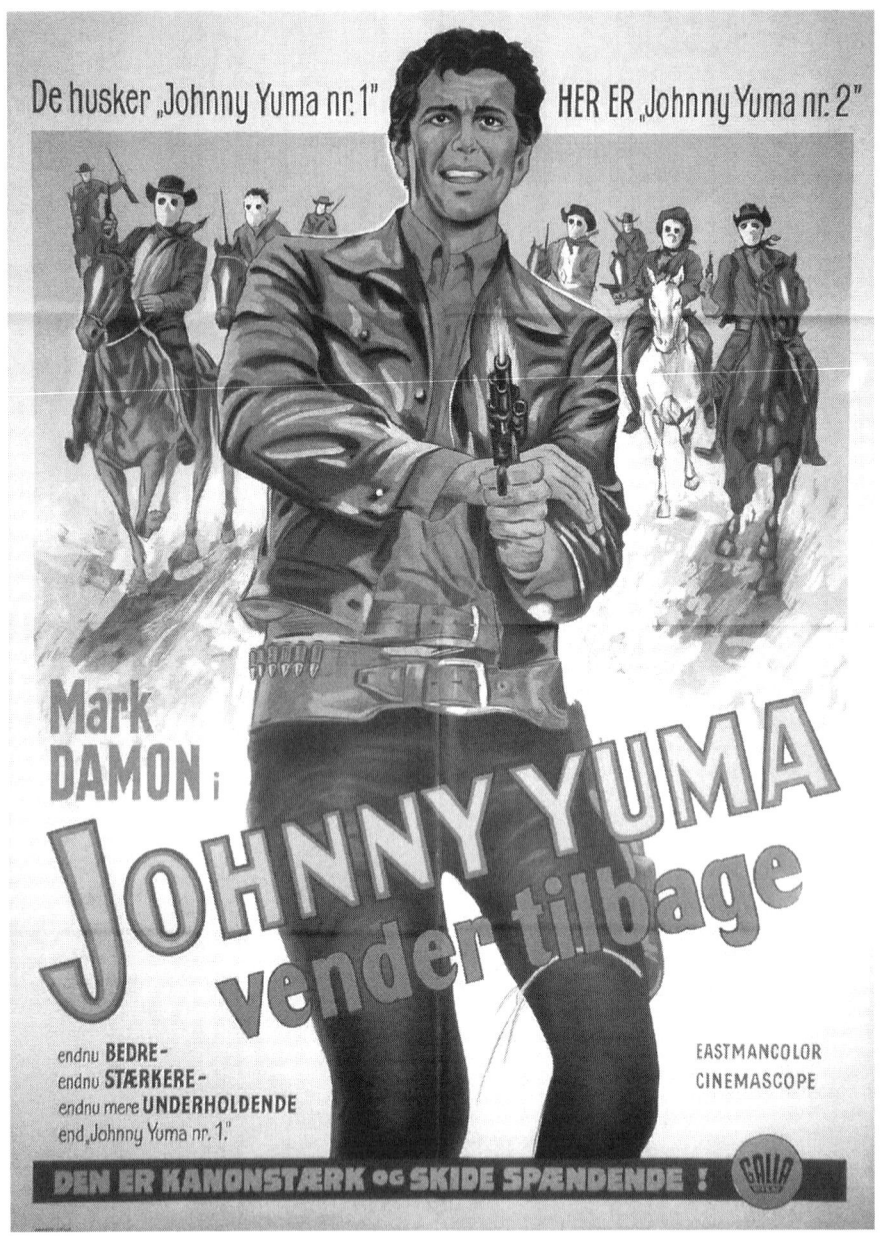

Scandinavian poster for **JOHNNY YUMA** (1966)

[1969][24] and Kent Osborne's **CAIN'S CUT-THROATS** [a.k.a. **CAIN'S WAY**, 1970]), whose specialty became playing leering, amoral sociopsychopaths in exploitation movies. The Vannucchi character's such a sadistic pig ("Find him! Even if you have to *torture* the entire town!") that he slaps, kicks and stomps a defenceless ten-year-old boy to death. But when the chips are down, Pedro's a coward who backs down from a potential fight with Dobkin as Carradine. In a fine dramatic scene between Damon and Dobkin, former accuses latter of being "bought" by Neri: not only his gun but also his integrity as a man. Final showdown in well-named Death City is expertly handled, with plenty of rooftop stunt-divers and wholesale destruction of both property and expendable extras. With a friendly warning cry of "Hey!" (*à la* George Hilton in Lucio Fulci's **MASSACRE TIME** [*Le colt cantarono la morte e fu...tempo di massacre*, 1966]), Damon blasts three men from behind while at least allowing them a fighting chance by tipping them off to his presence before making short work of them. When Vannucchi is about to do same to him (though minus the fair warning), Damon—

24 See *WC*#1, p.3

who cocks his Colt on his hipbone—lets him run out of ammo then lets him have it after first making him beg for mercy on his knees. (Talk about milking it for all it's worth!)

For one of the film's infrequent—if largely successful—attempts at comedy relief, when Neri later disrobes in full sight of its cage, her pet parrot becomes increasingly "excited", squawking uncontrollably and pecking at the bars. The scene is ridiculous and gratuitous, but admittedly amusing. (It has often been said that sarcasm is the lowest form of wit, but in our opinion parrot comedy generally falls a good deal lower—just witness the smartass squawker in Italo Alfaro's lowbrow oatcom **AND THEY SMELLED THE STRANGE, EXCITING, DANGEROUS SCENT OF DOLLARS** [*Sentivano uno strano, eccitante, pericoloso puzzo di dollari*, a.k.a. **CHARITY AND THE STRANGE SMELL OF MONEY**, 1973]!)

Yet another silver pocket watch plays a minor part in the plot of the present film. While not overly forceful, the trumpet-heavy Nora Orlandi/Robby Poitevin score compliments the action quite nicely. If you're in any way, shape or form a fan of spaghetti westerns, you could do far worse than this one, which easily falls somewhere within the Top 100 of the genre.

We'll leave the parting shot to Damon as Yuma: "Dying is an important thing. You only do it *once...*"

NOTES: In Hong Kong as of March '68, **JOHNNY YUMA** had grossed $748,338.30 (HK); which then translated to some $123,600 American. It was the only indie spaghetti western listed among a dozen other Hollywood, Euro and Hong Kong titles of various genres; actually coming in eighth below Lewis Gilbert's 007 megahit **YOU ONLY LIVE TWICE** (1967), Leone's **FOR A FEW DOLLARS MORE** (*Per qualche dollaro in più*, 1965), Robert Aldrich's **THE DIRTY DOZEN** (1967) and several local Shaw Brothers MA spectacles (including Chang Cheh's **THE ASSASSIN** [大刺客 / *Da ci ke*] and the same director's **THE ONE-ARMED SWORDSMAN** [獨臂刀 / *Du bei dao*, both 1967], both starring martial artist Jimmy Wang Yu and both grossing over $165,000 [US] apiece). **JOHNNY YUMA** was also a sizeable hit in Jamaica, as well as many other parts of the world (it presumably did fair trade in the USA too; it was released stateside theatrically by Atlantic Releasing/George Ross Pres./Clover Films, and later to US TV by Paramount). The film is unrelated to a US western teleseries, *The Rebel* (1959-62), wherein star Nick Adams played a character named Johnny Yuma. In 1967, Johnny Cash (co-star opposite Kirk Douglas of Lamont Johnson's partly-shot-in Spain Hollywood western sleeper **A GUNFIGHT** [1971]) recorded "The Rebel – Johnny Yuma" (sample lyrics: *"He wandered alone"* – *"panther-quick and leather-tough"* – *"He'd search his soul and gamble with death"*). Double-billed with "Dario Silvestri"/Marino Girolami's **BETWEEN GOD, THE DEVIL AND A WINCHESTER** (*Anche nel west c'era una volta Dio*, 1968), starring Richard Harrison, **JOHNNY YUMA** is available on domestic DVD from Wild East Productions of NYC.

1966, ITALY. D: ROMOLO GUERRIERI (ROMOLO GIROLAMI)
AVAILABLE FROM WILD EAST PRODUCTIONS

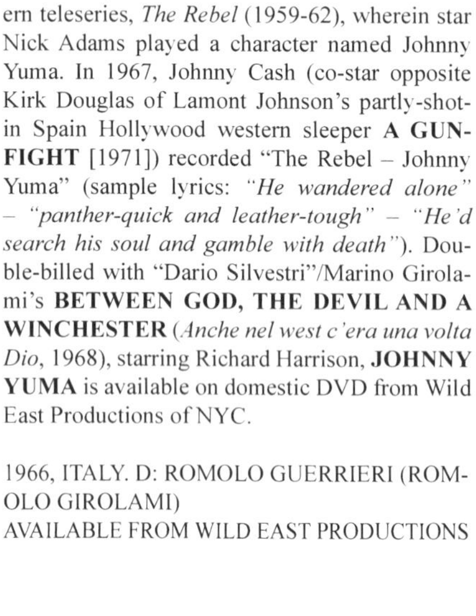

TEEN-AGE RIOT!

Vintage Juvie Movies reviewed by Steve Fenton

In 1950s America, there were only two things as scary as Commies and the A-Bomb: rock'n'roll and…juvenile delinquents! While "JD" movies were made both before and since, it wasn't until the '50s that they really first came into their own as an actual definable subgenre of exploitation cinema, having been inspired in large part by Marlon Brando's proto-biker flick **THE WILD ONE** *(1953, USA, D: Laslo Benedek) and to an even greater degree by ill-fated teen dream James Dean's troubled youth drama* **REBEL WITHOUT A CAUSE** *(1955, USA, D: Nicholas Ray). For the remainder of that decade, exploitative crime dramas featuring youthful antiheroic, antisocial misfits became prime fodder for the regional rural drive-in and urban grindhouse circuits. I shall irregularly be covering a number of archetypal examples in future issues; starting with these half-dozen here…*

LIVE FAST, DIE YOUNG
(a.k.a. LIVE FAST AND YOUNG)

Dialogue doozy: *"Only turkey-necks get into trouble!"*

A classically-titled JD drama from Universal-International Pictures, which, while a major studio that produced a number of key entries within the teenage-oriented genre, were not really known as major players within it, simply because much of their product was just too gosh-darn subdued and restrained compared to the output of more financially-strapped, less reputable outfits, who tended to push the envelope more in hopes of getting better returns on their investments while trying to make a name for themselves. Generally, the best Juvenile Delinquent cinema originated at the more sub-Hollywood independent studios (such as AIP and AA, and from even lower down in the indie hierarchy).

Jill (Norma Eberhardt, who also in '58 played the heroine of Paul Landres' moody vampire thriller **THE RETURN OF DRACULA**) is a social outcast at a Frisco high school. Laughed at by her peers and shunned by them like calculus homework, her grades have been suffering for it. Her 22-year-old big sister Kim (Mary Murphy) narrates the tale. Their father (Gordon Jones) is a loudmouth habitual boozer with anger management issues prone to haranguing his daughters (e.g., "I ain't gonna let ya sit around here on ya duff playin' phonograph records…"). True to his word, Pops graciously allows his eldest daughter Kim to go out and earn his beer money for him, this by slinging hash at a local greasy spoon while he sits back home on his big fat duff. She understandably doesn't want her impressionably idealistic baby sis Jill to drop out of school and suffer the same fate (i.e., a fruitlessly futile future).

Slamming her bedroom door behind her, Jill works off her anger at the whole world by listening to jazzy R'n'R instros—roughly the '58 equivalent of death metal—while feeling alienated and agitated but apathetic. "I don't gotta do *nothin'*!" she exclaims in double negative (clearly she must be flunking-out in English most of all). Leaving a scribbled note, Jill subsequently runs away from her un-fixably broken home (the sisters' mother had likewise skipped out on their deadbeat dad). Just before she hits the road, Jill lifts the last $20 of her big sis' folding money. In order to earn her room and board out in the big bad world all by her increasingly not-so-sweet little lonesome, Jill offers to clean Sam the rooming-house owner's place, an offer which spells nothing but T-R-O-U-B-L-E in big block letters (mostly for her). When he makes the moves on Jill—just as we were fully expecting he would—she is saved by the timely advent of Mary (Jamie O'Hara), a loose-living floozy who hits up drunks for liquor at the seedy neighbourhood drinkery. Catching on fast to the wicked ways of the world, Jill relieves a high-roller of the then-whopping sum of $160 ("This is like a *uranium mine*!"). Our misguided antiheroine shortly teams up with another wayward teenage belle named Mona (Dawn Richard), but a short while later comes to the conclusion that her cut of the take will be choicer if she operates solo rather than having a tag-partner on the payroll.

Cheesecake is restricted to a few chaste views of the sisters wearing their slips, relying on the sometimes loaded dialogue to speak—albeit only at a comparative whisper—what could not then be either explicitly told nor shown. Kim (or is it Mary?) proclaims with convincing vehemence, "I *hate* men!", and it is none-too-subtly implied by the script that she had been sexually molested at the tender age of 15 by one of her dad's drinking buddies (a Schlitz ad provides later product placement, adding to the sleazy sordidness of the milieu). To his eldest daughter, her no-account woman-hater of a father says accusingly, "You're a *tramp*, like Jill, like ya mother: like *all* o' them!" Elsewhere, dancing is blatantly equated with doing the "horizontal tango". After she hitches a ride Las Vegas-bound with a trucker named Jerry, Jill is impressed by his manly brawn ("I bet your arms could pack a punch like *missiles*!"). When he asks her how old she is, she promptly lies, "*Legal age.*" Having previously been described by someone as a "thumb-sucker", while riding in the cab of Jerry's rig the thumb-tripping Lolita bites and sucks her finger suggestively (hmmm, wonder what she might mean by that?). In another scene, top-billed Murphy as big sis Kim is befriended by one of second-billed Eberhardt as baby sis Jill's "workmates", who explains her lowly lot with "I got

Girl On The Loose: A leggy '50s cheesecake pose of Mamie Van Doren, and the US half-sheet poster for one of her trashiest psychotronic flicks

pregnant; he got drafted", a throwaway line which concisely and succinctly simplifies her tumultuous young life in a nutshell, in the process virtually trivializing it to the point of nothingness simply by her attitude.

While *en route* to Sin City, Jill must out of necessity seek temporary employment at a roadside joint inaptly known as "The Paradise". Back on the trail again, she is "interfered with" sexually by a motorist who gives the hitchhiking hottie a ride and would dearly love to drive her further (like, *all the way*) at the first opportunity. However, thwarting his plans, juicy juvie Jill's virtue is saved by a gang of benignant old hobos, who subsequently have a whip-round in order to raise bus-ticket money for her to continue on her merry way Vegas-ward. Intent on making a big score using her pre-womanly charms as a lure, jailbait Jill takes an old gambler to the aptly-named "Shady Side" Motel, where she purloins his $2,000 winnings and then further rubs his face in it by using his convertible for her getaway car, leaving him in the lurch, busted flat.

Working in league with two greasers, a blonde named Jackie—a Tuesday Weld/Irish McCalla-type played by Dorothy Provine, soon to be seen as **THE 30 FOOT BRIDE OF CANDY ROCK** (1959) opposite Lou Costello, flying solo from Bud Abbott—attempts to rip-off a couple of suckers, one of whom whips out a defensive straight razor. While lamming it, she makes Jill's big sis' acquaintance. After Kim introduces herself, Jackie asks sarcastically (as per certain celebrities of their day), "Kim Stanley, Kim Hunter or Kim Novak?" to which the other girl wittily replies, "I'm the *new* Kim. Nobody's discovered me yet", as if her rise to superstardom is assured, and only a question of time (say, the day after tomorrow at the latest). When Kim asks Jackie why she does what she does to get by, the latter answers simply and succinctly, "Beats workin'".

Upon later linking up with Jill's former ride Jerry the trucker (rhymes with…), Kim redoubles her search for her missing kid sis. But Jerry uses the same lines and makes the same moves on Kim as he had on Jill; however, being sexually uptight—and who can blame her with all these would-be silver-tongued Lotharios around!—Kim recoils from his touch, despite his sincere apologies.

Elsewhere in L.A., Jill's fence steers her to an antique shop which is in actuality merely a front for a cartel running stolen goods. Supporting player Mike "Touch" Connors (hero of Rog Corman's fab **DAY THE WORLD ENDED** [1955]) appears late in the game as a crooked businessman—also named Mike—whom Jill schmoozes (and coozes) at his luxurious penthouse. Again ably illustrating the double *entendres* lurking behind sometimes seemingly innocuous lines of dialogue, in her new-found elevated position within the underworld, Jill announces, "From now on, I only work from the *neck up*." Before you have time to even wonder quite what she meant by that, she becomes involved in the aptly-named Touch's robbery scheme: to steal a whole whack of "mellies" (i.e., diamonds, a.k.a. "About 150,000 dollars' worth of WOW!").

Determined to make up for lost time and follow her sinful sibling's lead by going bad herself—it makes a refreshing change for the *younger* sister to be a bad influence on her *older* one!—Kim volunteers to join Jill's scam, and fires-up her very first cigarette ever just to unofficially clinch it. Soft-touch Touch puts an elaborate plan into effect, involving a phony construction crew and a hot rod gang. However, in the eleventh hour, Kim—who may well have only been faking her recent voluntary fall from grace merely as a wily tactic—intercedes to foil the crummy crooks' heist and turn Jill in (for her own good, you understand). As the film ends, having only lived fast for a little while, rather than dying young Jill is instead placed on probation and ordered to undergo a psychiatric evaluation.

Illustrating the apathy of living under constant threat of having The Bomb drop smack-dab atop The American Dream and blowing it all to atoms at any moment, this film comes complete with a discernible undertow of Cold War anxiety, albeit not outright anti-Commie paranoia propaganda *per se*, more just a general tone of unease that permeates the proceedings.

Most of the incidental background music heard on radios and jukeboxes throughout **LIVE FAST, DIE YOUNG** (1958) is of the softer-edged jazz/rock instrumental variety. Not overly sensational, the film's end-result—despite its hoary and hokey "moral" resolution—is competently enough done, if rather flat and lacking in the more lurid thrills of something like **GUN GIRLS** (1957), say.

<u>NOTE:</u> It goes without saying that the sole connection between this film and Timothy A. Chey's 2008 Hollywood drama **LIVE FAST, DIE YOUNG** is its title.

1958, USA. D: PAUL HENREID
AVAILABLE FROM VIDEO BEAT

GIRLS TOWN
(a.k.a. THE WILD AND THE WICKED)

"Now, listen to me, girls / Watch your P's and Q's / Or you'll have the Girls Town Blues!"

These lyrics and others of the title theme are sung by a male vocalist. Just when you're thinking that a female voice might better suit the song considering the title, who should take over singing for the second half but star Mamie Van Doren herself. Performed in rock 'n' roll tempo to big-band jazz accompaniment, this song sets a fittingly trashy tone for what is to follow the opening titles.

Notorious trash producer Albert Zugsmith assembled a real psychotronic dream cast for **GIRLS** [sic] **TOWN** (1959), that's for sure and definite…

The motherless daughter of a known felon, peroxide blonde Silver Morgan (Mamie) is about to be raped by an overeager admirer named Chip out at Lovers' Lane. While she is seeking to evade her attacker, the dumb cluck falls over a cliff to his demise (*See!* A real actor substituted with a phony dummy!). Freddie (Mel Torme [!]…[make that !!]) subsequently finds Silver's lipstick at the scene of his gang buddy Chip's death, thus pegging her as the prime suspect for causing it. For passing bad cheques and committing several other infractions in direct violation of her probation—including physically assaulting a school teacher—incorrigible repeat offender Mamie, who's a *baaaad* grrrl, is suspected of murdering Chip, and while cops investigate the case she is for the time being incarcerated at an institution called Girls' Town (still more informally known as "Girlsville" or "Jailsville"). This minimum-security correctional facility—run by tough-as-nails if mostly soft-centered nuns—is not a reform school *per se* ("It's a home for girls who've had problems with the law"). There, along with other female residents, Mamie—here giving perhaps the most self-assured acting performance of her career—is forced to further her voluntarily-truncated formal education ("I don't wanna learn anything new, I know *too much* already!" she protests with a world-wise and -weary air).

Billed second, homely chinless wonder Torme—whose face disappears into his neck every time he opens his mouth…which is often—was evidently cast on account of his "cool cred" (such as it was) with the teenage consumer demographic, albeit here playing the heavy. His character is the leader of a gang of snotty hot-rodders known as "The Jaguars". From well-to-do families and born with silver spoons in their mouths, true to their name this gang of over-privileged rich brats—with a collective inflated sense of entitlement—all drive late-model Jags with both reckless disregard for the highway code and utter contempt for their perceived social lessers. A fierce rivalry exists between them and another local outfit called "The Dragons," who stem from less-privileged, blue collar social roots (i.e., the common working class, like the rest of us), and reflective of this all drive less-flashy wheels.

In his mid-thirties at the time and far better-known as a crooner than an actor, one can only wonder how many of his fans were thinking to themselves, "Don't give up your day job, Mel," while watching his performance here. During one sequence, Torme leads a rumble—complete with catfight—out at Malibu Lake. The jag-off Jaguars later compete wheel-to-wheel while draggin' against The Dragons. This results in a pretty crazy "no-hands" hot rod race down the LA storm drains, during which Torme's opponent is seriously injured in a wreck.

It develops that Silver's jailbait little sis Mary-Lee (aged only 15!) was the person present when Chip took a cliff-dive to his premature if not entirely undeserved doom. Afraid she'll testify against The Jags—towering pillars of the community who have their respectable reputations to uphold—Torme abducts Mary-Lee so as to ensure her silence. When Mamie rescues her, she and the other girls get real rough with the bad guys. As was expected right from the get-go (no spoiler here!), Mamie and her onscreen sister are cleared on all charges of wrongdoing, and everything ends happily…You were expecting some dark, downbeat resolution, perhaps? This is the '50s, FFS! People still believed in happy endings back then, though the odds of such bad gals as these living happily ever after no matter what the historical timeframe are decidedly slim indeed.

While Torme (some might say thankfully) doesn't get to sing here, fellow crooner/moonlighting actor Paul Anka does, down at a nightspot called The Cool Note. Playing one Jimmy Parlo, Anka's too-wholesome-to-live character is *almost* framed for chasing young stuff ("Contributing to the delinquency of a minor is a very serious offence!" says Mother Superior Veronica disapprovingly. But methinks the lady doth protest too much: what uptight post-menopausal RC nun wouldn't wanna stick her hand up some underage schoolgirl's skirt?!). Anka later goes at Torme with a baseball bat! Recent ex-**DAUGHTER OF DR. JEKYLL** (1957) Gloria Talbott plays Vita, an incorrigibly criminal bouncer's daughter doing time for using karate to roll a drunk. Secondary female lead Talbott is great as this bitchy shit-disturbing hellcat character, who provokes a dorm catfight after she steals Mamie's cigarettes, and really goes whole hog during the grand finale, laying beatings on whoever comes within swinging range; all this while uttering some pricelessly ludicrous lines of dialogue (e.g., "…go bingle your bongle!"; reminiscent of Russ Tamblyn's infamous "the way the bongo bingles" line in same producer Zugsmith's **HIGH SCHOOL CONFIDENTIAL** [1958], also starring Mamie).

And speaking of colorful wordage, at one point in the present film MVD is heard to exclaim, "You're in Queersville, man! You've *flipped*!" Other dialogue in "this crazy weenie-roast" drops such prime slang as "studs…daddy-o's…he-males…stags"; and let's not forget "…you dirty *skags*!" (latter being Mamie's heartfelt exclamation to her fellow GT inmates at a kangaroo court of gang debs).

Incidental background music (mostly jolly big-band jazz) was composed by Van Alexander. At the local make-out spot, a girl sings "I Love You" while Mamie and the other kids smooch without ever actually going so far as all-out heavy-petting, let alone getting to first base. The song "Wish It Were Me" was performed by Buck Ram; all the rest heard in the film were sung by the Paul Anka, whose velvet-lined pipes were made for such pop-pap as this. For one scene, Mamie ignores house rules by sneaking out after curfew to the nightclub to hear Anka—whom she sarcastically refers to as "King Groovy"—sing "Lonely Boy" (his big hit on ABC Records that summer). He later performs "It's Time to Cry" (his November '59 ABC single). Speaking of crying, his saccharin rendition of "Ave Maria" is guaranteed to leave not a single dry eye in the house…even hard-as-granite rounder MVD is moved to tears! Also appearing on the bill are The Platters, one of the most-filmed musical acts of the '50s (see also Corman's **CARNIVAL ROCK** [1957], etc). Oh yeah, and let's not forget Harold Lloyd, Jr. and Charles Chaplin, Jr., sons of the famous silent era comedians, which makes this a real popular culture grab-bag/time capsule, for sure.

With all this and more pop-cultural plop besides packed into it, what I don't get is, as of this writing, why the *fuck* does the vastly entertaining **GIRLS TOWN** only get a lousy "2.9" reading on the Sphincter Scale at the IMDb? Prime trash Americana doesn't get much primer or trashier than this! If one *Weng's Chop*per's meat is another one's poison, this here junk is pure cyanide!

1959, USA. D: CHARLES F. HAAS
AVAILABLE FROM VIDEO BEAT

A smokin' hot publicity pose of Mamie, taken to promote **GIRLS TOWN** (1959)

![Hot Car Girl poster — "She's HELL-ON-WHEELS...fired up for any thrill!" Starring Richard Bakalyan, June Kenney, John Brinkley, with Robert Knapp, Jana Lund, Sheila McKay.]

HOT CAR GIRL

A jalopy-jaunt down juvie-movie halls from Bernie Kowalski, director of the '50s monster schlockers **NIGHT OF THE BLOOD BEAST** (1958)[1] and **ATTACK OF THE GIANT LEECHES** (1959), both of which were AIP releases.

HOT CAR GIRL (1958) is by no means to be confused with Leslie H. Martinson's exceedingly similarly-titled **HOT ROD GIRL** (produced two years prior in '56). The present title was co-produced by the Corman Bros. (Roger and Gene) under the auspices of JD genre specialists Allied Artists (AA), a studio whose main competition in both the genre and drive-in product in general came from James H. Nicholson's and Samuel Z. Arkoff's then still-embryonic American International Pictures (AIP), for whom the Cormans also worked more famously within the same general period. It was scripted by another frequent Corman collaborator, writer-actor Leo Gordon (who performed both those duties on **THE CRY BABY KILLER** [1960]; famous as the screen debut of Jack Nicholson in the title role, a simpering, self-pitying homicidal JD).

For **HOT CAR GIRL**, broken-nosed pug-ugly "teenage" genre icon Richard "Dick" Bakalyan (1931-2015) stars on the top line as Duke Willis, a 20-year-old car thief who, instead of taking the high road to fame, fortune and happiness winds up caught in the fast lane (i.e., the highway to heck) straight to Nowheresville, the Ass-End of Beyond, U.S. of A.

In L.A., Duke Dick takes his romantic interest Peg Dale (June Kenney) out on a hot date to the Country Line Club, where for four bits a bottle, kids can order themselves an under-the-table "Orange Special" (actually soda-pop spiked with booze). Now, Duke may not exactly be the handsomest fella in town, but he's cool as they come, and good girl Peg likes his rough edges. As for Peg, an associate of Duke's opines, "She ain't only square—she's a *cube*!" To which Duke cockily and confidently responds, "So I'll round the corners off!" (How does that old saying go? Something about "trying to fit a square peg into a round hole"…)

At the hoppin', boppin' teen social, Duke and no-longer-quite-so-square Peg, having hit it off famously, symbolically "consummate" their relationship by accidentally tipping over a booze bottle on the tabletop, causing some of its contents to spill forth. Having all-too-willingly allowed herself to become drawn into the company of the "wrong crowd", Peg subsequently feels guilty after she puts-out for Duke. (And talk about an odd couple!)

With its stark naked chrome-plated motor, Duke's soft-topped, lead-footed custom '56 Ford heap sounds like about two-dozen Harley hogs all revving their engines at once. Ever-ready to peel out and lay rubber at a moment's notice, Duke impulsively drag-races on a public thoroughfare with a hot chick in a cool sports car. His street-racing opponent Janice, aptly-surnamed Wheeler (played by Jana Lund, from **HIGH SCHOOL HELLCATS** [1958][2]), is busted as culpable after a motorcycle cop is killed in the line of duty while attempting to chase the reckless racers down. Duke lights out for parts unknown, leaving Janice to take the rap for the crack-up he primarily caused, but for which she much more indirectly shares the blame. Before leaving the scene, he warns her not to squeal on him…or else.

Ed Nelson—here operating on the opposite side of the law than in his starring role as the ringleader of the **T-BIRD GANG** (1959)—plays a cop ("If we just find the punks that did it…") whose law-enforcing ambitions greatly outstrip his basic aptitude. An amusing scene occurs when, in collaboration with the other kids, Duke ("I *hate* cops") makes monkeys out of two police officers—Nelson included—by stealing their keys and locking the cops out of their cruiser, thus causing them acute public embarrassment. Even today (perhaps *more so* today in these times of an increased "police presence" in the USA) this scene is a real crowd-pleaser, so one can easily imagine all the real-life JDs in the theatre audience cheering at the screen upon its original release.

Doing his bit to help in apprehending the cop-killer(s?), Janice's well-heeled pops—Duke doesn't refer to her as "Miss Rich Britches" for nothing—offers a hefty reward for the real culprit's capture. Lt. Ryan (Robert Knapp) of the LAPD's Traffic Division wants whoever was responsible indicted for hit-and-run manslaughter. Fearing that they might be implicated in the crime by the fuzz along with him, Duke's cohorts Freddy (John Brinkley) and Micki (Sheila McKay) begin keeping their distance and going out of their way to avoid him (i.e., shunning him like the plague). When the jittery Janice threatens to cave and give him away to the cops, Duke responds in a fit of pique and panic by fatally breaking a bottle over her head, then, with Peg in tow, goes on a four-wheeled run for anywhere but there. Going nowhere fast—*real* fast—to make matters that much worse, Duke coldcocks a gas-pump attendant who IDs their licence plate. Reacting impulsively and instinctively without thinking things through properly first, Duke steals a gat (a.k.a. "piece," a.k.a. "heater" a.k.a. "rod") and speeds poor "devotedly dutiful" Peg towards not just his own self-destruction, but hers right along with him. A massive manhunt is mobilized, while Duke—gone kill-crazy and becoming progressively crazier with each passing moment as his stress levels increase (talk about "road rage"!)—rushes headlong towards his final destination. You know where that is as well as I do…cuz every last one of us suckers is bound to get there eventually. Duke just happens to be one of the lucky ones pointed out by the fickle finger of Fate to get there well in advance of the rest of us.

Bakalyan, a much-better-than-average actor with an offbeat charisma which makes him somehow likeable even when at his most hateful, conveys the ill-fated Duke's pathos very effectively. With a chip on his shoulder the size of a '57 Chevy engine block and a rap-sheet as long as both his legs laid end-to-end, after being busted for joyriding while still a juvenile offender, he had been subjected to some retributory police brutality. Hence his deep-seated mistrust of authority figures, especially those in law enforcement.

"Did you ever get a good look at a cop's badge?" asks Duke of his girl when his back's against the wall. "Right across the top it says 'Policeman'. By the time a crud's wearin' it three months, he thinks it says 'GOD'. I'd like ta tell 'em what *I think* the word should be…" He addresses this rather self-indulgent preach-speech—which runs longer than what I've transcribed here—not only to Peg, but also to we the far-from-innocent bystanders who just for being there have almost aided and abetted him in his crimes all along. Much like his propensity for beating his victims over their heads with blunt objects, so does he beat us over our own heads with his self-pity. But it works: we really *do* feel sorry for the poor misguided schmuck and wish things would—if only they could, which we know they can't—work out for him in the end! But it was already a foregone conclusion right at the very beginning that he was doomed to end bad-

---

1 See *Monster!* #17, p.33

2 See review on next page

ly, and in the worst way, too. How does William Blake's old poem go? "Some are born to sweet delight, some are born to endless night". You know what category Duke our antihero fits into right from the get-go. And speaking of endless night, there is very definitely a big sleep in our pitiable ne'er-do-well's immediate future; you can bank on it and collect the accrued interest.

At long last doing the honourable thing, Duke cuts Peg loose at the same cave in Bronson Canyon outside LA where Beverly Garland (**PROBLEM GIRLS** [1953], **SWAMP WOMEN** [1956]) met the walking, talking kooky cucumber monster in Corman's **IT CONQUERED THE WORLD** (1956). Cornered like a dirty rat by police marksmen, Duke takes the Cagney way out in a white-hot blaze of glory: tear-gassed and crying like a baby, he goes down shootin'. Indicating that he was by no means all bad, his penultimate gesture was to scribble off a note which posthumously fully exonerates his doting survivor Peg of any and all guilt. Ultimately—if we may read between the lines here more than we have done already—for all his earlier fervent apologies, Peg pegs him as little more than a hot-headed sociopath…a mere minor lay-by on the long, winding and sometimes slippery road of her life, which is only just beginning even as his comes to an abrupt and inglorious stop more surely than a dead-end street.

Heroine Miss Kenney's other JD jaunts include playing the lead of Rog Corman's **TEENAGE DOLL** and co-starring in his **SORORITY GIRL** (both 1957); the former was made for AA, the latter for AIP. In **HOT CAR GIRL**, XL-size grade-Z cult flick personality Bruno VeSota (who also appeared in Kowalski's above-noted **THE GIANT LEECHES**) here plays everyman Joe, the auto-theft ring's fence-*cum*-chop-shop proprietor (he went on to play a virtually identical part in **THE CHOPPERS** [1961], starring Arch Hall, Jr). When he becomes overstocked with hot car-radios, VeSota—*er*—"special orders" some trendy wire-spoked wheel-rims, which go for a then-hefty $100 per set. Needless to say, the car-strippers are more than happy to oblige him. Ms. McKay as Micki, the gang's Bohemian beat-chick member, wears horn-rimmed granny glasses for that pretentious pseudo-"intellectual" poseur look, but can hotwire a car with the best of 'em. As in many another genre entry, these JDs listen almost exclusively to jazz, and *soft* jazz at that (the score was provided by non-Latino Latin jazzman Cal Tjader [1925-1982]). At times evoking the compositions of sometime Corman musicmen Ronald Stein (**SORORITY GIRL**) and Fred Katz (**THE WASP WOMAN** [1959]), much of **HOT CAR GIRL**'s score consists of rapid drum staccatos echoed by bongo fury.

Consider this one of the top must-sees on your short-list of what's hot in Juvenile Delinquent cinema. If you can't relate to it nor feel it tug at both your heart-strings and short hairs, you either never were a JD or never will be. So are you a square or a wheel, Daddy-o? You decide which.

And that's all I'm sayin' on the matter. Get me?

1958, USA. D: BERNARD L. KOWALSKI
AVAILABLE FROM VIDEO BEAT

HIGH SCHOOL HELLCATS

Trailer copy: *"Teenage Girls…TANTALIZING… AND TERRORIZING!"*

Trailer narration: *"There's the devil to pay when high school hellcats and high school hotshots get together on an 'anything-goes' party!"*

"Those wild kids usually get what they deserve!" – So opines wholesome hero Mike about the "villains" of the present film, which might well be you or me, so don't knock 'em.

Yet another iconic JD potboiler from American International Pictures, sporting one of the most deliciously evocative exploitation movie titles of all time! Pure pulp hokum from start to finish, this movie wallows in cheezy teaze 'n' sleaze and loves every minute of it. You will too, you delinquent you; no need to try denying it, cuz we ain't buying it, y'hear!

As a rule, AIP flicks in the teenagers-gone-wrong genre (as with their fare in other genres too) tended to be more playful with so-called "traditional" gender roles and moral values than other, bigger studios. For example, here playing #1 Hellcat, co-star Jana Lund (also seen in Allied Artists' **HOT CAR GIRL** [1958]) exclaims regarding a substitute teacher assigned to one of their classes, "A man teaching Home Ec…? Ooooo-oooo, how *WI-I-I-ILD!*" One Miss Davis is there to teach a course on "Health and Physical Education": you guessed it: Sex Ed. class, during which—what else?!—all the growing girls wanna talk about is (quote) "*BOYS!*" So strong is the sexual suggestiveness in the air during this scene that you can almost smell the moistening female genitalia; that of Teach's and her students both. Or maybe it was just me reading too much into things again (yeah, it *could* be that…but I don't think so).

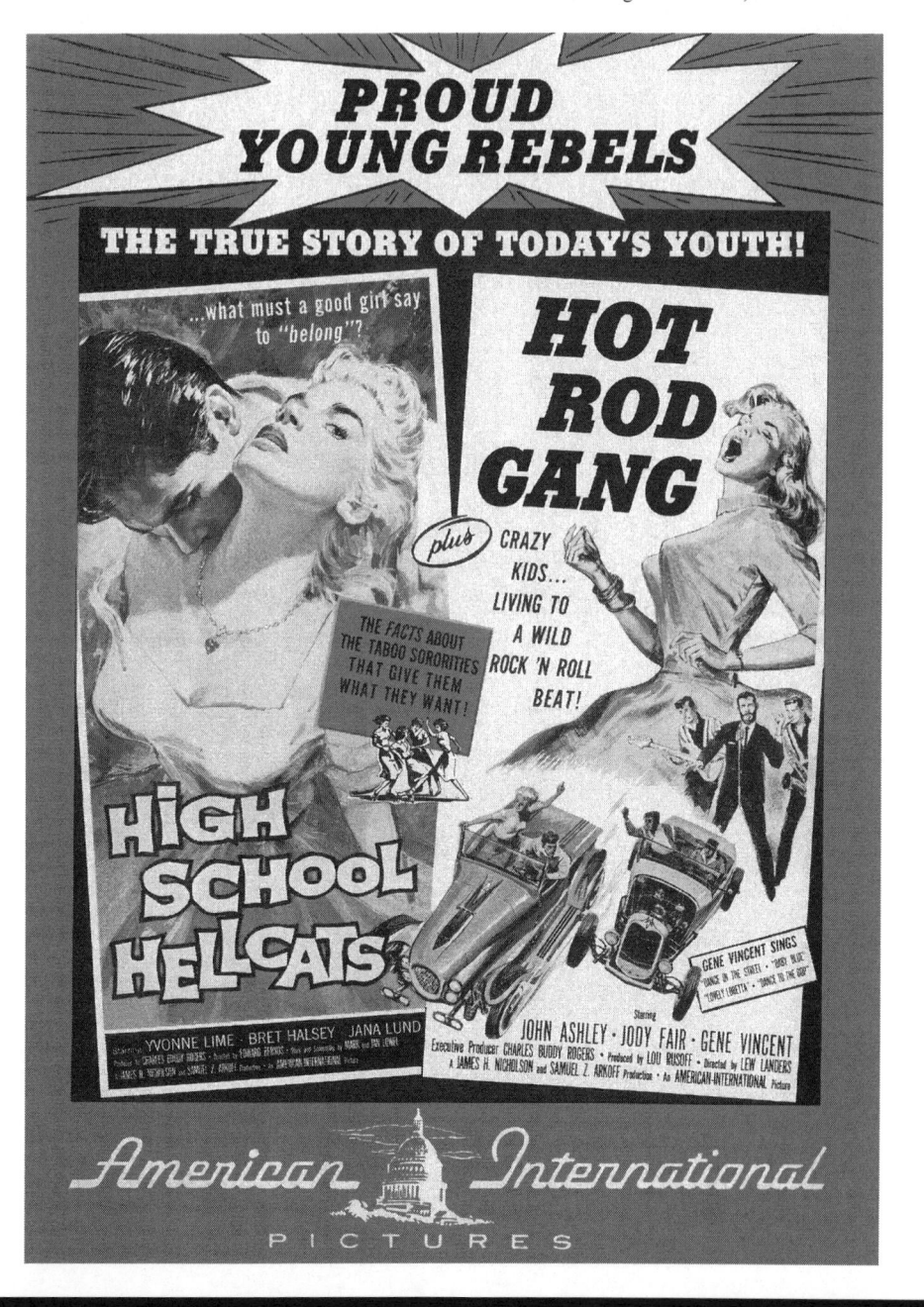

Starting things out in fine style on just the right footing, the film's memorable main title is seen written in chalk on a blackboard; which is then matter-of-factly wiped away by the sweeping eraser of a teacher. Right before this, Hellcat troublemaker Dolly was seen to hurl her stiletto point-first into the wall. Unfortunately, rather than a stinging rock 'n' roll rip-snorter, the ensuing title theme (by frequent AIP/Corman composer Ronald Stein) is instead bombastic big-band jazz, albeit perforated by electric guitar riffs and further punctuated by a twangy/jangly rockabilly solo. Hell, if all jazz was this rocked-up, I'd be a jazzman as well as a rocker!

In the girls' john of the title educational institution (complete with prominent "NO SMOKING" sign), titular, butt-puffing diabolical female felines—a gang of she-JDs who are the terrors of both their faculty and the student body alike—plan to initiate the new girl in school, Joyce Martin (the pert and perky Yvonne Lime, complete with bobbing ponytail; the actress also starred in such other choice AIP JD/drive-in fare as Gene Fowler, Jr.'s **I WAS A TEENAGE WEREWOLF** [1957] and David Bradley's **DRAGSTRIP RIOT** [1958]). "I think I'll start out with the 'slacks' test," announces Connie Harris (Lund), leader of the gang debs in the present film. "There's a gang in this class," announces Connie to new girl Joyce straight off, "*I'm* the boss." In a bit of wily feminine underhandedness, as per her earlier suggestion, Connie forces Joyce to transgress against the school's strict no-slacks-for-girls rule (after all, only *boys* wear pants; girls wear *skirts*, right? [*Sarcasm alert!*]). When Joyce later comes to school wearing slacks as "requested", she finds to her embarrassment—which was exactly the response Connie was hoping for—that all her other female classmates are—yep, you guessed it—wearing skirts instead. Sticking out like the proverbial sore thumb and feeling angry and hurt, Joyce cuts class.

Down at the local coffee shop, our harried heroine subsequently meets an inquisitive counter clerk named Mike Landers (genre fixture Brett Halsey, who was here billed with his first name shortened to "Bret"), who doesn't approve of (quote) "those other girls", who travel in packs and prey on those vulnerable lost lambs who have strayed off from the rest of the flock. A young adult electronic engineering student, Mike—an optimist who frequently uses upbeat adjectives like "swell"—is an orphan trying to make his way in the world by working at odd jobs to put himself through night school.

The Martins, Joyce's parents (Don Shelton and Viola Harris), are the typical "ideal" Middle American couple: dad, a lawyer, is the terminally overworked business-suit with no time to spare for his daughter other than to nag at her about her "improper" dress sense ("Those tight sweaters, and too much lipstick!"). When he catches her bobbing innocently—if to him indecently—about the house clad in only her slip, even though all the parts of her that shouldn't be showing *aren't*, Dad actually goes so far as to slap Joyce's face (hmmm, might there be some discreetly implied underlying incestuous tension going on here, perhaps?). In backlash, giving him a more figurative slap in the face in return, she later openly rebels against his imposed curfew. Mom, on the other hand, is more sympathetic to their sole progeny's pubescent plight…to a point, anyway. Trying to talk to her dad is like banging her head against a brick wall; while her mom's always too busy at her Bridge club to take much of an active role in their daughter's upbringing. Rather than raise her, they seem much more intent on simply keeping her down.

At the spooky abandoned movie cinema which serves as the gang's secret hideout, hopeful would-be inductee Joyce meets with the Hellcats to begin her initiation. "What a hellcat she's gonna make," spits Dolly with the utmost sarcasm regarding the newbie in their midst. Her social life and popularity depend on her being accepted as a member of this "elite" clique. However, Joyce quickly learns that there are a lot of *rules* to breaking the rules. And as for education? *Fuggettaboutit, square!* Average mark for a Hellcat is: why, straight *D's*, of course! ("We don't like eggheads…we don't like show-offs, and we don't like teacher's pets!"). She also better not dare hand in her homework completed nor on schedule either, or else face the consequences. Before long, the inevitable question arises: "Did you ever *steal*?" (i.e., "five-finger discount" jewellery).

During her initiatory interrogation, like seasoned alkies, her potential future gang-mates tipple liquor from bottles wrapped in brown paper bags.

Needless to say, straight-laced teetotaller Mike (whose portrayer Halsey typically played far-less-upstanding individuals than this during his JD phase; for instance, his socially irresponsible joyriding road-hog in William J. Hole, Jr.'s **SPEED CRAZY** [1959], another AA release likewise co-starring Ms. Lime) doesn't approve of the company Joyce has been keeping of late one bit. He blames—albeit not in as many words—her dysfunctional home life and poor communication with her folks for her need to look elsewhere (i.e., at her "Home away from home") for familial fulfillment. "You're beginning to sound exactly like my father!" exclaims Joyce later on after being preached at for the umpteenth time by the squeaky-clean Mike, who's so straightedge he's only about one corner shy of turning into Squaresville on a one-way ticket.

For the final part of her initiation, Joyce is ordered to "steal" a smirky-faced cool cat named Rip (Martin Braddock) from his steady girlfriend (rip Rip from both her arms and her heart, so to speak; albeit purely to satisfy a random whim of Connie's). To this end, Joyce invites him to a swinging wingding *sans* his steady ball-and-chain. Having achieved her (i.e., Connie's) objective by breaking the other couple up, Joyce passes her final test with flying colors…and they ain't various shades of pink! Our new novitiate having now been welcomed aboard as a full-fledged, card-carrying Hellcat, she seems a likely prospect to usurp the #2 spot in the pecking order currently jealously occupied by homely fellow hellion Dolly (if indeed beauty really does only run skin deep, poor Dolly's ran off and left her completely in the lurch!).

As per usual for this kind of "cautionary" tale, R'n'R music (albeit of only the pseudo kind) serves a purely peripheral function here. While the kids all listen to blaring rock 'n' roll records, Joyce only *pretends* to drink at a hard-boozin' house party (they break into the premises while the homeowners are away). When the lights go out, the big make-out session starts. However, the festivities come to an abrupt end when the tanked-up Connie unintentionally poops the party by "accidentally" falling to her death down the basement stairs, breaking her neck. Fearing parental/legal reprisals, the partiers conspire to hush-up the incident (an accident…or *not*?). Feeling the need to unburden her conscience about Connie's premature demise, Joyce very nearly spills the beans to the sensible Mike, who in an unrelated incident subsequently gets roughed-up by hot-rodders Rip and Freddy. "Alright, you punks, I'm taking you to the cops!" announces Mike after singlehandedly roughing them up worse and informally placing them under citizen's arrest.

Thanks to staunch role model (quote: "nice boy") Mike's persistent positive influence, Joyce ultimately promises to quit the 'Cats for keeps. However, of a distinctly different idea, the dotty Dolly (overplayed shrilly by Suzanne Sydney) lures the now joyful Joyce to the gang's old movie-house HQ, where she confesses the truth about the much-too-early late Connie's demise (not that we hadn't guessed as much already): It was Dolly herself who had caused their ex-leader's fatal fall. (*GASP!* Who knew?! Only everybody in the movie theater except for those smooching love-birds up there in the back row of the balcony who were understandably too busy to follow the plot.) Whilst attempting to stick

Joyce with her switchblade, the now completely hysterical—not to mention hysterically histrionic—Dolly falls to her own death over the theater balcony into the cheap seats. How's that for an ideal combination of just desserts and poetic justice?

So typical of the genre, many of the so-called "teens" here look more like 20-somethings (perhaps because they've been held back a few too many grades due to all those crappy marks?). Further symbolically underscoring their disdain for higher learning, smart-mouthed co-eds chuck books around the classroom.

HIGH SCHOOL HELLCATS (1958) is laden with JD thrills to spare; so be there or be square!

1958, USA. D: EDWARD L. BERNDS
AVAILABLE FROM M.G.M.

GIRLS ON THE LOOSE

Explosive dialogue: *"It's like playin' around with an H-bomb!"*

Again for Universal-International Pictures, director Paul Henreid also made **LIVE FAST, DIE YOUNG** (1958) that same year. Cast against her usual type, lead *femme fatale* Mara Corday—a mature woman by now, well into her twenties here—is better-known for playing wholesome if smolderingly sultry heroines in two prototypical/seminal "big bug" monster flicks of the time: namely Jack Arnold's **TARANTULA!** (1955) and Edward Ludwig's **THE BLACK SCORPION** (1957).

In Jamestown, a gang of masked, trench-coated armed robbers pull a $200,000 payroll stick-up at a bank. Upon thereafter removing their rubber "man-face" masks, the culprits are revealed to actually be—*GASP!*—young women in disguise. Having buried their swag-bag nearby for safekeeping, the girl gang—led by Vera Parkinson ('50s brunette glamor-puss Corday)—plan to let the loot lie in order for the heat to cool off for a two-year period before returning to reclaim it from its hiding place, then enjoy the avails of their ill-gotten gains with impunity...or so they hope. The robbery claimed more than merely monetary victims, as a security guard assaulted during its commission is left in a coma as a result. Lt. Bill Hanley (Mark Richman, who later became known as Peter Mark Richman [star of Gerd Oswald's cheapo 007 clone **AGENT FOR H.A.R.M.** [1966]) is the cop on the case of the missing 200-Gs.

Untrue to her name, Corday as Vera (meaning "truth") is an immoral hellcat who puts the blocks to the grocery delivery boy and rules her chicken coop with an iron hand (forget the velvet glove!). When a jittery fellow gang deb jeopardizes their schemes, Vera ("Thinking takes brains; just forget you've got them") causes the girl's "suicide" by gassing her. Not averse to contributing to the moral decline of her own kid sister Helen (Barbara Bostock), who is a fledgling nightclub chanteuse, Vera buys her a slinky, "skimpy" sequined evening gown to help liven-up her act. "Oh, I *can't* wear *this*," says Helen with great mock modesty. "I'd be thrown in jail for *indecent exposure!*" She performs barely competent, piano-driven lounge jazz: so don't expect any hot rock 'n' roll sounds here to blame the title chicks' immorality and sociopathic behavior on. Heard caterwauling on a pair of maudlin ditties (namely "I Was A Little Too Lonely" and "How Do You learn To Love?" [*GAG!*]), Bostock's vocals are truly horrendous to endure: even Mamie Van Doren could sing Babs under the table with her lips sewn shut—and that's saying something! Bostock's barefoot dancing to honky-tonk blues isn't much better, and the piano sounds out-of-tune to boot. Her severe lack of vocal talent leads us (i.e., me) to conjecture: for all her onscreen girl-next-door wholesomeness, might Babs perhaps have earned the part here by using her mouth for something other than merely "singing" with (note quotes)? After baby sis Helen begins to fall for the handsome young—if older than her—police lieutenant, her senior sibling Vera tries her best (i.e., worst) to keep them from forming a lasting pair-bond.

Described as someone who does too much "drinkin' an' thinkin'", although much more of the former than the latter, second-billed Lita Milan plays the not-so-sweet Marie, whose various social problems include heavy alcoholism and kleptomania, featuring "impulse buying" via the "five-finger discount" method ("My mother always said that shoplifting is one of the most *artistic* branches of crime"). In one scene she combines both those uncontrollable compulsions when she fills her pockets with mickeys of booze. While trying to pick flatfoot Richman's own pocket, Milan as Marie says to him, "You know, if it weren't for your *ears*, I would've sworn you were Frank Sinatra. I'm *CRAZY* about Frankie!" (And by the way, just for the record, Richman bears virtually *no* resemblance whatsoever to Ol' Blue Eyes other than for having his facial features arranged in roughly the same positions as his infinitely more famous "lookalike".)

Another of Vera's and Marie's fellow bad gals, Joyce (Abby Dalton, who had the year previous been seen in Roger Corman's **CARNIVAL ROCK** [1957]) runs her own massage parlor; although if this establishment *is* of the disreputable "rub 'n' tug" variety, the script greatly downplays the fact. However, purely in the interests of injecting some cheeze-sleaze, in the closest the film ever gets to a lesbian scene Dalton as Joyce does treat Milan as Marie to a relaxing "platonic" backrub. In another scene which is quite sexy in its own pointless way, for no apparent reason other than to up the cheesecake quotient, while dressed only in a bedsheet Milan licks her lips...*a lot*. Although, that said, any erotic content—this being a mainstream Universal picture and all, rather than more daring AIP (American International Pictures) or AA (Allied Artists) product—is very implicit indeed. As per usual, potential innuendo is conveyed by ambiguous dialogue, including Corday's exclamation "His name was *DICK*, and I was really gone on him!" (Hmmm, might that have been a double *entendre* or not? We wonder. Sometimes it's hard to tell.) In another example of potentially loaded dialogue, in regard to one of our title loose girls, someone who knows her says, "She's a normal, healthy girl who takes her *fun* where she finds it." Exactly what kind of "fun" is not specified, although the implication is obvious enough. In the classic exploitation way, screenwriters allow the dirty minds of we the viewers to read between the lines and fill in the blanks as we see fit (which is always fun to do!). And such big blanks as we draw here allow for a lot of wiggle-room in the imagination department!

Predicted miles in advance, one of the girl gang—namely Joyce—gets the idea in her pretty little head to filch all the swag for herself (a standard plot device used in innumerable gangster movies and westerns the world over). To this end she begins whittling down the opposition, beginning with Helen, who winds up in a coma after being knocked off a cliff by a car. When Marie thereafter demands her cut prematurely, she gets it...right in the back from Joyce's king-size penknife. When the expected confrontation between Joyce and Vera comes in the last act (**SPOILER ALERT!**), they fight, Vera is killed by Joyce, who then expires herself from her own injuries.

As befitting its title, **GIRLS ON THE LOOSE** (1958)'s dialogue brims with snarky cattiness and female tough-talk (e.g., "I'll ram these scissors right through you, you sick, ugly slob!" and the equally memorable, "Someday I'm gonna twist your spine till it *snaps*!"). All in all, though, this mostly amounts to pretty heavy-going stuff, and is recommended only for diehard JD enthusiasts who like their thrills cheap and easy, but none-too-sleazy.

1958, USA. D: PAUL HENREID
AVAILABLE FROM VIDEO BEAT

HIGH SCHOOL CAESAR

Title theme lyrics: *"High school Caesar / You know you ain't got a friend / And you're playin' a game / That you never can win / High school Caesar / You're gonna get it in the end!"* – *"You got the teachers on the run / The principal just bought a gun / But if he starts to mess around / Caesar's gang will have ta put him down!"*

One of the *very best* of the numerous **REBEL WITHOUT A CAUSE** (1955)-styled JD movies ever to emerge from the B leagues! Even if star John Ashley is generally better-known to many for his appearances in a series of cheap '60s Filipino horror movies, especially the *Blood Island* series[3], **HIGH SCHOOL CAESAR** (1960)—produced two years subsequent to his '50s horror camp classic **FRANKENSTEIN'S DAUGHTER** (1958)[4]—amounts to perhaps his most iconic role, in which he gives one of his most charismatic, self-assured and memorable performances of all.

Accompanied by the excellent no-frills and super-tough opening theme (written by John Neel and Oscar Nichols and sung by Ray Note recording artist Reggie Perkins), producer-director O'Dale

[3] See *Monster!* #5 (pp.57-64) and #6 (p.21)
[4] See *M!* #3, p.3

Ireland's credit is stylishly superimposed over the bloodied face of a youth in the process of being roughed-up and robbed by Ashley's leather-jacketed brat pack; this for refusing to buy into Caesar's on-campus "protection racket".

Mat Stevens (Ashley) and his preppie opponent Kelly Roberts (Lowell Brown) are both running in opposition for the prestigious position of Wilson High's student body president; an election for which Mat isn't above using strong-arm tactics—or any other means, be they fair or foul, for that matter—to ensure that he wins (like the song says, *"He's the cat that wants to rule / The biggest gangster in our school"*). To this end, his cronies rig the ballot, and Mat's victory seems certain.

As the way-too-overambitious Mat (that's with only a single t), who's out to make a dishonest buck every which way that he can at anybody's and everybody's expense, Ashley (*"He's so cool he's like a freezer / That's why we call him high school Caesar!"*) promises his teenage "constituents" a teen dance every Friday night which will only set them back 25 cents apiece ("Cokes for everybody!" he hucks). Math-master Mat sells correctly completed test papers in any subject for $10 a pop, and woe betide those who don't cough up the owed lucre on time. Despite his rough and rowdy ways at school however, at home Mat—where he is known more formally in the long-form of his Christian name as "Matthew"—maintains an angelic façade perhaps more befitting his Biblical namesake (the original Matthew was one of JC's apostles, in case you heathens don't know). A spoiled rich brat whose parents are always *in absentia*, a butler and maid at his beck and call substitute for actual parental figures; thus providing at least some kind of explanation/justification for his rampant sociopathic behaviour, if by no means any excuse for it.

In keeping with his "respectable" new social station, he trades in his leather jacket for a pristine white cardigan or sports coat. He sports a perfectly-primped D.A. (i.e., "duck's ass" = ducktail haircut) and drives his well-heeled daddy's big-winged Caddy, presumably with a valid license and all the proper insurance coverage. The only correspondence he receives from his parents is regular support cheques, however. Without overstating the obvious, the gritty script capably conveys the impression that Mat's thirst for patriarchal power stems from his nonexistent relationship with his never-present father. He nostalgically keeps his bronzed baby-booties atop his clock-radio, and cries in his pillow for affectionate parental company when dirty money fails to fill the gaping void in his materially full but emotionally barren life.

A massed road-race is proposed. The grand prize: a valuable gold coin once given to Mat by his seldom-seen dad. When Kelly, his political opponent for school prez wins the ballot, sour grapes sore loser Mat later runs the rightfully-elected winner's car off the road, causing its driver's death. Now a full-fledged murderer as well as a racketeer, Mat begins stepping-up his criminal campaign. However, wholesome hero Bob (Steve Stevens) helps organize the law-abiding students against the criminal kingpin in their midst. Mat and his cohort Cricket kidnap Wilson High student Wanda Anderson (Judy Nugent) and attempt to rape her. When she learns that Mat is the person responsible for Kelly's death, Wanda spills the beans, backed-up by Cricket's testimony. (**SPOILER ALERT!***) Having gathered at their hang-out "The Wagon" supposedly for the purpose of celebrating Mat's birthday, the kids—including his own gang members, The Bulldogs—all turn their backs on him *en masse* as if to deny his very existence (the old "Get thee behind me, Satan!" response). As a consequence of being collectively spurned by his peers, he begs for help and forgiveness for all his transgressions against them.

With a rousing start and a powerfully poignant finish, (**SPOILER ALERT!***) the film ends with Ashley as Mat reduced from big man on campus to a scared little boy, down on his knees weeping in the dirt and calling out for his father, who is, as-per-usual, nowhere to be seen. What do you think the moral message of all this is? That what goes around comes around, is what: so words to the wise. (As the theme lyrics told us right at the outset of the film, *"High school Caesar / You're gonna get it in THE END!"*)

<u>NOTES:</u> The wicked Reggie Perkins title track (music and lyrics by John Neel and Oscar Nichols) is up on YouTube for those who wanna give it a listen (*https://www.youtube.com/watch?t=2&v=p9zfQZx_J3w*). Originally released on the Ray Note label (#9), "High School Caesar" was backed with Perkins' lesser if still passably catchy tune "Date Bait Baby", the theme song of yet another JD'er, same director O'Dale Ireland's **DATE BAIT** (1960). While in **CAESAR** the school sock-hop "rocks" to lethargic bop 'n' stroll, the soundtrack also includes a great rockabilly track performed by Reggie Olson, entitled "Lookin' Waitin' Searchin' Hopin'", as well as Johnny Faire singing "I Fell for Your Line, Baby" (both on the Surf Records label). Also on Surf if not heard in the film, Faire cut both the classic, much-covered r-billy rave-up "Bertha Lou" (#5019) and "Betcha I Getcha" (#5024); that former title was memorably covered in the '80s by supreme garage trash r'n'r stylists Tav Falco's Panther Burns. Sound unheard, merely from the name of that latter Faire tune, you just know it's gotta be a real humdinger. On a related note, main theme singer Perkins also recorded "Saturday Night Party" on Gem Records (#1201). And lest we forget (not likely, Daddy-o!), John Ashley—who was a cool cat both on-screen and off it—himself recorded a number of decent '50s 'billy tunes; including such catchy cuts as "Born To Rock", "Hit and Run Lover", the Bo Diddley-esque "Mean Mean Woman" and the immortally-titled "Pickin' On the Wrong Chicken" (on Dot Records), all boasting his polished vocal stylings, which emulated Elvis without trying to be a slavish imitation (Ashley didn't quite have the range for that). Dressed as a beatnik, Ashley even got to perform with the great The Blue Caps (Gene Vincent's back-up band) in Lew Landers' **HOT ROD GANG** (1958), which also featured Vincent as well as Eddie Cochran. Most if not all the songs mentioned here are uploaded to YT, so by all means get surfin' on there and give 'em a spin! For those teeming millions out there who don't know what rockabilly was and is, it is and was that good old rock 'n' roll shite, rendered in its purest and most undiluted form (i.e., a revved-up combination of dirty-ass black blues and honky hick hillbilly). Okay, entry-level American roots music lesson over. Let's ditch this scene, cats.

1960, USA. D: O'DALE IRELAND
AVAILABLE FROM IMAGE ENTERTAINMENT

THE BOOKSHELF

WOOF!
Dog Eat Cinema Magazine #2
by Hans Minke & others
Cover price €6

Some days you feel like reading an entire reference book on the films you love and enjoy, while other days you just want something quick, to the point and entertaining. No deep thinking required; just good old fashioned sleaze to put a smile on your face and a tent in your pantaloons. *WOOF!* #2 is just that kind of 'zine: short and sweet with healthy doses of sleaze and oddball horror and exploitation, to boot. Nothing too complicated or bogged down with extra long, factoid-heavy articles to work your way through here—not that that's a bad thing but when you're looking to get in and out, articles like that tend to require more attention and time. Not so here. With about seven reviews (each taking about one page per), seven columns, one interview and a comic strip, *WOOF!* #2 doesn't stick around long enough to wear out its welcome.

The reviews are interesting, obviously written by knowledgeable fans with an appreciation for genre cinema, and the articles offer decent introductions to more obscure cinema. There's even some love to be had for the VHS collectors. The publication is filled with fantastic illustrations by various artists, many of a more mature, sexual nature, all lending *WOOF!* #2 a real underground feel. One could easily see purchasing a copy of this in an old-school tape rental shop, or off the rack in a hole-in-the-wall bookstore.

If I could offer this publication any constructive criticism, it would be that I felt some of the articles could have offered a *bit* more information on the topics they presented. Obviously with only 14 pages, there's not a ton that can be introduced in a page or so, but articles such as one focusing on Turkish westerns and another on werewolf films from around the world just needed a tad bit more to help introduce the uninitiated to such obscure and spanning subjects. Outside of that, the 'zine was well written, looked great and in my opinion is definitely worth checking out. I'm looking forward to issue #3 and have no doubt *WOOF!* is here to stay.

For those interested, both issues #1 and #2 can be purchased at *OMG-entertainment.nl* for a little over $6 US. Keep in mind this isn't the only magazine out there named *WOOF*, so be sure to use the link I provided and show Mr. Woof and crew your support! Print is back, and with endeavors like *WOOF!*, things are continuing to look up. ~ **Brian Harris**

omg-entertainment.nl/shop/product/woof-2/
woofmagazine@gmail.com

Screamland
Written by Harold Sipe / Illustrated by Hector Casanova
Image
Cover price $16.99

Imagine being an outcast all your life. Living on the outer rim of society. An outsider always looking in. Everyone counts you out because of your fucked-up appearance, or your cumbersome quirks, or whatever the revolting case may be. You are awkward. The rest of the "normal" world has branded you, rejected you, criticized and condemned you. You don't fit in. You're a leftover piece from the wrong puzzle. You're a grotesque monster. Quite fucking literally. You are the Frankenstein monster, or the Wolfman, and the neighborly knocks or your door are accompanied by torches and pitchforks, and the screams of peasants *not* asking for brown sugar but looking to decorate their fiefdom with the organs you've grown quite attached to. And despite those facts, you still have to find a way to fit in. To coexist in a world that wants you dead. But then, as chance would have it, comes the dawn of the silver screen, a silver lining in a cumulonimbus life. So what do *you* do? You slap a smile on that fucked-up mug of yours, and smile that lens-cracking smile for the camera, because you were born to be a fucking star!

And who would have guessed it, that the same people who feared you are now adoring you for bringing that fear into their lives. Your power is no longer in the form of bloodsucking brute force; it now comes from the mere fact that the morbid curiosity you call a face is being seen by millions on movie screens around the world. And the fact that you're undead means you can do this for-fucking-ever! So you sign your name on the dotted line, and get yourself a binding contract that says this agency will own you for the rest of life-withering eternity. Chained by a piece of fucking paper. Then one day, after years of being what you were fucking born to be, some dickbrain fuckwit goes and invents C-G-goddamnmuthafuckincocksuckin-I...and you're pretty much out of work. The legend is over. Pack your bags and go home to whatever shit-hole you crawled out of. What then? What happens when the stars fade, when the once great & feared monster becomes a joke, when the only work you can find comes in the form of Ed Wood casting you in monster pornos all donned in drag?

Screamland in a nutshell about just that. The tale of the Universal Monsters in the age of CGI, and it's a fun fucking hold-on-to-your fallopian-tubes (because nobody else will) ride.

The first trade focuses on:
 - Dracula...the closeted gay vampire, who wants to come out, but his agent

won't let him. He has to continue playing the ladies man despite the fact that in reality he likes the man-ass,
- A Hawaiian-shirt-wearing Frankenstein monster who has pretty much given up, and is just piloting through life on cruise control,
- A fat Wolfman whose image is now about as threatening as a dickless puppy with an ice cream cone, who survives only because of the convention circuit,
- And last but not least, the elusive, thought-to-be-involved-with-9/11 Mummy.

Each has a unique set of issues, and each leads a normal, somewhat boring life, but they all share in the fact that they happen to be monsters. After years of no work to speak of in the movie biz, their sexy agent Andrea finally lands them a chance to return to the box-office big screen. However the director is some punk trust-fund dick-cozy who is so into drugs he makes Smokey McCrackhead look like a nun's pussy-lips. Anyway, aforementioned fuck-stick is pissed off that his big budget video game to movie adaptation isn't big enough to get the glossy overused CGI effects we've all come to wipe our ass with, and is forced to use the real deal…dark gods forbid.

What I loved about this, other than its lightheartedness (and the fact it was fuckin' awesome), is that there was zero explanation. These monsters are inscribed so deeply into our subconscious and our culture that we accept that these legendary beasts exist. They don't need explanation or backstory because we know who they are. Don't get me wrong, you get to see snippets from their pasts in the form of small flashbacks, but not enough to interfere with the plot. For the most part it treats them as has-been stars of yesteryear, and instead focuses on their movie careers, and what they have to do to get by in this cut-throat, dog-eat-every-fuckin'-dog world of show business.

The writing had no business being this god damn good. It's funnier than a cock-eyed chimp in a pope hat riding a jackhammer in the shape of a dick, and god damn was it witty all the way through. It had me hooked from page one like I was a masochistic bluegill sunfish. It takes something we have known our entire lives and serves it up to us on a brand new platter, like the first time you eat sushi off the naked ass of a Twi'Lek. Now for the bad part…

The art…I hated it. It's just not for me. I am a sucker for detail; clean razor-sharp outlines, life-like shading, pristine eye-popping colors, and this just didn't feel like it had any of those. It wasn't a deal-breaker, and in the end made no difference, because the story itself was just fucking whip-cream on tits. As you flip through the pages you come across a cover done by *Chew*'s Rob Guillory, and your heart breaks and crumbles into powder, because you get a glimpse of what could have been. A moment's glance and you know he would have been perfect for this, even though you are fully aware that he's busier than a beaver with an oral fixation sketching out illustrations of Chogs and Cibopaths. I hate bashing art. I really do, because as I have stated many times in the past, I can't draw to save my panties. In fact, if aliens came down this minute and demanded, "Krys if you don't draw something better than a dick on a stick figures face, we are going to rectally-probe the shit out of you, and then go all cow mutilation on your sorry surgically-penetrated ass," (because god knows all aliens are intergalactic proctologists) all I would have to look forward to is an ass full of surgical equipment and then hopefully a quick death. But I know when something isn't to my tastes, and this wasn't my cup of Lady Grey.

Side Note: I really dug the snarky little jabs at CGI. While I'm not one of these soap box preachers protesting it like souls were hanging in the balance, I do prefer real practical FX in my horror movies over piss-poor, overused Computer Generated Images. So yeah, would I tell you to pick this up? Fuck yeah, I would! It's worth the read, worth the own, worth bringing to your grandma's grave instead of clichéd dead-in-a-day flowers. You will burn through its pages like that adorable fuckin' robot from **SHORT CIRCUIT** (1986). It's a fun ride—not gory mind you, so for those who really enjoy fucked-up gory things being looped from panel to panel, this may not be for you. For those who like to laugh, though, and love new spins on old favorites, this shit was made for you. Personally, I can't fuckin' wait to crack open volume 2 (whose art is infinitely better, too). ~ *Krys Caroleo*

NEXT ISSUE!
#8.5 – The 2015 Spooktacular Special!

COMING IN ISSUE #9:
Ghostly Possession Cinema of India
Holmes vs. Mars part 2
The Arthouse Insanity of Calvin Reeder
PollyGrind Revisited
Ed Wood Postmortem
Jean Rollin on VHS
More Bobby Suarez
Tons More Reviews & General Mayhem

Illustration by Megh

Viva la VHS!

The Forgotten Format Returns in This Selection of Excellent Books

by Adam Carl Parker-Edmondston

"Forgotten Format" may be a bit of a misleading title here, I admit. For collectors like myself, the format never really went away, it just became harder to get hold of, with stores around the world ceasing to stock the once-popular way of purchasing movies. DVD took its place, but as a format, VHS had a great run, going from 1976 to 2006. That is a whopping 30 years of tape-related joy. Whizz forward a few years and it seems the medium of showing movies this way is still going strong, being a more collector-based market now. It is odd and refreshingly exciting to think that in a time of instant streaming, collectors are still keeping the format alive and buying hard copies of movies. The heyday of the format was most certainly the '80s, but now in 2015 it could be an even more exciting time for VHS fans. There are numerous fanzines out there (Lunchmeat, Tape Mold, I Kill You Last and Blood Video, to name but a few) based solely around films on this format, music bands making '80s VHS-styled music (Horror Fiend), brand new and reissued VHS movies from specialty distributors (Sub Rosa, Secret Lair, VHShitfest and many, many more), documentaries (**REWIND THIS!** [2013], **ADJUST YOUR TRACKING** [2013] and **VHS FOREVER? PSYCHOTRONIC PEOPLE** [2014]), and books.

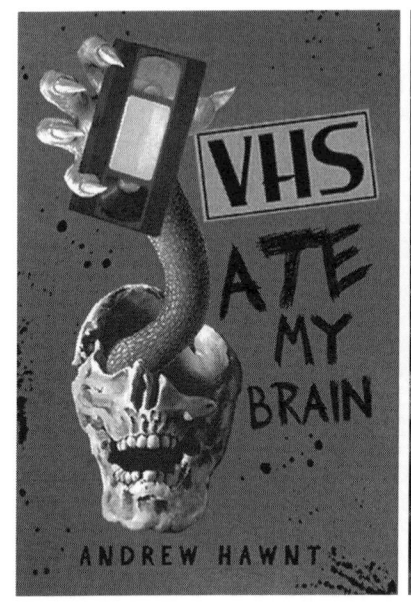

Now, it is the book aspect of the medium that I am looking at in this article. There are tons of books out there reviewing and looking at rare movies, some of which are VHS only. *Cinema Sewer* by Robin Bougie covers a wide variety of flicks, a lot of them focusing on adult cinema. *Rick Tremble's Motion Picture Purgatory* uses an inventive comic book format to review numerous films from all over the place, while you cannot go wrong with Chas Balun's classic *Gore Score* books, which focus on titles that have a bit of red on them. Similar to this you also have *The Official Splatter Movie Guide* by John McCarty, which does exactly what it says on the blood-splattered tin. Books that came out during the VHS era or look at a certain aspect of the culture are varied and vast, too. *Video Hunter's Guide* by Ron Swan, Joel Gunn and various authors helps to give key tapes a value, so collectors can get a rough idea of what to pay for their tapes, while *VHS Ate My Brain* is a look at all aspects of VHS culture, coming straight from the mind of fellow collector Andrew Hawnt. These are both recent releases, but books like *Sci-Fi on Tape* (James O'Neill) and *The Psychotronic Video Guide* (Michael J. Weldon) came out while VHS was still on shelves and are just as fascinating reads. Finally, we have books that focus on the Video Nasties era, when in the UK in the mid-'80s tapes were banned and video shop owners were even arrested for owning tapes the British Government deemed perverted. *See No Evil* by David Kerekes and David Slater looks at the entire sordid affair and breaks it down into key sections, while *Seduction of the Gullible* from *The Dark Side* magazine and written by John Martin takes a look at each film put on the governments banned list. There is even a 2014 graphic novel called *Video Nasty* by Mario Covone and Vasillis Logios. The comic is set in the UK in 1983 where a series of gruesome murders seem to be following some of the Video Nasty plots. A police inspector is sent on the case, while his superiors want the case blamed on the VHS, inspector David Gorely wants the truth. The truth, however, is not what you think. This graphic novel comes in a VHS case with some incredible artwork and postcards, too. For more details check out their Facebook page, and for the rest of the books try Amazon, as most can be bought there.

These are all great reads which give a very interesting and eclectic look at the VHS movies and genre as a whole. But one of the things that always grabs my attention with VHS tapes before I have even seen the shoddy acting, cheesy monsters and awesome synth sounds is, of course, the covers. Here is a gathering of a few key titles I have in my collection which I think will be of interest to fellow VHS collectors or just film fans alike.

Staying with the Video Nasties theme from before, we have a ton of books which showcase the lurid covers of these taboo movies. *The Dark Side* horror magazine has released numerous publications, two of which cover all the films put on the British Board of Film Classifications banning or worry list. *Video Nasties! From Absurd to Zombie Flesh-Eaters – A Collector's Guide to the Most Horrifying Films Ever Banned!* (1998) and *Video Nasties 2 – Banned: A Pictorial Guide to Movies That Bite!* (2001) are both by Alan Bryce, a gentleman who lived through this time of absurdity and has hands-on experience with the banning of video tapes. The first book takes a look at the original 75 titles put on the banned list, spread out over 164 pages. The size of the book is roughly the size of an actual opened-up VHS cover. Within the books glossy pages you get the VHS cover of the film in question, with the front and back both pictured. Then next to it you have a page filled with technical specs for the film (variant titles, cast, running time, etc.) and a short review by Mr. Bryce himself. All the classics you expect to see are here, like **THE EVIL DEAD** (1981), **POSSESSION** (1981), **THE BEAST IN HEAT** (1977) and many more. *Video Nasties 2* looks at some of the other titles which got the authority figures all hot under the collar, and this may be the more interesting book of the two, just because fans of VHS lore will no doubt know the original Nasties movies by heart already. Using the same format as the first book, we get to see such great-sounding titles as **THE AMAZING MR. NO LEGS** (1979)[1], **CATACLYSM** (1980), **MAN OF VIOLENCE** (1971) and **SCREAMTIME** (1986) explode from the page in glorious color. The only downside to these books is the fact their original release was limited edition only, though I believe you can pick them up via the UK Amazon site, but for at least £30.00 (about 45 US dollars). Volume 1 seems to be the hardest to get hold of, but volume 2 is on Amazon.com for around 20 dollars.

Following on from these, we have two other books which cover roughly the same ground in slightly different ways. *The Art of the Nasty* by Nigel Wingrove and Marc Morris (1998) covers all the films mentioned in the *Video Nasties* books, but condenses them into one handy coffee-table volume. The pictures of the VHS are obviously a lot smaller in this book, with some just been bigger than a thumb (and only the front covers are shown), but aside from the Nasties tapes, the book covers numerous other tapes which are of interest. Both authors have a background in adult-orientated movies, so it is no surprise that we get a section showing us some of the sleazy sexploitation movies that came out on tape. This section is of particular interest as a lot of these titles get missed out in documentaries and VHS-styled tomes. Films such as **GIRLS COME FIRST** (1975), **I'M NOT FEELING MYSELF TONIGHT!** (1976), **PUSSY TALK** (1975) and **WHAT SCHOOLGIRLS DON'T TELL** (1973) are just a few of the delights on show here.

Shock! Horror! Astounding Artwork from the Video Nasties Era by Francis Brewster, Harvey Fenton and Marc Morris (of *The Art of the Nasty* fame) was published in 2005 by FAB Press, a publishing company well-known for releasing books on the weird and wacky world of cinema and feature films. This book also covers all the Video Nasties (as you would expect from the title), but again only shows the front covers of the films. They are in a bigger size than *The Art of the Nasty*, though. The book is split into halves: the first focusing on just the cover art of these videos, while the second gives a look at the Video Nasties scare as well as a breakdown of the tapes in question, their rarity, etc. An interesting section at the back gives us a look at some of the alternative covers to some of the more popular titles. Much like Wingrove and Morris' book, this has a selection of titles that are not normally seen, such as **VAMPIRE HAPPENING** (1971), **E.T.N** (1967—the alternative cover for the video **NIGHT FRIGHT**, parodying **E.T. THE EXTRA-TERRESTRIAL** [1982]), **LEONOR** (1975) and **TRACK OF THE MOON BEAST** (1976). Both of these titles can be found on Amazon's US and UK sites (for around 20-30 dollars) and are more accessible than the Alan Bryce *Video Nasties* volumes.

Now, these books all cover just one small (yet important) part of VHS history. But there is so much more to VHS than just the Nasties era. These final books in this review focus on a hodgepodge of cool, bizarre and bonkers VHS covers, because let's face it, that's one of the main things we love about this format: it's variety. *VHS – Absurd, Odd and Ridiculous Relics from the Videotape Era* by Joe Pickett and Nick Prueher (2011) is one such book that focuses on some of the more absurd VHS releases out there. Anyone who has heard of The Found Footage Festival will know exactly what I mean. For those who haven't, you will be in for a treat when you get your peeps on this book. With chapters called "Leotards and Sweat", "Let's Learn", "Cats" and "Unusually Specific", you get a wide array of VHS covers that have to be seen to be believed! For me, these odd titles are a joy to find, but may not be to everyone's tastes. Hardcore horror, science fiction and fantasy collectors are going to find little of interest here, but fans of weird genre flicks or people who just fancy a laugh will get a buzz out of it. Some of my favorite VHS titles from this book are **BUNNETICS – THE BUTTOCKS WORKOUT** (1986), **HOW TO DATE GOD**, **HUNKS WITH HATS** (1993), **CAT ADVENTURE VIDEO** (1997) and **ALL-STAR TOPLESS ARM WRESTLING** (1989)! So if you like the sound of these, then this is the book for you. It can be purchased on the Found Footage Festival website (*foundfootagefest.com*).

Moving to the more traditional VHS rental covers now, we have *Portable Grindhouse – The Lost Art of the VHS Box* by Jacques Boyreau (2009), a book that will grab your attention straight away just because it comes in a slipcover which is actually picture of a blood-stained VHS on it! This book has a very brief introduction and then gets straight into the action. The book is sized once again like a VHS tape (a small-box one) and once again gives us the front and back covers of the tapes (always a bonus for me, as the back art can be just as good as the front). In no order at all, these tapes spring from the page into your face without missing a beat. Though I personally feel there were some odd choices in here (**VANISHING POINT** [1971] and **DICK TRACY** [1990] do not seem to fit in with the bulk of the titles) the rest of the entries more than make up for these slips. There are a ton of titles in here that I have never seen before. **DEATH PROMISE** (1977), **THE UNKNOWN COMEDY SHOW** (1987), **ALIEN MASSACRE** (1996; with a slightly bozz-eyed, gun-sporting woman on the front!), **BEAKS: THE MOVIE** (1987), **NINJA: AMERICAN WARRIOR** (1987) and **MONGREL** (1982) are all titles I desperately need in my collection, and it's all thanks to this book, because without it I would have had no idea they even existed! It can be found on Amazon, but for the quite frankly bonkers price of $56! The UK site has it at £26.00 (about $40 US).

20 Jahre Phantastische Videocover by Andreas Bethmann (1998) roughly translates to "*20 Years Fantastic Videocover*" is a German publication which just focuses on cover art from VHS from the '80s. You can see why I got excited when I found out about this book, right? With a book size slightly bigger than a big-box VHS release, it gives us two VHS covers per page with information about the film's release underneath each movie. As it's all in German, however, so it will be a tad tricky to decipher, but this book's visuals transcend any language barrier its text may have. There are some unique and incredible pieces of art on show here; some are variations on well-known movies (such as **MANIAC** [1980]), while others are movies I have never heard of! Sometimes it's tricky to tell if the movie is one I am actually familiar with because of the lack of text, but in most key features pop up in the art to let you know. Films such as **DAS TIER** (a.k.a. **THE ANIMAL**, 1982), **DIE GRUFT DER DAMONEN** (a.k.a. **THE CRYPT SLAYER**, 1982) and **AMPUTIERT** (a.k.a. **AMPUTATED**, 1983) have absolutely incredible covers—lord knows what the films are like, but man the covers are great. The German VHS art is very much in the vein of a lot of the low-budget flicks from the UK and US: cheesy and poorly drawn, with tons of exploitation aspects…and all very, very alluring because of it all. You will probably not be able to see some of these covers anywhere else other than here, so if you get chance I recommend checking this one out for sure. It seems to be on the German Amazon site, but I got mine of Ebay for $10 US so maybe check there too.

Finally, we come to the last book on this list, but certainly not least: Tom "The Dude" Hodge's book *VHS Video Cover Art* (2015). As well as being a stunning cover artist for movies such as **HOBO WITH A SHOTGUN** (2011) and **WOLF COP** (2014), he is also an avid VHS collector and has put together a collection of some of his own favorites from his vast collection. The cover looks amazing and has been drawn by Tom himself, and has him in '80s neon glory as VHS tapes fly all around him. As this is my field of collecting, I could not help myself when it came to checking to see which films I had of his in my own collection! Now, the book has only just become available and I have not yet obtained a copy, so I cannot give an in-depth review of it at this time, sadly. What I can see from photos online is that it is a smaller-sized volume, with I would imagine two VHS covers per page. Some of the tapes on show are great, though. Tom is a big fan of the painted-cover VHS art and we get some prime examples of various different types of work here, with titles like **LUST FOR FREEDOM** (1987), **WAR BUS** (1986), **THE BLACK COBRA** (1987), **SPOOKIES** (1986), **THE VIDEO DEAD** (1987) and **CELLAR DWELLER** (1988) all making an appearance, possibly for the first time. This is what I find exciting about this book, that it covers VHS from the UK, which have a different style than the US counterparts, some being quite epic pieces of art in their own right. This book can be found on Amazon and for people who want a glimpse into the world of UK or if you are in the UK and want to compare (like I have been doing) then this could be the title for you. With the popularity of VHS-related memorabilia seeming to grow each year, I doubt very much that this will be the last book brought out on the subject…heck, I feel inspired to whip out some from my own collection and bang them into print form! As a fan of movies, art and VHS I am hoping to see many more of these in the near future, so I very proudly shout from the rooftops with high hopes for the future, "*Viva la VHS!*"

---

1 See Michael Hauss' review on p.178

In Their Own Words:
Stars of the Golden Age of Porn tell it like it was

Book reviews by Louis Paul

What years are considered those of the Golden Age of Porn? I find it is debatable, but a safe answer would be 1972-1984. While some fine titles were released afterwards, it seems the best of the best movies in the genre seem to come from the above cited years. It has been well-documented that Porn's "Golden Age" began with the release of **DEEP THROAT** *in (1972), and subsequently,* **BEHIND THE GREEN DOOR** *(1972) and* **THE DEVIL IN MISS JONES** *(1973).*

After being kept behind locked doors and in bedrooms for much of mainstream America, sex was now out in the open. Charged by changing morals and the sexual freedoms that came along with the late 'Sixties counter culture changes and sexual revolution, sex was now on the big screen…even if it was not entirely legal in the early days.

Numerous police busts, trials and challenges within the Supreme Court really thrust the makers and actors of Golden Age porn films into the media spotlight and into daily headlines. Some were even threatened with jail time (and a few were imprisoned for various, albeit brief, times).

One particularly early Supreme Court ruling, *Miller vs. California*, cited that porno films lacked "Serious literary, artistic, political, or scientific value." Essentially, this led to a ban (overturned later in the courts) wherein local community police authorities claimed that the seizing of pornography (and in some cases, the destruction of both film and negatives) were protecting the local and legal standards, which were being upheld by such actions.

Fortunately, the earliest titles proved to be popular at the box-office, and the talent onscreen quickly garnered a following of fans. Even some Hollywood heavyweights gave support by appearing in the courtrooms when some of the more notorious trials took place (as in the case of actor Harry Reems, and others).

In time, pornography became unstoppable, and the '73 Supreme Court verdict was overturned, and literally hundreds (thousands, if you also include the many loops[1]) were made.

Why are the Golden Age movies considered the best of the pornographic motion pictures? For a variety of reasons. Some of the filmmakers came from various backgrounds (artists, writers, moonlighting Hollywood cameramen, sound people, and in some cases… directors, the latter three of course used pseudonyms so as not to jeopardize their "day jobs"). The people in front of the camera were (and frankly, had to be) uninhibited in their activities onscreen. Everything was laid bare, from emotions to in-your-face gynecological close-ups (and in some cases more than that with the very few titles released in 3D!). Suddenly, legs spread bare to reveal large moist wet female cavities that the men inserted their large penises into, and more. Well, to be frank, we are talking about theatrical distribution here, and that's what it was like to see these movies in theaters back in the day…on big screens. There's a percentage of people who are used to watching porn on their computers, laptops and handheld devices today that have never experienced what it was like viewing these movies in theaters. Let me tell you, it was nearly indescribable…and if you never have, you really missed something in the annals of cinema history.

Not every Golden Age title was a perfect form of this cinematic genre—far from it. But most of them, in their own way, succeeded in entertaining, and the best of them were more than pure stroke fodder for guys and gals.

True, some of the titles from the Golden Age were all that and more. Whether it was the subject matter, or the execution, or the unbridled passionate sex onscreen (well, the best of it, anyway), some of these titles have good reason to be remembered. Firstly, there's Gerard Damiano's **THE DEVIL IN MISS JONES**, wherein Georgina Spelvin (in a marvelous, uninhibited acting debut) plays a depressed, lonely spinster who attempts suicide only to make a deal with the devil to experience everything she denied herself and her libido (and a film he remade in sorts with **MEMORIES WITHIN MISS AGGIE** [1974]) with Deborah Ashira. Then there's Anthony Spinelli's **SEX WORLD** (1978), which remains a class act all the way. Going many steps further than Michael Crichton's science fiction movie **WESTWORLD** (1973), where our protagonists pay hefty sums of money to experience adventure and excitement in a world populated by robots overseen by zealous scientists, **SEX WORLD** takes a tour bus load of couples and singles to a place where they all get to ex-

---

1 The term *loop*, *loops*, or *porno loop* refers to short movies (originally shot on 8mm and Super 8mm, and later on 16mm film). Usually silent in the early days, these films had very brief running times (six minutes seemed to be an average length, but some were longer, a few shorter). Although the heyday for hardcore pornographic loops was in the late 1960s through the early 1980s, the form had existed for much longer, as far back as the earliest days of moving picture photography via privately filmed and traded shorts (obviously in black and white). Sexy footage of brief burlesque bits, and mini nudie shorts (usually filmed in a nudist colony) were also earlier forms of what later became the porno loops. It is interesting to note that some of the popular actors and actresses of the Golden Age who garnered audience popularity also started out in loops, and sometimes enterprising producers collected these short films and dubbed in sound (and, in some hilarious cases, used title cards instead) to cash in such popularity and release the combined footage into theaters as a new movie. Later loops did contain sound, but that didn't mean they were any better.

perience a libidinous overload, presumably with the aid of androids. Featuring an all-star cast of Golden Age actors like Kay Parker, Leslie Bovee, Sharon Thorpe, Desiree West, Annette Haven, Amber Hunt, and John Leslie, the film is buoyed by director Spinelli's deft directorial hand. Known as an actor's director within the genre who took time to craft the sultry sex onscreen as well as the characters they were playing and the situations they were in, nearly all of the films Spinelli directed in the Golden Age portion of his career (1971-1984) are above average. Some of them, such as **EASY** (1978), **NOTHING TO HIDE** (1981) and **TALK DIRTY TO ME** (1980), are considered classics of the genre today, and feature outstanding sex scenes…and plots. Not coincidentally, all three films also star or co-star Richard Pacheco. Which leads me to provide you with a list of what I think were the best actors who worked in porn's Golden Age: Pacheco, John Leslie, Jamie Gillis, Joey Silvera, Paul Thomas and Eric Edwards for the men. Georgina Spelvin, Kay Parker, Marilyn Chambers, Jennifer Welles, and Annette Haven for the ladies. Of course, tastes and opinions differ and vary as to personal favorites but I would be remiss to not list John Holmes, who I consider a naturalistic, if uneven actor (and although vilified by some for his acting, there's no denying his screen presence made more so with his extra-large long and thick 13-inch cock). Of all the men that appeared in the genre, John Holmes is the one name most synonymous with it. Having appeared in a well-documented hundreds (some say due to his appearances in numerous loops… thousands) of sex films, his rise to cult stardom when the Golden Age output was still shown in theaters is legendary. His fall is also well-documented, with a decline due to drug abuse, and a run-in with crime figures that saw him involved in a Manson-like massacre that led to him to prison and a further decline until he died of AIDS.

The Golden Age of Porn died out with the arrival of AIDS, and the ascent of the videocassette. In time, the theaters were phased out and/or closed due to lower attendance, and the productions became cheaper and shot on video. Some actors and actresses retired early, while others held on for a few more years.

Porn is of course everywhere today, as it was then. It's just more accessible via the methods I've noted earlier. Most of what you see is cheaply made, digitally shot quickies of a running time around 25 minutes at most. Longer, shot-on-film or -video titles still seem to be made in Europe, mostly Italy, France and some of the Baltic countries, but as an art form…we at least have the Golden Age titles to watch and re-watch as entertainment.

In recent years, there's been renewed interest in the Golden Age of Porn with some of its finest performers writing autobiographies, laying their souls bare in ways their "acting" performances could not. In addition there is also a highly recommended web site called The Rialto Report (*therialtoreport.com*) which highlights rare podcast interviews, and insightful articles.

I have been busy in recent months reading a number of books written by and about performers of the Golden Age of Porn and I wanted to share my thoughts with you.

The Devil Made Me Do It: A Memoir by Georgina Spelvin – Erotic Icon of the Seventies
by Georgina Spelvin
2008; Little Red Hen Books; 302 pp.

Georgina Spelvin is the stage name of Michelle Graham or Shelley Abels…or a dozen other names that she mentions from time to time in a game of "guess I want to keep my personal life private…sort of". One of the best actresses in the genre, besides her starring role in **THE DEVIL IN MISS JONES**, she can be seen in **SEX RITUALS OF THE OCCULT** (a.k.a. **HIGH PRIESTESS OF SEXUAL WITCHCRAFT**, 1973), **SLEEPY HEAD** (1973),

WET RAINBOW (1974), **THE PRIVATE AFTERNOONS OF PAMELA MANN** (1974), **3AM** (1975), **DESIRES WITHIN YOUNG GIRLS** (1977), **THE JADE PUSSYCAT** (1977), **EASY**, **TAKE-OFF**, **THE ECSTASY GIRLS** and **THE EROTIC ADVENTURES OF CANDY** (all 1978), **FOR RICHER, FOR POORER** (1979), **THE SEVEN SEDUCTIONS OF MADAME LAU** and **THE DANCERS** (both 1981), among other titles.

Georgina the name, according to our author, is a traditional theatrical pseudonym used by an actress who would want to remain anonymous. George Spelvin would be used by a male. Regardless, we all know her as Georgina, so let's refer to her as such. We all know Georgina as the original MILF. She owns that title hands down. As the suicidal Justine Jones in director Gerard Damiano's classic film **THE DEVIL IN MISS JONES**, she pulled something from herself very few actresses have managed to do. She embodied the role, which in a way mirrored that of the character she was playing. You believed Georgina *was* Justine. A frigid spinster ending her life who gets another chance (via the director in a cameo as the Devil) to experience unbridled lust and passion as never before. Georgina appeared in this movie along with Harry Reems and Marc Stevens (both in small roles), and delivered the goods, whether performing oral (a very interesting deep throat performance here), and whatever else the story requested, including a delirious three-way with an intense, emotional anal sequence.

In her book, Georgina writes little about appearing in a small role in **HIGH PRIESTESS OF SEXUAL WITCHCRAFT** alongside Marc Stevens (a handsome, long-haired actor who, like John Holmes, was well-endowed)—who became her friend in real life—and spends a good portion of the book introducing us to The Pickle Factory, a commune of artists and filmmakers who lived in a loft in New York City. Everyone at the Pickle Factory lived and worked together; the working part was the toughest, and according to Georgina, it was not as often as they hoped.

When they worked on documentaries for PBS as technicians (usually editing) the cash flowed, but not as much as they hoped. Otherwise, when the cash was low, things became dire. It was at this time that Georgina accepted small roles in films to make money. According to her, she didn't really know what was expected of her with **THE DEVIL IN MISS JONES**. She went to apply as a cook for the film crew (the shoot was expected to take one week, maybe longer), and then director Damiano asked her to read for a role…and it was the lead. Georgina was handed money for her own wardrobe and she shopped on New York's Lower East Side for the clothes, as what the prop person had was just underwhelming, and getting into the part was for her tantamount to becoming the star she always wanted to be.

Georgina was no stranger to the arts. She had been a child dancer, but her dreams of becoming a ballet star just didn't work out for her, so she eventually became a dancer in summer stock, Off Broadway, and Broadway shows. Her acting chops sharpened when she graduated to becoming the understudy for some of the bigger shows' leading ladies, and when the show would tour Middle America she had the leading role. After a succession of relationships and no passes at stardom, Georgina found herself vehemently against the Vietnam War and embracing the counterculture movement of the late 'Sixties. She was 37 when she appeared in **THE DEVIL IN MISS JONES**, a perfect age for the role, but much older than other actresses in a genre where the average age seemed to be 19-23.

Now that you know a little more about Georgina, let me say that I wished her book would have been more insightful about many of her other film roles (she mentions but two or three more). The bulk of the beginning introduces the reader to the Pickle Factory and Claire, a woman who also worked there, who not only became Georgina's sometime lover, but an actress who also appeared in a few titles (including **DIMJ**). We quickly segue into a quick recap of her stage career, and then we find Georgina deep into the throes of alcoholism and forced to perform cheesy burlesque routines in seedy theaters in towns way past their heyday. In fact, much of the book is devoted to her mother coming to her rescue and plying her with a concoction of cold soup and vodka, which Georgina sips between burlesque routines to keep her going in a decrepit Atlantic City theater that shows X-rated films by day and Georgina live at night.

Claire, Georgina's lover from the Pickle Factory flits in and out of her life and the two travel across the country to a commune on the West Coast, where Georgina briefly finds respite. However, after another few films, and she celebrates by drinking a pint of booze out of a paper bag and finds herself sitting on a curb near Christopher Street in NYC, her old co-star Marc Stevens (barely) recognizes her and signs her into a New York hospital for an emergency detox.

Former loves and friends from Georgina's old theater days (the pre-porno times) also flit in and out of her life, as she details her bouts with alcoholism and joining AA. In later years, Georgina writes about working as a desktop publisher for a Los Angeles-based company, which led to her self-publishing this book. Finding love in her early 'Seventies, the still-sprightly Ms. Spelvin holds great affection for the films she was in—and for fucking in them—and has, it seems, no remorse for appearing in them. I really would like to have read her write more about some of the Golden Age movies and the production of them. It's a quick read, and of course I learned things about Georgina Spelvin that I did not know beforehand, but I really cannot wholeheartedly recommend the book to someone looking for insightful recollections of many of the films she made during porn's heyday, because she just doesn't.

Bright Lights, Lonely Nights – The Memories of Serena, Porn Star Pioneer of The 1970s
by Serena Czarnecki
2015; Bear Manor Media; 382 pp.

If you've read this far then you probably know who Serena is. If you cannot recall her, she's the thin, fiery redheaded with fuck-me eyes known for a number of tantalizing roles in such genre fare as **HONEY PIE** (1975), **HOT HONEY** (1978), **MARILYN AND THE SENATOR** (1978), **BLONDE EMMANUELLE** (1978), **LUST AT FIRST BITE** (1978), **BLONDE IN BLACK SILK** (1979), **800 FANTASY LANE** (1979), **HEAVENLY DESIRES** (1979), **COED FEVER** (1980), **INSATIABLE** (1980), **MAI LIN VS. SERENA** (1980), **OLYMPIC FEVER** (1980), **SEDUCTION OF CINDY** (1980), and **SERENA – AN ADULT FAIRY TALE** (1980).

Serena, like many other adult film actresses started working in the adult film field by first posing nude for men's magazines, then in simulated sex scenes for same, graduating to full hardcore photography. She was a star who shined brightly, but briefly. Her tenure was the mid-1970s through the early 1980s. She has many fans, and has been through a lot. This new autobiography I found an interesting read because, unlike that of fellow Golden Age starlet Georgina Spelvin, Serena manages to pull you in and make you feel that you are with her as these things are taking place.

It's not all a pretty picture painted for onlookers, however. Serena has had a tough life. Self-diagnosed, and then professionally diagnosed with suffering from manic depression, among other things (she was finally diagnosed as bipolar), Serena lays bare everything for the readers. But beyond the lithesome sex bomb of the '70s and '80s, the now 65-year-old Serena proves to be talented as a multimedia artist (painting, and sculpture) and as a poet:

> Words, Words, Words
> From where do they spring?
> Why do they humble so?
> How did they gather in my
> Chest, in my mind.
> When you came so silent in the night.
>
> - Excerpt from "My Muse" by Serena

Painting herself as a "weird teenage hippie chick", Serena was always at odds with the world around her. Coming from suffering a number of mental illnesses that proved to be challenging and a family that tried to understand her, Serena took joy in intimate relationships. Her journey to porn starlet is paved with relationships and friendships made and lost, but (former adult film actor and activist) William Margold appears to be a satellite figure in her life that assisted her in her lifelong journey to be a stable emotional person. Unlike Georgina Spelvin's autobiography, which merely hints at but does not mention at all the numerous or noteworthy films she's appeared in, Serena notes all the highlights, whenever possible, despite suffering a serious accident not too long ago and being in a coma. She regained consciousness, but suffered a hair-raising number of years remembering—sometimes with the aid of others—her past life. In time, she regained over 90% of her memory, the rest filled out with remembrances from colleagues...the rest lost to time.

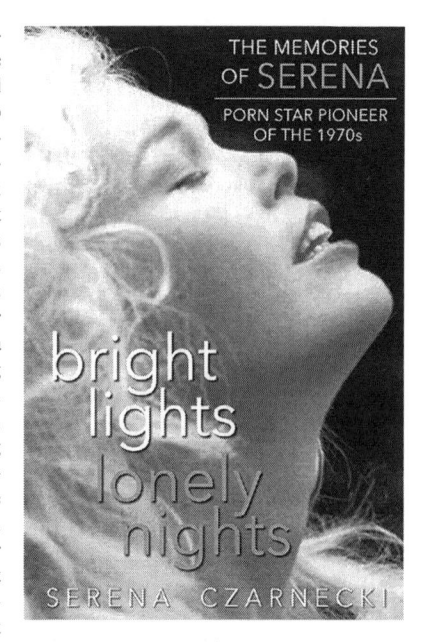

What there is is entertaining but bittersweet, as Serena battled a lifetime with mental illness, but under medical supervision and medication led a healthy, but abnormal, life.

> "You might think I was taken advantage of, but I didn't feel that way. I wanted cock. I wanted it without the problems, hang-ups and bullshit. Just cock. Big, small, thick, thin, what did I care? As long as it was hard, I wanted it inside me."

Amongst her film work, Serena also writes openly of her relationship and life with (fellow adult film star) Jamie Gillis, and how their dominant/submissive relationship was tailored well for the two of them, and how, when they added an additional partner (usually a female on coast-to-coast train trips) how they both managed to sate each other's desires:

> "He was fucking me from behind and I was non-chalantly eating chocolate. In our apartment, he would be fucking me while I was looking out the window talking to strangers on the street. I was in control. I controlled his orgasms and his cock. He was my total slave. I was his slut slave in turn."

Eventually, Serena and Jamie's relationship ended, but she writes often candid remembrances about a number of her co-stars like John Holmes:

> "His tool was so big it was more of a 'sight to see' than a real turn-on honestly. But I loved working with him. I'd be pliable in his hands because I trusted John would place me in that perfect position so that the (camera) lights hit me just so and that the lens saw what it needed to see."

As Serena's film work neared its end, she began a series of burlesque tours that took her to small towns in states like Massachusetts, and even sex clubs on Times Square in NYC:

> "I came out as China Girl to David Bowie's song. I wore an expensive kimono..."

Detailing her memorable two marriages, which were at the very least interesting experiences to read about, the one with her second husband, a voyeur who spent his lifetime earnings and wealth on Serena, takes a few rather unexpected twists and turns that I'll leave unsaid, best to be experienced by anyone who might be interested in reading about Serena and her life. Like Georgina Spelvin, Serena found what appears to be true love late in life, and devotes her time to her art, and to her fans, making public appearances to promote this book, and she seems to be on Facebook often. Finally, the book climaxes with several poems of an erotic nature and quite a few short stories...drawn from her life experiences? Perhaps.

John Holmes – A Life Measured In Inches
by Jennifer Sugar and Jill C. Nelson
2011; Bear Manor Media; 581 pp.

Most likely the definitive tome on the life of the man dubbed "The King", *A Life Measured In Inches* is a thorough, sometimes exhaustive and exhausting journey through the life of John Curtis Holmes and his many ups and downs. Told **RASHÔMON** (1950)-style via the remembrances of the surviving women in his life, and his many co-stars and filmmakers, an interesting portrait of a man with a huge cross to bear appears for all the world to read about.

A relatively quiet and pensive young man with an abnormally large penis, Holmes used this to his advantage once he figured out how his big dick would gain him unlimited and unbridled sex (which apparently he liked quite a lot, especially with smaller petite brunette women—in his own words, his favorite kind of woman and a huge turn-on for him). Struggling to make ends meet with his first wife, the gangly, rail-thin, afro-sporting redheaded Holmes tried his hand at posing in the nude for several magazines. In the late 1960s he was toe-to-toe with (later XXX male rival star) Rick Cassidy (who also did gay porn) in the amount of magazines he appeared in in simulated sexual situations. According to Bill Amerson (later a Holmes confidant, close [and, it appears, only trusted] friend):

> "It was the end of the day and in walked this really skinny kid with somewhat of an afro haircut. He didn't look like the type that we would use.[2] My partner said, 'Go ahead and take a Polaroid of him, anyway. Have him go into the back room, take off his clothes, take a Polaroid and say "Thank you, very much."' We went into the back room, he undressed and turned around. I had a Polaroid (camera) and I said, 'You are going to be star.' That's how I met John."

Holmes appeared in numerous pornographic loops, and with director Bob Chinn (with whom he frequently worked and hung out with, but according to Chinn, Holmes never revealed much of his inner thoughts) he created the "Johnny Wadd" series of films. Johnny Wadd being the big dick-swinging private eye adventurer who manages to screw nearly every female cast member in the movie…and oh yes, manages to find a missing valuable or foil the dastardly plans of the insidious villain of the flick. There are ten official *Johnny Wadd* titles in existence, and all but the last one was directed by Chinn. Several more exist but they either contain footage from other Holmes/Chinn movies, or are dubbed loops padded out to take advantage of the star and the popular character. Of the Holmes/Wadd titles (**JOHNNY WADD** [1970], **FLESH OF THE LOTUS** [1971], **BLONDE IN BLACK LACE** [1971], **TROPIC OF PASSION** [1972], **TELL THEM JOHNNY WADD IS HERE** [1976], **LIQUID LIPS** [1976], **THE JADE PUSSYCAT** and **CHINA CAT** [both 1977], and **BLONDE FIRE** [1978]), the best ones were **JADE PUSSYCAT** and **CHINA CAT**, because they show a clearly relaxed John Holmes easing into the role of a superstar…shortly before his slide downhill.

Authors Sugar and Nelson manage to coalesce an at-times scintillating (and at others, lurid) collection of remembrances into trying to piece together Holmes' life. Briefly touching on Holmes' own (and, most sources claim, fanciful) autobiography (finished by his wife, Laurie, who claimed the result was from numerous audio recordings that he made during the later years of his life), *Porn King: The Autobiography Of John C. Holmes* looks for other source material, even bringing in the policemen and federal agents who busted Holmes also adds more flavor to the story.

Unable to keep up with growing demand of stardom and popularity all because he had a huge cock, Holmes began to do huge amounts of cocaine, and then freebase crack. His addictions became so bad that he first borrowed money, and then stole possessions from friends (and even movie sets) due to his habit. It also affected his sexual performance on film, often leaving his big cock nothing more than a fleshy giant piece of sleeping meat that he would often try to gently shove into the waiting orifices of his female co-stars.

If nothing else, Holmes is universally painted by every single one of his female co-stars who are quoted in this book as being a gentle, patient lover both on- and off-screen. Fully aware of the size of his penis, most of his co-stars were in awe of him and wary to take him orally, vaginally, and in some cases… in the ass. But all praise his careful and patient manner, and most say they enjoyed it.

Some stories come to light that at the height of his screen popularity, Holmes was "servicing" many rich women (and, it is suggested, some men as well) and there are tales of him jetting off to some foreign place to have sex with them. (At the time) mature dancer, singer and actress Juliet Prowse is outed in the book as one of Holmes' rich socialite lovers.

The book takes a mean turn into Manson-like territory as Holmes' drug addictions see him hook up with some definitely sleazy types…both addicts and career criminals. He becomes involved in a scheme to rob a wealthy dealer who he's already befriended and hung out with, but the scene becomes violent and in retribution a bloody massacre takes place. Holmes' involvement in the latter, his refusal to name names, and admitted complicity lands him in prison for a time.

Clearly the most violent mass murder in California's history since the Manson killings, the Wonderland murders (so called because the house where the deed was done was located on Wonderland Avenue in Los Angeles) was a clear stamp on the forehead of Holmes, and upon his release he was dogged everywhere by the authorities, taking with him another petite lover, Dawn Schiller, as he crossed the country performing menial jobs.

Back into porn, he enjoyed a brief career resuscitation when he attempted to clean up from the drugs and alcohol…but he succumbed again. With the threat of AIDS looming, it is said that Holmes may have been infected by an appearance in a one-off film he appeared in that was gay-themed (although claims are made in the book that it was a female fan's ass that he was buggering onscreen). It was said that the money was good, but his health quickly took a turn for the worse, and his physical appearance became cadaver-like. He made two more films, in 1986 in Italy (**THE RISE AND FALL OF THE ROMAN EMPRESS** with Ilona Staller a.k.a. Cicciolina, the Italian porno starlet who later had a political career in office in Italy) and **THE DEVIL IN MR. HOLMES** (with former B-movie queen and *giallo* regular Karin Schubert) before returning to the states and experienced a severe health decline. Claiming to be suffer-

---
2   Amerson at the time was beginning to book "talent" for X-rated films.

ing from colon cancer, the often now-delirious Holmes married his then-companion Laurie Rose, and then was hospitalized shortly afterward.

As he lay in bed in a hospital, Holmes refused to reveal details about his involvement in the Wonderland murders, and died on March 13, 1988.

There are several unofficial and official documentaries on John C. Holmes, a few Hollywood movies (**WONDERLAND** [2003] starring Val Kilmer is one) and there is that Holmes autobiography that I mentioned; but if you really have an interest in what he may have been like in private and the demons that drove him to despair and finally to ruin, then I would recommend this book. Of course there's an alleged 2,500-plus feature films and loops out there as well…for some he will forever be "The King".

Hindsight: True Love & Mischief in the Golden Age of Porn
by Howie Gordon, a.k.a. Richard Pacheco
2013; Bear Manor Media; 684 pp.

Saving the best for last, here is a true surprise in the minor avalanche of books by and about Golden Age veterans. Pacheco (whose real name is Howie Gordon) reveals a surprisingly deft gift for writing, often invoking the spirits of literary giants like Philip Roth, John Updike, Joseph Heller, a splash of Norman Mailer, and oddly enough, the comedic wit of Woody Allen in his prime. Howie (or Richard, if you like) takes us back to his origins, his coming of age, both physically and spiritually, and recounts his days as an actor in hardcore films of the Golden Age. Using a witty style by sometimes ending chapters by discussing what we have read beforehand with an anonymous book agent (who wants him to write less about graphic sex) and God (who wants him to be honest and stay on track), it's like reading a satire of one's life as we go along. Howie knows ultimately that life is one big carnival; it all depends on what ride suits your fancy.

If you are not too familiar with Howie's well-known alter ego Richard Pacheco, here's a small list of some films where he was featured:

THE CANDY STRIPERS (1978), **EASY** (1978), **PIZZA GIRLS** (1979), **CANDY GOES TO HOLLYWOOD** (1979), **HOT LEGS** (1979), **HIGH SCHOOL MEMORIES** (1980), **INSATIABLE** (1980), **TALK DIRTY TO ME** (1980), **THE DANCERS** (1981), **NOTHING TO HIDE** (1981), **THE SEVEN SEDUCTIONS OF MADAME LAU** (1981), **VISTA VALLEY P.T.A.** (1981), **THE SEVEN SEDUCTIONS OF MADAME LAU** (1981), **IRRESISTIBLE** (1983), **UP 'N COMING** (1983), **THE RED GARTER** (1986), and **SENSUAL ESCAPE** (1991).

As played by Howie Gordon via his Pacheco pseudonym (or Dewey Alexander, another of his porn aliases), Pacheco rarely appeared threatening in the Golden Age porn films he made, and rather came across as a collegiate jock type, possibly an intellectual who just happened into the business. But the truth is, Howie came from a good family but was an overweight young boy and teenager who finally found his sexual initiation from his then-girl-of-his-dreams while still a teenager.

Hindsight guides us through his early years, then Howie's embracing of the late 'Sixties counterculture revolution and then joining the west coast-based Dragon's Eye Commune. It was there that he met Carly, who came from another traveling commune, and the two would eventually share a strong bond and eventually marry (many years later, they are still married and have several children).

Appearing in a campus-shot porno loop was Howie's first experience with porn, but he was always trying his hand at acting and joined the San Francisco Bay Area-based Magic Theatre ensemble and was a satellite when the Berkeley Blake Street Hawkeyes were in vogue. This avant-garde theatrical ensemble featured numerous talented actors, including Whoopi Goldberg, who became a lifelong friend (and who contributed the foreword to this book).

Then came a small, but important role in **THE CANDY STRIPERS** in 1978 (where he appeared as McKinley Howard), a film notorious then and today for its often-censored "fisting" scenes. Howie was afraid that he couldn't get an erection on the set, so sought other means to concentrate:

> "I was practicing getting hard-ons in my car as I drove over the Bay Bridge to the soundstage in San Francisco. And as soon as I got it up I'd stop as I didn't want to waste it. I just needed the confidence that I could do it. So, I'm riding along and whenever a truck was gonna pass, I'd cover myself up because they could look down into my car and see what I was doing. But, every now and then, I would miss one and they would

Ah, the life of an actor in the Golden Age. Wouldn't you like to be Howie/Richard? In the loving arms of Leslie Bovee and Serena.

see me. This made for some insane horn honking and some very amusing finger pointing."

Howie then appeared using the name Dewey Alexander in Anthony Spinelli's **EASY**. He had a still-legendary hot scene with co-star Jessie St. James. As a troubled, possibly violent student he blackmails masturbating teacher St. James into sex. It was one of the few times Howie wasn't playing such a nice guy, and although he was not fond of the character, the role brought him attention and more work.

He was selected as *Playgirl* magazine's "Man of the Year" in 1979 (he was already "Mr. November" in '78), and appeared in a tasteful nude photo layout for the women.

All during this period Howie would appear in a number of porn films as well as loops. The pay was low, but enough to keep him and his wife in comfort. As for Carly and her attitude towards his appearing in porno movies and fucking other women…as long as he kept it strictly to the work at hand she was fine with it—not ecstatic about it, but fine with it. Howie writes about having difficulties at times doing this. And how he would sometimes like to "rehearse" before an important scene was shot the next day, or how he could feel something more than professional empathy for a co-worker whom he was screwing before the cameras. Often Howie writes about the difficulties keeping an erection on a porno set…and what happens when it doesn't get hard.

There were fluffers (blow job girls who would be on standby to try to get people hard when this happened) on-set, but in his case, often it was recalling pivotal sensual moments from his teenage years.

Howie's stature as an "actor" in porn films meant he could be choosy (to a degree) when picking his next project, and sometimes negotiate his salary to his liking—something very few actors in the genre could afford to do. In later years, Carly would be the one arranging Howie's fees.

Working again with the director Anthony Spinelli (whose real name was Sam Weston), Howie used the Richard Pacheco pseudonym for the first time and mostly thereafter when appearing in Golden Age porn titles. **TALK DIRTY TO ME** is one of the most critically acclaimed movies of the genre and featured Pacheco and John Leslie as (respectively) Lenny and Jack, two good friends. Well, let me put it this way, Jack is a real ladies man, and Lenny, his best friend is always on the periphery of the action, never quite scoring with the women; he's pensive and thoughtful, and next to the balls-swinging lothario that Jack is…he might even seem a bit slow. The film did very well at the box-office and critically, even garnering notices in non-adult media.

NOTHING TO HIDE, also directed by Spinelli, was the follow-up to **TALK DIRTY TO ME**, and was even more of a success. Howie writes:

*"Make no mistake, **NOTHING TO HIDE** was still a porn movie. But for a minute there, we hijacked the crap and kicked it all into another direction. It gave a breath of fresh air to an industry mired in muck. And it gave hope that our sexual media might one day grow up."*

The film even featured an early use of a condom in the movie's penultimate sex scene between Pacheco (returning as Lenny) and Tigr, who played Karen, his love interest.

When Al Goldstein (publisher of *Screw* magazine) printed his top ten list of male actors in porn, he wrote that Pacheco was "the thinking girl's stud. If the roll calls for any amount of acting at all, Pacheco should be in it."

THE DANCERS was another big film of Pachecho's towards the latter part of his career, and he writes fondly of co-starring with—and getting to fuck—Georgina Spelvin. Both won Best Supporting Acting awards from adult entertainment awards media.

That same year, the adult film critics association awarded Pacheco as Best Actor (for **NOTHING TO HIDE**) and Supporting Actor (for **THE DANCERS**), something he is very proud of to this day.

Sprinkled throughout the hefty book are a number of entertaining bits about John Leslie (with whom Howie would have a strong friendship), and other male actors. One extraordinary story puts us right on the sidelines as John Holmes (in a latter day role) has an intense anal scene with Marilyn Chambers in **MARILYN CHAMBERS' PRIVATE FANTASIES** (1983, USA) that had onlookers watching and disbelieving as Chambers literally screamed and wailed with pleasure. I guess it was one of those "you had to be there" kind of moments, but Howie Gordon described it so perfectly, the reader does feel present.

Also revealed quite nakedly (no pun intended) are the emotional dangers involved with performing in adult movies, and how they can jeopardize or wreak havoc with personal lives, especially if you are married. Carly, Howie's wife is a rock, and despite some tenacious turns involving co-stars, especially Coleen Applegate and Shanna McCullough, his marriage has stayed steadfast and true.

Even when they had children, and pressure of a larger family, a new home, and the like presented itself, Howie writes how the threat of AIDS really made him want him to retire, but bills needed to be paid:

"Hey! I thought I had a great idea! I thought it was a career saver! I would pick out one actress to be my sex partner and we'd agree to only work exclusively with each other. It would be like a business marriage. We'd also agree to live monogamously in our private lives where our mates would agree to live monogamously too. In the way, the actress and I could continue our careers and yet still remain insulated against and other outside threat of a sexual transmission of AIDS".

But things didn't work out as planned, and Howie began to work less in the genre. However, he did work in a rare non adult film role in an Italian crime movie, originally titled **TRAGEDY**, alongside Joe Spinell. What was supposed to be a bit part turned larger as the filming continued, but the producers refused to pay beyond the scale of an "extra", and Howie walked. He still is in the film, and has a few photos of it in his book. Unable to find anything at all about the movie, my research revealed that this actually could be **IL CUGINO**

John Holmes personally inscribed this photo when they met on location for a movie Howie/Richard did together.

AMERICANO (a.k.a. BLOOD TIES, 1986), which also starred Brad Davis and Tony Lo Bianco.

As the 1980s came towards an end, the era of the videocassette was growing by leaps and bounds; theaters that showed hardcore movies were closing and only a handful remained...and there was the threat of AIDS as people in the business were dying. Howie still had to pay bills, and still wanted to act or be involved in the entertainment world he knew so well for so long:

> "I resumed my X-rated career, but the $1000-a-day jobs were all over. Everything was cheaper nowadays. Salaries had plummeted with the video revolution. As an actor, I was still offering to do a safe-sex scene, but there weren't many takers. Mostly I did non-sex roles for about $200 or $300 a day, whatever I could get. And there weren't a lot of those coming my way...both John Leslie and Anthony Spinelli used me as their assistant director..."

John Leslie died on December 5, 2010 of a heart attack, and his loss is deeply conveyed by Howie in the book; he even writes, "John Leslie was the best of us," referring to Leslie's abilities as an actor and a friend.

Howie Gordon ends his book, much as he started it, by reminding us that he is still here, and what drove him to his interest in sex in the first place:

> "I haven't died yet. I'm still here. And in order to finish this book, I want to tell you about forty-four years of foreplay...the hottest sex I ever had was in the ninth grade. Sally was the first girl I ever made out with."

Amazingly, Howie Gordon has not only made out with scores—perhaps hundreds—of women, but he got to fuck and have friendships with the likes of Jesie St. James, Kay Parker, Serena, Veronica Hart, Seka, Kelly Nichols, Marilyn Chambers...and, you name her...he did her. What a life, told in such a revealing, and often comical manner. He has a passion for storytelling, and in a way it must have been revelatory to sit back after he was done writing this memoir and look at it and go...wow, I did all that. Buy this book if you are interested in any way about the Golden Age of porn, or how X-rated movies (the best of them, anyway) were made back in the good old days.

Autographed copies of Howie's book are available at *hindsightbook.com*
Kindle versions available at *Amazon.com* and *BearManorBare.com*

Murderous Passions: The Delirious Cinema of Jesús Franco

Written by Stephen Thrower
Strange Attractor Press
Cover price £50

Has there ever been a more controversial filmmaker than Jess Franco? In terms of the healthy and often heated debate his work continues to inspire among cult movie buffs, I'd be willing to wager, "no". An insanely prolific filmmaker, Franco once described himself as a jazz musician who made films—and the description is actually quite helpful in appreciating the improvisational nature of so much of his work. Franco was born in Madrid on the 12th of May, 1930, and it was originally hoped that he would pursue a career in law—but the iconoclastic young man was much more drawn to music and movies, and eventually decided to settle on a career dabbling in the latter. He started off in the late 1950s making generally conventional and well-crafted mainstream movies. 1962's THE AWFUL DR. ORLOF (*Gritos en la noche*) brought him to the attention of horror buffs and it became something of a calling card; he would subsequently delve into more and more daring subject matter as the 1960s unfolded. He was hired by Orson Welles to direct the second unit on CHIMES AT MIDNIGHT (*Campanadas a medianoche*, 1965)—despite the best efforts of the Spanish producers to talk the mercurial actor/director out of doing so, as Franco was already regarded as an unpredictable sort—and from that moment forward, he appeared to become possessed by an insatiable desire to film, film and film. He finished out the decade with a series of films for British producer Harry Alan Towers, which enabled him access to bigger-name actors and higher-than-usual budgets (and accompanying theatrical exposure), but the 1970s saw him wandering into the wilderness, making offbeat movies of a very rough-and-ready nature and

A boyish Howie Gordon/Richard Pacheco & Marilyn Chambers on location for her scorching comeback film **INSATIABLE** *(1980).*

eventually embracing the sleazy excesses of hardcore pornography. In the 1980s, Franco—who had left his native Spain early on owing to problems with the strict Spanish censorship under Generalissimo Francisco Franco—finally returned to his homeland and continued his trend towards alternating offbeat, vaguely arty projects with hardcore porn. 1987's FACELESS (*Les prédateurs de la nuit*) was something of a throwback to THE AWFUL DR. ORLOF, and it offered him his biggest budget and name cast since the Harry Alan Towers years; its success helped to reintroduce him to a new generation of fans, but a string of similarly high(ish)-budget war dramas which followed did little to satisfy him artistically or commercially and he dropped off the map for several years before returning to the sex-and-horror field with KILLER BARBYS (a.k.a. VAMPIRE KILLER BARBYS, 1996). From there, Franco embarked on a long string of shot-on-video projects, many of which dealt with horror themes but were otherwise, for all intents and purposes, virtually unclassifiable. Franco died on April 2nd, 2013 due to complications from a stroke. There will never be another filmmaker quite like him—and whether that is a plus or a negative really depends on which side of the fence you're sitting on.

A great deal of ink has been spilled discussing Franco and his eclectic body of work. English-speaking readers have had a somewhat more limited exposure to in-depth studies, though the publication of *Obsession: The Films of Jess Franco* in 1993 was serious cause for celebration. Seen today, *Obsession* looks more than a little lacking, but it was an important step towards cataloging the confusing minefield that is Jess Franco's filmography, and it offered plenty of mouth-watering stills from films which were still hard as hell to actually see at that time. In 1999, the Glittering Images series offered up a photo-heavy tribute, *Jess Franco: El Sexo del Horror*, which also offered text in both Spanish and English. It corrected some mistakes found in *Obsession* and offered a slicker layout, with even more eye-catching illustrations to whet the appetite. In the ensuing years, there have been numerous magazine articles and retrospectives, but the only other English-friendly book of note was Jack Hunter's slim-but-worthy *Pornodelic Pleasures: Jess Franco Cinema*. All of these books were welcome and had merits worth celebrating, but they all managed to miss capturing the special magic that makes Franco's work so engaging for his passionate fan base. What they offered, more than anything, was a good sense of just how vast and difficult to catalog his body of work really is—here was a man who, at the height of his productivity, could manage to film a dozen movies a year…but this doesn't even begin to take into account the many alternate versions there are in existence for so many of these works. Confusing? Hell, yeah. As such, it is a minefield in need of a very special sort of a guide.

Happily, that guide has been found in the form of British writer Stephen Thrower. Thrower came to prominence in the genre scene with his books *Beyond Terror: The Films of Lucio Fulci* and *Nightmare USA: The Untold Story of the Exploitation Independents*, both published by FAB Press in the UK. Anybody who has read Thrower's earlier works knows that the man's passion is only exceeded by his flair for writing. Unlike many of the other authors in this field, Thrower knows how to convey enthusiasm without coming off like an amateur fanboy. His approach is serious, but not stuffy. He lays out the facts without coming off like an accountant. As such, when word got out that he was actually seeking to do the seemingly impossible and write an in-depth study of Franco and his cinema, it was clear that we were in for a very special treat indeed. And now that volume one of *Murderous Passions: The Delirious Cinema of Jesús Franco* is finally here, that optimism is more than rewarded; indeed, I would go so far as to say that even people who can't stand Jess and his movies will find this to be a very entertaining and eye-opening piece of writing.

Owing to the sheer volume of Franco's work, it's not surprising that the book had to be split in two. Indeed, to have tried and do it all in one go would have either resulted in a compromised overview or in a finished product which was so unwieldy that it would make for a real chore to slog through. Instead, Thrower, his research assistant/collaborator Julian Grainger and the publishers at Strange Attractor have elected to cover up until 1974 in this first volume; 1975 through 2013 will street sometime in 2016—which suddenly feels like a very long way away. If your tastes are anything like mine (which is to say, impeccable) you may well feel that all the really good stuff is covered in volume one—but let's not be too rash here, lest we forget some of the very fine work Jess would do for producer Erwin C. Dietrich in Switzerland or the many interesting movies he made for Golden Films Internacional upon his return to Spain, to say nothing of **FACELESS**, as well! In any event, I would be lying if I said that many of my absolute top favorite Franco films were made beyond 1974, so the contents of volume one are particularly well-suited to my tastes.

As one might expect from Thrower's previous books (to say nothing of his engaging interviews on several Franco DVDs and Blu-rays—when is somebody going to hire him to do a full-length commentary?), the writing is clear and incisive throughout. He provides a fascinating overview not only of Franco's work, but of the man himself. One of the things I was truly surprised to read was that Franco was doing well enough at one point in his career that he could afford to own homes in Paris and Rome, for example. Franco was a born storyteller, prone to telling tall tales, but Thrower and his collaborators have managed to sift through all the material and have offered up a very comprehensive portrait of Franco's background and the specific chronology of his filmography. Top marks go to Julian Grainger for his invaluable research work, which allows for much-improved-upon technical and cast credits, as well as some well-educated guesswork on production dates and the like. Thrower's flair for capturing the essence of the films he is discussing allows for an uncommonly astute analysis of Franco's many quirks and mannerisms. Elements often dismissed as sloppy and amateurish by other writers are taken into serious consideration, but happily Thrower is not one to simply make excuses for his idol: he truly dislikes some of Franco's films (including a couple I am rather fond of—here's to you, **LUCKY THE INSCRUTABLE** [*Lucky el intrépido*, 1967], and **CELESTINE, MAID AT YOUR SERVICE** [*Célestine... bonne à tout faire*, 1974]!) and he isn't afraid to point out where Franco sometimes succumbed to laziness, either. Another most welcome aspect of the book is the extensive use of quotations from contemporary reviews: due to the grubby nature of so many Franco films, one would be forgiven for thinking that they were made and then tossed onto a shelf to rot until somebody pirated copies for the home video market, but no—a lot of these films received real theatrical play dates and quite a few of them were reviewed, as well—and not always unfavorably, either!

In addition to Thrower's always highly readable prose, *Murderous Passions* also deserves ample praise for its stylish and reader-friendly layout and design. The folks at Strange Attractor have established themselves as a force to be reckoned with: their production values are every bit as good as those associated with FAB Press, for example, and the quality of the reproduction of the color and black-and-white stills and posters is simply splendid. Simply put, this is a gorgeous-looking tome.

Strange Attractor are offering two editions, both hardcover: in addition to the standard edition with an image of Lina Romay from **FEMALE VAMPIRE** (*La comtesse noire*, 1974) gracing the cover, there is also a special edition with an image from **THE DIABOLICAL DR. Z** (*Miss Muerte*, 1966) on the cover. As per the Strange Attractor website, the special edition perks are as follows: "Signed [by Stephen Thrower and Julian Grainger] and numbered Special Edition limited to 300 copies, in a cloth, foil blocked cover with inserted colour plate, plus limited 7″ vinyl disc of Franco music and a postcard set. The single contains three tracks from **LA COMTESSE PERVERSE** and **LE JOURNAL INTIME D'UNE NYMPHOMANE**, all by Roger Davy." Given my love of Franco, the special edition was a no-brainer, but it costs a little bit more, so your tolerance for the pricing may vary. I would say the special edition is a bargain, regardless, but be aware: owing to a global vinyl shortage, the special edition is not shipping outside of the UK until the publisher has the 7″ ready to ship with it—since I don't even own a record player, I told them to just skip the 7" with my order and they had the book delivered to me within a week.

In closing, *Murderous Passions* gets my vote as one of the best studies of a filmmaker I have ever had the pleasure of reading; I anticipate dipping in and out of it again for many years to come. Now bring on volume 2—I'm ready!
~Troy Howarth

The Roberts
Written by Justin Shady and Wayne Chinsing / Illustrated by Erik Rose
Image
Cover price $14.99

We all fear growing old, and losing our right to live the way we like. Becoming feeble in body and brittle in bone, with our helpless minds watching as the anatomy crumbles around it. Forced to live out the rest of our days playing bridge, shuffleboard and, like every retired member of my family, bocce ball. Constantly complaining about the temperature and those meddling kids, sharing old war stories, gluing our dentures to shit, and queefing dust, all on some shelf in the back of society's closet where the world can forget about us 'til we wither away and die in the concentration camps we call retirement homes, which are really nothing more than waiting rooms for the graveyard. "To keep old folks safe" they like to say, but really it's to keep them out of sight, hair, and mind when the children they raised can't stand to be bothered with them any longer. A way for their families to subdue the burden of guilt; letting their wallets do what their hearts couldn't.

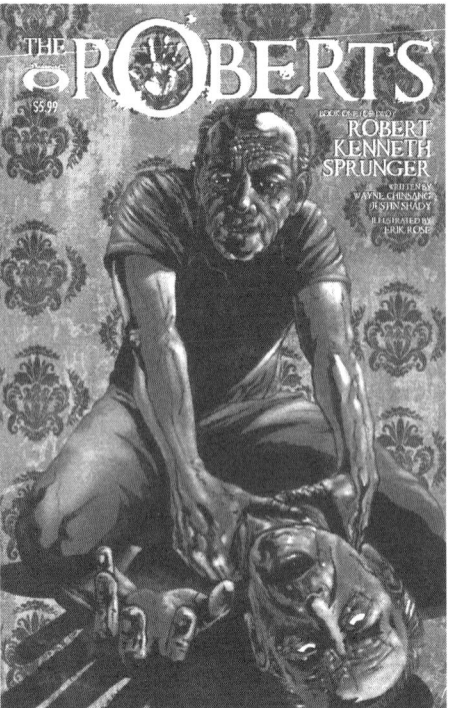

Think of how many times you went to visit a relative in a retirement hole and feared the staff was mistreating them, never once worrying about other dangers lurking behind pleasant-sounding monikers like Whispering Willows, Silent Meadows, Dying Hollow, or Withering Rose. But what of its other residents?

The Shady Lane Retirement Center for Elderly Adults is one such place, one that has been unwittingly harboring a secret of which even its denizens—and staff—are unaware. And in doing so answers the question: Where do serial killers go to retire? The ones that got away? The ones the law never caught up to? They have to go somewhere, right?

Shady Lane has a new resident, and with his entry, old needs resurface. Serial killers, much like assholes, never really retire. That would be like a bird resigning from flight, or a fish kicking the habit of breathing water. Some lunatics get lucky and never get caught, laying dormant like an undetonated bomb. But what happens when one has too much time on their idle hands, and a hobby that never loses its amusement? A tentative friendship is forged in Shady Lanes; one that will move past bridge and the courtroom exploits of Matlock. A friendship, that's more like a rivalry. One that spawns a blood-sample competition. And we get to watch as two of the world's most notorious serial killers reignite their reigns of terror straight out of a retirement camp.

I fucking loved this comic, put out by Image's Shadowline imprint (who also put out the amazing title *Morning Glories*), a label that has gone through more transitions than a Gameboy. I thought a comic about a bunch of old folks waiting around to kick the bucket might be boring, serial killers or no. Let's face it, it doesn't exactly sound like a fireworks display at a nitroglycerin plant. But I am officially willing to eat those words, even if it causes me literary acid reflux.

By now, if you've ever read anything I have ever written on comics, you should be accustomed to my love affair with black-and-white. Those monochromatic, often-overlooked gems that need no flashy colors to translate the importance of the story or detract from the seriousness of the plot, which are contrary to every rinse-and-repeat superhero saga in existence. And since this is a tale of an older generation, what better way to artistically display that than the good old black-and-white of the silver screen era.

This is Eric Rose's first time on a full-length mini-series, and it really shines when it's not dolled up with lurid colors. Look at any panel when it's penciled, and compare it after the inking process. There's (generally) no comparison. So it should come as no surprise that he is especially adept at shading. His outlines might seem a little clumsy at first, but are easily made up for with detailed gray tones. In my opinion those tones could even replace the outlines on most of the panels presented.

Story-wise it was fantastic; with subject-matter that's not only thought-provoking, but ultimately fascinating and original. Something to which you can truly say, "Holy McNipples, why did I never think of that?!" The mark of a truly great story. It's intriguing to see where murderers wind up after their capers are told; after the media moves on and society becomes interested in whatever celebrity is fucking whatever other celebrity. Evil never retires. It's an interesting concept that offers a glimpse into reignited bloodlusts. The narration will chokehold your attention from the first sentence, and the interaction between the home's occupants will keep you one "smilin' muthafucka" for the entire duration, especially when you consider some of the folks have certain ailments that play a particularly amusing role…and no, I'm not talking about pendulous labias and testicles, hilarious as they may be.

I have read the graphic novel three times over, and could probably gush about it for another 15 paragraphs. Every nuance is honestly worth mentioning, but I'll let you find that out for yourself. My only complaint came with the binding of the book. One of the pages was repeated, and the page that should have been next was missing, so I missed a page of story that I hope wasn't integral to the plot. I don't know if this was just in my copy of the TPB, or if this was a mistake of mass marketing proportions.[3]

Regardless, go the fuck out, and pick this the fuck up. Like a foreigner in a flea market might say in broken English while trying to sell you on an obvious knockoff: "It's the hot shit, man!" Anyway, this rates as WFA (Wayyy Fucking Awesome) on the Friendly Neighborhood Krys the Comic Chick Scale (which, by the way, isn't a real scale). ~ ***Krys Caroleo***

---

[3] Alas, it seems to be the latter, as my copy of the book has the same problem. But don't let that stop you from picking this awesome book up! – *ed.*

PARDON MY HYPERBOLE!

Comic & Graphic Novel reviews by Ralph Mathieu

Fragments of Horror
written and drawn by Junji Ito
Viz Media

Anyone who has read or even just looked at Junji Ito's manga masterworks, *Gyo*, *Uzamaki* and *Tomie*, already know that he is a true master of the horror genre. So a new collection of Ito's horror stories, *Fragments of Horror*, is reason enough to do a special H.P. Lovecraft dance. *Fragments of Horror* contains eight short horror stories, all perfect examples of how, in just a few pages, Ito can craft a story that will get under your skin and make you feel the horror that is happening to the characters in his stories. Junji Ito's art, with its crisp black line, is perfect in black and white and is simultaneously creepy, beautiful, and erotic. Merely looking at his art you will have gazed into the abyss…and you'll be happy to have done so.

Fight Club 2
written by Chuck Palahniuk and drawn by Cameron Stewart
Dark Horse Comics

Fight Club 2 is novelist Chuck Palahniuk's first foray into writing comic books, and he does this as if he has been writing in this medium for years. *Fight Club 2* is so titled because it is a continuation of characters and themes from his smash-hit novel *Fight Club*. One doesn't have to have read the novel or seen the movie to immediately become immersed into the world of Tyler Durden, a.k.a. Sebastian's subconscious, but if you have read the novel and/or watched the movie, you'll be even more rewarded by Palahniuk's comic follow-up. Here's a passage from the first issue that will illustrate what Palahniuk is doing with this comic (and really all of his writing):

> "Young people, they're so hungry to anchor themselves in the vast world. It's too bad that someone couldn't plant a bomb and explode all the worthless furniture stored inside Sebas-

tian's head…his cheap, mass-produced Ikea ideologies. His secondhand junk-store epiphanies and thrift-store political positions. Those bargain basement dreams—it's too bad a cleansing fire couldn't sweep them all away…making room for true enlightenment."

Cameron Stewart's art for *Fight Club 2* is also perfect, with his surface traditional "normal" linework that isn't constantly flashy, making the craziness and dramatic scenes even more potent when they happen.

The Spirit
written by Matt Wagner and drawn by Dan Schkade
Dynamite

The Spirit was a comic that Will Eisner created back in the early 1940s and was a long-running, much beloved comic strip. There have been many a creator and publisher that has taken a go at reviving the character, and although many of the creators that have done their versions/homages of *The Spirit* very lovingly, I don't think many of them did bring much different or could capture what Eisner's *The Spirit* was. All one has to know about the Spirit is that he is a crime-fighter and although there are some supernatural aspects to his origin, Spirit stories, are mostly straight-forward crime stories that have sprinklings of the fantastical (please do not see the Frank Miller **THE SPIRIT** [2008] movie from a few years ago, because although Miller has a love of Eisner's character and sequential art, his movie is so bad…seriously, it's not even fun to goof on).

So I've read many a *Spirit* comic book over the years and as I mentioned, none of them seemed to capture the essence of Eisner's *Spirit*. Well this looks to be corrected as Matt Wagner (writer and artist of such seminal creations as *Grendel* and *Mage*, and longtime writer of Vertigo's *Sandman Mystery Theater*) and artist Dan Schkade have come out firing on all cylinders with their excellent first issue of *The Spirit* titled "Who Killed the Spirt?" We don't see the title character at all in the first issue, as various characters are trying to find out what happened to him, but really the tone of this comic has *The Spirit* infused upon every page. And where did this artist, Dan Schkade, come from!? Schkade's art has the spirit (pun intended) of Eisner's art without being derivative, and colorist Brennan Wagner is equally up to being the exclamation mark upon this great creative team. Reading this first issue by Wagner and Schkade was one of the first times in the longest time I've been eagerly awaiting the next issue out of excitement rather than feeling I needed to read it because this is a seminal character.

Airboy
written by James Robinson and drawn by Greg Hinkle
Image

I was not prepared for how much I loved the new *Airboy* comic by James Robinson and Greg Hinkle. I've been a longtime enthusiast of Robinson's comic book writing, most notably in his long-running *Starman* comic for DC, which was as epic a look at the superhero genre as Neil Gaiman's *Sandman* was to the fantasy genre. *Airboy* was an aviator character first published during World War II for eleven years and has had a couple of other incarnations at other comic publishers before fading once again into obscurity. As James Robinson's *Airboy* comic begins, we very quickly see that this isn't really going to be a comic about the Airboy character, rather it's going to be Robinson's forum to deal with some of the strange pathways his life has taken (in the Hunter S. Thompson vein). Two issues into this new comic, we are treated to James Robinson's very unflattering look at himself as he tries to think of what he'll do with the Airboy character and he drags his artist, Greg Hinkle into his sordid "adventure" along the way. The fictional Airboy does appear in this comic at the end of the first issue, and in the second issue we see this character try to grasp what he is doing in this comic that is mostly about writer James Robinson. *Airboy* is very much a meta/breaking-the-fourth-wall creation, and is also very funny and dark—an obviously very personal look at what James Robinson has been going through the last few years.

Watch the Skies!
Monster! International is going to land real soon!
We promise!

Original pencils from Megh's cover art for this issue. For prints and commisions, contact *megh@artbymegh.com*

For more art and comics, please visit *artbymegh.com*

THE HOME FOR TRU
INDIE HORROR!
A PLAGUE SO PLEASANT
THE DEAD ARE THE ENDANGERED SPECIES
BLOOD SLAUGHTER MASSACRE
EBOLA ZOMBIES
ONCE THEY GET IN, YOU DON'T GET OUT!
HI-8
HORROR INDEPENDENT EIGHT
THE PERFECT HOUSE
HELLRAISER'S DOUG BRADLEY
SCREAM PARK
DEATH IS THE NEW ATTRACTION
SPECIAL ANNIVERSARY EDITION
SNUFF
A DOCUMENTARY ABOUT KILLING ON CAMERA
"EXTREMELY WELL PUT TOGETHER."
THE TURNPIKE KILLER
ALL ROADS LEAD TO DEATH
"YOU'RE GOING TO LOVE THE TURNPIKE KILLER. IT SCREAMS '80S HORROR."
WILDEYE RELEASING
wildeyereleasing.com

ABOUT THE CONTRIBUTORS...

Matthew E. Banks – is a graduate of University of Plymouth with a degree in English and Creative Writing. He lives in deepest, darkest Cornwall with his wife Samantha, who is an English Literature postgraduate. His main field of interest is the supernatural in all its manifestations, having published numerous ghost stories, classic horror film history, and research on Bela Lugosi. Matthew also likes *Doctor Who*, haunted houses and vampires, and regularly contributes to *We Belong Dead* Magazine, *Reflections* Magazine and *The Spectral Times*.

Stephen R. Bissette – a pioneer graduate of the Joe Kubert School, currently teaches at the Center for Cartoon Studies and is renowned for *Swamp Thing*, *Taboo* (launching *From Hell* and *Lost Girls*), "*1963*", *Tyrant*, co-creating John Constantine, and creating the world's second "24-Hour Comic" (invented by Scott McCloud for Bissette). He writes, illustrates, and has co-authored many books; his latest includes *Teen Angels & New Mutants* (2011), the short story "Copper" in *The New Dead* (2010), and he illustrated *The Vermont Monster Guide* (2009). His latest ebooks are *Bryan Talbot: Dreams & Dystopias* and the *Best of Blur* duo, *Wonders! Millennial Marvel Movies* and *Horrors! Cults, Crimes, & Creepers*.

Krys Caroleo – hates umbrellas, loves poking dead things with sticks, and 33 years ago ate her twin in utero to gain its powers and become the insane yet cuddly person she is today. She is a geek, but not the kind that bites the heads off of chickens…unless they piss her off.

Michael Elvidge – hails from Durham, Ontario, Canada where he has written and illustrated several 'zines and comics since the late 1990s. He grew up loving *Famous Monsters*, horror VHS rentals, and *Deep Red* Magazine. His work has also appeared in *Monster!*, *Broken Pencil* and even art galleries. When he's not working on horror movie reviews, art and comics, he's busy hosting a weekly Internet radio show about hard rock, punk and metal music, *The Coverage Radio Show*. You can find Michael on Facebook and Tumblr.

Steve Fenton – prefers to remain as much of a mystery to others as he is to himself.

Jeff Goodhartz – is a self-righteous and self-serving man of the people who has been watching and writing about Asian Cinema for far too long. His current 'blog is *Films from the Far Reaches* (as he's never above a shameless plug). He's quite shameless.

Brian Harris – has written for *Ultra Violent* magazine, *Exploitation Retrospect*, *Serial Killer* magazine, *Gorezone* magazine (UK) and *Hacker's Source* magazine. He's written nine books, four of which are still available, five are out-of-print. Brian has also run several websites including Joe Horror, Wildside Cinema, CineKult and Box Set Beatdown.

John Harrison – John Harrison is a freelance writer based in Melbourne, Australia. A regular contributor to *Monster!*, Harrison has written about Charles Manson for *Crime Factory* magazine, as well as in his own 2011 Headpress book *Hip Pocket Sleaze*. In 2004, he curated a season of Manson cinema for the Melbourne Underground Film Festival, and has written a chapter on vintage Manson-inspired pulp paperbacks for the upcoming book *Beat Girls, Love Tribes, and Real Cool Cats: Pulp Fiction and Youth Culture 1950-1980*, which is due to be published by Verse Chorus Press in May, 2016.

Michael Hauss – lives in Cincinnati, Ohio with his daughter and their two cats, Rotten Ralph and Fatty Boo-Boo. He has had articles published in various 'zines, and has been an exploitation film fanatic since his youth growing up in the frozen northeastern part of Ohio. He is a one-time member of the Gary Coleman fan club.

Troy Howarth – is the author of *The Haunted World of Mario Bava*. He keeps busy writing reviews for websites like *AV Maniacs* and *Eccentric Cinema* and has been published in magazines like *Absurd* in Denmark and *We Belong Dead* in the UK. The revised and expanded—and all-'round new and improved—edition of *The Haunted World of Mario Bava* is now available, and he also recently published an exhaustive study of the Italian thriller (the "*Giallo*") titled *So Deadly, So Perverse: 50 Years of Italian Giallo Films*. In addition to this, he's the co-author (with Chris Workman) of *The Tome of Terror*, a multi-volume encyclopedia of horror films which recently had its first installment published. His most recent book, *Splintered Visions*, about the films of Lucio Fulci, has just hit the stands, and he has agreements in place to follow-up with books on the peplum and *krimi* genres. Needless to say, this is a very busy period for him and he's very proud to be a part of *Weng's Chop*'s gallery of goons.

Andrew Leavold – is the director of the 2013 documentary **THE SEARCH FOR WENG WENG**, and the founder and co-owner of Trash Video, a writer and film critic, TV presenter, festival programmer, MC, agnostic evangelist and occasional guerrilla filmmaker.

Scott MacDonald – An avid fan of horror cinema since convincing an unsuspecting video store clerk to rent him **FRIDAY THE 13TH PART VII: THE NEW BLOOD** to him at the age of seven, Scott MacDonald has been devouring genre titles since. He's been making short genre films since he was a teenager, and has directed six which have played around the festival circuit. He is currently trying to finance an arthouse horror feature titled BAD REPUTATION. Scott writes for *EuroCultAV.com*, *DoomedMoviethon.com*, and *Fang of Joy* Magazine as well as *Fangoria.com*.

Ralph Mathieu – has been the owner of Alternate Reality Comics (4110 S. Maryland Pkwy. #8, Las Vegas, NV. 89119) since 1995. He's read comics since 1975, first picking up DC and Marvel titles such as *House of Mystery* and *Chamber of Chills*. Upon seeing ads for superhero comics in the aforementioned titles, he tried them out and had to buy them all. Nothing makes Ralph happier than owning Alternate Reality Comics where he get to find good homes for good comics and graphic novels and talk geek daily. Visit *alternaterealitycomics.net* or look up Alternate Reality Comics, Las Vegas on Facebook.

Megh – is an award-winning erotic artist whose work has been featured in the Museum of Sex, as well as having been archived in the Kinsey Library. She is a sometime fetish model for Muki's Kitchen (*mukiskitchen.com*) and Cannigals (*cannigals.com*), but she spends

Weng's Chop

most of her waking hours toiling away on her forthcoming and massively erotic graphic novel, *In the Land of Meat, Milk and Honey*. You can browse some of her archives at *artbymegh.com*. For prints and commissions, contact her at *megh@artbymegh.com*. Do not believe the stories told by the people chained in her basement—those people are liars.

Tim Merrill – When he isn't busy with his day gig as a lifeguard tending the lake of fire, Tim can usually be found pouring through the vaults, looking for the next AIP or Shaw Brothers eyegasm. He has written for *Asian Cult Cinema*, *Asian Eye* and the *Korean Herald*. Tim is proud to have had the opportunity to throw in on the bad ass greatness known only as *Weng's Chop*. He lives with his Peke protector Boo (a.k.a. Boocifer, Boozila), the mighty devil dog herself.

Eric Messina – can be found grinding out exploitation reviews for *theaterofguts.com* under the moniker Crankenstein. Theater of Guts was started in an effort to bring attention to the legacy of Chas Balun and *Deep Red* Magazine. The goal of the site is to review all of the titles in the VHS Bootleg catalog; past writers from *DR* have been interviewed and contributed reviews. He currently resides in Oakland Ca, with his wife Ami and dog Jack. TOG has a YouTube channel of parody trailers and video interviews, so check it out at "Trailers That Smell Skunkape".

Christos Mouroukis – was born in Italy and has an MA in Feature Film from Goldsmiths University of London. He has directed award-winning and internationally broadcasted short films and music videos. He writes about genre movies in Greek (for *horrorant.com*) and in English (for *Weng's Chop, Cinema Head Cheese*, and *Monster!*). He lives in Athens with his fiancée Faye, and their cats Arte and Franco.

Adam Parker-Edmondston – is a huge pop culture fan, especially monster movies and VHS. He writes for numerous websites including *Attack from Planet B*, *Cult Collective* and *Grizzly Bomb*, as well as regularly contributing to *WC*'s sister publication, *Monster!* Digest.

George Pacheco – has been writing professionally for well over a decade, working his way in the music industry as a fanzine editor and freelance scribe before graduating to contributing editor for the legendary *Metal Maniacs* magazine. George continues to write about music for such publications as *Outburn* and *Zero Tolerance* (UK) while focusing these days on film writing for *Weng's Chop*, *Rue Morgue*, *Video Watchdog* and the website *10kBullets*.

Louis Paul – has written for numerous fanzines and published his own, *Blood Times* (87-93). He has written several books including *Inferno Italia – Der Italienische Horrorfilm* (Bertler, Lieber, '98); *Serien Morden* (Bertler, Lieber, '00); *Film Fatales – Women in Espionage Films & Television 63-73* (McFarland, '02); *Italian Horror Film Directors* (McFarland, '05, '10); and *Tales from the Cult Film Trenches – Interviews with 36 Actors from Horror, Science Fiction and Exploitation Cinema* (McFarland, '07). Louis blames a 42nd Street double-bill of Umberto Lenzi's **ALMOST HUMAN** and the 3D porno **HARD CANDY** (with John Holmes) for disturbing his psyche for life.

Tim Paxton – has been publishing stuff about monsters since 1978, and currently lives to write about fantastic cinema from India. He is even considering publishing a book on the subject. What a knucklehead. Meanwhile ihe's happily keeping himelf busy with *MONSTER!*, *Monster! International*, *Weng's Chop*, and other such projects.

Steven Ronquillo – is a pretentious know-it-all who looks down on his fellow film fans and refuses to reveal his faves to them unless it makes him look good.

Richard Glenn Schmidt – is the author of *Giallo Meltdown: A Moviethon Diary*. He is the proprietor of *DoomedMoviethon.com* and *CinemaSomanmbulist.com* and co-host of *Hello! This is the Doomed Show*.

Matthew St. Cyr – is the author/host of the *Midnight Cinephile* website/podcast as well as staunch defender of trash cinema. He's a freelance writer for several magazines, author of several short stories and aspiring filmmaker, and is currently working on a new project called *Trash TV*.

Tony Strauss – has been writing about cinema in print and online for nearly two decades. His existence as that rarest and most annoying of creatures—an artsy-fartsy movie snob who loves trash cinema (yes, it's possible)—often leaves him as the odd man out in both intellectual and low-brow film discussions. Most movies that people describe as "boring" or "confusing" enthrall him, while the kinds of movies that are described as "non-stop action" usually bore him to tears. He has a BFA in Film, but don't hold that against him.

Anthony Thorne – is a proud Tasmanian who lives in Melbourne with his partner Hye Young and his 3-year-old son Sam. He used to write for *Fatal Visions*. Now he's training in 3D animation while he stockpiles reviews for a future spaghetti western book.

L. Thomas Tripp – is a longtime film fanatic and native of Las Vegas. He is currently pursuing a BA in creative writing at UNLV, and his love for film goes way back to 1985 when he first snuck in to the living room of his childhood home to watch the cable premier of the original **A NIGHTMARE ON ELM STREET**, something his mother did not want her eight-year-old son viewing. These days, not much surpasses his interest in literature, film, and writing.

Scott Wachtler – is the former Editor of the *Cambridge Chronicle*, and before that he was a journalist working for various newspapers (an ancient form of news delivery) in the Boston area for almost 10 years. He is the author of the recently-released true-crime eBook *Young Blood: Murder in the Woods* (available now at *Amazon.com*), about a former schoolmate now serving life in prison for killing his best friend. Scott's first foray into film criticism started innocently enough at age seven when he cried after hearing that his parents were taking him to see **STAR WARS**. He thought his parents said they were taking him to see a movie called **STAR AWARDS**. "I couldn't understand why they were taking a seven-year-old to the theater to see movie about stars getting awards?" he now says. "All of this confusion could have been prevented if only they had called it by its *real* title **STAR WARS: EPISODE IV: A NEW HOPE**. Jeez! Oh wait, it wasn't called that yet."

Bennie Woodell – is an independent filmmaker who lives in LA and has directed seven feature films. Ever since being a kid, he's enjoyed nothing more than action, horror, and exploitation films. He loves Hong Kong Cinema and wants to one day make a film there. Until then, you can find him on-set somewhere making beautiful violence, or at the movies being inspired…mainly the New Beverly, Egyptian, or Aero Theatre in Los Angeles.

David Zuzelo – is a full-time HorrorDad, a full-time Media Mangler and a full-time Trash Cinema Sponge. He is also a sometime 'blogger at Tomb It May Concern (*David-Z. blogspot.com*) and enjoys spewing words of sleazy musing across every publication that will have him. Check out his book *Tough To Kill-The Italian Action Explosion* and see just how many exploding huts he can endure, and still beg for more!

Printed in Great Britain
by Amazon.co.uk, Ltd.,
Marston Gate.